Awe for the Tiger,
Love for the Lamb

For she who daily walks the walk
As I do daily talk the talk,
my gaea

you animals who are so innocent, what have you done worthy of death?

  – Richard de Wyche, Bishop of Chichester, c. 1235

If thy heart be right, then will every creature be to thee a mirror of life, and a book of holy doctrine.

  – Thomas à Kempis, c. 1427

I pray, when a lion eats a man and a man eats an ox,
why is the ox made more for the man than the man for the lion?

  – Thomas Hobbes, 1641

The well-taught philosophic mind
To all compassion gives;
Casts round the world an equal eye
And feels for all that lives.

  – Anna Laetitia Barbauld, c. 1780

Boundless compassion for all living beings is the finest and surest guarantee of pure moral conduct …

  – Arthur Schopenhauer, 1841

Contents

Acknowledgments

A book of this nature must depend heavily on what others have done before. The following books have been of especial help in various degrees and in different parts of this volume: Jonathan Barnes, *Early Greek Philosophy*, London: Penguin, 1987; Richard Sorabji, *Animal Minds and Human Morals: The Origins of the Western Debate*, Ithaca: Cornell University Press, 1993. Each of these books is indispensable to understanding the Presocratic and classical mind, especially with regard to animals. Paul A.B. Clarke and Andrew Linzey, eds., *Political Theory and Animal Rights*, London: Pluto Press, 1990; Andrew Linzey and Tom Regan, eds., *Animals and Christianity: A Book of Readings*, London: SPCK, 1989; Lewis G. Regenstein, *Replenish the Earth: A History of Organized Religion's Treatment of Animals and Nature — Including the Bible's Message of Conservation and Kindness toward Animals*, New York: Crossroad, 1991, of great help for the first chapter; Mathias Guenther, *Tricksters and Trancers: Bushman Religion and Society*, Bloomington: Indiana University Press, 1999; Fleur Adcock and Jacqueline Simms, eds., *The Oxford Book of Creatures*, Oxford: Oxford University Press, 1995; Keith Thomas, *Man and the Natural World: Changing Attitudes in England 1500–1800*, London: Penguin, 1984, a monumental work of impeccable scholarship; E.S. Turner, *All Heaven in a Rage*, Fontwell: Centaur, 1992 [1964]; Roberta Kalechofsky, ed., *Judaism and Animal Rights: Classical and Contemporary Responses*, Marblehead, MA: Micah Publications, 1992; Richard D. Ryder, *Animal Revolution: Changing Attitudes toward Speciesism*, Oxford: Basil Blackwell, 1989, a work of original research containing material not found elsewhere; Dix Harwood, *Love for Animals and How It Developed in Great Britain*, New York: Privately Printed, 1928, a rare but brilliant book, especially helpful for the eighteenth century; Howard Williams, *The Ethics of Diet: A Catena of Authorities Deprecatory of the Practice of Flesh-Eating*, London: F. Pitman, 1883, a monument to the rigour, integrity, and depth of traditional scholarship; Jon Wynne-Tyson, *The Extended Circle: A Commonplace Book of*

Animal Rights, New York: Paragon, 1989 [1985], a work of immense dedication and labour, especially helpful for the final chapter; Roderick Frazier Nash, *The Rights of Nature: A History of Environmental Ethics,* Madison: University of Wisconsin Press, 1989, which puts a due emphasis, one sometimes overlooked, on the American contribution; James Rachels, *Created from Animals: The Moral Implications of Darwinism,* Oxford: Oxford University Press, 1991; John Vyvyan, *In Pity and In Anger,* Marblehead, MA: Micah, 1988 [London: Michael Joseph, 1969], and *The Dark Face of Science,* London: Michael Joseph, 1971, both invaluable for vivisection material; Joanna Cullen Brown, *Let Me Enjoy the Earth: Thomas Hardy and Nature,* London: Allison and Busby, 1990; Cecily Boas, ed., *Birds and Beasts in English Literature,* London: Thomas Nelson, 1926; Al-Hafiz B.A. Masri, *Animals in Islam,* Petersfield: The Athene Trust, 1989.

I have sometimes followed these authors, editors, and compilers, and have often been prompted by them. At the very least, they showed me where to start looking. Sometimes their signposts were the very goal. Of course, my sources have been far more diverse than those mentioned here, but without their particular yet multifarious stimuli this book would have been beyond my capacities. I have also drawn on, and elaborated, some of the sources used in my own previous writings.

My gratitude is also owed to many more, above all to those who are ever willing to discuss the development and state of animal welfare and animal rights literature with me, especially Lorna Chamberlain, Executive Director of the London Humane Society, my occasional co-author, and my treasured wife; David Fraser, NSERC Industrial Research Professor in Animal Welfare at the University of British Columbia, also my occasional co-author, and the recipient of most of my e-mail; and Mathias Guenther, Professor of Anthropology at Wilfrid Laurier University, my ever-stimulating power lunch companion. Joris and Dorothy Van Daele of London, Ontario, Ian Duncan of the University of Guelph, Barbara Noske of the University of Sydney, and Chien-hui Li, Fellow of Wolfson College, Cambridge, are also valued intellectual companions who provide a source of enjoyment as well as of self-questioning. Their views are so complex, stimulating, and mind- and heartfelt, that I cannot fail to be impressed by the variety of well-considered, albeit often conflicting, orientations which inform scholars of animal ethics.

I am especially indebted to Randy Malamud of Georgia State University and Walter Hogan of Eastern Michigan University who were not only very generous in their praise of an earlier draft of this book, which helped persuade UBC Press that publication was merited, but who also made a number of valuable suggestions for improvements which I have endeavoured to follow. While they are, of course, not responsible for the contents of this book, it would certainly have been a less satisfactory volume without their critiques. Finally, my editor, Randy Schmidt, is the editor every author would want – one who is wholeheartedly on the author's side in all those inconveniences which inevitably arise in the preparation of a book, even when the author gets a little testy.

An explanation is due for the lack of a bibliography. An extensive list of cited works was prepared but since all the books are given full bibliographic reference in the notes, environmental, space, and cost considerations prevailed.

A note on permissions: Extracts from "Essays" by Plutarch, translated by Robin Waterfield (Penguin Classics, 1992) © Robin Waterfield, 1992, and from *Piers the Ploughman* by William Langland, translated by J.F. Goodridge (Penguin Classics, 1959, revised edition 1966) © J.F. Goodridge, 1956, 1966, are reproduced by kind permission of Penguin Books Ltd.

Rod Preece, London, Ontario
Christmas Day, 2001

Introduction

My purpose in this book is to present some of the more compassionate and respectful attitudes toward our fellow creatures from the earliest writings to the opening decade of the twentieth century – after which, sensibilities to animals went into a period of modest decline and intellectual conceptions of animal capacities were dominated by the strictures of the Pavlovs and Piagets, before the great humanitarian revival of the 1970s. I have selected examples from the realm of myth, religion, poetry, philosophy, essays, novels, parliamentary proceedings, and other literature in a variety of forms. My criteria for selection have been threefold: (a) passages that are in and of themselves meritorious in expressing, or making the case for consideration of, animal well-being, animal interests, and/or animal rights; (b) passages that allow us to comprehend more readily the transformation from one level and form of sensibility to another; and (c) passages that have themselves stimulated further consideration of animal orientations.

In a book of this genre it is inevitable that the compiler will have left out much he would have wished to include – and perhaps much of value of which he was woefully ignorant. But it is to be hoped that the reader, the researcher, the browser, and the dabbler will find examples of the most significant, and perhaps even a few of the less significant, contributions to sensibilities toward animals in these pages. It is to be hoped, too, that there is abundant material here that even the most avid reader of animal welfare and animal rights literature will not have encountered before. In all traditions, perhaps especially in the Western tradition as a consequence of its ever-increasing technological capacities, it is almost as easy to find instances of cruelty, denigration and dismissal, as it is to find those portraits that elevate the human spirit at the same time as they elevate those beings with whom we share our threatened planet. This book, then, does not purport to represent a microcosm of the whole. Instead, it represents a microcosm of humanity's finer musings. I am convinced that by reflecting on, indeed revelling in, the more humane aspects of our traditions, we will find the inspiration to treat the world's fauna with the respect and consideration to which their inherent value entitles them.

The West and other closely related cultures have a more complex history than other cultures with regard to the treatment of animals because of the particular features of societal development, primarily in its technological dimensions. Aboriginal and Oriental cultures have, at least until recently, changed considerably less. Their attitudes and values have remained relatively consistent because the practical realities of their societies have remained relatively consistent, and this is, for them, a matter of pride. If one gets the values right first time there is no reason for a self-conscious change; indeed, there is every reason to resist it. Their philosophies thus show less variety. As a result I have concentrated my attention on the Western experience. This is not because the traditions of other societies matter less, or tell us less about the finer aspects of humanity's appreciation of animal worthiness. On the contrary, the West can learn, and sometimes has learned, from them, as they have from the West. However, because other traditions have experienced less of a cultural and ethical transformation, I have treated them, for the most part, in the first chapter alone. Thereafter, the passages are selected to illuminate the Western tradition.

What the selected passages share in common is a recognition that the human is not the only worthy animal, if indeed the human is worthy at all. It behoves us always to look beyond our own species when we are deciding in what kind of society we wish to live. The philosopher Mary Midgley has wisely described the appropriate ideal as "the mixed community," pointing out that "all human communities have involved animals."[1] The mixed community is one in which we recognize other beings as an integral part of the moral community, entitled to earnest consideration as the beings that they are with the needs that they have.

Despite the varieties of humanity's historical stages, each of which has influenced our attitudes in different ways, there has always been an underlying constant, at least in the minds of the compassionate. It is this constant that suffuses the ways in which more considerate humans have approached the complex practical ethical problems of everyday life with regard to our treatment of other species. It is what the eminent Swiss founder of the analytical school of psychology, Carl Gustav Jung, called "an unconscious identity with animals."[2] This resembles the conclusions of the eighteenth-century Franco-Swiss philosopher Jean-Jacques Rousseau who elevated feelings over reason and insisted that alongside our self-interest, we also have a natural compassion for others, including other animals.[3] Likewise, the early English proponent of the scientific method, Francis Bacon, claimed that our ethical deliberations naturally "take unto other living creatures."[4] And the late-nineteenth-century advocate of vegetarianism, Henry Salt, wrote of "one universal brotherhood" of *all innocent and beautiful life*."[5]

However much our ever changing economic, social, and scientific realities have affected our attitudes and behaviour toward animals, often harmfully, there remains inside each one of us, sometimes slumbering and waiting to be awakened, a primal sympathetic concern for other beings which has been a part of all human souls of whatever culture – albeit, in some eras, places, and individuals, a well-obscured part. The finest of the Lake Poets, William Wordsworth, called it "the primal sympathy! Which having been must ever be."[6] It is one of the moral demands of the primordial human spirit that lives eternally within us.

Unfortunately, it competes just as eternally with what the animal-embracing Russian novelist, Fyodor Dostoevsky, described as "a beast hidden within every man, a beast of rage, a beast of sensual inflammability."[7] In *The Brothers Karamazov* Dostoevsky also reminds us that beastliness is not a necessary characteristic of beasts: "people sometimes speak about the 'animal' cruelty of man, but that is terribly unjust and offensive to animals. No animal could ever be so cruel as a man, so artfully, so artistically, cruel."[8] As the renowned ethologist, Jane Goodall, has shown, chimpanzees can practise a "cruelty" which extends beyond any instinctive impulses they may possess.[9] And yet it is not so pernicious as human cruelty can be. Dostoevsky's "beast of sensual inflammability" is not the devil on the animal's shoulder. But nor, for Dostoevsky, is it an unalterable characteristic of humans either. Dostoevsky suggests that the potential for cruelty lies in every individual, but neither equally, nor consistently, nor inevitably. The magnanimous and the malevolent parts of the soul are universal. What reins in or liberates the one or the other are particular traditions, socialization, education, expectations, experience, and personal character, which in turn are affected by social, economic, political, ideological, scientific, and technological realities. If, for Dostoevsky, the "beast of rage" lives as a potential within every human, so too does the angel. And this book is the story of the angels, of those who rose to the heights their cultural and historical circumstances would allow. Or, at the very least, it is the story of those who kept the "beast" at bay long enough to allow the voice of primal sympathy to have the louder say.

Awe for the Tiger, Love for the Lamb

1
Animals in Myth and Religion

The stories of myth and religion reflect in part the cultural, social, political, and economic realities of the type of society in which they arise. The form of the society plays a significant role in moulding the consciousness of the people. We would thus expect rather different tales to emerge from hunter-gatherer, agricultural, and pastoral societies, and from expansionist urban state empires, such as those of the Maya, the Aztecs, and the Incas. Differing myths and differing religious parables are, in part, the consequences of differing everyday life experiences.

The ways in which animals are viewed and treated in a given society are thus influenced significantly by the practical realities of the human-animal economic relationship in that society. For example, we may acknowledge that in traditional Hindu India eating the cow was unacceptable in part because milk for consumption, calves for their labour, and cow dung for fuel and house-floor construction were deemed more valuable than beef.[1] If the Indian caste system, climate, and soil ensured there was inadequate fodder for an abundance of cattle, then the societal rules, expressed through religious edicts, must accord priorities. This should not persuade us, however, to ignore the fact that Brahmins and others refrained not only from the eating of beef but of all animal flesh. And such practices arose from the respect accorded to all living beings, primarily through the doctrine of reincarnation, which emphasized the kinship of all creatures. Indeed, while vegetarians are a decided minority in India, they are, by and large, deeply respected for their practices by those who are not themselves vegetarian. Economically driven societal organization is by no means all there is to a culture.

In some aboriginal societies, especially where the success of the traditional hunt was less than assured, animals were "worshipped," in the sense that they were prayed to, in order to induce their relatives, or their reincarnate selves emerged corporeally from the universal spirit, to return on a future occasion to ensure a continuing supply of animal food. Thus the "worship" was primarily for the benefit of the worshipper rather than any indication of adoration for the worshipped. Nonetheless, we should not fail to recognize that the skills, courage, strength, ingenuity, and fortitude of the prey, and of other animals which were not prey, induced an authentic respect for the animal realm. Animals faced the same trials and tribulations as humans and were entitled to a sympathetic appreciation in their perilous life journey.[2]

In the pastoral lands of the Bible we encounter injunctions to treat domesticated food animals with diligent care and concern. They will then be healthier and more productive animals, and will thereby improve the quality of human life. Caring for them is thus in part instrumental to human ends. But animals were recognized as different from human-devised instruments, such as the hoe and the plough. They were creatures of God, and as such were entitled to more than efficient treatment for human purposes. God permitted their consumption, at least after the Flood, but required that they be treated with a greater consideration than unconscious artifacts. They were breathing beings, not inanimate objects, and were thus entitled to a degree of moral consideration.[3]

It would then be unwarranted to imagine self-serving prudential considerations as the perennial determinants of human attitudes to animals. And that is true for aboriginal myths as well as Oriental and Western religions,[4] even though the particulars of each are decidedly different as a consequence of the widely differing everyday experiences occasioned by the multiplicity of societal and technological forms. To take but one example, the Talmud instructs the Jews to refrain from inflicting pain on any living creature.[5] Not only does that injunction reflect a general recognition of the entitlement of animals, whether domesticated, feral, or wild, to live free from human cruelty, but it can be seen to be a moral requirement at odds with the immediate self-interests of the predominant pastoralists and occasional hunters themselves. Animals are entitled to a significant degree of respect as the sentient beings they are, even though that entitlement constitutes a decided interference with human self-regarding convenience. If we must always look to the historical context to understand the particulars of the human-animal relationship, we must also look beyond it to understand the universal respectful elements of the human soul. All myths and religions extend consideration for the well-being of animals beyond merely self-serving prudential consideration, even though they always include those prudential considerations, and even though the interests of the adherents always exceed those of the animals. As Leo Tolstoy wrote with his customary wisdom, aplomb, and exaggeration, "religions differ in their external forms but are all the same in their basic principles."[6] Overdrawn perhaps, but the basic precept is fundamentally sound.

In the final analysis, human thoughts, sympathies, and inclinations are far more alike than dissimilar, however different the societies humans inhabit, and however different the forms through which the societal values are transmitted. The human is an animal who shares his human animality, his needs and basic values, with all his fellow humans. The culture may determine how the fundamental needs and values are pursued but does not determine what they are. These common human orientations encourage us to identify with the animals we encounter in myth, parable, fable, and story. And when we identify with those animals it is only a step to respect them for the beings they are and to feel a compassion for them in their travails.

In the selections that follow, the reader will find that however much societal forces impose themselves harmfully on animals, and however much some myths and tales distort animal reality, a natural compassion and respect for other species underlies the explicit or implicit imperatives imparted through myth and religion. And yet, in our cynical and secular age, it is commonplace to witness the derision of myth and religion. Myth is what its name is seen to imply: fable masquerading as reason. Religion is seen as an outdated superstition whose tenets have been undermined by science and philosophy. But we should listen carefully to that old saw that stories – and myth and religion are in an important sense stories – are lies which tell the truth.[7] Certainly they consist in part of parables and alle-gories, if not lies. Myth and religion, we may say, are philosophy by other, sometimes subtler, means.

Myth and religion teach us a manner of interpreting our experiences. They form, or at least inform, our values; stimulate our emotions; advise us how to act prudently and justly; and tell us who is equipped to undertake what action in what circumstances. They serve to infuse the human spirit and weld the societal bond. And they raise to the level of consciousness the permanent memories of the human soul. Evolution has selected us for practical tasks, not for the refinements of abstract thought.[8] Philosophy is not evolutionarily adaptive. Hence few are good at it. And those who are good at it are often led astray by the implications of their insightful but customarily, and almost necessarily, incomplete abstract intellectual schema. Myth and religion offer, as an at least sometimes wiser alternative, practical advice, often presented in the form of parables, tailored to the requirements of the society in which they arise.[9] Jean-Jacques Rousseau advised his philosophically over-optimistic Enlightenment colleagues that "a thinking man is a depraved being."[10] The intellect, Rousseau observed, has the capacity to lead us away from truths which intuitive feelings and early societal traditions readily impart.

Unfortunately, one of the difficulties of reporting oral myths is that there is no satisfactory way of determining how faithful are their current forms to their originals, or even whether there is an "original." Just as there are quite significant differences in the interpretation of the relationship of humans to animals between Genesis 1 and Genesis 2,[11] written by different persons perhaps centuries apart, so too there are different versions of aboriginal myths. As sagely said by !Unn/Obe, a Ju/Hoan woman of southern Africa, "Yes, of course, some people tell stories one way, some another. Perhaps it is because people sometimes separate for a while and go on telling stories. But in all these stories about the old times, people use different words and nouns for the same things. There are many different ways to talk. Different people just have different minds."[12] Different versions of the same stories, while containing significant similarities, will have variations that alter the message, sometimes slightly, sometimes rather more substantively. And just as Western philosophy altered over the centuries to incorporate the effects of newly emerging social and economic classes, increased secular education, and new technological capabilities, so too new aboriginal experiences in changing social, economic, and political conditions will have influenced their myths to incorporate a relevant response to those new conditions. Without a written record we lack the evidence to know what is old and what is new. And, as with the differences between Genesis 1 and Genesis 2, so too with aboriginal accounts, we do not know which versions more closely reflect the early mind of a people.

A part of the problem is that we have grounds for distrust when the myths are reported by those with an ideological axe to grind. A century and more ago the forms in which those myths were presented sometimes showed a lack of understanding of, and sympathy for, aboriginal culture. By contrast, since the middle of the nineteenth century, and most especially in recent decades, those myths have sometimes been manipulated to read as a telling critique of Western mores, particularly as a wiser alternative to Western environmental degradation. Thus, for example, the form in which the famous nineteenth-century environmentalist speech of Chief Seattle of the Duwamish is customarily reported is a 1970s invention of an American film director, bearing very little resemblance to early reports of that speech, which are not themselves without grounds for suspicion.[13] The version now customarily encountered corresponds far more to modern Western environmentalist ideals than to Amerindian forms of thought and expression. What we are offered is a distortion of the reality. If one wants to understand the import of aboriginal myth one must endeavour to be faithful to traditional forms of thought. Accordingly, several appealing legends have been omitted from this volume because I could not feel confident of their authenticity. Aboriginal myths contain both beauty and wisdom; they do not need to be distorted.

.As societal belief systems change to accommodate new eventualities, the prevailing stories are adjusted to meet the contingencies of the new circumstances. Thus when Christianity was adopted as the official religion of Rome, and then spread across Europe, it retained a number of earlier myths, yet Christianized, or denominationalized, and localized them. Thus were the holly, the maypole, and the Christmas tree incorporated into the Christian myth to hinder a psychological discord between the traditional and the new. One popular story was that after the Christian slave Androcles removed a thorn from the paw of a lion in distress, the pair became fast friends. Later Androcles was forced to engage a lion in combat in the Roman amphitheatre. The king of the beasts recognized his benefactor and greeted him with kindness. In Western Europe the story was transformed into a Catholic St. Jerome and the lion,[14] in Eastern Europe to an Orthodox St. Sergey and the bear.[15] The underlying moral message was that saintly persons would be compassionate to other species. As the Christian world later commercialized, then industrialized, different aspects of the Christian tradition were emphasized to encourage congruence between economic and religious imperatives. Just as with the Christian tradition, then, we can be confident that as societal circumstances altered in other societies, so their myths will have been adjusted to meet the needs of the changing popular consciousness and the permanent spirit of the people, although the changes will have been less than those that occurred in the West. All this should encourage us to be careful in the interpretation of any particular myth and what it means to society. And the further removed from contemporary consciousness and experience the myth is, the more circumspect we need to be.

We should not assume that treating animals well in myth or religion means that they were well treated in fact – in whatever culture. A medieval father may well have related the story of St. Jerome and the lion to the children of an evening before participating at a cockfight the next morning, more or less sanctioned by the clergy and held on Church property[16] – though the priests themselves were forbidden to attend by their bishops. Just as we recognize the New Testament exhortations to peace and altruism[17] as ideals rather than as a description of Christian practice, so too we must understand the moral implications of myth, fables, and stories as expressions of ideals. Nonetheless, we should also understand that the myth is often telling us how honourable people in fact behave, or are expected to behave. And given the greater congruence between myth and the everyday experience of aboriginal societies, we may expect their myths to come rather closer to practice than does Western religion to current Western norms. Nonetheless, throughout the vicissitudes of history and culture, we will be encouraged to find that there is something common to all experience: an awareness that when humans are at their best, and there are no countervailing pressures, they care for their fellow creatures.

In the first chapter the reader will find more commentary about the meaning of selected passages than in subsequent chapters. As we approach our own era, the quotations speak increasingly for themselves. In the earlier chapters, however, we are treating forms of thought and modes of expression that are no longer, or never have been, customary to the modern Western mind. The meanings of the more recent contributors to animal respect are more or less clear; the thoughts and ideals of those who are culturally or temporally distant from us are frequently opaque and require exposition. In the later chapters, the commentary is intended, by and large, to do little more than to place the ideas in their immediate historical, political, or social contexts, and to indicate the relationship between those ideas.

Amerindian Legends

I have selected two Cheyenne myths to represent the Amerindian way of life and thought, though there are significant variations in myths among Amerindian nations. One of the advantages of choosing Cheyenne myths is that they were collected at the Cheyenne Agency in Oklahoma in 1899 by representatives of the American Museum of Natural History. While there remains the perennial problem of expressing the self-identifying ideas of one culture in the language of another, and while we can feel confident that experience of European culture in general, and of European oppression of the Natives in particular, affected the substance of the myths to some degree, at least we can be sure the myths have not been altered in the last century to accommodate the experiences of new technology, changed societal norms, and the re-orientations engendered by the continuing clash of cultures.[18]

Even though Cheyenne myths stand as representations of Cheyenne experience, there is something common to all Amerindian thought that makes them representative of the tradition as a whole, despite the differences among nations. Moreover, choosing two myths from the same people allows one to appreciate both consistency and continuity. Within any culture each myth can be understood in part as a corroboration and elaboration of other myths, though there are occasional inconsistencies too, as with the Bible, the Qur'an, the Vedic Laws of Manu, and perhaps all such texts. The Cheyenne creation myth and the buffalo hunt myth are the tales chosen, the first serving in large part to *explain* the original ideals of the community, the second serving, *inter alia*, to *justify* the required new behaviour.

The Creation Myth of the Cheyenne

In the beginning the Great Medicine created the earth, and the waters upon the earth, and the sun, moon, and stars. Then he made a beautiful country to spring up in the far north. There were no winters, with ice and snow and bitter cold. It was always spring; wild fruits and berries grew everywhere, and great trees shaded the streams of clear water that flowed through the land.

In this beautiful country the Great Medicine put animals, birds, insects, and fish of all kinds. Then he created human beings to live with the other creatures. Every animal, big and small, every bird, big and small, every fish, and every insect could talk to the people and understand them. The people could understand each other, for they had a common language and lived in friendship. They went naked and fed on honey and wild fruits; they were never hungry. They wandered everywhere among the wild animals, and when night came and they were weary, they lay down on the cool grass and slept. During the days they talked with the other animals, for they were all friends.

The Great Spirit created three kinds of human beings: first, those who had hair all over their bodies; second, white men who had hair all over their heads and faces and on their legs; third, red men who had very long hair on their heads only. The hairy people were strong and active. The white people with the long beards were in a class with the wolf, for both were the trickiest and most cunning creatures in that beautiful world. The red people were good runners, agile and swift, whom the Great Medicine taught to catch and eat fish at a time when none of the other people knew about eating meat.

After a while the hairy people left the north country and went south, where all the land was barren. Then the red people prepared to follow the hairy people into the south. Before they left the beautiful land, however, the Great Medicine called them together. On this occasion, the first time the red people had all assembled in one place, the Great Medicine blessed them and gave them some medicine spirit to awaken their dormant minds. From that time on they seemed to possess intelligence and know what to do. The Great Medicine singled out one of the men and told him to teach people to band together, so that they all could work and clothe their naked bodies with skins of panther and bear and deer. The Great Medicine gave them the power to hew and shape flint and other stones into any shape they wanted ... into arrow- and spear-heads and into cups, pots, and axes ... The hairy people remained naked but the red people clothed themselves because the Great Medicine had told them to ...

After the red men had lived in the south for some time, the Great Medicine told them to return north, for the barren southland was going to be flooded. When they went back to that beautiful northern land, they found that the white-skinned and long-bearded people and some of the wild animals were gone. They were no longer able to talk to the animals, but this time they controlled all other creatures, and they taught the panther, the bear, and similar beasts to catch game for them. They increased in numbers and became tall and strong and active.

After several migrations, floods, and other ecological disasters:

The people returned to the south and lived as well as they could, in some years better, in others worse. After many hundreds of years, just before the winter season came, the earth shook, and the high hills sent forth fire and smoke. During that winter there were great floods. The people had to dress in furs and live in caves, for the winter was long and cold. It destroyed all the trees, though when spring came there was a new growth. The red men suffered much and were almost famished when the Great Medicine took pity on them. He gave them corn to plant and buffalo for meat, and from that time there were no more floods and no more famines.

The people continued to live in the south, and they grew and increased. There were many different bands with different languages, for the red men were never united after the second flood.

The descendants of the original Cheyenne had men among them who were magicians and with supernatural wisdom. They charmed not only their own people, but also the animals that they lived on. No matter how fierce or wild the beast, it became so tame that people could go up to it and handle it. The magic knowledge was handed down from the original Cheyenne who came from the far north ... ("Great Medicine Makes a Beautiful Country")[19]

The Cheyenne creation myth is one of the most illuminating legends from among the many thousands of aboriginal legends collected from around the world. The myth compilers Erdoes and Ortiz describe it as "this remarkable tale" in which "is stored the memory of much that has happened to the Cheyenne over many hundreds of years."[20] But it is much more than that too. It represents a universal history of humankind. The particulars may be different but, in essence, the human story is the same everywhere. And it is a story that includes the central elements of the human-animal relationship.

The similarity of the Cheyenne creation myth to many other stories of societal origins from around the world is astonishing. Many, perhaps all, peoples claim a special relationship between themselves and their Creator. Many view the site and conditions of their earliest communal memory as a paradise – a prelapsarian Eden – a place of primal perfection where humans, animals, and environment exist in idyllic harmony, where humans and animals speak to and understand each other, and are friends. There is no need of shelter or clothing.

All of these conditions are met in the Cheyenne myth. But we encounter them equally elsewhere, and not only in the tales of other Amerindian nations. In Japan *natsukashii* refers to an ideal earlier time that was conflict free, and to a yearning to return to the site of natural harmony. The Pitjantjara Aborigines of Australia revere *tjukurpa* – a dreamtime of mystical past harmonies. We find similar legends among the Bassari of West Africa and the Makritare of the Orinoco,[21] and in ancient India and China.[22] In the eighth-century-BC writings of Hesiod in Presocratic Greece we meet the first written idea of a Golden Age, a prior era of perfect peace revered in oral myth which did not brook the slaughter of our fellow creatures.[23] The theme was repeated by Empedocles, Plutarch, Porphyry, Virgil, and Tacitus among others. It was then taken up again in Boethius's sixth-century-AD *The Consolation of Philosophy*,[24] in Geoffrey Chaucer's "The Former Age" in the fourteenth century, and hinted at in Chaucer's *The Canterbury Tales* when he writes of "those far off days [when] All birds and animals could speak and sing."[25] In the early seventeenth century Shakespeare addressed it in *The Tempest*[26] and in the eighteenth century the mythical Golden Age was a common theme of the poets and essay writers.[27]

Most strikingly, we find a similar image not only in the Eden of Genesis but in the peaceable kingdom ideal of Isaiah 11 where "the wolf will live with the lamb, the panther lie down with the kid" and in Romans 8 where "the whole creation ... [which] has been groaning in labour pains ... might be freed from its slavery to corruption."[28] The early memories and ideals of humankind demonstrate some remarkable similarities with regard to our relationship to our original environment and our desire to recapture its innocence; and they are not yet entirely lost in the development of a civilization that removes us so far from them. A number of books and pamphlets advocating a vegetarian diet at the turn of the nineteenth century were based around them.[29] The societal tension between original nature and contemporary culture pervades all societies, though not all in the same degree.

In the Cheyenne creation myth the age of perfect environmental peace is destroyed by natural disasters. (One assumes, both from the context and for the sake of consistency with other myths, that the initial move south at the behest of the Great Medicine [called the Great Power in other versions] was a consequence of an early natural disaster not spelled out in the myth. Later catastrophes, most of which are not reproduced here, are explicit in the myth). Again, the cross-cultural similarities are remarkable. The flood story is found among the Sumerians, Babylonians, Hebrews, Hindus, Greeks, and others,[30] including other Amerindian nations.[31] Indeed, all societies will, one presumes, have retained a cultural memory of the floods occasioned by the end of the last Ice Age. These natural disasters are usually seen to prompt an altered human relationship to nature and to other species. It is notable that in the Cheyenne myth the wolf is as despised as the white man, and as despised as its traditional European counterpart too, as indicated not only by the fairy tale of *The Three Little Pigs* but by the philosopher Immanuel Kant who tells us that when we observe how great is the care animals give to their young it is difficult for us to be cruel in thought to them – and then adds: "even to a wolf."[32] Not all animals, or people, are equal for either the Europeans or the Cheyenne.

Having lived in peaceful harmony with the environment in "the state of nature," including with animals which would later become harmful to humans and human interests, so the myths indicate, humans were constrained to become carnivores – indeed, paradoxically, the Cheyenne express a cultural pride in having become the first human carnivores. They began to use animal skins for clothing and tent coverings, to cut down trees to provide fuel for fires and the framework for homes, and to live a life of reason rather than of nature or instinct – the Great Medicine gave the Cheyenne "medicine spirit to awaken their dormant minds. From that time on they seemed to possess intelligence." In Genesis too (9:3), it is only after the Flood that God grants the Jews the right to eat animals, presumably because the environmental changes occasioned by the Flood have rendered a vegetarian lifestyle impractical. And it is only after eating of the tree of knowledge that humans become creatures of rational thought. Whether there was such a vegetarian and environmentally harmonious period in early human history is still hotly contested; but what is clear is that the development of such myths indicates that many peoples felt that hunting and eating animals were activities which required a moral justification – or at least a permit from the Great Power. There is no need for a justification for behaviour that is considered in and of itself admirable, or even otherwise acceptable. Certainly, it is notable that after the floods humans no longer conversed with the animals but were their masters – the Cheyenne "controlled all other creatures" and in Genesis the animals "are placed in your hands." Once animal society was egalitarian, now it is hierarchical. Human culture and original nature are inextricably at odds, ensuring that there will be an ongoing tension between cultural aspirations and primordial ideals.

The message of so many traditions, exemplified by the Cheyenne creation myth, is of a now unattainable ideal in which humans, animals, and nature lived as one. The changes brought about, at least metaphorically, by the natural catastrophes have rendered that ideal impractical, or so the myths indicate. Thus, metaphorically, one was "no longer able to talk to the animals" – that is, human and animal interests were no longer in accord. Nonetheless, the initial harmony remained as an ideal to be approximated to the extent that the new circumstances would allow. Even those animals that now had to be killed were entitled to respect, especially for the sacrifice they had to make to permit humans to live.

While the Cheyenne creation myth is important for what it tells us about the Cheyenne attitude to animals and nature, it is also far more than that. It represents the human condition. It epitomizes the circumstances all humans have faced, and continue to face, with regard to the human-animal nexus. To understand the tensions that have underlain the attitudes toward our fellow animals throughout human history there is perhaps no better starting point than this Cheyenne creation legend.

The Cheyenne Legend of the Origins of the Buffalo Hunt

The buffalo formerly ate man. The magpie and the hawk were on the side of the people, for neither ate the other or the people. These two birds flew away from a council between animals and man. They determined that a race would be held, the winners to eat the losers.

The course was long, round a mountain. The swiftest buffalo was a cow called Nelka, "swift head." She believed she would win and entered the race. On the other hand, the people were afraid because of the long distance. They were trying to get medicine to overcome the fatigue.

All the birds painted themselves for the race, and since that time they have all
been brightly covered. Even the water turtle put red paint around his eyes. The
magpie painted himself white on head, shoulders and tail. At last all were ready for
the race, and stood in a row for the start.

They ran and ran, making loud noises in place of singing to help themselves run
faster. All small birds, turtles, rabbits, coyotes, wolves, flies, ants, insects, and snakes
were soon left far behind. When they approached the mountain the buffalo-cow
was ahead; then came the magpie, hawk and the people; the rest were strung out
along the way. The dust rose so quickly that nothing could be seen.

All around the mountain the buffalo-cow led the race, but the two birds knew
they could win, and merely kept up with her until they neared the finish line, which
was back to the starting place. Then both birds whooshed by her and won the race
for man. As they flew the course, they had seen fallen animals and birds all over the
place, who had run themselves to death, turning the ground and rocks red from
blood.

The buffalo then told their young to hide from the people, who were going out
to hunt them; and also told them to take some human flesh with them for the last
time. The young buffaloes did this, and stuck that meat in front of their chests,
beneath the throat. Therefore, the people did not eat that part of the buffalo, saying it is part human flesh.

From that day forward the Cheyenne began to hunt buffalo. Since all the friendly
animals were on the people's side, they are not eaten by people, but they do wear
and use their beautiful feathers for adornments.

Another version adds that when coyote, who was on the side of the buffalo, finished the race, the magpie, who even beat the hawk, said to coyote, "We will not
eat you, but only use your skin." ("How the Buffalo Hunt Began")[33]

The initial dictum of "How the Buffalo Hunt Began" is that the human
killing of animals for food is not a primordially natural behaviour but
requires a justification, and a justification is duly offered. The point is made
that nonhuman animals are not in harmony with each other either. Nature
has become in part a realm of conflict – it was not so prior to the natural
disasters – and in part a realm of continued symbiosis, of continued
mutual aid. There is an acknowledgment that humans are in some respects
the inferiors of other creatures, possessing the speed of neither the buffalo
nor the birds. In fact, if the Cheyenne are not to be the continued prey of
the buffalo, which are superior in strength as well as speed, they require
the assistance of other species that are "on the side of the people."

Of course, bison are ruminants not carnivores, and hence were never
predators, but for the Cheyenne, given the potential superiority implied
by the bisons' strength, speed, and size, their failure to devour humans
required an explanation. So too did the variety of animal and rock
colouration. Given the lack of biological, evolutionary, and geological
explanation, legends must be developed to allow the people to accommodate

the unexplained with their understanding. Indeed, it is a remarkable testimony to the similarity and continuity of human minds that even once scientific explanation was at hand, the Western public was still enthralled by alternative mythological explanations of natural phenomena. Rudyard Kipling's *Just So Stories* (1902) of "How the Whale got his Throat," "How the Camel got his Hump," "How the Rhinoceros got his Skin," and "How the Leopard got his Spots,"[34] for example, were no doubt read a great deal more often than Charles Darwin's *Origin of Species,* even though the *Origin* sold out its 1,250 copies on the first day of publication in 1859. One does not have to believe in the purported facts of myths, legends, and stories for them to be of value to the minds of a people – whether in the former British Empire or among the Cheyenne.

The rule that a small part of the buffalo must not be eaten serves as a reminder that in an ideal world there would be no conflict between the interests of the human and those of the buffalo. It serves too as a reminder that buffalo and humans are fellow animals, that eating a fellow animal is in small measure akin to cannibalism – hence the human flesh at the buffalo's throat – however much buffalo and human interests have now come to diverge, and however much flesh-eating is now acknowledged to be a justifiable practice.

The norm has its counterpart in Genesis 9:4 where, after the Jews were informed they may now consume meat, they were also told "you must not eat flesh with life, that is to say, blood in it." Blood was deemed the essence of life that may not be consumed. As with the Cheyenne, the Jews understood thereby that flesh-eating was not to be taken lightly, that humans and animals shared the spark of life in common, and that meat consumption was a right granted by the Creator in special circumstances, not a natural human right derived from human primordial nature.[35]

The Cheyenne buffalo hunt legend also offers an explanation of why even the young buffalo may be difficult to hunt. The buffalo parents have explained to their offspring the purpose of the hunters. The Cheyenne must thus learn the ways of the buffalo to hunt them not only successfully but also respectfully, for they have a human element within them.

Despite the conflicts of interest between predator and prey, there were still friendly animals and birds, those that did not need to be hunted for their meat or their hides. In these instances the symbiotic human-animal relationship of the time of conflict-free paradise remained in principle, but even here there is an acknowledgment that this relationship no longer existed in fact, for the "beautiful feathers" of the birds were taken for human decoration. To be sure, in the Cheyenne legend "Eagle War Feathers"[36] it is the eagles themselves who suggest their feathers be plucked to provide martial ornament. In fact, of course, the eagles did no such thing. But it was important to encourage among the Cheyenne a recognition of their obligations to their allies. Any deviation must be in compliance with the will of the friendly animals themselves. While this may be viewed as no more than a rationalization of Cheyenne self-interest – since, in fact, the eagles would object strenuously to being deprived of their protective feathers – it should also be recognized as an acknowledgment that the interests of other animals matter and that when we behave as our better selves we act in accordance with that principle.

It is notable that it is not the Cheyenne who have deemed it acceptable that the coyote be hunted for the hide alone, thus using only a part of the slaughtered animal. It is the magpie, the winner of the race on behalf of the Cheyenne, who punished the coyote for being "on the side of the buffalo." Nature is not itself at one, but is divided in enmity between the animals supporting the Cheyenne and those supporting the buffalo. The Cheyenne are thus not at odds with animated nature itself, only with a part of it, and that part, so the myth tells us, has only itself to blame. Again, the consistency with Western myth is striking. When Ovid accounts for the origins of Western flesh-eating in *Metamorphoses* he informs us the blame is laid on the pigs and the goats themselves. The pig: "is thought to have been the first victim to meet a well-deserved fate, because it rooted out the seeds with its upturned snout, and destroyed the hope of harvest. Then the goat, they say was sacrificed at Bachus' altars, as a punishment for having gnawed his vines. Both had themselves to blame."[37]

Cheyenne potential guilt differs from Western potential guilt for the use of only a part of the animal in that, according to the myth, it is one of the coyote's fellow nonhuman animals who has legitimized the hunting for the fur alone. The killing of our fellow creatures has been necessitated by the vicissitudes of our environmental history – the climate no longer permits humans to go naked – but it is deemed acceptable because other animals, not the Cheyenne themselves, so the myth says, have deemed it appropriate. Respect for nature remains, but the conflicts between humans and some animals have diminished, if not eradicated, the original mutual friendship. The essential message remains: animals are worthy of our respect, and we are obligated to many of them for their assistance in this life of conflict, filled with the demands of competing interests, among which human-animal competing interests are significant.

Thus the Cheyenne tales of creation and the beginning of the buffalo hunt provide a description of the moral context – the conflict between nature and culture, between sentiment and reality, between Eden and Arcadia, between primordiality and civilization – in which the human understanding of our responsibility to our fellow animals is played out.

Tales of the African Bushman
In reading aboriginal legends we will look in vain for explicit ethical pronouncements on our appropriate relationship to other species. The discourse of myth is not of that genre and if we do find explicit ethical

pronouncements included we can be confident they have been interpolated by a modern commentator with a point to make. Attitudes to animals can nonetheless be recognized as implicit within the traditional tales. And, of course, there are thousands of such tales to choose from. I have made the selections on the basis of how representative they are while trying to include examples of the different forms in which the stories are told.

The great French anthropologist Claude Lévi-Strauss wrote with regard to aboriginal society "Animals are good to think [with]."[38] People think their thoughts in substantial part through animal analogy stressing on the one hand our similarities, and on the other our differences, to other species. In *Tricksters and Trancers: Bushman Religion and Society*[39] the anthropologist Mathias Guenther has shown that African Bushmen epitomize that tradition of thinking. Some of their myths stress human-animal similarities with a corresponding respect for other species, others emphasize the particulars of a species which differentiates them from humans and colours attitudes toward them. The first story demonstrates in its entrancingly sonorous musical form that, whatever other differences there may be between humans and animals, in the final analysis all are equal in their mortality – a message also stressed in Ecclesiastes 3: "the fate of the human and the fate of the animal is the same: as the one dies, so the other dies."[40] Death is to be regretted and, for the Bushmen, it is the moon's immortality that is envied. The moon is speaking:

I die, I live; living, I come again;
I become a new moon.
Man dies; man, indeed, dies; dying he leaves his wife.
When I die, I return, living.
The gemsbock. The gemsbock dies, the gemsbock dies altogether.
  The hartebeest. The hartebeest dies, the hartebeest dies, altogether.
The she-ostrich. It dies, it indeed dies.
The kudu. The kudu indeed dies, and dying, it goes away.
The springbok. The springbok dies, and dying, it goes away forever,
Myself, I die; living again, I come back.
The korhaan [bustard]. The korhaan dies; the korhaan, dying, goes away.
The cat does [die]; it dies. The cat goes away, dying.
The jackal. The jackal dies; dying, the jackal goes away.
The lynx goes away, dying.
The hyena. The hyena dies, it goes away, dying, dying.
The eland dies. The eland dies and dying, it leaves.
Myself I die. Living again, I come back.
People see me; people say: "Look, the Moon does indeed lie here;
  it is grown, it is a Full Moon."
Things which are flesh must indeed die ...
(/Xam youth /A!kunta)[41]

All animals are alike in their mortality, and it is a matter of regret.

In the second myth the emphasis is on the distinction between predator and prey species, somewhat reminiscent of the Cheyenne "How the Buffalo Hunt Began," and on how each behaves according to unalterable species characteristics, which must be respected, as must the role of gender. Life for all, including humankind, is ordained by intrinsic nature, not by the will.

> Then the anteater [woman] says: "Springbok stand! The Lynx will kill you, for you are a springbok that eats grass ... Lynx stand! You eat springbok. Springbok stand! The lynx will catch you and eat you for you are a springbok ..."
>
> Then the hyena marries the female hyena, for the hyena feels that he is a hyena, who eats people. He therefore puts his children into a burrow, because he has married a female hyena. He brings to the hyena children, to the burrow, an ostrich. The hyena children then eat the ostrich ... Then the jackal becomes a jackal. He marries a female jackal, for he is a beast of prey. Once he was a man ...
>
> Then the silver-backed jackal marries a she-jackal. He puts the children into a hollow. For the strandwolf puts the strandwolf children into a hollow. For the strandwolf feels to marry a shestrandwolf who lives in a hollow.
>
> Then the aardwolf marries a she-aardwolf and because he realized that she lives in a cave he puts the aardwolf children into a cave. (//Kabbo, /Xam Bushman, Mowbray, Cape Province, 1871)[42]

In the final Bushman story we can recognize the complexity of myth in that, in contrast to the prey-predator distinction alone, the hare is singled out for special treatment. The hare plays the same role as the serpent in Genesis 3: "the snake was the most subtle of all the wild animals ... the snake tempted me," said Eve. For the Bushman it is the hare who is the beguiler, the deceiver, and the cause of human downfall. He deceives the moon, and in return all are condemned to death.

> When I told the hare about it – knowing that his mother was not dead but only asleep – the hare said no, his mother did not sleep, but his mother had really died. It was this that I became angry about, thinking that the hare might say: "Yes, my mother is asleep ... She lies sleeping; she will arise presently."
>
> If the hare had believed the Moon we, who are people, would have come to be like the Moon; we should not die, altogether. The Moon cursed us on account of the hare's doings, and we die, altogether. (Dia! Kwain, /Xam Bushman, Mowbray, Cape Province, 1871)[43]

To the Western mind, the selection of the hare to represent deception might at first sight appear puzzling. It is less so on reflection. Unlike many other prey animals, when the hare is hunted he appears lackadaisical, unconcerned, almost distracted. When approached, he shows no apparent awareness of danger, no preparation for flight, no frigid fright. At the very last moment he moves with disarming speed and dexterity, often escaping his predator, including his human predator, by his intricate manoeuvres. He is transformed in an instant from apparent tranquillity to energetic spontaneity. He is thus the great deceiver, the destroyer of hopes and expectations. He takes away what the hunter has decided is his. The hare is respected for his abilities, as is the serpent as the symbol of knowledge and wisdom in Genesis, but they are both denigrated for deceiving humans and bringing them great loss. Hence the Bushman has "hated the hare ever since"[44] and the Biblical snake is told (Genesis 3:14): "Accursed be you of all animals wild and tame!" The contrast between some animals and others and between animals in different roles is a pervasive theme of all cultures, both historically and currently.

The Zebra Story of the Shona of Zimbabwe

The zebra poem of the Shona of southeast Africa is of recent vintage but reflects a traditional Shona story and traditional Shona attitudes and values. For the Shona, zebras are not only beautiful and mysterious, they also symbolize peace and goodwill. They are recognized as the owners of the land they inhabit. Those who would take and use the land, the poem suggests, are infringing on the zebra's prerogative. It is only with the zebra's acquiescence that land use by humans is legitimate.

> Thank you, Zebra,
> Adorned with your own stripes,
> Iridescent and glittering creature,
> Whose skin is as soft as girls' is;
> One on which the eye dwells all day, as on the solitary cow of a poor man;
> Creature that makes the forests beautiful,
> Weaver of lines
> Who wear your skin for display,
> Drawn with lines so clearly defined;
> You who throw beads in patterns,
> Dappled fish
> Hatching around the neck of a pot;
> Beauty spots cut to rise in a crescent on the forehead,
> A patterned belt for the waist:
> Light reflected
> Dazzling the eyes.
> It is its own instinct, the Zebra's,
> Adorned as if with strings of beads around the waist as women are;
> Wild creature without anger or any grudge,
> Lineage with a totem that is nowhere a stranger,
> Line that stretches everywhere,
> Owners of the land.[45]

The Nigerian Elephant

Again, though modern in form, this Nigerian story is traditional in out-look. While the zebra represents beauty and grace, the elephant is saluted for his grandeur and power, of which the human can only stand in awe.

Elephant, opulent creature, elephant, huge as a hill even when kneeling:
Elephant, robed in honour, a demon, flapping fans of war:
Demon who splinters the tree branches, invading the forest farm:
Elephant, who disregards "I have fled to my father for refuge,"
Let alone "To my mother";
Mountainous animal, Huge Beast, who tears a man like a garment and hangs
   him up on a tree:
At the sight of him people stampede to a hill of safety:
My chant is a salute to the elephant.
Ajanaku, who treads heavily:
Demon who swallows bunches of palm-fruits whole, including the spikes:
Elephant, praise-named Laaye, massive blackish-grey creature:
Elephant, who single-handed makes the dense forest tremble:
Elephant, who stands sturdy and upright, who strolls as if reluctantly:
Elephant, whom one sees and points at with all one's fingers. The hunter's
   boast at home is not repeated when he really meets the elephant,
Ajanaku, who looks backwards with difficulty like a man with a stiff neck;
Elephant, who has a head pad but carries no load,
Elephant, whose burden is the huge head he balances:
Elephant, praise-named Laaye, "O death, please stop following me,"
This is part and parcel of the elephant's appellation.
Learn of the elephant, the waterman elephant,
Elephant, honour's equal, elephant who constantly swings his trunk like a
   fly-whisk,
Elephant, whose eyes are like water-jars,
Elephant, the greatest of wanderers, whose molar teeth are as big as
   palm-oil pits in Ijesaland.
Elephant, lord of the forest, praise-named Oriribobo,
Elephant, whose tusks are like shafts,
One of whose tusks is a porter's whole load, elephant, praise-named Otiko,
   with the mighty neck,
Elephant, whom the hunter sometimes sees face to face, elephant, whom the
   hunter at other times sees from the rear,
Elephant, who carries mortars, yet walks with a swaggering gait,
Primeval leper, animal treading ponderously.[46]

Nature's Law and the Aboriginal Way: An Australian Narrative

The following account of "nature's law" comes from Big Bill Neidjie, an elder of the Bunitj clan of the Australian Kakadu people. It is a late-twentieth-century expression of aboriginal values, although, again, the words reflect age-old values. However, their recent vintage allows us to see how Australian Aborigines distinguish between the tribal law they are exhorted to follow and their experience of the injunctions of Western law. For Australian Native peoples, indeed for Aboriginals generally, the appropriate way of life is heavily informed by tradition. Their belief is that the traditions of society reflect the wisdom of humans in their origins, especially with regard to nature and other species, as interpreted through the society's historical experiences. Thus the law looks backward to an undeviating conception of the right way to do things, originating in what they call "the dreamtime," a mystical Golden Age of a tribal past when all the great moral and practical questions were settled, including those of one's appropriate relationship to animals and nature. By contrast, European law is seen as ever-evolving and trying vainly to meet the contingencies of constantly changing practical realities and cultural norms.

Western conceptions were not, however, always entirely at odds with aboriginal notions. At one time in the early West, moral questions were settled by the edicts of the Ten Commandments, which Moses received from God, and which were said to be "inscribed by the finger of God." (Exodus 31:18). The Gospel of St. John opens: "In the beginning was the Word," that is, the appropriate way to act was settled at creation. A traditional Christian prayer informs us that, "as it was in the beginning, is now, and ever shall be ..." If the Western and aboriginal conceptions of law have diverged as a consequence of vastly differing historical experiences, we may still recognize a commonality that united them in a distant past. Indeed, toward the close of the eighteenth century, Edmund Burke was still admonishing his contemporaries to respect "the wisdom of ages," reminding them that "People will not look forward to posterity, who never look backward to their ancestors," and that "the sole authority" of constitutional law "is that it has existed time out of mind."

Just as it was in the now largely forgotten Western conception of the Golden Age, an Edenic paradise, so too in the Aborigine dreamtime all of nature is kin. Shakespeare's "One touch of nature makes the whole world kin" (Ulysses in *Troilus and Cressida,* 3, 3) is reminiscent of Australian aboriginal conceptions. For Bill Neidjie, all animals are alike in that humans and other species must struggle equally for survival. All are alike in that they must pursue their natural ends as the beings they are, always have been, and always will be. Knowing the difficulties we encounter in our own lives, we should respect other animals in theirs, for they face similar problems. It is thus that they are both our kin and our kindred travaillers.

Law never change ...
Always stay same.
Maybe it hard,
but proper one for all people.

Not like white European law ...
Always changing
If you don't like it, you can change.

Aboriginal law never change.
Old people tell us.
"You got to keep it."
It always stays ...

People look for food,
Animal look for food.
Lizard look, bird look,
We all same ...

This ground and this earth ...
Like brother and mother.

You know eagle?
Eagle our brother,
like dingo our brother.[47]

Oriental Traditions

Just as Jews, Christians, and Muslims find a common heritage in the Old Testament, so too do Jaina, Hindus, and Buddhists pay a common homage to many early East Indian religious writings. These writings are revered in all three traditions, though each lays greater stress on certain texts that they regard as their own. Nonetheless, as we shall see, despite the considerable variety of books, there are great similarities in content – indeed, frequent repetition to the point of duplication can be found.

Eastern religious traditions have described the appropriate relationship of human to nonhuman animal far more explicitly than we find in either the aboriginal or early Western traditions. Indeed, human duties toward other species are often expressed as explicit ethical pronouncements rather than implied in parables and legends. While it is possible to find instances of animal disdain in these traditions,[48] as in all traditions, the greater weight is emphatically on the side of a profound ethical responsibility. Nonetheless, it is not always easy to be confident of the precise content of some of those ethical pronouncements. In part, it is because of the difficulties of translation, or because sometimes the interpreters appear to want to include in their translations what they see as the implications of the passage translated instead of being content to let the passages speak for themselves. Three translations of the same passage from the *Ishopanishad* may serve to illustrate the problem:

1 The entire universe and everything in it, animate and inanimate, is His. Let us treat everything around us reverently, as custodians. We have no charter for dominion. All wealth is commonwealth. Let us enjoy, but neither hoard nor kill. The humble frog has as much right to live as we. (G. Naganathan)[49]

2 This whole universe must be pervaded by a Lord -/ Whatever moves in this moving [world]./ Abandon it, and then enjoy:/ Covet not the goods of anyone at all. (R.C. Zaehner)[50]

3 Behold the universe in the glory of God; and all that lives and moves on earth. Leaving the transient, find joy in the Eternal: set not your heart on another's possession. (Juan Mascaró)[51]

Reading Naganathan's version one imagines the passage to be primarily concerned with a profound compassion for the earth's creatures, including the least of animals. Zaehner's version suggests the passage is not concerned with our relationship to animated nature at all. And Mascaró does little more than remind us that we should recognize God's goodness in all his creation. Clearly, there are competing, and scarcely compatible, ways of viewing the same pronouncement. One must accordingly be wary of the interpretations sometimes put on certain Indian passages. Nonetheless, we should not fail to recognize that these traditional passages, taken as a whole, show a clear and decisive recognition of human responsibilities toward animals.[52]

The perfect devotee of the Lord is one who sees Atman [the principle of life] in all creatures as an expression of the Supreme Being and all beings as dwelling in the supreme spirit. (*Bhagavatam*)[53]

Ahimsa (Non-injury), truth, non-stealing, continence and non-possession are the five major vows which are concomitant to charitra (conduct). (*Yoga Shastra of Hemchandracharya*)[54]

Ahimsa — meaning avoidance from the infliction of injury or harm — is in origin a Jain principle, and the *Yoga Shastra* is a Jain text; but the principle was readily adopted by both Hindus and Buddhists in a pantheistic conception of God's presence in all creatures. *Ahimsa* applies to the treatment of all living creatures, if not with equal force, and may be said to constitute the core of Indian ethical thought in the same manner that the Golden Rule of Matthew 7:12 – "So always treat others as you would like them to treat you" – is deemed the central principle of Christianity.

Ahimsa is the highest dharma [religious principle, duty, or caste requirement], self-control, gift, penance, sacrifice, power, friend, happiness, truth [and] scripture. (*Mahabharata*)[55]

We bow to all beings with great reverence in the thought and knowledge that God enters into them through fractioning himself as living creatures. (*Mahabharata*)[56]

Everyone in the [meat] business, the one who cuts, the one who kills, the one who sells, the one who prepares, the one who offers, the one who eats; all are killers. (*Mahabharata*)[57]

As noted already, while only a relatively small proportion of Hindus and Buddhists are vegetarian by ethical or religious principle, such Eastern doctrines have encouraged even many meat-eaters to have a profound respect for those who eschew flesh. Yet the doctrine itself appears to be somewhat less than hard and fast, even for Brahmins. Thus, for example, in his *Hindu Ethics: A Historical and Critical Essay*, John Mackenzie has argued that the vegetarian principle was considerably weakened in practice through, for example, the Laws of Manu which he quotes as follows:

One may eat meat when it has been sprinkled with water, while Mantras were recited, when Brahmanas desire (one's doing it), when one is engaged (in the performance of a rite) according to the law, and when one's life is in danger.[58]

Again:

He who eats meat, when he honours the gods and manes, commits no sin, whether he has bought it, or himself has killed (the animal), or has received it as a present from others.[59]

Moreover, Mackenzie indicates there are limitations "to the doctrine of ahimsa" which

does not apply to the taking of lives in battle, or to the infliction of capital punishment. By qualifications such as these the force of the doctrine is very considerably weakened. The exceptions to the general principle that life should not be taken, and that the flesh of animals should not be eaten, were so many and of such diverse kinds, that we can believe it would be exceedingly difficult to determine whether a particular act was a breach of the law or not. We know that hunting and fishing continued in spite of all laws.[60]

All true enough – as exemplified by the story from the *Bhima Swarga* (below, pp. 25-6) – and a necessary corrective to those who would exaggerate the effectiveness of the doctrine. Nonetheless, *ahimsa* is an admirable principle and stands as a symbol of the ideal to be striven for. Moreover, there are many examples in Indian philosophies of the doctrine being taken to mean what it says.

The holy first commandment runs: not harsh but kindly be – and therefore lavish mercy on the louse, the bug and the gadfly. (*Pancatantra*)[61]

Whether it is the worm in the excrement or the beings in Indra's heaven, their love of life is the same, their fear of death is the same. (*Pancatantra*)[62]

All beings are fond of life: they like pleasure and hate pain, shun destruction, and like to live. To all life is dear. (*Acaranga Sutra*)[63]

He who harms animals has not understood or renounced deeds of sin. (*Acaranga Sutra*)[64]

May all beings look at me with a friendly eye, may I do likewise [in return], and may we look on each other with the eyes of a friend. (*Yajur Veda*)[65]

All beings tremble before danger, all fear death. When a man considers this, he does not kill or cause to kill. (*Dhammapada*)[66]

But although a man may wear fine clothing, if he lives peacefully; and is good, self-possessed, has faith and is pure; and if he does not hurt any living being, he is a holy Brahmin, a hermit of seclusion, a monk called a Bhikku. (*Dhammapada*)[67]

A man is not a great man because he is a warrior and kills other men; but because he hurts not any living being he in truth is called a great man. (*Dhammapada*)[68]

He who hurts not any living being, whether feeble or strong, who neither kills nor causes to kill – him I call a Brahmin. (*Dhammapada*)[69]

In the long course of samsara [flux], there is not one among living beings with form who has not been mother, father, sister, son or daughter, or some relative. Being connected with the process of taking birth, one is kin to all domestic animals, birds, and beings born from the womb. (*Lankavatara Sutra*)[70]

A bikkhu [monk] who has received ordination ought not intentionally to destroy the life of any living being down to a worm or an ant. (*Mahavagga*)[71]

What is religion? Compassion for all things which have life. What is happiness? To animals in this world, health. What is kindness? A principle in the good. What is philosophy? An entire separation from the world. (*Hitopadesa*)[72]

Are these flesh-eating humans who hunt the innocent deers, dwelling in forests and living on air, water, and grass, any better than curs? Why should the people who feel pain at the slightest prick of a thorn, attack the innocent animals with sharp pointed weapons? These cruel hunters destroy the life of these poor creatures for the sake of some momentary pleasure. If an animal faces danger of death he is terribly pained, then how much will he suffer when attacked with terrible weapons? (*Yogashastra*)[73]

Every creature in this world likes happiness and dislikes unhappiness; so we should not do unto others what one does not want others to do unto him. In other words one should never commit violence to other jivas [living beings]. (*Yogashastra*)[74]

With the three means of punishment, words, thoughts, and deeds, you shall not injure living things. (*Jaina Sutra*)[75]

All beings hate pain; therefore one should not kill them. This is the quintessence of wisdom: not to kill anything. (*Sutrakritanga*)[76]

All breathing, existing, living, feeling creatures should not be killed, nor treated violently, nor abused. All beings hate pain; therefore one should not kill them. This is the quintessence of wisdom: not to kill anything. (*Sutrakritanga*)[77]

(These) wise ones see the selfsame thing (*sama*)*
In a Brahman, wise and courteous,
　　As in a cow or an elephant
Nay, as in a dog or outcaste. (*Bhagavad Gita*)[78]

Nirvana that is Brahman is the lot
Of seers in whom (all) taint of imperfection is destroyed;
Their doubts dispelled, (all) self-controlled,
They take their pleasures in the weal
Of all contingent beings. (*Bhagavad Gita*)[79]

With self by Yoga integrated, (now) he sees
The self in all beings standing,
All beings in the self;
The same in everything he sees. (Bhagavad Gita)[80]

Who loves and worships (*bhaj-*) Me, embracing unity,
As abiding in all beings,
In whatever state he be,
That man of Yoga abides in me. (*Bhagavad Gita*)[81]

Let a man feel hatred for no contingent being,
Let him be friendly, compassionate.
Let him be done with thoughts of "I" and "mine,"
The same as in pleasure as in pain, long suffering ... (*Bhagavad Gita*)[82]

The following Balinese Hindu legend differs in form from the Hindu pronouncements of the mainland as well as being rather more ambivalent in its character.

[The Balinese Hindu clowns] Twalen and Mredah were so engrossed in their discussion that they almost missed an extraordinary sight: a demon was crossing the landscape of Hell in a flamboyant cart with wheels as gigantic as the demon himself.

"Look! Look! Just look at those two men pulling the cart and being whipped at the same time. God help me not to do what led them to this!" shrieked Mredah, who was a little lazy fellow. Mredah's voice had now become so shrill that Prince Bhima could no longer ignore what his servants were saying.

"I bet that's the punishment inflicted on those who have tortured the buffaloes and other animals for the fun of it," Twalen guessed.

"Like catching a dragonfly and ripping off its wings, to watch its reaction," Mredah broke in.

"That is correct," said Bhima in his usual cool, princely tone ...

---

* "That," i.e., the religious goal.

The servant-clowns witness a man about to be slain by a monster.

"What has *He* done?" asked Twalen, who couldn't figure out what terrible sins the poor man must have committed. Again, only Bhima was able to shed light on the situation.

"That man slaughtered animals without caring about the prescribed ritual," Bhima explained in his severe tone. "One should never forget that animals are human beings who have taken on other shapes and forms. After one has looked after an animal with care, then the creature should rightly give up its life for its master. But during the slaughtering, one should always repeat this *mantra*: "I am slaying you in order to free your soul. Do not take revenge on me." (*Bhima Swarga*)[83]

Confucianism

Confucius (K'ung Fu'tse) lived c. 551 BC to c. 479 BC.[84] The *Analects* is a book of his purported sayings and views, as well as of ancient Chinese philosophical and ethical commentary in general. There is, however, considerable dispute about its authenticity. Confucius's role is in several respects akin to that of Socrates in the Greek philosophical tradition – that of a profoundly revered thinker who wrote nothing himself and the interpretations of whose views are not entirely consistent.

Confucianism as a doctrine is a system of ethical precepts for the just governance and management of a society, the fundamentals of which are to be discovered in humanity's unadulterated moral intuitions. The doctrine treats humans as essentially social creatures, properly concerned with their own personal, moral, and intellectual development. Stressing filial relations, Confucianism concerns itself with the moral obligations involved at various levels of human interaction, emphasizing the differences between humans and "wild animals," which are customarily posited as the condition to be overcome. Nonetheless, a modest level of acknowledgement of our responsibilities to other species may be found within the tradition. One of the traditional stories told of Confucius concerns his support for animal sacrifice: "Tsekung wanted to do away with the ceremony of sacrificing the lamb in winter. Confucius said, 'Ah, Sze, you love the lamb, but I love the ritual.'"[85] While Confucius himself may have been more concerned with ritual traditions, it is clear that his disciple Tsekung recognized the worthiness of animal life.

In the traditional Chinese *Book of Songs*, which Confucius is said to have edited, we read: "the twittering yellow bird *rests* or alights on a little mound." Confucius is reported to have commented on that line: "When the bird *rests*, it knows where to rest. Should a human being be inferior to a bird in knowing where to *rest* (or even in knowing what to *dwell in*)?"[86] Confucius is acknowledging – perhaps even despairing at – the superiority of the bird's instinct in knowing what is appropriate to it, while humans in their ignorance will often make the wrong choice. Nonetheless, for Confucius, respect for relatives and for other species was of a decidedly different order: "Tsu-yu asked about filial piety. The master said, 'Nowadays, one who provides for (his parents) is called filial. But even dogs and horses are provided for. If there is no reverence – what is the difference?'"[87] This would appear to suggest that care and protection of animals is all well and good but they should be undertaken in a far different spirit from that of care for one's parents.

Clearly, evidence of Confucius's understanding of the appropriate human relationship to animals is both scanty and, in some instances, discouraging, if less than conclusive. The views of Mencius (c. 372 BC to c. 289 BC), Confucius's most influential disciple, are more readily discernible. "The superior man feels concern for creatures, but he is not benevolent to them. He is benevolent to the people but he does not love them. He loves his parents, is benevolent to the people and feels concern for creatures."[88] Our primary duty is toward immediate kin, secondarily to people in general, and thirdly to the animal realm. Mencius does not inform us of the relative weights to be given to these different interests but indicates only that the answer must lie in our answering the call of our natural endowment, that is, our conscience or intuition. "Mencius said, "Now as for his *ch'ing* (true essence), a man may become good – this is what I mean when I say (man's nature) is good. His becoming bad is not the fault of his endowment."[89]

Taoism

Taoism is chiefly, at least theoretically, derived from the *Tao-te-ching*, a book traditionally ascribed to Lao-tse, but almost certainly of third-century-BC vintage. It advocates the tao – the way – which is essentially quietist, culminating in mystical contemplation. By the fourth century AD it had in practice become heavily influenced by Mahayana Buddhism and had adopted many of its doctrines. While Taoism has generally avoided detailed commentary on the human-animal relationship, a few Taoists (or those influenced by Taoism), notably those suffused with philosophies of Indian extraction, have expressed the strongest ethical orientations to animals, though it would be inappropriate to consider them representative of Taoism in general.

Have a compassionate heart toward all creatures ... Even insects, grass and trees you must not hurt.[90]

Buy captive creatures and set them free. Hold fast to vegetarianism and abstain from taking life. Whenever taking a step, always watch for ants and insects ... Help people in distress as you would a fish in a dried up rut. Free people in danger as you would a sparrow from a fine net. Benefit living creatures and human beings.[91]

The Biblical Tradition

It is significantly more difficult to find explicit animal-considerate passages in the Jewish and Christian scriptures, especially the latter, than in Indian scriptures. Nonetheless, several Christian writers have insisted they are there to be found. For example, in *An Essay on Humanity to Animals* of 1798, Thomas Young, Anglican priest and Fellow of Trinity College, Cambridge, quoted passages from Exodus, Leviticus, Numbers, Proverbs, Jonah, St. Matthew, and I Corinthians to show that God cares for the animal realm and requires us to do likewise.[92] In her popular devout novel, *Agnes Grey* (1847), Anne Brontë interpreted both the Old and New Testaments as exhorting us to treat well of our fellow "sentient creatures."[93] And Victor Hugo in *Les Misérables* (1862) instructs us that "duty to all living creatures"[94] is one of the four duties of humankind according to the Gospel of St. Matthew. However, such doctrines have to be extracted painstakingly from the texts in most instances, and on some occasions with considerable ingenuity. Unlike the Eastern scriptures, only occasionally are they explicit and transparent. Indeed, some of the Biblical commentary on animals sounds like lessons in pastoral husbandry rather than general pronouncements on animal ethics.

In Ezekiel the message is that God looks after his people in the same manner that the good shepherd ought to look after his flock:

> For the Lord Yahweh says this: Look, I myself shall take care of my flock and look after it. As a shepherd looks after his flock when he is with his scattered sheep, so I shall look after my sheep. I shall rescue them from wherever they have been scattered on the day of clouds and darkness. I shall bring them back from the peoples where they are; I shall gather them back from the countries and bring them back to their own land. I shall pasture them on the mountains of Israel, in the ravines and in all the inhabited parts of the country. I shall feed them in good pasturage; the highest mountains of Israel will be their grazing ground. There they will rest in good grazing grounds; they will browse in rich pastures on the mountains of Israel. I myself shall pasture my sheep. I myself shall give them rest – declares the Lord Yahweh. I shall look for the lost one, bring back the stray, bandage the injured and make the sick strong. I shall watch over the fat and healthy. I shall be a true shepherd to them. (Ezekiel 34:11-16)

Other Biblical passages treat God's concern for his animal creation in a more explicit manner, indicating that earth was created as much for the benefit of wild animals and birds as for humans and their domestic flocks.

> In the ravines you [God] opened up springs,
> running down between the mountains,
> supplying water for all the wild beasts;
> the wild asses quench their thirst,
> on their banks the birds of the air make their nests,

they sing among the leaves.
From your high halls you water the mountains,
satisfying the earth with the fruit of your works:
for cattle you make the grass grow,
and for the people the plants they need,
to bring forth food from the earth ...
The trees of Yahweh drink their fill,
the cedars of Lebanon which he sowed;
there the birds build their nests,
on the highest branches the stork makes its home;
for the wild goats there are the mountains, in the crags the coneys find refuge.
(Psalms 104:10-14, 16-18)

There are a few passages, all from the Old Testament, which exhort us directly to give consideration to the animals.

If you see the donkey of someone who hates you fallen under its load, do not stand back; you must go and help him with it. (Exodus 23:5)

For six days you will do your work, and on the seventh you will rest, so your ox and your donkey may rest and the child of your slave-girl have a breathing space and the alien too. (Exodus 23:12)

You must not plough with ox and donkey together. (Deuteronomy 22:10)

The purpose of the injunction is to prevent harm to the animals.

You must not muzzle an ox when it is treading out the corn. (Deuteronomy 25:4)

The farmer is being told that the ox must not be deprived of a portion of the fruit of its labour. St. Paul repeats the doctrine verbatim in I Timothy 5:18.

The upright has compassion on his animals, but the heart of the wicked is ruthless. (Proverbs 12:10)

In Isaiah, God makes it clear how he regards the harming of His creatures from wanton cruelty in sacrifice.

Some slaughter a bull, some kill a human being, some sacrifice a lamb, some strangle a dog, some present an offering of pig's blood ... all these people have chosen their own ways and take delight in their disgusting practices ... They have done what I regard as evil, have chosen what displeases me. (Psalms 66:3-4)

The traditional King James version is even more powerful: "He that killeth an ox is as if he slew a man."

The benevolence of God toward His creatures is often repeated:

God had Noah in mind, and all the wild animals and all the cattle that were with him in the ark. (Genesis 8:1)

Yahweh, your faithful love is in the heavens, your constancy reaches to the clouds, your saving justice is like towering mountains, your judgments like the mighty deep. Yahweh, you support both man and beast. (Psalms 36:5-6)

HET: Yahweh is tenderness and pity, slow to anger, full of faithful love.
TET: Yahweh is generous to all, his tenderness embraces all his creatures.
YOD: All your creatures shall thank you, Yahweh, and your faithful shall bless you.
    (Psalms 145:8-10)

The similarity of human and animal is stressed in Ecclesiastes, in a manner reminiscent of Bushman myth.[95]

For the fate of human and the fate of animal is the same: as the one dies, so the other dies; both have the selfsame breath. Human is in no way better off than the animal – since all is futile. Everything goes to the same place, everything comes from the dust, everything returns to the dust. Who knows if the human spirit mounts upward or if the animal spirit goes down to the earth? (Ecclesiastes 3:19-21)

We can also read of humanity's need to learn from the animals, implying that there are respects in which the capacities of other species are superior to those of humanity, in a manner reminiscent of the Cheyenne legend of "How the Buffalo Hunt Began."[96] Indeed, when one makes such comparisons one can only be reminded of Wordsworth's dictum: we have all of us one human heart.[97]

You have only to ask the cattle, for them to instruct you, and the birds of the sky for them to inform you.
    The creeping things of the earth will give you lessons, and the fish of the sea provide you with an explanation: there is not one such creature but will know that the hand of God has arranged things like this. (Job 12:7-9)

According to Genesis, prior to the Flood, animals and humans lived without harm to each other, reminiscent of the golden age in the Cheyenne creation myth.[98]

"Look, to you I give all the seed-bearing plants everywhere on the surface of the earth, and all the trees with seed-bearing fruit; this will be your food. And to all the wild animals, all the birds of heaven and the living creatures that creep along the ground, I give all the foliage of the plants as their food." And so it was. (Genesis 1:29-30)

And if this was a long disappeared utopia it remained as an ideal to be regained at some point in the future.

The wolf will live with the lamb, the panther lie down with the kid, calf, lion and fat-stock beast together, with a little boy to lead them. The cow and the bear will graze, their young will lie down together. The lion will eat hay like the ox. The infant will play over the den of the adder; the baby will put his hand into the viper's lair. No hurt, no harm will be done ... (Isaiah 11:6-9)

When the day of reconciliation comes:

I shall make a treaty for [the people] with the wild animals, and the birds of heaven and the creeping things of the earth; I shall break the bow and the sword and warfare, and banish them from the country, and I will let them sleep secure. (Hosea 2:20)

And St. Paul tells us:

In my estimation, all that we suffer in the present time is nothing in comparison with the glory which is destined to be disclosed for us, for the whole creation is waiting with eagerness for the children of God to be revealed. It was not for its own purpose that creation had frustration imposed on it, but for the purpose of him who imposed it – with the intention that the whole creation might be freed from its slavery and corruption and brought into the same glorious freedom as the children of God. We are all aware that the whole creation, until this time, has been groaning in labour pains. (Romans 8:18-22)

Judaism

It is recognized all too infrequently that traditional Judaic pronouncements, especially those absent from the Bible, possess a solid animal ethic. In fact, one of the principles of the Torah: Bal Taschit – *do not destroy* – plays a similar role in Jewish thought to that of *ahimsa* in Jain, Hindu, and Buddhist thought. It is based on the idea that "the earth is the Lord's," that everything that exists belongs to Him, and that, correspondingly, we have no right to harm anything.[99] In the Talmud we read:

It is forbidden according to the law of Torah to inflict pain upon any living creature. On the contrary, it is our duty to relieve the pain of any creature, even if it is ownerless or belongs to a non-Jew.[100]

When horses, drawing a cart, come to a rough road or a steep hill, and it is hard for them to draw the cart without help, it is our duty to help them, even when they belong to a non-Jew, because of the precept not to be cruel to animals, lest the owner smite them to force them to draw more than their strength permits.[101]

Jews must avoid plucking feathers from live geese, because it is cruel to do so.[102]

Rejoicing cannot occur at an animal's expense.[103]

Animals are not to be penned up in stables on Shabbat.[104]

One who prevents an animal from eating when at work is punishable by flagellation.[105]

As the Holy One, blessed be He, has compassion upon man, so has He compassion upon the beasts of the field ... And for the birds of the air.[106]

Thou thinkest that flies, fleas, mosquitoes are superfluous, but they have their purpose in creation as a means of a final outcome ... Of all that the Holy One, blessed be He, created in His world, He did not create a single thing without purpose.[107]

The Talmud indicates further that heaven rewards those who show concern and compassion for nonhumans,[108] and that one should not have an animal unless one can feed it and care for it.[109] Another Hebrew doctrine is that "a good man does not sell his beast to a cruel person."[110]

According to the Book of Enoch, a Judaic text of perhaps around AD 150, probably earlier and most certainly based on earlier sources, it was only after the Flood that humans "began to sin against birds and beasts and reptiles and fish, and to devour one another's flesh and to drink the blood."[111] If God granted the right to eat meat after the Flood, clearly there were some who continued to regard flesh-eating as a "sin." Early Christians as well as Jews accepted the Book of Enoch as one of the holy scriptures.

The Jewish historian **Flavius Josephus** (AD 37-100), writing of the fundamental laws of the Mosaic code, observed: "It is not lawful to pass by any beast that is in distress, when it is fallen down under its burden, but to endeavour to preserve it, as having a sympathy with it in its pain."[112]

Islam

The primary Islamic scriptures are the Qur'an (Koran), the divine revelations of Allah to Mohammed, and the Hadith, the traditional wisdoms ascribed to Mohammed. Together they constitute the Shariah, the source of Islamic law. In the Qur'an Majeed we find the following pronouncements:

No kind of beast is there on earth, nor fowl that flieth with its wings, but is a folk like you; then unto their Lord shall they be gathered.[113]

A more modern, and more impressive, rendering of the statement is given as:

There is not an animal on earth, nor a bird that flies on its wings, but they are communities like you.[114]

Other animal sympathetic statements include:

There is no moving creature on earth but God provides for its sustenance.[115]

And the earth – He has assigned it to all living creatures.[116]

And the earth – He spread it out for all living beings, with its fruits, blossom-bearing palms, husk-coated grains, and fragrant plants.[117]

And the earth – we have spread out its expanse and cast on it mountains in stable equilibrium, and caused life of every kind to grow on it, justly weighed.[118]

In your own creation, as well as in the creation of all the animals pervading the earth, there are portents for those who believe.[119]

The Qur'an calls the cruel practices of those pagans who slit the ears of animals: "devilish acts."[120]

The pronouncements of the Hadith are more explicit than those of the Qur'an itself. Some scholars have, in fact, doubted the authenticity of some of the views ascribed to Mohammed in the Hadith, considering them representative of what the commentators wished Mohammed had said rather than what he did say. Yet even if such a view were valid, the purported sayings would indicate at the very least what humane Muslims believed appropriate and what they thought Mohammed himself would have espoused.

It behooves you to treat animals gently.[121]

Verily, there are rewards for our doing good to dumb animals.[122]

All creatures are like a family of God; and He loves the most those who are the most beneficent to His family.[123]

Everyone who shows clemency, even towards a mere bird under the knife, will find God's clemency towards him on Doomsday.[124]

There is a meritorious reward [*Thawab*] for every act of charity and kindness to every living creature.[125]

A good deed done to an animal is as meritorious as a good deed done to a human being, while an act of cruelty to an animal is as bad as an act of cruelty to a human being.[126]

There is no man who kills even a sparrow, or anything smaller, but God will question him about it.[127]

Avoid the seven abominations. And kill not a living creature, which Allah has made sacrosanct, except for a justifiable reason.[128]

The curse of God be upon him who exceedingly punishes any animal ... whoever has a horse and treats it well, will be treated well by God.[129]

Revel as we must in these admirable injunctions and principles from aboriginal, Oriental, Christian, Jewish, and Muslim sources, let us not imagine for a moment that these precepts reflect the practical realities of societies. They do, however, reflect the fact that these principles inform the way honourable people behave and the way all are instructed, if perhaps not expected, to behave.

2
The Classical World

There have been three primary influences on modern Western culture – the Judeo-Christian religious tradition, the Greco-Roman philosophical, legal, literary, and administrative traditions, and, perhaps rather less significantly, at least after the close of the Middle Ages, the prior mythological tradition of Europe onto which Christian and classical thought were grafted. Although there are earlier intimations of the Greek inspiration in the practices of the Middle East, it is Greek thought, beginning in the sixth century BC, which elevates individual reason as the route to knowledge, and applies reason self-consciously to the understanding of humans, animals, and nature, and to their relationship with one another. In classical Greece, reason seeks to replace myth and tradition as the source of wisdom.

The Greek philosophers sought to determine by the aid of their reason what distinguished humans from other beings. The consequence was a sense of ourselves as separate from nature and superior to its other constituent creatures. Aristotle (384 BC-322 BC), for example, perhaps the most learned, if not the most brilliant, of classical philosophers – he acknowledged Plato's unparalleled brilliance but thought it a potentially dangerous attribute – deemed the capacity for speech and reason, our planned organization of political communities, and the possession of a moral sense, to be the differentiating characteristics that made us more god-like than animal-like in our natures. Nonetheless, there was also a vigorous orientation in Greek, and later Roman, philosophy which emphasized our similarities to other species, our kinship with them, and our responsibilities toward them. It is this aspect of Greek and Roman thought which is presented in the passages selected for this chapter.

One should be wary of attempting to discern too much about the real attitudes to animals from the deliberations of philosophers. Although the notion of a human exclusivity was undoubtedly the overall victor in the intellectual battle, philosophers did not always win the war for the public mind either easily or overwhelmingly, especially to the extent that it influenced public behaviour. Contrasting European attitudes at the turn of the nineteenth century with those of the classical era, Helen Maria Williams advises us in her *Sketches on the State of Manners and Opinions in the French Republic to the End of the Eighteenth Century* (1801) that at one time

the codes of legislators were filled with regulations of mercy in favour of animals. The code of Triptolemus* may be cited as evidence of the estimation in which animals used for labour were held; and the agricultural Roman writers would lead us to think that the laws were more favourable to beasts than to men. We affect at present to look on Spartan manners with contempt; it were well if, in some cases, we studied Spartan humanity. The tribunal which condemned a boy to death for wantonly plucking out the eye of a bird pronounced a merciful judgment; animals were no longer mutilated, and infants' sports became less atrocious.[1]

We may not be persuaded by Williams's notion of "humanity," and we may conclude that her examples are not entirely representative. Thus, for example, Voltaire remarked in horror at the cruelties of the Roman Circus that the Romans "built their great masterpiece of architecture, the amphitheatre, for wild beasts to fight in." But we should certainly recognize that the apparent implications of an exclusively human-oriented ethic were not always followed – as witnessed by Xenocrates, head of Plato's Academy from 339 BC to 314 BC, who tells us that the Athenians punished a man for flaying a ram while alive. When Julius Caesar invaded Britain he found the Celts keeping hares, geese, and hens for enjoyment rather than food – a notion that did not seem to displease him.[2] We will encounter other illustrations of practical moral concern for animals in, for example, Plutarch's "Life of Marcus Cato"[3] and Cicero's letter to Marcus Marius.[4] Of greatest moment, however, was the assertion of the third-century Roman jurist Ulpian, primary author of the *Corpus Juris Civilis*[5] which laid much of the foundation for Roman law, that the *ius animalium* – "natural justice for animals" might be the most appropriate rendering – was a part of the *ius naturale* – natural law or natural justice.

Private law is threefold; it can be gathered from the precepts of nature, or from those of the nations, or from those of the city. Natural law is that which nature has taught all animals; this law indeed is not peculiar to the human race, but belongs to all animals ... From this law springs the union of male and female ... the procreation of children and their education ... the law of nations is that law which mankind observes. It is easy to understand that this law should differ from the natural, inasmuch as the latter belongs to all animals, while the former is peculiar to men.[6]

---

* Triptolemus was a legendary Greek hero. The code named in his honour was also commended by Plutarch and Porphyry as an example of Greek animal concern.

Perhaps the difference between some of the philosophy and some of the practice was, in part, because even those philosophers who, unlike Ulpian, emphasized human rational, political, and moral superiority, did not reject completely the significance of animals. Thus Aristotle, renowned for his view that "all animals must have been made by nature for the sake of men" (*Politics*, I, 8, 12), tells us: "in all natural things there is something wonderful ... in all [animals] there is something natural and beautiful" (*On the Parts of Animals*, I, 5) and that "just as in man we find knowledge, wisdom and sagacity, so in certain animals there exists some other potentiality akin to these" (*Historia Animalium* 588, A: 8). If the idea of human superiority in kind predominated among the classical philosophers, even those who proclaimed it most loudly recognized that other species possessed a certain level of worthiness. If humans mattered more, it did not imply to Greeks and Romans in practice that animals were without significance and devoid of moral consideration. In fact, the classical debate may best be understood to resemble the modern contest between the advocates of animal welfare and the proponents of animal rights – between those who acknowledged significant distinctions between humans and other species, while recognizing a considerable moral responsibility of humans toward other species, and those who emphasized the similarities and commended a more or less equal consideration in principle of all species.

Pre-Philosophical Greece

Our opening quotations are drawn from what are traditionally known as Homer's *Batrachomyomachia* – the famed battle of the mice and the frogs – and the *Homeric Hymns*, first written down in the eighth or seventh century BC, but based on earlier oral sources. Homer is, however, as much a myth as his purported compositions, for not only do we have little evidence of his life or his accomplishments – other than that he lived sometime in the eighth century BC or so, somewhere in the region of Smyrna in Asia Minor – but far more variety is attributed to his genius than would have been likely for an individual mind. It was, in fact, the German scholar F.A. Wolf (1759-1824), writing in the 1780s, who first argued that Homer's works were an anthology rather than the wisdom of a single poet, a view now commanding more or less universal ascription. *Homeric Hymns* is thus more of a historical context for the poems than an attribution. They may be regarded as an integral part of a Greek tradition that provided an impetus to Greek philosophy, or, at least, one side of it.

In the *Batrachomyomachia* we read that the poem's purpose was:

> to show
> How bravely did both frogs and mice bestow
> In glorious fight their forces, even the deeds
> Daring to imitate of earth's giant seeds.[7]

Their bravery paralleled that of human courage in battle. In the "Hymn to Apollo" we learn "of goodly horse so brave a breed" and of "the haughty neighs of swift-hooved horse"[8] – the horse was certainly the most favoured animal, but others received a certain due. In the "Hymn to Hermes" we encounter "a herd of oxen with brave heads endowed"[9] and in the "Hymn to Venus" it is the wolves, lions, leopards, and deer:

> Whose sight so pleased that ever as she passed
> Through every beast a kindly love she cast.[10]

The Mother of the Gods "loves dreadful lions' roars and wolves' hoarse howls."[11]

The Odyssey, whence the following short extract, is the mythological masterpiece traditionally ascribed to Homer. Believed by his family and friends to be dead, Odysseus returns from the Trojan wars and subsequent adventures, and is recognized by none but his faithful dog Argos.

And lo, a hound raised up his head and pricked his ears, even where he lay, Argos, the hound of Odysseus, of the hardy heart, which of old himself had bred, but had got no joy out of him, for ere that he went to sacred Ilios. Now in time past the young men used to lead the hound against wild goats and deer and hares; but as then, despised he lay (his master being afar) in the deep dung of mules and kine, whereof an ample bed was spread before the doors, till the thralls of Odysseus should carry it away to dung therewith his wide demesne. There lay the dog Argos full of vermin. Yet even now when he was ware of Odysseus standing by, he wagged his tail and dropped both his ears, but nearer to his master he had not now the strength to draw. But Odysseus looked aside and wiped away a tear that he easily hid from Eumaeus,* and straightway he asked him, saying: "Eumaeus, verily this is a great marvel, this hound lying here in the dung. Truly he is goodly of growth, but I know not certainly if he have speed with this beauty, or if he be comely only, like as are men's trencher dogs that their lords keep for the pleasure of the eye."

Then didst thou make answer, swineherd Eumaeus: "In very truth this is the dog of a man that has died in a far off land. If he were what once he was in limb and in the feats of the chase, when Odysseus left him to go to Troy, soon wouldst thou marvel at the sight of his swiftness and his strength. There was no beast that could flee from him in the deep places of the wood, when he was in pursuit; for even on a track he was the keenest hound. But now he is holden in an evil case, and his lord hath perished far from his own country, and the careless women take no charge of him ..."

But upon Argos came the fate of black death even in the hour that he beheld Odysseus again, in the twentieth year.[12]

---

* Eumaeus was Odysseus's swineherd, who had failed to recognize his master on arrival and who was still unaware of the stranger's identity.

Anacreon was a lyric poet of Teos, a Greek colony in Asia Minor, who wrote c. 500 BC. The verses traditionally ascribed to him are now recognized as not being the work of the genuine Anacreon and are instead known as the Anacreontea; at least some of the poetry is thought to be contemporaneous.

The following two poems may be said to exemplify the humanitarian thought of the era:

The Grasshopper

Grasshopper thrice happy! who
Sipping the cool morning dew,
Queen-like chirpest all the day
Seated on some verdant spray;
Thine is all whate'er earth brings,
Or the earth with laden wings;
Thee, the ploughman calls his joy,
'Cause thou nothing dost destroy:
Thou by all art honour'd; all
Thee the spring's sweet prophet call;
By the Muses thou admir'd,
By Apollo art inspir'd,
Ageless, ever-singing good,
Without passion, flesh or blood;
Oh how near thy happy state
Comes the gods to imitate![13]

The Dove

Whither flies my pretty dove?
Whither, nimble scout of Love?
From whose wings perfumes distil,
And the air with sweetness fill.
Is't to thee which way I'm bent?
By Anacreon I am sent
To Rhodantha, she who all
Hearts commands, Love's general.
I to Venus did belong,
But she sold me for a song
To her poet; his I am,
And from him this letter came,
For which he hath promis'd me
That ere long he'll set me free.
But though freedom I should gain,
I with him would still remain;
For what profit were the change,

Fields from tree to tree to range,
And on hips and haws to feed,
When I may at home pick bread
From his hand, and freely sup.[14]

Both poems reflect themes which recur for centuries: animals that are harmless to human interests are easier to appreciate, and that there is an ongoing dispute over whether domestication and human companionship are more beneficial to some animals than life in the wild.

Greek Presocratic Philosophers

The writings of few of the Presocratic philosophers have survived. Consequently, we know their work only by their reputation and by what slightly later philosophers reported as their views and their arguments. Not all of the later reports are compatible with one another. Accordingly, extracts have been selected from those works regarded by classical scholars as being the most reliable.

Pythagoras

Pythagoras was born at Samos in Asia Minor around 570 BC and emigrated to the Greek colony of Croton in southern Italy around the age of 30, where he lived until apparent hostility with some of the citizens persuaded him to move to the nearby city of Metapontium. He is chiefly renowned for his contributions to mathematics and musical harmony[15] – though many doubt he made much of a contribution at all. However, few doubt his belief in metempsychosis (reincarnation) and vegetarianism, and many of those known as the Pythagoreans followed him faithfully in this respect.

Given his espousal of metempsychosis, the question has been legitimately raised as to whether his concern for the treatment of animals and his refusal to eat flesh arose out of a compassion for his fellow animals or for the humans whose souls were now inhabiting the bodies of the animals – a question also raised about Hindu and Buddhist reincarnationists. Whatever Pythagoras's own view – and the available evidence suggests he cared for animals *qua* animals – his contemporary and later followers made the concern for the animals themselves much more explicit. "The Pythagorean Diet" was the customary term for vegetarianism until the mid-nineteenth century when the term "vegetarian" was coined. In the early twentieth century the Irish dramatist George Bernard Shaw tried in vain to introduce the term "Shelleyism" – after the poet Percy Bysshe Shelley. But the rather misleading term "vegetarian" – misleading in that vegetarians eat far more than vegetables alone – has prevailed. "[I]t became very well known to everyone that [Pythagoras] said, first, that the soul is immortal then that it changes into other kinds of animals; and further that at certain periods whatever has happened happens again, there being nothing absolutely new, and that all living beings belong to the same kind. Pythagoras seems to have been the first to introduce these doctrines into Greece" (Porphyry, *Life of Pythagoras*, 19).[16]

While Porphyry's understanding of Pythagoras's philosophy may be said to be the standard view, we should bear in mind that Porphyry was writing over seven centuries after the Samian's death, and thus could rely only on later sources. Porphyry (c. AD 234 to c. AD 305) was born at Tyre in modern day Lebanon, once a Greek colony but by Porphyry's day part of the Roman empire. Later he moved to Rome where he studied under the Neoplatonist philosopher Plotinus, who first systematized the idea of the Great Chain of Being, which played a dominant role in the understanding of the human relationship to animals from the medieval period until the nineteenth century, and in some respects to the very present. Porphyry has been described with justice as the most significant Greek contributor to the animal welfare debate. We shall meet the writings of Porphyry and Plotinus later in this chapter.[17] Pythagoras's apparent claim that "all living beings belong to the same kind" became the central issue of the classical era with regard to our responsibilities to animals. "Pythagoras believed in metempsychosis and thought that eating meat was an abominable thing, saying that the souls of animals entered different animals after death" (Diodorus, *Universal History*, 10, 6, 1-3).[18]

Diodorus lived in the first century BC. He was born at Agyrium in Sicily, later moving first to Alexandria, then to Rome. His *Universal History*, originally in 40 books, many of which have been lost, is regarded as uncritical and unreliable. Nonetheless, he seems to have depicted Pythagoras accurately. Pythagoras's view, according to Diodorus, was that souls moved from animal to animal as well as from human to animal and vice versa. The refusal of flesh would therefore appear to imply the non-eating of animal, and not merely human, souls.

What [Xenophanes*] says about [Pythagoras] goes like this:

And once when he passed a puppy that was being whipped they say he took pity on it and made this remark: "Stop, do not beat it; for it is the soul of a dear friend. I recognized it when I heard the voice." (Diogenes Laertius, *Lives of the Philosophers*, 8, 36)[19]

Diogenes lived around the third century AD, but nothing is known of his life. It is his account that has prompted some to suggest that Pythagoras was concerned only with the souls of humans rather than with the animals now in possession of those souls.

---

* Xenophanes, c. 570 BC to c. 480 BC, founder of the Eliatic school of thought.

Empedocles

From the Greek colony at Acragas in Sicily, Empedocles (c. 495 BC to c. 435 BC) was a Pythagorean who wrote in verse, primarily on nature and on sacrifice. He emphasized the similarities between animals and would appear to have been the first to condemn animal sacrifice on the grounds of its inhumanity to the slaughtered animals. There is, however, considerable uncertainty among classical scholars as to the authenticity of some of the views attributed to him.

Pythagoras and Empedocles and the rest of the Italians* say that we have a fellowship not only with one another and the gods but also with the irrational animals. For there is a single spirit which pervades the whole world as a sort of soul and which unites us with them. That is why, if we kill them and eat their flesh, we commit injustice and impiety, inasmuch as we are killing our kin. Hence these philosophers urged us to abstain from meat. (Sextus Empiricus, *Against the Mathematicians*, 9, 127-9)[20]

Sextus Empiricus, a Greek scholar of around the second or third century AD, is an important figure in the development of philosophical skepticism. We shall encounter more of his writing later in the chapter.[21] The idea of "fellowship" with the animals (also expressed as kinship, community, or belongingness) is an extension of the idea of being of the same "kind" as the animals, and, again, is central to the debate about animal respect. It is here dressed in the concept of the universal spirit or universal soul of which each individual soul, whether human or animal, is seen to be a part. The idea of abstaining from meat "inasmuch as we are killing our kin" has its counterpart in Hinduism's *Mahabharata* (13) where we read "the meat of other animals is like the flesh of one's own son." The idea of a universal spirit, from which all souls come and to which all return, is also found among the Inuit and many other aboriginal societies.

The reference to "the irrational animals" should not be taken to imply that the Pythagoreans thought of animals as lacking reason. The use of the phrase is no more than a concession to contemporary idiom. In fact, we will encounter the phrase on a few occasions in the succeeding pages. In all these instances, no negative judgment on animal reason is to be inferred.

For Empedocles says that here too† Love and Strife predominate by turns over men and fish and beasts and birds. He writes as follows:

This is plain in the bulk of mortal members; sometimes by Love they all come together into one, limbs which the body acquires when life is thriving at its peak,

---

* That is, the Greek followers of Pythagoras, many of whom resided in Greek colonies in Italy.
† That is, in our own world, as opposed to the heavens.

sometimes again divided by evil Conflicts, each wanders apart along the shores of life. So too is it with plants and fish of the watery halls, and beasts of the mountain lairs and flying gulls. (Simplicius, *Commentary on the Physics,* 1124, 9-18)[22]

Simplicius was a pagan Neoplatonist scholar, who flourished between c. AD 500 and c. AD 540. He was educated in Alexandria, lived later in Persia and Greece, and is best known for his commentaries on Aristotle. Empedocles is here giving a decided emphasis to the view that all of nature is one, psychologically as well as physically.

Empedocles uses the word [ktilos] of tame and gentle things
    All were gentle and amenable to men,
    Both beasts and birds, and kindness glowed.
(Scholiast to Nicander, *Theriaca,* 452)[23]

"Scholia" are marginal notes added to early texts by later readers. Nicander was a didactic poet of around the second century BC. Empedocles was here, one assumes both from the words and for consistency with other of his statements, commenting on the human-animal relationship in the Golden Age. There is a notable similarity with the ideas expressed in the Cheyenne "Creation Myth."[24]

By such [vegetal] offerings nature and every sense of the human soul was pleased. [As Empedocles taught:]
But with the foul slaughter of the bulls their altars were not washed, but this was the greatest defilement among men: to bereave of life and eat the whole limbs. (Porphyry, *On Abstinence from Animal Food,* 2, 27)[25]

As everyone somehow surmises, there is by nature a common justice and injustice ... This is what Empedocles says about not killing animate creatures: it is not the case that this is just for some and not just for others.
    But, a law for all, through the broad
    air it endlessly extends and through the boundless light.
    (Aristotle, *Rhetoric,* 1373b, 6-9, 14-17)[26]

Empedocles's universal moral which prohibits the killing of animals corresponds to the Jain principle of *ahimsa.*[27]

Heraclitus
Heraclitus (flourished c. 500 BC) came from Ephesus in Asia Minor. He is best remembered for the doctrine that everything is in flux, nothing is permanent. His is the famous saying that "it is not possible to step into the same river twice." He also subscribed to the doctrine of a universal soul to which the spirits of all beings return.

Dry dust and ash ... should be put in the poultry run so that birds can sprinkle themselves with it; for this is how they wash their feathers and wings, if we are to believe Heraclitus of Ephesus who says that pigs wash in mud and farmyard birds in dust or ashes. (Columella, *On Agriculture*, 8, 4, 4)[28]

A first-century-AD Latin author, born at Cadiz, Columella wrote on farming matters. Heraclitus's advice would appear to be the earliest recorded instance of the idea that each animal ought to be treated according to the specific needs of its species, the idea which is, indeed, the very foundation of modern animal welfare science. We should at least acknowledge the advice as that of Heraclitus if Columella intends us to understand the first and last parts of his statement to apply to the Presocratic approach. In his *Works and Days* of the eighth century BC, Hesiod wrote at length on farming matters, but his advice was directed primarily to the interests of the farmers, whereas Heraclitus's (or Columella's) is directed to the interests of the animals.

Democritus

Apparently the most prolific of the Presocratic philosophers, Democritus (c. 460 BC to c. 370 BC) was born in northern Greece at Abdera. He was reputedly the first to suggest that everything was composed of atoms and obeyed deterministic natural laws. He also expressed a high opinion of animated nature.

Perhaps we are foolish to admire animals for their learning, although Democritus asserts that we are their pupils in all the most important things – of the spider in weaving and healing, of the swallow in building, of the song birds (the swan and the nightingale) in singing. (Plutarch, *Whether Land or Sea Animals are Cleverer*, 20, 974A)[29]

Along with Porphyry, Plutarch (c. AD 45 to c. AD 120; born Chaeronea, northern Greece) is the most significant classical contributor to animal ethics. His writings are reported at some length later in the chapter.[30]

Diogenes of Apollonia

Said to be the last of the Presocratic natural philosophers, Diogenes of Apollonia (flourished c. 430 BC) believed that *nous* (intelligence) was responsible for the movement of air, which was the basic element of which all else was composed. Simplicius is here reporting the views of Diogenes.

Humans and other animals, inasmuch as they breathe, live by the air. And this is for them both soul and intelligence ... and if this departs, they die and their intelligence is lost ... The souls of all animals are indeed the same. (Simplicius, *Commentary on the Physics*, 152)[31]

However much we may question Diogenes of Apollonia's understanding of physiology, we should notice his recognition that animals and humans share breath, soul, and intelligence – indeed the spark of animate life – in common. Whereas a number of later philosophers (Aristotle, for example) emphasize that which separates humans from animals, Diogenes, in common with most of the Presocratics, lays stress on that which unites them.

Later Greek and Roman Thinkers

Plato
The most profound of the classical Greek philosophers, Plato (c. 427 BC to c. 347 BC) conceived of the essential unity of politics and ethics via an idealized conception of justice. He wrote, *inter alia*, the *Republic, Statesman, Laws, Phaedo, Symposium, Thaetatus, Phaedrus*, and *Timaeus*. On at least two occasions in his writings he adopted an explicitly Pythagorean stance – in Book 10 of the *Republic* and in the *Phaedo* – affirming metempsychosis (the transmigration of souls) and thus acknowledging a kinship between humans and other species. There is, however, a distinct hierarchy in Plato's conception of animal value with, perhaps surprisingly, the ant and the bee, because of their gentle and social natures, being placed closest to the human at the apex, well ahead of their more structurally complex and/or predatory brethren. Nonetheless, it is notable that animals in general are of sufficient stature for Plato that some humans will choose to become animals rather than remain human while some animals will choose a human existence.

Having praised the superiority of Pythagoras over Homer, Plato relates a story of transmigration:

The spectacle, [the unnamed prophet] said, was worthy to behold, in what manner the several souls made choice of their life; for it was both pitiful and ridiculous and wonderful to behold, as each for the most part chose according to the habit of their former life. For he told that he saw the soul which was formerly the soul of Orpheus making choice of the life of a swan, through hatred of womankind, being unwilling to be born of woman on account of the death he suffered from them. He saw likewise the soul of Thamyris, making choice of the life of a nightingale, and he saw like wise a swan turning to the choice of human life, and other musical animals, in like manner, as is likely. And that he saw one soul, in making its choice, chuse the life of a lyon, and that it was the soul of Telamonian Ajax, shunning to become a man, remembering the judgment given with reference to the armour. Then next he saw the soul of Agamemnon, and that this one, in hatred also of the human kind, on account of his misfortunes, exchanged it for the life of an eagle ... And that in like manner the souls of wild beasts went into men, and men again into beasts. (Plato, *Republic,* Book 10)[32]

[T]hey may be supposed to be fixed in the same natures which they had in their former life. What natures do you mean, Socrates?

I mean to say that men who have followed after gluttony, and wantonness, and drunkenness, and have no thought of avoiding them, would pass into asses and animals of that sort. What do you think?

I think that exceedingly probable.

And those who have chosen the portion of injustice, and tyranny, and violence, will pass into wolves or hawks and kites: – whither else we can suppose them to go?

Yes; that is doubtless the place for natures such as theirs.

And there is no difficulty, he said, in assigning to all of them places answering to their several natures and propensities?

There is not, he said.

Even among them some are happier than others; and the happiest both in themselves and their place of abode are those who have practised the civil and social virtues which are called temperance and justice and are acquired by habit and attention without philosophy and mind.

Why are they the happiest?

Because they may be expected to pass into some gentle and social nature which is like their own, such as that of bees and ants, or even back again into the form of man, and just and moderate men spring from them. (Plato, *Phaedo*)[33]

Clearly, these are two quite different versions of transmigration. In the first the destination depends on choice; in the second it is determined by merit. The first expresses a greater human–animal similarity than the second, though even in the second certain species are worthy. For Plato, there are good and bad humans, and good and bad animals. The primary difference is that, at least in the *Phaedo*, human goodness corresponds to individual character while animal goodness corresponds to species character.

Plutarch

Plutarch is most famous for his *Lives,* parallel biographies of many renowned and lesser figures of classical Greece and Rome, and also for his *Essays*, or *Moralia* as they used to be more commonly called, which were dissertations on such topics as "Moral Progress," "Anger," and "Contentment," as well as three essays on animals, their natures, and our responsibilities toward them. Plutarch may be said to set the tone for his arguments with this single sentence, citing the poet Brion (c. 100 BC). "Boys throw stones at frogs for fun, but the frogs don't die 'for fun,' but in sober earnest" (Plutarch, *Whether Land or Sea Animals are Cleverer,* 965 A-B).[34]

In his "Life of Marcus Cato," an eminent Roman statesman, Plutarch discusses our responsibilities toward domesticated species and some of the more salutary aspects of the Greek tradition.

[W]e may extend our goodness and charity even to irrational creatures; and such acts flow from a gentle nature, as water from an abundant spring. It is doubtless the part of a kind-natured man to keep even worn-out horses and dogs, and not only take care of them when they are foals and whelps, but also when they are grown old. The Athenians when they built their Hecatompedon* turned those mules loose to feed freely which they had observed to have done the hardest labour. One of these (they say) came once of itself to offer its service, and ran along with, nay, and went before, the teams which drew the wagons up to the acropolis, as if it would encourage them to draw more stoutly; upon which there passed a vote that the creature should be kept at the public charge even till it died. The graves of Cimon's horses, which thrice won the Olympian races, are yet to be seen close by his old monument. Old Xanthippus, too (amongst many others who buried the dogs they had bred up), entombed his which swam after his galley to Salamis, when the people fled from Athens, on the top of a cliff, which they call the Dog's Tomb to this day. Nor are we to use living creatures like old shoes or dishes, and throw them away when they are worn out or broken with service; but if it were for nothing else, but by way of study and practice in humanity, a man ought always to prehabituate himself in these things to be of a kind and sweet disposition. As to myself, I would not so much as sell my draught ox on the account of his age, much less for a small piece of money sell a poor old man, and to chase him, as it were, from his own country, by turning him not only out of the place where he has lived for a long while, but also out of the manner of living he has been accustomed to, and that more especially when he would be as useless to the buyer as to the seller. (Plutarch, "Life of Marcus Cato")[35]

We should, Plutarch opines, treat our animals well for their own sake, but if we cannot then we should do so in order to improve our own characters. Moreover, we should employ the same considerations toward our animals as we should toward our human servants, even if not to the same degree.

In the following story from Plutarch, which is intended to demonstrate the superiority of animal over human life, and which is based loosely on the tenth book of Homer's *Odyssey*, some Greek warriors have been captured by the enchantress Circe and transformed into swine. Odysseus tries to persuade their spokespig, Gryllus, to desire their reconversion into humans.

Gryllus [to Odysseus]: ... what you're scared of is people changing from a worse state to a better one ... you're trying to persuade us, whose lives are filled with countless advantages ... to sail away with you after having changed back to human beings, when there is no creature worse off than a human being ... Let's start with the virtues, which you humans obviously pride yourselves on: you consider yourselves superior to animals in morality, intelligence, courage and all the other virtues. Now, you're really clever, Odysseus, so answer this question of mine. You see, I once overheard you telling Circe about the Cyclope's land and

---

* Temple of Hecate, goddess of witchcraft.

how it is never ploughed and never sown at all, but is such good and innately generous land that it spontaneously yields produce of every kind. So my question is: which do you prefer, the Cyclope's land or harsh Ithaca, which supports only goats and which grudgingly gives its farmers a return on their considerable efforts and hard labour, a return that is small in quantity, poor in quality and of low value? ...

Odysseus: ... Although my own native land occupies a higher place in my heart and my affection, my acclaim and admiration go to the Cyclope's land.

Gryllus: So we'll say that this is how it is: the most intelligent man in the world expects to value and appreciate different things from those that he is drawn to and loves. And I assume your answer is also relevant to the mind, given that the same goes for it as the land: the better mind is that which produces its spontaneous crop, so to speak, of virtue without involving hard work.

Odysseus: I grant you that assumption as well.

Gryllus: Well, you're now admitting that the animal mind is better equipped by nature for the production of virtue, and is more perfect. I mean without being instructed or schooled – without being sown or ploughed, as it were – it naturally produces and grows whatever kind of virtue is appropriate to a given creature.

Odysseus: Virtues in animals, Gryllus?

Gryllus: Yes, virtues of every kind, more than you'd find in the greatest human sage. Let's start with courage if you like, which is a particular source of pride to you ... when animals fight with one another or with you humans, they do not employ tricks and stratagems; they rely in their battles on blatant, bare bravery backed up by genuine prowess ... You don't find animals begging or pleading for mercy or admitting defeat. Cowardice never led a lion to become enslaved to another lion, or a horse to another horse ... if you think that you humans are superior to animals where courage is concerned, then why do your poets use as epithets for the best fighters "wolf-spirited," "lion-hearted" and "of boar-like" bravery? Why do none of them describe a lion as "human-hearted" or a boar as "of man-like bravery"? ... animals draw on pure passion in their fights, whereas for you humans it is diluted with rationality ...

Animals ... have minds which are completely inaccessible to and unapproachable by alien feelings and lifestyles ... They keep their distance from elegance and extravagance in their way of life, and assiduously protect their self-restraint from their better self-government by restricting the number of the desires which live with them and by forbidding entry to extraneous ones ... [A]nimals' intelligence refuses to accommodate any expertise which has no point or purpose; and it doesn't regard the necessary skills as matters to be imported from others, or as things to be taught for money ... but rather it generates the necessary skills on the spot, out of itself, as if they were native and natural products ...

You see, if you reply with the truth – that nature is their teacher – then you're attributing animals' intelligence to the source of all authority and skill.

And if you want to deny the name of reason or intelligence to what animals have, then it is time for you to try to find a more attractive and distinguished name for it, since there is no doubt that the faculty it constitutes is both practically better and more impressive than human intelligence. Ignorance and lack of information play no part in it; rather it is a self-taught and self-sufficient faculty. And this is not a sign of weakness, but is because of the strength and perfection of its natural virtue that it does without any educational contribution that external agents might make of its intelligence ...

In case you're not convinced we [animals] can learn skills, then listen while I demonstrate that we even teach them. For instance, hen partridges teach their chicks to avoid danger by concealing themselves – to lie on their backs and hold a clump of earth in front of themselves with their claws. And consider storks: you can see them on the roofs, the mature ones in attendance instructing those which are tentatively learning to fly. Nightingales give singing lessons to their chicks, and those which are caught while they are still young and are brought up in captivity by humans don't sing very well, as they've been separated from their teacher too soon ...

Odysseus: ... Do you claim that even sheep and donkeys are rational?

Gryllus: My dear Odysseus, these are precisely the ones to provide very strong evidence of the fact that animals' nature is not lacking in reason and understanding. A given tree is not more or less mindless than any other tree; they are all equally unconscious, because none of them has a mind. Analagously, a given creature would not give the impression of being intellectually less alert and quick than any other creature, if they did not all have reasoning and understanding, but in varying degrees. (Plutarch, "On the Use of Reason by 'Irrational' Animals")[36]

The above selection constitutes some one-fifth of Plutarch's essay, all of which is devoted to the demonstration of animal superiority over humans. Similar, if not so extensive, arguments are to be found in the writings of Xenophon, Philo of Alexandria, Ovid, and Seneca. The purpose of such argument was perhaps in general less to demonstrate animal superiority than to chide humans for their hubris in imagining themselves the superior species entitled to use animals at their whim.

In his essay "Whether Land or Sea Animals are Cleverer" Plutarch discusses the sentience, rationality, and attributes of animals in general and certain species in particular.

For nature, which, they rightly say, does everything to some purpose and to some end,* did not create the sentient creature merely to be sentient when something [untoward] happens to it. No, for there are in the world many things friendly to it, many also hostile; and it could not survive for a moment if it had not learned to give the one sort a wide berth while freely mixing with the other. It is, to be sure,

---

* The argument is originally that of Aristotle in the *Politics* 1, 8, 12: "nature makes nothing purposeless or in vain."

sensation that enables each creature to recognize both kinds; but the acts of seizing or pursuing that ensue upon the perception of what is beneficial, as well as the
eluding or fleeing of what is destructive or painful, could by no means occur in
creatures incapable of some sort of reasoning and judging, remembering and
attending. Those beings, then which you* deprive of all expectation, memory,
design, or preparation, and of all hopes, fears, desires or griefs – they will have no
use for eyes or ears either, even though they have them. Indeed, it would be better to be rid of all sensation and imagination that has nothing to make use of it,
rather than to know toil, and distress and pain while not possessing any means of
averting them.

There is, in fact, a work of Strato, the natural philosopher, which proves that it is
impossible to have sensation at all without some action of the intelligence ...

In general, then, the evidence by which the philosophers demonstrate that
beasts have their share of reason is their possession of purpose and preparation and
memory and emotions and care for their young and gratitude for benefits and hostility to what has hurt them; to which may be added their ability to find what they
need and their manifestation of good qualities, such as courage and sociability and
continence and magnanimity.

Plutarch follows this introduction with descriptions of the particular
virtues of a lengthy list of specific species. The following may be taken as
representative examples:

It is impossible to relate in full detail all the methods of production and storage
practised by ants, but it would be careless to omit them entirely. Nature has, in
fact, nowhere else so small a mirror of greater and nobler enterprises. Just as you
may see greater things reflected in a drop of clear water, so among ants there exists
the delineation of every virtue.

Love and affection are found, namely [in] their social life. You may see, too, the
reflection of courage in their persistence in hard labour. There are many seeds of
temperance and many of prudence and justice.

... even to this day the Thracians, whenever they propose crossing a frozen river,
make use of a fox as an indicator of the solidity of the ice; if she perceives by the
sound that the stream is running close underneath, judging that the frozen part has
no great depth, but is only thin and insecure she stands stock still and, if she is permitted, returns to the shore; but if she is reassured by the absence of noise, she
crosses over. And let us not declare this is a nicety of perception unaided by reason;
it is, rather, a syllogistic conclusion developed from the evidence of perception:
"What makes noise must be in motion; what is in motion is not frozen; what is not
frozen is liquid; what is liquid gives way" ...

And what music, what grace, do we not find in the natural, untaught warbling
of birds! To this the most eloquent and musical of our poets bear witness when they
compare their sweetest songs and poems to the singing of swans and nightingales.

---

* That is, Plutarch's philosophical adversaries, whom he is addressing.

... it is not easy to find naturally clever animals doing anything which illustrates merely one of their virtues. Their probity, rather, is revealed in their love of offspring and their cleverness in their nobility; then, too, their craftiness and intelligence is inseparable from their ardour and courage. (Plutarch, "Whether Land or Sea Animals are Cleverer")[37]

In his early and incomplete essay "On the Eating of Flesh" Plutarch complains of the inconsiderate treatment of food animals and advocates a vegetarian diet on the grounds of sparing the animals the cruelties inflicted on them and also of saving humanity from its meat-eating degradation.

Can you really ask what reason Pythagoras had for abstaining from flesh? For my part I rather wonder both by what accident and in what state of soul or mind the first man who did so, touched his mouth to gore and brought his lips to the flesh of a dead creature, he who set forth tables of dead, stale bodies and ventured to call food and nourishment the parts that had a little before bellowed and cried, moved and lived. How could his eyes endure the slaughter when the throats were slit and hides flayed and limbs torn from limb? How could his nose endure the stench? How was it that the pollution did not turn away his taste, which made contact with the sores of others and sucked juices and serums from mortal wounds? ...

You call serpents and panthers and lions savage, but you yourselves by your own foul slaughter, leave them no room to outdo you in cruelty; for their slaughter is their living, yours is a mere appetizer.

It is certainly not lions and wolves that we eat out of self-defence; on the contrary, we ignore these and slaughter harmless, tame creatures without stings or teeth to harm to us, creatures that, I swear, Nature appears to have produced for the sake of their beauty and grace ...

But nothing abashes us, not the flower-tinting of the flesh, not the cleanliness of their habits or the unusual intelligence that may be found in the poor wretches. No, for the sake of a little flesh we deprive them of sun, of light, of the duration of life to which they are entitled by birth and being. Then we go on to assume that when they utter cries and squeaks their speech is inarticulate, that they do not, begging for mercy, entreating, seeking justice, each one of them say, "I do not ask to be spared in case of necessity; only spare me your arrogance! Kill me to eat, but not to please your palate!" Oh, the cruelty of it! What a terrible thing it is to look on when the tables of the rich are spread, men who employ cooks and spicers to groom the dead! And it is even more terrible to look on when they are taken away, for more is left than has been eaten. So the beasts died for nothing! There are others who refuse when the dishes are set before them and will not have them cut or sliced. Though they did spare the dead, they did not spare the living. (Plutarch, "On the Eating of Flesh")[38]

Cicero

Marcus Tullius Cicero (106 BC–43 BC), a renowned statesman and essayist, was by repute the greatest Roman orator. He wrote essays on a wide variety of topics, including "On Friendship," "On Duty," and "On Old Age." He has little to say about consideration for animals other than the following enlightening comment in a letter to a friend on the public's attitude to the treatment of animals in the Roman Circus.

[W]hat pleasure can a cultivated man get out of seeing a weak human being torn to pieces by a powerful animal or a splendid animal transfixed by a hunting spear? Anyhow, if these sights are worth seeing, you have seen them often, and we spectators saw nothing new. The groundlings [those of inferior rank] showed much astonishment thereat, but no enjoyment. There was even an impulse of compassion, a feeling that the monsters had something human about them. (Cicero to Marcus Marius, from Rome, late August 55 BC, *Letters to Friends [ad familiares]*, 7, 1)[39]

Lucretius

Titus Lucretius Carus (c. 100 BC to c. 55 BC) was a Roman poet whose personal life is obscure. In his magnum opus, *On the Nature of the Universe* (*de rerum natura*), he wrote of the earth as a living, breathing animal, much in the vein of some modern Gaia theorists.[40] He added his voice to those who insist we can, and do, learn from the animals. On several occasions he indicates either that humans lack by nature capacities possessed by other species or suggests that humans may once have had them but lost them through disuse. In the following sentence he describes the human indebtedness to birds: "Men learnt to mimic with their mouths the trilling notes of birds long before they were able to enchant the ear by joining together in tuneful song" (Lucretius, *On the Nature of the Universe*, 5, 13, 80-2).[41] In the most moving passage of his writings, Lucretius sympathizes with the cow deprived of her offspring, acknowledging a maternal instinct of the same nature in cattle as in humans.

Outside some stately shrine of the gods incense is smouldering on the altar. Beside it a slaughtered calf falls to the ground. From its breast it breathes out a hot stream of blood. But the bereaved dam, roaming through green glades, scans the ground for the twin-pitted instrument of familiar feet. Her eyes roll this way and that in search of the missing young ones. She pauses and fills the leafy thickets with her plaints. Time and again she returns to the byre, sore at heart with yearning for her calf. Succulent osiers and herbage fresh with dew and her favourite streams flowing level with their banks – all these are powerless to console her and to banish her new burden of distress. The sight of other calves in the lush pastures is powerless to distract her mind or relieve her distress. (Lucretius, *On the Nature of the Universe*, 2, 352-66)[42]

Philo of Alexandria

Commenting on the verse in the book of Exodus (34:26) that forbids the boiling of a slaughtered kid in its mother's milk, Jewish philosopher Philo of Alexandria (c. 20 BC to c. AD 50), also known as Philo Judaeus, was aroused to passion as well as compassion in his denunciation of the practice. "The man who seethes the flesh of any one of them in the milk of its own mother is exhibiting a terrible perversity of disposition and exhibits himself as wholly destitute of that feeling, which of all others, is most indispensable to, and most nearly akin to a rational soul, namely compassion."[43]

Seneca

The Roman Stoic philosopher and playwright Seneca (c. 4 BC to c. AD 65) was born in Spain, lived in Rome as a successful administrator, and is best known for his *Essays on Morals* and his *Letters on Morals* to Lucillus, whence this extract on the virtues of vegetarianism.

Inasmuch as I have begun to explain to you how much greater was my impulse to approach philosophy in my youth than to continue it in my old age, I shall not be ashamed to tell you what ardent zeal Pythagoras inspired in me. Sotion* used to tell me why Pythagoras abstained from animal food, and why, in later times, Sextius† did also. In each case the reason was different, but it was in each case a noble reason. Sextius believed that man had enough sustenance without resorting to blood, and that a habit of cruelty is formed whenever butchery is practised for pleasure. Moreover, he thought we should curtail the sources of our luxury; he argued that a varied diet was contrary to the laws of health, and was unsuited to our constitutions. Pythagoras, on the other hand, held that all beings were interrelated and that there was a system of exchange between souls which transmigrated from one bodily shape to another. If one may believe him, no soul perishes or ceases from its functioning at all, except for a tiny interval – when it is being poured from one body into another. We may question at what time and after what seasons of exchange the soul returns to man, when it has wandered through many a dwelling-place; but meantime, he made men fearful of guilt and parricide, since they might be, without knowing it, attacking the soul of a parent and injuring it with knife or with teeth – if, as is possible, the related spirit be dwelling temporarily in this bit of flesh! When Sotion had set forth this doctrine, supplementing it with his own proofs, he would say: "You do not believe that souls are assigned, first to one body then to another, and that our so-called death is merely a source of abode? You do not believe that in cattle, or in wild beasts, or in creatures of the deep, the soul of him who was once a man may linger? You do not believe that nothing on this earth is annihilated, but only changes its haunts?

And that animals also have cycles of progress and, so to speak, an orbit for their souls, no less than heavenly bodies, which revolve in fixed circuits? Great men have put faith in this idea; therefore, while holding to your own view, keep the whole question in abeyance in your mind. If the theory is true, it is a mark of purity to

---

* Sotion was a Pythagorean contemporary of Seneca.
† "Sextius" refers to Quintus Sextius the Elder, renowned for declining an honour from Julius Caesar.

refrain from eating flesh; if it be false, it is economy. And what harm does it do you to give such credence? I am merely depriving you of food which sustains lions and vultures."

I was imbued with this teaching, and began to abstain from animal food; at the end of a year the habit was as pleasant as it was easy. I was beginning to feel that my mind was more active. (Seneca, *Ad Lucilium Epistulae Morales,* Letter 58)[44]

Eventually, Seneca returned to meat-eating. But the letter, along with that from Cicero, is a useful reminder that even the Stoics, by general repute the least animal sympathetic of the classical thinkers, were sometimes persuaded that the interests of animals mattered.

Pliny the Elder
Pliny the Elder (Gaius Plinius Secundus) was born at Novum Comum in northern Italy and lived from AD 23 to 79. His remarkable *Natural History* has much to tell us about animals, most of it, unfortunately, unenlightening. In his pages we meet 300-feet-long eels, 150-feet-long sharks, three-acre whales, religious elephants, merciful lions, and an octopus that climbed trees. Such was the animal lore of his time. Nonetheless, he adds his voice to those who would warn humans against an overweening pride in their own excellence.

All other animals know their own natures ... Man, however, knows nothing unless by learning ... No creature's life is more fragile; none has a greater lust for everything; none a more confused sense of fear or a fiercer anger ... not even sea-monsters and fish act cruelly, except against different species. But man, I swear, experiences most ills at the hands of his fellow men ...

The elephant is the largest land animal and is closest to man as regards intelligence, because it understands the language of its native land, is obedient to commands, remembers the duties it has been taught, and has a desire for affection and honour. Indeed, the elephant has qualities rarely apparent even in man, namely honesty, good sense, [and] justice ...

Among all insect species the pride of place is reserved for bees ... What is especially astonishing, they have manners more advanced than those of other animals, whether wild or tame. Nature is so great that from a tiny ghost-like creature she has made something incomparable. What sinews or muscles can we compare with the enormous efficiency and industry shown by bees? What men, in heaven's name, can we set alongside these insects which are superior to men when it comes to reasoning? (Pliny the Elder, *Natural History*)[45]

Ovid
Publius Ovidus Naso (43 BC–AD 18), Roman poet, was celebrated for his verse treatises on love, but the *Metamorphoses* was his mythological creative masterpiece. The following legend of human love for an animal takes place in the groves of Orpheus, the celebrated Thracian musician of Greek

mythology, of whom it was said that the sounds of his lyre were so enchanting they could soothe the wild animals, make the trees dance, and calm the waters. Ovid was also a primary source for the image of Pythagoras (in Book 15 of the *Metamorphoses*) but few scholars place much faith in the historicity of Ovid's account and it has accordingly, albeit with qualms, been omitted here.[46] Of course, being an explicit part of Greek mythology, the story of Cyparissus is not subject to the same tests.

There was once a magnificent stag, sacred to the nymphs who live in the fields of Carthea, whose branching antlers cast deep shade over its head ... This stag was quite without fear, and its natural timidity forgotten, used to visit people's houses and hold out his neck, even to strangers to be stroked. But the person who was most attached to it was Cyparissus, the handsomest of the Cean boys. He used to lead it to fresh grazing, or to the waters of some crystal spring, and wove wreaths of different kinds of flowers to hang upon its horns. Sometimes he sat on its back, like a horseman on his horse, and gleefully guided the animal's soft mouth this way and that, by means of scarlet reins.

One summer day at noon, when the curving arms of the shore-loving crab were being scorched by the heat of the sun, the stag was tired, and lay down to rest on the grassy ground, finding coolness in the shade of the trees. There Cyparissus unwittingly pierced it with his keen javelin. When he saw his friend cruelly wounded and dying, the boy resolved to die himself. Phoebus* said all he could to comfort him, chiding him and telling him his grief should be moderate in proportion to its cause. Still the boy groaned and begged as a last gift from the gods, that he should be allowed to go on mourning forever. Now, as his blood drained away, by reason of his endless weeping, his limbs began to change to a greenish hue, and the hair which lately curled over his snowy brow bristled and stiffened, pointing upwards in a graceful crest toward the starry sky. Sadly, the God Apollo sighed: "I shall mourn for you," he said, "while you yourself will mourn for others, and be the constant companion of those in distress."

Such was the grove which Orpheus had drawn around him, and now he sat in the midst of a gathering of wild creatures, and a host of birds. (Ovid, *Metamorphoses*, Book 10)[47]

Marcus Aurelius

Military general, Stoic philosopher, and Roman emperor, Marcus Aurelius (AD 121–80) is noted for his *Meditations* which remained required reading for the educated gentleman until the late nineteenth century. He is certainly not one of those who elevated the status of animals. In fact, he was foremost among the Stoics in maintaining their traditional (but not universal) belief that only humans are rational, social, and capable of, and hence entitled to, justice. He follows Aristotle in believing that the "lower"

---

* Phoebus is another name for Apollo, one of the highest of the Olympian gods.

animals exist for the sake of humans. Nonetheless, he regards cruelty to animals as quite unacceptable. The reality is that even the Stoics, those customarily depicted as the least animal considerate of classical philosophers, find an at least somewhat respected place for the animals in their cosmologies.

Is it not plain that the inferior exist for the sake of the superior? but the little things which have life are superior to those which have not life, and to those which have life the superior are those which have reason ...

As to the animals which have not reason, and generally all things and objects, do thou, since thou have reason and they have none, make use of them with a generous and liberal spirit. But toward human beings, as they have reason, behave in a social spirit ...

All things are little, changeable, perishable. All things come from thence, from that universal ruling power either directly proceeding or by sequence. And accordingly the lion's gaping jaws, and that which is poisonous, and every harmful thing, as a thorn, as mud, are after-products of the grand and beautiful. Do not then imagine that they are of another kind from that which thou dost venerate, but form a just opinion of the source of all ...

Take care not to feel toward the inhuman, as they feel toward men ...

A spider is proud when he has caught a fly, and [a human] when he has caught a poor hare, and another when he has taken a little fish in a net, and another when he has taken wild boars, and another when he has taken bears ... Are these not robbers ...? (*The Meditations of the Emperor Marcus Aurelius*)[48]

We should behave toward our fellow humans with a sense of common kinship, and toward the "lower" animals with generosity and liberality, in sufficient degree that it would seem to exclude hunting and fishing. Marcus Aurelius might have thought to inquire whether his own court physician, Galen, who dissected pigs and apes for anatomical research, was not equally a robber.

Aelian

Claudius Aelianus (c. AD 170 to c. AD 230), born at Praeneste in Italy, was a Roman citizen who, like many of his countrymen, wrote in Greek. *On the Characteristics of Animals* was his most important work. As with other natural histories of the period, it is filled with zoological and ethological absurdities. Nonetheless, it also contains stories of compassion and respect.

A certain Byzantine, Leonidas by name, declares that while sailing past Aeolia he saw with his own eyes at the town called Porosolene a tame Dolphin which lived in the harbour there and behaved towards the inhabitants as though they were personal friends. And further he declares that an aged couple fed this foster-child, offering it the most alluring baits. What is more, the old couple had a son who was brought up along with the Dolphin, and the pair cared for the Dolphin and their own son, and somehow by dint of being brought up together the man child and the fish* gradually came without knowing it to love one another, and, as the oft-repeated tag has it, "a super-reverent counter-love was cultivated." So then the Dolphin came to love Porosolene as his native country and grew as fond of the harbour as his own home, and what is more, he repaid those who had cared for him what they had spent on feeding him. And this was how he did it. When fully grown, he had no need of being fed from the hand, but would now swim further out, and as he ranged abroad in his search for some quarry from the sea, would keep some to feed himself, and the rest he would bring to his "relatives." And they were aware of this and were even glad to wait for the tribute which he brought. This then was one gain; another was as follows. As to the boys so to the Dolphin his foster-parents gave a name, and the boy with the courage born of their common upbringing would stand upon some spot jutting into the sea and call the name, and as he called would use soothing words. Whereat the Dolphin, whether he was racing with some oared ship, or plunging and leaping in scorn of all the other fish that roamed in shoals about the spot, or was hunting under stress of hunger, would rise to the surface with all speed, like a ship that raises a great wave as it drives onward, and drawing near to his loved one would frolic and gambol at his side; at one moment would swim close by the boy, at another would seem to challenge him and even induce his favourite to race with him. And what was more astounding, he would at times even decline the winner's place and actually swam second, as though presumably he was glad to be defeated. (Aelian, *On the Characteristics of Animals*, 2, 6)[49]

Sextus Empiricus

Sextus Empiricus was a second- or third-century-AD Greek skeptic philosopher who found the reasoning of the Stoics on animal irrationality itself irrational.

Now according to those Dogmatists who are, at present, our chief opponents – I mean the Stoics – internal reason is supposed to be occupied with the following matters: the choice of things congenial and the avoidance of things alien; the knowledge of the arts contributing thereto; the apprehension of the virtues pertaining to one's proper nature and of those relating to the passions. Now the dog – the animal upon which, by way of example, we have decided to base our argument – exercises choice of the congenial and avoidance of the harmful, in that it hunts after food and sinks away from a raised whip. Moreover, it possesses an art which supplies what is congenial, namely hunting. Nor is it devoid even of virtue; for certainly if justice consists in rendering to each his due,† the dog, that welcomes

---

* That is, the dolphin; the traditional Greek distinction was between animals of the land and animals of the water, not between mammals and fish.
† Plato's definition of justice in the *Republic*.

and guards its friends and benefactors but drives off strangers and evil-doers, cannot be lacking in justice. But if he possesses this virtue, then, since the virtues are interdependent, he possesses also all the other virtues; and these, say the [Stoic] philosophers, the majority of men do not possess. That the dog is also valiant we see by the way he repels attacks, and intelligent as well, as Homer too testified* when he sang how Odysseus went unrecognized by all the people of his own household and was recognized by the dog Argos, who neither was deceived by the bodily alterations of the hero nor had lost his original apprehensive impression, which indeed he evidently retained better than the men. And according to [the Stoic philosopher] Chrysippus, who shows special interest in irrational animals, the dog even shares in the far-famed "Dialectic."† This person [Chrysippus], at any rate, declares that the dog makes use of the fifth complex indemonstrable syllogism‡ when, on arriving at a spot where three ways meet, after smelling at the two roads by which the quarry did not pass, he rushes off at once by the third without stopping to smell. For, says the old writer [Chrysippus], the dog implicitly reasons thus: "The creature went either by this road, or by that, or by the other; but it did not go by this road or by that: therefore it went by the other." Moreover, the dog is capable of comprehending and assuaging his own sufferings; for when a thorn has got stuck in his foot he hastens to remove it by rubbing his foot on the ground and by using his teeth. And if he has a wound anywhere, because dirty ones are hard to cure whereas clean ones heal easily, the dog gently licks off the pus that has gathered. Nay more, the dog admirably observes the prescription of Hippocrates [the renowned physician of Cos] rest being what cures the foot, whenever he gets his foot hurt he lifts it up and keeps it as far as possible free from pressure. And when distressed by unwholesome humours he eats grass by the help of which he vomits what is unwholesome and gets well again. If, then, it has been shown that the animal upon which, as an example, we have based our argument not only chooses the wholesome and avoids the noxious, but also possesses an art capable of supplying what is wholesome, and is capable of comprehending and assuaging its own sufferings, and is not devoid of virtue, then – these being the things in which the perfection of internal reason consists – the dog will be thus far perfect. (Sextus Empiricus, *Outlines of Pyrrhonism*, 1.14)[50]

It should be noticed once again that the view of the Stoics as unfriendly to animals is put in question; and this time by the words of their most eminent philosopher, save for Zeno. On the question of reason, Stoics in general would appear to argue that few men possess reason, and in this respect most men are like other species. Their opponents argue that most men possess reason and other species share in this capacity. On both accounts most men and most animals are similar.

---

* In the *Odyssey*, 17, 300. See p. 37.
† That is, the Stoic system of logic.
‡ The syllogism has the form: either A or B or C exists; but neither A nor B exists; therefore C exists.

Plotinus

Plotinus (c. AD 205 to c. AD 270) was born in Egypt but lived in Rome from AD 244, where he founded a Neoplatonist school noted for its asceticism, including vegetarianism. The significance of Plotinus lies in his systematization of the earlier Greek idea of the Great Chain of Being, which became, according to the great historian of ideas, Arthur O. Lovejoy, "one of the half-dozen most potent and persistent presuppositions in Western thought,"[51] extending its influence well into the nineteenth century and beyond. The kernel of the idea is that there is a hierarchy of beings from the deities through spiritual beings, humans, other mammals, and crustacea to the lowest insects, all deserving of respect as the beings that they are. Some later thinkers used the idea to stress the proximity between species and to elevate the status of the animals, others to proclaim human superiority and the relative insignificance of other species.

The animals and plants share in reason and soul and life ... the formative principle did not make everything gods but some gods, some spirits (a nature of the second rank), then men and animals after them in order, not out of grudging meanness but by a reason containing all the rich variety of the intelligible world ...

We must conclude that the universal order is for ever something of ... [j]ustice and wonderful wisdom ... from the evidence of what we see in the All, how this order extends to everything, even to the smallest, and the art is wonderful which appears, not only in the divine beings but also in the things which one might have supposed providence would have despised [for] their smallness, for example, the workmanship which produces wonders in rich variety in ordinary animals, and the beauty of appearance which extends to the fruits and even the leaves of plants ...

[T]here is no blame attaching to the production of plants because they have no sense-perception, nor in the case of other animals because they are not like men: to blame anyone for this would be the same as asking, "Why are men not what gods are?"

[We] ought not to inquire whether one thing is less than an other but whether it, as itself, is sufficient; for all things ought not to have been equal.

[I]t would not have been right for all things to have been cut off from each other, but they had to be made like each other, in some way at least. (Plotinus, *Enneads*, 3)[52]

Porphyry

A student of Plotinus in Rome, the Greek scholar Porphyry edited his teacher's works and wrote his biography (as well as one on Pythagoras), composed an influential tome on Aristotle's logical system (*Eisagoge*), and contributed a book *On Abstinence from Animal Food* that is increasingly recognized as perhaps the primary classical work related to animal ethics.[53]

We shall pass on ... to the discussion of justice; and since our opponents [the Stoics] say that this ought only to be extended to those of similar species, and on this account deny that irrational animals can be injured by men, let us exhibit the true, and at the same time Pythagoric opinion, and demonstrate that every soul which participates of sense and memory is rational. For this being demonstrated, we may extend, as our opponents will also admit, justice to every animal ...

Since, however, with respect to reason, one kind, according to the doctrine of the Stoics, is internal, but the other external, and again, one kind being right, but the other erroneous, it is requisite to explain of which of these two, animals, according to them, are deprived. Are they therefore deprived of right reason alone? Or are they entirely destitute both of internal and externally proceeding reason?

They appear, indeed, to ascribe to brutes an entire privation of reason, and not a privation of right reason alone. For if they merely denied that brutes possess right reason, animals would not be irrational, but rational beings, in the same manner as nearly all men are according to them. For, according to their opinion, one or two wise men may be found in whom alone right reason prevails, but all the rest of mankind are depraved; though some of these make a certain proficiency, but others are profoundly depraved, and yet at the same time, all of them are similarly rational ... If, however, it be requisite to speak the truth, not only reason may plainly be perceived in all animals, but in many of them it is so great as to approximate to perfection ...

Since ... that which is vocally expressed by the tongue is reason, in whatever manner it may be expressed, whether in a barbarous or a Grecian, a canine or a bovine mode, other animals also participate of it that are vocal; men, indeed, speaking conformably to the human laws, but other animals conformably to the laws which they received from the Gods and nature. But if we do not understand what they say, what is this to the purpose? For the Greeks do not understand what is said by the Indians, nor those who are educated in Attica the language of the Scythians, or Thracians, or Syrians; but the sound of the one falls on the ear of the other like the clangour of cranes, though by others their vocal sounds can be written and articulated, in the same manner as ours can by us ... The like also takes place in the vocal sounds of other animals. For the several species of these understand the language which is adapted to them ...

The difference, indeed, between our reason and theirs, appears to consist, as Aristotle somewhere says,[54] not in essence, but in the more and the less; just as many are of the opinion, that the difference between the Gods and us is not essential but consists in this, that in them there is a greater, and in us a less accuracy, of the reasoning power. And, indeed, so far as pertains to sense and the remaining organization, according to the sensoria and the flesh, every one nearly will grant that these are similarly disposed in us, as they are in brutes. For they not only similarly participate with us of natural passions, and the motions produced through these, but we may also survey in them such affections as are preternatural and morbid. No one, however, of a sound mind, will say that brutes are unreceptive of the reasoning power, on account of the difference between their habit of body and ours, when he sees that there is a great variety of habit in man, according to their race, and the nations to which they belong and yet, at the same time, it is granted that all of them are rational ...

It does not follow, if we have more intelligence than other animals, that on this account they are to be deprived of intelligence; as neither must it be said, that partridges do not fly, because hawks fly higher ...

[B]rutes are rational animals, reason in most of them being indeed imperfect, of which, nevertheless, they are not entirely deprived. Since, however, justice pertains to rational beings, as our opponents say, how is it possible not to admit, that we should also act justly toward brutes? For we do not extend justice to plants, because there appears to be much in them which is unconnected with reason ...

[T]o compare plants ... with animals, is doing violence to the order of things. For the latter are naturally sensitive, and adapted to feel pain, to be terrified and hurt; on which account also they may be injured. But the former are entirely destitute of sensation, and in consequence of this, nothing foreign, or evil, or hurtful, or injurious can befall them ... And is it not absurd, since we see that many of our own species live from sense alone, but do not possess intellect and reason, and since we also see, that many of them surpass the most terrible of wild beasts in cruelty, anger, and rapine, being murderous of their children and their parents, and also being tyrants, and the tools of kings, to fancy that we ought to act justly toward these, but that no justice is due from us to the ox that ploughs, the dog that is fed with us, and the animals that nourish us with their milk, and adorn our bodies with their wool? Is not such an opinion most irrational and absurd? ...

[I]f God fashioned animals for the use of men, in what [manner] do we use flies, lice, bats, beetles, scorpions, and vipers? ... And if our opponents should admit that all things are not generated for us, and with a view to our advantage, in addition to the distinction which they make being very confused and obscure, we shall not avoid acting unjustly, in attacking and noxiously using those animals which were not produced for our sake ... I omit to mention, that if we define, by utility, things which pertain to us, we shall not be prevented from admitting, that we were generated for the sake of the most destructive animals, such as crocodiles ... and dragons.[55] For we are not in the least benefited by them; but they seize and destroy men that fall in their way, and use them for food; in so doing acting not at all more cruelly than we do, excepting that they commit this injustice through want and hunger, but we through insolent wantonness, and for the sake of luxury, frequently sporting in theatres, and in hunting slaughter the greater part of animals. And by thus acting, indeed, a murderous disposition and a brutal nature become strengthened in us, and render us insensible to pity: to which we may add, that those who first dared to do this, blunted the greatest part of lenity, and rendered it inefficacious ...

[S]ince animals are allied to us, if it should appear, according to Pythagoras, that they are allotted the same soul that we are, he may justly be considered impious who does not abstain from acting unjustly toward his kindred. Nor because some animals are savage, is their alliance to us to be on this account abscinded. For some men may be found who are no less, and even more malefic than savage animals to their neighbours, and who are impelled to injure any one they may meet with, as if they were driven by a certain blast of their own nature and depravity. Hence also, we destroy such men; yet we do not cut them off from an alliance to animals of a mild nature. Thus, therefore, if likewise some animals are savage, these, as such, are to be destroyed, in the same manner as men that are savage;[56] but habitude or alliance to other and wilder animals is not on this account to be abandoned. But neither tame nor savage animals are to be eaten; as neither are unjust men.

He ... who admits that he is allied to all animals, will not injure any animal ... since justice consists in not injuring anything, it must be extended as far as to every animated nature* ... when reason governs ... man will be innoxious towards everything. For the passions being restrained, and desire and anger wasting away, but reason possessing its proper empire, a similitude to a more excellent nature immediately follows. (Porphyry, *On Abstinence from Animal Food)*[57]

---

* A doctrine that corresponds to the *ahimsa* of the Jaina.

3
The Dark Ages

The Dark Ages corresponds roughly to the Middle Ages, that period in Western European history from the collapse of the western Roman Empire, beginning toward the end of the fourth century, until the revival of classical secular learning in the Renaissance, stimulated in part via Arabic and Jewish sources, which broke out hesitantly in Italy in the thirteenth century and pervaded all of Europe by the sixteenth.

While the sobriquet "Dark Ages" is less in vogue today, it was once the customary term to apply to a time of economic and technological stagnation in which the prosperity and erudition promised by the Greco-Roman heritage succumbed to what was thought of as the barbaric millennium. The term has lost its currency because we know that Charlemagne, at the turn of the ninth century, was promoting the revival of classical learning, primarily, but not solely, among the clergy – though perhaps not with the greatest of success. Furthermore, by the eleventh century, the European population was once again increasing, and trade, and consequently wealth, were slowly returning. Nonetheless, it is not until toward the end of the medieval period that we encounter a yearning for secular knowledge, the practice of the fine arts, and a sufficiently thriving economy to afford the luxuries of scholarship, science, and art on a grand scale.

All this had an impact on the treatment of, and understanding of, our relationship to the animal realm – but not always to the advantage of the animals. On the one hand, animal experimentation was an acceptable practice in classical Rome, most famously by Galen, court physician to the emperor Marcus Aurelius, who dissected apes and pigs to further the understanding and functions of the body.[1] Following the Roman defeats at the hands of the reputed barbarians – usually considered complete by the loss of the palace of Soissons in AD 627 – animal experimentation ceased by and large until the sixteenth century. The Greeks and Romans had been using animal power since the first century BC, often quite cruelly, for grinding grain via the "hourglass" mill and the water mill, raising water by capstan in a geared bucket chain, crushing both olives and metal ore in an edge-runner mill, and even for kneading dough. With the sacking of Rome, and the ensuing collapse of the imperial administration in the colonies, much of the technology was lost and the animals were spared their excessive labours.

On the other hand, popular medicine was often in the hands of reputed witches and other amateur physicians – admittedly little, if at all, less competent than those who were trained[2] – sometimes imposing alarming barbarities on animals to acquire their purportedly curative organs. In Shakespeare's *Macbeth* (4. 1) the witches concoct their potion from toad, snake, newt, frog, bat, dog, blindworm, lizard, owlet, wolf, shark, goat, and tiger parts. Even if, as we may readily imagine, this recipe is many times more complex than was customary, it nonetheless reflects the medicinal abuse of animals in the Middle Ages. In addition, religious learning became so directed to the importance of the afterlife and insignificance of the mundane that the debate about the ethics of animal use, which played a lively role in classical thought, was largely forgotten. Indeed, many of the major manuscripts were lost or destroyed; others were relegated to the dusty monastery library shelves where they were customarily consulted only if they were seen to have a bearing on heavenly matters. In actuality, the animals were at least sometimes treated better by practising Christians than by their pontificating brethren, leading the historian W.E.H. Lecky to conclude of monastic farming that "it represents one of the most striking efforts made in Christendom to inculcate a feeling of kindness and pity towards the brute creation."[3] Thus Ruth Burtt testifies:

> The records of the monasteries often show a marked consideration for their working beasts on the part of monastic landlords and this is notably so in the large estates owned by the great abbeys.
>
> Thus 13th century rules, laid down by the Abbey of St. Peter, Gloucester, expressly state that the servants of their manors are to take care of the oxen, making sure that the mangers in each stall contain a night's food for each team, and they are to plough without injuring or distressing the beasts.[4]

Also in the thirteenth century, Walter of Henly's husbandry manual recommended that working animals should not be "overloaded or overworked, or overridden or hurt."[5] In part this was to ensure their productivity; and in part to treat them as the sentient beings they were recognized to be. They could be distressed only if they posssessed feelings.

When one notices the cruelties it is easy to be misled about the countervailing sympathies for animals. Thus, for example, John Passmore commented on a fourteenth-century Japanese writer who opposed the caging of wild birds, observing that such sensibility "could certainly not be matched in European writers of the same period."[6] In fact, in the thirteenth century, as W.E.H. Lecky pointed out in 1869, St. James of Venice "was accustomed to buy and release the birds with which Italians used to play by attaching them to strings, saying that 'he pitied the little birds of the Lord,' and his tender charity recoiled from all cruelty, even to the most diminutive of animals."[7] In the fifteenth century, Leonardo da Vinci, whose *Notebooks* are replete with the most profound animal sympathy, purchased caged birds from Florentine market vendors, and, as his first biographer Giorgio Vasari informs us, "he let them fly away, restoring them to their lost liberty."[8] Vasari not only reported this behaviour, he deemed it an admirable aspect of Leonardo's character and evidently expected his sixteenth-century readers to concur. Practice and precept were often at odds, in both Japan and Europe.

The dearth of classical learning permitted the old myths to flourish, and new ones to be coined, in which we find, at least in some measure, an emphasis on, delight in, and respect for, the world of nature. And even some of the theologians found time to provide a respected place for the animals in their cosmologies, especially those who managed to escape the narrow confines of much theological learning and listened a little to the myths sung by the bards – which were often about the lives of the saints themselves, and sometimes of their love for animals. As Andrew Linzey has estimated, more than two-thirds of the saints demonstrated "a practical concern for, and befriending of, animals."[9] If much of today's literature on the history of animal welfare thinking tells a dismal tale of animal disrespect in the Middle Ages, it is because the authors pay too much attention to medieval intellectual abstractions and not enough to the myths in which the common people revelled.

If this, then, was the Dark Ages for those who regard the human as the progressive animal, involved in continuous intellectual and technological development, distancing itself from the "inferior creatures" incapable of "self-improvement," it was also an age that was, overall and with notable exceptions, perhaps not quite so sombre for the animals, at least in historical comparison. Medieval myth laid the groundwork for later European poetry and literary prose that played a major role in raising the status of nonhuman species.

Of course, animals were often treated atrociously, as they have been throughout human history. But that must be understood by comparison with the equally appalling treatment of humans. Animal treatment is always most readily understood in the context of cultural attitudes in general. If serfs were treated by and large as inferior creatures, in effect as if another species, the attitude to animals could scarce be expected to be any better. In his admirable, yet largely unknown, *Love for Animals and How It Developed in Great Britain,* Dix Harwood explains:

[S]ince men could be extremely cruel to a political or religious enemy, it is not to be expected that a common criminal or a beast would escape lightly.

In 1279, while Edward I was king, two hundred and eighty Jews were hanged for clipping coins. The custom of pressing to death for refusal to plead was introduced in the next century. And sometimes as much as four or five hundred pounds weight was placed on a man's body before he cried for mercy. A traitor was first half-killed by slow strangulation; and while he still lived his entrails were snatched out and flung into the fire before his expiring eyes. The body was then quartered and distributed to various gates and gibbets for birds to pluck at ... From the time when the Danes plucked out the eyes and sliced off the noses, ears, and upper lips, England has been accustomed to horrors ... Legalized boiling in oil did not offend the public until 1547 ... For centuries branding was a common punishment ... The rack flourished on the continent from the dark ages to the time of Voltaire ... Men were quartered and torn with red hot pincers ... [or] were impaled on iron stakes. The hearts of men thus became greatly hardened – a deplorably rapid process ... Animals could certainly not be expected to escape lightly in a world where gibbets stood at every crossroads and where the greatest men of the realm tossed a golden gratuity to the axman and laid their heads on the block in the gray courtyard of the tower.

Compared to what men were made to suffer, the persecution of a captive bull or bear seems almost pardonable and at least comprehensible.[10]

We should, then, scarcely be surprised that animals were condemned to death, or other punishment, for purportedly criminal behaviour, a not uncommon judicial procedure, especially in France, and known to continue in Switzerland until the onset of the twentieth century.[11] But if this was a travesty of justice, it also indicates to us that the Middle Ages recognized a greater human–animal similarity than was common later. Animals were deemed capable of accepting responsibility for their antisocial behaviour, which implied that they possessed both a degree of rationality and a moral sense. Moreover, in medieval art there is a common recognition that animals have been treated unjustly in this life. As Boria Sax has explained, the

traditional roles of human beings and animals are reversed in Hell. Fantastic animals ... hunt, herd, cook ... and eat people, just the way people have done to animals on earth. This reversal reflects the discomfort that people have doubtless always felt about their treatment of animals.[12]

This chapter is divided into two sections: myth, and theology and philosophy. While myths do not evaluate our appropriate relationship to the animal realm in a philosophical manner, they often express an awe, an affection, and a relationship which elevates the animal in the public mind. As to philosophical theology, while we may say the official attitude of the Church was, at best, ambivalent toward other species, a number of the less, and a few of the more, prominent luminaries of Christian doctrine expressed a devout concern for God's creation and human responsibilities toward it.

In a diligent account of medieval Christian attitudes, Richard D. Ryder mentions, *inter alia*, St. Jerome being portrayed as an ethical vegetarian, St. Columba as ordering his monks to care for an exhausted crane, St. Walaric as having a rapport with the birds of the woods, St. Neot as saving hares and stags from hunters, and St. Aventine as acting in a similar manner. St. Godric of Finchdale is reported to have rescued birds from snares, St. Carileff to have protected a bull from the royal hunt, and St. Monacella to have saved a hare from the hounds, as did St. Anselm and St. Isidore.[13] Whether or not such stories were true is far less important than the fact that the prevalence of such accounts in the Middle Ages indicates that a mark of great worthiness was the caring for our animal relations, especially when they were oppressed.

Myth

In mainland European myth, swans and horses are treated with special favour; in Celtic myth, land birds customarily have pride of place. In the tale of *Gudrun,* the eponymous heroine is aided by a swan in her quest for her lover. Lohengrin, too, is assisted by a swan in his search for the Holy Grail. Swan-maidens come to the aid of the princess in the *Nibelungenlied.* In the knightly romances surrounding the reign of Charlemagne we encounter many valiant horses that enjoy a special relationship with their riders and are seen to be as courageous as the human heroes.

Apart from horses and swans, we find faithful magpies in league with Krake against her errant lover in the Norse *Ragnar Lodbrok Saga.* The poem *Ortnit* tells of a faithful dog that mourns the death of his master. And the epic German legend of *Parzival* displays, at least ultimately, a compassion for the birds we find more commonly as the focus of Celtic myth.

Wolfram von Eschenbach

Wolfram von Eschenbach (c. 1170-1220) was a roving knight and one of the greatest of the German minnesinger. His *Parzival* ranks as one of the finest epic stories of the medieval period.

[The young Parzival] was raised in the countryside of Soltane, far from the land of his birth, and he was denied his royal heritage with one exception. He crafted for himself a bow and little arrows with which he shot numerous birds.

Yet whenever he shot a bird, whose song had been so ringing before, he would cry and tear out his hair. So handsome and proud by nature, he washed himself every morning in the stream that flowed through the meadow, and lived free from all cares but one. It was the song of the birds above that tormented him and drove him weeping to his mother who asked what had brought about his sorrow in the fields. Yet for a long time he would not tell her, as is customary among children.

One day she noticed him staring up at the trees where the birds were singing and realized it was the birds' sweet singing which had brought about his suffering, as a consequence of his royal lineage. Without good reason, she turned her bitterness against the birds and desired to put an end to their singing. She summoned her ploughmen and peasants to capture the birds and throttle them. Yet many managed to escape death and sang as merrily as before.

Whereupon the child asked his mother what evil the birds had occasioned them and begged mercy for the birds immediately. In reply his mother kissed him on the mouth, wondering what right she had to break the commandment of Almighty God. "Why," she asked herself, "should the birds be made to suffer because of me ... ?"

Stand tall, and rise yet taller, [Parzival], remembering that your heart's first duty is compassion for the oppressed. Save them from suffering with goodwill and kindness. (Wolfram von Eschenbach, *Parzival,* 118-19, 170)[14]

No doubt von Eschenbach thought Parzival's first duty to the oppressed was toward fellow-humans. Yet there is clearly an honoured place for the birds too.

The Legend of Alexander the Great

In medieval legends Alexander the Great (356 BC-323 BC; King of Macedon and conqueror of much of Asia) was a popular hero, if rather less frequently regaled than King Arthur and his knightly court. Written about a century after *Parzival, The Wars of Alexander* makes much of the relationship between the hero and his famous horse Bucephalus.

At one point during a desert campaign, horses and knights are poisoned by the water of a tainted river. The compassionate warriors, we are told, were "troubled more for the harm of their beasts than their own." Alexander's love for his horse is expressed resoundingly at Bucephalus's death: "The hero gazes on his steed and sees his breath fail. He sighs exceeding sore and weeps sadly. For [Bucephalus] had stood him in stead, in battles full hard, had won him worship in war and saved him from many a peril. The king casts his eye on the corpse and says, 'Farewell, my fair fool, thou failed me never. Shall now thy flesh by worms or birds be eaten? Nay, the lord forbid.'" (*The Wars of Alexander*)[15]

Piers Ploughman

The Vision of William concerning Piers the Ploughman, a fourteenth-century allegorical alliterative unrhymed poem, very probably composed, at least in the main, by William Langland, is both a social satire and a commendation of the simple Christian life, in which, *inter alia,* we should learn from other creatures.

Then Nature approached me, calling me by name; and he bade me take heed, and gather wisdom from all the wonders of the world. And I dreamt that he led me out onto a mountain called Middle-Earth, so that I might learn from all kinds of creatures to love my Creator. And I saw the sun and the sea, and the sandy shores, and the places where birds and beasts go forth with their mates – wild snakes in the woods, and wonderful birds, whose feathers were decked with many colours. And I could also see man and his mate, in poverty, and in plenty, in peace and war; and I saw how men lived in happiness and misery both at once ...

And I perceived how surely Reason followed all the beasts, in their eating and drinking, and engendering of their kinds . ...

And I beheld the birds in the bushes building their nests, which no man with all his wits, could ever make. And I marvelled to know who taught the magpie to place the sticks in which to lay her eggs and breed her young; for no craftsman could ever make such a nest hold together, and it would be a wonderful mason who could construct a mould for it.

And yet I wondered still more at other birds – how they concealed their eggs secretly on moors and marshlands, so that men could never find them; and how they hid them more carefully still when they went away, for fear of the birds of prey and of wild beasts ... And when I saw all these things I wondered what master they had, and who had taught them to rear their houses so high in the trees, where neither man nor beasts could reach their young ...

Yet the thing that moved me most, and changed my way of thinking, was that Reason ruled and cared for all the beasts, except only for man and his mate; for many a time they wandered ungoverned by Reason. (William Langland, *Piers the Ploughman*)[16]

Rinaldo and Bayard

Among the medieval legends portraying an intimate and mutually respectful relationship between horse and rider is the *Volsunga Saga* where we can read of the comradeship between Sigurd and Grani. We find elsewhere El Cid's faithful charger Babieca being held in great honour. Veillantif, Roland's steed "of mighty heart," received frequent praise in *Chansons de geste;* Papillon, or Beiffror in other accounts, is Ogier the Dane's majestic mount "famed for his skill and wisdom"; in the *Ettin Langshanks,* Dietrich's noble equine companion saves him from death. In Thomas Chestre's *Lanval,* Blanchard is a horse of marvellous attainment, as is the magical horse of "The Squire's Tale" in Chaucer's *Canterbury Tales.* Perhaps the most famous of medieval horses is Bayard, in some accounts originally the mount of Aymon who, after several adventures in which the horse is the source of the knight's valour, passes Bayard to his youngest son Renaud or Rinaldo. In other accounts, Bayard is the gift of Charlemagne to Aymon's sons in common. And there were yet others, differing considerably in their detail and the prominence of the role assigned to Bayard, but often they begin with a contest for mastery between the horse and his future master.

The version we shall follow is that of Thomas Bullfinch who, in 1863, told the legends of Charlemagne based on the fifteenth-century Italian accounts collected and related by Pulci, Boiardo, and Ariosto, which, in turn, were founded on oral myths that had been around in ever-changing form since at least the tenth century. The moral of the story in its human-animal dimension relates to the responsibilities acquired in a special relationship, the conflicts that arise when responsibilities to crown, kin, and equine companion are at odds, and the torment and penance endured for having sacrificed the worthy animal.

The purpose of the first part of the story is to explain how exceptional both Rinaldo and Bayard were, and hence worthy of each other in their common courage, unequalled by others, which resulted in their mutual friendship. If Rinaldo succeeded ultimately in subduing Bayard it was not because he was the more courageous; it took the efforts of two brave humans to overcome the horse, one of whom was killed in the attempt, and even then Rinaldo's victory was "by chance."

Rinaldo took his way to the forest of Arden celebrated for so many adventures. Hardly had he entered it when he met an old man, bending under the weight of years, and learned from him that the forest was infested with a wild horse, untamable, that broke and overturned everything that opposed his career. To attack him, he said, or even to meet him, was certain death. Rinaldo, far from being alarmed, showed the most eager desire to combat the animal ...

To win this wonderful horse it was necessary to conquer him by force or skill; for from the moment when he should be thrown he would become docile and manageable. His habitual resort was a cave on the borders of the forest; but woe to anyone who would approach him unless gifted with strength and courage more than mortal. Having told this the man departed ...

Rinaldo plunged into the forest, and spent many days in seeking Bayard, but found no traces of him. One day he encountered a Saracen knight, with whom he made acquaintance, as often happened to knights, by first meeting him in combat. This knight, whose name was Isolier, was also in quest of Bayard. Rinaldo succeeded in the encounter ...

Rinaldo and Isolier, now become friends, proceeded together to the attack of the horse ... A bright bay in color (whence he was called Bayard), with a silver star in his forehead, and his hind feet white, his body slender, his head delicate, his ample chest filled out with swelling muscles, his shoulders broad and full, his legs straight and sinewy, his thick mane falling over his arching neck – he came rushing through the forest, regardless of rocks, bushes, or trees, rending everything that opposed his way, and neighing defiance.

He first descried Isolier, and rushed upon him. The knight received him with lance in rest, but the fierce animal broke the spear, and his course was not delayed by it for an instant. The Spaniard* adroitly stepped aside, and gave way to the rushing tempest. Bayard checked his career, and turned again upon the knight, who had already drawn his sword. He drew his sword, for he had no hope of taming the horse; that, he was satisfied, was impossible.

---

* In the medieval era much of Spain was Muslim. Hence Isolier is introduced as both a Saracen and a Spaniard.

Bayard rushed upon him; fiercely rearing, now on this side, now on that. The knight struck him with his sword, where the white star adorned his forehead, but struck in vain, and felt ashamed, thinking that he had struck feebly, for he did not know that the skin of the horse was so tough that the keenest sword could make no impression upon it.

Whistling fell the sword once more, and struck with greater force, and the fierce horse felt it, and drooped his head under the blow, but the next moment turned upon his foe with such a buffet that the Pagan fell stunned and lifeless to earth.

Rinaldo, who saw Isolier fall, and thought that his life was reft, darted towards the horse, and with his fist gave him such a blow on the jaws that the blood tinged his mouth with vermillion. Quicker than an arrow leaves the bow the horse turned upon him, and tried to seize his arm with his teeth.

The knight stepped back, and then, repeating his blow, struck him on the forehead. Bayard turned, and kicked with both his feet with a force that would have shattered a mountain. Rinaldo was on his guard, and evaded his attacks, whether made with head or heels. He kept at his side avoiding both; but, making a false step, he at last received a terrible blow from the horse's foot, and at the shock almost fainted away. A second such blow would have killed him, but the horse kicked at random, and a second blow did not reach Rinaldo, who in a moment recovered himself. Thus the contest continued until by chance Bayard's foot got caught between the branches of an oak. Rinaldo seized it and putting forth all his strength and address, threw him to the ground. No sooner had Bayard touched the ground than all his rage subsided. No longer an object of terror he became gentle and quiet, yet with dignity in his mildness.

The paladin* patted his neck, stroked his breast, and smoothed his mane, while the animal neighed and showed delight to be caressed by his master. Rinaldo, seeing him now completely subdued, took the saddle and trappings from the other horse, and adorned Bayard with the spoils.

We are subsequently entertained by fifty pages of adventures before being informed that Bayard's gentle nobility is reserved only for the benefit of a few, and certainly not for Sacripant. According to Boiardo's and Ariosto's *Orlando* poems, Sacripant is a king of Circassia who is in love with Angelica, who is also loved – vainly – by Rinaldo. Bayard's loyalty to Rinaldo is portrayed and the story points out that kind treatment of an animal will result in corresponding generosity on the animal's part. Moreover, Bayard is seen as an animal "gifted with wonderful intelligence" – there is no notion of "irrational animals" here.[17]

In silence [Sacripant] mounted the horse of Angelica, taking the lady behind him on the croup, [the rump] and rode away in search of a more secure asylum. Hardly had they ridden two miles when a new sound was heard in the forest, and they

---

* That is, Rinaldo; so called because his rank entitled him to stature at Charlemagne's court.

perceived a gallant and powerful horse, which, leaping the ravines and dashing aside the branches that opposed his passage, appeared before them, accoutred with a rich harness adorned with gold.

"If I may believe my eyes, which penetrate with difficulty the underwood," said Angelica, "that horse that dashes so stoutly through the bushes is Bayard, and I marvel how he seems to know we have the need of him, mounted as we are both on one feeble animal." Sacripant, dismounting from the palfrey,* approached the fiery courser, and attempted to seize his bridle, but the disdainful animal, turning from him, launched at him a volley of kicks enough to have shattered a wall of marble. Bayard then approached Angelica with an air so gentle and loving as a faithful dog could show his master after a long separation. For he remembered how she had caressed him, in Albracca. She took his bridle in her left hand, while with her right she patted his neck. The beautiful animal, gifted with wonderful intelligence, seemed to submit entirely. Sacripant, seizing the moment to vault upon him, controlled his curvetings,† and Angelica, quitting the croup of the palfrey, regained her seat.

Rinaldo appears on the scene and a battle ensues:

one fighting on foot, the other on horseback. You need not, however, suppose that the Saracen king found any advantage in this; for a young page, unused to horsemanship, could not have failed more completely to manage Bayard than did this accomplished knight. The faithful animal loved his master too well to injure him, and refused his aid as well as his obedience to the hand of Sacripant, who could but strike but ineffectual blows, the horse backing when he wished him to go forward, and dropping his head and arching his back, throwing out with his legs, so as almost to shake the knight out of his saddle. Sacripant, seeing that he could not manage him, watched his opportunity, rose on his saddle, and leapt lightly to earth; then, relieved from the embarrassment of the horse, renewed the combat on more equal terms.

Having won the fight, Rinaldo endures another hundred pages of adventures in which he loses and regains Bayard more than once, his brothers are captured and rescued, and Rinaldo's castle is laid under siege by the Emperor Charlemagne. Bayard's consummate loyalty finds no match in the behaviour of Rinaldo. In the end it is Bayard, not Rinaldo, who is the hero of the legend.

The distress in Rinaldo's castle for want of food grew more severe every day, under pressure of the siege. The garrison were forced to kill their horses, both to save the provision they would consume, and to make food of the flesh. At last all the horses were killed except Bayard, and Rinaldo said this to his brothers, "Bayard

---

* A palfrey is a fine but small lady's horse suitable for gentle riding but inferior to the *equus magnus*, the warhorse, which stood some 17 or 18 hands.
† Curvetings are horses' leaps with forelegs raised together.

must die, for we have nothing else to eat." So they went to the stable and brought out Bayard to kill him. But Alardo said, "Brother, let Bayard live a little longer; who knows what God may do for us?" Bayard heard these words, and understood them as if he was a man, and fell on his knees, as if he would beg for mercy. When Rinaldo saw the distress of his horse his heart failed him, and he let him live.

Just at this time Aya, Rinaldo's mother, who was the sister of the Emperor, came to the camp, attended by knights and ladies, to intercede for her sons. She fell on her knees before the king, and besought him that he would pardon Rinaldo and his brothers; and all the peers and knights took her side, and entreated the king to grant her prayer. Then said the king, "Dear sister, you act the part of a good mother, and I respect your tender heart, and yield to your entreaties. I will spare your sons their lives if they submit implicitly to my will."

When Charlot* heard this he approached the king and whispered in his ear. And the king turned to his sister and said, "Charlot must have Bayard, because I have given the horse to him. Now go, my sister, and tell Rinaldo what I have said."

When the Lady Aya heard these words she was delighted, thanked God in her heart, and said, "Worthy king and brother, I will do as you bid me." So she went into the castle, where her sons received her most joyfully and affectionately, and she told them the king's offer. Then Alardo said, "Brother, I would rather have the king's enmity than give Bayard to Charlot, for I believe he will kill him." Likewise said all the brothers. When Rinaldo heard them he said, "Dear brothers, if we may win our forgiveness by giving up the horse so be it. Let us make our peace, for we cannot stand against the king's power." Then he went to his mother and told her they would give the horse to Charlot, and more, too, if the king would pardon them, and forgive all that they had done against his crown and his dignity. The lady returned to Charles [Charlemagne] and told him the answer of his sons.

When the peace was thus made between the king and the sons of Aymon, the brothers came forth from the castle, bringing Bayard with them, and, falling at the king's feet, begged his forgiveness. The king bade them rise, and received them into favour in the sight of all his noble knights and counsellors, to the great joy of all especially of the Lady Aya, their mother. Then Rinaldo took the horse Bayard, gave him to Charlot, and said, "My lord and prince, this horse I will give to you; do with him as to you seems good." Charlot took him, as had been agreed upon. Then he made the servants take him to the bridge, and throw him into the water. Bayard sank to the bottom, but soon came to the surface again and swam, saw Rinaldo looking at him, came to land, ran to his old master, and stood by him as proudly as if he had understanding, and would say, "Why did you treat me so?" When the prince saw that he said, "Rinaldo, give me the horse again, for he must die." Rinaldo replied, "My lord and prince, he is yours without dispute," and gave him to him. The prince then had a millstone tied to each foot, and two to his neck, and made them throw him again into the water. Bayard struggled in the water, looked up to his master, threw off the stones, and came back to Rinaldo.

---

* Charlot is an ahistorical duplicitous son of Charlemagne.

When Alardo saw that, he said, "Now must thou be disgraced for ever, brother, if thou give up the horse again." But Rinaldo answered, "Brother, be still. Shall I for the horse's life provoke the anger of the king again?" Then Alardo said, "Ah, Bayard! What a return do we make for thy true love and service!" Rinaldo gave the horse to the prince again, and said, "My lord, if the horse comes out again I cannot return him to you any more, for it wrings my heart too much." Then Charlot had Bayard loaded with the stones as before, and thrown into the water; and commanded Rinaldo that he should not stand where the horse would see him. When Bayard rose to the surface he stretched his neck out of the water and looked round for his master, but saw him not. Then he sank to the bottom.

Rinaldo was so distressed for the loss of Bayard that he made a vow to ride no horse again all his life long nor to bind a sword to his side, but to become a hermit. He resolved to betake himself to some wild wood, but first to return to his castle to see his children and to appoint to each his share of his estate.[18]

In abject distress at his perfidy to Bayard, Rinaldo becomes a devout and holy recluse, is martyred, and later sanctified. Who could doubt from such a story that in the medieval era there was sincere respect for at least certain animals on certain occasions?

Mabinogeon

The *Mabinogeon*, sometimes *Mabinogion*, are Welsh popular tales, written versions of which were secreted in British libraries prior to the printing era, but largely forgotten until the mid-nineteenth century when they were collected and translated by Lady Charlotte Guest. They are associated with the legends of King Arthur and told through the lives of Welsh heroes.

We are initially entertained by the customary Celtic delight in birds, expressed by Kynon, a Welsh knight of King Arthur's court:

presently the sky became clear, and with that, behold the birds lighted upon the tree and sang. And truly, Kay, I never heard any melody equal to that, either before or since. And ... I was most charmed with listening to the birds ...

Again:

Then the birds descended upon the tree. And the song of the birds was far sweeter than any strain they had heard before.

One of the *Mabinogeon's* literary delights is a variant of the story of Androcles, with the Welsh knight Owain of King Arthur's court in the role of Androcles. In this version, reminiscent of the myth of "How the Buffalo Hunt Began"[19] and a French edition of the story – Chrétien de Troyes's *Yvain, or the Knight with the Lion*[20] – nature's animals are divided on different sides.

And as he journeyed he heard a loud yelling in a wood. And it was repeated a second and a third time. And Owain went towards the spot, and beheld a craggy mound, in the middle of the wood, on the side of which was a grey rock. And there was a cleft in the rock, and a serpent was within the cleft. And near the rock stood a black lion, and every time the lion sought to go thence the serpent darted towards him to attack him. And Owain unsheathed his sword, and drew near the rock; and as the serpent sprung out he struck him with his sword and cut him in two. And he dried his sword, and went on his way as before. But behold the lion followed him, and played about him, as though it had been a greyhound that he reared.

They proceeded thus throughout the day, until the evening. And when it was time for Owain to take his rest he dismounted, and turned his horse loose in a flat and wooded meadow. And he struck fire, and when the fire was kindled, the lion brought him fuel enough to last for three nights. And the lion disappeared. And presently the lion returned, bearing a fine large roebuck.

After the pair had eaten:

Owain laid himself down to sleep; and never did sentinel keep stricter watch over his lord than the lion that night over Owain.

Later Owain is accosted in defence of Luned, a young woman whom Owain's assailants are trying to have put to death:

And they attacked Owain, and he was hard beset by them. And with that, the lion came to Owain's assistance, and the two got the better of the young men. And they said to him, "Chieftain, it was not agreed that we should fight save with thyself alone, and it is harder for us to contend with yonder animal than with thee." And Owain put the lion where Luned had been imprisoned, and blocked up the door with stones. And he went to fight with the young men as before. But Owain had not his usual strength, and the youths pressed hard upon him. And the lion roared incessantly at seeing Owain in trouble. And he burst through the wall, until he found a way out, and rushed upon the young men and instantly slew them. So Luned was saved from being burned.

Much later in the legend we encounter Gurhyr Gwalstat who is able to converse with the animals and who thereby helps the knights rescue Mabon. It is clear that the animals are not thought to be "dumb" but to possess a language of their own which only a few gifted humans can comprehend.

His followers said unto Arthur, "Lord, go thou home, thou canst not proceed with thy host in quest of such small adventures as these." Then said Arthur, "It were well for thee, Gurhyr Gwalstat, to go upon this quest, for thou knowest all languages, and art familiar with those of the birds and beasts. Though, Eidoel, oughtest likewise to go with thy men in search of thy cousin. And, as for you, Kay and Bedwyr, I have hope of whatever adventure ye are in quest of, that ye will achieve it. Achieve ye this adventure for me."

They went forward until they came to the Ousel* of Cligrwi. And Gurhyr abjured her, saying, "Tell me if thou knowest aught of Mabon, the son of Modron, who was taken three nights old from between his mother and the wall?" And the Ousel answered, "When I first came here, there was a smith's anvil in this place, and I was then a young bird; and from that time no work has been done upon it, save the pecking of my beak every evening; and now there is not so much as the size of a nut remaining thereof; yet during all that time I have never heard of the man for whom you inquire. Nevertheless, I will do that which is fitting that I should for an embassy from Arthur. There is a race of animals who were formed before me, and I will be your guide to them."

The story continues repetitively in this vein through stag to eagle to salmon.

"As much as I know I will tell thee. With every tide I go along the river upward, until I come to the walls of Gloucester, and there have I found such wrongs as I never found elsewhere; and to the end that ye may give credence thereto, let one of you go hither upon each of my two shoulders." So Kay and Gurhyr Gwalstat went upon the two shoulders of the Salmon, and they proceeded until they came unto the wall of the prison; and they heard a great wailing and lamenting from the dungeon. Said Gurhyr, "Who is it that laments in this house of stone?" "Alas! it is Mabon, the son of Modron, who is here imprisoned; and no imprisonment was ever so grievous as mine."[21]

Arthur is summoned, the fight to release Mabon is fought, Kay and Bedwyr are transported to the dungeon by the salmon, and, thanks to the help from the animals, Mabon is rescued.

Irish Myth

There are numerous Irish folk-tales that dwell on compassion for the earth's creatures and a delight in the wonders of nature.[22] The legend selected is based on an eighteenth-century rendering of a medieval myth about St. Kieran, reputedly the first Irishman to embrace the Christian faith.

One day that [Kieran] was in Clare there it was that, he being at the time but a young child, he made a beginning of his miracles; for in the air right over him a kite came soaring and, swooping down before his face, lifted a little bird that sat upon her nest. Compassion for the little bird took Kieran, and he deemed it an ill thing to see it in such plight; thereupon the kite turned back and in front of Kieran deposited the bird half dead, sore hurt; but Kieran bade it rise and be whole. The bird arose; and by God's favour went whole upon its nest again ...

Later, in the region of Ely:

Kieran began to dwell as a hermit ... When first Kieran came hither he sat down under a tree's shade; but from the other side of the trunk rose a wild boar of great

---

* An ousel is a small black thrush with a white crescent on its breast.

fury which, when he saw Kieran, fled and turned again as a tame servitor to him, he being by God rendered gentle. Which boar was the first monk that Kieran had there; and moreover went to the wood to pull wattles and thatch with his teeth by way of helping on the cell* ... And out of every quarter in which they were of the wilderness irrational animals came to Kieran: a fox, namely, a brock [badger], a wolf and a doe, which were tame to him, and as monks, humbled themselves to his teaching and did all that he enjoined them.[23]

As in so much medieval thought, the inherent desire is to overcome the iniquities of nature (as in Isaiah 11:6-9),[24] to exemplify the Biblical doctrine that the animals, too, worship their creator, and to show that the chosen of God enjoy a special relationship with the animal realm, each treating the other with affection and respect.

Medieval Theology and Philosophy

The Christian theologian Arnobius (fl. fourth century) taught rhetoric at Sicca Venria in north Africa during the reign of the Roman emperor Diocletian. He composed the seven books known as *Adversus nationes* or *Adversus gentes* early in the century in which, *inter alia*, he emphasized human-animal similarities.

Will you, laying aside [all] partiality, consider in the silence of your thoughts that we are creatures quite like the rest, or separated by no great difference? For what is there to show that we do not resemble them? Or what excellence is in us, such that we scorn to be ranked as creatures? Their bodies are built on bones, and bound closely together by sinews; and our bodies are in like manner built upon bones, and bound closely together by sinews. They inspire the air through the nostrils, and in breathing expire it again; and we in like manner draw in the air, and breathe it out with frequent respirations. They have been arranged in classes, female and male; we, too, have been fashioned by our Creator into the same sexes; and we are born from sexual embraces, and are brought forth and sent into our life from our mothers' wombs. They are supported by eating and drinking, and get rid of the filth which remains by the lower parts; and we are supported by eating and drinking, and that which nature refuses we deal with in the same way. Their care is to ward off death-bringing famine, and of necessity to be on the watch for food. What else is our aim in the business of life, which presses so much upon us, but to seek the means by which the danger of starvation may be avoided, and carking anxiety be put away?

They are exposed to disease and hunger, and at last lose their strength by reason of age. What then? Are we not exposed to these evils, and are we not in like manner weakened by noxious diseases, destroyed by wasting age? But if that, too, which is said in the more hidden mysteries is true, that the souls of wicked men on leaving their human bodies, pass into cattle and other creatures, it is [even] more

---

* That is, to help build Kieran's monastery.

clearly shown that we are allied to them, and not separated by any great evil, since it is on the same ground that both we and they are said to be living creatures, and act as such.

But we have reason, [one will say], and excel the whole race of dumb animals* in understanding. I might believe this was quite true, if all men lived rationally and wisely, never swerved aside from their duty, abstained from what is forbidden, and withheld themselves from baseness, and [if] no one through folly and the blindness of ignorance demanded what is injurious and dangerous to himself. I should wish, however, to know what this reason is, through which we are more excellent than all the tribes of animals.

[Is it] because we have made for ourselves houses, by which we can avoid the cold of winter and heat of summer? What! Do not the other animals show forethought in this respect? Do we not see some build nests as dwellings for themselves in the most convenient situations; others shelter and secure [themselves] in rocks and lofty crags; others burrow in the ground, and prepare for themselves strongholds and lairs in the pits which they have dug out? But if nature, which gave them life, had chosen to give to them also hands to help them, they too would, without doubt, raise lofty buildings and strike out new works of art.

Yet, even in those things they make with beaks and claws, we see that there are many appearances of reason and wisdom which we men are unable to copy, however much we ponder them, although we have hands to serve us dextrously in every kind of work. (Arnobius, *Adversus nationes*, 2, 16-17)[25]

Lactantius

Lactantius (c. AD 240-320), was born in north Africa, but little else is known of his life. His *Divinae institutiones* (Divine Precepts) was the first systematic account in Latin of the Christian attitude to life. Again, there is an emphasis on human-animal similarities, including reason, though humanity is alone in possessing a religious nature – a criterion which was still being offered as the primary human-animal distinction by Edmund Burke in the late eighteenth century.

The highest good of man ... is in religion alone. For the other things, even those which are thought proper to man, are found in other animals also. For when they discern and distinguish their own voices among themselves by proper notes, they seem to speak together. Some type of laughing also appears in these, since by a stroking of the ears and a contraction of the mouth and a movement of the eyes into frolicsomeness, they either laugh at men or at each other. What of their mates and their own offspring? Do they not bestow on them something like mutual love and indulgence? They surely have a providence, for they look out for things for themselves for the future and they lay away foods. Signs of reason are also caught

---

* That is, creatures who are unable to communicate with humans. The use of "dumb" as a synonym for stupid is a twentieth-century innovation.

in many. For when they seek useful things for themselves, beware evil, avoid danger, and prepare hiding places for themselves opening out to several exits, certainly they manifest an understanding of something. Can anyone deny that there is reason in them when often they delude man himself? (Lactantius, *Divinae institutiones*, 3, 10)[26]

Athanasius

St. Athanasius (c. AD 293-373) was born at Alexandria in Egypt and was the chief defender of Christian orthodoxy against Arianism – the denial of the consubstantiality of Christ, hence the doctrine of the Trinity. His *De incarnatione* (The Incarnation of the Word of God) was completed c. AD 335.

The omnipotent and perfectly holy word of the Father is present in all things and extends His power everywhere illuminating all things visible and invisible, containing and enclosing them in Himself; He leaves nothing deprived of His power, but gives life and protection to everything, everywhere, to each individually and to all together. (Athanasius, *De incarnatione*)[27]

Although most Christian interpreters would be inclined to deny it, Athanasius's view approximates the Indian pantheistic sense of creation.

Basil of Caesarea

St. Basil the Great (c. AD 329-379) was born at Caesarea, where he eventually became bishop. His writings stemmed from his practical concerns as monk, pastor, and Church leader. In his *Hexaemeron* (Six Days) Basil wrote of the beauties of the world as a reflection of the splendour of God.

And for these also, O Lord, who bear with us the heat and burden of the day, we beg Thee to extend Thy great kindness of heart, for Thou hast promised to save both man and beast, and great is Thy loving kindness, O Master. (Prayer of Saint Basil of Caesarea)[28]

The Earth is the Lord's and the fullness thereof, O God, enlarge within us the sense of fellowship with all living things, our brothers the animals to whom Thou gavest the earth as their home in common with us. We remember with shame that in the past we have exercised the high dominion of man with ruthless cruelty, so that the voice of the earth, which should have gone up to Thee in song, has been a groan of travail. May we realise that they live, not for us alone, but for themselves and for Thee, and that they love the sweetness of life. (*The Liturgy of Saint Basil*)[29]

This is perhaps the first explicit statement of the view that animals are ends in themselves. Basil's animal appreciation is reflective of Eastern Christendom in general, as can be gleaned from the *Book of Needs* of the Russian Church.[30]

John Chrysostom

St. John Chrysostom (c. AD 347–407) was born at Antioch in modern day Syria and became Archbishop of Constantinople. He is most noted for his homilies in general and his *Homilies on Genesis* in particular.

The Saints are exceedingly loving and gentle to mankind, and even to brute beasts … Surely, we ought to show them great kindness and gentleness for many reasons, but, above all, because they are of the same origin as ourselves. (St. John Chrysostom, Homily XXIX, 471, *Homilies on the Epistle to the Romans*)[31]

Chrysostom's words stand as a valuable reminder to those who imagine erroneously that Darwinism wrought a fundamental revolution in animal ethics by proclaiming our common animal origins. Not only were inchoate evolutionary conceptions present at least as early as the Sumerians but Chrysostom is here indicating that our common origins are the primary basis for our responsibilities toward animals.

Augustine of Hippo

St. Augustine of Hippo (AD 354–430) is one of the greatest of the Fathers of the Roman Catholic Church. He was Bishop of Hippo in north Africa. His best-known writings are *The City of God* and his *Confessions*. While he denied immortal souls to animals and insisted on a great human superiority over the animal realm, he nonetheless recognized a measure of the significance of animals and our responsibilities toward them.

Every form of life, both great and small, every power both great and small, every well-being both great and small … above all those that run through all, being spiritual and corporal, every mode, every species, every order – both great and small – all these are from God. (St. Augustine, *De natura boni*, 12, 16)[32]

[L]iving creatures show their love of bodily peace by their avoidance of pain, and by their pursuit of pleasure to satisfy the demands of their appetites they demonstrate their love of peace and soul. In just the same way, by shunning death they indicate quite clearly how great is their love of peace in which soul and body are harmoniously united. (St. Augustine, *The City of God*, Book xix, ch. 14)[33]

I remember … when I had determined to try for a prize in poetry at the theatre [in my youth] that a certain fortune-teller asked what I would give him in order to win; but I, detesting and abominating these foul mysteries, replied "that though the crown were of an undying lustre, I would not permit a fly to be killed to gain me the victory." For [the fortune-teller] would have killed some living creatures, and by such honours appeared to render the devils propitious … this evil also I repudiated. (St. Augustine, *Confessions*, Book 4, ch. 3)[34]

Thou, [God], didst not make all things equal, therefore all things are [as they are]; for each is good in itself, and all very good together, because our "God made all things very good." (St. Augustine, *Confessions*, Book 7, ch. 12)[35]

Augustine is here indicating a subscription to the idea of the Great Chain of Being.[36]

Kevin

Of noble Leinster lineage, St. Kevin (died c. AD 618) was founder of the abbey of Glendalough in County Wicklow, Republic of Ireland. He is reputed to have enjoyed a special relationship with nature and refused a celestial offering of the levelling of four hills for the foundation of his monastery, saying:

I have no wish that the wild creatures on those mountains should be sad because of me.[37]

Guthlac

St. Guthlac (c. AD 673-716) was an early Anglo-Saxon visionary and saint, who, according to his contemporary St. Felix, was able to summon the wild birds at his call and have them feed from his hand. Guthlac is reported to have said: "Hast thou never learned in Holy Writ that he who led his life after God's will, the wild beasts and the wild birds have become more intimate with him?"[38]

John of Salisbury

Scholastic philosopher, Bishop of Chartres, friend and biographer of Thomas à Becket, and by repute the greatest scholar of his age, John of Salisbury (c. 1110-80) wrote both the *Policraticus*, an exemplary treatise on government, and the *Metalogicus*, a discussion of the intellectual controversies of the era. In his *De nugis curialium* (Trifles of the Court) he criticized the aristocratic practices of his day, noting how hunting demeaned humanity.

In our time hunting and hawking are esteemed the most honourable employments, and most excellent virtues, by our nobility; and they rank it the height of worldly felicity to spend the whole of their time in these diversions; accordingly they prepare for them with more solicitude, expence, and parade than they do for war; and pursue the wild beasts with greater fury than they do the enemies of their country. By constantly following this way of life, they lose much of their humanity, and become as savage, nearly, as the beasts they hunt. (John of Salisbury, *De nugis curialium*, I, iv)[39]

While Salisbury's concern is with the degradation of the aristocracy rather than the interests of the animals they hunt, it is nonetheless significant that the hunting of animals is seen to degrade the hunter through killing for glory.

Walter Map

In all probability Welsh by extraction, Walter Map (c. 1140 to c. 1209) studied at the University of Paris and became Archdeacon of Oxford. His

De nugis curialium – there is no connection with Salisbury's work of the same title – was written c. 1200 and reflects his recognition of the degeneracy of humanity as exemplified by courtly life. "Now how comes it that we men have degenerated from our original beauty, strength and force, while other living creatures in no way go astray from the grace first given to them? ... The creatures of earth, sea and air – everything except man – rejoice in the life and powers with which they were created. They, it seems, have not fallen out of their maker's favour" (Walter Map, *De nugis curialium*, I, i).[40]

Richard de Wyche
St. Richard de Wyche (c. 1197-1253) studied at Oxford and Cambridge before being ordained. He became Bishop of Chichester in 1244. It was said of him that when "he saw poultry or young animals being conveyed to his kitchen (he never ate meat himself) he would say half-sadly, half-humorously": "Poor, innocent little creatures: if you were reasoning beings and could speak you would curse us. For we are the cause of your death, and what have you done to deserve it?"[41]

Thomas Aquinas
One of the primary theologians of the Catholic Church, and the greatest of the Scholastic philosophers, St. Thomas Aquinas (1225-74) was a prolific author whose most renowned works are the *Summa contra Gentiles* (1258-60) and the *Summa Theologica* (1267-73). His lasting contribution to social thought was his development of the concept of natural law, which is still influential in secular as well as religious philosophy today.

Although Thomas insists on kindness to animals, his overall attitude is less than considerate of their significance. However, the importance of the contributions of the "angelic doctor" lies less in their arguments than in alerting us to the significance of what he is arguing against. One does not normally argue against a view that has few adherents. Thus, if the opposition to killing animals and to the treatment of animals as ends in themselves – the two primary thrusts of the Thomist argument – were commonly-held opinions, then the medieval sympathy for animals was considerably greater than we customarily conclude.

In the *Summa Theologica* (Part II, Question 64, Article 1) Aquinas discusses "Whether it is unlawful to kill any living thing." He concludes there "is no sin in killing a thing for the purpose for which it is." For Aquinas the lower lives exist for the sake of the higher and thus animals exist for humans and are not ends in themselves. In Part II, Question 65, Article 3, he asks "Whether Irrational Creatures also Ought to be Loved out of Charity" to which he offers a Stoic response:

Charity is a kind of friendship. Now the love of friendship is two fold: first, there is the love for the friend to whom our friendship is given, secondly, the love for those good things we desire for our friend. With regard to the first, no irrational creature can be loved out of charity; and for three reasons. Two of these reasons refer in a general way to friendship, which cannot have an irrational creature for its object: first because friendship is towards one to whom we wish good things. While properly speaking, we cannot wish good things for an irrational creature, because it is not competent, properly speaking, to possess good, this being proper to the rational creature which, through its free-will, is the master of its disposal of the good it possesses ... Secondly, because all friendship is based on some fellowship in life ... Now irrational creatures can have no fellowship in human life which is regulated by reason. Hence friendship with irrational creatures is impossible, except metaphorically speaking. The third reason is proper to charity, for charity is based on the fellowship of everlasting happiness, to which the irrational creatures cannot attain. Therefore we cannot have the friendship of charity towards an irrational creature.

Of course, Thomas is neither promoting nor even countenancing cruelty to animals. He follows this passage immediately with the assertion: "Nevertheless, we can love irrational creatures out of charity, if we regard them as the good things that we desire for others, in so far, to wit, as we wish for their preservation, to God's honour and man's use; thus too does God love them out of charity."[42]

Elsewhere we find St. Thomas declaring: "It is God's custom to care for all His creatures, both the greatest and the least. We should likewise care for creatures, whatsoever they are, in the sense that we use them in conformity with the divine purpose, in order that they may not bear witness against us in the Day of Judgment."[43] Clearly, if the animals may bear witness against us for the wrongs we have committed to God's creatures, then cruelty to animals is a wrong in and of itself.

If Aquinas deemed it theologically important to oppose both vegetarianism and the belief that animals are their own beings with their own purposes, as Augustine had done eight centuries earlier against the vegetarian Manicheans, then the force of those beliefs must still have been felt in the thirteenth century. Indeed, writing to the Cambridge Platonist Henry More in 1649, René Descartes declared his view of animals as machines "not so much cruel to animals as it is favourable to men (those men not attached to the Pythagorean superstition), whom it absolves from suspicion of crime when they eat animals."[44] Clearly, both in the thirteenth and seventeenth centuries eating animals was almost universally practised but still occasioned a concern over whether one actually had a moral right to do so.

While Aquinas refers to the animals as "irrational creatures" he does not mean they are devoid of reason but rather that rationality is not their primary characteristic – "All animals by their natural instincts have a participation of prudence and reason," he tells us (*Summa Theologica*, 96, 1, Reply to Objection 4). And he allows animals souls, but not of the eternal variety – which makes one wonder how they come to be waiting to expose our sins on Judgment Day! In the final analysis, for Aquinas, following Aristotle and the Stoics, our responsibilities to our fellow animals are diminished because we cannot share a sense of community with them, a fellowship, which, he imagines, must be reserved for our fellow human beings.

Maimonides and Medieval Judaism

Medieval Judaism contained similar competing ideas to those of medieval Christianity. The tradition of the kaballah which arose in the early medieval era – and which was still influencing Christianity in the seventeenth century via such admirers as Robert Fludd and John Milton[45] – stressed the unity of all life and recognized the transmigration of souls, but allowed for flesh consumption on the ground of the elevation of the animal's soul.[46] From a Jewish source in tenth-century Baghdad one could read that "The animal has not been created in order that evils should be inflicted upon it but in order that good should be done to it."[47] Another medieval Hebrew work, *Sefer Chasidim* (The Book of the Pious), tells us to: "Be kind and compassionate to all creatures that the Holy One, blessed be He, created in this world. Never beat nor inflict pain on any animal, beast, bird, or insect. Do not throw stones at a dog or a cat, nor kill flies or wasps."[48]

The most esteemed of medieval Hebrew philosophers was Moses Maimonides, or Moses ben Maimon (1135-1204), a rabbi born in Spain, who wrote in Arabic on a great variety of topics, including medicine. His *Guide for the Perplexed* examined the principles of Biblical and Jewish thought. He was imbued with Aristotelean philosophy and exerted a significant influence on Christian, as well as Jewish, attitudes in the Middle Ages and the Renaissance. Among his animal compassionate pronouncements are the following:

It is prohibited to kill an animal with its young on the same day, in order that people should be restrained and prevented from killing the two together in such a manner that the young is slain in the sight of the mother; for the pain of animals under such circumstances is very great. There is no difference in this case between the pain of man and the pain of other living beings.[49]

There is no difference between the worry of a human mother and an animal mother for their offspring. A mother's love does not derive from the intellect but from the emotions, in animals just as in humans.[50]

We should not learn cruelty and should not cause unnecessary and useless pain to animals but should lean toward compassion and mercy.[51]

The Law enjoins that the death of the animal should be the easiest. It is not allowed to torment the animal by cutting the throat in a clumsy manner, by pole-axing, or by cutting a limb while the animal is still alive.[52]

[T]hose who go to hunt [animals] and kill birds ... violate the commandment that forbid us to wantonly destroy [God's creation].[53]

The Islamic Tradition in the Medieval Era

Of course, Islam is itself a religion that emerged in the early Middle Ages. Consequently, all the quotations from the Qur'an and the Hadith included in the first chapter are medieval.[54] Moreover, most of the later medieval statements are explanatory reiterations of the holy edicts. Accordingly, we shall append here statements from only two sources. It should be noted, however, that even though Islam changed relatively little in the Middle Ages, it had a significant influence on European thought at that time, specifically with reference to attitudes to animals, which, as we shall see in the writings of Francis Bacon, Alexander Pope, and Richard Steele, affected European attitudes in later centuries.[55]

The first quotation is from Al-Hazen in the eleventh century and is of particular interest in its similarity to the Great Chain doctrine of Plotinus[56] and bears comparison with the later expression of that doctrine by John Locke.[57]

In the region of existing matter, the mineral kingdom comes lowest, then comes the vegetable, then the animal, and finally the human being. By his body he (man) belongs to the material world, but by the soul he appertains to the spiritual or immaterial. Above him are only the purely spiritual beings – the angels – above whom only is God: thus the lowest is combined by a chain of progress to the highest.[58]

Be like a bee; anything he eats is clean, anything he drops is sweet and any branch he sits on does not break . ... A savage and ferocious beast is better than a wicked and tyrant ruler. (Immam Hazrat Ali, *Maxims of Ali,* seventh century)[59]

He who takes pity on a sparrow and spares its life, Allah will be merciful on him on the last Day of Judgment. (Al-Tabarani transmitting the thought of Mohammed)[60]

Francis of Assisi

Many Christian saints were elevated as a consequence of their relationship to animals, the most famous being St. Francis (c. 1182-1226). Among many others, we might take note of St. Thecla, a first-century follower of St. Paul, who was purportedly befriended by lions sent by her enemies to devour her, and who later defended her against a bear; Blaise, patron saint of sick cattle, gave sanctuary to wild beasts; Gall, patron saint of birds, shared his cave-dwelling with a bear; Harvey charmed animals with his music and is invoked to protect flocks and herds. The renowned St. Francis stands in good company.

Given his reputation, it is perhaps surprising that St. Francis wrote little about animals. In fact, his relationship to nature and the animals is better known through the reports of his actions and what his followers wrote about him. St. Francis did, however, have a few words of his own to contribute.

Praise be to Thee my Lord with all Thy creatures ... Praise be to Thee my Lord for Brother Wind, for air and clouds, clear sky and all the weathers through which Thou sustainest all Thy creatures. O bless and praise my Lord all creatures, who thank and serve Him in deep humility. (St. Francis, *The Canticle of the Creatures,* 1225)[61]

Be conscious, O man, of the wondrous state in which the Lord God has placed you, for He created you and formed you in the image of His beloved Son according to the body, and to his likeness according to the spirit. And [yet] all the creatures under heaven, each according to his nature, serve, know, and obey their Creator better than you. (St. Francis, *Admonitions*)[62]

He who possesses Holy Obedience:

... is subject and submissive to all persons in the world
and not to humans only
but even to all beasts and wild animals
so that they may do whatever they want with him
inasmuch as it has been given to them from above
by the Lord.
(St. Francis, *Salutation of the Virtues,* 16-18)[63]

Thomas of Celano

Thomas was a contemporary of St. Francis and a member of the Franciscan order. He wrote the first two biographies of St. Francis.

St. Francis came to a certain place near Bevagna where a very great number of birds of various kinds had congregated, namely doves, crows, and some others popularly called daws.* When the most blessed servant of God saw them, being a man of very great fervor and great tenderness towards lower and irrational creatures, he left his companions in the road and went eagerly toward the birds. When he was close enough to them, seeing that they were waiting expectantly for him, he greeted them in his usual way. But, not a little surprised that the birds did not rise in flight, as they usually do, he was filled with great joy and humbly begged them to listen to the word of God ... from that day on, he solicitously admonished all birds, all animals, and reptiles, and even creatures that have no feeling, to praise and love their Creator, for daily when the name of the Savior had been invoked, he saw their obedience by personal experience. (Thomas of Celano, *First Life of St. Francis,* Bk. I, ch. xxi)

[H]e called all creatures *brother,* and in a most extraordinary manner, a manner never experienced by others, he discerned the hidden things of nature with his sensitive heart ... (*First Life,* Bk. I, ch. xxix)

He removed from the road little worms, lest they be crushed under foot; and he ordered that honey and the best wines be set out for the bees, lest they perish from

---

* Mullachia, a crow-like bird.

want in the cold of winter. He called all animals by the name *brother*, though among all the kinds of animals he preferred the gentle ...

[T]hat original goodness that will be one day *all things in all* already [shone] forth in this saint *all things in all*. (*Second Life*, Bk. I, ch. cxxxiv, 165)[64]

Bonaventure

As a boy, St. Bonaventure (c. 1217-74) knew St. Francis and attributed his desire to become a friar to him. He became a leading medieval theologian, Minister General of the Franciscan order, and Cardinal Bishop of Albano. We may well be skeptical of some of the stories he told of Saint Francis (many of which were borrowed more or less verbatim from Thomas of Celano). In the following extract from St. Bonaventure's biography of St. Francis the least believable tales have been omitted. The biography's significance lies in its reflection of what Bonaventure sees as the ideal relationship to animated nature of a truly saintly person, and of what he expects his audience to find truly admirable in such a person.

When he considered the primordial source of all things, he was filled with even more piety, calling creatures, no matter how small, by the name of brother or sister, because he knew they had the same source as himself ...

When Francis was traveling near the city of Siena, he came upon a large flock of sheep in a pasture. When he greeted them kindly, as he was accustomed to do, they all stopped grazing and ran to him, lifting their heads and fixing their eyes on him. They gave him such a welcome that the shepherds and friars were amazed to see the lambs and even the rams frisking about him in such an extraordinary way.

Another time at St. Mary of the Portiuncula the man of God was offered a sheep, which he gratefully accepted in his love of that innocence and simplicity which the sheep by its nature reflects. The pious man admonished the little sheep to praise God attentively and to avoid giving any offence to the friars. The sheep carefully observed his instructions, as if it recognized the piety of the man of God. For when it heard the friars chanting in the choir, it would enter the church, genuflect without instructions from anyone before the altar of the Virgin, the mother of the Lamb, as if it wished to greet her ...

Another time at Greccio a live hare was offered to the man of God, which he placed on the ground and let it go free to where it wished. But when the kind father called, it ran and jumped into his arms. He fondled it with warm affection and seemed to pity it like a mother. After warning it gently not to let itself be caught again, he let it go free. But as often as he placed it on the ground to run away, it always came back to his father's arms, as if in some secret way it perceived the kind feeling he had for it. Finally, at the father's command, the friars carried it away to a safer place far from the haunts of men.

In the same way on an island in the lake of Perugia a rabbit was caught and offered to the man of God. Although it fled from everyone else, it entrusted itself to his hands and his heart as if to the security of its home. When he was hurrying across the Lake of Rieti to the hermitage of Greccio, out of devotion a fisherman offered him a waterfowl. He took it gladly and opened his hands to let it go, but it did not want to. He prayed for a long time with his eyes turned toward heaven. After more than an hour, he came back to himself as if from another realm and gently told the bird to go away and praise God. Having received his permission with a blessing, the bird expressed its joy in the movements of its body, and flew away. Once on the same lake in a similar way he was offered a large live fish which he addressed as brother in the usual way and put it back into the water by the boat. The fish played about in the water in front of the man of God; and as if it were attracted by his love, it would not go away from the ship until it received from him his permission with a blessing ...

When he was ill at Siena, a nobleman sent him a live pheasant he had recently caught. The moment it saw and heard the holy man, it was drawn to him with such affection that it would in no way allow itself to be separated from him. Many times it was placed outside the friar's place in the vineyard so that it could go away if it wanted. But every time it ran right back to his father as if it had always been reared by him. Then it was given to a man who used to visit God's servant out of devotion but it absolutely refused to eat, as if it were upset at being out of the sight of the devoted father. It was finally brought back to God's servant, and as soon as it saw him, showed signs of joy and ate heartily.

When he went to the hermitage of La Verna to observe a forty-day fast in honor of the Archangel Michael, birds of different kinds flew around his cell, with melodious singing and joyful movements, as if rejoicing at his arrival, and seemed to be inviting and enticing the devoted father to stay. (Bonaventure, *The Life of Saint Francis*)[65]

Perhaps these stories read more like myth than biography or theology. Whatever they are, they reflect what was expected to be the reverence of a holy man for the creatures of his Creator.

Bestiaries

Medieval bestiaries remain at least in part an unsolved puzzle. They were illustrated moralizing treatises on beasts whose popularity, it has been repeatedly said, was exceeded only by that of the Bible. This fact itself reflects a continuing fascination with the animal realm, but does not indicate how the bestiaries are to be interpreted. They were derived, it would appear, from a single ancient original by Physiologus ("Naturalist"), a Greek scholar from around the second century, whose work contained many biological absurdities, including the *fact* that leopards have sweet-smelling breath. Over the centuries, much new information, and frequently further absurdities, was added to the bestiaries, sometimes replicated in the gargoyles that adorned medieval churches and public buildings.

The bestiaries were used by the clergy to impart moral and Biblical lessons to the congregation. Some began their sermons with the quotation from the Book of Job (12:7-9) on how we should learn from the beasts.[66] Yet the implications of the bestiaries remains unclear: were animals wise and capable creatures from whom humans had much of value to learn, merely a convenient means of imparting lessons by analogy, or creatures created by God for human use, one of which was human edification? It is probable that different compilers, and different pedagogical users, perceived the animals in different ways according to their own sensibilities. Certainly, the animals were portrayed with different emphases in different bestiaries, and sometimes within a particular bestiary, on occasion as wise creatures, on occasion as foolish ones, and on occasion as wise in some respects and foolish in others.[67]

Richard Rolle of Hampole

Richard the Hermit (d. 1349) was a Yorkshire recluse who was educated briefly at Oxford, but apparently preferred the solitude of a religiously contemplative life to that of a cleric. The following story, written by Richard, is in the bestiary mode though not from a bestiary itself. It is certainly reflective of how animals were used in bestiaries to teach moral lessons. Whether the story truly reflects a respect for the bee or treats the bee as a mere means of instruction is left to the judgment of the reader. Even though Richard's (and, for that matter, Aristotle's) knowledge of animal behaviour is decidedly rudimentary, and occasionally downright wrong, it is clear that the bee is presented as being superior in some respects to many humans.

The bee has three aspects to her nature. One is that she is never idle, and finds no good in those who will not work, but casts them out and puts them away. Another is that when she flies she takes soil in her feet so that she will not be easily raised too high by the blowing of the wind. The third is that she keeps her wings clean and bright.

Thus righteous men who love God are never in idleness. That is so whether they labour, pray, or think, or read, or do other good works; or whether they chastise idle men, and show they deserve to be excluded from the repose of heaven, on the ground they will not work here. They take soil; that is, they hold themselves to be worthless and dirty, so that they be not puffed up with vanity and pride. They keep their wings clean; that is, they fulfill the two commandments of charity in good conscience, and they have other virtues, uncontaminated with the filth of sin and unclean pleasure.

Aristotle said that the bees will fight against those who wish to take their honey. So should we fight against devils who endeavour to steal our honey of pure life and of grace. For many there are, who are unable to keep moderation in love toward friends, kin and strangers. They love them too much, setting their thoughts unrighteously on them; or they love them too little, if they do not all they would have done unto themselves. Such people cannot fight for their honey, for the devil turns it to worms, and makes their souls often full of bitterness in anguish and grief, and occupied with other worthless thoughts and other wretchedness. For they are so involved in earthly friendship that they will not fly into the love of Jesus Christ, in which they may forget the love of all those who live on the earth.

Wherefore, accordingly, Aristotle says that some birds are strong in flight, and can pass from one land to another. Some are weak in flight, on account of heaviness of body, and because their nest is not far from the earth. So it is of those who turn to the service of God. Some are strong in flight, for they fly from earth to heaven, where their thoughts dwell, and where they delight in God's love, and have no thought of the love of the world. Some are unable to fly from this world, but the way of their hearts is in the delight of the love of men and women, and they come and go, now in one way, now in another. And in Jesus Christ they can find no sweetness, or, if on occasion they feel they ought, it is too little and too short, for other thoughts within them bring them no constancy. For they are like a bird that is called an ostrich or stork, that has wings, which cannot fly because of the burden of its body. So they have understanding, and they fast, and keep vigil, and seem holy in men's sight, but they may not fly to the love and contemplation of God for they are filled with other affections and vanities. (Richard the Hermit, *The Nature of the Bee*)[68]

It would be appropriate to close this chapter with several quotations whose meanings are a lot clearer than the bestiaries and bestiary-style analogies.

Catherine of Siena

The visionary and advocate of Church reform, St. Catherine of Siena (1347-80) found a religious basis for the love of animals:

The reasons why God's servants love His creatures so deeply is they realise how deeply Christ loves them. And it is the very character of love to love what is loved by those we love.[69]

Bridget of Sweden

Founder of the Order of the Most Holy Saviour, St. Bridget of Sweden (c. 1300-73) wrote *The Revelations of Saint Bridget*, which was formally approved by the Council of Basle in 1431. It contains the following instance of animal sympathy. "Let a man fear, above all, me, his God, and so much the gentler will he become towards my creatures and animals, in whom, on account of me, their Creator, he ought to have compassion; for to that end was rest ordained on the Sabbath."[70]

Bernardine of Siena

A Franciscan who followed in the footsteps of the order's founder, St. Bernardine of Siena (1380-1444) was convinced of the moral superiority of animals. "Look at the pigs who have so much compassion for each other

that when one of them squeals, the others will run to help ... And you children who steal the baby swallows. What do other swallows do? They all
gather together to try to help the fledglings ... Man is more evil than the
birds."[71]

Geoffrey Chaucer
In the Prologue to *Canterbury Tales* (c. 1387) Chaucer (c. 1340-1400)
wrote of the Prioress, perhaps a trifle sentimentally:

> As for her sympathies and tender feelings,
> She was so charitably solicitous
> She used to weep if she but saw a mouse
> Caught in a trap, if it were dead or bleeding.
> And she had little dogs she would be feeding
> With roasted flesh, or milk, or fine white bread.
> And bitterly she wept if one were dead
> Or someone took a stick and made it smart;
> She was all sentiment and tender heart.[72]

Unduly sentimental or not, animal sympathy was what was expected of
a person of sensibility.

Dives et Pauper
Dives et Pauper – in essence meaning "The Wealthy and the Poor" – is a
moral treatise, probably of late-fourteenth-century vintage, and certainly
composed no later than 1410. Keith Thomas has said of the following
extract that it "is a notable passage and a very embarrassing one to anybody
trying to trace some development in English thinking about animal cruelty. For here at the very beginning of the fifteenth century we have a clear
statement of a position which differs in no respect whatsoever from that of
most eighteenth-century writers on the subject."[73]

When God forbade man to eat flesh, he forbade him to slay beasts in any cruel way,
or out of any liking for shrewness. Therefore, He said, "Eat ye no flesh with blood
(Gen. IX), that is to say, with cruelty for I shall seek the blood of your souls, at the
hands of all beasts." "That is to say: I shall take vengeance for all the beasts that are
slain out of cruelty of soul and a liking for shrewness." For God that make all hath
care of all, and He will take vengeance upon all that misuse His creatures. Therefore, Solomon saith, "that He will arm creatures in vengeance on their enemies"
(Sap.* V); and so men should have thought for birds and beasts and not harm them
without cause, in taking regard they are God's creatures. Therefore, they that out
of cruelty and vanity behead beasts, and torment beasts or fowl, more than is
proper for men's living, they sin in case full grievously.[74]

* Book of Wisdom.

4
The Renaissance

Renaissance is literally a rebirth – a rebirth of classical art, architecture, technology, and, generally, classical modes of literary, philosophical, and scientific thought. It was the age of Copernicus, Galileo, Kepler and Newton, Bacon and Descartes, Dante, Leonardo da Vinci, Michelangelo, and Shakespeare. But the Renaissance built on established classical knowledge, developing new modes, techniques, perspectives, and imagination of its own; and, in some cases, advancing a rigorously scientific, and sometimes rationalist, approach to knowledge in general.

Whereas the thought of the Middle Ages was first and foremost religious, with at least one eye cast continuously toward eternity, Renaissance thought increasingly fixed the other eye firmly on the mundane. Life on earth became an acknowledged, although not the sole, end in itself – Thomas Aquinas had already tentatively affirmed it in the latter part of the thirteenth century – and not merely a preparation for heaven, as Augustine had insisted. In the Renaissance – which will be treated, a trifle arbitrarily, as lasting from the close of the fifteenth century to the final decades of the seventeenth century – secular knowledge once again became an accepted desideratum.

Aristotle had begun his *Metaphysics* with the claim that "all men by nature have a desire to know."[1] Thomas Hobbes confirmed the adage in *Leviathan:* "Man is distinguished, not only by his reason; but also by this singular passion from other animals ... which is a lust of the mind, that by a perseverance of delight in the continual and indefatigable generation of knowledge, exceeds the short vehemence of any carnal pleasure." Nonetheless, the Renaissance was still an age of diversity and not everyone welcomed the revelations and re-orientations. While the novelties were glorified by some, they were denounced by others, and reinterpreted and nuanced by yet others who recognized that the new hubris, an unctuous faith in the wonders of human accomplishment, persuaded many to deem their own species "more perfect," as François Fénelon, theologian

Archbishop of Cambrai, termed it, and to diminish the significance of the interests of the other animals with whom we share our terrestrial home.[2]

If the new scientific age succeeded in providing a preliminary understanding of the orbits of the planets, the general laws of mechanics, and of scientific method, it did not always proceed very far in our knowledge of the animal realm – a notable exception being Leonardo da Vinci's studies. To be sure, the bestiaries were slowly replaced with "scientific" treatises on animals, but they left almost as much to be desired as the bestiaries themselves. In Konrad Gesner's *Historia Animalium* (in five volumes between 1551 and 1587) we still encounter the satyr (a woodland spirit man-beast), and several of Physiologus's imaginings are repeated. In Ulisse Aldrovandi's fourteen-volume *Natural History* (beginning in 1599) a harpy – part bird, part woman – is duly described in detail. Edward Topsell's *History of Four-Footed Beasts* (1607) contains a sphinx, dragons, and basilisks (reptiles that can kill a man with a look but are harmless to women), while his 1655 *Historia naturalis de quadrupedibus* portrays an Indian zebra and three kinds of unicorn. By the end of the period, the University of Leiden's Indian Cabinet Hall proudly housed a winged cat, the hand of a mermaid, and a monster hatched from a hen's egg (that is, a cockatrice). It was indeed the age of science, but science can provide understanding only when its data correspond with reality. And to the extent that justifiable sympathies are dependent on appropriate factual knowledge, misinformation is likely to pervert those sympathies. Still, the Renaissance provided some significant elaborations of compassion and respect, and even some significant measure of improved scientific understanding of the anatomy of animals, if rather less of their ethology.

Leonardo da Vinci

Customarily acknowledged as the quintessential Renaissance man, Leonardo (1452-1519) was not only one of the world's greatest painters, but also contributed to our understanding of physics and biology, of the potential for human flight and submarine travel, and of the relationships between time, space, sound, music, painting, sculpture, and architecture. He studied the movements of animals in great detail, in order to be able to represent them in his sketches and paintings with accuracy and understanding, as evidenced by his remarks in the scientific and artistic sections of his notebooks. Whether it was as a consequence of these meticulous studies, or some prior predilection of his compassionate spirit – almost certainly more of the latter – Leonardo not only drew and painted animals with consummate appreciation of their characters, but acted the part throughout his life as well. Even when he was analyzing the relationship between force and weight, his mind turned to animals with a ready appreciation of their reality. "The spirit of the sentient animals moves through the limbs of their bodies and when the muscles are responsive, it causes them to swell, and as they swell they shorten and in shortening they pull the tendons that are joined to them."[3]

That animals are creatures of spirit, sentience, and will is, for Leonardo, demonstrated by empirical observation – but not so for late Renaissance thinkers such as René Descartes and Nicolas Malebranche who imposed a predetermined conceptual schema on the objects of investigation. Leonardo studied them with diligence and with respect for their empirical realties.

Despite the empirical bases of his scientific and artistic work, Leonardo still delighted in repeating and elaborating the animal fables current at least since Aesop and Aristophanes. No age entirely replaces another; nor does the empirical orientation of the scientific mind always obscure our preternatural love of myth and fable – perhaps they become especially fascinating when we know they are not "true." Here are just two of the many fables told by Leonardo to amuse his friend Beatrice d'Este:

The lamb sets an example in kindness and humility. When given as food to a caged lion, it will approach as gently as its own mother, and very often it happens that lions go hungry rather than harm the little lambs.

The lizard is friendly to man. When it sees a man asleep and a snake nearby, it will fight the snake, and if it realizes that the snake is the stronger, it will scamper across the face of the man and wake him up so that he can save himself.[4]

There are times when the importance of the moral lesson and the charm of the tale exceed faithfulness to animal reality.

Throughout Leonardo's notebooks compassion for oppressed animals is pronounced. (The authenticity of the first quotation, while impressive, has been subject to some dispute.)

I have from an early age abjured the use of meat, and the time will come when men such as I will look upon the murder of animals as they now look upon the murder of men.[5]

Of asses which are beaten
O Indifferent nature, whereof art thou so partial, being to some of thy children a tender and benignant mother, and to others a most cruel and pitiless stepmother? I see thy children given into slavery to others, without any sort of advantage, and instead of remuneration for the services they have done, they are repaid by the severest suffering, and they spend their whole life in benefiting their oppressor.

Of bees
And many will be cruelly robbed of their stores and their food, and will be cruelly submerged and drowned by folks devoid of reason. O justice of God! Why dost thou not awake to behold thy creatures thus abused?

Of sheep, cows, goats, and the like
From countless numbers will be taken away their little children and the throats of these shall be cut, and they shall be quartered most barbarously.

Of animals that are eaten
The rat was being besieged in its dwelling by the weasel which with continual vigilance was awaiting its destruction, and through a tiny chink was considering its
great danger. Meanwhile the cat came and suddenly seized hold of the weasel and
forthwith devoured it. Whereupon the rat, profoundly grateful to its deity, having
offered up some of its hazel-nuts in sacrifice to Jove, came out of its hole in order
to repossess itself of the lately lost liberty, and was instantly deprived of this and of
life itself by the cruel claws and teeth of the cat.[6]

Leonardo is giving expression to one of the predominant ideas of the
Renaissance: that nature is neither an ideal nor a salvation, but is a cruel
force that must be dominated and suppressed if justice is to be achieved.
He glories in the beauties of nature, but is repelled by its indifference to
justice. It is not merely human cruelty to animals that repels him, but
"the cruel claws" of animal reality, even if they are ordained by nature. His
thoughts were later echoed by Charles Darwin who wrote in equal exas-
peration of "the clumsy, wasteful, blundering, low and horridly cruel works
of nature." If we are to understand human domination of nature we must
recognize that it is only in part a control and domination out of human
self-interest. It is also in part a reaction against the iniquities of the natural
laws of inter-species competition.

Nonetheless, for Leonardo, human cruelty is more intolerable than
other animal cruelty, because, however much it is predicated on nature, it
is ultimately a consequence of deliberate choice.

Of shoe soles made from leather
In many parts of the country you can see men walking about on the skins of large
beasts.

Of candles made of beeswax
[The bees] give light to divine service – and for this they are destroyed.

Of knives with handles made of ram's horns
Here we see the horns of certain beasts fitted to sharp iron, which is then used to
take the lives of their own kind.

Of mule bells placed too close to the mule's ear
In many parts of Europe, one hears instruments large and small, making all sorts of
sounds, to the great torment of those who hear them most closely.

Of asses
Here the hardest labour is repaid by hunger and thirst, pain and blows, goads and
curses, and loud abuse.

Of a fish served with its roe
Endless generations of fish will be lost because of the death of this pregnant one.

Of slaughtered oxen
Behold – the lords of great estates have killed their own labourers.[7]

As with St. Francis, we may best recognize Leonardo's compassion for animals by the statements of his contemporaries. In 1550 Giorgio Vasari, himself an important Florentine painter and architect, wrote nine volumes on *The Lives of the Most Eminent Painters, Sculptors and Architects*. Among his accolades for the "truly marvelous and celestial" man, as Vasari calls Leonardo, he offers us the following:

He was so pleasing in conversation that he attracted to himself the hearts of men. And although he possessed, one might say, nothing and worked little, he always kept servants and horses, in which latter he took much delight, and particularly in all the other animals, which he managed with the greatest love and patience; and this he showed when often passing by the places where birds were sold, for, taking them with his own hand out of their cages, and having paid to those who sold them the price that was asked, he let them fly away into the air, restoring them to their lost liberty. For which reason nature was so pleased to favour him, that, wherever he turned his thought, brain and mind, he displayed such divine power in his works, that, in giving [the animals] their perfection, no one was ever his peer in readiness, vivacity, excellence, beauty, and grace.[8]

In Vasari's view, Nature is so enamoured with those who are considerate of the interests of animals that to them she will grant privileges that she withholds from others.

Martin Luther

Instigator of the Reformation, Martin Luther (1483-1546) posted his famous ninety-five theses on the door of the castle church at Wittenberg in 1517. Excommunicated from the Catholic Church for his heretical views, he appears to have allowed for animals' immortal souls – though perhaps not in quite the same form as human souls. He certainly allows them some kind of afterlife in a manner reminiscent of the Qur'an, which George Sale, the first translator of the Qur'an into English (1734), interpreted to mean "irrational animals will also be restored to life at the resurrection, that they may be brought to judgment, and have vengeance taken on them for the injuries they did on another while in the world."[9] Thereafter they will, it would appear, be rendered harmless and be redeemed.

In response to a little girl who asked him whether her recently deceased pet dog would now be in heaven, Luther replied:

We know less of what that other world is like than this little girl knows of the empires or powers of this world. But of this we are sure, the world to come will be no empty, lifeless waste ... God will make new heavens and a new earth. All poisonous and malicious and hurtful creatures will be banished there, all that our sin has ruined. All creatures will not only be harmless, but lovely and joyful, so that we might play with them. The suckling child shall play on the hole of the asp and the weaned child shall put his hand on the cockatrice's den.* Why, then, should there not be little dogs in the new earth, whose skin might be as fair as gold, and their hair as bright as precious stones.[10]

Erasmus

Desiderius Erasmus (c. 1466-1536), an important Catholic figure in the Reformation controversy, was born in Rotterdam. He is often referred to as the first of the great humanist thinkers, and one of the most eminent of the early transalpine Renaissance figures. His humanism did not deter his appreciation of animal interests, for he found the ritual of hunting among humankind's most inveterate follies.

The man who, when he sees a pumpkin, supposes it's a woman, will be called crazy because not many people take part in that kind of delusion. But when another man swears that his wife, whom he shares with half his neighborhood, is more chaste that Penelope,[†] and so flatters himself to the top of his bent, nobody calls him mad, because it's recognized as the common fate of husbands. The same sort of fidelity afflicts those who prefer before everything else the chase of wild beasts, and say they get indescribable delight from the blast of hunting horns and the howling of hounds. I expect such people think even dog turds smell of cinnamon. But what pleasure is there in slaughtering animals in whatever numbers? Killing bulls and sheep is a job for common butchers, but cutting up a wild animal, forsooth, is permitted only to a man of noble birth. Baring his head, on bended knee, using a special knife (for it would be a sacrilege to use any other), he makes the ritual gestures, and then cuts off certain prescribed pieces in an exactly prescribed order. Meanwhile a hushed circle stands around, watching the ceremony as if it were a brand-new discovery, though they've seen it a hundred times before. If one of them happens to be given a little scrap of meat he feels himself exalted as by a new accession of nobility. And so when they have finished dissecting and devouring the dead beast, what have they accomplished except to degrade themselves into beasts while imagining they are living the life of kings. (Desiderius Erasmus, *The Praise of Folly* [Encomium moraliae] [1509])[11]

As with the very similar argument of John of Salisbury in the twelfth century, there is far more concern with the degradation of the hunter than with the plight of the hunted animal.[12] And certainly there is none of the deep sensibility of Leonardo. Nonetheless, there is a decided sense that the killing of animals without "necessity" is an unwholesome and degrading activity. The life of the animal has intrinsic value.

---

* The reference is to Isaiah 11:8.
† Odysseus's (Ulysses') wife, famed for her fidelity during her husband's twenty-year absence.

Thomas More

A martyred Catholic saint, Sir Thomas More (1478-1535) was a scholar of great repute as well as being lord chancellor to Henry VIII. Almost certainly influenced by Erasmus – More and Erasmus were friends, fellow humanist thinkers, and *The Praise of Folly* was dedicated to More – he took up the hunting theme in a more explicit way, with regard to compassion for the hunted animal rather than mere abhorrence for the hunters, in his famed *Utopia*, which apparently met with nothing but praise from Erasmus.

Having ridiculed foolish honours, empty nobility, and the amassing of wealth for its own sake, More continues:

To these foolish pleasures [the worthy inhabitants of Utopia] add gambling, which they have heard about, though they've never tried it, as well as hunting and hawking. What pleasure can there be, they say, in throwing dice on a playing table? If there were any pleasure in the action, wouldn't doing it over and over again make one tired of it? What pleasure can there be in listening to the barking and howling of dogs – isn't it a rather disgusting noise? Is any more pleasure felt when a dog chases a hare than when a dog chases a dog? If what you really want is slaughter, if you want to see a creature torn apart under your eyes you ought to feel nothing but pity when you see the little hare fleeing from the hound, the weak creature tormented by the stronger, the fearful and timid beast brutalized by the savage one, the harmless hare killed by the cruel hound. And so the Utopians, who regard this whole activity of hunting as unworthy of free men, have accordingly assigned it to their butchers ... In [the Utopians'] eyes, hunting is the lowest thing even butchers can do. In the slaughterhouse, their work is more useful and honest, since they kill animals only out of necessity; whereas the hunter seeks nothing but his own pleasure from killing and mutilating some poor little creature. (Thomas More, *On the Best State of a Commonwealth and on the New Island of Utopia*, Bk. 2 [1516])[13]

John of the Cross

More in than of the Renaissance, St. John of the Cross (1542-91) was a Spanish mystic and poet who suffered under the Inquisition, but retained enough compassion to find the animal realm "all clothed with beauty and dignity." His sensibility to animals pervades his writing but is at its zenith in his *Spiritual Canticle* of 1584.

According to Saint Paul, the Son of God is the brightness of His glory and the image of His substance. It must be known, then, that God looked at all things in the image of His son alone, which was to give them their natural being, to communicate to them many natural gifts and graces and to make them finished and perfect, even as He says in Genesis these words: God saw all the things that He had made and they were very good. To behold them and find them very good was to make them very good in the Word, His Son. And not only did He communicate to them their being and their natural graces when He beheld them, as we have said. But also in this image of His son alone, He left them clothed with beauty, communicating to them supernatural being. This was when He became man, and thus exalted man in the beauty of God, and consequently exalted all the creatures in Him, since in uniting Himself with man He united Himself with the nature of them all. Wherefore said the same Son of God: *Si ego exaltatus fuero a terra, omnia trahem ad me ipsum.* That is, I, if I be uplifted from the earth will draw all things unto Me. And thus in this lifting up of the Incarnation of His Son, and in the glory of His resurrection according to the flesh, not only did the Father beautify the creatures in part, but we can say He left them all clothed with beauty and dignity. But, besides all this, speaking now somewhat according to the sense and affection of contemplation, in the vivid contemplation and knowledge of the creatures, the soul sees with great clearness that there is in them such abundance of graces and virtues and beauty wherewith God endowed them, that, as it seems to her, they are all clothed with natural beauty, derived from and communicated by that infinite supernatural beauty of the image of God, Whose beholding of them clothes the world and all the heavens with beauty and joy; just as he does also the opening of His hand, whereby as David says: *Imples omne animal benedictione.* That is to say: Thou fillest every animal with blessing. (St. John of the Cross, *Spiritual Canticle* [1584])[14]

As with Luther, but far more emphatically, St. John of the Cross believes animals to possess immortal souls. Moreover, unlike for Fénelon, humans are not "more perfect." Animals are "finished and perfect." St. John of the Cross is beginning a tradition of thought which finds considerable resonance in the words of such later luminaries as Leibniz and Goethe.

Montaigne

There was more to the Renaissance than art, science, and theology. There was also the flourishing of the finest literature among the dramatists, poets, and essayists. Perhaps the most notable essayist was Michel Eyquem, seigneur de Montaigne (1533-92), who wrote "Of Freedom of Conscience," "That to Philosophize is to Learn to Die," "Of the Education of Children," "Of Cannibals," and much else beside. He held that there is: "a kind of respect and a general duty of humanity which tieth us ... unto brute beasts that have life and sense, but even to trees and plants ... unto men we owe justice, and to all other creatures ... grace and benignity ... there is a certain commerce and mutual obligation between them and us."[15]

In his "Apology for Raymond Sebond" (c. 1580) Montaigne addresses the question of the supposed superiority of humans and inferiority of other species. Throughout the essay he follows, sometimes without attribution, the arguments of Plutarch, Pliny, Democritus, and others of the classical period whom we have already met. Those arguments, and much else, have been omitted here.

Presumption is our natural and original malady. The most vulnerable and frail of all creatures is man, and at the same time the most arrogant ... It is by the vanity of this ... imagination that he equals himself to God, attributes to himself divine characteristics, picks himself out and separates himself from the horde of other creatures, carves out their share to his fellows and companions the animals, and distributes among them such portions of faculties as he sees fit. How does he know by the force of his intelligence, the secret internal stirrings of animals? By what comparison between them and us does he infer the stupidity that he attributes to them? ...

Plato, in his picture of the golden age under Saturn, counts among the principal advantages of the man of that time the communication he had with the beasts; inquiring of them and learning from them, he knew the true qualities and differences of each one of them; whereby he acquired a very perfect intelligence and prudence, and conducted his life far more happily than we could possibly do. Do we need a better proof to judge man's impudence with regard to the beasts? ...

The defect that hinders communication between them and us, why is it not just as much ours as theirs? It is a matter of guesswork whose fault it is that we do not understand each other; for we do not understand them any more than they do us. By this same reasoning they may consider us beasts, as we consider them ...

Moreover, what sort of faculty of ours do we not recognize in the actions of animals? Is there a society regulated with more order, diversified into more charges and functions, and more consistently maintained than that of the honeybees? Can we imagine so orderly an arrangement of actions and occupations as this to be conduced without reason and foresight?

Some by these signs and instances inclined,
Have said that bees share in the divine mind
And the ethereal spirit. (Virgil) (*Georgics*, bk. 4, lines 263-5)

Do the swallows that we see on the return of spring feretting in all the corners of our houses search without judgment, and choose without discrimination, out of a thousand places, the one which is most suitable for them to dwell in? And in that beautiful and admirable texture of their buildings, can birds use a square rather than a round figure, an obtuse rather than a right angle, without knowing the properties and their effects? Do they take now water, now clay, without judging that hardness is softened by moistening? Do they floor their palace with moss or with down, without foreseeing that the tender limbs of their little ones will lie softer and more comfortable on it? Do they shelter themselves from the rainy wind and face their dwelling toward the orient without knowing the different conditions of those winds and considering that one is more salutary to them than the other? Why does the spider thicken her web in one place and slacken it in another, use this sort of knot, now that one, unless she has the power of reflection, and thought, and inference?

We recognize easily enough in most of their works, how much superiority the animals have over us and how feeble is our skill to imitate them. We see, however, in our cruder works, the faculties that we use; and that our soul applies itself with all its power; why do we not think the same of them? Why do we attribute to some sort of natural and servile inclination those works which surpass all that we can do by nature and art? Wherein, without realizing it, we grant them a very great advantage over us, by making Nature, with maternal tenderness, accompany them and guide them as by the hand in all the actions and comforts of their life; while us she abandons to chance and to fortune, and to seek by art the things necessary for our preservation, and denies us at the same time the power to attain, by any education and mental straining, the natural resourcefulness of the animals: so that their brutish stupidity surpasses in all conveniences all that our divine intelligence can do ...

We are neither above nor below the rest; all that is under heaven, says the sage, incurs the same law and the same fortune.
All things are bound by their own chains of fate. (Lucretius)[16]

There are certain affectionate leanings which sometimes arise in us without the advice of our reason, which come from an unpremeditated accident that others call sympathy: the animals are as capable of it as we are. We see horses forming a certain familiarity with one another, until we have trouble making them live or travel separately; we see them apply their affection to a certain color in their companions, as we might to a certain type of face, and when they encounter this color, approach it immediately with joy and demonstrations of good will, and they take a dislike and hatred of some other color. Animals, like us, exercise choice in their amours and make a certain selection among females. They are not exempt from jealousies, or from extreme and irreconcilable envy ...

[T]he very share of the favors of nature that we concede to the animals, by our own confessions, is much to their advantage. (Montaigne, "Apology for Raymond Sebond" [c. 1580])[17]

Of course, the "scientific" mind will insist Montaigne is guilty of the unpardonable sin of anthropomorphism; and undoubtedly he is. But we should recall that evolutionary theories have not only demonstrated our common origins but imply that we should consider humans and other animals to be in all respects alike unless, and to the extent that, differences are rigorously demonstrated. The onus is on those who would disavow Montaigne to demonstrate in what respects he errs.

Shakespeare

"The swan of Avon," as Ben Jonson dubbed William Shakespeare (1564–1616), expressed compassion for the objects of the hunt, trapped birds, overworked horses, and even insects. He rarely wrote pieces specifically about animals, but they appear frequently, usually in short bursts, in his poetry and plays, sometimes reflecting his ready understanding of the natural order.

For example, in *Measure for Measure* (1.4) he describes the lapwing's elaborate mating display, and in *Macbeth* (2.3) he shows an awareness of the rarity that a barn owl may bring down a falcon, and sometimes he demonstrates a profound sympathy for the animals, even for what would have been seen as the meanest of them.

> The sense of death is most in apprehension.
> And the poor beetle that we tread upon,
> In corporal sufferance finds a pang as great
> As when a giant dies.
> (Isabella in *Measure for Measure,* 3.1 [c. 1605])

In *As You Like It* a duke has been usurped by his brother and is in exile in the forest of Arden, attended by French lords, including "melancholy Jaques," a man of sensibility.

> *Duke S.:* Come shall we go and kill us venison?
> And yet it irks me, the poor dappled fools,
> Being native burghers of this deserted city,
> Should in their own confines with forked heads
> Have their round haunches gor'd.
> *First Lord:* Indeed, my lord,
> The melancholy Jaques grieves at that;
> ... as he lay along
> Under an oak, whose antique root peeps out
> Upon the brook that brawls along this wood:
> To the which place a poor sequester'd stag,
> That from the hunter's aim had ta'en a hurt,
> Did come to languish; and, indeed, my lord,
> The wretched animal heav'd forth such groans,
> That their discharge did stretch his leathern coat
> Almost to bursting; ...
> *Duke S.:* But what said Jaques?
> Did he not moralize this spectacle?
> *First Lord:* O, yes, into a thousand similes,
> First, for his weeping in the needless stream;
> "Poor deer," quoth he,"thou mak'st a testament
> As worldlings do, giving thy sum of more
> To that which had too much": Then being alone,
> Left and abandoned of his velvet friends;
> "Tis right," quoth he; "this misery doth part
> The flux of company"; Anon, a careless herd,
> Full of the pasture, jumps along by him,
> And never stays to greet him; "Ay," quoth Jaques,
> "Sweep on, you fat and greasy citizens;
> 'Tis just the fashion: Wherefore do you look
> Upon that poor and broken bankrupt there?"

Thus most invectively he pierceth through
The body of country, city, court,
Yea, and of this our life; swearing that we
Are mere usurpers, tyrants, and what's worse,
To fright the animals and to kill them up,
In their assign'd and native dwelling-place.
(*As You Like It,* 2.1 [c. 1600])

Jaques's dismay is directed not only at the hunter tyrants who have usurped the rights of the stag in his own domain, but also at the insouciance of the fellow deer who have passed him by.

So doth the swan her downy cygnets save,
Keeping them prisoner underneath her wings.
(Earl of Suffolk in *Henry VI,* Part I, 5.3 [c. 1592])

One touch of nature makes the whole world kin ... (Ulysses in *Troilus and Cressida,*
3.3 [c. 1600])

Marcus: Alas, my lord, I have but kill'd a fly.
Titus: But how, if that fly had a father and mother?
How would he hang his slender gilded wings
And buzz lamenting doings in the air
Poor harmless fly!
That with his pretty buzzing melody,
Came here to make us merry, and thou hast kill'd him.
(*Titus Andronicus,* 3.2 [c.1593])

In Shakespeare's early poem *Venus and Adonis* he expresses sympathy for the hunted hare. "Wat" is a colloquialism for the hare. Venus is speaking.

"And when thou hast on foot the purblind hare,
Mark the poor wretch, to overshoot his troubles
How he outruns the wind, and with what care
He cranks and crosses with a thousand doubles:
     The many musets through the which he goes
     Are like a labyrinth to amaze his foes.

"Sometimes he runs among a flock of sheep,
To make the cunning hounds mistake their smell
And sometimes where earth-delving conies keep,
     To stop the loud pursuers in their yell,
     And sometimes sorteth with a herd of deer;
     Danger deviseth shifts; wit waits on fear:

"For there his smell with others being mingled,
The hot scent-snuffing hounds are driven to doubt,

Ceasing their clamorous cry till they have singled
With much ado the cold fault clearly out;
   Then they do spend their mouth: Echo replies,
   As if another chase were in the skies.

"By this, poor Wat, far off upon a hill,
Stands on his hinder legs with a listening ear,
To hearken if his foes pursue him still:
Anon their loud alarums he doth hear;
   And now his grief may be compared well,
   To one sore sick that hears the passing-bell.

"Then shalt thou see the dew-bedabbled wretch
Turn and return, indenting with the way;
Each envious briar his weary legs doth scratch,
Each shadow makes him stop, each murmur stay;
   For misery is trodden on by many,
   And being low never relieved by any."

Even the snail, like the beetle in *Measure for Measure*, is acknowledged a sentient creature:

Or, as the snail, whose tender horns being hit,
Shrinks backward in his shelly cave with pain,
And there, all smother'd up, in shade doth sit,
Long after fearing to creep forth again.
(*Venus and Adonis* [c. 1593])[18]

It is often suggested that Shakespeare's sensitivity to animals is most unusual, perhaps even unique, for his age. It is, however, worth reflecting on whether Shakespeare would have enjoyed his immense popularity in his own day if he were not expressing views acceptable to, if not already shared by, his audience.

John Donne

Poet, essayist, and divine, John Donne (1572-1631) is regarded as the greatest of the metaphysical poets. His prose writings, primarily on religious and moral topics, include *Devotions* (1624), which contains the immortal line: "No man is an Island, entire of Itself." His best-known poetical works are *An Anatomy of the World* (1611) and *Of the Progress of the Soul* (1612). His poem *Metempsycosis* contains the following words of sympathy for the life of the unfortunate fish. It should be noted, however, that since the subject was the rather recondite one of the transmigration of souls some commentators have been convinced the poem was less than in earnest. Certainly, metempsychosis was taken seriously by few – but by considerably more than is commonly recognized. Donne may have been more in earnest than some imagine, certainly with regard to the injustices to fish if not to the soul's peregrinations.

> Is any kind subject to rape like fish?
> Ill unto man, they neither do nor wish:
> Fishers they kill not, nor with noise awake,
> They do not hunt, nor strive to make a prey
> Of beasts, nor their young sons to bear away;
> Fowls they pursue not, nor do undertake
> To spoil the nests industrious birds do make;
> Yet them all these unkind kinds feed upon,
> To kill them is an occupation.
> And laws make fasts and lents for their destruction.[19]

Francis Quarles

Supporter of the divine right of kings, and author of moral and religious verse, Francis Quarles (1592-1644) complained of human excesses in the use of animal food in his *Enchiridion* of 1640:

> The birds of the air die to sustain thee
> The beasts of the field die to nourish thee;
> The fishes of the sea die to feed thee.
> Our stomachs are their common sepulchre.
> Great God! With how many deaths are our poor lives patched up!
> How full of death is the life of momentary man![20]

He added:

> Take no pleasure in the death of a creature; if it be harmless or useless, destroy it not; if useful, or harmful, destroy it mercifully.[21]

George Wither

Of considerable fame in his own day, although now largely forgotten, George Wither (1586-1667) was a poet and satirical pamphleteer (for which he earned a few months in Marshalsea prison). He was one of numerous poets of his era whose verses reflected a sympathy for animals in their frequent misuse by humans. The horse was particularly esteemed and pitied.

> And though I know this creature lent
> As well for pleasure as for need;
> That I the wrong thereof prevent,
> Let me still carefully take heed.
> For he that wilfully shall dare
> That creature to oppress or grieve,

Which God to serve him doth prepare
Himself of mercy doth deprive.

And he or his unless in time
They do repent of that abuse,
Shall one day suffer for his crime;
And want such creatures for their use.
(George Wither, "When We Ride for Pleasure" [1641])[22]

Margaret Cavendish

Margaret Cavendish (c. 1624-74), the Duchess of Newcastle, wrote plays, poetry, and essays on science, philosophy, and nature. She was one of the first women authors to venture into print. She described herself as "tender-natured, for it troubles my conscience to kill a fly and the groans of a dying beast strike my soul." Like Montaigne, she wondered whether other species possessed forms of knowledge unattained by humankind.

For what man knows whether fish do not know more of the nature of water, and ebbing and flowing and the saltness of the sea? Or whether birds do not know more of the nature and degrees of air, or the causes of tempests? Or whether worms do not know more of the nature of the earth and how plants are produced? Or bees of the several sorts of juices and flowers than men? ... Man may have one way of knowledge ... and creatures another way, and yet other creatures' manner or way may be [as] intelligible and instructive to each other as Man's. (Margaret Cavendish, *Philosophical Letters* [1664])[23]

It was, however, in her poetry that her sensibilities flourished. In "A Moral Discourse between Man and Beast" she gives the advantage in different respects to each. In "Of the Ant" she praises their communal ownership, their industrious endeavours, and their superiority in lacking the worst human passions. She penned two poems on the cruelties of hunting, one on the stag and one on the hare, both in 1653. In *The Hunting of the Hare* she provides us with a fulsome description of the emotions of the chase, the wiles of the wretched hare and the cruelty of the dogs, and the greater cruelty of their masters, before concluding:

Yet man doth think himself so gentle, mild,
When he of creatures is most cruel wild.
And is so proud, thinks only he shall live,
That God a god-like nature did him give.
And that all creatures for his sake alone,
Was made for him to tyrannize upon.
(Margaret Cavendish, *Poems and Fancies* [1653])[24]

John Milton

John Milton (1608-74) wrote in favour of the reformation of the Episcopalian Church, divorce on the grounds of incompatibility, and freedom of publication, arguing in his *Areopagitica* that through open and honest discussion truth would emerge. Whether humans were eternally ensouled Milton doubted; but if humans were, then so were other animals. "There seems ... no reason why the soul of man should be made an exception to the general law of creation. For ... God ... infused the breath of life into other living beings also; ... every living thing receives animation from one and the same source of life and breath."[25]

Today Milton is best remembered for his poetry, including *L'Allegro, Il Penseroso, Comus, Paradise Lost,* and *Paradise Regained.* Immediately prior to the following extract from *Paradise Lost,* considered by many the greatest epic poem in the English language, Adam bemoans his solitude, being without a partner of his species, when the "inferior" animals have been given mates by God. The "Universal Lord" replies:

> What call'st thou solitude, is not the earth
> With various living creatures and the air
> Replenished, and all these at thy command
> To come and play before thee? Know'st thou not
> their language and their ways? They also know,
> And reason not contemptibly; with these
> Find pastime, and bear rule; thy realm is large.
> (Milton, *Paradise Lost,* Bk. 8, 3 [1677])

Even though other species are at Adam's command, they are still rational creatures, worthy of belonging to the human community, if not, ultimately, capable of sharing in it fully with humans.

Molière

Jean Baptiste Poquelin Molière (1622-73), one of the greatest French classical playwrights, wrote *Le Tartuffe, L'Avare, Le Misanthrope,* and *Le Malade Imaginaire,* among other dramas. In this extract from *L'Avare* (The Miser) Molière expresses contempt for those who disregard the well-being of their animals. The coachman's compassion includes feeding the horses from his own meagre provisions.

Maître Jacques [the coachman and factotum]: ... You were saying ...?

Harpagon [the miser]: That my carriage needs to be cleaned and my horses got ready to drive to the fair.

Maître Jacques: Your horses, sir? My word, they're in no condition at all to walk. I won't tell you that they're down on their litter, the poor beasts don't have any, and it would be no way to talk; but you make them observe such austere fasts that they are nothing any more but ideas or phantoms or shadows of horses.

Harpagon: They're sick indeed! They don't do anything.

Maître Jacques: And because they don't do anything, sir, don't they need to eat anything? It would be much better for them, poor creatures, to work a lot and eat likewise. It breaks my heart to see them so emaciated; for the fact is I have such a tender feeling for my horses that when I see them suffer, it seems to be happening to me. Every day I take things out of my own mouth for them; and, sir, it's a sign of too harsh a nature if a man has no pity on his neighbor. (Molière, *The Miser,* 3.1 [1668])

As with Shakespeare, we can be confident that Molière's audience sympathized with him in his denigration of those who failed to treat their animals with kindness and generosity. When Molière writes of the horses' suffering seeming to happen to him he approaches the theme of empathy with animals later elaborated by Rousseau.[26]

John Evelyn and Samuel Pepys

The two great diarists of the seventeenth century, John Evelyn (1620-1706) and Samuel Pepys (1633-1703), made passing comments on certain "sports," reflecting what was increasingly the attitude of the educated and the polite. Thus Evelyn:

I was forc'd to accompanie some friends to the Bear-garden &c: Where was *Cock-fighting, Dogfighting, Beare & Bull baiting,* it being a famous day for all these butcherly Sports, or rather barbarous cruelties: The Bulls did exceedingly well but the Irish Wolfe dog exceeded, which was a tall Gray-hound, a stately creature in deede, who beat a cruell Mastife: One of the Bulls tossed a Dog full into a Lady's lap, as she sate in one of the boxes at a Considerable height from the *Arena:* There were two poore dogs killed; & so all ended with the Ape on horse-back, & I most heartily weary, of the rude & dirty passetime ... (John Evelyn, *Kalendarium,* 16 June 1670)[27]

Herein we witness the eternal human paradox: the event is recognized for what it is – a "rude and dirty" pastime – the treatment of the animals is appropriately depicted – "butcherly Sports" with "barbarous cruelties" – yet Evelyn is sufficiently entertained to take sides in the contests, to describe the combatants in glowing terms, and, while remaining appalled, remaining nonetheless.

In his *Diary* for 1665 Pepys tells us that he met a great crowd of hunters at Deptford: "and a great many silly stories they tell of their sport, which pleases them mightily and me not at all, such is the different sense of pleasure in mankind."[28] The cockpit was no better:

I did go to Shoe Lane to see a cocke-fighting at a new pit there, a sport I was never at in my life; but Lord! To see the strange variety of people, from Parliament man[29] ... to the poorest 'prentices, bakers, brewers, butchers, draymen, and what not; and all these fellows one with another in swearing, cursing, and betting. I soon had enough it, and yet I would not but have seen it once, it being strange to observe the nature of these poor creatures ... (Samuel Pepys, *Diary,* 21 December 1663)[30]

Like Evelyn, Pepys wrote of animal sports as "a very rude and nasty pleasure" (*Diary,* 4 August 1665). Again the paradox: a "rude and nasty" diversion, indeed: "yet I would not but have seen it once." Of course, we cannot be sure whether the observation "of these poor creatures" which is apparently so entertaining refers to the spectators or the animals. In 1696 the historian **Richard Tutbury** hid behind no paradox, declaring that "bull-running is a sport of no pleasure, except such as take pleasure in beastliness and mischief."[31]

George Fox

Founder of the Society of Friends (Quakers), George Fox (1624-91) was a seeker of spiritual enlightenment. He set out for the West Indies and America in 1671 to spread the gospel, and with considerable effect. His was an ascetic view of life, with compassion for all the oppressed, whether human or nonhuman. His perception of the relationship of humans to animals had a profound impact on later Quaker views, both with regard to their abomination of cruelty and their sympathy for vegetarianism.

"Away with you," say the professors and teachers of the world, "you [Quakers] are a company of madmen, you are not fit to live upon the earth."

"Ay, but," say the serious people, "you are the madmen that destroy the creation, and the creatures of God upon your lust, and the lusts of your eye, the lusts of the flesh, and the pride of life, which is not of the Father, but of the world, by which you destroy the Father's works, and the prime of the creatures, which were given forth to be used by the wisdom, by which they were created to the glory of the Creator" ...

And here is the devil the king of pride, that murderer, that leads people to consume and destroy the creatures upon their lusts, for his lusts they do; and so you are more like fools, that are slaves to the devil, who is out of the truth, that leads you to destroy the works, and creatures, and creation of God, and all your want [lack] is of God, for you want God, and his wisdom to order you ...

[Fashion] is our liberty, say the professors and teachers of the world, and all is ours, and it is the saint's liberty; nay, this is the liberty of the flesh, and the king of pride's kingdom, in his dominion in the earth; destroying the creatures, and devouring the creatures, and this liberty is your own bondage, who are servants of corruption ... (George Fox, *The Serious People's Reasoning and Speech, with the World's Teachers and Professors* [c. 1673])[32]

[L]iberty is a natural right, and every creature would have its natural right,* its liberty; and Christ gives liberty, and breaks the bonds asunder: and where the spirit of the Lord rules, there is liberty; but where it is quenched, there is bondage, and not liberty, that bondage that causeth the whole creation to groan, which the creature waited to be delivered from, into the glorious liberty of the sons of God, by Christ ... †

---

* This would appear to be the first application of the doctrine of natural rights to animals, not long after the idea had first been applied to humans in the mid-seventeenth century.

† The reference is to Romans 8:22.

What wages doth the Lord desire of you for this earth that he giveth to you teachers and great men, and to all the sons of men, and all creatures, but that you give him the praises, and honour, and the thanks, and the glory; and not that you should spend the creatures upon your lusts, but to do good with them; you that have much to them that have little; and so to honour God with your substance; for nothing brought you into the world, nor nothing you shall take out of the world, but leave all creatures behind you as you found them, which God hath given to serve all nations, and generations. (George Fox, *To All Sorts of People in Christendom* [c. 1673])[33]

Thomas Tryon

An English Anabaptist essayist, Thomas Tryon (1634-1703) did not begin writing until the age of 48. He then produced *Pythagoras: His Mystick Philosophy Reviv'd; Dreams and Visions;* as well as *The Way to Save Wealth, shewing how a Man may live plentifully for Two-pence a Day,* and a host of minor works on herbs and health in general. It was, however, his contribution to our responsibilities to the animal realm which were most memorable.

The inferior creatures groan under your cruelties. You hunt them for your pleasure, and overwork them for your covetousness, and kill them for your gluttony, and set them to fight with one another till they die, and count it a sport and a pleasure to behold them worry one another.

Man's duty, he added, was

as it best tends to the helping, aiding and assisting beasts to the obtaining of all the advantages their natures are by the great, beautiful and always beneficent creator made capable of. (*Philotheos Physiologus* [that is, Thomas Tryon], "Friendly Advice to the Gentlemen Planters of the East and West Indies" in *The Country-man's Companion* [1683])[34]

As the voice of the birds, Tryon asks:

But tell us, O men! We pray you to tell us what injuries have we committed to forfeit? What laws have we broken, or what cause given you, whereby you can pretend a right to invade and violate our part, and natural rights, and to assault and destroy us, as if we were the aggressors, and no better than thieves, robbers and murderers, fit to be extirpated out of creation. From whence did thou (O man) derive thy authority for killing thy inferiors, merely because they are such, or for destroying their natural rights and privileges. (Philotheos Physiologus, "The Complaints of the Birds and Fowls of Heaven to their Creator for the Oppressions and Violences Most Nations on Earth do Offer Them," in *The Country-man's Companion* [1683])[35]

This would appear to be the second reference to the idea of natural rights for animals, and perhaps rather closer to current usage than that employed by George Fox.[36]

In his *Wisdom's Dictates* of 1691 Tryon made his vegetarian message abundantly clear:

[V]iolence and killing either Man or Beasts is as contrary to the Divine Principle as light is to darkness ... Man's Soul nor Body can ever be at rest or peace, until he do suffer the inferior creatures to have and enjoy that Liberty and quiet they groan to be delivered into ... Refrain at all times from such Foods as cannot be procured without violence and oppression. For know that all the inferior Creatures when hurt do cry and send forth their complaints to their Maker or grand Fountain whence they proceeded. Be not insensible that every Creature doth bear the Image of the great Creator according to the Nature of each, and that He is the Vital Power in all things. Therefore let none take pleasure to offer violence to that life, lest he awaken the fierce wrath and bring danger to his own soul.[37]

Francis Bacon

The early age of science witnessed a growing confidence in the human capacity to control nature and bend it to suit human will. Philosopher, essayist, and statesman Francis Bacon (1561-1626) is customarily assigned the dubious compliment of being the one, as William Leiss wrote in his *Domination of Nature,* "to formulate the conception of human mastery over nature much more clearly than had been done and to assign it a prominent role in men's concerns."[38] A pervasive, if erroneous, assumption today is that the human control of nature was always undertaken at the expense of the animal realm. In fact, many who subscribed to that control thought it of potential benefit to the animals as well as to humans. As we saw in the words of Leonardo, nature could not be a moral standard[39] but must be controlled if justice is to be achieved. As late as the turn of the twentieth century, the dramatist George Bernard Shaw, who pronounced himself "a vegetarian on humanitarian and mystical grounds" and who had "never killed a fly or a mouse vindictively or without remorse" could also welcome the change "from the brutalizing torpor of nature's tyranny over Man into the order and alertness of Man's organized dominion over nature."[40] Bacon's belief, perhaps as unduly optimistic as Shaw's, was that there was room for the promotion of both human and animal interests in a human controlled environment.

Goodness I call the habit, and goodness of nature the inclination. This of all virtues and dignities of mind is the greatest, being the character of the deity; and without it man is a busy, mischievous thing, no better than a kind of vermin. *Goodness* answers to the theological virtue, *charity,* and admits no excess, but error. The desire of power in excess caused the angels to fall; the desire of knowledge in excess caused man to fall; but in *charity* there is no excess, neither can angel or man come in danger by it. The inclination of goodness is imprinted deeply in the nature of man; insomuch that, if it not issue towards men, it will take unto other living creatures; as it is seen among the Turks ... who ... are kind to beasts, and give alms to dogs and birds. (Francis Bacon, "Of Goodness and Goodness of Nature," *Essays*, 13 [c.1597])[41]

Clearly, for Bacon, not only do we have a moral responsibility toward the animal realm, but there are strict limits to humanity's capacity to control nature wisely. Bacon's statement, incidentally, is among the first to recognize Muslim kindness to animals, a belief which was almost proverbial in Britain by the early eighteenth century.

In the *De Dignitate et Augmentis Scientarium* (Of the Dignity and Advancement of Learning) of 1627 Bacon discussed Biblical proverbs in general, including that of Proverbs 12:10.

A righteous man regardeth the life of his beast, but the tender mercies of the wicked are cruel.

Explanation:
There is implanted in man by nature a noble and excellent spirit of compassion that extends itself to the brutes which by the divine ordinance are subject to his command. This compassion therefore has a certain analogy with that of a prince toward his subject. Moreover, it is most true, that the nobler a spirit is, the more objects of compassion it has. For narrow and degenerate spirits think that these things concern them not; but the spirit which forms a nobler portion of the use has a feeling of communion with them. Whence we see that under the old law there were many commandments not so much ceremonial as institutions of mercy; as was that of not eating the flesh with the blood thereof.[42]

Pierre Gassendi and Cartesianism's Detractors

The French philosopher René Descartes (1596-1650) argued that animals were no more than "beast machines," entirely devoid of reason, and, at least as far as moral significance is concerned, of sentience too.[43] It is a common assumption that Descartes's argument was widely accepted in the scientific community. In fact, only a handful or so of British scientists subscribed to the theory – notably Kenelm Digby, though some have doubted even his commitment. However, many certainly found it a convenient, if unexpressed, justification for the vivisection they practised. Even in France, where automataic Cartesianism proved significantly more persuasive, rumblings against his doctrines were not uncommon.

Some philosophers were explicit in their rejection of Cartesian principles. The Cambridge Platonist Henry More (1614-87) wrote to Descartes on 11 December 1648, denouncing "the internecine and cutthroat idea you advance in *[The Discourse on] Method* which snatches life and sensibility away from all the animals."[44] At the turn of the next century both the naturalist John Ray and the philosopher John Locke, among others, were equally condemnatory. The Tory politician and philosopher Viscount Bolingbroke averred that the common man would continue to believe that there was a marked difference between the town bull and the parish clock, despite those philosophers who thought of animals as sophisticated watches.

It was, however, left to the French priest, mathematician, scientist, and logician Pierre Gassendi (1592-1655) to reply in detail. Already in the Preface to his earliest work, *Exercises in the Form of Paradoxes in Refutation of the Aristoteleans* (1624), he advises us that "I restore reason to the animals; I find no distinction between the understanding and the imagination." In the body of the work he argues that it is simply an assumption, a prejudice, to deny reason to the animals: "the nature of an animal is no more known than is man's" (2, sec. 5, subsec. 4), and that the animal reasons from experience in the same manner as a human: "all ... knowledge is in the senses or derived from them" (2, sec. 6, subsec. 2).[45] This he wrote before Descartes elaborated his principles in the *Meditations*, which denied reason to the animals definitively. Gassendi responded privately to Descartes, expressing what he called his "Doubts." Descartes responded publicly with considerable vitriol, which provoked Gassendi to respond in print − without his customary philosophical restraint − with what he now called his "Rebuttals," together with Descartes's comments on Gassendi's original position.

In the *Second Meditation*, Descartes had written: "I may by chance look out of a window and notice some men passing in the street, at the sight of whom I do not fail to say that I see men ... and nevertheless what do I see from this window except hats and clothes ...? But I judge that they are men, and thus I comprehend, solely by the faculty of judgment which resides in my mind, that which I believed I saw with my eyes." Such a faculty of judgment, such a capacity for reasoning, he allowed only to humans. Gassendi responded:

For while you deny that any dog has a mind and leave him with only an imagination, [the dog] also perceives that a man, or his master, is hidden under the hat and clothes, and even under a variety of different forms. You skilfully glossed over the force of this argument and merely said that "relying on you know not what argument, I had affirmed as certain that a dog judged in the same way we did." Now obviously you had seen the argument; nor is the experience of occurrences similar to the one at stake unknown to you; but since you had nothing to answer, you went on a detour and once again slipped away under a flood of ink saying: "unless it is that when you see that [the dog] is made of flesh, you believe that all things that are in you are in it." Then again, you add this, "But I, who notice no mentality in the dog, think that nothing like the things that I recognize in the Mind will be found in the dog." Is it not true that if you think the existence of a mentality is evidenced by your realization that there is a man underneath when you see nothing but his hat and clothes, and if likewise a dog realizes that there is a man underneath when he sees nothing but his hat and clothes, is it not true, I say, that you should also think that the existence of a mentality like yours is evidenced by the dog? (Pierre Gassendi, *Metaphysical Colloquy,* Rebuttal to Meditation 2, Doubt 7 [1641])[46]

For Gassendi, the rationality of animals had immediate implications concerning our responsibilities toward them: "There is no pretence for saying that any right has been granted us by [moral] law to kill any of those animals which are not destructive or pernicious to the human race."[47] In response to a letter from his friend Johann van Helmont, Gassendi made a good case for vegetarianism, though there is no evidence that he followed his own prescriptions:

Man lives very well upon flesh, you say, but, if he thinks this food to be natural to him, why does he not use it as it is, as furnished to him by Nature? But, in fact, he shrinks in horror from seizing and rending living or even raw flesh with his teeth, and lights a fire to change its natural and proper condition ...

What is clearer than that man is not fitted for hunting, much less for eating, other animals? In one word, we seem to be admirably admonished by Cicero that man was destined for other things than for seizing and cutting the throats of other animals. If you answer that, "that may be said to be an industry ordered by Nature, by which such weapons are invented," then, behold! it is by the very same artificial instrument that men make weapons for mutual slaughter. Do they [say] this at the instigation of Nature? Can a use so noxious be called *natural?* Faculty is given by Nature, but it is our own fault that we make a perverse use of it.[48]

Influenced in many respects by Descartes's general philosophy, British idealists nonetheless refused to countenance the notion of animals as automata, or, at the very least, to treat them as though they were. Thus, for example, **Henry More** (1614-87), who influenced Isaac Newton's scientific work and emphasized the mystical and theosophic aspects of Platonism, continued his epistolary remonstrance to Descartes:[49]

But I beg you, most penetrating man, since it is necessary by this argument of yours, either to deprive animals of their sense or to give them immortality, why should you rather set up inanimate machinery than bodies motivated by immortal souls, even though that may have been least consonant with natural phenomena so far discovered? In this, indeed, the most learned ancients judged and approved; take Pythagoras, Plato, and others. Certainly the persistent idea is present in all the works of Plato, and has given courage to all Platonists. Nevertheless, such a remarkable genius has been reduced to these straits, that, if one does not concede immortality to the souls of brutes, then all animals are of necessity inanimate machines.[50]

Henry More opts for immortal animal souls.

Clergyman and philosopher **John Norris** (1657-1711), whose philosophy was an uncomfortable amalgam of Malebranche and Plato, seems almost convinced by the Cartesian doctrine but refuses to accept the practical implications of that doctrine with regard to the treatment of animals.

To conclude now with a Word or two, concerning the *Treatment* of Beasts. Tho' it is my Opinion, or if you will, my Fancy, that Reason does most favour that side which denies all Thought and Perception to brutes, and resolves those Movements of theirs which seem to carry an appearance of it (because *like* those which we exert by Thought) into mechanical Principles, yet, after all, lest in Resolution of so abstruse a Question our Reason should happen to deceive us, as 'tis easy to err in the Dark, I am so far from incouraging any practices of Cruelty, upon the bodies of these Creatures, which the Lord of the Creation has (as to the moderate and nec-essary use of them) subjected our Power, that on the contrary I would have them used and treated with as much tenderness and pitiful regard, as if they had all that Sense and Perception, which is commonly (tho' I think without sufficient Reason) attributed to them. Which equitable Measure, they that think they really have that Perception, ought in pursuance of their own Principle, so much the more *Consci-entiously* to observe. (John Norris, *An Essay towards the Theory of the Ideal or Intelli-gible World* [1701], pt. II, ii)[51]

A veritable Pascal's wager for animals! We cannot be sure that animals are sentient, but, in the absence of certainty, morality and prudence require an assumption in its favour.

Authority on the brain and nervous system, and Sedleian Professor of Natural Philosophy at Oxford University, **Thomas Willis** (1621-75) puzzled over the Cartesian doctrine of soul, and concluded: "For granting to the Soul one Vital Portion living in the Blood, to be a certain inkindling of it, and another Sensitive, to be only an heap of Animal Spirits every-where diffused thorow the Brain and Nervous Stock; it follows from hence, that Brutes have a soul Co-extended to the whole Body and Parts not only many and distinct, but after a manner dissimilar" (Thomas Willis, "Of the Soul of Brutes" in *Dr. Willis's Practice of Physick* [1684]).[52] Perhaps not the most lucid, or even transparent, piece of English prose, but the rejection of Cartesianism is clear enough.

Pierre Bayle

The French philosopher Pierre Bayle (1647-1706) provided the most com-plete survey of historical views on animal souls in the article "Rorarius"[53] in his *Historical and Critical Dictionary* (1697). Bayle's own view, he acknowledges, is essentially that of the German philosopher Gottfried Wilhelm Leibniz, though Bayle hopes to add some clarity to the Leib-nizian view. Bayle starts with an assertion entirely at odds with what one customarily reads of the Western tradition today: "For a long time people have maintained that beasts do have a rational soul."[54] For Bayle, Carte-sianism and Thomism are aberrations in the Western tradition.

Bayle cites the Jesuit priest Ignace Pardies from his *De la connoissance des bêtes:*

If you once grant that beasts without any spiritual soul are capable of thinking, of goal-directed action, of foreseeing what is to come, of remembering what has happened, of profiting from experience by the particular reflections they make on it; why will you not say that men are capable of performing their functions without any spiritual soul? After all, the operations of men are no different from those that you attribute to beasts. If there is any difference, it is only one of degree. And thus all you could say will be that the soul of man is more perfect than that of beasts because it remembers better than they do, thinks with more reflection, and foresees with more assurance.[55]

While Pardies is using this argument against animal rational souls, Bayle considers animals to possess all the characteristics described and thus, he believes, the argument demonstrates that animals belong in the same spiritual category with humans.

The Cartesian has no sooner overthrown, ruined, annihilated the view of the Scholastics concerning the soul of beasts,* than he finds out that he can be attacked with his own weapons and can be shown that he has proven too much; and that if he reasons logically, he will give up views that he cannot give up without becoming an object of ridicule and without admitting the most glaring absurdities. For where is the man who would dare to say that he is the only one who thinks and that everybody else is a machine?[†56]

[W]e clearly conceive that an unextended substance which can have sensation is capable of reasoning; and consequently, if the soul of beasts is an unextended substance, capable of sensation, it is capable of reasoning. It is then of the same species as man's soul ...

Leibniz' s hypothesis ... leads us to believe, (1) that God, at the beginning of the world, created the forms of all bodies and, hence, all the souls of beasts, (2) that these souls have existed ever since that time, inseparably united to the first organized body in which God placed them ... there remains the biggest question, namely, what becomes of these souls or forms when either the animal dies or the unity of the organized substance is destroyed? And it is this that is most puzzling, insofar as it does not even seem slightly reasonable for the souls to remain uselessly in a chaos of confused matter. This made me decide finally that there was only one reasonable view to adopt; and that is the theory of the conservation of not only the soul, but also of the animal itself and of its organic machine ...[57]

Richard Overton
More famous as a revolutionary Leveller, Cromwellian intriguer, and radical Presbyterian than as an animal advocate, Richard Overton (fl. 1642-49)

* In essence, the Scholastic view was that it is a material, non-rational, and mortal soul.
† Solipsism (that is, the belief that the self is the only knowable, hence existent, thing) is often considered a consequence of the Cartesian dictum: *cogito ergo sum* (I think therefore I am).

expressed the kind of animal respect increasingly common among evangelicals in the later seventeenth century. The views of Ambroise Paré (1510-90), French army surgeon and author, whose most famous work was *On Monsters and Marvels* to which Overton refers, and with which he concurs, indicate that the Darwinian notion that animals possess all the attributes of humans in vestigial or complete form – human and animal differences are of degree and not of kind – was current in Europe more than two centuries prior to the publication of the *Origin of Species* (1859). It is remarkable how many books on the history or philosophy of animal welfare and animal rights encourage the notion that such ideas are developed by Darwin and that he was responsible for transforming our conception of the human moral relationship to the animal realm. Even if Paré's ethology is hopelessly inadequate, the moral principle on which it is based corresponds with that of Charles Darwin in *The Descent of Man*.

[The principles of life] are general to the whole Creation ... so that, as Solomon says, man has no preeminence above a beast, even one thing befalleth them ...

As Ambrose Parey says, ... if we will diligently search into [animals'] nature, we shall observe the impressions of many virtues: ... magnanimity, prudence, fortitude, clemency, docility, love, carefulness, providence; yea, knowledge, memory &c. is common to all brutes, the affections and passions of the mind, all [man's qualities] good and bad, and every faculty he has, is to be found more or less among them. And Parey further says, they are of quick sense, observant of the rites of friendship and chastity, they submit themselves to the discipline of man, they have taught man many things, &c.

The hare is eminent for memory, the dog for apprehension and fidelity, the serpent for wisdom, the fox for subtlety, the dove for charity and innocence, the elephant for docility, modesty and gratitude. Pliny said [the elephant] comes near the understanding of man[58] ... the ape is eminent for imitation and understanding, the turtle for love, the crocodile for deceit, the lamb for patience, the wasp for anger &c., and for his five senses [man] is by them excelled ...

[A]ll other creatures as well as man, shall be raised and delivered from death at the resurrection. (Richard Overton, *Man's Mortality* [1643])[59]

And the homologies, physical, emotional, and spiritual, entailed a corresponding obligation: "If your neighbour's ox, or his ass were in a ditch, it is a shame to pass by and not to help ..." (Richard Overton, *The Baiting of the Great Bull of Basham* [1649]).[60]

Obiter Dicta

So far in this chapter we have concentrated on some principal figures of the Renaissance and its aftermath, noting the remarks of those who are better known for other contributions to Western thought than their animal sympathies. The exceptions are those such as Cavendish and Tryon whose attention was drawn in the first instance to the plight of animals and the merit of our compassion for them. There are, however, a number of relatively minor, and one or two hitherto unmentioned although fairly significant, figures who made telling remarks, usually in passing, and whose words reflect an important dimension of the psyche of the sixteenth and seventeenth centuries.

The Puritan theologian **Philip Stubbes** (1555-1610) claimed in his *Anatomy of Abuses* of 1583 that he had "never read of any in the volume of the Sacred Scriptures that was a good man and a hunter."[61] He continued:

What Christian Heart can take pleasure to see one poor beast to rent, tear, and kill another, and all for his foolish pleasure? And although they be bloody beasts to mankind, and seek his destruction, yet we are not to abuse them, for his sake who made them, and whose creatures they are. For notwithstanding that they be evil to us, and thirst after our blood, yet are they good creatures in their own nature and kind, and made to set forth the glory, power and magnificence of our God, and for our use, and therefore for his sake we ought not to abuse them.[62]

In like vein we read from the polymath **Thomas Draxe**: "Let us in no wise curse, ban [interdict], blame or misuse any of the poor Creatures, knowing that if there be any defect or untowardness in their nature, or any want of duty and observance in them, towards us, our sin hath been and is the cause and occasion of it" (Thomas Draxe, *The Earnest of Our Inheritance* [1613]).[63]

Voltaire reported that the most eminent of the new scientists, **Sir Isaac Newton** (1642-1727), found:

it a frightful inconsistency to believe that animals feel and at the same time cause them to suffer. On this point his morality was in accord with his philosophy. He yielded with repugnance to the barbarous custom of supporting ourselves upon the blood and flesh of beings like ourselves, whom we caress, and he never permitted in his own house the putting of them to death by slow and exquisite methods of killing for the sake of making the food more delicious. The compassion which he felt for other animals culminated in true charity for men. (Voltaire, *Eléments de la Philosophie de Newton* [1738])[64]

Sir Matthew Hale (1609-76), Chief Justice of the Court of King's Bench, wrote that

The end of man's creation was that he should be the viceroy of the great God of heaven and earth in this inferior world, his steward, villicus,* bailiff or farmer of this godly farm of the lower world.

It was thus that mankind was

invested with power, authority, right, dominion, trust and care, to correct and abridge the excesses and cruelties of the fiercer animals, to give protection and

---

* Estate overseer.

defence to the mansuete* and useful, to preserve the species of diverse vegetables,†
to improve them and others, to correct the redundance of unprofitable vegetables,
to preserve the face of the earth in beauty, usefulness and fruitfulness. (Matthew
Hale, *The Primitive Organization of Mankind* [1677])[65]

Hale's exegesis is an elaboration of the notion that the dominion over
nature and its constituent creatures is to be undertaken for the improvement and benefit of the environment and the animals. Lord Chief Justice
Hales also thought consideration for animals an appropriate part of practical life:

I ever thought that there is a certain degree of justice due to the creatures as well
as from man to man, and that an excessive use of the creature's labour is an injustice, for which we must account. I have, therefore, always esteemed it a part of my
duty, and it has invariably been my practice, to be merciful to my beasts; and upon
the same account I have declined all cruelty to any of God's creatures. Where I had
the power, I have prevented it in others. I have abhorred those sports that consist
in torturing them; and if any noxious creatures must be destroyed, it has been my
practice to do this with the least torture or cruelty, ever remembering, that,
although God has given us dominion over his creatures, yet it is under a law of justice, prudence, and moderation, otherwise we should become tyrants, and not
lords over God's creatures.[66]

In 1679, **W. Howell** advised in his *The Spirit of Prophecy:* "That there are
some footsteps of reason, some strictures and emissions of ratiocination in
the actions of some brutes, is too vulgarly known and too commonly
granted to be doubted."[67] Vulgarly, and wisely, known perhaps, but sometimes denied too by those who proclaimed a science superior to those with
the vulgar knowledge of common sense and the intuitions.

Sir Philip Sidney (1554-86), author of the famed *Arcadia*, published
posthumously by his sister in 1590, urged mankind in his poetry (published 1595) to respect God's trust in human dominion and to practise it
with discretion:

But yet, O man, range not beyond thy need;
Deem it no glory to dwell in tyranny.
Thou art of blood, joy not to make things bleed;
Thou fearest death; think they are loath to die ...
And you poor beasts, in patience bide your hell.[68]

The diarist John Evelyn mentioned a sermon he heard delivered by a
Dr. Stradling in London on 9 April 1677 on Romans 8:22[69]

---

* Tame, gentle.
† That is, vegetation in general.

showing how even the creatures should enjoy a manumission* and as much felicity as their nature is capable of, when at the last day they shall no longer groan for their servitude to sinful man.[70]

In 1683, the Anglican Dean of Winchester **Richard Meggott** preached on the similarities of all animals:

Even in that which we pretend our peculiar prerogative, ratiocination, [the animals] seem to have a share ... Their knowledge extendeth not only to simple objects, but it is evident by the subtlety and docility,[†] which is so wonderful in many of them, even to propositions, assumptions and deductions. (Richard Meggott, *A Sermon Preached at Whitehall* [1683])[71]

During the Cromwellian Protectorate, such "sports" as bear-baiting cock-fighting and cock-throwing were outlawed in public. An early Puritan, **Robert Bolton** (1572-1631) of Blackburn, who, according to the *Dictionary of National Biography*, had a "sustained popularity" in his day, helped set the stage for such edicts.

Bathe not thy recreations in blood: Refresh not thy tired mind with spectacles of cruelty: Consider, 1. How God himself out of tenderness and pity, would not have his people feed upon the flesh of Beasts with the blood, lest thereby they should be fleshed to cruelty, and inured to behold rueful objects without horror. And dost thou think then, he will allow thee to feed thine eye and fancy with their bloody torturing and tearing one another to pieces? 2. With what brutish swageness thou dejects and debases humanity, below the inhumanity of beasts. No beast, they say, takes contentment in the hurting of any other, except in the case of hunger or anger. They satisfy their appetites and rage sometimes with cruelty and blood; but their eyes and fancies never. 3. That men bloodily minded towards harmless beasts, discover our natural propension to cruelty. (Robert Bolton, *Some Generall Directions for a Comfortable Walking with God* [1625])[72]

Bolton deemed it sinful to "take delight in the cruel tormenting of a dumb creature," or to revel in "the bleeding miseries of that poor harmless thing which in its kind is much more and far better serviceable to its Creator than thyself."[73] A few years later, **Edmund Ellis,** a clergyman who suffered equally under the Commonwealth and the Restoration for his espousal of unpopular causes, added to Bolton's view. In *The Opinion of Mr. Perkins, Mr. Bolton and Others concerning the Sport of Cock-Fighting* (Perkins being the author of *Cases of Conscience* [1632], which had adopted a rather more moderate stance than that of Bolton), Ellis wrote,

[Y]et I am not afraid to make known to the world that I cannot imagine how any man, whilst he is actually like unto God, the Father of Mercies, can possibly delight

---

* That is, should be set free from slavery.

† Their ability to learn from instruction.

and recreate himself, in seeing his fellow-creatures (which are infinitely less inferior to us, than we are to our, and their Creator) so subtle and active to destroy each other. Having this opinion of the sport of cock-fights, and seeing it frequently used in the country where I live, no man, that I can hear of, opposing it as actually sinful, I could not retain the confidence I have, that I am, indeed, a faithful servant of the great God in the gospel of His Son, and a true lover of the souls of men, if I should not venture to oppose it myself.[74]

Writing around the same time as Robert Bolton, another Puritan, **William Hinde** (1569-1629), perennial curate of Bunbury in Cheshire, opined: "I think it utterly unlawful for any man to take pleasure in the pain and torture of any creature, or delight himself in the tyranny which the creatures exercise, one over another, or to make a recreation of their brutish cruelty which they practise one upon another." (William Hinde, *A Faithfull Remonstrance of the Happy Life and Holy Death of John Bruen* [c. 1625])[75]

Fellow sectarian **Thomas Edwards** (fl. 1640s) was more emphatic in his recognition of human and animal similarities. "God loves the creatures that creep on the ground as well as the best saints; and there is no difference between the flesh of a man and the flesh of a toad" (Thomas Edwards, *Gangraena*, I, 20 [1646]).[76]

A radical ranter, **Jacob Bottomley,** writing mid-century, added a pantheistic touch: "I see God in all creatures, man and beast, fish and fowl and every green thing from the highest cedar to the ivy on the wall; and that God is the life and being of them all."[77]

A later dissenter, **Edward Bury,** (fl. 1670s), deemed it "no doubt lawful" to kill animals for food "but to sport ourselves in their death seems cruel and bloody: suppose thou heardest such a poor creature giving up the ghost to speak after this manner (for it is no absurdity to feign such a speech), 'Oh man, what have I done to thee ... I am thy fellow creature'" (Edward Bury, *The Husbandman's Companion* [1677]).[78]

The Presbyterian minister **John Flavel** (c. 1630-91) a "voluminous and popular author," according to the *Dictionary of National Biography,* summed up the thinking of dissenting Protestantism in commenting on an overworked horse:

What has this creature done that he should be
Thus beaten, wounded and tired out by me?
He is my fellow-creature.
(John Flavel, *Husbandry Spiritualised* [1699])[79]

Those who cannot imagine that supposedly misanthropic English Puritans could really respect and care for their "fellow-creatures" are wont to quote **Thomas Babbington Macaulay**'s famous barb that the seventeenth-century "Puritan hated bear-baiting, not because it gave pain to the bear but because it gave pleasure to the spectators. Indeed, he generally contrived to enjoy the double pleasure of tormenting both spectators and bear."[80] The above quotations indicate emphatically that the Whig historian's statement tells us more about the Whig than the Puritan mentality.

While there would appear to be no notable American contributions to the animal welfare debate at this early date, it was nonetheless a matter very much on the minds of the New England Puritan colonists, as exemplified in the Massachusetts Bay Colony *The Body of Liberties* of 1641, prepared by the Reverend **Nathaniel Ward.**

Of the Brute Creature.
Liberty 92.
No man shall exercise any Tyranny or Cruelty toward any brute creature which are usually kept for man's use.

Liberty 93.
If any man shall have occasion to lead or drive Cattle from place to place that is far off, so that they may be weary, or hungry, or fall sick, or lame. It shall be lawful to rest or refresh them, for a competent time, in any open place that is not corn, meadow, or enclosed for some peculiar purpose.[81]

A fitting close to this chapter is a few famous lines from **Andrew Marvell** (1622-78), one of the finer English metaphysical poets, together with a few less well-known but equally worthy lines from John Wilmot, a somewhat obscure aristocrat, but a no less instructive poet.

The Nymph complaining for the death of her Faun
The wanton Troopers riding by
Have shot my Faun, and it will dye.
Ungentle men! They cannot thrive
To kill thee! Thou neer didst alive
Them any harm; alas, nor cou'd
Thy death yet do them any good.
I'm sure I never wisht them any ill;
Nor do I for all this; nor will

But if my simple Pray'rs may yet
Prevail with Heaven to forget
Thy murder, I will Joyn my Tears
Rather than fail. But O my fears!
It cannot dye so. Heaven's King
Keeps register of everything:
And nothing may we use in vain.
Ev'n Beasts must be with justice slain.

Else men are made their *Deodands.**
Though they should wash their guilty hands
In this warm life-blood, which doth part
From thine, and wound me to the Heart,

Yet could they not be clean; their Stain
Is dy'd in such a Purple Grain.
There is not such another in
The World to offer for their Sin.[82]

John Wilmot (1647-80), second Earl of Rochester, included these lines in his *Satyr* (c. 1675), which is not only a human-animal comparison that bodes better for the animal but bears in its opening lines some resemblance to Book 10 of Plato's *Republic.*[83]

Were I (who to my cost already am
One of those strange prodigious Creatures *Man)*
A Spirit free, to choose for my own share,
What Case of Flesh, and Blood, I pleas'd to weare,
I'd be a *Dog,* a *Monkey,* or a *Bear,*
Or any thing but that vain *Animal,*
Who is so proud of being rational.
The senses are too gross, and he'll contrive
A Sixth, to contradict the other Five;
And before certain instinct, will preferr
Reason, which Fifty times for one does err ...

For all his Pride and his Philosophy,
'Tis evident, *Beasts* are in their degree
As wise at least, and better far than he.
Those *Creatures,* are the wisest who attain,
By surest means, the ends at which they aim ...

Whose Principles, most gen'rous are, and just,
And to whose *Moralls,* you wou'd sooner trust.
Be judge your self, I'le bring it to the test,
Which is the basest *Creature Man,* or *Beast?*
Birds, feed on *Birds, Beasts,* on each other prey,
But Savage *Man* alone, does *Man* betray:
Prest by necessity, they Kill for Food;
Man undoes *Man,* to do himself no good.[84]

---

* Forfeits. In medieval law, when a death had been caused, whatever caused the death was subject to forfeit.

5
The Enlightenment

The Enlightenment refers to the mainstream of eighteenth-century European and American intellectual thought up to the time of the French Revolution. Built on the scientific and literary foundation of the Renaissance and its consequent development, it was an age of increasing religious skepticism, empiricism, and rationalism – at least among secular intellectuals. Above all, it was an era marked by supreme confidence in the abilities of rational men to solve all the puzzles of the universe. The attitude of "advanced" thinkers was that, if science had shown the way to understand the laws of the physical world, the application of those rational, scientific principles to human social, political, and ethical questions would produce similar certainties. There was now nothing beyond human comprehension or capacity. Mystery, doubt, and unfathomable complexity were all swept away, or, at least, swept under the carpet.

Of course, as with any age, there were nonconformists. Some rejected the extremes to which other Enlightenment thinkers would go. Others, notably the representatives of the established churches, thought the ideas of an increasingly rejected past still contained much wisdom. And yet others recognized that the overweening confidence in human reason ignored sentiments, sensibilities, and primordial common sense, especially, though from widely differing perspectives, Jean-Jacques Rousseau, Edmund Burke, and many Dissenters.

Where did the animals stand in such an epoch? One might have expected the glorification of the human intellect to encourage a dismissal of animal interests and well-being – and among some it undoubtedly did. But it also promoted a healthy interest in the study of nature, which in turn stimulated a welcome recognition of animal complexities – even though progress was often slow. By the end of the century most naturalists still failed to recognize the reality of bird migration and mermaids were still commonly sighted, though there was at least an increasing awareness of the unity of life, as Giovanni Borelli had demonstrated in Italy in 1680 when he showed that the same laws governed the wings of birds, the fins of fish, and the legs of insects. Moreover, the governing idea of the Enlightenment was that humans behaved in accordance with the same permanent natural laws that determined all animal behaviour. To be sure, human hubris hindered the idea from being taken too literally, and grounds for human exclusivity were constantly sought – and not infrequently found. Nonetheless, there remained the earnest endeavour to develop a logical system to provide a rigorous basis for understanding all behaviour, and on which a scientific basis for ethics could be predicated. This despite Utilitarians from the skeptic David Hume, who found an answer in probability, to the rationalist Jeremy Bentham, who found an answer in an abstract system which, he claimed, permitted him to legislate for the whole world from the recesses of his study. Significantly, the method of each allowed a significant place for the animals. The place of the animal was assured in the lexicons of philosophers.

Yet in reality David Hume, Jeremy Bentham, and other animal-sympathetic philosophers were adding little more than intellectual sophistication to some practical achievements and the dictates of intuition, indicating that earlier, or less philosophically derived, compassions had already suffused by degree the public mind. At most, they were building a philosophical edifice in which to house prior recognitions. If Britain had to wait until the early nineteenth century for national animal welfare legislation – the Protectorate ordinance of 1654 outlawing cock-fighting and the like applied only to public events and had become obsolete with the restoration of the monarchy – some municipalities were quicker off the mark. Chester, in northwest England, had already prohibited bear-baiting in 1596 during the reign of Elizabeth I – a decree later ignored – and in 1653 Maidstone, southeast England, banned, as "cruel and un-Christianlike," cock-throwing (that is, throwing objects at poultry tied to a stake, customarily practised at Shrovetide as a burst of exuberance before the deprivations of Lent). By the closing decades of the eighteenth century the general legislation now widely mooted was already unnecessary in some parts of Britain, where bull- and bear-baiting, and cock- and dog-fighting, were little more than an unpleasant memory. Writing in 1801, George Nicholson mentioned the counties of Shropshire and Staffordshire, and particular towns in Suffolk and Cheshire, as regions where bull-baiting continued. It was an occasional "entertainment" too at northern wakes' fairs. In some other jurisdictions it had fallen into disrepute or was out of fashion. Birmingham had prohibited it by bylaw in 1774. Cock- and dog-fighting were still rife in London, but the capital banned the former spectacle before national legislation was enacted. In 1781 London's Smithfield Market was put under statutory surveillance and by 1786 slaughterhouses were regulated. More humane methods of slaughter were being avidly sought and countless pages were devoted to developing a less deadly manner of bee-keeping – Daniel Wildman's *A Complete Guide for the Management of Bees,* just one of a host of books advocating more humane husbandry methods, went through thirteen editions between 1775 and 1798. However, it was only in 1851 that an effective system, a readily removable frame in the hive, was generally implemented.

By the end of the eighteenth century even those who opposed animal welfare legislation did so predominantly on prudential grounds regarding the purposes of legislation, the availability of the common law to meet non-emergency situations, a concern with jurisdictional issues, or because they saw the proposed measures as an undue interference in the private lives of the lower classes, while leaving unaffected the upper-class "sports" of hunting, shooting, angling, and horse-racing. Many, even more than in our own times, remained addicted to "sport" hunting, even though as early as 1603 a preacher at St. Paul's cathedral had advised the congregation there would be no hunting or hawking in heaven.

The ideas and values of the Enlightenment era altered the educated mind significantly, if not yet all of the public face. The general tenor of the views we encounter in this chapter contributed to those early, if far from complete, practical advances – which is neither to ignore nor downplay the fact that many continued to treat other species as mere instruments of human purposes.

John Ray

Among the first to develop a systematic classification of the animal and vegetable realms, assisted by his student Francis Willughby and many clerical and lay associates, John Ray (1627-1705) helped set the tone for eighteenth-century naturalist thought. Writing in 1691, he advised the coming generation:

It is a generally received Opinion that all this visible world was created for Man; that Man is the end of Creation, as if there were no end of any Creature but some way or other to be serviceable to man. This opinion is as old as *Tully* [Cicero] ... But though this be vulgarly received, yet Wise Men nowadays think otherwise. Dr. More [the Cambridge Platonist] affirms "The Creatures are made to enjoy themselves, as well as to serve us, and that it's a gross piece of Ignorance and Rusticity to think otherwise." And in another place, "This comes only out of Pride and Ignorance or a haughty Presumption, because we are encouraged to believe, that in some sence, all things are made for Man, therefore to think that they are not all made for themselves. But he that pronounceth this, is ignorant of the Nature of Man, and the Knowledge of Things. For if a good Man be merciful to his Beast, then surely a good God is Bountiful and Benign, and takes pleasure that all his Creatures enjoy themselves that have Life and Sense, and are capable of Enjoyment." For my part, I cannot believe that all things in the world were so made for Man, that they have no other use ...

I believe there are many Species in Nature, which were never yet taken notice of by Man, and consequently of no Use to him, which yet we are not to think were Created in vain; but it's likely (as the Doctor [More] saith) to partake of the over-flowing Goodness of the Creator, and enjoy their own beings. But though in this sence it be not true, that all things were made for Man: yet thus far it is, that all the Creatures in the world may be some way or other useful to us, at least to exer-cise our Wits and Understandings, in considering and contemplating of them, and to afford us Subject of Admiring and Glorifying their and our Maker. (John Ray, *Wis-dom of God Manifested in the Works of the Creation* [1691])[1]

John Locke
If Ray set the tone for naturalists, the way for philosophy was set by the founder of British empiricism and foremost of the early liberal thinkers, John Locke (1632-1704). He relied initially on the postulates of the Great Chain of Being first systematized some fourteen hundred years before but still popular at the close of the seventeenth century.

There are some brutes, that seem to have as much knowledge and reason as some that are called men; and the animal and vegetable kingdoms are so nearly joined, that if you will take the lowest of the one, and the highest of the other, there will scarce be perceived any great difference between them; and so on until we come to the lowest and most inorganical parts of matter; we shall find everywhere that the several *Species* are linked together, and differ but in almost insensible degrees. (John Locke, *An Essay Concerning Human Understanding,* 1690)[2]

While some earlier examples of Great Chain reasoning tended to emphasize human distinctiveness, the idea was now used predominantly to stress human-animal similarities. For Locke these similarities had implications for compassion toward our fellow creatures.

Cruelty.   One thing I have frequently observed in children, that when they have got possession of any poor creature, they are apt to use it ill; they often torment and treat very roughly young birds, butterflies, and such other poor animals which fall into their hands, and that with a seeming kind of pleasure. This, I think, should be watched in them; if they incline to any such cruelty, they should be taught the contrary usage; for the custom of tormenting and killing of beasts will, by degrees, harden their minds even towards men; and they who delight in the suffering and destruction of inferior creatures, will not be apt to be very compassionate or benign to those of their own kind ... Children should from the beginning be bred up in an abhorrence of killing or tormenting any living creature, and be taught not to spoil or destroy anything, unless it be for the preservation or advantage of some other that is nobler ... I think people should be accustomed from their cradles to be ten-der to all sensible [that is, sentient] creatures, and to spoil or waste nothing at all. This delight they take in doing of mischief, whereby I mean spoiling of any thing to no purpose, but more especially the pleasure they take to put any thing in pain that is capable of it, I cannot persuade myself to be any other than a foreign [that is, contrary to nature] and introduced disposition, a habit borrowed from custom and conversation. (John Locke, *Some Thoughts Concerning Education* [1693])[3]

Locke's further view that it was repugnant to waste food that could sustain a wild creature became increasingly persuasive. This is not to say the practice was widely established, either then or now. It is one thing to accept the legitimacy of a moral pronouncement and quite another to embody it in one's culture. Today, cruelty to animals is almost universally proscribed, but frequently practised. Locke understood that it was part of a sound educational system to attempt to eradicate cruelty to animals, a view often reiterated throughout the eighteenth and nineteenth centuries, resulting in the establishment of humane education organizations.

Alexander Pope

Although the naturalists and the philosophers contributed to the recognition of animals as worthwhile beings in themselves, with their own purposes, characters, excellences, and fulfilments, it was in the literary genre that respect and compassion for animals were most handsomely expressed – in poetry, novels, and occasional essays.

Both a Catholic and a Tory – allegiances rarely thought of as conducive to extended animal sympathies – Alexander Pope (1688-1744) became famous for *The Rape of the Lock* (1714), *The Dunciad* (1728-43), and *An Essay on Man* (1734). Like John Locke he subscribed to the Great Chain doctrine but drew even more emphatic conclusions from it.

Vast chain of being! which from God began,
Natures ethereal, human, angel, man,
Beast, bird, fish, insect, what no eye can see,
No glass can reach; from infinite to thee,
From thee to nothing ...

Connects each being, greatest with the least;
Made beast in aid of man, and man of beast;
All serv'd, all serving: nothing stands alone:
The chain holds on, and where it ends, unknown.

Thus then to man the voice of Nature spake:
"Go, from the creatures thy instructions take:
Learn from the birds what food the thickets yield;
Learn from the beasts the physic of the field
Thy arts of building from the bee receive;
Learn of the mole to plough, the worm to weave ...
And hence let reason, late, instruct mankind ..."
(Alexander Pope, *An Essay on Man* [1734])[4]

Pope stresses the interdependence of all beings, the priority of certain animal instincts, and the view that reason should supplement, not replace, instinct. It was in an article in the *Guardian* that he had earlier drawn the moral implications of such conceptions, while acknowledging a human superiority he downplayed in the *Essay on Man*.

I cannot think it extravagant to imagine, that mankind are no less in proportion accountable for the ill use of their dominion over the creatures of the lower ranks of beings, than for the exercise of tyranny over their own species. The more entirely the inferior creation is submitted to our power, the more answerable we should seem for our mismanagement of it; and the rather, as the very condition of nature renders these creatures incapable of receiving any recompense in another life for their ill-treatment in this. It is observable of those noxious animals, which have qualities most powerful to injure us, that they naturally avoid mankind, and never hurt us unless provoked or necessitated by hunger. Man, on the other hand, seeks out and pursues even the most inoffensive animals on purpose to persecute and destroy them.

Pope then refers to the theme of Montaigne, discussed earlier, and continues:

We should find it hard to vindicate the destroying of any thing that has life, merely out of wantonness; yet in this principle our children are bred up, and one of the finest pleasures we allow them is the license of inflicting pain upon poor animals; almost as soon as we are sensible what life is ourselves, we make it a sport to take it from other creatures. I cannot but believe a very good use might be made of the fancy which children have for birds and insects. Mr Locke* takes notice of a mother who permitted them to her children, but rewarded or punished them as they treated them well or ill. This was no other than entering them betimes into a daily exercise of humanity, and improving their very diversion to a virtue.

I fancy, too, some advantage might be taken of the common notion, that it is ominous or unlucky to destroy some sorts of birds, as swallows or martins; this opinion might arise from the confidence these birds seem to put in us by building under our roofs; so that it is a kind of violation of the laws of hospitality to murder them. As for robin-red-breasts in particular, it is not improbable they owe their security to the old ballad of the Children in the Wood. However it be, I do not know, I say, why this prejudice, well improved and carried as far as it would go, might not be made to conduce to the preservation of many innocent creatures, which are now exposed to the wantonness of an ignorant barbarity ...

When we grow up to men, we have another succession of sanguinary sports; in particular, hunting. I dare not attack a diversion which has such authority and custom to support it; but must have leave to be of opinion, that the agitation of that exercise, with the example and number of the chasers, not a little contribute to

* That is, John Locke in his *Some Thoughts Concerning Education* (1693).

resist those checks, which compassion would naturally suggest in behalf of the animal pursued ...

But if our sports are destructive, our gluttony is more so, and in a more inhuman manner. Lobsters roasted alive, pigs whipped to death, fowls sewed up, are testimonies to our outrageous luxury. Those who (as Seneca expresses it) divide their lives betwixt an anxious conscience and a nauseated stomach, have a just reward of their gluttony in the diseases it brings with it; for human savages, like other wild beasts, find snares and poison in the provisions of life, and are lured by their appetite to their destruction. I know nothing more shocking or horrid than the prospect of one of their kitchens covered with blood, and filled with the cries of creatures expiring in tortures. It gives one an image of a giant's den in a romance, bestrewed with the scattered heads and mangled limbs of those who were slain by his cruelty.

Pope then takes his readers on an excursion into Plutarch's opinions, followed by some historical examples of humanity to animals. He continues:

I remember an Arabian author [Tell'amed, a Muslim scholar], who has written a treatise to show, how far a man supposed to have subsisted on a desert island, without any instruction, or so much as the sight of any other man, attain the knowledge of philosophy and virtue. One of the first things he made him observe is, that universal benevolence of nature in the protection and preservation of its creatures. In imitation of which, the first act of virtue he thinks his self-taught philosopher would of course fall into is, to relieve and assist all the animals about him in their wants and distresses.

Ovid is next cited at some length, first in Latin, then in John Dryden's translation of Book 15 of the *Metamorphoses*.

The sheep was sacrificed on no pretence,
But meek and unresisting innocence,
A patient useful creature, born to bear
The warm and woolly fleece that cloth'd her murderer;
And daily to give down the milk she bred,
A tribute for the grass on which she fed.
Living, both food and raiment she supplies,
And is of least advantage when she dies.
How did the toiling ox his death deserve;
A downright simple drudge and born to serve.
O tyrant! With what justice canst thou hope
The promise of the year, a plenteous crop,
When thou destroy'st thy lab'ring steer, who till'd,
And ploughed with pains, thy lest ungrateful field;
From his yet reeking neck to draw the yoke,
That neck, with which the surly clods he broke;

And to the hatchet yield thy husbandsman,
Who finish'd autumn, and the spring began?
...
What more advance can mortals make in sin
So near perfection, who with blood begin?
Deaf to the calf that lies beneath the knife,
Looks up, and from her butcher begs her life;
Deaf to the harmless kid, that ere he dies
All methods to secure thy mercy tries,
And imitates in vain the children's cries.

Returning to his own voice, Pope suggests:

Perhaps that voice or cry so nearly resembles the human, with which Providence has endued so many different animals, might purposely be given them to move our pity, and prevent those cruelties we are too apt to inflict on our fellow-creatures. There is a passage in the book of Jonas,* when God declares his unwillingness to destroy Nineveh, where methinks that compassion of the Creator, which extends to the meanest ranks of his creatures, is expressed with wonderful tenderness – "Should I not spare Nineveh that great city, wherein are more than six score thousand persons" – "and also much cattle?" And we have in Deuteronomy a precept of great good nature of this sort, with a blessing in form annexed to it, in these words: "If thou shalt find a bird's nest in the way, thou shalt not take the dam with the young: but thou shalt in any wise let the dam go, that it may be well with thee, and that thou mayst prolong thy days."

To conclude, there is certainly a degree of gratitude owing to those animals that serve us. As for such as are mortal or noxious,† we have a right to destroy them; and for those that are neither of advantage nor prejudice to us, the common enjoyment of life is what I cannot think we ought to deprive them of. (Alexander Pope, "On Cruelty to the Brute Creation" [sometimes called "Against Barbarity to Animals"], *Guardian*, 61, 21 May 1713)[5]

Pope was a friend of the vivisector Dr. Stephen Hales, but in a conversation recorded by another friend, Joseph Spence, he protested against the surgeon's practice.

S[pence]. I shall be very glad to see Dr. Hales, and always love to see him, he is so worthy a man. P[ope]. Yes, he is a very good man, only I'm sorry he has his hand so imbued with blood. S. What! he cuts up rats! P. Ay, and dogs too (With what emphasis and scorn he spoke it.) Indeed, he commits most of those barbarities with the thought of being of use to man; but how do we know that we have a right to kill creatures that we are so little above as dogs for our curiosity, or even for some use to us? (Joseph Spence, *Anecdotes, Observations and Characters*)[6]

---
* Jonah.
† That is, lethal or harmful.

Spence also reported a conversation that suggests that Pope may no longer have held the same view of the animals' lack of immortal souls that he expressed in his "On Cruelty to the Brute Creation." Spence opened the conversation by speculating that dogs possess reason.

P. So they have to be sure. All our disputes about that, are only disputes about words. Man has reason enough only to know what is necessary for him to know; and dogs have just that too. S. But then they must have souls too; as unperishable in their nature as ours? P. And what harm would that be to us?[7]

In his poem *Windsor Forest* (1713) Pope expressed his quiet disgust for the fowler:

See! from the brake the whirring pheasant springs,
And mounts exulting on triumphant wings:
Short is his joy; he feels the fiery wound,
Flutters in blood, and panting beats the ground.
Ah! what avail his glossy, varying dyes,
His purple crest, and scarlet-circled eyes,
The vivid green his shining plumes unfold,
His painted wings, and breast that flames with gold?
Nor yet, when moist Arcturus clouds the sky
The woods and fields their pleasing toils deny.
To plains with well-breath'd beagles we repair,
And trace the mazes of the circling hare:
(Beasts, urged by us, their fellow-beast pursue,
And learn of man each other to undo)
With slaughtering guns the unwearied fowler roves,
When frosts have whiten'd all the naked groves;
Where doves in flocks the leafless trees o'ershade,
And lonely woodcocks haunt the watery glade.
He lifts the tube, and levels with his eye;
Straight a short thunder breaks the frozen sky:
Oft, as in airy rings they skim the heath,
The clam'rous lapwings feel the leaden death;
Oft, as the mounting larks their notes prepare,
They fall, and leave their little lives in air.[8]

The *Tatler*

Some three years prior to Pope's *Guardian* article, the *Tatler* ran two articles, one devoted in part, the other in whole, to the issue of cruelty to animals. Their authorship has not been conclusively established, though the second is very probably by essayist, playwright, and editor **Richard Steele** (1672-1729). In the 27 December 1709 issue we read, as an exemplary contrast to an instance of cruelty: "I am extremely pleased, to see his younger brother carry an universal benevolence toward every thing that has life. When he was between four and five years old, I caught him weeping over a beautiful butterfly which he chanced to kill as he was playing with it; and I am informed that this morning he has given his brother three half pence (which was his whole estate) to spare the life of a tomtit."[9] This set the tone for an article a few weeks later that begins with a petition against the Shrovetide practice of cock-throwing:

> Upon delivery of this petition, the worthy gentleman who presented it, told me the customs of many wise nations of the east, through which he had travelled; that nothing was more frequent than to see a dervees [a dervish, a Muslim friar] lay out a whole year's income in the redemption of larks and linnets that had unhappily fallen into the hands of bird-catchers; that it was also usual to run between a dog and a bull to keep them from hurting one another, or to lose the use of a limb in parting a couple of furious mastiffs. He then insisted upon the ingratitude and disingenuity of treating in this manner a necessary and domestick animal, that has made the whole house keep good hours, and called up the cook-maid for five years together. What would a Turk say, continued he, should he hear that it is a common entertainment in a nation which pretends to be one of the most civilised in Europe, to tie an innocent animal to a stake, and put him to an ignominious death, who has perhaps been the guardian and proveditor [provider] of a poor family, as long as it was able to get eggs for its mistress?
>
> I thought what this gentleman* said was very reasonable; and have often wondered, that we do not lay aside a custom which makes us appear barbarous to nations much more rude and unpolished than ourselves. Some French writers have represented this diversion of the common people much to our disadvantage, and imputed it to a natural fierceness and cruelty of temper; as they do some other entertainments peculiar to our nation: I mean those elegant diversions of bull-baiting and prize-fighting, with the like ingenious recreations of the bear garden. I wish I knew how to answer this reproach which is cast upon us, and excuse the deaths of so many innocent cocks, bulls, dogs and bears, as have been set together by the ears, or died untimely deaths only to make us sport ... The virtues of tenderness, compassion and humanity are those by which men are distinguished from brutes, as much as by reason it self; and it would be of the greatest reproach to a nation to distinguish it self from all others by any defect in these particular virtues. For which reasons, I hope that my dear countrymen will no longer expose themselves by an effusion of blood, whether it be of theatrical heroes, cocks, or any other innocent animals, which we are not obliged to slaughter for our safety, convenience,† or nourishment. Where any of these ends are not served in the destruction of a living creature, I cannot but pronounce it a great piece of cruelty, if not a kind of murder. (*Tatler,* 16 February 1710)[10]

---

* Identified only as a Pythagorean; that is, a vegetarian.
† That is, in accordance with nature, such as the provision of clothing.

The *Spectator*

Essayist **Eustace Budgell** (1686-1737), who was a regular contributor to the *Tatler*, *Spectator*, and *Guardian*, as well as a critic of the incumbent administration in the pages of the *Craftsman*, described a hunt in some detail in which Richard Steele's invented character, Sir Roger de Coverley, manages to enjoy the hunt while sparing the hare.

[T]he poor hare ... was now quite spent, and almost within the reach of her enemies; when the huntsman getting forward, threw down his pole before the dogs. They were now within eight yards of that game which they had been pursuing for almost as many hours; yet on the signal before-mentioned they all made a sudden stand, and though they continued opening as much as before, durst not once attempt to pass beyond the pole. At the same time Sir Roger rode forward, and alighting, took up the hare in his arms; which he soon after delivered up to one of his servants with an order, if she could be kept alive, to let her go in his great orchard; where it seems he has several of these prisoners of war, who live together in a very comfortable captivity. I was highly pleased to see the discipline of the pack, and the good nature of the knight, who could not find in his heart to murder a creature that had given him so much diversion. (*Spectator,* 13 July 1711)[11]

Essayist, poet, editor, and statesman, **Joseph Addison** (1662-1719), a close associate of Richard Steele, and cousin of Eustace Budgell, found at least some vivisection inexcusable.

Is it not wonderful that the love of the parent should be so violent [forceful] while it lasts. And that it should last no longer than is necessary for the preservation of the young?

The violence of this natural love is exemplified in a very barbarous experiment; which I shall quote at length, as I find it in an excellent author, and hope my readers will pardon the mentioning such an instance of cruelty, because there is nothing can so effectually shew the strength of that principle in animals of which I am here speaking. "A person who was well skilled in dissections opened a bitch, and as she lay in the most exquisite tortures, offered her one of her young puppies, which she immediately fell a licking; and for the first time seemed insensible of her own pain. On the removal, she kept her eye fixed on it, and began a wailing sort of cry, which seemed rather to proceed from the loss of her young one, than the sense of her own torments." (*Spectator,* 18 July 1711)[12]

Addison is reported to have claimed: "True benevolence, or compassion, extends itself through the whole of existence and sympathises with the distress of every creature capable of sensation."[13]

Henry Fielding

One of the first English novelists, Henry Fielding (1707-54) made passing remarks of esteem for his fellow-creatures in his novels. Thus, in *Joseph Andrews* (1742) he describes the lion as a "magnanimous beast"[14] while in

Amelia (1751) he arouses our sympathy for the father by telling us he "was a great lover of birds and strictly forbad the spoiling of their nests."[15] It was, however, in his periodical writings that he expressed his compassion forthrightly. As a stipendiary magistrate, as well as an author, Fielding offered the following eye-witness account of a reunion between a donkey and his owner, following the animal's theft and recovery, and the prosecution of the thief.

"Sir, this is my ass," [avowed the owner], "I should know him among all the asses in the world, as he would know me, wouldst thou not poor Duke? Sir, we have lived together these many years, ay that we have, as a man and wife, as a man may say; for, Sir, I love my ass as my wife; the best twenty horses in the world, no, nor a king's ransom to boot, should not buy my poor ass. Poor Duke! ... we shall never part more, I hope, whilst I live."

Then followed a scene of tenderness between the man and the ass, in which it was difficult to say, whether the beast or its master gave tokens of the higher affection. (*Covent-Garden Journal,* 22 February 1751-2)[16]

Fielding also penned a paean to the horse:

Standing the other day in Fleet Street with my son ... I observed, with great indignation, an ill-looking fellow most cruelly lashing a pair of starved horses, who laboured to the utmost of their power to drag on a heavy burthen. And, as they were prevented from making greater haste, even had they been able, by the coaches which were before them, this gentleman must have exercised his arm for nothing more than his own innocent* diversion, at the expense of the skins of those poor unhappy beasts.

As I look on myself to have been sent into the world as a general blessing, that I am endowed with so much strength and resolution to redress all grievances whatsoever, and to defend and protect the brute creation, as well as my own species, from all manner of insult and barbarity, which, however exercised, is, after the several edicts I have published, no less than a most impudent opposition to my authority, I had certainly pulled the fellow from his box, and laid my little finger on him, had my son not interposed, and begged me not to raise a disturbance, by punishing him there: for that he had marked his [licence] number, and that I might find him at my leisure. Whether the fellow saw my brows knit at him, a sight very few people are able to endure, I can't tell, but he began to withhold his whipping, and suffered me to be persuaded by my son, especially as there were some ladies in his coach, whom I would by no means have ventured to frighten by such an execution.

My son Tom told me, as we pursued our walk that he had a facetious† acquaintance ... who professed the Pythagorean principles, and affirms that he believes [in]

---

* Naive, unknowing, wasted.
† Agreeable, amusing.

the transmigration of souls. This gentleman, as Tom informed me, comforts himself on all such occasions with a persuasion that the beasts he sees thus abused have formerly been themselves ... coachmen; and that the soul of the then driver will in his turn pass into the horse and suffer the same punishment which he so barbarously inflicts on others. But to pass by such whimsical opinions, I have often thought that the wisdom of the legislature would not have been unworthily employed in contriving some law to prevent those barbarities which we so often see practised on these domestic creatures. A boy should, in my opinion, be more severely punished for exercising cruelty on a dog or a cat, or any other animal, than for stealing a few pence or shillings, or any of those lesser crimes which our courts of justice take notice of ...

...

The history of a hero hath been scarce thought complete without some description of his horse; the horses of Alexander[17] and Caesar are consecrated to fame with their riders. It is reported of the latter, that he would stoop to take up his master, though he would condescend to take no other on his back. Indeed, I have known a horse, who hath not belonged to a hero, who would be rid by none but his owner.

Romance generally acquaints us with the names and virtues of the horse as well as the hero. Thus, the famous Cid's horse was called Balieca and that great renowned knight Don Quixote thus expresses himself in favor of Rozinante: "Thou wise enchanter, whoever thou art, who shall chronicle these achievements, I desire thee not to forget my good horse Rozinante, mine eternal and inseparable companion in all my travels and adventures."[18] Nor do I think it possible to read that excellent history without conceiving a very great affection for that renowned beast ... and I think it may be observed to their reputation, that all great personages ancient and modern, have chosen to communicate their graces to posterity by equestrian statues.

...

And whether we observe the great beauty of this animal, its swiftness, its strength, the obedience which it pays to man, with its great usefulness on all occasions, how much it contributes to health, to business, to diversion; and lastly, how often the lives of men have been preserved by the remedies which the swiftness of the horse hath timely conveyed to them, we shall see great reason for the utmost affection we can show them in return. (*Champion*, 22 March 1739-40)[19]

While Steele thought it appropriate to organize a petition to stop cock-throwing in 1710, thirty years later the conception of law had changed sufficiently, if not yet decisively, and Fielding could promote legislative measures as the appropriate remedy for cruelty to animals. It would appear that he was the first to do so since the Protectorate days of the 1650s.

Fielding's animal sympathies are a little more guarded in his novels, but they are there. There is a memorable example in *Joseph Andrews* when a hunted rabbit scurried past:

It was, however, so weak and spent, that it fell down twice or thrice on the way. This afflicted the tender heart of poor Fanny, who claimed, with tears in her eyes, against the barbarity of worrying a poor defenceless animal out of its life, and putting it to the extremest torture for diversion ... The hounds were now very little behind their poor reeling, staggering prey, which, fainting almost at every step, crawled through the wood, and had almost got round to the place where Fanny stood, when it was overtaken by its enemies, and being driven out of the covert, was caught, and instantly torn to pieces before Fanny's face, who was unable to assist it with any aid more powerful than pity.[20]

Fielding also wrote an amusing burlesque in his *Miscellanies* (1743)[21] on some of the inanities of contemporary vivisection. He found, it would appear, some animal experimentation to be of little or no practical value (other than to the vanity of the researcher). Researchers were indifferent to the lives of the animals being dissected, and, worse, they encouraged repetition of experiments that would be a waste of life even if the experiments were valuable in themselves. As the piece is a parody, however, with very specific and immediate political and experimental relevance, to reproduce the text here would be more confusing than enlightening. Nonetheless, other castigations of the period are illuminating. In 1801 George Nicholson reported the following mid-eighteenth-century account in *On the Primeval Diet of Man*, but without indicating its source (and which I have been unable to locate). The report concerns the experiments of Browne Langrish (d. 1759), a physician whose avowed purpose was "to discover a safe and easy Method of dissolving Stone in the Bladder." He failed in his attempts; the animals died in vain.

It is impossible to read the experiments of Browne Langrish, read before the Royal Society, and published in 1746, under the title of *Physical Experiments on Brutes,* without sensations of horror. After the injection of various corrosive menstruums into the bladders of dogs, they were hung, for the sake of examination; but others died in the most dreadful convulsions. The stomach of a dog was cut out whilst alive, in order to try whether the liquor *Gastricus* would be coagulated by it. But the most dreadful of his experiments are those made on dogs to ascertain by what means the fumes of sulphurs destroy an animal body. He cut asunder the windpipes of dogs, so that the fumes could not reach the lungs, and then fixing the head through a hole in the wainscot he proceeded to the most wanton of experiments. The miserable creatures foamed at the mouth, roared hideously, or died in excruciating torture. This author, in the winding up of one part of his work, talks of the *pleasure,* variety and usefulness of his experiments! In the manner these privileged tyrants sport away the lives and revel in the agonies and tortures of creatures, whose sensations are as delicate, and whose natural right to an unpainful enjoyment of life is as great as that of man.[22]

The respectable *Monthly Review* was equally caustic in reviewing a book by John Caverhill on *Experiments on the Cause of Heat in Living Animals.*

Caverhill (d. 1781) was a Scottish physician and author of *A Treatise on the Cause and Cure of Gout*. According to the 1885 edition of the *Dictionary of National Biography* (vol. II, 285), "he conducted a large number of barbarous experiments on rabbits." The *Monthly Review* was not alone in its outrage at his excesses of animal experimentation.

[W]e claim no small degree of merit with our readers in having, for their information, read the numerous and cruel experiments related in this pamphlet throughout; the perusal of which was attended with a continual shudder at the repeated recital of such a number of instances of the *most deliberate* and *unrelenting* cruelty, exercised on several scores of rabbits, in order to ascertain the truth of a strange and exaggerated hypothesis. At every page we read of awls stuck between the vertebrae ... and into the spinal marrow of living rabbits, who exhibit, at the time, every symptom of exquisite pain, and live ten, twelve, and even nineteen days afterwards: their bladders sometimes bursting, in consequence of their losing the power of expelling the urine accumulated in them, unless when the unfeeling operator, not out of tenderness, but to protract the miserable life of the suffering animal as long as possible, in order to render the experiment more complete, thought proper to press it out from time to time, with his hands. But we spare the sensibility of our readers, which must be already hurt by this brief relation of these *immoral* experiments: for surely there are *moral* relations between man and his fellow-creatures of the brute creation. (*Monthly Review*, September, 1770)[23]

Jonathan Swift
Throughout his satirical writings, Jonathan Swift (1667-1745), Anglican Dean of St. Patrick's, Dublin, elevated animals over humans. It is, however, a matter of dispute whether Swift intended his comments to be taken literally, or whether they were little more than a convenient device for ridiculing human hubris and damning the machinations of Whig politicians.

Certainly, his work involves a significant degree of satirical exaggeration. Nonetheless, since his poem "To Mr. Congreve"[24] of 1693 contains a critique of vivisection on behalf of the animals, we can be confident that his estimation of the animals was sincere, if expressed in a deliberately exaggerated form. As Ricardo Quintana has written, commenting on "To Mr. Congreve": "Since the Restoration scientific enthusiasm had been the object of all kinds of jibes from playwrights and satirists ... In [those scientists] it seemed the balance of common sense had been upset; a flaw had split their judgment from end to end. How else could be explained their trivial passion for natural curiosities and their nasty habit of dissecting animals dead and alive? Now Swift was among the most relentless enemies of the new science; to him the virtuosos symbolized modern madness in one of its acutest forms."[25] Certainly, as with Aristotle,[26] Dostoevsky,[27] and Tolstoy,[28] among others, Swift believes no animal can fall as low as can humans.

It is in "A Voyage to the Country of the Houyhnhnms" of *Gulliver's Travels* that Swift elevates the animals and castigates the human race most emphatically. It is a land where the horses – Houyhnhnms – govern and where the humans – Yahoos – are treated as an inferior species, only of value to the extent that they are instrumental to the purposes of horses. Clearly, Swift is asking his readers to compare the estimation of "inferior animals" by the Houyhnhnms with their own evaluation and treatment of horses. If Houyhnhnms think of humans from the perspective of their own prejudiced interests, so too do humans judge and treat horses from the perspective of their own prejudices. Moreover, Swift shows that those characteristics that humans claimed raised them above the beasts could be just as readily used to demean them. A few extracts will give the flavour of Swift's story, but a reading of the text in its entirety is necessary to appreciate the breadth of Swift's message.

I owned, that the Houyhnhnms among us, whom we called *horses,* were among the most generous and comely animal we had, that they excelled in strength and swiftness, and when they belonged to persons of quality, employed in travelling, racing, or drawing chariots, they were treated with much kindness and care, till they fell into diseases, or became foundered in the feet, but then they were sold, and used to all kind of drudgery till they died, after which their skins were stripped and sold for what they were worth, and their bodies left to be devoured by dogs and birds of prey. But the common race of horses had not so good fortune, being kept by farmers and carriers and other mean people, who put them to greater labour, and fed them worse. I described as well as I could, our way of riding, the shape and use of a bridle, a spur, and a whip, of harness and wheels. I added that we fastened plates of a certain hard substance called *iron* to the bottom of their feet. To preserve their hoofs from being broken by the stony ways on which we often travelled.

My master [a Houyhnhnm], after some expressions of great indignation wondered how we dared to venture upon a Houyhnhnm's back, for he was sure that the weakest servant in his house would be able to shake off the strongest Yahoo, or by lying down, and rolling upon his back, squeeze the brute to death. I answered that our horses were trained-up from three or four years old to the several uses we intended them for; that if any of them proved intolerably vicious, they were employed for carriages; that they were severely beaten while they were young, for any mischievous tricks; that the males, designed for the common use of riding or draught, were generally *castrated* about two years after their birth, to take down their spirits, and make them more tame and gentle; that they were indeed sensible of rewards and punishments ...

[I]t is impossible to express his noble resentment at our savage treatment of the Houyhnhnm race, particularly after I had explained the manner and use of *castrating* horses among us, to hinder them from propagating their kind, and to render them more servile ... He said I differed from other Yahoos, being more cleanly, and not altogether so deformed, but in point of real advantage, he thought I differed for the worse. That my nails were of no use either to my fore or hinder feet; as to my fore-feet, he could not properly call them by name, for he never observed me to walk upon them; that they were too soft to bear the ground; that I generally went with them uncovered, neither was the covering I sometimes wore on them of the same shape, or so strong as that on my feet behind. That I could not walk with any security, for if either of my hinder feet slipped, I must inevitably fall. He then began to find fault with other parts of my body, the flatness of my face, the prominence of my nose, mine eyes placed directly in front, so that I could not look on either side without turning my head: that I was not able to feed myself, without lifting one of my fore-feet to my mouth: and therefore nature had placed those joints to answer that necessity. He knew not what could be the use of the several clefts and divisions in my feet behind; that these were too soft to bear the hardness and sharpness of stones without a covering made from the skin of some other brute; that my whole body wanted a fence against heat and cold, which I was forced to put on and off every day with tediousness and trouble ...

There was nothing which rendered the Yahoos more odious, than their undistinguished appetite to devour everything that came in their way, whether herbs, roots, berries, the corrupted flesh of animals, or all mingled together ...

As these noble Houyhnhnms are endowed by Nature with a general disposition to all virtues, and have no conceptions or ideas of what is evil in a rational creature, so their grand maxim is to cultivate *Reason,* and to be wholly governed by it. Neither is *Reason* among them a point problematical as with us, where men can argue with plausibility on both sides of a question, but strikes you with immediate conviction, as it must needs do where it is not mingled, obscured, or discoloured by passion and interest. (Jonathan Swift, "A Voyage to the Country of the Houyhnhnms," *Gulliver's Travels,* pt. 4, chs. 4, 5, 7, 8)[29]

In "The Beasts' Confession" Swift employs apes, wolves, pigs, and asses to symbolize the worst aspects of humanity and concludes:

When Beasts could speak, (the Learned say
They still can do so every Day) ...
Our Author's Meaning, I presume, is
A Creature *bipes et implumis;*[30]
Wherein the Moralist design'd
A Compliment on Human-Kind:
For, here he owns, that now and then
Beasts may *degen'rate* into Men.[31]

Samuel Johnson

Chief director of the literary tastes of his generation, editor of the finest literary journals, influential author and lexicographer, and as much a Tory as Pope and Fielding though neither a Catholic like the first nor a skeptic like the second, Samuel Johnson (1709-84) found animal experimentation a repulsive reflection of an uncontrolled human arrogance. While Pope condemned experimentation on dogs, and Fielding parodied the practice in general, Johnson gave it a vituperative broadside. He referred to vivisection as the work of "a race of men who have practised tortures without pity, and related them without shame, and are yet suffered to erect their heads among human beings."[32] In an article in *The Idler* he complained:

Among the inferiour professors of medical knowledge, is a race of wretches, whose lives are only varied by varieties of cruelty; whose favourite amusement is to nail dogs to tables and open them alive; to try how long life may be continued in various degrees of mutilation, or with the excision or laceration of the vital parts; to examine whether burning irons are felt more acutely by the bone or tendon; and whether the more lasting agonies are produced by poison forced into the mouth or injected into the veins.

It is not without reluctance that I offend the sensibility of the tender mind with images like these. If such cruelties were not practised it were to be desired they should not be conceived, but since they are published every day with ostentation, let me be allowed once to mention them, since I mention them with abhorrence ... the anatomical novice tears out the living bowels of an animal, and styles himself physician, prepares himself by familiar cruelty for that profession which he is to exercise upon the tender and helpless ...

What is alleged in defence of these hateful practices, every one knows, but the truth is, that by knives, fire and poison, knowledge is not always sought, and is very seldom attained. The experiments that have been tried are tried again; he that burned an animal with irons yesterday, will be willing to amuse himself with burning another tomorrow ... It is high time that universal resentment should arise against these horrid operations, which harden the heart, extinguish those sensations which give man confidence in man, and make the physician more deadly than the gout or stone. (*The Idler*, 5 August 1758)[33]

Johnson also showed his sensibility to animals when he claimed: "It is very strange, and very melancholy, that the paucity of human pleasures should persuade us ever to call hunting one of them."[34]

There were, however, limits to his compassion, shown when his friend and biographer **James Boswell** remonstrated against what had become a popular opinion.

[Johnson]: "There is much talk of the misery we cause to the brute creation; but they are recompensed by existence. If they were not useful to man, and therefore protected by him, they would not be nearly so numerous." [Boswell] "This argument is to be found in the able and benignant Hutchinson's* 'Moral Philosophy.' But the question is, whether the animals who endure such sufferings of various kinds for the service and entertainment of man, would accept of existence upon the terms on which they have it." (James Boswell, *The Life of Samuel Johnson* [1791])[35]

* Boswell meant "Hutcheson."

It is reflective of the tenor of the times that Johnson would observe there was "much talk of the misery we cause to the brute creation."

Christopher Smart

In his famed biography of Johnson, Boswell described the "fondness which he showed for animals which he had taken under his protection." Hodge, Johnson's cat, was the primary recipient of the benevolence. However, perhaps none has captured the cat with the grace, charm, and wit of the insanely devout (clinically speaking) Christopher Smart (1722-71), who claimed that animals and birds were "fellow subjects of th'eternal king" and that humanity to animals was a matter of some moment:

> Tho' these some spirits think but light,
> And deem indifferent things
> Yet they are serious in the sight
> Of CHRIST, the King of Kings.[36]

"God," he wrote, "be merciful to all dumb creatures in respect of pain."[37] It was in his fragmented poem *Jubilate Agno* that he tells us most about Jeoffroy his cat. But before he reached his beloved companion he offers us page after page of animal compassion. He opens the poem with:

> Rejoice in God, O ye Tongues; give the glory to the Lord, and the Lamb.
> Nations, and languages, and every Creature, in which is the breath of Life.
> Let man and beast appear before him, and magnify his name together.
> Let Noah and his company approach the throne of Grace, and do homage to the Ark of their Salvation.

We are then offered over a hundred lines of blessings for the animals of the ark (including many, as Smart recognizes, who were not there). In the second part of the fragmented poem he delights us with the virtues of many animals before he arrives at Jeoffroy.

> For having consider'd God and himself he will consider his neighbour.
> For if he meets another cat he will kiss her in kindness.
> For when he takes his prey he plays with it to give it a chance.
> For one mouse in seven escapes by his dallying ...
> For he is of the tribe of Tiger ...
> For he is an instrument for the children to learn benevolence upon.
> For every house is incompleat without him & a blessing is lacking in the spirit ...
> For he is of the lord's poor and so indeed is he called by benevolence perpetually – poor Jeoffroy! ...
> For he is good to think on, if a man would express himself neatly ... [38]

It is in this last quoted line that Smart inaugurates the recognition of the principle that, in the later words of anthropologist Claude Lévi-Strauss: "animals are good to think [with]."[39]

Laurence Sterne

While it was horses for some and cats for others, the novelist and cleric Laurence Sterne (1713-68) showed special favour to the ass, in both *A Sentimental Journey* and *Tristram Shandy*.

> When the mourner [of the dead ass] got thus far on his story, he stopped to pay nature her tribute – and wept bitterly.
>
> He said, Heaven had accepted the conditions [of a vow he had made], and that he had set out from his cottage with the poor creature, who had been a patient partner on his journey – that it had eat the same bread with him all the way, and was unto him a friend.
>
> Everybody who stood about, heard the poor fellow with concern – La Fleur offered him money. – The mourner said he did not want it – it was not the value of the ass – but the loss of him – The ass, he said, he was assured loved him – and upon this told them a long story of the mischance upon their passage over the Pyrenean mountains which had separated them from each other three days; during which time the ass had sought for him as much as he had sought for the ass, and that they had neither scarce eat or drank till they met.
>
> Thou hast one comfort, friend, said I, at least, in the loss of thy poor beast; I'm sure thou hast been a merciful master to him. – Alas! said the mourner, I thought so, when he was alive – but now that he is dead I think otherwise, – I fear the weight of myself and my afflictions together have been too much for him – they have shortened the poor creature's days, and I fear I have them to answer for. – Shame on the world! said I to myself – Did we love each other, as this poor soul but loved his ass – 'twould be something ... (Laurence Sterne, *A Sentimental Journey through France and Italy,* "Nampont: The Dead Ass," 1768[40])

> Now, 'tis an animal (be in what hurry I may) I cannot bear to strike – there is a patient endurance of sufferings, wrote so unaffectedly in his looks and carriage, which pleads so mightily for him, that it always disarms me; and to that degree, that I do not like to speak unkindly to him: on the contrary, meet him where I will – whether in town or country – in cart or under panniers – whether in liberty or bondage – I have ever something civil to say to him on my part ... with an ass I can commune for ever. (Laurence Sterne, *The Life and Opinions of Tristram Shandy, Gentleman* [1760])[41]

Sterne also showed compassion for both birds and flies. Writing about the confinement of the Bastille in Paris, and accepting it initially as just another and necessary prison, he tells us:

> I was interrupted in the hey-day of this soliloquy with a voice I took to be of a child, which complained "it could not get out." – I looked up and down the passage, and seeing neither man, woman, or child, I saw it was a starling hung in a little cage. – "I can't get out – I can't get out." said the starling.
>
> I stood looking at the bird: and to every person who came through the passage it ran fluttering to the side towards which they approached it, with the same

lamentation of its captivity. – "I can't get out," said the starling – God help thee!, said I, but I'll let thee out, cost what it will; so I turned about the cage to get to the door; it was twisted and double twisted so fast with wire, there was no getting it open without pulling the cage to pieces – I took both hands to it.

The bird flew to the place where I was attempting the deliverance, and thrusting his head through the trellis, pressed his head against it, as if impatient – I fear, poor creature! said I, I cannot set thee at liberty – "No," said the starling – "I can't get out – I can't get out," said the starling.

I vow, I never had my affections more tenderly awakened; or do I remember an incident in my life, where the dissipated spirits, to which my reason has been a bubble, were so suddenly called home. Mechanical as the notes were, yet so true to nature were they chanted, that in one moment they overthrew all my systematic reasonings upon the Bastile; and I heavily walked upstairs, unsaying every word I had said in going down them.

Disguise thyself as thou wilt, still slavery! said I – still thou art a bitter draught; and though thousands in all ages have been made to drink of thee, thou art no less bitter on that account. (Laurence Sterne, *A Sentimental Journey,* "The Hotel de Paris" [1768])[42]

In a trying moment the author determined to maintain his temper and avowed:

"never to give the honest gentleman a worse word or a worse wish than my uncle Toby gave the fly which buzz'd about his nose all dinner time, – 'Go, – go, poor devil,' quoth he, – 'get thee gone, – why should I hurt thee? This world is surely wide enough to hold both thee and me.'" (Laurence Sterne, *Tristram Shandy* [1759])[43]

John Gay

Poet and playwright, John Gay (1685-1732) is best known for *The Beggar's Opera* (1728). His poetry expresses a consistent appreciation for animal suffering. In the first cited piece "shambles" is the traditional term for the slaughterhouse and "quills" are the feathers from geese, which, along with the spines from porcupines, were used as writing implements, fishing-floats, and toothpicks. In Britain all, or almost all, bees were killed at the collecting of the honey until the mid-nineteenth century.

In him ingratitude you find,
A vice peculiar to the kind.
The sheep, whose annual fleece is dy'd
To guard his health, and serve his pride,
Forc'd from his fold and native plain,
Is in the cruel shambles slain.
The swarms who, with industrious skill,
His hives with wax and honey fill,

In vain whole summer days employ'd,
Their stores are sold, the race destroy'd.
What tribute from the goose is paid!
Does not her wing all science aid,
Does it not lovers' hearts explain,
And drudge to raise the merchant's gain?
What now rewards this general use?
He takes the quill and eats the goose! ...
(John Gay, "The Philosopher and the Pheasants," *Fables* [1722])[44]

Against an elm a sheep was ty'd;
The butcher's knife in blood was dy'd;
The patient flock, in silent fright,
From far beheld the horrid sight:
A savage Boar, who near them stood,
Thus mock'd to scorn the fleecy brood.
   All cowards should be serv'd like you.
See, see, your murd'rer is in view;
With purple hands and reeking knife
He strips the skin yet warm with life:
Your quarter'd sires, your bleeding dams,
The dying bleat of harmless lambs
Call for revenge. O stupid race!
Thy heart that wants revenge is base.
   I grant, an ancient Ram replys,
We bear no terror in our eyes,
Yet think us not of soul so tame,
Which no repeated wrongs inflame;
Insensible of ev'ry ill,
Know, those who violence pursue
Give to themselves the vengeance due,
For in these massacres they find
The two chief plagues that waste mankind.
Our skin supplys the wrangling bar,
It wakes their slumbering sons to war,
And well revenge may rest contented,
Since drums and parchment were invented.
(John Gay, "The Wild Boar and the Ram," *Fables* [1722])[45]

In the following verse on the mistreatment of transport horses, "Samian" refers to Pythagoras, who was born at Samos in Asia Minor, and "Hackney" is a form of passenger coach.

The lashing Whip resounds the Horses strain,
And blood in Anguish bursts the swelling vein.

O barb'rous Men! your cruel Breasts asswage;
Why vent ye on the gen'rous Steed your rage?
Does not his service earn your daily Bread?
Your Wives, your Children, by his Labours fed!
If, as the *Samian* taught, the Soul revives,
And, shifting Seats, in other Bodies lives,
Severe shall be the brutal Coachman's Change,
Doom'd in a *Hackney* Horse the Town to range:

Carmen, transform'd, the groaning Load shall draw,
Whom other Tyrants, with the Lash, shall awe.
(John Gay, *Trivia*, "Of Walking Streets by Day" [1716])[46]

Anne Finch

Anne Finch, Countess of Winchilsea (1661-1720), was a prolific poet whose verses occasionally touched on her appreciation for animals and the injustices they suffered.

When the loos'd Horse now, as his Pasture leads,
Comes slowly grazing thro' th' adjoining Meads,
Whose stealing Pace, and lengthen'd Shade we fear,
Till torn up Forage in his Teeth we hear:
When nibbling Sheep at large pursue their Food,
And unmolested Kine rechew the Cud;
When Curlews cry beneath the Village-walls,
And to her straggling Brood the Partridge calls;
Their short liv'd Jubilee the Creatures keep,
Which but endures whilst Tyrant-Man dost sleep.
(Anne Finch, "A Nocturnal Reverie" [c. 1709-13])[47]

John Dyer

John Dyer (c. 1700-58) was a Welsh poet and Anglican minister who wrote *Irregular Ode* and *Grongar Hill*, as well as *The Fleece*, whence these lines.

Ah! ne'er let may he
Glory in wants which doom to pain and death
His blameless fellow creatures. Let disease,
That wasted hunger, by destroying live;
And the permission use with trembling thanks,
Meekly reluctant: 'tis the brute beyond;
And gluttons ever murder when they kill.
Ev'n to the reptile every cruel deed

Is high impiety. Howe'er not all,
Not of the sanguinary tribe are all;
All are not savage. Come ye gentle Swains,
Like Brama's healthy sons on Indus' banks,

Whom the pure stream and garden fruits sustain,
We are the sons of Nature; your mild hands
Are innocent.
(John Dyer, *The Fleece* [1757])[48]

With *The Fleece* we move from the Muslim of Turkey to the Hindu of
India as the standard with whom to contrast Europeans unfavourably in
their sensibilities to animals.

James Thomson

James Thomson (1700-48) was a Scottish poet, author of *The Seasons*
(1726-30) and *The Castle of Indolence* (1748). It is in *The Seasons* that his
sensibilities toward animals are most pronounced, and which is thought by
some, notably Dix Harwood, to have revolutionized our attitudes toward
animals by treating sensibilities toward them from a rural rather than an
urban perspective.[49]

... but you, ye Flocks,
What have you done, ye peaceful People! What
to merit Death? You who have given us Milk
In luscious Streams, and lent us your own Coat
Against the Winter's Cold? And the plain Ox
That harmless, honest, guileless Animal,
In what he has offended? He whose toil,
Patient, and ever ready, clothes the Land
With all the Pomp of Harvest, shall he bleed,
And, struggling, groan beneath the cruel Hands
Ev'n of the clown he feeds? And that, perhaps,
To swell the Riot of the autumnal Feast,
Won by his labour? ... [50]

... when, returning with her loaded bill,
Th' astonished mother finds a vacant nest,
By the hard hand of unrelenting clowns
Robb'd, to the ground the vain provision falls;
Her pinions ruffle, and low-drooping scarce
Can bear the mourner to the popular shade;
Where, all abandoned to despair, she sings
Her sorrows through the night, and on the bough

Sole sitting; still, at every dying fall,
Takes up again her lamentable strain
Of winding woe, till, wide around, the woods
Sigh to her song, and with her wail resound ... [51]

Ah see where robb'd, and murder'd, in that Pit
Lies the still heaving Hive! At evening snatch'd
Beneath the cloud of Guilt-concealing Night,
And fix'd o'er sulphur; while, not dreaming Ill,
The happy People in their waxen cells
Sat tending public Cares, and planning Schemes
Of Temperance, for Winter poor, rejoic'd
To mark, the full-flowing round, their copious Stores,
Sudden the dark oppressive Steam ascends.

And, us'd to milder Scents, the tender Race,
By thousands tumbled from their honeyed Domes,
Convolv'd, and agonizing in the Dust.
And was it then for This you roam'd the Spring,
Intent, from Flower to flower? for this you toil'd,
Ceaseless, the burning Summer-Heats away?
For this in Autumn search'd the blooming Waste,
Nor lost one sunny Gleam? for this sad Fate?
O Man! tyrannic Lord! how long, how long,
Shall prostrate Nature groan beneath your Rage,
Awaiting renovation? When oblig'd,
Must you destroy? Of their ambrosial Food

Can you not borrow, and in just Return,
Afford them shelter from the wintry Winds;
Or, as the sharp Year pinches, with their Own
Again regale them on some smiling Day?
See where the stony Bottom of their Town
Looks desolate and wild, with here and there
A helpless Number, who the ruin'd State
Survive, lamenting weak, cast out to death.[52]

William Cowper

William Cowper (1731-1800) was a popular, if eccentric and sometimes disturbed, poet, whose works include *The Task* (1785) and *The Diverting History of John Gilpin* (1787). His verses reflect both his attachment to animals and his advocacy of our responsibilities toward them.

Detested sport,
That owes its pleasure to another's pain!
That feeds upon sobs and dying shrieks
Of harmless nature ...
Well, – one at least is safe. One sheltered hare
Has never heard the sanguinary yell
Of cruel man exulting her woes.
Innocent partner of my peaceful home,
Whom long years' experience of my care
Has made at last familiar, she has lost
Much of her vigilant instructive dread,
Not needful here, beneath a roof like mine.
Yes, – thou mayest eat thy bread, and lick the hand
That feeds thee; thou mayest frolic on the floor
At evening, and at night retire secure
To thy straw couch, and slumber unalarmed.
For I have gained thy confidence, have pledged
All that is human in me to protect
Thine unsuspecting gratitude and love.
If I survive thee I will dig thy grave;
And when I place thee in it, sighing say,
I knew at least one hare that had a friend.
(William Cowper, *The Task,* Bk. III, "The Garden" [1785])[53]

Cowper was a friend to many animals, but most notably to the hares he tamed and about whom he wrote in the *Gentleman's Magazine,* 28 May 1784.

It is no wonder that my intimate acquaintance with these specimens of the kind has taught me to hold the sportsman's amusement in abhorrence; he little knows what amiable creatures he persecutes, of what gratitude they are capable, how cheerful they are in their spirits, what enjoyment they have of life, and that, impressed as they seem with a peculiar dread of man, it is only because man gives them a peculiar cause for it.[54]

He was, however, a friend to more than companion animals:

I would not enter on my list of friends
(Tho' grac'd with polish'd manners and fine sense
Yet wanting sensibility) the man
Who needlessly sets foot upon a worm ...
An inadvertent step may crush the snail
That crawls at evening in the public path,
But he that has humanity, forewarn'd,
Will tread aside, and let the reptile live ...

In the spacious field.
There they are privileged. And he that hunts
Or harms them there, is guilty of a wrong,
Disturbs th' economy of nature's realm,
Who, when she form'd, design'd them an abode.
(William Cowper, *The Task,* Bk. VI, "The Winter Walk at Noon" [1785])[55]

Among Cowper's various animal writings were his translations from some of **Vincent Bourne**'s Latin poems in his *Poematia* of 1734. This piece, for example, on the glow-worm, may have inspired Cowper's famous line about the man who "needlessly sets foot upon a worm":

Perhaps indulgent Nature meant,
   By such a lamp bestow'd,
To bid the traveller as he went,
   Be careful where he trod:
Nor crush a worm, whose useful light
   Might serve, however small,
To shew a stumbling stone by night,
   And save him from a fall.[56]

Cowper also expressed his animal sympathies clearly in a letter he wrote to James Hurdis, Professor of Poetry at Oxford (13 June 1791).

I am glad that your amusements have been so similar to mine; for in this instance too I seemed to have need of somebody to keep me in countenance, especially in my attention and detachment to animals. All the notice that we lords of the creation vouchsafe to bestow on the creatures, is generally to abuse them: it is well therefore that here and there a man should be found a little womanish, or perhaps a little childish, in the matter, who will make some amends, by kissing, and coaxing, and laying them in one's bosom ... You remember the little ewe lamb, mentioned by the prophet Nathan;* the prophet perhaps invented the tale for the sake of its application to David's conscience; but it is more probable that God inspired him with it for that purpose. If he did, it amounts to a proof that He does not overlook, but on the contrary much notices such little partialities and kindness to his *dumb* creatures, as we, because we are articulate, are pleased to do.[57]

Oliver Goldsmith
Renowned for his play *She Stoops to Conquer* (1773) and his novel *The Vicar of Wakefield* (1766), Oliver Goldsmith (c. 1730-74) was sufficiently interested in animal matters to write *An History of Earth and Animated Nature* (1774), based largely on the natural history studies of Buffon. He did, however, have a number of points of his own to make, telling us of a vixen who had defended her cub valiantly against hounds and that he "was

---

* 2 Samuel:12.

not displeased to hear that this faithful creature escaped;" of the ass, that it is "the most gentle and quiet of all animals;" of the caged bird that sings less sweetly precisely because it is caged: "it is but the mirth of a little animal, insensible of its unfortunate situation; it is the landscape, the grove, the golden break of day, the contest on the hawthorn, the fluttering from branch to branch, the soaring in the air, and the answering of its young, that gives the bird's song its true relish."[58]

In *The Hermit: A Ballad* (1766) we find the following lines:

> No flocks that range the valley free,
>   To slaughter I condemn;
> Taught by the Power that pities me,
>   I learn to pity them.[59]

It was, however, in his *The Citizen of the World* (1762), where a purported visitor from China is describing European customs, that he was most fulsome:

> The better sort here pretend to the utmost compassion of every kind; to hear them speak, a stranger would be apt to imagine they could hardly hurt the gnat that stung them. They seem so tender, and so full of pity, that one would take them for the harmless friends of the whole creation, the protectors of the meanest insect or reptile that was privileged with existence. And yet would you believe it, I have seen the very men who have thus boasted of their tenderness, at the same time devouring the flesh of six different animals tossed up in a fricassee. Strange contrariety of conduct. They pity and they eat the objects of their compassion ...
>
> Man was born to live with innocence and simplicity, but he has deviated from nature; he was born to share the bounties of heaven, but he has monopolised them; he was born to govern the 'brute creation'; but he has become their tyrant. If an epicure now shall happen to surfeit on his last night's feast, twenty animals the next day are to undergo the most exquisite tortures in order to provoke his appetite to another guilty meal. Hail, O ye simple, honest bramins of the east, ye inoffensive friends of all that was born to happiness as well as you: you never sought a short-lived pleasure from the miseries of other creatures. You never studied the tormenting arts of ingenious refinement; you never surfeited upon a guilty meal.[60]

A number of other prominent literary figures of the era made their animal concerns apparent, but more as asides than primary orientations. Thus, for example, **Daniel Defoe** (c. 1660-1731): "What rapes are committed upon nature, making the ewes bring lambs all the winter, fattening calves to a monstrous size, using cruelties and contrary diets to the poor brute to whiten its flesh for the palates of the ladies!" (Daniel Defoe, *The Complete English Tradesman* [1726]).[61]

Scottish novelist **Tobias Smollett** (1712-71), author of *Roderick Random* (1748) and *Peregrine Pickle* (1751), as well as a popular *History of England*

(1757), bemoaned his experience of southern France where one could travel: "without hearing the song of a blackbird, thrush, linnet, gold-finch or any other bird whatsoever. All is silent and solitary. The poor birds are destroyed, or driven for refuge into other countries, by the savage persecution of the people, who spare no pains to kill, and catch them for their own subsistence." (Tobias Smollett, *Travels through France and Italy* [1766])[62]

William Shenstone (1714-63), landscape gardener and poet, is best remembered for *The Schoolmistress* (1742). In his *A Pastoral Ballad: Hope* (1743) he condemned the common practice of robbing birds' nests.

> I have found a gift for my fair;
> I have found where the wood-pigeons breed:
> But let me that plunder forbear,
> She will say 'twas a barbarous deed:
> For he ne'er could be true, she averr'd,
> Who could rob a poor bird of its young;
> And I loved her the more when I heard
> Such tenderness fall from her tongue.[63]

His friend, the Anglican clergyman and poet **Richard Jago** (1715-81), took the same approach in his "Elegy on the Goldfinches."

> O Plunderer Vile! O more than adders fell!
>   More murderous than the cat, with prudish face;
> Fiercer than kites in whom the furies dwell,
>   And thievish as the cuckoo's pilfering race.[64]

In *Edge-Hill, or the Rural Prospect delineated and moralized* (1767) he wrote of the hunted "tim'rous hare":

> But that poor trembling wretch!
> "Who doubts if now she lives," what hath she done;
> Guiltless of blood, and impotent of wrong.[65]

In **Henry Brooke**'s *Fool of Quality* (1777) a boy rescues a poor cock from the customary Shrovetide pastime, and is asked by his benefactor: "Why, my love, did you venture your life for a silly cock? Why did I? Repeated the Child! why, sir, because he loved me. The stranger, then, stopping back, and gazing on him with eyes of tender admiration – May heaven forever bless thee, my little angel, he exclaimed, and continue to utter from thy lips the sentiment that it inspires."[66]

An anonymous article in the *Gentleman's Magazine* in 1736 repeated the by now increasingly common criticism of hunting: "A poor Animal is in the most cowardly manner, *overpower'd* by Numbers, *run down* and *kill'd*; and for what Purpose? The Sportsmen do not eat venison! Is the poor Animal's *Fright*, *Flight* and *Death* then, the Pleasure they take all the fatigue for? Surely this can be no *manly* diversion. Would any of 'em singly

have attacked the Buck, it would more have had the Appearance of *it ...
Killing* can never be a *Pleasure* to a *human Breast*, since seeing anything
suffer, gives us a Part in the *Sensation.*"[67]

It is notable that this emphasis on empathy comes a quarter of a century before Rousseau's groundbreaking statement and over half a century
before Jeremy Bentham's famous statement that the relevant question
for moral consideration is "Can they *suffer?*"[68]

Joseph Butler

There is an oft-repeated claim in the literature on the history of animal
rights that Christianity denies souls to animals.[69] And certainly many
Christians have subscribed to that doctrine, including, at least on one
occasion, the compassionate Alexander Pope, who thought that, as a
consequence, we owed animals an even greater responsibility during their
lives.[70] In fact, however, the question of animal souls has a lengthy and
controversial history. Among early Christians, Origen and Arnobius
ascribed immortal souls to animals. Later, Luther (apparently), St. John
of the Cross, Henry More and the Cambridge Platonists, Bayle and Leibniz,
and numerous Dissenters, including George Fox, concurred. The status
of the soul is unclear in the writings of Milton, Fludd, and Overton, but
whatever it might have been, it was similar for humans and animals,
and all would be resurrected. In the eighteenth century, the question
became a matter of sometimes heated public debate. As a consequence of
the increasing recognition and acknowledgment of human-animal similarities, and the increasing awareness, based in part on the fact of those
similarities, that we owed them compassion and consideration, divines
found it increasingly difficult to find criteria on which God might have
differentiated.

In "the Age of Reason," as the Enlightenment was later called, Bishop
Thomas Watson despaired of his century that "there was never an age
since the death of Christ, never one since the commencement of this
history of the world, in which atheism and infidelity have been more generally confessed." In the "Advertisement" to his *The Analogy of Religion,
Natural and Revealed, to the Constitution and Course of Nature* (1736)
Joseph Butler (1692-1752), later Bishop of Durham, allowed that "many
persons" had ceased to look on Christianity as a subject of legitimate rational inquiry, indeed that "it is now discovered to be fictitious."[71] Yet even if
they maintained their religious beliefs enthusiastically, against what they
saw as the nefarious intellectual tenor of the times, Joseph Butler and
like-minded clerics were also influenced by the rising tide of concerns for
the dominance of reason in debate, including theological debate, and for
the frequently neglected rights of animated nature. In the case of Joseph
Butler, the matter was of the most serious consequence for Christian, or
at least Anglican, understanding of the human-animal relationship. His

Analogy of Religion was the most widely read and influential anglophone theological work of the century, and remained required reading for Oxford and Cambridge undergraduates for over a century. Since it was in the opening pages of the *Analogy* that Butler declared there were no rational grounds for denying souls to animals – even his undergraduate readers would probably have perused the first chapter or so – the claim, if certainly not accepted unequivocally, now had to be entertained as a legitimate hypothesis at the very least. Butler wrote of "the natural immortality of brutes" and argued his case from "probability" which "is the very guide of life."[72]

[W]e find it to be a general law of nature in our own species, the same individuals, should exist in degrees of life and perception, with capacities of action, of enjoyment and suffering, in one period of their being, greatly different from those appointed them in another period of it. And in other creatures the same law holds. For the differences of their capacities and states of life at their birth (to go no higher) and in maturity; the change of worms into flies, and the vast enlargement of their locomotive powers by such change; and birds and insects bursting their shell, their habitation, and by this means entering into a new world, furnished with new accommodations for them, and finding a new sphere of action assigned them – these are instances of this general law of nature. Thus all the various and wonderful transformations of animals are to be taken into consideration here ...

[T]here can no probability be collected from the reason of the thing, that death will be their destruction: because their existence may depend upon somewhat in no degree affected by death; upon somewhat quite out of reach of this king of terrors. So there is nothing more certain, than that *the reason of the thing* shows us no connection between death and the destruction of living agents. Nor can we find any one thing throughout the whole *analogy of nature,* to afford us even the slightest presumption, that animals ever lose their living powers; much less, if it were possible, that they lose them by death: for we have no faculties wherewith to trace any beyond or through it, so as to see what becomes of them. This event removes them from our view. It destroys the *sensible* proof, which we had before their death, of their being possessed of living powers, but it does not appear to afford the least reason to believe that they are then, or by that event, deprived of them.

And our knowing that they were possessed of these powers, up to the very period to which we have faculties capable of tracing them, is itself a probability of their retaining them beyond it. (Joseph Butler, *The Analogy of Religion, Natural and Revealed, to the Constitution and Course of Nature,* ch. 1 [1736])[73]

John Wesley

John Wesley (1703-91), the vegetarian founder of Methodism – the most rapidly growing Protestant denomination of the eighteenth and nineteenth centuries – had no doubts about animal souls or our responsibilities to our fellow-creatures, even though he thought they would continue to be tormented until the Resurrection. God, we are told, in a sermon on Romans 8:29-30, directs us to be tender of even the meaner creatures; to show mercy to these also. "Thou shalt not muzzle the ox that treadeth out the corn." – A custom which is observed in the eastern countries even to this day. And this is by no means contradicted by St. Paul's question: "Doth God take care of oxen?" Without doubt he does. We cannot deny it, without flatly contradicting his word. The plain meaning of the Apostle is, Is this all that is implied in the text? Hath it not a farther meaning? Does it not teach us, we are to feed the bodies of those whom we desire to feed our souls? Meantime it is certain, God "giveth grass for the cattle," as well as "herbs for the use of men" ...

What was the original state of the brute creatures, when they were first created? ... it is certain these, as well as man, had an innate principle of self-motion; and that, at least, in as high a degree as they enjoy it at this day. Again: They were endued with a degree of understanding; not less than that they are possessed of now. They also had a will, including various passions, which likewise they still enjoy: And they had liberty, a power of choice, a degree of which is still found in every living creature ...

What then is the barrier between men and brutes? the line which they cannot pass? It was not reason. Set aside that ambiguous term. Exchange it for that plain word, understanding: And who can deny that brutes have this ...

But will "the creature," will even the brute creation, always remain in this [present] deplorable condition? God forbid that we should affirm this; yea, or even entertain such a thought! While "the whole creation groaneth together," (whether men attend or not), their groans are not dispersed in idle air, but enter into the Ears of him that made them.

Nothing can be more express. Away with vulgar prejudices, and let the plain word of God take place. They "shall be delivered from the bondage of corruption, into glorious liberty," – even a measure, according as they are capable – of "the liberty of the children of God" ...

To descend to a few particulars: the whole creation will, then, undoubtedly, be restored, not only to the vigour, strength and willingness which they had at their creation, but to a far higher degree of each than they ever enjoyed. They will be restored, not only to that measure of understanding they had in paradise, but to a degree of it much higher than that, as the understanding of an elephant is beyond that of a worm. And whatever affections they had in the the garden of God, will be restored with vast increase; being exalted and refined in a manner which we ourselves are not now able to comprehend. The liberty they then had will be completely restored, and they will be free in all their motions. They will be delivered from all irregular appetites, from all unruly passions, from every disposition that is evil in itself, or has any tendency to evil.

Thus in that day, all the vanity to which they are now helplessly subject will be abolished; they will suffer no more, either from within or without; the days of their groaning are ended. (John Wesley, "The General Deliverance," in *Sermons on Several Occasions* [1788])[74]

In discussing the problem of evil in the same sermon, he concluded:

They could not sin, for they were not moral agents. Yet how severely do they suffer! – yea, many of them, beasts of burden in particular, almost the whole time of
their abode on earth; so that they can have no retribution here below. But the
objection vanishes away, if we consider that something better remains for them
after death for these poor creatures also; that these, likewise, shall one day be
delivered from this bondage of corruption, and shall then receive an ample amends
for their present sufferings.

One more excellent end may undoubtedly be answered by the preceding considerations. They may encourage us to imitate Him whose mercy is overall his
works. They may soften our hearts towards the meaner creatures, knowing that the
Lord careth for them. It may enlarge our hearts towards those poor creatures.[75]

Methodists, and indeed the evangelical party within the English
Mother Church, began to gain a reputation for showing mercy to the
beasts and deeming them eminently worthy of moral consideration, even
though the animals themselves were usually thought incapable of moral
action.

John Hildrop

Some who argued the case for animal souls, notably John Hildrop and
Richard Dean, extended their studies to develop a general and explicit case
for compassion toward animals, while Butler did little more than lay down
a general principle and Wesley went into few details. Reverend Hildrop,
Oxford D.D. and Anglican rector, offered a Swiftian insistence that
human depravity could never be matched by other species.

Shew me any one species of animals more ridiculous, more contemptible, more
detestable, than are to be found among the silly, the vicious, the wicked part of
mankind. Are apes and monkeys more ridiculous or mischievous creatures than
some who are to be found in the most polite assemblies? Is a *poor dog* with four
legs, who acts agreeably to his nature, half so despicable as a *sad dog* with two,
who with high pretensions to reason, virtue, and honour, is every day guilty of
crimes for which his brother dog would be doomed to hanging? Is a swine that
wallows in the mire half as contemptible as a drunkard or a temperance? What is
the rage of tigers, the fierceness of lions, the cruelty of wolves and bears, the
treachery of cats and monkeys, when compared with the cruelty, the treachery, the
barbarity of mankind? The wolf and the tiger, that worry a few innocent sheep,
purely to satisfy hunger, are harmless animals when opposed to the rage and fury
of conquerors, the barbarity and cruelty of tyrants and oppressors, who uninjured,
unprovoked, lay whole countries to waste, turn the most beautiful cities into ruins,
and sweep the face of the earth before them like an inundation or devouring fire.[76]

Reason and revelation, Hildrop tells us: "declare it to be a breach of natural justice, and indication of a cruel and unnatural temper, to abuse or

oppress [animals], to increase the miseries and aggravate the sufferings of these innocent unhappy creatures, and to add, by our barbarity, to the weight of that bondage to which they are made subject to our disobedience, to put them to unnecessary labours, to punish them with immoderate severities, or with-hold from them those necessary refreshments which their state and condition requires" (John Hildrop, *Free Thoughts upon the Brute Creation* [1742]).[77]

In his *A Lapse of Souls in a State of Pre-existence, the only Original Sin and Ground Work of the Gospel Dispensation* (1766), fellow Anglican clergyman **Capel Berrow** (1715-82) also wondered why animals suffer. "Wherefore all those agonizing pains and miseries heaped on an helpless offspring of Divine Providence? Are they not flesh and blood? Do *they* not, as well as *we*, know what sorrow means? And were they brought into a painful existence for nought but the service, or rather, for little else than to gratify the pride, the wantonness, the cruelty of Man? – What! one being created under *the foreseen* certainty of its being made *miserable* solely for the use or pleasure of another."[78]

Richard Dean

Richard Dean (1727-78) was a schoolteacher and Anglican minister in Middleton, Lancashire. His two-volume *Essay on the Future Life of Brutes, introduced with Observations upon Evil, its Nature and Origins* (1767), was a general study of animal ethics, despite its rather misleading title. Rather than emphasizing primarily the depravity of humankind, Dean stressed the virtues of other species and discussed their implications for human behaviour toward them. While many before had commented on animal pain and suffering, Dean was perhaps the first to make it the focal point of his thesis.

If it be allowed that brute animals are more than mere machines, have an intelligent principle residing within them, which is the spring of their several actions and operations, men ought to use such methods in the management of them, as are suitable to a nature that may be taught, instructed and improved to his advantage; and not have recourse to force, compassion and violence. Brutes have sensibility; they are capable of pain, feel every bang, and cut or stab, as much as man himself, some of them perhaps more, and therefore they should not be treated as stocks or stones. It is lamentable to think that any occasion should be given for remarks of this sort, when the world is possessed of so many superior advantages, when mankind exceed the pitch of former ages in the attainments of science. But the fact is notorious, maugre* all the privileges we enjoy under the improvements of natural reason and the dispensation of religious light; cruelty is exercised in all its hideous forms and varieties. Animals are everyday perishing under the hands of barbarity

---

* In spite of.

without notice; without mercy; famished, as if hunger was no evil; mauled, as if they had no sense of pain; and hurried about incessantly from day to day, as if excessive toil was no plague, or extreme weariness was no degree of suffering. Surely the sensibility of brutes entitles them to a milder treatment than they usually meet with from hard and unthinking wretches. Man ought to look on them as creatures under his protection, and not as put in his power to be tormented. Few of them know how to defend themselves against him as well as he knows how to attack them. For a man to torture a brute, whose life God has put into his hands, is a disgraceful thing, such a meanness of spirit as his honour requires him to shun. If he does it out of wantonness, he is a fool, and a coward; if for pleasure, he is a monster. Such a mortal is a scandal to his species, and ought to have no place in human societies but as a hangman or a butcher. (Richard Dean, *An Essay on the Future Life of Brutes* [1767])[79]

Dean was verbalizing the message of **William Hogarth**'s 1751 didactic engravings of *The Four Stages of Cruelty*, showing how pain inflicted on animals was itself an abomination and led to further cruelties against humans. "The four stages of cruelty," Hogarth wrote, "were done in the hopes of preventing in some degree that cruel treatment of poor Animals which makes the streets of London more disagreeable to the human mind than anything whatever, the very describing of which gives pain ... there is no part of my works of which I am so proud, and in which I feel so happy because I believe the publication of them has checked the diabolical spirit of barbarity, which, I am sorry to say, was once so prevalent in this country ... I had rather, if cruelty has been prevented by the four prints, be maker of them than of the [Raphael] cartoons."[80]

In *Light of Nature Pursued* (1754) **Abraham Tucker** (1705-74), writing under the pseudonym of Edward Search, confirmed the potential immortality of the animal's soul:

Upon occasion of the divine care extending to the smallest things, I shall venture to put in a word on behalf our younger brethren of the brutal species ... Since then, as well by God's special injunctions as by His ordinary Providence, he calls upon creatures for their labours, their sufferings, and their lives, in the progress of His great work the Redemption, why should we think it an impeachment of His equity, if He assigns them wages for all they undergo in this important service? Or an impeachment of His power and His wisdom, if such wages accrue to them by certain stated laws of universal nature running through both worlds.

In what manner the compensation is operated would be needless and impossible to ascertain: perhaps they stand only one stage behind us in the journey through matter, and as we hope to rise from sensitivo-rational creatures to purely rational, so they may be advanced from sensitive to sensitivo-rational. And when our nature is perfected, we may be employed to act as guardian angels for the improvement of their new faculties, becoming lords, and not tyrants, of our new world, and exercising government by employing our superior skill and power for the benefit of the governed: by which we may comprehend how much they have an interest of their own in everything relative to the forwarding of our Redemption.[81]

James Granger

James Granger (1723-76) was Vicar of Shiplake in Oxfordshire and esteemed author of *A Biographical History of England from Egbert the Great to the Revolution* (of 1688). In 1772, he published a sermon he had delivered to his congregation on Proverbs 12:10,[82] entitled *An Apology for the Brute Creation, or Abuse of Animals Censured*. He was the butt of Dr. Johnson's famous quip: "The dog is a whig. I do not like much to see a whig in any dress, but I hate to see a whig in a parson's gown."

Granger's reference in the following extract to the "Hell of Horses" is to Robert Burton's oft-quoted proverb from *The Anatomy of Melancholy* of 1621: "England is a paradise for women and hell for horses."[83]

How often is [the horse] whipped, spurred, battered and starved to death? What a piteous spectacle is his lean, hide-bound, scarred and maimed carcase, thus miserably disfigured by man, before he is dismembered and devoured by dogs ... It hath been observed that there is no country on the face of the earth that is not totally sunk in barbarism where the beast is so ill-treated as it is in our own; hence England is proverbially "the Hell of Horses." Our humanity hath also with great appearance of reason been called in question by foreigners on account of our barbarous customs of baiting and worrying animals and especially that cruel and infamous sport still practised among us on Shrove Tuesday.

To overcome these cruel practices, Granger invoked once again the pain principle: "the great law of humanity, which comprehends every kind of being that hath the same acute sense of pain [which] man finds in his own frame." By directing his "discourse" to "such as have the care of horses, and other useful beasts; but also for children, and those that are concerned in forming their hearts" Granger hoped to reduce the everyday suffering he witnessed and to make humane education a regular part of a national educational system.[84]

Humphry Primatt

Cambridge graduate and Vicar of Swardeston in Norfolk, Humphry Primatt (c. 1735 to c. 1778) argued his case for duty toward our fellow creatures almost entirely on Biblical and Christian principles. While he denied immortal souls to animals, like Alexander Pope he believed that, as a consequence, we owe them a greater responsibility in the here and now. Like Dean and Granger, he emphasized animal susceptibility to pain.

[W]e are all susceptible and sensible of the misery of pain; an evil, which, though necessary in itself and wisely intended as the spur to incite us to self-preservation, and to the avoidance of destruction, we nevertheless are naturally adverse to, and shrink back at the apprehension of it. Superiority of rank or station exempts no creature from the sensibility of pain, nor does inferiority render the feelings thereof the less exquisite. Pain is pain, whether it be inflicted on man or beast; and the creature that suffers it, whether man or beast, being sensible of the misery of it while it lasts, suffers *evil;* and the sufferance of evil, unmeritedly, unprovokedly, where no offence has been given, but merely to exhibit power or gratify malice, is cruelty and injustice in him that occasions it ...

Let me intreat thee then, O courteous Christian reader, by all that is amiable, just, and good; let me intreat thee for God's sake, for Christ's sake, for man's sake, for beast's sake, yea, and for thine own sake, *put on ... bowels of mercies, kindness, humbleness of mind, meekness.* Make it your business, esteem it your duty, believe it to be the ground of your hope, and know that it is that which the Lord doth require of thee – *to do justly, and to love mercy, and to walk humbly with thy God.* See that no brute of any kind, whether intrusted to thy care, or coming in thy way, suffer through thy neglect or abuse. Let no views of profit, no compliance with custom, and no fear of the ridicule of the world, ever tempt thee to the least act of cruelty or injustice to any creature whatsoever. But let this be your invariable rule, everywhere, and at all times, to *do unto others as, to their condition, you would be done unto.* (Humphry Primatt, *The Duty of Mercy and the Sin of Cruelty to Brute Animals,* chs. 1, 5 [1776])[85]

Emanuel Swedenborg

Swedish scientist, religious prophet, and mystic, Emanuel Swedenborg (1688-1772) wrote prolifically about the animal realm in his early scientific period. After "heaven was opened" to him in 1745 he turned his attention to spiritual matters, but always found a place for the animals in his cosmology, arguing, for example, that birds have their knowledge of the things appropriate to them, including an understanding of the seasons, because they have remained true to their primordial nature and not perverted that nature by reason. By contrast, humans have pursued the path of reason at the expense of their souls. Swedenborg had a profound influence on William Blake.[86]

[A]ll things of the created universe are recipients of the Divine Love and the Divine Wisdom ... the Divine is in each and every thing of the created universe ...

I heard several about me in the spiritual world talking together, who said they were quite willing to acknowledge that the Divine is in each and every thing of the universe, because they behold therein the wonderful works of God, and these are the more wonderful the more interiorly they are examined. And yet, when they were told that the Divine is actually in each and every thing of the universe, they were displeased; which is a proof that although they assert this they do not believe it. They were therefore asked whether this cannot be seen simply from the marvelous power which is in every seed, of producing its own vegetable form in like order, even to new seeds; also because in every seed an idea of the infinite and eternal is presented; since there is in seeds an endeavour to multiply themselves and to fructify infinitely and eternally? Is not this evident also in every living creature, even the smallest? In that there are in it organs of sense, also brains, a heart, lungs, and other parts; with arteries, veins, fibers, muscles, and the activities proceeding therefrom; besides the surpassing marvels of animal nature, about which whole volumes have been written. All these wonderful things are from God ...

Animals of every kind have limbs by which they move, organs by which they feel, and viscera by which these are exercised; these they have in common with man. They have also appetites and affections similar to man's natural appetites and affections; and they have inborn knowledges corresponding to their affections, in some of which there appears a resemblance to what is spiritual, which is more or less evident in beasts of the earth, and birds of the air, and in bees, silk-worms, ants, etc. From this it is that merely natural men consider the living creatures of the kingdom to be like themselves, except in the matter of speech ...

All animals, great and small, derive their origin from the spiritual in the outmost degree, which is called the natural ...

From [the remarkable lives of bees] and others very similar to them in the brute creation, the confessor and worshiper of nature confirms himself in favor of nature, while the confessor and worshiper of God confirms himself from the very same things in favor of the Divine; for the spiritual man sees in them spiritual things and the natural man natural things, thus according to his character. (Emanuel Swedenborg, *Divine Love and Wisdom*, secs. 57, 59, 60, 61, 346, 355 [1763])[87]

American Commentary

We know of little American writing before the final decade of the eighteenth century that deals directly with respect for our fellow animals, but occasional asides reflect the attitudes that inspired the Massachusetts Bay Colony ordinance of 1641. New England clergyman **Solomon Stoddard** advised his congregation that: "Men have not the command of their own compassions; their compassion doth prevail whether they will or no, and they are forced to neglect their own interest to relieve others in distress; and this compassion is not only to friends, but to strangers ... yea, to brute creatures also."[88]

Writing in his brother's newspaper at the age of sixteen, **Benjamin Franklin** (1706-90) referred to that "natural compassion ... to ... Fellow-Creatures" that brings "Tears at the Sight of an Object of Charity, who by a bear [sic] Relation of his Circumstances" seems "to demand the Assistance of those about him." No doubt Franklin had fellow humans uppermost in mind, but since he was at this time a vegetarian, converted by the arguments of Thomas Tryon,[89] and since, even after returning to flesh-eating as he announced proudly in his *Autobiography*, he "never went a-fishing or Shooting,"[90] fellow animals are sure to have been included in his dictum.

Quaker leader **John Woolman** (1720-72) was among the first to speak out against slavery in America. His religious writings refer, only occasionally but certainly with passion, to the interests of the animals: "[S]uch Buildings, Furniture, Food and Raiment, as best answer our Necessities, and are the least likely to feed that selfish Spirit which is our Enemy, are the most acceptable to us. In this State the mind is tender, and inwardly watchful, that the Love of Gain draw us not into any Business which may weaken our Love to our Heavenly Father, or bring unnecessary Trouble to any of his Creatures" (John Woolman, *On the Right Use of the Lord's Outward Gifts*).[91]

Again, while the primary consideration would be fellow humans, the comments in his journal would leave us with little doubt that our fellow animals were also included in his general principles.

(c. 1732): Another thing remarkable in my childhood was, that once as I went to a neighbour's house, I saw on the way, a Robbin sitting on her nest, and as I came near she went off, but having young ones, flew about, and with many cries expressed her Concern for them. I stood and threw stones at her, till one striking her she fell down dead. At first I was pleas'd with the Exploit, but after a few minutes was seized with Horror, at haveing in a sportive way kild an Innocent Creature while she was carefull of her young. I beheld her lying dead, & thought those young ones for which she was so carefull must now perish for want of their dam to nourish them; and after some painfull consideration on the subject, I climbed up the Tree, took all the young birds, and killed them supposing that better than to leave them to pine away and die miserably; and believ'd in this case, that scripture proverb was fulfilled, "the tender mercies of the wicked are Cruel." I then went on my errand, but for some hours, could think of little else but [the Cruelties I had committed and was much troubled.]

(c. 1740): I ... was early convinced in my own mind that true Religion consisted in an inward life, wherein the Heart doth Love and Reverence God the creator, and learn to Exercise true Justice and Goodness, not only toward all men, but also toward the Brute Creatures. That as the mind was moved by an inward Principle to love God as an invisible, Incomprehensible Being, by the same principle it was moved to love him in all his manifestations in the Visible world. That as by his breath the flame of life was kindled in all Animal and Sensible creatures, to say we love God as unseen, and at the same time Exercise cruelty toward the least creature moving by his life, or by life derived from Him, was a Contradiction in itself.

(c. 1772): In Observing their dull appearance at Sea, and the pineing sickness of some of [these birds], I once remembered the Fountain of goodness, who gave being to all creatures, and whose love extends to that of careing for the Sparrows, and believe where the love of God is verily perfected, & the true Spirit of government watchfully attended to a tenderness to all creatures made Subject to us

will be experienced & a care felt in us that we do not lessen the Sweetness of life in the animal Creation, which the great Creator intends for them under our government.[92]

French Commentary
Both **François Marie Arouet de Voltaire** (1694-1778) and Jean-Jacques Rousseau (1712-78) were avid proponents of a vegetarian diet on ethical grounds, though it is doubtful that their practices conformed to their advocacy. Nonetheless, there can be no doubting their compassion toward their fellow animals. Thus Voltaire, renowned author of *Candide* (1759) and *The Century of Louis XIV* (1751), writes as a deist – God is the great geometrician – against the Cartesians, Thomists, and others:

How pitiful, how impoverished, to have said that animals are machines lacking knowledge and feeling, which always conduct themselves in the same manner, which learn nothing, improve nothing, etc. What! The bird which builds his nest in a semi-circle when he attaches it to a wall, a quarter circle when built on a corner, and a full circle in a tree, this bird does everything in the same manner? The hunting dog which you have trained for three months, does he not know at the end of this period more than he knew prior to your instructions? The canary to which you teach a tune, does he repeat it forthwith? Do you not spend a considerable time in instructing him? Have you not noticed that he makes mistakes and corrects them?

Is it because I speak to you that you judge me to have feelings, memory, ideas? Very well! I shall not speak to you. You will see me enter my home with an afflicted look, search anxiously for a document, open the desk in which I recall having shut it, and read it with pleasure. You will conclude that I have evinced the feeling of affliction and that of pleasure, that I have memory and knowledge.

Extend the same judgment to a dog who cannot find his master, who seeks him in the streets, crying sadly, who enters the house, feeling disturbed and anxious, who mounts and descends, who goes from room to room, who finally finds the master he loves in his study, and who testifies to his joy by the softness of his voice, by his bounds, by his fawning.

The barbarians seize this dog, who so prodigiously surpasses man in affection; they nail him to a table, and vivisect him to show you the mesenteric veins. You discover in him all the same organs of sentience which are in you. Answer me, mechanist, has nature arranged all these springs of sentience in order that he should not have feelings? Has he nerves in order to be impassive? Do not presume there to be such an insolent contradiction in nature. (Voltaire, "Bêtes," *Dictionnaire philosophique* [1764])[93]

Voltaire's lesser-known *Traité sur la tolérance* (Treatise on Toleration) (1763) is equally emphatic about human-animal similarities.

[I]t is said that God made a compact with Noah and all the animals; yet he nonetheless allowed Noah *to eat all that had life and movement;* he excluded only the blood which he forbad to be consumed. God added "that he would wreak vengeance on all the animals which spilt human blood."* One may infer from these passages, and from several others, what all antiquity has always thought up to the very present, that the animals have a certain level of cognition. God did not make a compact with trees and stones, which lack sentience; but he did with the animals, which he deigned to endow with feelings often more refined than our own, and with certain ideas necessary to those feelings. It is for this reason that he requires us to eschew the barbarism of feeding on their blood, because, in fact, blood is the source of life, and consequently of sentience. Deprive an animal of its blood and its organs cannot function. Thus it is with consummate reason that the Scriptures tell us in a hundred places that the soul – that which is termed the *sentient soul*:† – lies in the blood; and this conception is so natural it has existed among all peoples.

It is upon this conception that the compassion we owe all animals is founded ... there have always been peoples who have been scrupulous in this practice: this principle endures in the peninsula of India; all the Pythagoreans in Italy and Greece abstained constantly from eating flesh. In his book on *Abstinence* Porphry reproached his disciple‡ for having left his group solely to satisfy his barbarous appetite.

It seems to me that those who have the audacity to believe animals no more than machines have renounced the light afforded by nature. There is a manifest contradiction in conceiving God to have given animals all the organs of sentience while maintaining that he did not give them sentience.

It seems to me equally that they must never have observed animals if they cannot recognize their needs expressed in differing tones, their suffering, joy, fear, love, anger, and all their differing sentiments; it would be very strange if they could express so well what they cannot feel.[94]

Charles Louis de Secondat, baron de la Brede et de Montesquieu, more commonly known as simply **Montesquieu** (1689-1755), jurist and political philosopher, who wrote the *Lettres persanes* (1721) and *De l'Esprit des lois* (The Spirit of the Laws) (1748), made a similar point earlier and more succinctly, if much less powerfully: "By the allurement of pleasure [animals] preserve the individual, and by the same allurement they preserve the species. They have natural laws, because they are united by sensation ... association would quickly follow from the very pleasure one animal feels at the approach of another of the same species ... [there is a] sense or instinct which man possesses in common with brutes ..." (Montesquieu, *The Spirit of the Laws*, Bk. 1, sec. 2).[95]

In the *Discourse on the Origin and Foundations of Inequality among Men* (1754), **Jean-Jacques Rousseau** tells us in his discussion of natural law in the Preface that,

---

* Genesis 9:5.
† In Hebrew *nephesh chayah* – living soul.
‡ Firmus Castricius.

as long as [man] does not resist the inner compulsion of compassion, he will never do harm to another man, or even to another sentient being, except in those legitimate cases where, since his own preservation is involved, he is obliged to give preference to himself. By this means, the old debate concerning the applicability to animals of natural law can be put to an end, for it is clear that, bereft of understanding and liberty, they cannot recognize this law, but since they share to some extent in our nature by virtue of the sensibility with which they are endowed, it will be thought they must also participate in natural right, and that man is bound by some kind of duty towards them. It seems, in fact, that if I am obliged to do no harm to my fellow man, it is less because he is a rational being than because he is a sensitive being, since sensitivity is a quality which is common to man and beast and should at least give the beast the right not to be needlessly mistreated by the man.[96]

In Part One of the *Discourse on Inequality*, Rousseau continues: "we observe every day the repugnance of horses to tread a living body under foot, and an animal does not, without some uneasiness, pass close by a dead member of its own species ... the sorrowful lowing of cattle entering a slaughterhouse bespeaks the impression of the horrible spectacle which confronts them."[97] In Rousseau's view, "compassion is a natural sentiment"[98] for both humans and animals. However, it is in *Emile, or On Education* (1762) that Rousseau has most to tell us about the human relationship to other species: "Men be humane. This is your first duty. Be humane with every station, every age, everything which is not alien to man. What wisdom is there for you save humanity?"[99] The question, then, is whether animals are "alien to man," and, for Rousseau, the answer is in the negative.

Emile ... will begin to have gut reactions at the sounds of complaints and cries, the sight of blood flowing will cause him an ineffable distress before he knows whence come this new movement within him ...

Thus is born pity, the first sentiment that touches the human heart according to the order of nature. To become sensitive and pitying, the child must know that there are beings like him who suffer what he has suffered, who feel the pains he has felt, and that there are others whom he ought to conceive of as being able to feel them too. In fact, how do we let ourselves be moved by pity if not by transporting ourselves outside of ourselves and identifying with the suffering animal, by leaving, as it were, our own being to take on its being. It is not in ourselves, it is in him that we suffer. Thus, no one become sensitive until his imagination is animated and begins to transport him out of himself.[100]

There is probably no finer statement of the capacity for human kinship with animals. Indeed, while there have been earlier intimations, this is the first passage in which there is an explicit call not merely for sympathy with other animals but for empathy with them too.

A naturalist and a novelist, heavily influenced by Rousseau, **Jacques-Henri-Bernardin de Saint-Pierre** (1737-1814) wrote *Études de la nature* (1784), an attempt to prove the existence of God from the wonders of nature, as well as being a critique of the politics of his day. It included the story of *Paul et Virginie*, published separately in 1788, and one of the earliest and certainly the most successful of the books on the return to nature theme, going through more than 150 reprints. *Voeux d'un solitaire* (Prayers of a Hermit) (1789) was an extension of his earlier naturalist studies, and *Suite des Voeux d'un solitaire* (Sequel to the Prayers of a Hermit), whence this extract, an apologia for his inaction during the revolutionary period and a critique of contemporary policy and custom.

It is insufficient to attend to the physical needs of the peasantry, one must also assuage their customs. Our rustics are often barbaric, and it is their education which is the sole cause; often they beat their asses, their horses, their dogs, and even their wives, because that was how they were treated in their childhood ...

Thus they must be led to abandon their barbaric sports, the fruit of their cruel education. One sport, among others, that I find deplorable, is that in which they take a live goose by the neck, and engage in its destruction by each in turn throwing sticks at it. During this protracted agony, lasting several hours, the poor animal flays its feet in the air, to the great satisfaction of the brutal tormentors, until the most accomplished among them succeeds in breaking its vertebrae, causing its battered carcass to fall to the ground; he then carries it off in triumph to eat with his companions. Thus passes into their blood the substance of an animal which has died enraged. These ferocious and imbecilic festivities frequently occur on chateau grounds or church property, without the lord or the priest taking the trouble to voice any opposition; the latter will often prohibit any dancing to girls while allowing the boys to torment innocent birds. Thus it is that in our towns they turn away women wearing hats from their churches, while they greet men bearing swords with respect. Many deem it a great sin to attend the Opera, yet watch with pleasure a bull, man's fellow labourer, being ripped apart by a pack of dogs. To the detriment of the weak, everywhere barbarism is a virtue to those who hold mercy to be a crime.

Cruelty exercised towards animals is but an apprenticeship for cruelty toward mankind. I have researched whence arise these appalling peasant customs of tormenting geese, innocent and useful birds ...

Whatever the cause maybe, the authorities must abolish these inhuman sports and substitute for them sports which exercise both the body and the soul ... [which have] such power to refine the spirit.[101]

Georges Louis Leclerc, comte de Buffon (1707-88) was the Keeper of the Jardin du Roi (later Jardin des Plantes) and devoted his life to the writing of the monumental forty-four volume *L'Histoire naturelle* (1749-1804), at the time the greatest work of natural history ever produced. A defender of the right to consume flesh, nonetheless he believed it had been taken to excess. In his nineteenth-century study on the historical development of vegetarianism, Howard Williams found the following extract from *L'Histoire naturelle* convincing but bemoaned the fact that "unhappily, Buffon seems to have considered himself as holding a brief to defend his clients, the flesh-eaters"[102] and thus failed to remain consistent to his argument, having demonstrated clearly that "Flesh is not a better nourishment than grains or bread":

> Man knows how to use, as a master, his power over [other] animals. He has selected those whose flesh *flatters his taste.* He has made domestic slaves of them. He has multiplied them more than Nature could have done. He has formed innumerable flocks, and by the cares which he takes in propagating them he *seems* to have acquired the right of sacrificing them for himself. But he extends that right *much beyond* his needs. For, independently of those species which he has subjected, and of which he disposes at his will, he makes war also upon wild animals, upon birds, upon fishes. He does not even limit himself to those of the climate he inhabits. He seeks at a distance, even in the remotest seas, new meats, and entire Nature seems scarcely to suffice for his intemperance and the inconsistent variety of his appetites.
>
> *Man alone consumes and engulfs more flesh than all other animals put together. He is, then, the greatest destroyer, and he is so more by abuse than by necessity.* Instead of enjoying with moderation the resources offered him, in place of dispensing them with equity, in place of repairing in proportion as he destroys, of renewing in proportion as he annihilates, the rich man makes his boast and glory in *consuming* all his splendour in destroying in one day, at his table, more material *(plus de biens)* than would be necessary for the support of several families. He abuses equally other animals and his own species, the rest of whom live in famine, languish in misery, and work only to satisfy the immoderate appetite and the still more insatiable vanity of this human being who, *destroying others by want, destroys himself by excess.*[103]

Third Earl of Shaftesbury

Anthony Ashley Cooper, third Earl of Shaftesbury (1671-1713), was a Whig politician and political philosopher whose most memorable work, *Characteristics of Men, Manners, Opinions, Times* (1711), was greatly admired by Hume, Montesquieu, Herder, and Babbitt.[104] Its theme was that in aesthetics, politics and ethics alike, the right path lay in a delicate equipoise between the interests of the community and the self. However, the moral community was not merely local, or even human (though it was that primarily) but included animals as creatures against which the practice of "unnatural passions" – that is, those that did not contribute to the common welfare – was a crime. Already in *The Moralists* (1709), later included in *The Characteristics*, he had surveyed the various orders of the world and concluded: "These rural meditations are sacred ... I sing of nature's order in created beings, and celebrate the beauties which resolve in thee, the principle of all beauty and perfection." Serpents, savage beasts, and poisonous insects were "beauteous in themselves ... a dunghill or heap of any seeming vile and horrid matter" was sufficient to demonstrate Nature's beauty.[105]

In *An Inquiry Concerning Virtue or Merit of the Characteristics* he added the moral implications, condemning those who showed

unnatural and unhuman delight in beholding torments, and in viewing distress, calamity, blood, massacre and destruction, with a peculiar joy and pleasure ... To see the sufferance of an enemy with cruel delight may proceed from the height of anger, revenge, fear and other extended self-passions, but to delight in the torture and pain of other creatures indifferently, natives or foreigners, of our own or another species, kindred or no kindred, known or unknown, to feed, as it were, on death, and be entertained with dying agonies – this has nothing in it accountable in the way of self-interest or private good ..., but is wholly and absolutely unnatural, as it is horrid and miserable.[106]

If we feel today that Shaftesbury might be stating the obvious, we must recall that public attendance at hangings of condemned criminals was still a form of popular entertainment and the savageries of the cock-pit were to continue for another century and a quarter. In Shaftesbury's day they were still considered by some a diversion worthy of gentlemanly interest. Shaftesbury's writings are thought by many to inaugurate the cult of sensibility.

Bernard Mandeville

Dutch by birth and education, Bernard Mandeville (1670-1733) moved to England in 1692. *The Fable of the Bees* (1714, 1723, 1728), based on his 1705 poem "The Grumbling Hive," was his most renowned work. The excerpts are from his interpretative "Remarks" on the poem. A lion is speaking:

'Tis only Man, mischievous Man that can make Death a Sport. Nature taught your Stomach to crave nothing but Vegetables; but your violent Fondness to change, and greater eagerness after Novelties, have prompted you to the Destruction of Animals without Justice or Necessity, perverted your Nature and warp'd your Appetites which way soever your Pride or Luxury have call'd them ...

Man feeds on the Sheep that clothes him, and spares not her innocent young ones, whom he has taken into his Care and Custody. If you tell me the Gods made Man Master over all other Creatures what Tyranny was it then to destroy them out of Wantonness? ... A single Lion bears some sway in the Creation, but what is a single Man? A small and inconsiderate part. A trifling Atom of one great Beast.* What

---

* Hobbes's *Leviathan*, which was a colossus composed of individual humans, forming a new organism.

Nature designs she executes, and 'tis not safe to judge of what she purpos'd, but from the Effect she shews. If she had intentioned that Man, as Man from a Superiority of Species, should lord it over all other Animals, the Tiger, nay, the Whale and the Eagle, would have obey'd his Voice.[107]

Mandeville now speaks with his own voice, rather than through the lion:

[W]hen to soften the Flesh of Male Animals, we have by Castration prevented the Firmness their Tendons and every Fibre would have come to without it, I confess, I think it ought to move a human Creature when he reflects upon the cruel Care with which they are fatned for Destruction. When a large and gentle Bullock, after having resisted a ten times greater force of Blows, than would have killed his Murderer, falls stunn'd at last, and his arm'd Head is fastn'd to the ground with Cords; as soon as the wide Wound is made, and the Jugulars are cut asunder, what Mortal can without Compassion hear the painful Bellowings intercepted by his Blood, the bitter Sighs that speak the Sharpness of this Anguish, and the deep sounding Grones with loud Anxiety fetch'd from the bottom of his strong and palpitating Heart; Look on the trembling and violent Convulsions of his Limbs; see while his reeking Gore streams from him, his Eyes become dim and languid, and behold his Strugglings, Gasps and last Efforts for Life, the certain Signs of his approaching Fate? When a Creature has given such convincing and undeniable Proofs of the Terrors upon Him, and the Pains and Agonies he feels, is there a follower of *Descartes* so inur'd to Blood, as not to refute, by his Commiseration, the Philosophy of that vain Reasoner? (Bernard Mandeville, *The Fable of the Bees* [1714])[108]

Ironically, in his college dissertation, Mandeville had maintained the Cartesian doctrine "bruta non sentiunt" – animals lack sentience – a thesis then contested on the European mainland by La Fontaine, Spinoza, Gassendi, and Bayle, among others. His *Fable of the Bees* was a volte-face of sufficient moment that it persuaded Joseph Ritson (1752-1803) to become a vegetarian.[109]

David Hume

Scottish nominalist, skeptic, and early utilitarian philosopher, David Hume (1711-76) considered animals to differ from humans in the degree of their rational, moral, and aesthetic senses, but believed that human and animal differences were only of degree and not of kind. His *Treatise of Human Nature* (1739-40) contains short chapters on "Of the Reason of Animals," "Of the Pride of Animals," and "Of the Love and Hatred of Animals."

[N]o truth appears to me more evident, than that beasts are endow'd with thought and reason as well as men ... 'Tis from the resemblance of the external actions of animals to those we ourselves perform, that we judge their internal likewise to resemble ours ... reason is nothing but a wonderful and unintelligible instinct in our souls, which carries us along a certain train of ideas, and endows them with particular qualities, according to their particular situations and relations ... [110]

Every thing is conducted by springs and principles, which are not peculiar to man, or any one species of animals ... Love in animals, has not only for its object animals of the same species, but extends itself farther, and comprehends almost every sensible and thinking being ... 'Tis evident that *sympathy*, or the communication of passions, takes place among animals, no less than among men. Fear, anger, courage and other affections are frequently communicated from one animal to another, without their knowledge of that cause, which produc'd the original passion. Grief likewise is receiv'd by sympathy; and produces almost all the same consequences, and excites the same emotions as in our species. The howlings and lamentations of a dog produce a sensible concern in his fellows. And 'tis remarkable, that tho' almost all animals use in play the same member, and nearly all the same action as in fighting: a lion, a tyger, a cat their paw; an ox his horns; a dog his teeth; a horse his heels: Yet they most carefully avoid harming their companion, even tho' they have nothing to fear from his resentment; which is the evident proof of the sense brutes have of each other's pain and pleasure.[111]

In the *Enquiry Concerning the Principles of Morals* of 1751 Hume drew the relevant moral conclusion: "we should be bound by the laws of humanity to give gentle usage to these creatures." Strictly speaking, Hume is not at this point referring to animals *per se* but to an imaginary "species of creature intermingled with men." However, in the following paragraph he adds: "This is plainly the situation of men, with regard to beasts."[112]

Henry St. John, Viscount Bolingbroke

Disgraced Tory statesman and author of *The Idea of a Patriot King* (1749) and *Essays on Human Knowledge* (1751), Lord Bolingbroke (1678-1751), like Gassendi, Locke, Hume, and others before him, thought animals more rational than many gave them credit for. In consternation at Hobbes (and by implication, and with greater reason, Descartes)[113] he exclaimed:

Absurd and impertinent vanity! We pronounce our fellow animals to be automates, or we allow them instinct, or we bestow graciously upon them, at the utmost stretch of liberality, an irrational soul, something we know not what but something that can claim no kindred to the human mind. We scorn to admit them into the same class of intelligence with ourselves, though it is obvious, among other observations easy to be made, and tending to the same purpose, that the first inlets, and the first elements of their knowledge, and of ours, are the same. (Lord Bolingbroke, *Essay the First, Concerning the Nature, Extent and Reality of Human Knowledge*)[114]

Later in the same essay Bolingbroke adds:

As these animal systems come to be more and more sensible to us, and as our means of observing them increase, we discover in them, and according to their different species, or even among individuals of the same species, in some more, in others fewer, of the same appearances, that denote a power of thinking in us from the lowest conceivable degrees of it, up to such as are not far, if at all remote, from those in which some men enjoy it. I say some men, because I think it indisputable that the difference between the intellectual faculties of different men is often greater than that between the same faculties in some men and some other animals.[115]

Elsewhere he comments:

Other animals seem to act more agreeably to the laws, each of his own nature, and more uniformly than man, by that secret determination of the will which is knowable only by its effects, like every other kind of force, which we call instinct, and which may answer in natural influences, to that which the divines call grace in those that they suppose to be supernatural. This influence, whatever it be, is, I think, more extensive and more durable in other animals than in us. It serves them in more particulars, and seems to have the sole direction of their conduct through life.[116]

How astonished the clergy would have been to find that which they deemed graciously supernatural to be the natural property of animals!

David Hartley

Physician and philosopher, David Hartley (1705-57) conceived of all mental phenomena as sensations arising from the vibrations of the white medullary substance of the brain and spinal cord – a doctrine known as "associationism." This rendered humans and animals essentially alike, and highlighted implications for our consumption of animals.

With respect to animal Diet, let it be considered, that taking away the Lives of Animals in order to convert them into Food does great Violence to the Principles of Benevolence and Compassion. This appears from the frequent Hard-heartedness and Cruelty found among those Persons whose Occupations engage them in destroying animal Life, as well as from the Uneasiness which others feel in beholding the Butchery of Animals. It is most evident, in respect of the larger Animals, and those with whom Mankind have a familiar intercourse – such as Oxen, Sheep, and domestic Fowls. These Creatures resemble us greatly in the Make of the Body in general, and in that of the particular Organs of Circulation, Respiration, Digestion, &c; also in the Formation of their Intellects, Memories and Passions, and in the Signs of Distress, Fear, Pain, and Death. They often likewise win our Affections by the Marks of peculiar Sagacity, by their Instincts, Helplessness, Innocence, nascent Benevolence, &c. And if there be any Glimmering of the Hope of an Hereafter for them, if they should prove to be our Brethren and Sisters in this higher Sense, in Immortality as well as Mortality, in the permanent Principle of our Minds as well as in the frail Dust of our Bodies, if they should be partakers of the same Redemption as well as of our Fall, and be members of the same mystical Body, this would have a particular Tendency to increase our Tenderness for them. (David Hartley, *Observations on Man, His Frame, His Duty and His Expectations* [1749])[117]

Adam Smith

Contrary to his popular image as an advocate of individual self-interest, Scottish philosopher, economist, and historian Adam Smith (1723–90) theorized about the natural sociality and benevolence of humankind. The animals, too, were recipients of that natural beneficence.

[B]efore any thing can be the proper object of gratitude or resentment, it must not only be the cause of pleasure or pain; it must likewise be capable of feeling them. Without this other quality, those passions cannot vent themselves with any sort of satisfaction upon it. As they are excited by the causes of pleasure and pain, so their gratification consists in relating those sensations upon what gave occasion to them; which it is no purpose to attempt upon what has no sensibility.

Animals, therefore, are less improper objects of gratitude and resentment than inanimate objects. The dog that bites, the ox that gores, both of them are punished. If they have been the causes of the death of any person, neither the public nor the relations of the slain, can be satisfied, unless they are put to death in their turn; nor is this merely for the security of the living, but in some measure, to revenge the injury of the dead. Those animals, on the contrary, that have been remarkably serviceable to their masters, become the objects of a very lively gratitude ...

But though animals are not only the causes of pleasure and pain, but also are capable of feeling those sensations they are still far from being complete and perfect objects of gratitude or resentment; and those passions still feel there is something wanting in their entire gratification. (Adam Smith, *The Theory of Moral Sentiments* [1759])[118]

Until the final sentence Smith appears to be arguing that animals should be treated as morally responsible for their actions in the same way that humans are, reminiscent of how some medieval European courts treated accused animals. If, on the other hand, they are "far from being the perfect objects of gratitude and resentment" then the case for treating them as entirely responsible for their felonies diminishes or disappears. The question for the modern animal rights ethicist must be whether animals can be objects of gratitude for their beneficent acts without being objects of resentment for their injurious acts.

Edmund Burke

Anglo-Irish political writer and Whig parliamentarian Edmund Burke (1729–97) is most famous for his support for the American colonies during their conflict with Britain, and for his development of conservative philosophy in his opposition to the French Revolution. It was, however, in his writings on aesthetics that he expressed his animal sympathies.

Humankind is "attached to particulars by personal *beauty*. I call beauty a social quality; for when women and men, and not only they, but when other animals give us a sense of joy and pleasure in beholding them (and there are many that do so), they inspire us with sentiments of tenderness and affection toward their persons; we like to have them near us, and we enter willingly into a kind of relation with them; unless we should have strong reason to the contrary." (Edmund Burke, *A Philosophical Enquiry into the Origin of Our Ideas of the Sublime and Beautiful* [1756])[119]

William Paley

Theologian and political philosopher, William Paley (1743-1805) is best known for his extremely influential *Natural Theology; or Evidence for the Existence and Attributes of the Deity* (1802), in which he developed the theory from design, the view that the universe manifests divine forethought and testifies to an intelligent creator. It was, however, in his earlier *Principles of Moral and Political Philosophy* (1785) that he questioned whether we have a moral right to consume other creatures, concluding that we would not have such a right were it not for Biblical authority. It was Howard Williams's view in *The Ethics of Diet* that Paley's "ultimate refuge in an alleged biblical authority (forced upon him, apparently, by the necessity of his position rather than by personal inclination) confirms rather than weakens his preceding candid admissions ..."[120]

By the General Rights of mankind, I mean the rights which belong to the species collectively; the original stock, as I may say, which they have since distributed among themselves.

These are, 1 [a] right to the fruits or vegetable produce of the earth.

The insensible parts of the creation are incapable of injury; and it is nugatory to inquire into the right where the use can be attended with no injury. But it may be worth observing, for the sake of an inference which will appear below, that, as God had created us with a want and desire for food, and provided things suitable by their nature to sustain and satisfy us, we may fairly presume, that he intended we should apply these things to that purpose.

2 A right to the flesh of animals.

This is a very different claim from the former. Some excuse seems necessary for the pain and loss which we occasion to brutes, by restraining them of their liberty, mutilating their bodies, and, at last, putting an end to their lives (which we suppose to be the whole of their existence) for our pleasure or conveniency.

The reasons alleged in vindication of this practice are the following: that the several species of brutes being created to prey upon one another affords a kind of analogy to prove that the human species were intended to feed upon them; that if left alone they would over-run the earth, and exclude mankind from the occupation of it; that they are requited for what they suffer at our hands, by our care and protection.

Upon which reasons I would observe that *the analogy* contended for is extremely lame since brutes have no power to support life by any other means, and since we have, for the whole human species might subsist entirely upon fruits, pulse, herbs and roots, as many tribes of Hindoos actually do. The two other reasons may be valid as far as they go, for, no doubt, if man had been supported entirely by vegetable food, a great part of those animals which die to furnish his table, would never have lived; but they by no means justify our right over the lives of brutes to the extent in which we exercise it. What danger is there, for instance, of fish interfering with us, in the occupation of their element? or what do *we* contribute to their support or preservation?

It seems to me that it would be difficult to defend this right by any arguments which the light and order of nature afford; and that we are beholden for it to the permission recorded in scripture, Gen. IX, 1,2,3 ...

Wanton, and, what is worse, studied cruelty to brutes, is certainly wrong, as coming within none of these reasons ... From reason then, or revelation, or from both together, it appears to be God Almighty's intention, that the products of the earth, should be applied to the sustenation of human life. Consequently all waste and misapplication of these productions is contrary to the Divine intention and will; and therefore wrong, for the same *reason* as any other crime is.[121]

Immanuel Kant

One of the greatest figures in philosophy, Immanuel Kant (1742-1804) wrote numerous profound metaphysical treatises, including *Critique of Pure Reason* (1781), *Prolegomena to Future Metaphysics* (1783), and *Critique of Practical Reason* (1788). Among his many original and epochal contributions to philosophy was the development of the categorical imperative, according to which each person is entitled to be treated as an end in himself or herself and never as a mere means. In Kant's view, however, since animals lacked consciousness they could not be ends in themselves but were instead mere means to human ends. Not surprisingly, Kant has met with a spirited disapproval from animal welfarists and rightists alike. Nonetheless, Kant was not without his animal sympathies.

The following extract is from lecture notes taken by his students (or perhaps their amanuenses) and were thus not prepared by Kant for publication. They should therefore be treated with a degree of caution, although they are consistent with general principles he expressed throughout his works.

Animal nature has analogies to human nature, and by doing our duties to animals in respect of manifestations which correspond to manifestations of human nature, we indirectly do our duty towards humanity. Thus, if a dog has served his master long and faithfully, his service, on the analogy of human service, deserves reward, and when the dog has grown too old to serve, his master ought to keep him till he dies. Such action helps to support us in our duties toward human beings, where they are bounden duties. If then any acts of animals are analogous to human acts and spring from the same principles we have duties toward the animals because thus we cultivate the corresponding duties toward human beings. If a man shoots his dog because the animal is no longer capable of service, he does not fail in his duty to the dog, for the dog cannot judge, but his act is inhuman and damages in himself that humanity which it is his duty to show towards mankind. If he is not to stifle his human feelings, he must practise kindness towards animals, for he who is cruel to animals becomes hard also in his dealings with men. We can judge the heart of a man by his treatment of animals. Hogarth[122] depicts this in his engravings. He shows how cruelty grows and develops. He shows the child's cruelty to animals, pinching the tail of a dog or cat; he then depicts the grown man in his cart running over a child; and lastly, the culmination of cruelty in murder. He thus brings home to us in a terrible fashion the rewards of cruelty, and this should be an impressive lesson to children. The more we come in contact with animals and observe their behaviour, the more we love them, for we see how great is their care for their young. It is then difficult for us to be cruel in thoughts even to a wolf. Leibniz used a tiny worm for the purposes of observation, and then carefully replaced it with its leaf on the tree so that it should not come to any harm through any act of his. He would have been sorry – a natural feeling for a human man – to destroy such a creature for no reason ... A master who turns out his ass or his dog because the animal can no longer earn its keep manifests a small mind. (Immanuel Kant, "Duties towards Animals and Spirits," *Lectures on Ethics* [c. 1780])[123]

While the reasons for Kant's insistence on kindness to animals will not satisfy animal liberation, rights, or welfare philosophers, it is worthy of note that much of the behaviour he applauds and approves does not fall far short of what many of greater sensibility would advocate.

Soame Jenyns

A British parliamentarian and Commissioner of the Board of Trade, Soame Jenyns (1704-87) wrote on a variety of topics, including *The Art of Dancing: A Poem* (1727) and *A View of the Internal Evidence of the Christian Religion* (1776). His condemnation of the animal orientations of human civilization was no less effective than that of Swift:

The laws of self-defence undoubtedly justify us in destroying those animals who would destroy us; who injure our properties, or annoy our persons; but not even these, whenever their situation incapacitates them from hurting us. I know of no right which we have to shoot a bear on an inaccessible island of ice, or an eagle on the mountain's top whose lives cannot injure us, nor deaths procure us any benefit. We are unable to give life, and therefore ought not wantonly to take it away from the meanest insect without sufficient reason; they all receive it from the same benevolent hand as ourselves, and have therefore an equal right to enjoy it. Tho' civilization may, in some degree, have abated the native ferocity of man, it is not extirpated; the most polished are not ashamed to be pleased with scenes of barbarity and to the disgrace of human nature, to dignify them with the name of SPORTS. They arm cocks with artificial weapons, which nature had kindly denied to their malevolence, and, with shouts of applause and triumph, see them plunge into each other's hearts; they view with delight the trembling deer and defenceless hare, flying for hours in the utmost agonies of terror and despair, and at last, sinking under fatigue, devoured by merciless pursuers; they see with joy the beautiful pheasant and harmless partridge drop from their flight, weltering in their blood, or perhaps perishing with wounds and hunger, under the cover of some friendly thicket to which they have in vain retreated for safety; they triumph over the unsuspecting fish, whom they have decoyed by an insidious pretence of feeding, and drag him from his native element by a hook fixed to, and tearing out, his entrails; and, to add to all this, they spare neither labour nor expense to preserve and propagate these animals, for no other end but to multiply the objects of their persecution. What name should we bestow on a supreme being, whose whole endeavours were employed, and whose whole pleasure consisted in terrifying, ensnaring, tormenting, and destroying mankind? whose superior faculties were exerted in fomenting animosities against them, in contriving engines of destruction, and inciting them to use them in maiming and murdering each other? whose power over them was employed in assisting the rapacious deceiving the simple, and oppressing the innocent? who, without permission or advantage, should continue from day to day, void of all pity and remorse, thus to torment mankind for diversion, and at the same time endeavour with his utmost care to preserve their lives, and to propagate their species, in order to increase the number of victims devoted to his malevolence, and be delighted in proportion to the miseries he occasioned? I say what name detestable enough could we find for such a being? yet if we impartially consider the case, and our immediate situation, we must acknowledge that, with regard to inferior animals, just such a being is man. (Soame Jenyns, "On Cruelty to Animals," in *Disquisitions on Several Subjects*)[124]

Jenyns had no doubts about the animal's immortal soul. Indeed, he even countenanced metempsychosis. God, he wrote,

has given many advantages to Brutes, which Man cannot attain to with all his superiority ... we are not so high in the scale of existence as our ignorant ambition may desire ...

Is not the justice of God as much concerned to preserve the happiness of the meanest Insect which he has called into being, as of the greatest Man that ever lives? are not all creatures we see made subservient to each others uses? and what is there in Man, that he only should be exempted from the common fate of all created Beings? ...

The certainty therefore of a future state, in which we, and indeed all Creatures endowed with sensation, shall somehow or other exist, seems (if all our notions of Justice are not erroneous) as demonstrable as the Justice of their Creator ...

But the pride of man will not suffer us to treat this subject [of the transmigration of souls] with the seriousness it deserves; but rejects as both impious and ridiculous every supposition of inferior creatures ever arriving at its own imaginary dignity, allowing at the same time the probability of human nature being exalted to the angelick, a much wider and more extraordinary transition, but yet such a one as may probably be the natural consequence, as well as the reward of a virtuous life; nor is it less likely that our vices may debase us in the servile condition of inferior animals, in whose forms we may be severely punished for the injuries we have done to Mankind when amongst them, and be obliged in some measure to repair them, by performing the drudgeries tyrannically imposed upon us for their service. (Soame Jenyns, *A Free Inquiry into the Nature and Origin of Evil* [1757])[125]

Other contemporaries also showed a measure of respect for our fellow animals. Thus, the editor of Bishop Richard Cumberland's *A Treatise of the Laws of Nature* (1727):

The Author's scheme had been more complete had he included ... benevolence towards brutes ... because we can't imagine but that the Deity takes pleasure in the happiness of all his creatures that are capable thereof ... A truly benevolent man yet receives pleasure even from the happiness of the brute creation.[126]

In his posthumous *System of Moral Philosophy* (1755), **Francis Hutcheson** (1694-1746) tells us that brutes "have a right that no useless pain or misery should be inflicted upon them"[127] and that the right to slaughter animals for food was "so opposite to our natural compassion of the human heart that one cannot think an express grant of it by revelation was superfluous."[128]

The deist recluse **William Wollaston** asserted in *The Religion of Nature Delineated* (1724) that humankind ought to take animals into moral account "in proportion to their several degrees of apprehension." He added: "There is something in human nature, resulting from our very make and constitution, which renders us obnoxious to the pains of others, causes us to sympathise with them, and almost comprehends us in their case. It is grievous to see (and almost to hear of) any man, or even any animal what-ever, in torment."[129]

John Balguy, the Anglican Archdeacon of Westminster to whom Butler's *Analogy* was dedicated, could not be persuaded that animals themselves were capable of virtue. Nonetheless, like everyone else by this time he was convinced "there is no reason to doubt, but Brutes, as they are capable of being treated by us mercifully or cruelly, may be the *Objects* either of virtue or vice."[130]

6
The Utilitarian and Romantic Age

The Enlightenment spawned two competing modes of viewing the world: Utilitarianism and Romanticism. The Utilitarians provided the logical extension of Enlightenment thought, regarding all behaviour as self-interested, but, anticipating the theories of the criminologist Cesare Beccaria, proclaiming enlightened self-interest as the path to "the greatest happiness of the greatest number," a phrase coined in Britain by the Unitarian Joseph Priestley in his *Essay on Government* (1768). The maximization of pleasure and the minimization of pain were the appropriate motives for every action, and each policy and legislative proposal was to be judged by an arithmetical calculation of its contributions to that end: what Jeremy Bentham called the "felicific calculus."

The Romantics, however, rejected what they saw as the unidimensional conceptions of the Utilitarians, proclaiming instead diversity, the passions, the unfathomable mysteries, an intuitive moral sense, the wonders of nature, and the virtue of the common man. "The essential passions of the heart," wrote Wordsworth, "find a better soil" among the humble and rustic – the Romantics replaced competition and individualism with community, which, according to the Utilitarians, was a mere figment of the intellectual imagination – "The Community is a fictitious *body*," avowed Bentham. To beauty the Romantics added the sublime, an awe of nature that respected the weeds as well as the roses, the beetle as well as the lion. Thus Wordsworth in *The Prelude* (1805): "Each shrub is sacred, and each weed divine." To sympathy they added empathy – though the term had not yet been coined – not merely a respect for, but an identity with, our fellow creatures. Of course, not all Romantics laid equal stress on these elements. Moreover, there were two distinct aspects to Romanticism, a radical Rousseauian variant, as with Shelley, Byron, and Blake – despite Blake's hatred of Rousseau's secularism – and a more conservative strain derived ostensibly from Burke, though almost certainly by extending his aesthetical, and perhaps even political, principles to a point where Burke would have scarce recognized his influence. The Lake Poets, Wordsworth, Coleridge, and Southey, numbered themselves among the Burkean adherents.[1] Some of the Gothic Romantics, such as Ann Radcliffe in her novels, managed to find an explicit and equal place for Rousseau and Burke, an unlikely yet not entirely antithetical juxtaposition.[2] (Radcliffe's estate also helped save the early SPCA from a financial crisis.)

Despite their competing, indeed antagonistic, frameworks of thought, Utilitarians and Romantics alike were able to offer the animals an honourable place in their schema, the former deeming animal pleasures and pains worthy of consideration along with those of humans, the latter relying more on a direct compassion for the very lives of their fellow sentient beings. In fact, the differing modes of expression of the Utilitarians and the Romantics served to obscure their common humanity. Philosophy, after all, is in part a raising to the level of consciousness what we already feel in our souls – "guts," if one prefers – and providing those intuitions with a formal means of expression which allows us to order and comprehend them better. Often our expressions are by degree controlled by the mode of conceptualization we have selected, the ideology by which we have been convinced or to which we have been converted. But what we deem appropriate in practice is less subject to that control. Thus, while Utilitarians and Romantics expressed their values in widely differing forms, they continued to share a common humanity, a common respect for the well-being of other species – except, of course, those whose self-interests remained unenlightened, those whose intuited moral sense was tainted by rationalization, and those who were successfully socialized to ignore the gentle and primeval stirrings in their breasts.

Jeremy Bentham

Jeremy Bentham (1758-1832), a writer on jurisprudence and political philosophy, summed up previous eighteenth-century animal ethical thought, much of which had stressed the importance of pain and suffering endured by the animals, in a footnote made famous by the animal liberationists. In his *Introduction to the Principles of Morals and Legislation* (1789) he reasoned that if "the blackness of the skin" does not give us a right to exploitation, neither does the number of legs, the degree of reason, or the capacity for conversation. "The day may come when the rest of the animal creation may acquire those rights which never could have been withheld from them but by the hand of tyranny ... A full grown horse or dog is beyond comparison a more rational as well as a more conversible animal, than an infant of a day or a week or even a month old. But suppose the case were otherwise, what would it avail? The question is not, can they *reason*? nor can they *talk*? but, can they *suffer*?"[3]

In *The Principles of Penal Law* (1811) Bentham averred: "It ought to be lawful to kill animals, but not to torment them. Death by artificial means, may be made less painful than natural death: the methods of accomplishing this deserve to be studied and made an object of policy. Why should the law refuse its protection to any sensitive being? The time will come when humanity will extend its mantle over everything which breathes."[4] And the law would change in time, even if not to the extent or degree many would have wished. The changes would be implemented around the same time as, and often earlier than, the legal moves to extend the franchise, to provide legislative protection for children, women, and factory workers, and to abolish slavery and the slave trade. If the new legislative reformers put humans first in their intentions, they often succeeded earlier on animal welfare issues. Certainly, Bentham was far less persuaded than Voltaire, Rousseau, Mandeville, Thomson, Hartley, or even Paley, that it was inappropriate to kill animals for food, but he followed Henry Fielding in calling for legislative reforms to provide for animal protection.[5]

Johann Wolfgang von Goethe

Like many other nations, Germany was giving greater intellectual consideration to the nonhuman realm by the close of the eighteenth century. For example, the Catholic Coadjutor (*Suffragan*) Bishop of Mainz, C.T. von Dalberg, argued in his *Von den Wahren Grenzen der Wirksamkeit des Staats in Beziehung auf seine Mitglieder* (1793) (On the True Limits of the State's Action in Relation to its Members) that the state may neither command nor permit unnecessary tormenting or wasteful destruction of the nonhuman creation, whether animal, vegetable, or mineral.[6]

None, however, gave these matters as much consideration as did Germany's most celebrated mind, Johann Wolfgang von Goethe (1749-1832). Perhaps the most complete polymath since Leonardo[7] and Athanasius Kircher (1602-80), Goethe was not only Germany's finest dramatist but was also an accomplished novelist and poet, and undertook extensive research in physics, botany, and zoology. His best-known works are perhaps *Faust*, in which he developed, parenthetically almost, a rudimentary theory of evolution which he had first mooted in the 1780s,[8] *Dichtung und Wahrheit* (Poetry and Truth), and *Die Leiden des Jungen Werthers* (The Sorrows of Young Werther), but it was in his minor poems that he most advanced the cause of animals.

In his c. 1785 poem "Das Göttliche" (Divinity) Goethe tells us that the difference between man and animals can be reduced to the possession of an explicit ethical sense alone:

For that alone
Distinguishes him
From all beings
That we know.[9]

In *Faust* he acknowledged animals his "brothers" ("You" is the deity):

You lead the ranks of living creatures before me
To teach me to know my brothers
Of the still bush, of the air and water.[10]

It was, however, in his c. 1803 poem "Metamorphose der Tiere" (Metamorphosis of Animals), on which he had been working intermittently since around 1799, that he combined his primary art with the conclusions of his research into animal anatomy, and advanced in novel form the principle of animal continuity, something he had discovered as early as 1783 in the writings of Leibniz. Goethe gave the idea of the Great Chain, of animal continuity, a new emphasis that elevated the status of animals beyond the efforts of Locke, Pope, and Leibniz who had employed the Chain concept to similar animal-friendly purposes. While avowing the Kantian categorical imperative, Goethe, who thought of himself as intellectually close to Kant,[11] more so than any other of his contemporaries, is at the same time denying Kant's view of the human as the only genuinely conscious animal and as the sole purposeful end in itself. In contrast to Kant, Leibniz had allowed all beings, within their allotted place in the scale, the right to say "I." Goethe affirms Leibniz, but draws the ranks of the scale ever tighter, asserting explicitly for the first time in the Kantian language of the categorical imperative that each animal is an end in itself.

The poem has to be understood in the context of prevailing thought, and not only that of Leibniz and Kant, but also of Spinoza, Blumenbach, von Humboldt, and Dalberg, at the very least.[12] It is a powerful indictment of those who conceived of animals as incompletely formed humans, and those who thought of humans as "more perfect" than other animals. Goethe accepts that Nature has bestowed her gifts more generously on the most complex creatures, but nonetheless he insists that each animal is fully formed for its own ends, is itself a completeness, a perfection, and hence a purpose in itself. It is perfectly formed as the being that it is with the needs that it has. Each animal is a *Zweck*, a purposeful whole, an end in itself. If humans have greater capacities for thought than do other species, it is only an accident of nature's bounty and not something for which humans deserve credit or applause. All animals come from a single archetype – again we witness the evolutionary idea in rudimentary form – and all possess certain advantages. All animals, humans included, are constrained to be nothing other than that for which nature constructed them. All animals, for Goethe, have their own limited natures that prevent the energy they use to develop teeth, for example, from being used to develop horns on the head, for example. Within that necessity there lies freedom. Life is a tension between will and form, but when they are in conflict form will prevail. The idea of "will" as the force of biological change was a popular one. It played a role in Lamarck's theory of evolutionary "transformism," developed in 1801 and extended in 1809, and an even greater role in

Erasmus Darwin's evolutionary theories of the closing years of the eighteenth century. Goethe stood in opposition to them, and has, of course, been vindicated by history.

Metamorphosis of Animals

Be prepared, and dare to climb the last step
To this summit; proffer me your hand and freely open your
Eyes onto the broad field of nature. Her goddess
Distributes the rich gifts of life, but feels no such
Concerns as do mortal mothers to secure their
Progeny's nourishment; she does not find it seemly:
For doubly she appointed the highest law, limited
Every life, gave it measured need, and unmeasured talent.
To be sure, in her distribution she quietly favoured
The merry efforts of the children of multiple needs;
Untaught, they pursue their determined end.

Each animal is an end in itself, it emerges fully formed
From Nature's loins, and produces perfect offspring.
All its limbs are formed in accord with eternal laws,
And the most unusual form preserves the secret of the primal pattern.
Thus is every mouth skilled at seizing food which is
Appropriate for the body, even if it is weakly and toothless
Or is as powerfully dentured as the jaw; in each case
An appropriate organ dispatches the food to the other body parts.
As well, each foot, whether long or short, moves
In harmony with the purpose of the animal and its needs.
Thus is full, pure health passed on to the children from the mother
For all parts of the body are in harmony and efficient for living.
And the way of life reacts powerfully on the forms of all
In return. Thus is orderly development demonstrated,
Yielding to change from externally operating forces.
Yet within is found the power of the more noble creatures
Though bound by the holy limits of life's generation.
No god extends these boundaries, nature respects them.
For only thus limited was perfection ever possible.

Yet within a spirit appears to struggle mightily
To break through the boundaries, to create capricious
Forms wilfully; yet what it begins it begins in vain.
For even though it exerts itself on those limbs
To equip them powerfully, in response do other limbs
Already wither; the burden of over-balance
Destroys all attempts at beauty of form and all pure movement.

If you see a special advantage somehow granted
To any one creature, ask yourself likewise in what manner
It suffers a deficiency in some other respect; and if you
Seek with inquiring mind, there
You will find the key to all development.
For no animal whose upper jaw is fully lined
With teeth had borne a horn on its forehead,
And for this reason is the eternal mother quite
Unable to horn lions, though she were to muster all of her might.
For she has insufficient power to plant both rows of teeth and to promote antlers
   and horns.[13]

According to Goethe's biographer, Nicholas Boyle, after 1783, for Goethe, "the supreme religious issue is not the relation between men and gods ... but the relation between man and animals."[14] As a result of his botanical investigations, he had written "Metamorphosis of Plants" in 1789, in which he expressed the conviction that all plants are formed – metamorphosed – from a single archetype. His conception of the human-animal relationship is analogous. "Metamorphosis of Animals" could be interpreted as the culmination of the search stimulated by what Goethe referred to in *The Sorrows of Young Werther* as "the wonderful feeling with which my heart embraces Nature"[15] – even if in the "Metamorphosis of Animals" his pre-Darwinian conceptions hinder our appreciation of his dedication. Certainly, Goethe's cosmology is a complex and dated one, and only fully comprehensible in its historical context, but his elevation of animals as ends in themselves is paramount in the history of animal ethics. Any barriers to the recognition of animal worthiness that had been erected by Kant's philosophy were now removed, although there remained an acknowledgment of the importance of the Kantian revolution in language, conception, and imperative.

Johann Gottfried von Herder

Associate of Goethe, and philosophical leader in the *Sturm und Drang* (Storm and Stress) movement, Herder (1744-1803) thought of humans as possessing a cultural and organic superiority over other species. However, in his *Ideen zur Philosophie der Geschichte der Menschheit* (Ideas for a Philosophy of Human History) (1784-91) he expressed a view similar to that of Goethe, an intimate colleague of his at Weimar, in opposition to the notion that humans had perfected the capabilities of other species.

The human species has been praised for possessing in the most perfected form all the powers and capabilities of every other species. This is patently untrue. Not only is the assertion incapable of empirical proof; it is also logically insupportable, for it is self-contradictory. Clearly, if it were true, one power would cancel out the other and man would be the most wretched of creatures. For how could man at one and the same time bloom like a flower, feel his way like the spider, build like the bee, suck like the butterfly, and also possess the muscular strength of the lion, the trunk of the elephant and the skill of the beaver? Does he possess, nay does he comprehend, a single one of those powers, with that intensity, with which the animal enjoys and exercises it? ...

No creature, that we know of, has departed from its original organization or has developed in opposition to it. It can operate only with the powers inherent in its organization, and nature knew how to devise sufficient means to confine all living beings to the sphere allotted to them.[16]

For Herder, if humans have their superiorities, so too do other animals.

William and Dorothy Wordsworth

One of the early leaders of English Romanticism, William Wordsworth (1770-1850) was a prolific poet whose reputation in the latter part of his life was no less than it is today. Both his love of nature and his compassion for animals pervade his writings. If today we tend to think of poetry as a pretty appurtenance, a flight of fantasy, it is important to recall that prior to the twentieth century poetry was considered a most appropriate form of advancing a moral or political argument. Indeed, in the nineteenth century, British parliamentary debates, including those on animal welfare, were replete with quotations from the poets, particularly Wordsworth, to demonstrate the worthiness of the cause. Shelley was justified in calling poets the "unacknowledged legislators."

Wordsworth's *Hart-Leap Well* of 1800 is written in two parts. The first tells the traditional tale of the knightly hunter's purported respect for the stag he hunts and slays. The second reports Nature's revenge for the cruelty inflicted on one of her own.

The Shepherd stopped, and that same story told
Which in my former rhyme I have rehearsed.
"A jolly place," said he, "in times of old!
But something ails it now: the spot is curst ...

"There's neither dog nor heifer, horse nor sheep,
Will wet his lips within that cup of stone;
And often times, when all are fast asleep,
The water doth send forth a dolorous groan.

"Some say that here a murder has been done,
And blood cries out for blood: but for my part,
I've guessed, when I've been sitting in the sun,
That it was all for that unhappy Hart.

"What thoughts must through the creature's brain have past!
Even from the topmost stone, upon the steep,

Are but three bounds – and look, Sir, at this last –
O Master! it has been a cruel leap.

"For thirteen hours he ran a desperate race;
And in my simple mind we cannot tell
What cause the Hart might have to love this place,
And come and make his death-bed near the well.

"Here on the grass, perhaps asleep he sank,
Lulled by the fountain in the summer-tide;
This water was perhaps the first he drank
When he had wandered from his mother's side.

"In April here beneath the flowering thorn
He heard the birds their morning carols sing;
And he perhaps, for aught we know, was born
Not half a furlong from that self-same spring.

"Now, here is neither grass nor pleasant shade;
The sun on drearier hollow never shone;
So will it be, as I have often said,
Till trees and stones and fountain, all are gone."

"Grey-headed Shepherd, thou hast spoken well;
Small difference lies between thy creed and mine;
This Beast not unobserved by Nature fell;
His death was mourned by sympathy divine.

"The Being that is in the clouds and air,
That is in the green leaves among the groves,
Maintains a deep and reverential care
For the unoffending creatures whom he loves ...

"One lesson, Shepherd, let us two divide,
Taught both by what she shows, and what conceals;
Never to blend our pleasure or our pride
With sorrow of the meanest thing that feels."[17]

Hart-Leap Well is a spot in Yorkshire, named, according to local lore, after the hunt which Wordsworth describes in part one of the poem.

Wordsworth's general appreciation of the animal realm is captured in a short extract from his remarkable *Ode: Intimations of Immortality from Recollections of Early Childhood*, written around 1803-6.

Ye blessèd Creatures, I have heard the call
Ye to each other make; I see
The heavens laugh with you in your jubilee;
My heart is at your festival.
My head hath its coronal,
The fulness of your bliss, I feel – I feel it all.[18]

Following the death of the beloved family pet, Music, Wordsworth's
compassion and admiration for animals found expression in "Tribute"
(published in 1807).

We grieved for thee, and wished thy end were past;
And willingly have laid thee here at last;
For thou hadst lived till every thing that cheers
In thee had yielded to the weight of years;
Extreme old age had wasted thee away,
And left thee but a glimmering of the day;
Thy ears were deaf, and feeble were thy knees, –
I saw thee stagger in the summer breeze,
Too weak to stand against its sportive breath,
And ready for the gentlest stroke of death.
It came, and we were glad; yet tears were shed;
Both man and woman wept when thou were dead;
Not only for a thousand thoughts that were,
Old household thoughts, in which thou hadst thy share;
But for some precious boons vouchsafed to thee,
Found scarcely anywhere in like degree!
For love, that comes wherever life and sense
Are given by God, in thee was most intense;
A chain of heart, a feeling of the mind,
A tender sympathy, which did thee bind
Not only to us Men, but to thy Kind:
Yea, for thy fellow-brutes in thee we saw
A soul of love, love's intellectual law: –
Hence, if we wept, it was not done in shame;
Our tears from passion and from reason came,
And, therefore, shalt thou be an honoured name![19]

The essence of Wordsworth's sensibility to animals is found in his
"Lines left upon a Yew-tree" (1795). The closing stanza reads:

If Thou be one whose heart the holy forms
Of young imagination have kept pure,
Stranger! henceforth be warned; and know that pride,
Howe'er disguised in its own majesty,
Is littleness; that he who feels contempt

For any living thing hath faculties
Which he has never used; that thought with him
Is in its infancy. The man whose eye
Is ever on himself doth look on one,
The least of Nature's works, who might move
The wise man to that scorn which wisdom holds
Unlawful, ever. O be wiser, Thou!
Instructed that true knowledge leads to love;
True dignity abides with him alone
Who, in the silent hour of inward thought,
Can still suspect, and still revere himself,
In lowliness of heart.[20]

Dorothy Wordsworth (1771-1855) – "Wordsworth's exquisite sister," Coleridge called her – kept an enthralling diary of her life with her brother at Alfoxden and Grasmere. While many animals are described in her writing, it was the birds which most captured her affection.

Tuesday, 15th [June, 1802]   I spoke of the little Birds keeping us company – and William told me that very morning a bird had perched upon his leg. He had been lying very still and had watched this little creature, it had come under the Bench where he was sitting and then flew up to his leg; he thoughtfully stirred himself to look further at it and it flew onto the apple tree above him. It was a little young creature, that had just left its nest, equally unacquainted with man and unaccustomed to struggle against storms and winds. While it was upon the apple tree the wind blew about the stiff boughs and the Bird seemed bemazed and not strong enough to strive with it. The swallows come to the sitting-room window as if wishing to build but I am afraid they will not have the courage for it, but I believe they will build at my room window. They twitter and make a bustle and a little chearful song hanging against the panes of glass, with their soft white bellies close to the glass, and their forked fish-like tails. They swim round and round and again they come. – It was a sweet evening ...

Saturday 19th   The swallows were very busy under my window this morning ... The shutters were closed, but I hear the Birds singing. There was our own Thrush shouting with an impertinent shout – so it sounded to me. The morning was still, the twittering of the little Birds was very gloomy. The owls had hooted a ¼ of an hour before, now the cocks were crowing ...

Friday 25th   When I rose I went just before tea into the garden. I looked up at my Swallow's nest and it was gone. It had fallen down. Poor little creatures they could not be more distressed than I was. I went upstairs to look at the Ruins. They lay in a large heap upon the window ledge; these Swallows had been ten days employed in building their nest, and it seemed to be almost finished. I had watched them early in the morning, in the day many and many a time and in the evenings when it was almost dark. I had seen them sitting together side by side in their unfinished nest both morning and night. When they first came about the window they used to hang against the panes, with their white Bellies and their forked tales looking like fish, but then they fluttered and sang their own little twittering song. As soon as the nest was broad enough, a sort of ledge for them they sate both mornings and evenings, when William was at Eusemere, for more than an hour. Every now and then there was a feeling motion in their wings, a sort of tremulousness and they sang a low song to one another.

At this point a page has been torn from the diary, covering three days. Unfortunately, it will have included Dorothy Wordsworth's description of the first efforts at rebuilding the nest.

[*Tuesday, 29th June*]   It is now 8 o'clock I will go and see if my swallows are on their nest. Yes! there they are side by side looking down into the garden. I have been out on purpose to see their faces ...

Tuesday, 5th July   The swallows have completed their beautiful nest ...

On 9 July Dorothy and William were due to leave Grasmere for a visit to London and she was forced to leave her swallow neighbours.

Thursday 7th   The Swallows stole in and out of their nest, and sate there *whiles* quite still, *whiles* they sung low for 2 minutes or more at a time just like a muffled Robin ... I must leave them the well the garden the Roses, all Dear creatures!! they sang last night after I was in bed – seemed to be singing to one another, just before they settled to rest for the night. Well, I must go. Farewell.[21]

Samuel Taylor Coleridge
Poet, critic, theologian and philosopher, and close friend of Charles Lamb and the Wordsworths (though also occasionally a bitter enemy of William), Samuel Taylor Coleridge (1772-1834) is today best remembered for "The Rime of the Ancient Mariner," *Kubla Khan*, and *Biographia Literaria*. A Lake Romantic like Wordsworth and Southey, Coleridge too delighted in the world of nature and its creatures.

Like Sterne before him, Coleridge showed a special concern for the denigrated ass.

To a Young Ass: Its Mother being tethered near it
Poor little Foal of an oppressed race!
I love the languid patience of thy face:
And oft with gentle hand I give thee bread,
And clap thy ragged coat, and pat thy head.
But what thy dulled spirits hath dismay'd,
That never thou dost sport along the glade?
And (most unlike the nature of things young)
That earthward still thy moveless head is hung?

Do thy prophetic fears anticipate,
Meek child of misery! thy future fate?
The starving meal, and all the thousand aches
'Which patient Merit of the Unworthy takes'?
Or is thy sad heart thrill'd with filial pain
To see thy wretched mother's shortened chain?
And truly, very piteous is *her* lot –
Chain'd to a log within a narrow spot,
Where the close-eaten grass is scarcely seen,
While sweet around her waves the tempting green!

Poor Ass! thy master should have learnt to show
Pity – best taught by fellowship of Woe!
For much I fear that *He* lives like thee,
Half famish'd in a land of Luxury!
How *askingly* its footsteps hither bend?
It seems to say, "And have I then *one* friend?"
Innocent foal! thou poor despis'd forlorn!
I hail thee *Brother* – spite of the fool's scorn!
And fain would take thee with me in the Dell
Of peace and mild Equality to dwell,
Where Toil shall call the charmer Health his bride,
And laughter tickle Plenty's ribless side!
How thou wouldst toss thy heels in gamesome play,
And frisk about, as lamb or kitten gay!
Yea! And more musically sweet to me
Thy dissonant harsh bray of joy would be,
Than warbled melodies that soothe to rest
The aching of pale Fashion's vacant breast![22]

In "The Rime of the Ancient Mariner" (1797-1800) Coleridge makes frequent allusion to his animal sympathies.

Part IV

By the light of the Moon he beholdeth
God's creatures of the great calm

Beyond the shadow of the ship,
I watched the water snakes;
They moved in tracks of shining white,
   And when they reared, the elfish light
Fell off in hoary flakes.

Within the shadow of the ship,
I watched their rich attire:
Blue, glossy green, and velvet black,
They coiled and swam; and every track
Was a flash of golden fire.

Their beauty and their happiness	O happy living things! no tongue Their beauty might declare: A spring of love gushed from my heart,
He blesseth them in his heart	And I blessed them unaware: Sure my kind saint took pity on me, And I blessed them unaware.
The spell begins to break.	The self-same moment I could pray; And from my neck so free The Albatross fell off, and sank Like lead into the sea.

Part VII

*And to teach by his own example, love
  and reverence to all things that
  God made and loveth.*
	Farewell, farewell! but this I tell
	To thee, thou Wedding-Guest!
	He prayeth well, who loveth well
	Both man and bird and beast.
	He prayeth best, who loveth best
	All things both great and small;
	For the dear God who loveth us,
	He made and loveth all.[23]

In discussing the Socinian creed in *A Lay Sermon* (1817) Coleridge expressed sympathy for the view that animals possessed immortal souls – a matter about which Wordsworth had no doubts – and he acknowledged the inferior moral character of humans. He also recognized human reason as but another form of instinct, comparable to the instincts of other species.

[I]f it should be asked, why this resurrection, or re-creation is confined to the human animal, the answer must be – that more than this has not been revealed. But some have added, and in my opinion much to their credit, that they hope, it may be the case with the Brutes likewise, as they see no sufficient reason to the contrary. And truly upon *their* scheme I agree with them ... [Men] are *on the whole* distinguished from other Beasts incomparably more to their *disadvantage,* by Lying, Treachery, Ingratitude, Massacre, Thirst of Blood, and by Sensualities which both in sort and degree it would be libelling their Brother-beasts to call *bestial,* than to their advantage by a greater extent of Intellect. And what indeed, abstracted from the Free-will, could this intellect be but a more shewy instinct? of more various application indeed, but far less secure, useful, or adapted to its purposes, than the instinct of Birds, insects, and the like.[24]

Robert Southey

Robert Southey (1774-1843) became Poet Laureate in 1813, being succeeded on his death by Wordsworth. He is best remembered for his biographies of Lord Nelson (1813) and John Wesley (1820) but his poems *The Battle of Blenheim* and *The Holly Tree* also retain their appeal. Southey may be thought to have had greater affection for nature as a whole than for its constituent creatures, but in, for example, "To Contemplation" (1797) he clearly delights in "The Red-breast on the blossom'd spray" which "Warbles with her latest lay," "the dull beetle's drowsy flight," "the horn-eyed snail" creeping "o'er his long moon-glittering trail" and the "living light" of "the glowworms."[25] It is in his mournful "On the Death of a Favourite Old Spaniel" (1797) that his affection is seen at its most intense.

And they have drown'd thee then at last! poor Phillis!
The burthen of old age was heavy on thee,
And yet thou should'st have lived! what tho' thine eye
Was dim, and watch'd no more with eager joy
The wonted call that on thy dull sense sunk
With fruitless repetition, the warm Sun
Would still have cheer'd thy slumber, thou didst love
To lick the hand that fed thee, and tho' past
Youth's active season, even Life itself
Was comfort. Poor old friend! most earnestly
Would I have pleaded for thee: thou hadst been
Still the companion of my childish sports,
And, as I roam'd o'er Avon's woody cliffs,
From many a day-dream has thy short quick bark
Recall'd my wandering soul. I have beguil'd
Often the melancholy hours at school,
Sour'd by some little tyrant, with the thought
Of distant home, and I remember'd then
Thy faithful fondness: for not meant the joy,
Returning at the pleasant holydays,
I felt from thy dumb welcome. Pensively
Sometimes have I remark'd thy slow decay,
Feeling myself change too, and musing much
On many a sad vicissitude of Life!
Ah poor companion! when thou followedst last,
Thy master's parting footsteps to the gate
That clos'd for ever on him, thou didst lose
Thy truest friend, and none was left to plead
For the old age of brute fidelity!
But fare thee well! Mine is no narrow creed,
And he who gave thee being did not frame

The mystery of life to be the sport
Of merciless man! there is another world
For all that live and move – a better one!
Where the proud bipeds, who would fain confine
INFINITE GOODNESS to the little bounds
Of their own charity, may envy thee![26]

Southey also wrote of cats that

A house is never perfectly furnished for enjoyment unless there is a child in it rising three years old, and a kitten rising six weeks. Kitten is in the animal world what the rosebud is in the garden; the one the most beautiful of all young creatures, the other the loveliest of all opening flowers.[27]

That his was not, indeed, "a narrow creed" restricted to humans and companion animals, Southey made clear when he described Portuguese bull-fighting (in which the animal is taunted but not killed) as "a damnable sport"[28] and when he complained that a "bittern was shot and eaten at Keswick" by a young Cambridge student "for which shooting I vituperate him in spirit whenever I think of it."[29] And, like Wordsworth, he readily accepted that animals share in any afterlife that might exist.

Lord Byron

George Gordon, Lord Byron (1788-1824), was both the darling and the scourge of his generation. He was a social outcast for his putative sexual relationship with his sister, for his religious skepticism, and for his life of dissipation; but he was also admired for his poetry – and begrudgingly for his bravado. Among his more famous works are *Childe Harold's Pilgrimage* (1812) and *Don Juan* (1819-24), a lyric poem filled with cynicism and abhorrence of convention.

Byron's love for his dog Boatswain was legendary. Boatswain's epitaph ran:

Near this spot
Are deposited the remains of one
Who possessed Beauty without vanity,
Strength without insolence,
Courage without Ferocity,
And all the Virtues of man without his Vices.
This Praise, which would be unmeaning Flattery
If inscribed over human ashes,
Is but a just tribute to the memory of
Boatswain, a Dog,
Who was born at Newfoundland, May 1803
And died at Newstead Abbey, 18 Nov, 1808[30]

The "Inscription" to Boatswain was as condemnatory of man as laudatory of the dog.

When some proud son of man returns to earth,
Unknown to glory, but upheld by birth,
The sculptor's art exhausts the pomp of woe,
And storied urns record who rest below:
When all is done, upon the tomb is seen,
Not what he was, but what he should have been:
But the poor dog, in life the firmest friend,
The first to welcome, foremost to defend,
Who labours, fights, lives, breathes for him alone.
Unhonour'd falls, unnoticed all his worth,
Denied in heaven, the soul he held on earth,
While man, vain insect! hopes to be forgiven,
And claims himself a sole exclusive heaven.
Oh man! thou feeble tenant of an hour,
Debased by slavery or corrupt by power,
Who knows thee well must quit thee with disgust,
Degraded mass of animated dust!
Thy love is lust, thy friendship all a cheat,
Thy smiles hypocrisy, thy words deceit!
By nature vile, ennobled but by name,
Each kindred brute might bid thee blush for shame.
Ye! who perchance behold this simple urn,
Pass on – it honours none you wish to mourn:
To mark a friend's remains these stones arise;
I never knew but one, – and here he lies.
(Inscription on the tomb of a favourite Newfoundland dog buried at Newstead
    Abbey, 1808)[31]

In *Cain* (1821) Byron expressed sympathy for the serpent, and for the animals that must die because of human sin in the Garden of Eden. Moreover, he sides emphatically with Cain against his brother on the issue of sacrifice because it entails the cruel and unnecessary killing of an animal. In *Don Juan* (1823), Byron takes up the cause of the fish.

And angling too, that solitary vice,
Whatever Isaac Walton sings or says,
The quaint, old, cruel coxcomb in his gullet
Should have a hook, and a small trout to pull it.[32]

Byron was following **Thomas Young,** who had written in *An Essay on Humanity to Animals* (1798): "It must be observed that fishing with any *living* bait, is to be condemned for the same reason as fishing with the worm: in all such instances we torture *two* animals at once for our amusement; in others, only *one.*"[33]

Likewise, **Charles Lamb,** of *Tales from Shakespeare* (1807) and *Essays of Elia* (1820-5) fame, wrote in 1799 of anglers as "patient tyrants, meek inflictors of pangs intolerable, cool devils."[34] Two minor poets had offered similar strictures. One, **John Bidlake,** Oxford D.D. and schoolmaster, tells us in "The Sea" (1796):

> Cruel delight! From native beds to drag
> The wounded fools, and spoil their silv'ry scales
> And spotted pride, writh'd on the tort'rous hook,
> In patient suff'rance dumb ... [35]

The other, the satirist **John Wolcot** (1738-1819), writing under the pseudonym of Peter Pindar, is disturbed that he "cannot meet the lamb-kin's asking eye" knowing the cruel fate in store for her. Nor can he abide violence to birds and their nests. But his greatest sorrow is for the fish.

> And you, O natives of the flood, should play
> Unhurt amid your chrystal realms, and sleep
> No hook should tear you from your loves away;
> No net surrounding fork its fatal sweep ... [36]

Ann Radcliffe expressed the same sentiment in *The Mysteries of Udolpho* (1794): "A basket of provisions was sent thither, with books and Emily's lute; for fishing tackle [M. St. Aubert] had no use, for he never could find amusement in torturing or destroying."[37]

William Blake

A prophetic visionary influenced by the devout Emanuel Swedenborg and the mystical Jakob Boehme, William Blake (1757-1827) stressed the spirit of the imagination and the authority of the passions. He was both an engraver of the majestic and a poet of the sublime. His works are sometimes almost unfathomable, but he had a profound influence on the Romantic mind. He hints to his readers that he can see in life's experience things that less gifted humans can never fully comprehend. Fortunately, much, though not all, of his writing about animals is more accessible to the average reader. To be sure, in the *Book of Thel* (1789) Blake offers us an enigmatic account of the Great Chain, emphasizing the communal spirit from the earthworm, and the very clay in which the worm lives, all the way to the seraphim. On the plates for the series of engravings *For Children: The Gates of Paradise* he stresses a mystical kinship: "I have said to the Worm: Thou art my mother and my sister."[38] The "Auguries of Innocence" is, however, far less opaque.

> A Robin Red breast in a Cage
> Puts all Heaven in a Rage.
> A Dove house fill'd with Doves & Pigeons
> Shudders Hell thro' all its regions.
> A dog starv'd at his Master's gate

Predicts the ruin of the State.
A Horse misus'd upon the Road
Calls to Heaven for Human blood.
Each outcry of the hunted Hare
A fibre from the brain does tear.
A Skylark wounded in the wing,
A Cherubim does cease to sing.
The Game Cock clip'd & arm'd for fight
Does the Rising Sun affright.
Every Wolf's & Lion's howl
Raises from Hell a Human Soul.
The wild Deer wand'ring here & there
Keeps the Human Soul from care ...
He who shall hurt the little Wren
Shall ne'er be belov'd by Men.
He who the Ox to wrath has mov'd
Shall never be by woman loved.
The wanton Boy that kills the Fly
Shall feel the Spider's enmity.
He who torments the Chafer's sprite
Weaves a bower in endless Night ...
Kill not the Moth nor Butterfly
For the Last Judgment draweth nigh.[39]

As in the *Book of Thel*, Blake stresses the unity of life in "The Fly."

Little Fly,
Thy summer's play
My thoughtless hand
Has brush'd away.

Am not I
A fly like thee?
Or art not thou a man like me?

For I dance
And drink & sing.
Till some blind hand
Shall brush my wing.

If thought is life
And strength and breath,
And the want
Of thought is death.

Then am I
A happy fly
If I live
Or if I die.[40]

Blake's most famous poem "The Tyger" expresses human incomprehension of the mind of the deity, as well as absolute awe at the mysterious diversity of the animal realm. He leaves us wondering how both the tiger and the lamb could be designed by the same author.

Tyger, Tyger, burning bright
In the forests of the night,
What immortal hand or eye
Could frame thy fearful symmetry?

In what distant deeps or skies
Burnt the fire of thine eyes?
On what wings dare he aspire?
What the hand dare seize the fire?

And what shoulder, & what art,
Could twist the sinews of thy heart?
And when thy heart began to beat,
What dread hand? & what dread feet?

What the hammer? what the chain,
In what furnace was thy brain?
What the anvil? what dread grasp
Dare its deadly terror's clasp?

When the stars threw down their spears
And water'd heaven with their tears,
Did he smile his work to see?
Did he who made the lamb make thee?

Tyger, Tyger, burning bright
In the forests of the night,
What immortal hand or eye
Did frame thy fearful symmetry?[41]

Blake's recognition is that while we have love for the lamb it is awe we feel for the tiger. Implicit in his message is that predators and prey have different needs and purposes. As he wrote in *The Marriage of Heaven and Hell* (1793), "One Law for the Lion & Ox is Oppression."[42] Again, as with Leonardo, the incompatibilities of all life, however holy, is, to borrow

Wordsworth's words, "beyond human estimate." Nonetheless, as he avowed at the close of *Visions of the Daughters of Albion*, Blake believed all life is sacred.

> "And trees & birds & beasts & men, behold their eternal joy!
> "Arise, you little glancing wings, and sing your infant joy!
> "Arise, and drink your bliss, for every thing that lives is holy."[43]

In the *Book of Thel* he adds: "every thing that lives/Lives not alone, nor for itself."[44]

Whereas Goethe treats individual animals as ends in themselves, for Blake the greater emphasis is on community and belonging: We all live for each other. This bears comparison with the claim of the Scottish master storyteller of Romanticism, Walter Scott, that he had "a fellowship with the sheep and lambs."[45]

Percy Bysshe Shelley

Author of *Queen Mab* (1813) and *Prometheus Unbound* (1820), Percy Bysshe Shelley (1792-1822) was, by consensus, one of the greatest English poets. A perusal of his verse might suggest an author with a greater love for love, beauty, politics, and poetry itself, than for animals, or perhaps even humans, but his prose tells another story. Converted to vegetarianism, perhaps by John Frank Newton or Joseph Ritson,[46] he penned two pamphlets against the eating of flesh (the second not being published until the twentieth century) in which he argued that vegetarianism was natural to humans, that it promoted health and longevity, and that it permitted food animals to escape the consequences of their harmful domestication and wild animals the cruelties inflicted upon them by human predators. In the first pamphlet, *A Vindication of Natural Diet: being One of a Series of Notes to Queen Mab, A Philosophical Poem*, he wrote:

> Prometheus, (who represents the human race) effected some great change in the condition of his nature, and applied fire to culinary purposes; thus inventing an expedient for screening from his disgust the horrors of the shambles ... It is only by softening and disguising dead flesh by culinary preparation, that it is rendered susceptible of mastication or digestion; and that the sight of its bloody juices and raw horror, does not excite intolerable loathing and disgust. Let the advocate of animal food, force himself to a decisive experiment on its fitness, and as Plutarch recommends, tear a living lamb with his teeth, and plunging his head into its vitals, slake his thirst with the steaming blood; when fresh from the deed of horror let him revert to the irresistible instincts of nature that would rise in judgment against it, and say, Nature formed me for such work as this. Then, and only then, would he be consistent ...
>
> Is it to be believed that a being of gentle feelings, rising from his meal of roots, would take delight in sports of blood ...

[He who is] unvitiated by the contagion of the world ... will hate the brutal pleasures of the chase by instinct; it will be a contemplation full of horror and disappointment to his mind, that beings capable of the gentlest and most admirable
sympathies, should take delight in the death-pangs and last convulsions of dying
animals ...

NEVER TAKE ANY SUBSTANCE INTO THE STOMACH THAT ONCE HAD LIFE.[47]

It is unfortunate that Shelley's second, undated, and untitled piece, but
called by his editors *On the Vegetable System of Diet*, remained unpublished
until the twentieth century, and remains largely unknown, for it is altogether a more persuasive piece than the first. While Shelley repeats some
of what he had argued in the first pamphlet, he adds a new gloss.

It demanded surely no great profundity of anatomical research to perceive that
man has neither the fangs of a lion nor the claws of a tiger, that his instincts
are inimical to bloodshed, and that the food which is not to be eaten without the
most intolerable loathing until it is altered by the action of fire and disguised by the
addition of condiments, is not that food for which he is adapted by his physical
conditions. The bull must be degraded into an ox, the ram into the wether by an
unnatural and inhuman operation.*

... Sows big with young are indeed no longer stamped upon [to death] and suck-
ing pigs roasted alive; but lobsters are slowly boiled to death and express by their
inarticulate cries the dreadful agony they endure; chickens are mutilated and
imprisoned until they fatten, calves are bled to death that their flesh may appear
white: and a certain horrible process of torture furnishes brawn for the gluttonous
repasts with which Christians celebrate the anniversary of their Saviour's birth.
What beast of prey compels its victims to undergo such protracted, such severe
and such degrading torments? The single consideration that man cannot swallow
a piece of raw flesh would be sufficient to prove that the natural diet of the human
species did not consist in the carcases of butchered animals ...

Those who are persuaded of the point which is the object of this enquiry to
establish, are bound by the most sacred obligations of morality to adopt in practice
what he admits in theory ...

The very sight of animals in the fields who are destined to the axe must encourage obduracy if it fails to awaken compassion. The butchering of harmless animals
cannot fail to produce much of that spirit of insane and hideous exultation in which
the news of a victory is related altho' purchased by the massacre of a hundred
thousand men. If the use of animal food be in consequence, subversive to the
peace of human society, how unwarrantable is the injustice and the barbarity
which is exercised toward these miserable victims. They are called into existence by
human artifice *that they may drag out a short and miserable existence of slavery and
disease, that their bodies may be mutilated, their social feelings outraged.* It were
much better that a sentient being should never have existed, than that it should
have existed only to endure unmitigated misery.

---

* That is, castration, also condemned in the first essay.

Shelley here added a footnote to his concluding sentence: "The attachment of animals to their young is very strong. The monstrous sophism that beasts are pure unfeeling machines and do not reason scarcely requires a confutation."[48]

In *Prometheus Unbound* Shelley acknowledged that harm is in the first instance not always the consequence of cruel intent. He has Prometheus say:

> It doth repent me: words are quick and vain;
> Grief for a while is blind, and so was mine,
> I wish no living thing to suffer pain.[49]

In "Love's Philosophy" (1819) he avowed a universal spirit shared by all beings.

> Nothing in the world is single;
> All things by a law divine
> In one spirit meet and mingle ... [50]

In *The Revolt of Islam* (1817) he again condemns flesh-eating.

> Never again may blood of bird or beast
> Stain with its venomous stream a human feast,
> To the pure skies in accusation steaming.[51]

Robert Burns

Written sometimes in dialect, the poetry of Robert Burns (1759-96) has become broadly popular. "Flow Gently Sweet Afton," "My Heart's in the Highlands," "Tam O'Shanter," and "The Cotter's Saturday Night" are no less stirring today than in the late eighteenth century. In "To a Mouse" Burns acknowledges that technological advances have increased the human capacity to dominate and harm other species, but it is a capacity for which he has significant regret. In the poem "brattle" means "scamper," "pattle" means "plough staff."

To a Mouse, On turning her up in her Nest, with the Plough, November, 1785

> Wee, sleeket, cowran, tim'rous *beastie,*
> O, what a panic's in thy breastie!
> Thou need na start awa sae hasty,
>   Wi' bickering brattle!
> I wad be laith to rin an' chase thee,
>   Wi' murd'ring *pattle!*
>
> I'm truly sorry Man's dominion
> Has broken Nature's social union,
> An' justifies that ill opinion,
>   Which makes thee startle,

At me, thy poor, earth-born companion,
An' *fellow-mortal!* [52]

We encountered love for companion animals in the verse of Christopher Smart, William Wordsworth, Robert Southey, and Lord Byron, among others. In "Poor Mailie's Elegy" Burns's companion is neither cat nor dog but a ewe. The Bardie, that is bard, in the poem is Burns himself. "Dowie" is "sad."

Poor Mailie's Elegy
It's no the loss o warl's gear,
That could sae bitter draw the tear,
Or make our *Bardie,* dowie, wear
    The mourning weed:
He's lost a friend and neebor dear,
    In *Mailie* dead.

Thro' a' the town she trotted by him;
A lang half-mile she could descry him;
Wi' kindly bleat, when she did spy him.
    She ran wi' speed:
A friend mair faithfu' ne'er came nigh him.
    Than *Mailie* dead ... [53]

In "On Seeing a Wounded Hare" Burns added outrage to his sympathy for animals.

Inhuman Man! curse on thy barbarous art
    And blasted be thy murder-aiming eye;
    May never pity soothe thee with a sigh
Nor ever pleasure glad thy cruel heart!

Go live, poor wand'rer of the wood and field!
    The bitter little that of life remains:
    No more the thickening brakes and verdant plains
To thee a home, or food, or pastime yield.[54]

George Crabbe

Originally trained as a physician, George Crabbe (1754-1832) took up poetry, composing *The Library* (1781), *The Village* (1783), *The Parish Register* (1807), and *Tales of the Hall* (1819). His descriptions of rural life are a stern and grim rebuke to those who had written nostalgically of country life as an unbroken idyll – for example, Oliver Goldsmith in *The Deserted Village*. Crabbe depicts peasant life in the gruesome rawness of its poverty and its human cruelties, and has little time for the niceties of ethical considerations for animals when there is so little done to assuage the conditions of the rural poor. Yet, reflective of educated opinion in general, he found cock-fighting deplorable. There were some who found bull- and bear-baiting anathema and yet they could tolerate cock-fighting because they deemed it to be in the very nature of the cock.

> Here his poor Bird th' inhuman cocker brings,
> With spicy food th' impatient spirit feeds,
> And shouts and curses as the battle bleeds.
> Struck through the brain, depriv'd of both his eyes,
> The vanquish'd bird must combat till he dies;
> Must faintly peck at his victorious foe,
> And reel and stagger at each feeble blow:
> When fall'n, the savage grasps his dabbled plumes,
> His blood-stained arms, for other deaths assumes;
> And damns the craven fowl, that lost his stake,
> And only bled and perish'd for his sake.[55]

The long and hard fight for legislation against cruel "sports" was under-way when *The Parish Register* was written. Despite previous opposition, the new law, once passed, enjoyed widespread acceptance. The *Lincoln Gazette* referred to "this relic of feudal barbarism"[56] and the *Stamford Mercury* (the town of Stamford had remained the most vociferous opponent of legislation) wrote of "an unlawful and barbarous custom,"[57] while the *Monthly Review*, the *European*, the *London Magazine*, and, most especially, the *Gentleman's Magazine* had long offered support.

Sarah Trimmer

If Romantic verse was the stentorian voice of the "unacknowledged legislators," Utilitarian prose was no less emphatic and no less persuasive. It may even have been more powerful, for if verse swelled the heart, the prosaic spelled out the reasons, the details, and the remedies more easily. Prompted by the authoritative voice of John Locke on the importance of education to eliminate cruelty, some of the most effective animal welfare literature was directed to the instruction of the young.

Several books in the last quarter of the eighteenth century were thus oriented, including Thomas Percival's *A Father's Instructions* (in three parts, 1775-1800), Anna Laetitia Barbauld's hymns and fables, Sarah Trimmer's tales, including her *Fabulous Histories Designed for the Instruction of Children Respecting their Treatment of Animals* (1786), Thomas Day's *The History of Sandford and Merton* (in three parts, 1783-9) and *The History of Little Jack* (1788), and Mary Wollstonecraft's *Original Stories from Real Life* (1788). If these books are, in general, uniformly mawkish and sententious, they are at least instructive of the benevolent and industrious ideals they hoped to implant in contemporary youth.

Sarah Trimmer (1741-1810) was the most popular of these writers, who, if occasionally excessively sentimental, nonetheless had important points to make against the credulous. Commenting on the *Learned Pig*, famous in London at that time, she offers the kind of advice we customarily hear today with regard to circuses.

"And do you think, mamma," said Harriet, "that the Pig knows the letters and can really spell the words?" "I think it possible, my dear, for the Pig to be taught to know the letters one from the other, and that his keeper has some private sign by which he directs him to each that are wanted; – but that he has an idea of *spelling* I can never believe, nor are animals capable of attaining human sciences, because, for these, human faculties are requisite; and no art of man can *change* the nature of any thing, though he may be able to improve that nature to a certain degree, or at least call forth to view, the powers which would be hidden from us, because they would only be exerted in the intercourse of animals with each other. As far as this can be done by familiarizing them, and showing them such a degree of kindness as is consistent with our highest obligations, it may be an agreeable amusement, but will never answer any important purpose to mankind; and I would advise you, Harriet, never to give countenance to those people who show what they call *learned* animals; as you may assure yourself they exercise great barbarities upon them, of which starving them almost to death is likely among the number." (Sarah Trimmer, *Fabulous Histories* [1786], later known as *The History of the Robins*)[58]

In her *Easy Introduction to the Knowledge of Nature* (1782) Trimmer condemned cock-fighting in particular and "barbarous sports" in general.

Oh, Henry! I hope you will never take pleasure in such barbarous sports, I could tell you many stories of the bad consequences of cock-fighting, which has frequently been the ruin of those who were fond of it; but I hope God·will preserve you from this and all other sins.[59]

Thomas Day

Thomas Day (1748-89) was an English social reformer, an associate of Erasmus Darwin with Rousseauian sympathies, a supporter of the American Revolution, an adamant opponent of the slave trade, and an advocate for the small farmer. Losing political influence, largely because of his personal eccentricities, he turned to writing educational books in which the treatment of animals played a prominent role. The flavour of his instruction may be gleaned from the following extracts from *The History of Little Jack* (1788).

In his walks over the common, [the old man] one day found a little kid that had lost its mother, and was almost famished with hunger: he took it home to his cottage, fed it with the produce of his garden, and nursed it till it grew strong and vigorous. Little Nan (for that was the name he gave it) returned his cares with gratitude, and became as much attached to him as a dog. All day she browsed upon the herbage that grew around his hut, and at night reposed upon the same bed of straw with her master. Frequently did she divert him with her innocent tricks and gambols. She would nestle her little head in his bosom, and eat out of his hand part of his scanty allowance of bread; which he never failed to divide with his favourite. The old man often beheld her with silent joy, and in the innocent effusions of his heart, would lift his hands to heaven, and thank the Deity that, even in the midst of poverty and distress, had raised him up one faithful friend.

Little Jack comes adventitiously on the scene, is instructed in the old man's sense of virtue, and later:

Another love of Jack's, which now discovered itself, was an immoderate love of horses. The instant he was introduced into the stable, he attached himself so strongly to these animals, that you would have taken him for one of the same species, or at least a near relation ... In respect of the animals trusted to his care, he not only refrained from using them ill, but was never tired with doing them good offices.

When a nefarious "young gentleman" runs a monkey through with his sword, "Jack, who was not of a temper to see calmly such an outrage committed upon an animal whom he considered as his friend, flew upon him like a fury, and, wresting the sword out of his hand, broke it into twenty pieces."[60]

In his better-known and more influential *The History of Sandford and Merton* (1783-9), Day turns first to the insects.

Once, indeed, Harry was caught twirling a cockchafer round, which he had fastened by a crooked pin to a long piece of thread, but then this was through ignorance and want of thought: for as soon as his father told him the poor helpless insect felt as much, or more than he would do, were a knife thrust through his hand, he burst into tears, and took the poor animal home, where he fed him during a fortnight on fresh leaves; and when he was perfectly recovered, turned him out to enjoy liberty and fresh air. Ever since that time, Harry was so careful and considerate, that he would step out of the way for fear of hurting a worm, and employed himself in doing kind offices to all the animals in the neighbourhood. He used to stroke the horses as they were at work, and fill his pockets with acorns for the pigs: if he walked in the fields, he was sure to gather green boughs for the sheep, who were so fond of him, that they followed him wherever he went. In the winter-time, when the ground was covered with frost and snow, and the poor little birds could get no food, he would often go supperless to bed, that he might feed the robin-redbreasts. Even toads and frogs, and spiders, and such kind of disagreeable animals, which most people destroy wherever they find them, were perfectly safe with Harry: he used to say they had a right to live as well as we, and that it was cruel and unjust to kill creatures only because we did not like them.[61]

Mary Wollstonecraft

A reader of *A Vindication of the Rights of Men* (1790) or *A Vindication of the Rights of Woman* (1792), the first written against Burke, the second against Rousseau, would scarce recognize the famed humanitarian and feminist Mary Wollstonecraft (1759-97) in her 1788 text, *Original Stories from Real Life*. In her highly regarded later political works, Wollstonecraft is philosophical, perceptive, sophisticated, and occasionally profound. In the *Original Stories* she is sentimental to a fault and, despite her insistence on kindness to animals, the gulf she describes between humans and animals is far greater than any we find expressed by the Romantic poets. Indeed, none of the sense of kinship we find in Thomas Day is present; there is merely a sense of duty. Nonetheless, there is every reason to believe that most people, both then and now, would come closer in their animal-regarding beliefs to Wollstonecraft than to the Romantics.

In *Original Stories* we encounter what is customary for the genre: chapters on the benefits of prayer, religious devotion, charity, appropriate "Behaviour to Servants," and on "Idleness produces Misery." Significantly though, Wollstonecraft deems the elimination of cruelty to animals so central to virtue that the first three chapters are devoted to "The Treatment of Animals." No other topic receives such lengthy consideration.

Mrs. Mason asked how she dared to kill any thing, but to prevent it hurting her? ... You have already heard that God created the world, and every inhabitant of it. He is then called the Father of all creatures; and all are made to be happy. He made those snails you despise, and caterpillars, and spiders; and when he made them, did not leave them to perish, but placed them where the food that is most proper to nourish them is easily found. They do not live long, but *their* Father, as well as your's, directs them to deposit their eggs on the plants that are fit to support the young, when they are not able to get food for themselves. And when such a great and wise Being has taken care to provide every thing necessary for the meanest creature, would you dare kill it, merely because it appears, as you think, ugly?

Observe these ants, they have a little habitation in yonder hillock; they carry food to it for the winter, and live very snug in it in cold weather. The bees, too, have comfortable towns, and lay in a store of honey to support them when the flowers die, and snow covers the ground: and this forecast is as much the gift of God, as any quality you possess.

Do you know the meaning of the word Goodness? I see you are unwilling to answer. I will tell you. It is, first, to avoid hurting any thing; and then, to contrive to give as much pleasure as you can. If any insects are to be destroyed, to preserve my garden from desolation, I have it done in the quickest way. Domestic animals that I keep, I provide the best food for, and never suffer them to be tormented; and this caution arises from two motives: – I wish to make them happy; and as I love my fellow-creatures [that is, fellow-humans] still better than them, I would not allow those I have any influence over, to grow habitually thoughtless and cruel, and by these means lose the greatest pleasure life affords, – that of resembling God, by doing good.

A boy shoots a pair of birds.

Take up the hen; I will bind her wing together; perhaps it will heal. As to the other, though I hate to kill it, I must put it out of pain; to leave it in its present state would be cruel; and, avoiding an unpleasant situation myself, I should allow the bird to die by inches, and call this treatment tenderness, when it would be weakness or selfishness. Saying so, she put her foot on the bird's head, turning her own the other way.[62]

Wollstonecraft's husband **William Godwin** (1756-1836) wrote the *Enquiry Concerning Political Justice* in 1793 – later a stimulus to anarchist thought – followed by his novels: *Adventures of Caleb Williams* (1794), *St. Leon* (1799), and *Fleetwood* (1805). In *Fleetwood* he abjured hunting.

I was inaccessible to the pitiful ambition of showing before a gang of rural squires, that I had a fine horse, and could manage him gracefully ... I have still further and more direct reason for my rejection of the sports of the field. I could not with patience regard torture, anguish and death, as the sources of my amusement. My natural temper, or my reflective and undebauched habits as a solitaire, prevented me from overlooking the brutality and cruelty of such pursuits. In very early youth I had been seduced first by a footman of my father, and afterward by my tutor, to join an excursion of angling. But after a short trial, I abjured the amusement forever; and it was one among the causes of the small respect I entertained for my tutor, that he was devoted to so idle and unfeeling an avocation.[63]

Priscilla Wakefield

Writing a few years later, the Quaker philanthropist Priscilla Wakefield (1751-1832), author of reputable works on botany, insects, and travel, addressed the children for whom she was now writing in quite different terms from those of Wollstonecraft. In her epistolary *Instinct Displayed* (1811) she tells her correspondent: "it will give you pleasure to see how far the animal feelings can approach to the moral virtue peculiar to rational and responsible beings; and what a union of the most affectionate and the most hostile qualities, can exist in the same creature, both springing from a noble, generous disposition."[64]

She finds "a charm ... throughout all the tribes of animated nature" and relates countless stories of a horse that protected a smaller dog from a larger one, of rats that "show a degree of pity and sagacity nearly equal" in protection of their relatives, of a peacock anxious for his companion, and the like. Her naturalist observations, while often acute, will be described by many as unduly anthropomorphic. Nevertheless they reflect a profound compassion.

The whole of her lengthy book employs the precepts of the chain argument, showing how alike are humans and other animals, and what responsibilities we consequently owe them.

The distinctions between reason and instinct are difficult to ascertain: to define their exact limits has exercised the ingenuity of the most profound philosophers, hitherto without success. Nor can the learned agree as to the nature of that wonderful quality, that guides every creature to take the best means of preserving its species by the most admirable care of its progeny. Some degrade the hidden impulse to a mere mechanical operation; whilst others exalt it to a level with reason, that proud prerogative of man. There are, indeed, innumerable gradations of intelligence, as of the other qualities with which the animal kingdom is endowed; in like manner as the different orders of beings approach each other so closely, and are so curiously united by links, partaking of the nature of those above and those below, that it requires a discerning eye to know what rank to assign them. Thus, quadrupeds and birds are assimilated to each other by the bat; the inhabitants of the waters to those of the land, by amphibious animals; animals to vegetables, by the leaf-insect, and by plants that appear to have sensation; and animate to inanimate, by the oyster, the molluscae, and sea anemones.

Reason and instinct have obvious differences; yet the most intelligent animals, in some of their actions, approach so near to reason, that it is really surprising how small the distinction is.[65]

In the final analysis, for Wakefield, animals possess intelligence and sagacity, and, if not the ineluctable "reason," then qualities which are equally admirable and barely distinguishable.

Jean Paul Friedrich Richter

Jean Paul was the pseudonym of the German novelist, Johann Paul Friedrich Richter (1762-1825). He combined Fichtean idealism with the Romanticism of *Sturm und Drang* in his writings. Among his romances are *Hesperus* (1795) and *Leben des Quintus Fixlein* (Life of Quintus Fixlein) (1796). *Levana* (1807), whence this extract, is a treatise on education.

Love in the child, as in the animal, exists as an instinct; and this central fire frequently, but not always, breaks through its outer crust in the form of compassion. A child is often indifferent, not merely to the sufferings of animals, and to those of persons unconnected with himself, (except when the cry of pain finds an echo in his own heart,) but even to those of relatives ... But the sun comes and warms the world; the superabundance of power becomes love; the strong stem encloses and protects the pith; the teasing lad become the affectionate young man ... there is not so much need to ingraft the buds of affection, as to remove the moss and briers of selfishness which hide them from the sun.[66]

For Richter the potential lies already within and needs only to be exploited.

[T]each a child to consider all animal life sacred, – in short, give him the heart of a Hindoo, not the heart of a Cartesian philosopher.

I hear speak of something higher than compassion for animals, though of that also. Why has it been long remarked that children's cruelty to animals predicts cruelty to men ... ? It is certain that, unless associated with other things, the little human being can only sympathize with those sufferings which speak in tones similar to his own. Consequently, the unusual cry of a tortured animal sounds to him like the strange and amusing howl of the inanimate wind; but, as he sees life and voluntary motion, and even attributes to them inanimate forms, he sins against life when he separates them as though they were but machinery. Life itself should be sacred; every life, irrational as well as any other ...

The so-called instinct of animals – this ass which perceives the angel's presence sooner than the prophet* ought to be regarded as the greatest miracle of creation, and also as the key and index to all other miracles; in so much as the riddle of the universe resembles those riddles which both describe the riddle and signify it. Animals should be rendered familiar to children in every possible way ... The prejudice which values life by the yard – why, then, are not elephants and whales ranked higher than ourselves? – disappears by the contemplation of the infinity which is the same in every living creature, and, like, an infinite series of numbers, is increased by no finite additions; which is not affected, for instance, by the two million joints of a centipede, or how many thousand muscles of the willow-caterpillar ...

To the child's eye, admit all living things into the human family; so the greater reveals to him the less. Breathe a living soul into everything ...

I do not refer to any mere empty exercise of compassion in the school of others' sufferings, but to an exercise of religion in the consecration of life, of the deity ever present in the trees and the human brain. The love of animals, like maternal love, arises from no expectation of reciprocated advantage, still less from selfishness, and has the further advantage of always finding an object on which to manifest itself.

Oh! the beautiful time will come, must come, when the beast-loving Brahmins shall dwell in the cold north and make it warm; when the heart, having rejected its worst and cruellest sins, shall also lay aside those which slowly poison it; when man, who now honors the multiform part of humanity, shall also begin to spare, and finally to protect, in the present, the animated ascending and descending scale of living creatures, so as to no more to offer to the Great First Cause the hateful sight of its, it is true thickly veiled, but wide-extended animal suffering.[67]

The Naturalists
Priscilla Wakefield related that the "harmonious beauty of creation, and the interesting objects it presents, have been my delight since childhood ..."[68] Her method of study was not, however, that of those today known as "natural philosophers." For most of those who are now so designated, the

---

* Balaam's ass. Numbers 22.

removal, collecting, dissecting, pickling, and stuffing of insects, birds, and quadrupeds must be seen as a limitation to their respect for the animals they so assiduously studied – and so often killed. The prevailing belief among them was that while animals should otherwise be respected, the "sacrifice" of a few individuals was an eminently worthwhile price to pay for the acquisition of knowledge.

Two of the most prominent of this burgeoning number of naturalists were **Gilbert White** (1720-93) and **Erasmus Darwin** (1731-1802). White was Vicar of Selborne in Hampshire and produced the first detailed study of the fauna and flora of a parish. He was an avid "sportsman," claiming it to be "impossible ... to extinguish the spirit of sporting, which seems to be inherent in human nature,"[69] though he castigated "unreasonable sports-men," who contravened what he deemed humane practices, and com-plained of those who were exterminating "a nobler species of game [than partridges] ... the heathcock, black game or grouse." And while he acknowledged "the chain of beings" and regretted the gap of "another beautiful link in it"[70] – the red deer whom the hunters had driven from the locality to, no doubt, safer pastures – at best there is ambivalence about White's humanitarianism. Still, he clearly revelled in the objects of his study, even if his behaviour did not match his wonder.

I was much taken with the [tortoise's] sagacity in discerning those that do it kind offices; for, as soon as the good old lady comes in sight who has waited on it for more than thirty years, it hobbles towards its benefactress with awkward alacrity; but remains inattentive to strangers. Thus not only *"the ox knoweth his owner, and the ass his master's crib,"* but the most abject reptile and torpid of beings distin-guished the hand that feeds it, and is touched with the feelings of gratitude![71]

One may recoil at the depiction of "abject reptiles" but the value of the studies of these new naturalists was that they could not fail to demonstrate the essential human-animal similarities – a discovery which in turn influ-enced their own attitudes.

There is a wonderful spirit of sociality in the brute creation, independent of sexual attachment: the congregating of gregarious birds in the winter is a remarkable instance.

Many horses, though quiet with company, will not stay one minute in a field by themselves: the strongest fences cannot restrain them. My neighbour's horse will not only not stay by himself abroad, but he will not bear to be left alone in a strange stable without discovering the utmost impatience, and endeavouring to break the rack and manger with his fore feet. He has been known to leap out a stable-window, through which dung was thrown, after company; and yet in other respects he is remarkably quiet ... Oxen and cows will not fatten by themselves; but will neglect the finest pasture that is not recommended by society. It would be needless to instance sheep, which continually flock together.

But this propensity seems not to be confined to animals of the same species; for we know a doe still alive, that was brought up from a little fawn with a dairy of cows; with them it goes a-field, and with them it returns to the yard. The dogs of the house take no notice of this deer, being used to her; but, if strange dogs come by, a chase ensues; while the master smiles to see his favourite securely leading her pursuers over hedge, or gate, or stile, till she returns to the cows, who with fierce lowings and menacing horns, drive the assailants out of the pasture.

Even great disparity of kind and size does not always prevent social advances and mutual fellowship. For a very intelligent and observant person has assured me that, in the former part of his life, keeping but one horse, he happened also on a time to have but one solitary hen. These two incongruous animals spent so much of their time together in a lonely orchard, where they saw no creature but each other. By degrees an apparent regard began to take place between these two sequestered individuals. The fowl would approach the quadruped with notes of complacency, rubbing herself gently against his legs; while the horse would look down with satisfaction, and move with the greatest caution and circumspection, lest he should trample on his diminutive companion. Thus by mutual good offices, each seemed to console the vacant hours of the other.[72]

Erasmus Darwin was a practising physician, inventor, botanist, and poet before becoming a student of the animal world. Nonetheless, he considered animals capable of entering into contracts, the rejection of which was sometimes used to deny that animals were entitled to justice or could have rights. And, as he wrote in *The Temple of Nature*, man:

Should eye with tenderness all living forms,
His brother-emmets, and his sister-worms.[73]

Darwin was a prominent member of a Birmingham scientific society, and also of a Lichfield literary group, which included Thomas Day and his protégé Anna Seward. His two major works were a long poem, *The Botanical Garden* (1789-91), in which he expounded the classification system of Linnaeus, and *Zoonomia* (1794-6), a prose work in which he developed a rudimentary theory of evolution. He argued the case that animals learn from experience rather than acting on instinct, and that their emotions are analogous with human emotions.

An ingenious philosopher has lately denied, that animals can enter into contracts, and thinks this an essential difference between them and the human creature: but does not daily observation convince us that they form contracts with each other, and with mankind? When puppies and kittens play together, is there not a tacit contract, that they will not hurt each other? And does not your favourite dog expect you should give him daily food for his services and attention to you? And thus barters his love for your protection? In the same manner that all contracts are made amongst men, that do not understand each others arbitrary language. (Erasmus Darwin, *Zoonomia* [1794], I, 169)[74]

Even though Erasmus Darwin failed to recognize the role of natural selection in evolution, and mistakenly allowed a major role for will, nonetheless he understood evolution perhaps better than anyone prior to his grandson Charles. Certainly, he left little doubt that humans and animals were of the same origin.

Would it be too bold to imagine, that in the great length of time since the earth began to exist, perhaps millions of ages before the commencement of the history of mankind, would it be too bold to imagine, that all warm-blooded animals have arisen from one living filament, which THE GREAT FIRST CAUSE endued with animality, with the power of acquiring new parts, attended with new propensities, directed by irritations, sensations, volitions, and associations, and thus possessing the faculty of continuing to improve by its own inherent activity, and of delivering down those improvements by generation to its posterity, world without end. (*Zoonomia*, I, 509)[75]

A lesser naturalist than White or Darwin, **William Jones of Nayland** (1726-1800) was more emphatic in his denunciation of cruelty.

Cruelty to dumb animals is one of the distinguishing vices of low and base minds. Wherever it is found, it is a certain mark of ignorance and meanness; a mark which all the external advantages of wealth, splendour, and nobility, cannot obliterate. It is consistent neither with true learning nor true civility. (William Jones, *Zoologia Ethicae*)[76]

Anna Seward (1757-1809), who was known as the "Swan of Lichfield," wrote in sympathy with the ideas of her friend Darwin, but also captured the spirit of Hildrop, Dean, and Wesley.

But since full oft the pangs of dire disease,
    Labour, and famine, add oppression hard,
From cruel Man, the blameless victims seize;
    Of Heavenly Justice they may claim reward.
Has God deprived animals of immortal souls?
Ah, no! the great Retributory Mind
    Will recompense and may perhaps ordain
Some future mode of being, more refin'd
    Than ours, less sullied with inherent stain;
Less torn by passion, and less prone to sin,
    Their duty easier, trial less severe,
Till their firm faith, and virtue prov'd, may win
    The wreaths of Life in yon Eternal Sphere.[77]

Herman Daggett

If we ignore the Dorillites – who flourished in Vermont in the 1790s, eschewing the eating of flesh and the wearing of clothes made from animals – a rare American voice proclaiming the rights of animals in this era was Herman Daggett (1766-1832), who delivered an oration on those rights at Providence College, Yale, in 1791. Although a scarce voice, it was yet a stentorian and unqualified one. And no doubt it evoked sympathetic sentiments among many in his audience.

The design of my appearing in public, at this time, is to say a few things in favour of a certain class of beings, whose rights have seldom been advocated, either from the pulpit, from the stage, or from the press. I mean the inferior animals.

The cruelty and injustice, with which this class of beings has been treated, by their boasted superiors in the human race, is too notorious to need a particular recital. In general their welfare and happiness has been looked upon as a matter of very little importance, in the system; and in our treatment of them, hardly to be regarded ...

[T]he lower order of sensible beings, are considered as moving in a very different sphere, and belonging to a community of a very different nature from that of ours; so far different, that the feelings of benevolence, are, commonly, not at all interested in their favor.

A well known circumstance, which attends some of these animals, contributes, not a little, to confirm us in the truth of this observation. For those of them who are tamed, and domesticated by us, immediately become the objects of our kind regards. And our sensibility is deeply wounded, when they are abused. But where there is no such relation, by which they are distinguished from the common herd, to use a phrase denoting cruelty, they are treated like brutes. Without the least regard to justice, we commonly treat them in that manner, which we suppose, will make them conduce most to our own advantage; and subject them, in all things, to what happens to be our pleasure. Though sometimes, it must be acknowledged, that our malevolence towards them, is of a disinterested nature, and they are tormented only for the sake of the unnatural pleasure, which is taken in doing it.

Now, in order to determine, in what light, these animals ought to be considered, and how they ought to be treated, let us carefully attend to a few things, of known and acknowledged truth, with regard to the objects of our benevolence. And here I think it is past dispute, that all beings, capable of happiness belong to that number. Let their circumstances or characters, dispositions or abilities, color or shape, be what they may; if they are sensible beings, and capable of happiness, they ought to be the objects of our benevolent regards ... We may, and ought to have a true regard for all beings, according to their real worth, and to wish them well, according to their capacity for enjoyment ...

But lest this mode of reasoning be judged too nice, let us call into view a rule of judging, instituted by a divine Philanthropist, and oracle of wisdom, in the days of ... [Tiberius Julius] Caesar. That we do to others as we would have them do unto us; i.e. in a change of circumstances ... Let this rule, therefore, be faithfully applied, in every case, and cruelty to animals would no longer be indulged.

God has appointed to all his creatures, a certain sphere to move in, and has granted them certain privileges, which may be called their own. If we judge impartially, we shall acknowledge that there are the rights of a beast, as well as the rights of man. And because man is considered as the Lord of this lower creation, he is not thereby licensed to infringe on the rights of those below him any more than a King or Magistrate, is licensed to infringe on the rights of his subjects. If the Governor of the universe has given us liberty to prepare animal food; or, if the rights of these creatures, in certain instances interfere with the rights of others, or with the rights of men, so as thereby to become forfeited; we may, in such cases, take away their lives, or deprive them of their privileges, without the imputation of blame. And I know of nothing in nature, in reason, or in revelation, which obliges us to suppose, that the unalienated rights of a beast, are not as sacred, and inviolable, as those of a man: or that the person, who wantonly commits an outrage upon the life, happiness or security of a bird, is not really as amenable, at the tribunal of eternal justice, as he, who wantonly destroys the rights and privileges, or injuriously takes away the life of one of his fellow creatures of the human race.[78]

The great protagonist of *The Rights of Man*, **Thomas Paine** (1737-1809) preferred to write of our duties toward the animals rather than their inherent rights. In *The Age of Reason* (1794) he argued that

the moral duty of man consists in imitating the moral goodness and beneficence of God, manifested in the creation toward all his creatures. That seeing, as we daily do, the goodness of God to all men to practise the same toward each other; and consequently, that everything of persecution and revenge between man and man, and everything of cruelty to animals, is a violation of moral duty.[79]

David Williams

Welsh dissenting minister, founder of the Royal Literary Fund and, like Erasmus Darwin, an associate of Benjamin Franklin, David Williams (1738-1816) wrote *inter alia Lectures on Education* (1785) and *Lectures on Political Principles* (1789). Apparently stimulated by Jonathan Swift's story of the Houyhnhnms and the Yahoos, Williams wrote these lines:

Where pain and pleasure, happiness and misery are concerned, there the obligations of morality are concerned; and a man who is not merciful to the animals in his power, whatever his pretensions may be to reason and religion, is, in truth, of a narrow understanding and a bad heart. What shall we say, then, of that morality, that religion, and that policy, which admits of the cruelties we see daily exercised on creatures, we derive benefit and pleasure from every moment of our lives. Those animals which assist our labour, relieve our fatigues, and contribute to our pleasures, are often committed into the hands of men, who seem to be actually inferior to them in every quality both of mind and body.

No person who could divest himself of the prejudices attached to outward form, on being shown an animal cast in one of the most beautiful molds of nature:

docile, apprehensive,* intelligent, faithful, cheerful, and generous in his services – at the same time being shewn a brute in human form who is the delegate of avaricious cruelty in extorting his utmost labour. – If he were impartially to attend to the whole conduct of the one, and the whole conversation and conduct of the other, and were told that one of them had an intelligent immortal soul, designed for happiness here and in heaven, and that the other would terminate his existence with this life, he would certainly imagine the horse to be the immortal being; and the man too well rewarded by the grave or annihilation. The remains of barbarity, which still continue in our treatment of animals, are a reproach to our natures; to all our moral, philosophical, and religious pretensions; and to those forms of government and principles of police,† which we ignorantly and vainly extol as the most excellent and perfect which can be imagined. (David Williams, *Lectures on Political Principles* [1789])[80]

John Oswald

The last decade of the eighteenth century and first decade of the nineteenth century were witness to a number of books designed to promote animal well-being, often with a subsidiary purpose of advocating either vegetarianism, then in vogue, or the virtues of a particular species, customarily the horse, or the need for legislative protection of animals – sometimes in combination.

A devotee of Hinduism and Rousseau, and an avid supporter of the French Revolution, John Oswald (d. 1793) published the first of such books in 1791: *The Cry of Nature; or, an Appeal to Mercy and Justice on Behalf of the Persecuted Animals*. He claimed that, with the advent of the revolution, "the barbarous governments of Europe" were being superseded by "a better system of things" and that "the day is beginning to approach when the growing sentiment of peace and goodwill towards men, will also embrace, in a wide circle of benevolence, the lower orders of life." His purpose, he wrote, was to lessen the sum of animal misery in the world for "of all creatures the essence is the same."[81]

Within us there exists a rooted repugnance to the spilling of blood; a repugnance which yields only to custom, and which even the most inveterate custom can never entirely overcome ... [82]

What then shall we say? Vainly planted in our breast, is this abhorrence of cruelty; this sympathetic affection for every animal? Or, to the purpose of nature, do the feelings of the heart point more unerringly than all the elaborate subtilty of a set of men, who, at the shrine of science, have sacrificed the dearest sentiments of humanity?

---

* That is, capable of apprehending.
† That is, policy.

Ye sons of *modern science,* who court not wisdom in her walks of silent meditation in the grove, who behold her not in the living loveliness of her works, but expect to meet her in the midst of obscenity and corruption; ye who dig for knowledge in the depth of the dunghill, and who hope to discover wisdom enthroned among the fragments of mortality, and the abhorrence of the senses; ye that with ruffian violence interrogate trembling nature, who plunge in her maternal bosom, the butcher knife, and, in quest of your nefarious science, the fibres of agonizing animals delight to scrutinize ... Barbarians! To these very bowels I appeal against your cruel dogmas; to these bowels, fraught with mercy, and entwined with compassion; to these bowels which nature hath sanctified to the sentiments of pity and gratitude; to the yearnings of kindred, to the melting of tenderness of love! ... [83]

But come, ye men of scientific subtilty, approach and examine with attention this dead body. It was late a playful fawn, which, skipping, and bounding on the bosom of the parent earth, awoke, in the soul of the feeling observer, a thousand tender emotions. But the butcher's knife hath laid low the delight of a fond dam, and the darling of nature is now stretched in gore upon the ground. Approach, I say, ye men of scientific subtilty, and tell me, tell me, does this ghastly spectacle whet your appetite? Is the steam of gore grateful to your nostrils, or pleasing to the touch, the icy ribs of death? But why turn ye with abhorrence? Do you then yield to the combined evidence of your senses; or with a species of rhetoric, pitiful as it is perverse, will you still persist in your endeavour to persuade us, that to murder an innocent animal, is not cruel or unjust; and that to feed upon the corpse, is neither filthy nor unfit?[84]

Alas! Let my tears – alas! for a poor innocent that hath done thee no harm, which, indeed, is incapable of harm, let the tears of nature plead! Spare, spare, I beseech thee by every tender idea; spare my eternal bosom the unutterable anguish which there the cries of agonizing innocence excite, whether the creature that suffers be a lambkin or a man. See the little victim how he wantons unconscious of coming fate, the up-lifted steel he views, innocent and engaging as the babe, that presses, playful, the bosom of her, in whom thy bliss is complete. Why shouldst thou kill him in the novelty of life; why ravish him from the sweet aspect of the sun, while yet, with fresh delight, he admires the blooming face of things? ... is compassion then so great a crime? ... [85]

Even the animal sacrifices of times past were preferable to the barbarities of modern civilization. Oswald describes what he sees as "the decency with which, at first, the devoted victims were put to death."

But when man became perfectly civilized, those exterior symbols of sentiments, with which he was now feebly if at all impressed, were also laid aside. Formerly sacrificed with some decorum to the plea of necessity, the animals were now with unceremonious brutality destroyed, to gratify the unfeeling pride or wanton cruelty of men. Broad barefaced butchery occupied every walk of life; every element was ransacked for victims; the most remote corners of the globe were ravished of their inhabitants, whether by the fastidious gluttony of man their flesh was held grateful to the palate, whether their blood could impurple* the pall of his pride, or their spoils add a feather to the wings of his vanity: and while nature, while agonizing nature, is tortured by his ambition, while to supply the demands of his perverse appetite she bleeds at every pore, this imperial animal exclaims; ye servile creatures! why do ye lament? why vainly try, by cries akin to the voice of human woe, my compassion to excite? Created solely for my use, submit without a murmur to the decrees of heaven, and to the mandates of me; of me the heaven-deputed despot of every creature that walks, or creeps, or swims, or flies in air, on earth, or in the waters which encompass the earth. Thus the fate of the animal world has followed the progress of man from this sylvan state to that of civilization, till the gradual improvements of art, on this glorious principle of independence, have at length placed him free from every tender link, free from every lovely prejudice of nature, and an enemy to life and happiness through all their various forms of existence ...[86]

But now the revolution offers humankind emancipation from all historical ills.

May the benevolent system spread to every corner of the globe; may we learn to recognize and to respect in other animals the feelings which vibrate in ourselves; may we be led to perceive that those cruel repasts are not more injurious to the creatures whom we devour than they are hostile to our health, which delights in innocent simplicity, and destructive of our happiness, which is wounded by every act of violence, while it feeds as it were on the prospects of well being, and is raised to the highest summit of enjoyment by the sympathetic touch of social satisfaction.[87]

The voice of nature, so dear to Oswald's heart, also spoke loudly to **Friedrich Schiller** (1759-1805), author of the *Sturm und Drang* play *Die Räuber* (The Robbers) (1781), an attack on political tyranny. In his poem "Der Alpenjäger" (The Hunter of the Alps), the mountain spirit protects the afflicted animal with his godly hands. "Must you bring death and misery up here to me?" he cries. "The earth has room for all. Why must you persecute my flock?"[88]

John Lawrence

A writer on farming and politics, but above all on matters pertaining to the horse, John Lawrence (1753-1829) was the author of the influential *A Philosophical and Practical Treatise on Horses and on the Moral Duties of Men toward the Brute Creation* (1796-8).

Writing under the pseudonym of John Scott in *The Sportsman's Repository* (1820) – despite his proclaimed humanitarianism to animals he was an avid hunter and proponent of meat-eating – Lawrence offered a criticism of that "general unfeeling foolery, under the guise of sensibility,

---

* Give royal quality to.

which includes an aversion to taking away the lives of deserted or aged and diseased dogs and cats in the same people who feast without reluctance or remorse upon the flesh of the finest, happiest and healthiest animals duly slaughtered for the purpose!"[89]

In his chapter "On the Rights of Beasts" in his *Philosophical and Practical Treatise on Horses*, Lawrence argued the case for the rights of animals and for their legal protection. Indeed, his was one of the most influential voices in bringing about Britain's early animal welfare legislation.

The barbarous, unfeeling, and capricious conduct of man to the brute creation, has been the reproach of every age and nation. Whence does it originate? ... We are to search for the cause of this odious vice, rather in custom, which flatters the indolence of man, by saving him the trouble of investigation, and in the defect of early tuition, than in a natural want of sensibility in the human heart, or in the demands of human interest.

It has ever been, and still is, the invariable custom of the bulk of mankind, not even excepting legislators, both religious and civil, to look upon brutes as mere machines; animated yet without souls; endowed with feelings, but utterly devoid of rights; and placed without the pale of justice. From these supposed defects, and from the idea, ill understood, of their being created merely for the use and purposes of man, have the feelings of beasts, their lawful, that is, natural interests and welfare, been sacrificed to his convenience, his cruelty, or his caprice.

It is but too easy to demonstrate by a series of melancholy facts, that brute creatures are not yet in the contemplation of any people, reckoned within the scheme of general justice; that they reap only the benefit of a partial and inefficacious kind of compassion. Yet it is easy to prove, by analogies drawn from our own, that they also, have souls; and perfectly consistent with reason, to infer a gradation of intellect, from the spark which animates the most minute mortal exiguity, up to the sum of infinite intelligence, and feeling, necessarily imply rights. Justice, in which are included mercy, or compassion, obviously refer to sense and feeling. Now is the essence of justice divisible? Can there be one kind of justice for men, and another for brutes? Or is feeling in them a different thing to what it is in ourselves? Is not a beast produced by the same rule, and in the same order of generation with ourselves? Is not his body nourished by the same food, hurt by the same injuries; his mind actuated by the same passions and affections which animate the human breast; and does not he also, at last, mingle his dust with ours, and in like manner surrender up the vital spark to the aggregate, or fountain of intelligence? Is this spark, or soul, to perish because it chanced to belong to a beast? Is it to become annihilate? Tell me, learned philosophers, how that may possibly happen.

If you deny unto beasts their rights, and abandon them to the simple discretion of man, in all cases, without remedy, you defraud them of those benefits and advantages, acceded to them by nature herself, and commit a heinous trespass against her positive ordinances, as founded on natural justice. You deprive them, in great measure even of compassion. But previous to an attempt to vindicate the rights of animals, it is no doubt necessary to determine, specifically, in what they consist. They arise then, spontaneously, from the conscience, or sense of moral obligation in man, who is indispensably bound to bestow upon animals, in return for the benefit he derives from their services, "a good and sufficient nourishment, comfortable shelter, and merciful treatment; to commit no wanton outrage upon their feelings, whilst alive, and to put them to the speediest and least painful death, when it shall be necessary to deprive them of life." ... [90]

The grand source of the unmerited and superstitious misery of beasts, exists, in my opinion, in a defect in the constitution of all communities. No human government, I believe, has ever recognized the *jus animalium,** which surely ought to form a part of the jurisprudence of every system, founded on the principles of justice and humanity ... Experience plainly demonstrates the inefficacy of mere morality to prevent aggression, and the necessity of coercive laws for the security of rights. I therefore propose, that the Rights of Beasts, be formally acknowledged by the state, and that a law be framed upon that principle, to guard and protect them from acts of flagrant and wanton cruelty, whether committed by their owners or others. As the law stands at present, no man is punishable for an act of the most extreme cruelty to a brute animal, but upon the principle of an injury done to the property of another; of course the owner of a beast has the tacit allowance of the law to inflict upon it, if he shall so please, the most horrid barbarities ... [91]

A law of this nature would effectually sweep away all those hellish nuisances, miscalled sports; such as the baiting and torturing animals to death, throwing at cocks, hunting tame ducks, sometimes with a wretched owl fastened to their backs, eating live cats, and the like; in which savage exercitations, the unnatural and preposterous idea is fostered and encouraged, that one animal can derive sportive and pleasing sensations, from witnessing the lingering tortures and excruciated sensibility of another.[92]

A good portion of Lawrence's work is devoted to cruelty to post, cart, racing, and other horses. The same theme was addressed by **Helen Maria Williams** (1767-1827), a prolific essayist and poet who devoted her attention to French affairs.

Can no law succour that wretched horse, worn to the bone from famine and fatigue, lashed by his cruel tyrant into exertion beyond his strength, while he drags in some vile vehicle six persons beside his merciless owner? For myself, I confess, that at the view of such spectacles the charm of nature seems suddenly dissolved – to me the fields lose their verdure, and the woods their pleasantness – nor is my indignation confined to the unrelenting driver of these loaded machines; I consider the passengers who tacitly assent to the pain he inflicts, as more than his accomplices in his barbarity.[93]

Horses were indeed the central humanitarian concern throughout the nineteenth century, but they were used extensively as work implements

---

* See p. 35.

by humans. Not only were a number of the earliest legislative proposals devoted to protection for horses, but when the Toronto Humane Society published its aims and objectives in 1888 the first ten pages on animal abuse were devoted to "Cruelty to Horses." Of the list of thirteen prevalent cruelties the "Society will seek to prevent," two are generic, five refer to animals other than the horse – only one to dogs and none to cats – and the remainder refer specifically to the horse.

Thomas Young

Reverend Thomas Young, Fellow of Trinity College, Cambridge, was primarily a publisher of sermons, including *Christ's Resurrection: A Sermon* (1811) and *Christ's Righteousness: A Sermon* (1811). In 1798 he wrote *An Essay on Humanity to Animals*, prefaced by a lengthy poem to the same end by his Trinity College colleague, Reverend C. Hoyle. Following Aquinas, John of Salisbury, Hogarth, Daggett, and others,[94] he takes the view that cruelty to animals leads to cruelty to humans.

It being allowed then, that cruelty to animals has a strong tendency to render us cruel towards our own species, we can have little difficulty in concluding, that this alone is a sufficient reason why we should abstain from it. And by a similar argument, we may conclude, that it is our duty to cultivate humanity toward animals. I do not mean that humanity only, which consists in a mere abstinence from persecution; but that operative humanity, which exerts itself in positive acts of kindness, and which, not content barely to rescue animals from pain, wishes, although it find them happy, to leave then still more abundantly gratified. Humanity, such as this, would undoubtedly tend to render us more humane towards mankind.[95]

Young argues further that humanity is owed to other species on the grounds of their sensibility, as a requirement of the Scriptures, from our own enlightened self-interest, and to build human character. He treats most contemporary issues – cruelty in "sports," including hunting, shooting, and fishing, in which he is especially critical of his fellow clergy, cruelty to horses, the malpractices of bee-keeping, where he is particularly concerned with the development of more humane methods, and vivisection, which he accepts as legitimate but only if eminently worthwhile ends are in view. His words on "The Article of Eating" are representative of his approach.

A man of humane disposition will not easily taste of a dish, in which cruelty has been mingled. It is true, *he* did not inflict the torture, his feelings would not have permitted him; but it was perhaps inflicted on his account, or if not, he ought at least to shew his disapprobation of the cruel art, by strictly abstaining from the meats it has infected.

Most men, I suppose, esteem it a duty which they owe to God, to beg his blessing upon the food of which, through his bounty, they are about to partake. But how absurdly impious it is to beg his blessings upon a table which is furnished out in part by the abuse of his bounty, and the torture of his creatures! For my own part, I could not join in such a grace, and far from expecting a blessing, should be more apt to dread a curse, upon such a table.[96]

He offers further culinary advice to those who "have made some progress in humanity."

There is something shocking in the idea of a man swallowing alive at one sitting thirty or forty animals so large as an oyster. The advocates for oyster-eating indeed generally argue, that the oyster is instantaneously killed by cutting it away from its shell. But, in the first place, it seems improbable that life can be entirely driven out of the body of an animal by any wound, in so short a time as generally intervenes betwixt the opening of an oyster, and it being swallowed, and in the next place, it has been, I believe, observed by the microscope that in an oyster detached from both its shells, the circulation of juices had not entirely ceased at the distance of twenty-four hours after.

The same person will perhaps restrain from lobsters, because they are too often put into the water before it be hot, and so left to suffer all the anguish of boiling gradually, writhing, and making a most piteous noise.

Such a person as this of whom we are speaking, will not be apt to make his supper upon larks. When he sees them placed upon the table, he will be apt to reflect what would have been their employment, had they been suffered to live till another spring; how much they would have added to the pleasures of that season, taking advantage of its earliest gleams to welcome its approach; how they would have cheered the plowman's toil; how enlivened his own walks with their sprightly and cheerful song!

He will be far from holding out any temptation to the boy to range the heath, in order to rob the plover of her eggs. He will not be able to bear the thought of giving anguish to the breast even of a single bird, in order to satisfy, not the calls of hunger, but the capricious and petulant demands of a childish and disgraceful luxury ... [97]

A man who has made a tolerable progress in humanity, will adopt, and even bear in mind, the principle of increasing, as far as lies, within his power, the quantity of pleasure in the world, and diminishing that of pain; he will establish this to himself as a constant and inviolable rule of action, and in carrying it into practice he will not overlook one created thing that is endowed with faculties capable of perceiving pleasure and pain.[98]

Young's remarks on bee-keeping and vivisection will be enlightening to those interested in the origins of animal welfare science. His advice with regard to the former is to investigate practices of other, warmer, countries where the death of the bees is avoided, and to undertake research to find more humane apiarian methods. In the latter case, he accepts vivisection where the advances to medical knowledge are unequivocal, but rejects the practice in other instances. Unfortunately, he is willing to allow the researchers to judge what constitutes those advances.

George Nicholson

Printer, compiler, traveller, and advocate for women, George Nicholson (1760-1825) produced a remarkable compendium of much previous vegetarian and animal welfare literature in 1801, entitled *On the Primeval Diet of Man; Arguments in Favour of Vegetable Food; On Man's Conduct to Animals, &c. &c.* While most of the book repeats earlier writers from Porphyry, Plutarch, and Montaigne, to Cowper, Lawrence, and Young, Nicholson does apparently add a few snippets of his own,[99] predominantly from the perspective of a Rousseauian vegetarian simplicity.

Among Butchers, and those who qualify the different parts of animals into food, it would be easy to select persons much further removed from those virtues which would result from reason, consciousness, sympathy, and animal sensations than any savage on the face of the earth. In order to avoid all the generous and spontaneous sympathies of compassion, the office of shedding blood is committed into the hands of a set of men who have been educated in inhumanity, and whose sensibility has been blunted and destroyed by early habits of barbarity. Thus men increase misery in order to avoid the sight of it; and because they cannot endure being obviously cruel themselves, or commit actions which strike painfully on their senses, they commission those to commit them who are formed to delight in cruelty, and to whom misery, torture, and shedding of blood is an amusement. They appear not once to reflect, that WHATEVER WE DO BY ANOTHER WE DO OURSELVES ... [100]

In our conduct to animals, one plain rule may determine what form it ought to take, and prove an effectual guard against an improper treatment of them: – a rule universally admitted as the foundation of moral rectitude; TREAT THE ANIMAL WHICH IS IN YOUR POWER, IN SUCH A MANNER, AS YOU WOULD WILLINGLY BE TREATED WERE YOU SUCH AN ANIMAL. From men of imperious temper, inflated by wealth, devoted to sensual gratifications, and influenced by fashion, no share of humanity can be expected. He who is capable of enslaving his own species, of treating the inferior ranks of them with contempt or austerity, and who can be unmoved by their misfortunes, is a man formed of the materials of a cannibal, and will exercise his temper on the lower orders of animal life with inflexible obduracy. No arguments of truth or justice can affect such a hardened mind.

Even persons of more gentle natures, having been long initiated in corrupt habits, do not readily listen to sensations of feeling; or, if the principles of justice, mercy, and tenderness, be admitted, such principles are merely theoretical, and influence not their conduct ...[101]

Joseph Ritson

The antiquarian Joseph Ritson (1752-1803) first espoused vegetarianism at the age of 20, having been convinced by Mandeville's comments on castration and animal slaughter in *The Fable of the Bees*.[102] In 1802 he published *An Essay on Animal Food as a Moral Duty*, which, like Nicholson's book, is an erudite compilation of the arguments of previous writers. He argues, from a host of sources, that our primeval diet was vegetarian, that it is neither natural nor necessary to consume animal food, which is the cause of cruelty, ferocity, and human sacrifices, and that the consumption of flesh is pernicious to our body while a vegetable diet promotes health and increases our capabilities. Like Nicholson, he adds a few words of his own to his compendium.

Of those who argue that Nature lays creatures "under the necessity of devouring one another," he asks "Who is this female personification, 'Nature,' what are 'her' principles, and where does 'she' reside?"[103]

> The *sheep* is not so much "design'd" for the *man,* as the *man* is for the *tyger;* this animal being naturally carnivorous, which man is not; but *nature* and *justice,* or *humanity,* are not, allways, one and the same thing ...[104]

> If god made *man,* or there be any *intention* in *nature,* the life of the *louse,* which is as natural to him as his frame of body, is equally sacred and inviolable with his own.

> If the benefit resulting from justice or inhumanity be a sufficient reason or apology for its commission, a man will be equally justifiable in taking away the life of another, his friend, parent, or child, as in the death, on that account, of any inferior animal, and even more in proportion as the benefit attain'd was greater ...

> [T]here is neither evidence nor probability, that any one animal is "intended" for the "sustenance" of another, more especially by the privation of life. The lamb is no more "intended" to be devoured by the wolf, than the man by the tyger or other beast of prey, which experiences equally "the agreeable flavour of his flesh," and "the wholesome nutriment it administers to their stomachs"; nor are many millions of animals ever tastëed by man: such reasoning is perfectly ridiculous! ...

> Man, in a state of nature, would, at least, be as harmless as an ourang-outang.[105]

John Frank Newton

In 1811 John Frank Newton wrote *Return to Nature*, an argument in favour of returning to the primordial state of humanity. Shelley cites the work frequently in his vegetarian pamphlets. While almost all the book is devoted to the benefits of a vegetarian diet, and from a health rather than ethical perspective, he includes a few passages of a more general ethical interest. Writing, presumably, against the reasoning of Thomas Robert Malthus (in his *An Essay on the Principle of Population* [1798]), who had contended that poverty and distress are unavoidable, since population increases by geometrical ratio while the means of subsistence increase by arithmetical ratio, Newton avers:

> A writer on population of some celebrity has contended that the destructive operations of whatever sort by which men are killed off or got rid of, are of so many

blessings and benefits, and he has the triumph of seeing his doctrines pretty widely disseminated and embraced; although no point can be more clearly demonstrable than that the earth might contain and support at least ten times the number of inhabitants that are upon it.[106]

But only, of course, if humans cease to be carnivores. He concludes, relating the war against animals to the wars of nations:

So long as men are compassionate to the degree that they cannot hear a fly struggling in a spider's web without emotion, it never can be reasonably maintained that it is their natural impulse to wound and kill the dumb animals, or to butcher one another in what is called *the field of honour.*[107]

7
The Legislative Era

The first half of the nineteenth century witnessed the role of Shelley's "unacknowledged legislators," who had done so much to improve public sensibility, being replaced by that of the acknowledged legislators. Stirred to action by the advocacy of John Lawrence[1] and others, the British parliament debated no fewer than eleven animal welfare Bills between 1800 and 1835, nine of which were defeated, usually in close votes. In 1822 an act was passed against cruelty to horses and cattle, in the main, and in 1835 a Bill to outlaw bull-, bear-, and badger-baiting, and cock- and dog-fighting, was enacted with little opposition. These were followed by acts protecting dogs against cruelty (1839 and 1854) and a further measure extending the prohibition against certain blood sports (1849). Early opponents conceded that the "sports" were, indeed, "savage," but they argued that baiting and animal fights instilled courage in the population (a contention common since the reign of Elizabeth I at least); that the proposed measures were unenforceable or an undue interference in private predilections; that the existing common or statute law was adequate to deal with cases of public mischief; that no emergency situation existed which would render the common law insufficient; that the proposed measures would prohibit lower class amusements while leaving the diversions of the upper classes unaffected; or that encouraging extensive legislation into new areas of public policy would foster a spirit of Jacobinism and the undermining of respect for public order. It is worth remembering that the harbinger of liberalism, John Locke, had insisted in 1690, in the *Second Treatise on Government*, that if fewer laws were passed, the less the natural rights of citizens would be violated, and the radical Joseph Priestley argued in 1786, in his *Essay on Government*, that governments should not interfere "without the greatest caution, in things that do not immediately affect the lives, liberty or property of the members of the community." Authority needed to be controlled, not given freer rein. While each of these points resonated in the early debates, they were heard less and less frequently as the years passed, and almost never after mid-century. The mind of a nation had been transformed.

While Britain was the first to enact national parliamentary legislation to protect animals in general,[2] similar moves were afoot elsewhere, though customarily at the state or municipal level. As an independent state of the German Confederation, Hamburg issued a proclamation against animal cruelty in 1825, though it was more a statement of general principle than an ordinance or law, especially since it provided no penalties for breach.

Cruelty to animals undermines the foundations of morality and should be restrained by a definite law. Unfortunately, it cannot be denied that this evil is abroad among us. We see it daily before our eyes in various forms: in the nefarious and heartless mistreatment of horses, and of cattle for slaughter; in coarse viciousness towards domestic animals; in the cruelties which children are permitted to inflict upon all sorts of creatures without reprimand from their criminally indifferent parents – and indeed even in many truly inhuman experiments made in connection with scientific investigations in themselves of no importance.[3]

What is significant about this "statement of intent," as we might call it, is that it appears to be the first move toward controlling animal experimentation, something not finally dealt with until the last quarter of the nineteenth century, and beginning in Britain. Less ambitious legislation was, however, passed in Hamburg in 1841, and indeed throughout much of the German Confederation between 1830 and 1844. In 1828 New York made cruelty to horses, cattle, and sheep a misdemeanour, followed by Massachusetts, Connecticut, and Wisconsin in 1838, though the statutes appear to have been rarely enforced.

In Britain some continued to argue the case for specific exclusions from general legislation. For example, the bull was considered so mighty a creature it could not be included in the demeaning concept of "cattle." Cock-fighting was defended by some who opposed bull- and bear-baiting and other forms of animal "sport," since the cock possessed by nature a warring instinct, an "invincible courage." It was born to, and loved to, fight. Fox-hunting was (and by many still is) deemed legitimate, for, as eighteenth-century commentators had opined, the fox was "a subtle, pilfering foe," a "conscious villain," "the nightly robber of the fold," and "a noxious beast"; and this remained the view of many who considered themselves enlightened on animal issues. Both sides of the legislative debate encouraged people to make informed decisions. The relevant material was reprinted frequently to keep the issues constantly before the public mind, usually on the occasion of the preparation of a new Bill to be presented to Parliament. Humphry Primatt's *Duty of Mercy* (see p. 159) was reprinted twice, in an abridged form in 1821, and in full in 1831, with notes by the Reverend Arthur Broome (who became the first Secretary of the Society for the Prevention of Cruelty to Animals), specifically in support of the new legislative proposals. Thomas Young's *Essay* (see pp. 217-18) reappeared, also abridged, in 1804, 1809, and 1822 as new legislative proposals were about to appear. And John Lawrence's *Philosophical Treatise* (see pp. 215-16) was also in great demand. Few parliamentary issues have received such thorough public scrutiny.

It was also a period in which the poets continued to tout their animal-respecting wares, the essayists fulminated against animal cruelty, and the philosophers refined their points about animal pain and suffering. Yet there was rather less such philosophical writing than in the eighteenth century. The points had been made, and were, on the whole, convincing. There appeared relatively little new to say, at least on the by now less contested issues; and writers like to be original. On the other hand, much needed to be done to improve the conditions for animals. What was new was twofold. This was the era of the novel and, in general, the novelists possessed the sensibilities that had once been the prime province, though not sole prerogative, of the Romantic poets. From a practical perspective, even more important was the founding of the (later Royal) Society for the Prevention of Cruelty to Animals (SPCA) in 1824. While its initial task was to enforce legislation, it soon encompassed public education and advocacy.

Richard Brinsley Sheridan

Author of the dramatic masterpieces *The Rivals* (1775) and *School for Scandal* (1777), Richard Brinsley Sheridan (1751-1816) gave few indications of his animal sympathies in his plays. However, he became a Whig Member of Parliament in 1780, and, as one of the foremost orators of his time, was eloquent in his support of the first legislative attempt to outlaw bull-baiting, introduced by Sir William Pulteney in 1800. In response to the view that blood sports encourage valour in the population – this was the period of the Napoleonic wars – Sheridan wondered caustically in the debate whether the Spanish predilection for bull-fighting rendered them more valiant than the British. In his view bull-baiting produced as much civil as military aggression, and was not even a battle among equals.

Why, every instance of bull-baiting is an instance of renewed ferocity in the manners of the people. Do not those engaged in those sports prepare the dogs for the purpose by much previous instruction? and differing from other barbarous games, is not the animal pinned, and the dogs let loose on his sides, while he is denied the means of defence? Yet this is the sport which fires the martial spirits and confirms the native courage of Englishmen! The contrary is the truth. However, if the Right Honourable Secretary* should ever be present at a baiting, no doubt he would turn the bull loose, which certainly would be an effectual mode of raising the gallant pride of a warlike populace.[4]

* Tory statesman George Canning, who had ridiculed the Bill.

For Sheridan, both the bull and the people were losers in a baiting. The Bill was narrowly lost in the Commons by 43 votes to 41.

Robert Southey (see pp. 190-1) was equally caustic about Parliament's failure to understand the nature of animals who were treated as objects of amusement. In "The Dancing Bear" he laments:

> [W]e are told all things were made for man;
> And I'll be sworn there's not a fellow here
> Who would not swear 'twere hanging blasphemy
> To doubt that truth. Therefore, as thou wert born,
> Bruin, for Man, and Man makes nothing of thee
> In any other way – most logically
> It follows thou wert born to make him sport;
> That that great snout of thine was form'd on purpose
> To hold a ring; and that thy fat was given thee
> For an approved pomanium! To demur
> Were heresy. And politicians say
> (Wise men who in the scale of reason give
> No foolish feelings weight) that thou art here
> Far happier than thy brother bears who roam
> O'er trackless snow for food ... Besides
> 'Tis wholesome for thy morals to be brought
> From savage climes into a civilised state,
> Into the decencies of Christendom.
> Bear, Bear! It passes in the Parliament
> For excellent logic, this![5]

Thomas Erskine

Thomas Erskine (first Baron Erskine) (1750-1823), lawyer, Whig parliamentarian, Lord Chancellor (1806-7), and an intimate friend of Sheridan and Charles James Fox, the Whig leader, took up the legislative cudgel on behalf of the animals. In 1807 he published privately a strange yet delightful pamphlet: *An Appeal in Favour of the Agricultural Service of Rooks*. This was the first unambiguous intimation of his humanitarian spirit, for it was only a few years later that he came to support the emancipation of slaves. Still, as the *Dictionary of National Biography* informs us, he already had many pets, including a dog, a goose, and even two leeches; and he introduced his dog to his clients at consultations. In 1809, he moved the Prevention of Cruelty to Animals Bill, which passed the Lords, apparently persuaded by Erskine's eloquent conviction, but was lost by 37 votes to 27 in the Commons. He introduced another Bill in the following session, but he later withdrew it. In his final years he was also the primary proponent in the Upper House of Richard ("Humanity Dick") Martin's successful Bill of 1822, for which Martin was eulogized by the poet Thomas Hood as "Thou Wilberforce of hacks!" The SPCA recognized Lord Erskine as the primary force behind Parliament's eventual change of opinion and published his legislative speeches. On the second reading of his Bill on 15 May 1809 Erskine argued:

Nothing is more notorious than that it is not only useless, but dangerous, to poor suffering animals, to reprove their oppressors, or to threaten them with punishment. The general answer with the addition of bitter oaths and increased cruelty, is "What is that to you?" If the offender be a servant, he curses you, and asks "Are you my master?" and if he be the master himself, he tells you that the animal is his own. The validity of this most infamous and stupid defence, arises from the defect in the law which I seek to remedy. Animals are considered as property only. To destroy or abuse them, from malice to the proprietor, or with an intention injurious to his interest in them is criminal, but the animals themselves are without protection; the law regards them not substantively; they have no rights.[6]

In the same speech, he observed that

For every animal which comes in contact with Man, and whose powers, and qualities, and instincts, are obviously constructed for his use, Nature has taken the same care to provide, and as carefully and as bountifully as for Man himself, organs and feelings for its own enjoyment and happiness. Almost every sense bestowed upon Man is equally bestowed upon them – seeing, hearing, feeling, thinking, the sense of pain and pleasure, and passions of love and anger, sensibility to kindness, and pangs from unkindness and neglect, are inseparable characteristics of *their* natures as much as of *our own*.[7]

Erskine was already asserting an important part of what Charles Darwin took such scientific pains to demonstrate over sixty years later in *The Descent of Man*. He acknowledged human dominion, but a restricted one in light of animal sensibilities:

We are too apt to consider animals under the dominion of man in no view but that of property; whereas the dominion granted to us over the world is not conceded to us absolutely. It is a dominion in trust; and we should never forget that the animal over which we exercise our power has all the organs which render it susceptible of pleasure and of pain. It sees, it hears, it smells, it tastes. It feels with acuteness. How mercifully, then, ought we to exercise the dominion entrusted to our care![8]

Lewis Gompertz

Jewish philanthropist, inventor of devices to minimize the burden to animals, and advocate of the oppressed whether enslaved, female, impoverished, or brute being, Lewis Gompertz (1779-1861) was one of the founders, and second Secretary, of the SPCA. He was a vegetarian, indeed almost a vegan, who refused to wear leather or silk, would not ride in a coach on account of the suffering to horses, and abominated hunting and animal experimentation. He wrote two significant books on animal protection: *Moral Inquiries on the Situation of Man and Brutes* (1824) and *Fragments in Defence of Animals* (1852), the second discussing vivisection and whale hunting, along with what were then the more customary topics. The first was written in response to some of the disappointments experienced in the judicial interpretations of Martin's Act of 1822, advocating new and more extensive measures. For its day, it was one of the most progressive and complete of tracts, though he acknowledged at the end having only just encountered Thomas Young's *Essay on Humanity to Animals* "containing many [subjects which Gompertz had] omitted, and also corroborating several sentiments we have expressed."[9] In the opening chapter, he acknowledged his era as being an ameliorative one:

[F]ortunate have been the efforts of genius and of virtue in increasing the happiness and in improving the character of man ... The time may, we trust, not be far distant, when all men will treat each other as brothers; when each individual will participate in the good of his neighbour, and add sympathy instead of reproach to his sufferings and failings, of whatever nature they may happen to be ...

The dreadful situation of the brute creation, particularly of those which have been domesticated, claims our strictest attention. Let every mind capable of reflection, direct it for a moment to that of the horse and the ass, by whose exertions we (in the present state of things) derive so much advantage; and let their cases be examined by a judgement unbiased by habit. We are indeed so accustomed to their excruciating sufferings, that they fail of exciting the attention even of the benevolent, who concur in the idea that a horse was created to be whipped on its almost bare skin, simply to compel it to perform the labour that purpose or caprice of his master may require; and in doing which so many persons take delight, to the utmost of what the nature of the animal can support.

The elegant appearance of some of our horses, and the health they seem to possess, naturally incline us to suppose them to be in a state of enjoyment. But how many of these elegant animals are destroyed monthly, and daily, by our stage-coachmen, postillions, etc., who only calculate on their own profits! Besides, it must be recollected that it requires very great sufferings, and time, to effect much change in the figure of an animal in the prime of life; and a view of their whole lives will also lead to a very different impression. When the young horse is first receiving his education, he is immediately taught to be suspicious and fearful by the torture it commences with, and by the different mutilations he is then subjected to; the very possession of their tails and ears has been deemed too great an indulgence; and sometimes the mere amputation of the former will not suffice, the stump must also undergo the operation of nicking.[10] This consists in making several cuts across the inside of the stump, which is then kept strained towards the back of the animal, so as to prevent it from ever afterwards lying in its natural position. They are then, after suffering still greater mutilations, *broken-in,* as it is termed, in a manner the severity of which is of course according to the disposition of their tutors; to the difficulty with which they understand the signs of men, whose language they are unacquainted with; and to the aversion they very naturally and justly evince at being enslaved and ill-treated. They are, however, at last, by dint of punishment, made subservient to our use. They have then two thick irons placed in their mouths, by which they are controlled; these are occasionally pulled and jerked by their drunken drivers with their whole force, notwithstanding that one of them acts by a lever to increase its power. The sides of their mouths and tongues are said frequently to get between these two irons, and to be wounded by them, as is sometimes indicated by their bleeding. They are then incessantly flogged, spurred, and over-exerted, to set off their master's equipage, for the amusement of his servants, or some other unworthy purpose, till they lose a great part of their strength and beauty, and are afterwards sold to some stageman, hackney-coachman, etc., by whom, besides being half-starved, they are worse treated because their strength is less, till they become unfit for any purpose but a dust-cart for a scavenger, or perhaps for a dealer in horse flesh, who takes care to get his last penny out of them, and who frequently finds it to his interest to finish by working them to death.

This is the unexaggerated state of the generality of the horses of *humane* Englishmen. They are even very many of them still suffering more, and which are continually to be seen in our hackney coaches, etc., adding lameness to their other calamities; and which, after having had their eyes cut out by strokes of the whip, are, by fear of chastisement, compelled to go too quickly, and in the greatest dread, over ground they cannot see, and without giving any proof of their relying on the guidance of their drivers.

It is strange that persons who would shudder at the idea of even *seeing* a human being flogged, think nothing of witnessing or even inflicting themselves like punishment on dumb animals. They seem to think it of no importance, because they are used to it; and truly do they suffer every day and continually, what we should think a severe trial for half an hour ...

Who can dispute the inhumanity of the sport of hunting ... of pursuing a poor defenceless creature for mere amusement, till it becomes exhausted by terror and fatigue, and of then causing it to be torn to pieces by a pack of dogs? From what kind of instruction can men, and even women, imbibe such principles as these? How is it possible they can justify it? And what can their pleasure in it consist of? Is it not solely in the agony they can produce to the animal? They will pretend that it is not, and try to make us believe so too – that it is merely in the pursuit. But what is the object of their pursuit? Is there any other than to torment and destroy? ...

Forbid it that we should give assent to such tenets as these! That we should suffer for one moment or reason to be veiled by such delusions! But on the contrary let us hold fast every idea, and cherish every glimmering of such kind of knowledge, as that which shall enable us to distinguish between *right* and *wrong,* what is due to one individual – what to another.[11]

After nine chapters in like vein on different topics, Gompertz comes to his peroration.

> Even to mankind the effects of this Bill, when properly amended, may be expected to be highly beneficial, as cruelty is cruelty under whatever colouring it may appear; and whether exercised on a man or a fly, cruelty is still cruelty. It matters not whether the victim be furnished with two legs or with four, with wings, with fins, or with arms; where there is sensation, there is subject for cruelty, and in proportion to the degree of sensation will its actions operate.
>
> Cruelty, then, always being the same, how terrible must be the result of encouraging it in any instance!
>
> It is too evident that the passion for it being once excited, soon extends itself beyond the bounds prescribed, and objects of the brute creation alone do not satisfy its cravings; human beings then become the sacrifice, and tyranny and bloodshed the result.[12]

Gompertz's faith in humanity's improved character and its potential to encompass the brute creation in its compassion may strike our cynical age as unduly optimistic, reflective of nineteenth-century utopianism. Yet his faith was not entirely without empirical foundation. Increased sensibility had been a growing part of moral expectations ever since the time of Shaftesbury at the onset of the eighteenth century. In 1816 the Royal Society had refused membership to Dr. Wilson Philip because of his animal experimentation excesses. Several prominent magazines, the *European Magazine*, *Monthly Review*, the *London Magazine*, and the *Gentleman's Magazine* included, were wholeheartedly behind new legislation, which seemed increasingly likely of success, avidly promoted by dissenting Christians and philosophical Utilitarians, but also supported enthusiastically by a significant body of established clergy. Even the staid *Times*, which a few years previously opposed the bull-baiting Bill as an undue interference in private lives, was now emphatic in its opposition not only against bull-baiting, but against other forms of animal "entertainment," too. On the occasion of a notorious lion bait in 1825, *The Times* described the spectacle as "this extremely gratuitous as well as disgusting exhibition of brutality." It condemned: "the torture of a noble lion with the full consent and for profit of a mercenary being who had gained large sums of money by hawking the poor animal about the world and exhibiting him. It is vain, however, to make any appeal to humanity where none exists or to expiate on mercy, justice and retribution hereafter when those whom we strive to influence have never heard that language in which alone we can address them."[13]

If economic laissez-faire had ever actually been deemed to promote the public good more effectively than did legislation, it was no longer in vogue. The *Morning Post* ran a leading article on behalf of the lion against the owners of his canine persecutors: "The majestic Master of the Forest, true to his invincible character when fairly roused in his own defence, shook the vile brutes 'like dewdrops from his noble main' [sic]; thus satisfactorily proving the futility of any future attempts of the same cruel and barbarous description."[14] If the *Post* could not spell, it certainly could pronounce.

New pro-animal books and pamphlets became increasingly common. In 1826 Sir **Richard Phillips,** the vegetarian publisher of the *Leicester Herald,* wrote *Golden Rules of Social Philosophy* in which he applied the Biblical maxim to "any sentient or suffering being" including "the meanest of animals."[15] The Gloucester surgeon, and President of the local RSPCA, **Ralph Fletcher** wrote in his *A Few Notes on Cruelty to Animals* (1842) that we should show respect for "the interest and feelings of every sentient being that holds life."[16]

William Youatt

The veterinarian William Youatt (1776-1847) wrote *The Obligations and Extent of Humanity to Brutes* (1839), arguing, as had his utilitarian mentor Jeremy Bentham, that the only standard of judgment of an action concerning humans or animals should be its "increasing or diminishing the general sum of enjoyment." He opened his book with a chapter on the "Obligations of Humanity to Animals as founded on the Scriptures," perhaps the most complete historical examination of Biblical sources. In his succeeding chapter "On the Duty of Humanity to Animals" he held out great hopes for the effects of the new legislation:

> [W]ill any of those who act as ill-humour or passion prompt tell us what code of law, human or divine, permits them to use their dumb slaves with brutality? Will they tell us on what principle there should exist an acknowledged right in favour of man, and none with regard to the inferior animal? Is common feeling a different thing in the human being and the brute?
>
> These are questions, however, which need not be farther urged. The law of the land has begun to recognize the *jus animalium.* It will no longer permit the claim of property to be urged against it. It will permit no man to use even his own with injustice and cruelty. It has entered on this new and glorious career of legislation; and it is to be hoped that it will pursue its course until the brute receives, in return for the benefits which it bestows on man, "sufficient nourishment, and merciful treatment, and a death as little painful as circumstances will permit."[17]

For Youatt, there are important differences between humans and animals, but they are always matters of degree and never of kind.

> No one can doubt the existence of imagination in the brute. We perceive it in his dreams; he runs, he hunts, he fights while the external senses are asleep. When the sportsman is preparing for his excursion, what is it but the anticipation of the pleasures of the field that animates his dog, and produces the most boisterous ebullitions of joy? When the hunter starts at a distant cry of the hounds – every

motion and every attitude telling how eager he is to break away – what is this but the vivid recollection of past, and the anticipation of future pleasure?

The brutes, then, are evidently possessed of attention, and memory, and association, and imagination. The difference between the biped and his quadruped slave is in degree, and not in kind ... [18]

But we are told, or used to be told, that the brute is the slave of instinct alone. As for the term *instinct,* I never could affix a definite meaning to it; – I would substitute the word *propensity,* which I can understand ... There are propensities in every animal to associate together for mutual comfort and protection, and for the continuance of their species; and there is the strongest of all propensities or instincts, – the devotion of the parent to the rearing and happiness of the child ... [19]

Dr. [Erasmus] Darwin [in his *Zoonomia*] used to tell a curious story of a wasp. As he was walking one day in his garden he perceived a wasp upon the gravel walk with a fly almost as large as itself, which it had just caught. Kneeling down in order to observe the manoeuvres of the murderer, he saw him distinctly cut off the head and the body; and then, taking up the trunk, to which the wings still remained attached, he attempted to fly away. A breeze of wind, however, acting upon the wings of the fly, turned the wasp around, and impeded or forbad his progress. Upon this, he alighted again on the gravel, deliberately sawed off one wing, and then the other, and having thus removed the cause of his embarrassment, he flew off with his booty.

Could any process of reasoning be more perfect than this? ... Here is a perfect course of reasoning.[20]

Youatt emphasizes his conclusion with regard to the nature of animals. "*They are all perfect in their way.* Their propensities and their reasoning powers are precisely what they should be."[21]

John Styles

Anglican clergyman and Doctor of Divinity, John Styles (1782-1849) won the £100 prize offered by the SPCA "for the best Essay on the obligations of humanity as due to the brute creation" with his 1839 book *The Animal Creation: Its Claims on Our Humanity Stated and Enforced.* Some of the volume constitutes a defence of Christian theology, both natural and revealed, and some a defence of respectful flesh-eating; most is devoted to the condemnation of a litany of cruelties practised against animals. Civilization is not the answer, Styles avers, but rather "Practical Christianity." "The most abhorred barbarities inflicted on men and animals prevailed at those periods of its history when the human intellect had reached its highest attainments, and society had received all the polish that the fine arts and letters, and philosophy could confer upon it ... from all this worldliness we must be totally severed."[22]

As true Christians, Styles argues, we would oppose inflicting sartorial cruelties on horses, countenancing vivisection, and a whole host of other invasive practices. It was probably this practical outlook that recommended his essay to the SPCA as much as his devout commitment to Christianity. His victory in the contest is perhaps somewhat surprising – Youatt also entered – in that Styles's section on the avoidance of luxury in meat-eating is plagiarized, in good part verbatim, from Thomas Young's 1798 *Essay*.[23] One must assume the SPCA jury did not notice.

The practical measures that would do most to promote animal well-being were organized by Styles as follows:

CO-OPERATION, forming societies, and maintaining correspondence with branch divisions and active and influential individuals through every part of the country; securing funds, and opening channels for their prompt, energetic, and successful application; are among the first duties of the friends of humanity. These different societies should offer prizes for improvements in slaughtering, in the construction of market carts, and the different vehicles which are used for the conveyance of cattle, and for any other object which may be secured by exciting emulation in the minds of those to whose care animals are intrusted, for the purpose of relieving them from the sufferings which they endure from custom and habit, and the operation of a barbarous system of treatment. Individuals co-operating with these associations should, upon principle and uniformly, refuse to hire cabs and hackney coaches that are drawn by lean horses; they should also reprove acts of cruelty, and spare neither time nor exertion to bring the perpetrators to justice ...

Associations like those for which we plead are absolutely necessary for the purposes of enforcing the law, watching the conduct of those who are exposed to the temptation of offending, diffusing knowledge, exciting attention, and awaking and employing the energy of virtuous and holy principle ...

LEGISLATION must still be the business of humanity. The operation of the existing law upon the popular mind has been most salutary; still much remains to be done to secure the community against the guilt and disgrace of suffering torture to be inflicted on any creature that has a right to its protection. A very large proportion of the evil it is not possible for the law to reach. The pits, and the rings, and the most glaring of the miscellaneous barbarities have been arrested in their progress. Bull-baiting is making its last struggle; and though one of the inspectors of the Animals' Friend Society very narrowly escaped being murdered, as reported in a Birmingham newspaper a few months since; yet at Stamford* it has nearly been suppressed, chiefly by the efforts of the Society for the Prevention of Cruelty. The pits are extinct; though premises are still hired for the purpose of badger-drawing, dog-fighting, and similar enormities, in the retreats of low ale-houses and places difficult of access. The cruelties of the slaughter house, the knacker-yard, that in spite of law, and recent regulations still continue, and the thousand nameless tortures inflicted on horses, asses, and dogs, which are scarcely checked, require still further legislative interference. We want a law on the subject, clear,

---

* Stamford was the site of one of the more notorious traditional bull-baits.

precise, comprehensive, compulsory as to punishment, and which would defy evasion ...

The general EDUCATION of the people in useful knowledge is among the indispensable remedies of cruelty and the many other evils that afflict the social state ... by education, we do not mean merely storing the intellect with the principles of science and the manual arts. We include in education mental and moral discipline. The intellect and the heart must be cultivated together. Obedience is doubly secured when men not only bow to the authority of the laws, but acknowledge their reasonableness; when they feel that to be human and to abstain from every act of cruelty, is not only lawful, but right. Education ought to be directed especially to the cultivation of kindly sentiments towards the inferior creatures.[24]

John Clare

The nature poet John Clare (1793-1864) was renowned for a while in the 1820s for his *Poems Descriptive of Rural Scenery* (1820) and *The Village Minstrel* (1821). He was declared insane in 1837 and committed to an asylum. In recent decades his poetry has come to be appreciated once again. Just before badger-baiting was outlawed in 1835 he wrote in sympathy of the animal's unmerited plight:

Badger

When midnight comes a host of dogs and men
Go out and track the badger to his den,
And put a sack within the hole, and lie
Till the old grunting badger passes by.
He comes and hears – they let the strongest loose.
The old fox hears the noise and drops the goose.
The poacher shoots and hurries from the cry,
And the old hare half wounded buzzes by.
They get a forked stick and bear him down
And clap the dogs and take him to the town,
And bait him all day with many dogs,
And laugh and shout and fright the scampering hogs.
He runs along and bites at all he meets:
They shout and hallo down the noisy streets.

He turns about to face the loud uproar
And drives the rebels to their very door.
The frequent stone is hurled where'er they go;
When badgers fight, then every one's a foe.
The dogs are clapt and urged to join the fray;
The badger turns and drives them all away.
Though scarcely half as big, demure and small,
He fights with dogs for hours and beats them all.

The heavy mastiff, savage in the fray,
Lies down and licks his feet and turns away.
The bulldog knows his match and waxes cold,
The badger grins and never leaves his hold.
He drives the crowd and follows at their heels
And bites them through – the drunkard swears and reels.

The frighted women take the boys away,
The blackguard laughs and hurries on the fray.
He tries to reach the woods, an awkward race,
But sticks and cudgels quickly stop the chase.
He turns agen and drives the noisy crowd
And beats the many dogs in noises loud
He drives away and beats them every one,
And then they loose them all and set them on.
He falls as dead and kicked by boys and men,
Then starts and grins and drives the crowd agen;
Till kicked and torn and beaten out he lies
And leaves his hold and cackles, groans, and dies.[25]

It is difficult to imagine a more effective paean to the courage of the badger, and it is one that must have aroused sympathy in all but the most hardened.

In general, Clare was a friend to the more readily forgotten: the baited badger rather than the bull and bear, the wren rather than the commonly eulogized nightingale, the dowdy sparrow rather than the radiant swallow, the fly rather than the purity of one's ale. In his unpunctuated nature notes (c. 1825) he wrote:

When I was a boy I kept a tamed cock sparrow 3 years   it was so tame that it would come when calld & flew where it pleasd when I first had the sparrow I was fearful of the cat killing it so I used to hold the bird in my hand toward her & when she attempted to smell of it I beat her   she at last would take no notice of it & I ventured to let it loose in the house   they were both very shoy at each other at first & when the sparrow ventured to chirp the cat would brighten up as if she intended to seize it but she went no further than a look or a smell at length she had kittens & when they were taken away she grew so fond of the sparrow as to attempt to caress it   the sparrow was startled at first but came to by degrees & venturd so far as at last to perch upon her back   puss would call for it when out of sight like a kitten & would lay mice before it the same as she would for her own young & they always lived in harmony so much the sparrow would even take away bits of bread from under the cat's nose & even put itself in a posture of resistance when offended as if it reckoned her no more than one of its kind ... [26]

In an entertaining piece on flies (c. 1845), Clare described how they made themselves at home, sipping the tea and beer, how they are allowed every liberty, and concluded: "they are the small or dwarfish portion of our own family, and so many fairy familiars that we know and treat them as one of ourselves."[27]

In 1833 the Society for the Promotion of Christian Knowledge published *Insects and their Habitations: A Book for Children*, which carried something of the same message, if in a rather less secular and kinship vein.

It is a sin against God who created both them and you, to inflict unnecessary suffering upon any one of his creatures. Ask yourselves too, how you would like such treatment, from one stronger than yourself. If you meet a beetle or caterpillar, step aside, and do not wantonly crush it. And should you see a poor earth-worm, lying in the dusty path, parched with the sun, and too much exhausted to regain his home, extend a kind hand to help him, and place him on the nearest cool and moist ground. He is a harmless little creature, though not pleasing to the eye or agreeable, but he is God's workmanship; and while you are thankful for being endowed with reason, and with an immortal soul, let the inferior creatures enjoy their lives while they may.[28]

Mary Shelley

Daughter of Mary Wollstonecraft and William Godwin, and wife of Percy Shelley, Mary Shelley (1797-1851) was the author of *Frankenstein: the Modern Prometheus* (1818), and four other novels written after the early death of her husband by drowning. The subtitle to *Frankenstein*, often omitted, is the key to her most enduring story and indicates its relevance to the modern animal rights and environmental debates. The book is about the dangers of scientific and technological intrusion into the natural order, and the preference for rustic simplicities over intellectual pretensions, for natural animality over the refinements of culture. At no point does Shelley discuss animal issues directly, but they are frequently addressed as asides. It is notable that her "daemon" was a vegetarian who showed more kindness to animals than did most of his human acquaintances. "Alas! why does man boast of sensibilities superior to those apparent in the brute; it only renders them more necessary beings. If our impulses were confined to hunger, thirst, and desire, we might be nearly free; but now we are moved by every wind that blows and a chance word or scene that the word may convey to us ..."[29]

The daemon comments on the traditional fable in which an ass tries to gain his master's affection by imitating the behaviour of a lap-dog but is beaten for his behaviour. "It was as the ass and the lap-dog; yet surely the gentle ass whose intentions were affectionate, although his manners were rude, deserved better treatment than blows and execration ... my chief delights were the sight of the flowers, the birds, and all the gay apparel of summer ... My food is not that of man; I do not destroy the lamb and the kid to glut my appetite; acorns and berries afford me sufficient nourishment."[30] In her Rousseauian "return to nature" novel *The Last Man* (1826) she continued her critique of civil society. And, reminiscent of the Kieran legend,[31] Rousseauian natural compassion plays its role in the rescue of a small bird threatened by a predator. "A robin red-breast dropt from the frosty branches of the trees, upon the congealed rivulet; its panting breast and half-closed eyes shewed that it was dying: a hawk appeared in the air; sudden fear seized the little creature; it exerted its last strength, throwing itself on its back, raising its talons in impotent defence against its powerful enemy. I took it up and placed it on my breast. I fed it with a few crumbs from a biscuit; by degrees it revived; its warm fluttering heart beat against me ..."[32] Shelley does not comment on how this interference in nature differs from that of her scientist, Victor Frankenstein. The paradoxical reality of the human soul lies in its sympathizing with Shelley in her contradictions. She defends the weak against the strong. Nature glorifies the strong in its crushing of the weak.

She concludes with her evaluation of the human animal: "Our name was written 'a little lower than the angels,' and behold, we were no better than ephemera. We had called ourselves the 'paragon of animals,' and lo! we were a 'quintessence of dust' ... Truly we were not born to enjoy, but to submit, and to hope."[33]

Charles Waterton

If once the elegies were predominantly to horses, dogs, cats, and nightingales, improved naturalist awareness and extending sensibilities soon found a place for the traditionally less favoured species, as we saw, for example, in the writings of John Clare.[34] Traveller and naturalist Charles Waterton (1782-1865) wrote *Essays in Natural History* (1838) – of which Charles Dickens had a well-thumbed copy, with pencilled notes in the section on ravens[35] – and *Wanderings in South America, the North-west of the United States and the Antilles in the Years 1812, 1816, 1820 and 1824* (1825), whence this extract on his experience with a sloth whom he surprised during his sojourn in Demerara (Guyana) in 1820:

As soon as we got up to him he threw himself upon his back, and defended himself in gallant style with his fore-legs. "Come, poor fellow," said I to him, "if thou hast got into a hobble to-day, thou shalt not suffer for it: I'll take no advantage of thee in misfortune; the forest is large enough both for thee and me to rove in: go thy ways up above, and enjoy thyself in these endless wilds; it is more than probable thou wilt never have another interview with man. So fare thee well." On saying this, I took a long stick which was lying there, held it for him to hook on, and then conveyed him to a high and stately mora. He ascended with wonderful rapidity, and in about a minute he was almost at the top of the tree.[36]

Barron Field (1786-1846), lawyer and erstwhile theatrical critic of *The Times*, associate of Lamb, Wordsworth, and Coleridge, was Judge of the Supreme Court of New South Wales from 1817-24. While in Australia he wrote *First Fruits of Australian Poetry* (1819) which included just two poems: "Botany Bay Flowers" and "Kangaroo," whence this extract, written to counter the common view that the marsupial was an aberration of nature.

> Thou yet art not incongruous,
> Repugnant or preposterous.
> Better proportion'd animal,
> More graceful or ethereal,
> Was never followed by the hound,
> With fifty steps to thy one bound.
> Thou can'st not be amended: no;
> Be as thou art; thou art best so.[37]

Alexander Pushkin

Along with Gogol, reputed father of the Russian novel, Alexander Pushkin (1799-1837) proved a worthy forerunner of Dostoevsky and Tolstoy as animal-compassionate storytellers. Poet and dramatist as well as novelist, Pushkin was moved by the beauty of the Crimean and Caucasian wilderness and the heroes of Russian history. In *Dubrovsky* (1833) he describes the agony, confusion, and merriment occasioned by a village fire.

> At that moment a new apparition attracted his attention: a cat was running about the roof of the burning barn, not knowing where to jump. Flames were on all sides of it. The poor creature mewed plaintively for help; the small boys yelled with laughter, watching the animal's despair.
>
> "What are you laughing at, you little devils?" the blacksmith said to them angrily. "Aren't you ashamed? One of God's creatures perishing, and you little fools pleased about it!" – and putting a ladder against the burning roof he climbed up to save the cat. It understood his intention and with grateful eagerness clutched at his sleeve. The blacksmith, half scorched, descended with his burden.[38]

The Brontës

Charlotte (1816-55), Emily (1818-48), and Anne (1820-49) were daughters of an Anglican clergyman, living in isolated Haworth, Yorkshire, yet possessing a worldly wisdom rarely matched by those who inhabited the great cities. Sensibility to animals pervades their striking novels. For example, we read in **Charlotte**'s *Shirley* (1849) of how her character would select a soothsayer to consult. In preference: "Neither man nor woman, elderly nor young: – [but] the little Irish beggar that comes barefoot to my door; the mouse that steals out of the cranny in the wainscot; the bird that in frost and snow pecks at my window for a crumb; the dog that licks my hand and sits beside my knee."[39]

Later, she describes the admirable Farren and Miss Helstone:

They took a similar interest in animals, birds, insects, and plants: they held similar doctrines about humanity to the lower creation; and had a similar turn for minute observation on points of natural history. The nest and proceeding of some ground-bees, which had burrowed in turf under an old cherry-tree, was one subject of interest: the haunts of certain hedge-sparrows, and the welfare of certain pearly eggs and callow fledglings another.

Had "Chambers Journal" existed in those days, it would certainly have formed Miss Helstone's and Farren's favourite periodical ... both would have put implicit faith, and found great savour in its marvellous anecdotes of animal sagacity.[40]

There is much besides which reflects Charlotte's respect for animated nature, but nothing with quite the pathos of this description of the setting sun. "The grey church and greyer tombs look divine with this crimson gleam on them. Nature is now at her evening prayers: she is kneeling beside those red hills. I see her prostrate on the great steps of her altar, praying for a fair night for mariners at sea, for travellers in deserts, for lambs on moors, and unfledged birds in woods."[41]

In **Anne** Brontë's *Agnes Grey* (1847) we encounter the incorrigible child Tom, and are reminded that an interest in nature does not guarantee a respect for it.

I observed on the grass about his garden certain apparatus of sticks and cord, and asked what they were.

"Traps for birds."

"Why do you catch them?"

"Papa says they do harm."

"And what do you do with them, when you catch them?"

"Different things. Sometimes I give them to the cat; sometimes I cut them in pieces with my penknife; but the next I mean to roast alive."

"And why do you mean to do such a horrible thing?"

"For two reasons; first to see how long it will live – and then to see what it will taste like?"

"But don't you know it is extremely wicked to do such things? Remember, the birds can feel as well as you; and think, how would you like it yourself?"

"Oh, that's nothing! I'm not a bird, and I can't feel what I do to them."

"But you will have to feel it sometime, Tom – you have heard where wicked people go to when they die; and if you don't leave off torturing birds, remember you will have to go there, and suffer just what you have made them suffer."

"Oh, pooh, I shan't. Papa knows how I treat them; and he never blames me for it; he says it's just what *he* used to do when *he* was a boy. Last summer he gave me a nest full of young sparrows, and he saw me pulling off their legs and wings, and heads, and never said anything, except that they were nasty things, and I must not let them soil my trousers; and Uncle Robson was there too, and he laughed, and said I was a fine boy."

"But what would your mamma say?"

"Oh she doesn't care – she says it's a pity to kill the pretty singing birds, but the naughty sparrows, and mice and rats I may do what I like with. So now, Miss Grey, you see it is *not* wicked."

"I still think it is, Tom; and perhaps your papa and mamma would think so too, if they thought much about it. However," I internally added, "they may say what they please, but I am determined you shall do nothing of the kind, as long as I have the power to prevent it."[42]

After several other instances of animal cruelty, Miss Grey kills some fledglings out of compassion to prevent their being further tormented by Tom. Tom's mother remonstrates with the governess.

"I am sorry, Miss Grey, you should think it necessary to interfere with Master Bloomfield's amusements; he was very much distressed about your destroying the birds."

"When Master Bloomfield's amusements consist in injuring sentient creatures," I answered, "I think it is my duty to interfere."

"You seem to have forgotten," said she calmly, "that the creatures were all created for our convenience."

I thought the doctrine admitted some doubt, but merely replied – "If they were, we have no right to torment them for our amusement."

"I think," said she, "a child's amusement is scarcely to be weighed against the welfare of a soulless brute."

"But, for the child's own sake, it ought not to be encouraged to have such amusements," answered I, as meekly as I could to make up for such unusual pertinacity. "Blessed are the merciful, for they shall obtain mercy."

"Oh, of course! but that refers to our conduct towards each other."

"The merciful man shows mercy to his beast," I ventured to add.

"I think *you* have not shown much mercy," replied she, with a short, bitter, laugh; "killing the poor birds by wholesale, in that shocking manner, and putting that boy to such misery, for a mere whim."

I judged it prudent to say no more.[43]

And finally:

A little girl loves her bird ... Why? Because it lives and feels, because it is helpless and harmless. A toad, likewise, lives and feels, and is equally helpless and harmless, but though she would not hurt a toad, she cannot love it like the bird, with its graceful form, soft feathers, and bright, speaking eyes.[44]

Of the three sisters, it was, however, **Emily** who was closest to the animals. In **Elizabeth Gaskell**'s *Life of Charlotte Brontë* (1857), written just two years after the eldest sister's untimely death (she was the last sister to die), Gaskell has more to say about Emily's attitude to animals than Charlotte's or Anne's.

Soon after [Charlotte] came back to Haworth in a letter to one of the household where she had been staying, there occurs this passage: – "Our poor little cat has been ill two days, and is just dead. Emily is sorry." These few words relate to points in the character of the two sisters, which I must dwell upon a little. Charlotte was more than commonly tender in the treatment of all dumb creatures, and they, with that fine instinct, so often noticed, were invariably attracted towards her. The deep and exaggerated consciousness of her personal defects – the constitutional absence of hope, which made her slow to trust in human affection, and consequently slow to respond to any manifestation of it – made her manner shy and constrained to men and women, and even to children ... But not merely were her actions kind, her words and tones were ever gentle and caressing, toward animals: and she quickly noticed the least want of care or tenderness on the part of others towards any poor brute creature ...

The feeling, which in Charlotte partook of something of the nature of an affection, was, with Emily, more of a passion. Some one speaking of her to me, in a careless kind of strength of expression, said "she never showed regard to any human creature; all her love was reserved for animals." The helplessness of an animal was its passport to Charlotte's heart; the fierce, wild, intractability of its nature was what often recommended it to Emily. Speaking of her dead sister, the former told me that from her many traits in Shirley's character were taken; her way of sitting on the rug reading, with her arm around her rough bull-dog's neck; her calling to a strange dog, running past, with hanging head and lolling tongue, to give it a merciful draught of water, its maddened snap at her, her nobly stern presence of mind, going right into the kitchen, and taking up one of Tabby's red-hot Italian irons to sear the bitten place, and telling no one, till the danger was well nigh over, for fear of the terrors that might beset their weaker minds. All this, looked upon as well-invented fiction in "Shirley," was written by Charlotte with streaming eyes; it was the literal true account of what Emily had done. The same tawny bull-dog (with his "strangled whistle"), called "Tartar" in "Shirley" was "Keeper" in Haworth parsonage, a gift to Emily.

Emily is constrained to punish Keeper for a peccadillo (excessively by modern standards). Still, Gaskell informs us:

The generous dog owed her no grudge; he loved her dearly ever after; he walked first among the mourners to her funeral; he slept moaning for nights at the door of her empty room, and never, so to speak, rejoiced, dog-fashion, after her death. He, in his turn, was mourned over by the surviving sister. Let us hope somehow, in half Red Indian creed, that he follows Emily now; and, when he rests, sleeps on some soft white bed of dreams, unpunished when he awakens to the land of shadows.

Now we can understand the force of the words, "Our poor little cat is dead. Emily is sorry."[45]

Alphonse de Lamartine

It was in the first half of the nineteenth century that animal respect infiltrated French literature in a consistent manner, notably among the poets. Poet, novelist, historian, and statesman, Alphonse de Lamartine (1790-1869) – briefly head of the provisional government after the February Revolution of 1848 – was perhaps too interested in melancholia, affairs of the heart, religion, and politics to devote very much attention to animals in his poetry and novels. But in *Les Confidences* (1848) Lamartine described his vegetarian predilections. Having explained the orientation of his early education from his mother, based on the principles of Rousseau and Bernardin de Saint-Pierre, he added:

It was in accord with this system that she raised me. My education was a second-hand philosophical education corrected and softened by motherhood.

In practice this education was derived substantially from Pythagoras and [Rousseau's] *Emile.*

Accordingly, the greatest simplicity of dress and the most rigorous frugality of food constituted its foundation. My mother was convinced, a conviction I share, that killing animals in order to feed on their flesh and blood is one of the weaknesses of the human condition; that it is one of those curses inflicted on mankind, either by his fall from grace, or by the hardening of the heart through his own perversity. She believed, a belief which I share with her, that the custom of hardening the heart towards the most gentle animals, our companions, our helpers, here on earth, our brethren in work and even in affection, that these sacrifices, blood lusts, and the sight of palpitating flesh, both brutalize the person and harden the instincts of the heart. She believed, and I believe it too, that this food, appearing more succulent and remedial, contained irritants and putrefactions which turned the food sour and shortened man's life-span. As evidence in favour of abstinence from flesh, she would cite the numerous peoples of India, who denied themselves every living being, and the robust and healthy pastoral peoples, and even our industrious rural workers, who work more, live simpler and longer lives, and who eat meat perhaps ten times in their lives. She never allowed me to partake until I was thrown pele-mele into school life. To rid my desire for it, had I ever had one, she did not reason with me but employed that instinct which resonates with us better than logic.

I had a lamb, a gift from a peasant from Milly, which I had taught to follow me everywhere, like a most loving and faithful dog. We loved each other with that first passion which children and young animals naturally have for each other. One day the cook said to my mother in my presence: "Madame, the lamb is fat; the butcher has come to ask for it; should I give it to him?" I cried out. I threw myself on the lamb. I demanded to know what the butcher wanted with it; and what was a butcher. The cook replied that he was a man who killed lambs, sheep, small calves, and lovely cows for money. I could not believe it. I begged my mother. And readily got mercy for my friend. Some days later, my mother, who was going into town, took me with her, and brought me, as if by accident, to the butcher's yard. I saw men with naked and bloody arms, who were slaughtering an ox; others were cutting the throats of calves and sheep; yet others were carving their still palpitating limbs. Rivulets of blood steamed here and there on the pavement. A profound compassion, mingled with horror, came over me, and I asked that we pass by quickly. The thought of those horrible and disgusting scenes, the obligatory foretaste of one of the meat platters that I saw served up at the table, caused me to loathe animal food and dread butchers. Despite the necessity of conforming to the customs of society, where [in my political career] I could be found eating what everyone else eats, I retained a rational repugnance for cooked flesh, and have always found it difficult not to view the butcher's trade as sharing something with that of bureaucrats. I thus lived until I was twelve years of age on bread, dairy products, vegetables, and fruit. My health was no less robust, my growth no less rapid, and perhaps it was as a result of this diet that I acquired those pure traits, that refined sensibility, and that quiet serenity of humour and character that I have maintained to this day.[46]

George Sand

Feminist author who demanded for women the same sexual liberties enjoyed by men, paramour successively of Sandau, Musset, and Chopin, George Sand (1804-76) wrote novels which both please and perplex the modern animal rights enthusiast, though in reality her paradoxes reflect no more than the contradictions of her age.

In her first non-collaborative novel, *Indiana* (1831), she first indicates her understanding of the nature of a pointer's relationship to its master.

The only cheerful affectionate face in the group was that of a handsome hunting dog, a large pointer, which had stretched its head out on the knees of the seated man. It had a remarkable long body, stout hairy legs, a pointed fox-like nose, and an intelligent face bristling with untidy hairs; behind them like two topazes gleamed two large, tawny eyes. Those hunting dog's eyes, so bloodthirsty and sinister in the ardour of the hunt, now expressed a feeling of indefinable melancholy and tenderness, and when the master, the object of all that instinctive love which is sometimes superior to rational affections, stroked the silvery coat of the handsome dog, the animal's eyes glistened with pleasure and its long tail swept the hearth rhythmically, scattering the ashes on the patterned floor.

Although the eponymous Indiana is an avid hunter she shows her compassionate side when: "M. Delmare, sitting on the porch steps, is killing swallows in flight. Indiana seated at her loom by the drawing room table, leans forward from time to time to look sadly at the Colonel's cruel pastime in the courtyard."

It is, however, in a letter she writes that the fullness of her sensibility is evidenced. "I have more faith than you have. I serve the same God but I serve him better and with a purer heart. Yours is the god of men, the king, the founder, and protector of your race [males]; mine is the God of the universe, the creator, the support, and hope of all creatures. Yours has made everything for you alone; mine has made all species for each other. You think yourselves masters of the world, I think you are only its tyrants ... God doesn't want the creatures of His hands to be oppressed and crushed ..."[47] To be sure, Sand is more concerned with the oppression of women than that of animals, but nonetheless "all species" are made "for each other." In *The Master Pipers* (1852), the muleteer recognizes and acts on the interests of his charges, even when they counter his own interest to make speed. "When he had eaten enough for the moment, Huriel asked me to pack the rest of the food and added: 'If you're tired, my dears, you can take a nap here, for our animals need us to let the heat of the day go by. This is the time when the flies are fiercest, and in the groves the animals can rub and shake themselves as they please.'"

Moreover, Sand understands that different species have different needs. "The mole loves its dark cave as the bird loves its nest in the tree tops and the ant would laugh in your face if you tried to convince her that there are kings whose palaces are finer than her little nest."[48] In contrast, *The Master Pipers* also features a sanguine description of a mule-beating and Sand emphasizes the differences between humans and other species rather than the similarities.

Jules Michelet

Regarded as the greatest French historian of the late Romantic school, Jules Michelet (1798-1874) was the author of the multi-volume *L'Histoire de France* (1833-67), *Le Peuple* (1846), and *Jeanne d'Arc* (1853). He also wrote Romantic impressions of world cultural history, nature, and life, including *La Bible de l'humanité* (The Bible of Humanity) (c. 1865) and *L'Oiseau* (The Bird) (1856). In *The Bible of Humanity* he addresses "The Redemption of Nature."

One is never saved alone. Man does not deserve his salvation but by the salvation of all. The animal also has its rights before God. "The animal! Mysterious! Immense world of dreams and silent griefs! Without language, too many visible signs express these griefs. All nature protests against the barbarity of man who disowns, degrades, and tortures his inferior brother."

This sentence which I wrote in 1848 has frequently recurred to me ...

No one can evade death either for himself or others. But mercy demands at least that none of those short-lived creatures should die without having lived, and loved, and transmitted through love its little soul, and performed that sweet duty which the tenderness of God imposes, "to have had the divine moment."

Hence the beautiful and really pious beginning of the [Hindu] *Ramayana* is this exquisite outburst of Valmiki upon the death of a poor heron, in which utterance he weeps: "O, hunter, may thy soul never be glorified in all the lives to come, for thou hast stricken that bird in the sacred moment of love!" ... the Indian genius, the richest and most prolific, knows neither the little nor the great, but generously embrace the whole as a universal brotherhood, as if all possessed but one soul.[49]

It was, however, in *The Bird* that Michelet's animal sympathies were given their most complete expression.

Without waiting for human listeners, and with all the greater security, the nightingale had still chanted in the forest his sublime hymn. And for whom? For her whom he loves, for his offspring, for the woodlands, and, finally, for himself, his most fastidious auditor ...

For the first time I perceived the seriousness of human existence when it is no longer surrounded by the grand society of innocent beings whose movements, voices, and sports are, so to speak, the smile of creation ... all natural history I had begun to regard as a branch of the political. Every living species, each in its humble right, striking at the gate and demanding admittance to the bosom of democracy. Why should their elder brothers repulse them beyond the pale of those laws which the universal Father harmonizes with the law of the world? ...

What is required for its protection? To reveal the bird as a *soul,* to show that it is a *person* ...

... science ... cannot study unless it kills; the sole use which it makes of a living miracle is, in the first place, to dissect it. None of us carry into our scientific pursuits that tender reverence for life which nature rewards by unveiling to us her mysteries ... [50]

Behold, then, the nest is made, and protected by every prudential means which the mother can devise. She rests upon her perfected work, and dreams of the new guest which it shall contain tomorrow.

At this hallowed moment, ought not we, too, to reflect and ask ourselves what is it that this mother's bosom contains?

A soul? Shall we dare to say that this ingenious architect, this tender mother, has a *soul?*

Many persons, nevertheless, full of sense and sympathy, will denounce, will reject this very natural idea as a scandalous hypothesis.

Their heart would incline them towards it; their mind leads them to repel it; their mind, or at least their education; the idea which, from an early age, has been impressed upon them.

Beasts are only machines, mechanical automata; or if we think we can detect in them some glimmering rays of sensibility and reason, those are solely the effect of *instinct.* But what is instinct? A sixth sense – I know not what – which is undefinable, which has been implanted in them, not acquired by ourselves – a blind force which acts, constructs, and makes a thousand ingenious things without their being conscious of them, without their personal activity counting for aught.

If it is so, this instinct would be invariable, and its works immovably regular, which neither time nor circumstances would ever change ...

Ah, if she be a machine, what am I myself? and who will then prove that I am a person? If she has not a soul, who will answer to me for the human soul?

Open your eyes to the evidence. Throw aside your prejudices, your traditional and derived opinions. Preconceived ideas and dogmatic theories apart, you cannot offend Heaven by restoring a soul to the beast. How much grander the Creator's work if he created persons, soul, and will, than if he has constructed machines!

Dismiss your pride, and acknowledge a kindred [spirit] in which there is nothing to make a devout mind ashamed. What are these? They are your brothers.[51]

The translator of *The Bird*, **W.H. Davenport Adams** had published his own book *The Bird World* in 1878, the year before he undertook the translation. Although he does not allow the bird an immortal soul, he sees all the finest human attributes and aspirations symbolized in the creature.

The bird has always been a favourite with man; and in parable, legend, myth, and song, almost invariably occurs in connection with picturesque and romantic association. In the fable of the Greek as in the saga of the Norsemen, in the polished odes of the Latin as in the more spontaneous lyrics of the English, it is the image of all that is light, and innocent, and graceful. Especially is it the embodiment of human aspiration; of the desire of the human heart, when oppressed with the burden and the mystery of this unintelligible world, to take to itself wings, and flee away, and be at rest. Poised in the air on equal wings, it is the type of self-reliance and independence. Swooping downwards with arrowy rush on some doomed prey, it is an emblem of power. Clinging to the partner of its little nest, it is the type of love. Carolling in the sunshine of the early morning, it is the symbol of praise.

Davenport Adams followed this with quotations from the poetry of Spenser, Herbert, Tennyson, Wordsworth, Shelley, Keats, and Webster, before adding:

It is not difficult to understand why between Man and the Birds so close a fellowship should exist. We are drawn towards most of them by their comparative helplessness; but more, perhaps, by the singular conditions of their existence. They are the children of the air, and enjoy the possession of an attribute we covet, – the capacity of flight. We see them rising to heaven's gate on outstretched wings, and hovering far away among the blue until the eye can scarce distinguish each floating speck; and we are filled with a sense of envy. How lightly and gracefully they pass from tree to tree, or skim the surface of the waters in search of their insect prey; or cleave the air with rushing pinions, as if bent on some mission of urgent speed! The facility and elegance of their movements is not less admirable than the beauty of their form.

But everything about the birds seems adapted to engage our interest. Most of them attract by the glowing colours of their plumage, which in exquisite brilliancy and subtle harmony, surpass the finest efforts of human artists. Others charm by the sweetness of their song, which is always distinct and characteristic – so that the notes of the lark are easily distinguished from those of the blackbird. Others invite attention by the marvellous ingenuity displayed in the construction of their nests; others, by the care and foresight with which they provide for their offspring. Then the variety of family and sub-family is marvellously rich. Some species are so tender and frail as to appeal at once to our sympathies and command our protection; others are so fierce and strong as to compel our admiration and surprise.[52]

Charles Baudelaire

Dying in obscurity, his poems denounced as at best decadent, at worst licentious if not obscene, Charles Baudelaire (1821-67) produced his most famous collection of poetry as *Les Fleurs du mal* (The Flowers of Evil) in 1857. There were several later editions with additions. Today he is recognized as one of the first French poets to transcend the didactic limitations of the Romanticism of his own age. His poetry reflects his compassion for the captured albatross and the concern he felt for the swan deprived of water, but it is "Cats" which best embodies a different genre of sensibility, as well as representing cats in a more insightful manner than had been the custom.

> Fervent lovers and austere scholars
> Both love, in their mature season,
> The powerful gentle cats, pride of the house,
> Which like them are sensitive of the cold and sedentary.
>
> Friends of science and ecstasy,
> They search for silence and the horror of darkness;
> Erebus would have taken them for his funeral steeds,
> If they could bend their pride to slavery.
>
> While dreaming they take the noble attitudes
> Of great Sphinxes stretched out in the heart of the desert,
> Which seems to sleep in endless revery;
>
> Their fecund loins are full of magic sparks,
> And specks of gold like fine sand,
> Add vague stars to their mystical eyeballs.[53]

Honoré de Balzac

Honoré de Balzac (1799-1850) was one of the most prolific and most frequently read of French novelists. Much in the manner of Thomas Hobbes, Balzac stressed the self-interested similarities between humans and other species, more to bring humans down to size than to elevate the animals, a thesis in which he was followed by Emile Zola (1840-1902) in *La Bête humaine* and other novels. In the general preface (1842) to his series of novels and short stories known as *La Comédie humaine*, Balzac informs his readers:

> The leading idea of this human comedy came to me at first like a dream ... The idea came from the study of human life in comparison with the life of animals ...

There is but one animal. The Creator used one and the same principle for all organized being.

An animal is an essence which takes external form, or, to speak more correctly, takes the difference of its form from the centres or conditions in which it comes to its development. All zoological species grow out of these differences. The announcement and pursuit of this theory, keeping it as he did in the harmony with preconceived ideas of the Divine Power, will be the lasting glory of Geofroy Saint-Hilaire,* the conqueror of Cuvier[†] in this particular branch of science, – a fact recognized by Goethe in the last word which came from his pen.[54]

Because of his popularity, Balzac did more than the theologians, scientists, philosophers, and natural scientists he cites in his cause – Swedenborg, Saint-Martin, Leibniz, Buffon, Bonnet, and Needham – to persuade the French public that there is one primeval form from which all of animality is derived. The difference between animals, including human animals, must always be less than the similarities.

Arthur Schopenhauer

Among the philosophers of the legislative era, three stand out in their contributions to the debate on our relationship with, and obligations to, other species: Arthur Schopenhauer (1788-1860), the German philosopher of the will; John Stuart Mill (1806-73), the utilitarian who introduced quality, as opposed to mere quantity, of pleasure into the greatest happiness principle; and Auguste Comte (1798-1857), the influential French founder of the philosophy of Positivism.

Already in his early and philosophically most important work, *Die Welt als Wille und Vorstellung* (The World as Will and Idea) of 1819, Schopenhauer gives a suggestion of the role which animals would play in his later philosophy.

[The other-regarding man] sees that the distinction between himself and others, which to the bad man is so great a gulf, only belongs to a fleeting and illusive phenomenon. He recognizes directly and without reasoning that the in-itself of his own manifestation is also that of others, the will to live, which constitutes the inner nature of everything and lives in all; indeed, that this applies also to the brutes and the whole of nature, and therefore he will not cause suffering even to a brute.[55]

Later, imbued with Brahminism and Buddhism – if not to the extent of refraining from the consumption of meat – and equally imbued with a distaste for Judaism, Christianity, and Islam, Schopenhauer treated human responsibilities to animals, the importance of animal welfare legislation, and the role of animal protection societies in his *Über das Fundament der*

---

* An early proponent of the theory of evolution.
[†] Stout defender of the fixity of species.

Moral (On the Basis of Morality) of 1841 (second edition 1860). The central theme is a critique of Kant's view that the possession of reason is the criterion of being entitled to moral consideration. Schopenhauer insists that, to the contrary, it is the possession of will, the will to live, rather than reason. He acknowledges that the sum of "the condition of clear recollection, circumspection, foresight, intention, the planned co-operation of many, the State, trades, arts, sciences, religions and philosophies ... strikingly distinguishes man's life from that of the animal."[56] However, he adds:

general morality [is] outraged by the proposition [of Kant] that beings devoid of reason (hence animals) are *things* and therefore should be treated merely as *means* that are not at the same time an *end.* In agreement with this, it is expressly stated in [Kant's] *Metaphysical Principles of the Doctrine of Virtue,* section 13, that "man can have no duty to any beings except human"; and then it says in section 17 that "cruelty to animals is contrary to man's duty to *himself,* because it deadens in him the feeling of sympathy for their sufferings, and thus a natural tendency that is very useful to morality in relation to *other human beings* is weakened." ... [animals] are mere "things," mere *means* to any ends whatsoever. They can therefore be used for vivisection, hunting, coursing, bullfights, and horse-racing, and can be whipped to death as they struggle with heavy carts of stone. Shame on such a morality ... that fails to recognize the eternal essence that exists in every living thing, and shines forth with inscrutable significance from all eyes that see the sun![57]

By contrast, for Schopenhauer:

Every action refers to, and has as its ultimate object, a being susceptible to weal and woe ... If it is to have moral worth, its motive cannot be an egoistic claim, direct or indirect, near or remote.[58] ... [This is] the Only Genuine Moral Incentive ... justice as a genuine voluntary virtue certainly has its origin in compassion ... Boundless compassion for all living beings is the firmest and surest guarantee of pure moral conduct, and needs no casuistry ... Tastes differ, but I know of no finer prayer than the one which ends old Indian dramas ... It runs: "May all living beings remain free from pain."[59]

He then applies the principle he has adduced.

Since compassion for animals is so intimately associated with goodness of character, it may be confidently asserted that whoever is cruel to animals cannot be a good man. This compassion also appears to have sprung from the same source as the virtue that is shown to human beings has. Thus, for example, persons of delicate feelings, on realizing that in a bad mood, in anger, or under the influence of wine, they unnecessarily or excessively, or beyond propriety, ill-treated their dog, horse, or monkey – these people will feel the same remorse, the same dissatisfaction with themselves as is felt when they recall a wrong done to human beings, where it is called the voice of reproving conscience. I recall having read of an Englishman who, while hunting in India, had shot a monkey; he could not forget the look which the dying animal gave him, and since then had never again fired at monkeys. Similarly William Harris, a true Nimrod,* in 1836 and 1837 traveled far into the interior of Africa merely to enjoy the pleasure of hunting. In his book, published in Bombay in 1838, he declared how he shot his first elephant, a female. The next morning he went to look for the dead animal; all the other animals had fled from the neighborhood except a young one, who had spent the night with his dead mother. Forgetting all fear, he came toward the sportsmen with the clearest and liveliest evidence of inconsolable grief, and put his tiny trunk round them in order to appeal to them for help. Harris says he was then filled with real remorse for what he had done, and felt as if he had committed a murder. We see this English nation of fine feelings distinguished above all others by a conspicuous sympathy for animals, which appears at every opportunity, and has been strong enough to induce the English, in spite of the "cold superstition" that other wise degrades them, to repair by legislation the gap their religion has left in morality ... in Europe a sense of the rights of animals is awakening, in proportion to the slow dying and disappearing of the strange notions that the animal world came into existence simply for the benefit and pleasure of man. Such notions result in animals being treated exactly like things, for they are the source of their rough and quite ruthless treatment in Europe ... To the glory of the English, then, let it be said that they are the first nation whose laws have quite seriously protected even the animals from cruel treatment. The ruffian must actually make amends for having committed an outrage on animals, even when they belong to him. Not content with this, the English have voluntarily formed in London a Society for the Prevention of Cruelty to Animals. By private means and at considerable expense, it does a great deal to counteract the tortures that are inflicted. Its emissaries are secretly on the watch to appear later and denounce the torturers of dumb sensitive creatures, and everywhere their presence is feared.[60][†]

John Stuart Mill

The tensions in the writings of John Stuart Mill (1806-73) are a trifle disconcerting, if not so pronounced as among some others. He appears to demean animals in the opening pages of *Utilitarianism* (1863), when he avows: "it is better to be a human being dissatisfied than a pig satisfied"[61] – and certainly he appears, in proclaimed defence of utilitarianism, to disavow the utilitarian idea of having pleasures, happiness, or satisfaction

---

* Nimrod was a descendent of Cush, who is recorded as a mighty hunter. See Genesis 10:8 and I Chronicles 1:10.
† At this point, in the second edition of 1860, Schopenhauer adds a lengthy footnote on the success of Lewis Gompertz's Society of Animal Friends in enforcing the legislation and the efforts of *The Times* in impugning the character of the daughter of a Scottish baronet who had taken a knife to her horse. He refers also to the "praiseworthy efforts" of a Hofrath (Court Counsellor), Herr Perner, who was devoting his attention to instituting an animal protection society in Germany and of the existence of an Animals' Friends Society in Pennsylvania.

count as the very criterion of goodness. Nonetheless, in 1868 he expressed dissatisfaction at the restrictive approach of the RSPCA and declined the offer of a Vice-Presidency "while it is thought necessary or advisable to limit the society's operations to the offences committed by the uninfluential classes of society,"[62] citing pigeon-shooting exhibitions, fox-hunting, and the use of feathers and furs for fashion as instances of the Society's failure to act against the pastimes of the prosperous. Mill was also active in the campaign against vivisection.

In *The Principles of Political Economy* (1848), Mill had earlier argued in favour of further legislation to protect animals, expressing dissatisfaction at the lack of seriousness with which existing legislation treated crimes against animals.

The reasons for legal intervention in favour of children, apply not less strongly to the case of those unfortunate slaves and victims of the most brutal part of mankind, the lower animals. It is by the grossest misunderstanding of the principles of liberty, that the infliction of exemplary punishment on ruffianism practised towards these defenceless creatures, has been treated as meddling by government with things beyond its province; an interference with domestic life. The domestic life of domestic tyrants is one of the things which it is the most imperative on the law to interfere with; and it is to be regretted that the metaphysical scruples respecting the nature and source of the authority of government, should include many warm supporters of laws against cruelty to animals, to seek for a justification of such laws in the incidental consequences of the indulgence of ferocious habits to the interests of human beings, rather than in the intrinsic merits of the case itself. What it would be the duty of a human being, possessed of the requisite physical strength, to prevent by force if attempted in his presence, it cannot be less incumbent on society generally to repress. The existing laws of England on the subject are chiefly defective in the trifling, almost nominal, maximum, to which the penalty even in the worst cases is limited.*[63]

In defending fellow utilitarian Jeremy Bentham's principle of utility against the Kantian onslaught of the theologian Dr. Whewell, Mill argued in 1874:

There is no great stretch of hypothesis in supposing that in proportion as mankind are aware of the tendencies of actions to produce happiness or misery, they will like and commend the first, abhor and reprobate the second ...

This then is Dr. Whewell's noble and disinterested ideal of virtue. Duties, according to him, are only duties toward ourselves and our like.

We are to be humane to them, [according to Dr. Whewell] because we are human not because we and they alike feel animal pleasures ... The morality which

---

* Fourteen days in prison or forty shillings fine.

depends upon the increase of pleasure alone, would make it our duty to increase the pleasure of pigs or of geese rather than that of men, if we are sure that the pleasures we could give them were greater than the pleasures of men ...

It is not only not an obvious, but to most persons not a tolerable doctrine, that we may sacrifice the happiness of men provided we can in that way produce an overplus of pleasure to cats, dogs, and hogs.

Having analyzed Whewell's claim with regard to what most persons find tolerable by comparison with the former treatment of "black men ... in the Slave States of America" and the treatment of serfs in feudal Europe, arguing that what is culturally accepted is not necessarily what is justifiable, Mill concluded:

Nothing is more natural to human beings, nor, up to a certain point in cultivation, more universal, than to estimate the pleasures and pains of others as deserving of regard exactly in proportion to their likeness to ourselves. These superstitions of selfishness had the characteristics by which Dr. Whewell recognizes his moral rules; and his opinion on the rights of animals shows that in this case he is at least consistent. We are perfectly willing to stake the whole question on this one issue. Granted that any practice causes more pain to animals than it gives pleasures to man; is that practice moral or immoral? And, if exactly in proportion as human beings raise their heads out of the slough of selfishness, they do not with one voice answer "immoral," let the morality of the principle of utility be for ever condemned.[64]

John Stuart Mill has reversed himself. Contrary to what he wrote in *Utilitarianism*, on the principle of utility he now wishes to maintain, it must indeed be better to be a pig satisfied than a human being dissatisfied.

Auguste Comte

In the Positivist writings of Auguste Comte (1798-1857), the respect and admiration for other species is concentrated largely on those animals he deems capable of a symbiotic relationship with humans, predominantly certain "higher" mammals. His view of the potential human-animal relationship is perhaps unique – indeed, most of his contemporaries, including many who adhered to his general philosophy, were skeptical, though John Stuart Mill commended him for it. Comte's estimation of animal capacity, especially of inter-species sociability, exceeds anything we have hitherto encountered. Animals, he asserts, are capable of progress, thought, social life, and inter-species altruism. In his *Theory of the Great Being* (1854), he argued:

Our conception of the constitution of the Great Being remains defective unless we associate with man all the animal races which are capable of adopting the common motto of all the higher natures: *Live for Others*. Without the animals, the Positive Synthesis could but imperfectly form the permanent alliance of all voluntary agents to modify the external conditions of our life so far as they are modifiable ... Political action recognizing [the benevolent instincts] as supreme, is enabled to carry out the largest plans, by bringing all our practical remedies to bear on the direct improvement of man's condition upon earth, in concert with the animal races which, as sympathetic, are justly associated with Humanity.[65]

In *Theory of the Future of Man* (1854) Comte adds that human control of nature through technology will improve the lot of animals as well as humankind.

[I]n Western industry we have reached the point of considering it barbarous to use men as a weight or motive power; all purely mechanical services, not merely statical but dynamical, we project out of ourselves, by the aid of a judicious employment of machines. Hence a simultaneous advance both in personal dignity and in social utility, as we can avail ourselves of the mental and moral value inseparable from the humblest children of Humanity, but previously lost to the race and painful to the individual. Our progress in this respect too often stops short at the substitution of animals for men, not sufficiently using inorganic forces. The better use will have as consequences, respect for our voluntary [animal] assistants and increased use of the blind forces of nature, the vast power inherent in which should suffice us did we but know how to use it; for instance, did we know how to employ to better purpose the immense force of the tide. From the animals as from men, we should demand not merely automatic service, as opposed alike to economy and morality. When we have learnt to avail ourselves of the heart and intelligence of our [animal] allies to such a degree as to entrust them with the main superintendence of inorganic forces, we shall find a better use for human agents thus set free, and be able to develope on a large scale the sense of fraternity upon earth.[66]

In the same volume, Comte opposes animal (and human) dissection.

To such an extent can reasoning take the place of observation, that most anatomical laws can be deduced from physiological conceptions with as much ease as was the duality of the cerebral organs, indicated by the fact of double vision, and by our instinct of symmetry. As salutary for the instinct as for the heart, the discipline of synthesis will make us shrink from substituting animals for men [in vivisection], the priesthood of Sociocracy more even than the priesthood of Theocracy being disposed to insist upon the constant respect of our [animal] auxiliaries.[67]

His general principles are elaborated in his primary thesis on *The System of Positive Philosophy, or Treatise on Sociology, Instituting the Religion of Humanity* (1851, begun in 1830).

[T]he happiness of living for others is not entirely monopolised by Man. Many animals possess it likewise, and indeed give evidence of a higher degree of sympathy than our own, although the practical results of it are not so great as with us. In

these higher races* a careful distinction should be made between social and domestic feeling ... The social sympathies have no deep influence except with races anal-
agous to the canine; and in these the conjugal and parental affections are weak ...

Under theological systems the highest aspirations of men were to live ultimately
with gods or angels. Is it strange that a dog or a horse should seek to associate
themselves with beings of a higher order than themselves? Pride alone could deter
any being from a connection so sure to satisfy his noblest sympathies. Here then in
the animal kingdom is the first spontaneous form of the great sociological principle
that all permanent union between independent beings must rest upon Love.

Thus although Egoism is the more ordinary basis of unity amongst animals, there
are still many races which approximate through Altruism to unity of a nobler and
more beautiful kind, and also more complete and more durable ... For such animals
should be regarded henceforward as accessory members of the Great Being, a title
to which they have a far higher claim than many useless members of the human
race who have never been anything but a burden to Humanity. Those who doubt
this should think of the privation that Humanity would suffer even now by the loss
of these subordinate allies ...

The true dignity of human life will be reasserted as a practical and philosophic
truth. The reality and the utility which distinguish Positivism both imply the ele-
mentary feelings of universal brotherhood shall be extended to all beings found
worthy to associate with Man. And we shall be benefited by the addition no less
than they; for it will give a purer and more vivid character to the sympathies which
we desire to encourage. In promoting this result the new priesthood [of Positivism]
will soon be supported by popular feeling, which even in Christian times always
resisted the orthodox view as absurd and egotistical. A remodelled education will
thus establish the true estimate of the [animal] social races as allies indispensable to
our researches and occupations ... Varying the candid expression of a hero who
knew what ambition was, we may say that it is better to be the first of animals than
the lowest of angels.

Animal Unity will thus gradually establish itself by the same process as Human
Unity.[68]

If we are today surprised at Comte's expectations of animals we should
recall one of the founding principles of the London Zoological Society in
establishing the Regent's Park Zoo in London in 1826. A primary purpose
was the "introducing and domesticating of new Breeds or Varieties of Animals ... likely to be useful in Common Life." Its only success in domestication was the golden hamster!

Ralph Waldo Emerson
Following the British example of 1822, the state of New York enacted
anti-cruelty legislation in 1828, with Massachusetts next in 1836, and

---

* That is, species.

with Connecticut and Wisconsin in 1838. A number of other states quickly followed suit. These statutes, even though their enforcement was by and large neglected, reflected the growing concern for responsibilities to animals and awe for nature, exemplified in both the American transcendentalist movement and the interest in communal projects such as the Brook Farm experiment, designed to provide a unity between human and nature.

Transcendentalism's most eloquent advocate was the poet and essayist Ralph Waldo Emerson (1803-82), ably assisted by, among others, Bronson Alcott and Margaret Fuller. Henry David Thoreau and Nathaniel Hawthorne were loosely attached. The co-operative community of Brook Farm (1841-47), stimulated by Coleridge and Southey's planned but abortive Susquehanna project and the communitarian ideals of the French Romantic socialist Charles Fourier, was an attempt to provide a practical basis for the transcendentalists' ideas on vitality in religious thought and emotion, and their opposition to slavery and oppression of all kinds.

Influenced by meetings with Wordsworth and Coleridge, combined with his own Platonic idealism and immersion in the mystical writings of Swedenborg and the Oriental sacred books, Emerson produced the bible of transcendentalism's orientation to animals and nature in his famous essay of 1836, *Nature*.

Neither does the wisest man extort her secret, and lose his curiosity by finding out all her perfection. Nature never became a toy to a wise spirit. The flowers, the animals, the mountains, reflected the wisdom of his best hour, as much as they had delighted the simplicity of his childhood ...[69] The lover of nature is he whose inward and outward senses are still truly adjusted to each other, who has retained the spirit of infancy even into the era of manhood ... the primary forms, as the sky, the mountain, the tree, the animal, give us a delight *in and for themselves* ...[70] Nature stretches out her arms to embrace man, only let his thoughts be of equal greatness ...[71] There seems to be a necessity in spirit to manifest itself in material forms; and day and night, river and storm, beast and bird, acid and alkali, preexist in necessary Ideas in the mind of God, and are what they are by preceding affections in the world of spirit ...[72] A life in harmony with Nature, the love of truth and justice, will purge the eyes to understand her text ... Space, time, society, labor, climate, food, locomotion, the animals, the mechanical forces, give us sincerest lessons, day by day, whose meaning is unlimited. They educate both the Understanding and the Reason ... every animal function from the sponge up to Hercules, shall hint or thunder to man the laws of right and wrong, and echo the Ten Commandments ... The chaff and the wheat, weeds and plants, blight, rain, insects, sun – it is a sacred emblem from the first furrow of spring to the last stack which the snow of winter overtakes in its fields ...[73] Who can estimate ... [h]ow much industry and providence and affection we have caught from the pantomime of brutes? ... Each creature is only a modification of the other; the likeness in them is more than difference, and their radical law is one and the same ... as we degenerate ... [w]e are as much strangers in nature, as we are aliens from God. We do not understand the notes of birds. The fox and the deer run away from us; the bear and the tiger rend us.[74]

Emerson follows, among others, Borelli, Leibniz, Erasmus Darwin, and Goethe, and precedes Balzac and Charles Darwin, in his understanding that "Each creature is only a modification of the other ... their radical law is one and the same." He recognizes that in our historical development we have alienated ourselves from our fellow creatures, and he understands that we delight in animated nature, not as instrument, but as animals "in and for themselves."

In his poetry Emerson extolled several species, including the bee and the titmouse. In "The Humble-Bee" we read:

Wiser far than human seer,
Yellow-breeched philosopher!
Seeing only what is fair,
Sipping only what is sweet,
Thou dost mock at fate and care,
Leave the chaff, and take the wheat.[75]

Of the titmouse, he writes:

And I affirm the spacious North
Exists to draw thy virtue forth,
I think no virtue goes with size;
The reason of all cowardice
Is, that men are overgrown,
And, to be valiant, must come down
To the titmouse dimension.[76]

Nathaniel Hawthorne

Renowned novelist and short-story writer, Nathaniel Hawthorne (1804–64) participated in the Brook Farm experiment, but found it not to his personal taste. *The Blithedale Romance* (1852) is based on that experience. However, in *The House of the Seven Gables* (1851), he expresses many of the "return to nature" ideals of Brook Farm. He pursues, for example the Isaiah 11 ideal of the peaceable kingdom.[77]

Phoebe found an unexpected charm in this little nook of grass, and foliage, and aristocratic flowers, and plebeian vegetables. The eye of Heaven seemed to look down into it, pleasantly, and with a peculiar smile; as if glad to perceive that Nature, elsewhere overlooked, and driven out of the dusty town, had there been able to retain a breathing-place. The spot acquired a somewhat wilder grace, and yet a very gentle one, from the fact that a pair of robins had built their nest in the pear-tree, and were making themselves exceedingly busy and very happy, in the dark intricacy of its boughs. Bees, too – strange to say – had thought it worth their while to come hither, possibly from the range of hives beside some farm-house, miles away. How many aerial voyages might they have made, in quest of honey, or honey-laden, betwixt dawn and sunset! Yet late as it now was there still arose a pleasant hum out of one or two of the squash blossoms, in the depths of which these bees were plying their golden labor ...

Nor must we forget to mention a hen-coop, of very reverend antiquity, that stood in the farther corner of the garden, not a great way from the fountain. It now contained only Chanticleer,* his two wives, and a solitary chicken ...

The girl ran into the house to get some crumbs of bread, cold potatoes, and other such scraps as were suitable to the accommodating appetite of fowls. Return-ing, she gave a peculiar call, which they seemed to recognize. The chicken crept through the pales of the coop, and ran with some show of liveliness to her feet; while Chanticleer and the ladies of his household regarded her with queer, sidelong glances, and then croaked one to another, as if communicating their sage opinions of her character ...

"Here, you odd, little chicken!" cried Phoebe. "Here are some nice crumbs for you!"

The chicken, hereupon, though almost as venerable in its appearance as its mother – possessing, instead, the whole antiquity of its progenitors, in miniature – mustered vivacity enough to flutter upward and alight on Phoebe's shoulder.

"This little fowl pays you a high compliment!" said a voice behind Phoebe ...

"The chicken really treats you like an old acquaintance," continued he, in a quiet way, while a smile made his face pleasanter than Phoebe at first fancied it. – "Those venerable personages in the coop, too, seem very affably disposed. You are lucky to be in their good graces so soon! ..."

"The secret is," said Phoebe smiling, "that I have learned to talk with hens and chickens."[78]

In *The American Notebooks* a calf is being taken to the fair to be sold. "He was a prettily behaved urchin and kept thrusting his hairy muzzle between William and myself, apparently wishing to be stroked and petted. It was an ugly thought, that his confidence in human nature, and Nature in gen-eral, was so ill rewarded by cutting his throat and selling him in quarters. This, I suppose, has been his fate before now."[79] In *The Artist of the Beau-tiful* (1844) Hawthorne condemns the catching of a butterfly and argues that the greatest artistic work can never match the real beauty of nature.

[Owen Warland] wasted the sunshine, as people said, in wandering through the woods and fields and along the banks of streams. There, like a child, he found

---

* That is, a rooster. "Chanticleer" was the proper name of the cock in the medieval leg-end of Reynard the Fox and appeared later in the same guise in Chaucer's *Canterbury Tales*.

amusement in chasing butterflies or watching the motions of water insects. There was something truly mysterious in the intentness with which he contemplated those living playthings as they sported on the breeze or examined the structure of an imperial insect whom he had imprisoned. The chase of butterflies was an apt emblem of the ideal pursuit in which he had spent so many golden hours; but would the beautiful idea ever be yielded to his hand like the butterfly that symbolized it? Sweet, doubtless, were these days, and congenial to the artist's soul. They were full of bright conceptions, which gleamed through his intellectual world as the butterflies gleamed through the outward atmosphere, and were real to him, for the instant, without the toil, and perplexity, and many disappointments of attempting to make them visible to the sensual eye. Alas that the artist, whether in poetry or whatever other material, may not content himself with the inward enjoyment of the beautiful, but must chase the flitting mystery beyond the verge of his ethereal domain, and crush its frail being in seizing it with a material grasp ...

He had lost his faith in the invisible, and now prided himself, as such unfortunates invariably do, in the wisdom which rejected much that even his eye could see, and trusted confidently in nothing but what his hand could touch.[80]

Owen's artistic appreciation is reawakened by the butterfly. "[T]his creature of the sunshine had always a mysterious mission for the artist – had reinspired him with the former purpose of his life. Whether it were pain or happiness that thrilled through his veins, his first impulse was to thank Heaven for rendering him again the being of thought, imagination and keenest sensibility that he had long ceased to be."[81] The artist then spends years creating a jewelled replica of a butterfly, which is itself capable of simulated flight, and which is then irreparably damaged by a child. "And as for Owen Warland, he looked placidly at what seemed the ruin of his life's labor, and which was yet no ruin. He had caught a far other butterfly than this. When the artist rose high enough to achieve the beautiful, the symbol by which he made it perceptible to mortal senses became of little value in his eyes while his spirit possessed itself in the enjoyment of reality."[82]

Another of the Concord sages, **Margaret Fuller**, put the peaceable kingdom and butterfly messages together when she averred that our goal must be to secure "that spontaneous love for every living thing, for man and beast and tree, which restores the golden age."[83]

William A. Alcott

Educator and physician, William A. Alcott (1798-1859), a cousin of the transcendentalist Bronson Alcott, was a prolific author whose *Vegetable Diet* (1848) was one of the most eloquent arguments for vegetarianism at that time.

The destruction of animals for food, in its details and tendencies, involves so much of cruelty as to cause every reflecting individual – not destitute of the ordinary sensibilities of nature – to shudder ...

It must be obvious that the custom of rendering children familiar with the taking away of life, even when it is done with a good degree of tenderness, cannot have a very happy effect. But, when this is done, not only without tenderness or sympathy, but often with manifestations of great pleasure, and when children, as in some cases, are almost constant witnesses of such scenes, how dreadful must be the results!

In this view, the world, I mean our own portion of it, sometimes seems to me like one mighty slaughterhouse – one grand school for the suppression of every kind, and tender, and brotherly feeling – one grand process of education to the entire destitution of all moral principle – one vast scene of destruction to all moral sensibility, and all sympathy with the woes of those around us. Is it not so?

I have seen many boys who shuddered, at first, at the thought of taking the life, even of a snake, until compelled to do it by what they conceived to be duty, and who shuddered still more at taking the life of a lamb, a calf, a pig, or a fowl! And yet I have seen these same boys, in subsequent life, become so changed, that they could look on such scenes not merely with indifference, but with gratification. Is this change of feeling desirable? How long is it after we begin to look with indifference on pain and suffering in brutes, before we begin to be less affected than before by human suffering? ...

How shocking it must be to the inhabitants of Jupiter, or some other planet, who had never before witnessed these sad effects of the ingress of sin among us, to see the carcasses of animals, either whole or by piecemeal, hoisted upon our very tables before the faces of children of all ages, from the infant at the breast, to the child of ten or twelve, or fourteen, and carved, and swallowed; and this not merely once but from day to day, through life! What could they – what would they – expect from such an education of the young mind and heart? What, indeed, but mourning, desolation, and woe!

On this subject the First Annual Report of the American Physiological Society thus remarks – and I wish the remark might have its due weight on the mind of the reader:

"How can it be right to be instrumental in so much unnecessary slaughter? How can it be right, especially for a country of vegetable abundance like ours, to give daily employment to twenty thousand or thirty thousand butchers? How can it be right to train our children to behold such slaughter? How can it be right to blunt the edge of their moral sensibilities, by placing before them, at almost every meal, the mangled corpses of the slain; and not only placing them there, but rejoicing while we feast upon them?" ...

How can the Christian, with the Bible in hand, and the merciful doctrines of its pages for his text, "Teach me to feel another's woe," – the beast's not excepted – and yet, having laid down that Bible, go at once from the domestic altar to make light of the convulsions and exit of a poor domestic animal? ...

The usual apology for hunting and fishing, in all their various and often cruel forms – whereby so many of our youth, from the setters of snares for birds, and the anglers for trout, to the whalemen, are educated to cruelty, and steeled to every virtuous and holy sympathy – is, the necessity of the animals whom we pursue for food. I know, indeed, that this is not, in most cases, the true reason. It serves as an apology. They who make it may often be ignorant of the true reason, or they or others may wish to conceal it; and, true to human nature, they are ready to give every reason for their conduct, but the real and most efficient one.[84]

Henry David Thoreau

Henry David Thoreau (1817-62) was described by Nathaniel Hawthorne as "a young man with much of wild original nature still remaining in him ... and nature, in return for his love, seems to adopt him as her special child, and shows him secrets which few others are allowed to witness."[85] Having befriended Emerson, living as a member of his household on two occasions, Thoreau edited the transcendentalist journal *The Dial* before building a cabin at Walden Pond, near Concord, Massachusetts, in 1845, where he lived for over two years. *Walden; or Life in the Woods* (1854), based on his experiences there, is his best-known work and an American classic, though his essay on *Civil Disobedience* is almost as widely read, and it inspired Gandhi, among other emergent leaders, to escape the yoke of imperialism.

Paradox, tension, ambivalence, even contradiction, lie at the very heart not just of Thoreau's writings but of his very soul. As with Rousseau, it is a self-conscious, self-aware ambivalence, both about himself and the very nature of humankind – a tension between the Edenic, Arcadian, and cultured consciousness. The "Edenic" part of the soul embraces a peaceful, compassionate, innocent, and vegetarian life; the "Arcadian" element yearns for a courageous, industrious, valorous, adventurous, and carnivorous life; the cultured soul delights in progress, books, learning, the arts, and the finesse of civilization. All three are present in Thoreau. Indeed, it is a contradiction all humans experience, at least subliminally, but which few of us grasp. Perhaps no one has expressed the tension with the precision and self-recognition of Thoreau – maybe Rousseau and the Indian Nobel literature laureate Rabindranath Tagore excepted[86] – and in a manner which leaves the advocate of animal rights perplexed, but not without the hopes which Thoreau himself expresses.

In *Walden*, Thoreau tells us "no nation that lived simply in all respects, that is, no nation of philosophers, would commit so great a blunder as to use the labor of animals." Yet it is not for the sake of the animals but out of fear that one "should become a horse-man or herds-man merely[87] ... husbandry is degraded with us, and the farmer leads the meanest of lives. He knows nature but as a robber ... "[88] In common with Karl Marx and Herbert Marcuse, Thoreau's concern is to prevent a human one-dimensionality. He espouses a Rousseauian primitivism when he avers "Simplicity, simplicity, simplicity! I say, let your affairs be as two or three, and not a hundred or a thousand, and keep your accounts on your thumb nail."[89] On the one hand, he comments that "whether we should live like baboons or like men is a little uncertain,"[90] and, on the other hand, he tells: "What recommends commerce to me is its enterprise and bravery ... Commerce is unexpectedly confident and serene, alert, adventurous, and unwearied."[91] On the one hand, he is a lover of books and learning, and, on the other, tells us of the much admired Alek Therien: "his thinking was so primitive and immersed in his animal life, that, though more promising than a merely learned man's, it rarely ripened to any thing which can be reported."[92]

A list of Thoreau's delights is revealing:

As I sit at my window this summer afternoon, hawks are circling above my clearing; the tantivy of wild pigeons, flying by twos and threes athwart my view, or perching restless on the white-pine boughs behind my house, gives a voice to the air; a fish-hawk dimples the glassy surface of the pond and brings up a fish; a mink steals out of the marsh before my door and seizes a frog by the shore; the sedge is bending under the weight of the reed-birds flittering hither and thither; and for the last half hour I have heard the rattle of railroad cars, now dying and then reviving like the beat of a partridge, conveying travellers from Boston to the country.[93]

A love of the simplicities of Arcadian nature and the technological complexity of smoggy steam locomotion all in one breath!

It is, however, in the chapter on "Higher Laws" that the self-conscious ambivalence is most apparent.

As I came home through the woods with my string of fish, trailing my pole, it being now quite dark, I caught a glimpse of a woodchuck stealing across my path, and felt a strange thrill of savage delight, and was strongly tempted to seize and devour him raw; not that I was hungry then, except for that wilderness which he represented. Once or twice, however, while I lived at the pond, I found myself ranging the woods, like a half-starved hound, with a strange abandonment, seeking some kind of venison which I might devour, and no morsel could have been too savage for me. The wildest scenes had become unaccountably familiar. I found in myself, and still find, an instinct toward a higher, or, as it is named, spiritual life, as do most men, and another toward a primitive rank and savage one, and I reverence them both. I love the wild not less than the good. The wildness and adventure that are in fishing still recommended it to me. I like some days to take rank hold on life and spend my day more as the animals do. Perhaps I have owed to this employment and to hunting, when quite young, my closest acquaintance with Nature. They early introduce us to and detain us in scenery with which otherwise, at that age, we should have little acquaintance. Fishermen, hunters, woodchoppers, and others, spending their lives in the fields and woods, in a peculiar sense a part of Nature themselves, are often in a more favorable mood for observing her, in the intervals of their pursuits, than philosophers or poets even, who approach her with expectation. She is not afraid to exhibit herself to them. The traveller on the prairie is naturally a hunter ... He who is only a traveller learns things at second-hand and by the halves, and is poor authority. We are most interested when science reports what these men already know practically or instinctively, for that alone is a true *humanity,* or account of human experience ...

Almost every New England boy among my contemporaries shouldered a fowling piece between the ages of ten and fourteen; and his hunting and fishing grounds were not limited like the preserves of an English nobleman, but were more bound-less even than those of a savage. No wonder, then, that he did not oftener stay to play on the common. But already a change is taking place, owing, not to an in-creased humanity, but to an increased scarcity of game, for perhaps the hunter is the greatest friend of the animals hunted, not excepting the Humane Society.

Moreover, when at the pond, I wished sometimes to add fish to my fare for vari-ety. I have actually fished from the same kind of necessity that the first fishers did. Whatever humanity I might conjure up against it was all factitious, and concerned my philosophy more than my feelings. I speak of fish only now, for I have long felt differently about fowling, and sold my guns before I went to the woods. Not that I am less humane than others, but I did not perceive that my feelings were much affected. I did not pity the fishes nor the worms. This was habit. As for fowling, dur-ing the last years I carried a gun my excuse was that I was studying ornithology, and sought only new or rare birds. But I confess I am now inclined to think that there is a finer way of studying ornithology than this. It requires so much attention to the habits of birds, that, if for that reason only, I have been willing to omit the gun. Yet notwithstanding the objection on the score of humanity, I am compelled to doubt if equally valuable sports are ever substituted for these; and when some of my friends have asked me anxiously about their boys, whether they should let them hunt, I have answered, yes – remembering that it was one of the best parts of my education, – *make* them hunters, though sportsmen only at first, if possible, mighty hunters at last, so that they shall not find game large enough for them in this or any vegetable wilderness, – hunters as well as fishers of men. Thus far I am of the opinion of Chaucer's nun, who

> "yave not of the text a pulled hen
> That saith that hunters ben not holy men"*

There is a period in the history of the individual, as of the race, when the hunters are the "best men," as the Algonquins called them. We cannot but pity the boy who has never fired a gun; he is no more humane, while his education has been sadly neglected. This was my answer with respect to those youths who were bent on this pursuit, trusting they would soon outgrow it. No humane being, past the thoughtless age of boyhood, will wantonly murder any creature, which holds its life by the same tenure that he does. The hare in its extremity cries like a child. I warn

---

* "He did not rate that text at a plucked hen/Which said that hunters are not holy men." In fact, this statement refers to the monk, not the nun, in the Prologue to the *Canterbury Tales.*

you, mothers, that my sympathies do not always make the usual *philanthropic* distinctions.

Such is oftenest the young man's introduction to the forest, and the most original part of himself. He goes thither as a hunter and fisher, until at last, if he has the seeds of a better life in him, he distinguished his proper objects, as a poet or naturalist it may be, and he leaves the gun and fish-pole behind. The mass of men are still and always young in this respect. In some countries a hunting parson is no uncommon sight. Such a one might make a good shepherd's dog, but he is far from being the Good Shepherd. I have been surprised to consider that the only obvious employment, except wood-chopping, ice-cutting, or the like business, which ever to my knowledge detained at Walden Pond for a whole day any of my fellow-citizens, whether fathers or children of the town, with just one exception, was fishing. Commonly they did not think that they were lucky, or well paid for their time, unless they got a long string of fish, though they had the opportunity of seeing the pond all the while. They might go there a thousand times before the sediment of fishing would sink to the bottom and leave their purpose pure; but no doubt such a clarifying process would go on all the while. The governor and his council faintly remember the pond, for they went a-fishing there when they were boys; but now they are too old and dignified to go a-fishing, and so they know it no more forever. Yet they expect to go to heaven at last. If the legislature regards it, it is chiefly to regulate the number of hooks to be used there; but they know nothing about the hook of hooks with which to angle for the pond itself, impaling the legislature for a bait. Thus even in civilized communities, the embryo man passes through the hunter stage of development.

I have found repeatedly of late years, that I cannot fish without failing a little in self-respect. I have skill at it, and like many of my fellows, a certain instinct for it, which revives from time to time, but always when I have done I feel that I would have been better if I had not fished. I think that I do not mistake. It is a faint intuition, yet so are the first streaks of morning. There is unquestionably this instinct in me which belongs to the lower orders of creation; yet with every year I am less of a fisherman, though without more humanity or even wisdom; at present I am no fisherman at all. But I see that if I were to live in a wilderness I should again be tempted to become a fisher and hunter in earnest. Beside, there is something essentially unclean about this diet and all flesh ... The practical objection to animal food in my case was its uncleanliness; and, besides, when I had caught and cleaned and cooked and eaten my fish, they seemed not to have fed me essentially, it was insignificant and unnecessary, and cost more than it came to. A little bread or a few potatoes would have done as well with less trouble and less filth. Like many of my contemporaries, I had rarely for many years used animal food, or tea, or coffee, &c.; not so much because any ill effects which I had traced to them, as because they were not agreeable to my imagination. The repugnance to animal food is not the effect of experience, but is an instinct. It appeared more beautiful to live low and fare hard in many respects; and although I never did so, I went far enough to please my imagination. I believe that every man who has ever been earnest to preserve his higher or poetic faculties in the best condition has been particularly inclined to abstain from animal food, and from much food of any kind ... [94]

It may be vain to ask why the imagination will not be reconciled to flesh and fat. I am satisfied that it is not. Is it not a reproach that man is a carnivorous animal? True, he can and does live, in great measure, by preying on other animals; but this is a miserable way, – as any one who will go to snaring rabbits, or slaughtering lambs, may learn, – and he will be regarded as a benefactor of his race who shall teach man to confine himself to a more innocent and wholesome diet. Whatever my own practice may be, I have no doubt that it is a part of the destiny of the human race, in its gradual improvement, to leave off eating animals, as surely as the savage tribes have left off eating each other when they came in contact with the more civilized.

If one listens to the faintest but constant suggestions of his genius, which are certainly true, he sees not to what extremes, or even insanity, it may lead him; and yet that way, as he becomes more resolute and faithful, his road lies. The faintest assured objection which one healthy man feels will at length prevail over the arguments and customs of mankind. No man ever followed his genius till it misled him. Though the result were bodily weakness, yet perhaps no one can say that the consequences were to be regretted, for these were a life in conformity to higher principles. If the day and night are such that you greet them with joy, and life emits a fragrance like flowers and sweet-scented herbs, is more elastic, more starry, more immortal, – that is your success. All nature is your congratulation, and you have cause momentarily to bless yourself. The greatest gains are far from being appreciated. We easily come to doubt if they exist. We soon forget them. They are the highest reality. Perhaps the facts most outstanding and most real are never communicated by man to man. The true harvest of my daily life is somewhat as intangible and indescribable as the tints of morning or evening. It is a little star-dust caught, a segment of the rainbow which I have clutched ...

We are conscious of an animal in us, which awakens in proportion as our highest nature slumbers. It is reptile and sensual, and perhaps cannot be wholly expelled; like the worms which, even in life and health, occupy our bodies. Possibly we may withdraw from it, but never change its nature. I fear that it may enjoy a certain health of its own; that we may be well, yet not pure ... [95]

Nature must be hard to overcome, but she must be overcome.[96]

Clearly, if secondarily, for Thoreau as for Leonardo, Bacon, Charles Darwin, and Shaw,[97] nature is not, at least ultimately, the criterion of the good, but is she who must be both obeyed, to the degree necessary, and overcome, to the degree possible.[98]

More generally though, Thoreau's self-analysis does a great deal to allow us to understand the psychology of the Edenic vegetarian, the Arcadian hunter's relationship to nature, the contemporary hunter's rationalization of respect for the animals he kills, and the tensions and potentialities which arise with modernity. This does not mean that Thoreau's philosophy is compelling – even if there is something welcome in the honesty of its "realism." Moreover, it has always struck me as singularly odd that the deeply humanitarian Henry Salt[99] would find so much to commend in Thoreau. It does, however, suggest that, unmatched by any previous and few subsequent writers, he offers us the opportunity to understand the historical dynamic of our relationship to other species, which is a prerequisite of a profound humanitarian philosophy. If there is an ultimate message, it is that modern civilization does not discard humanity's historical experience, but retains it as a conflicting series of primal memories to bedevil one's equally primordial compassion.

8
The Darwinian Age

For the RSPCA the Victorian era was largely a period of consolidation in which most of the Society's innovations were concentrated on encouraging the promotion of kindness, especially among children via a wealth of rather sentimental, but probably effective, publications.[1] From having been the prime mover in the animal protection movement it became an increasingly staid, and on occasion rather complacent, organization. Britain's initiative was followed, with the founding of humane societies in the United States, continental Europe, and the countries of the British Empire. In fact, the United States, stimulated by the pioneering writings of the transcendentalists, led the way in uniting the concern for the well-being of animals with a concern for the protection of the environment, or at least a wiser use of it.

In the realm of ideas, the primary stimulus – metamorphosis, many have deemed it – which affected, both scientifically and ethically, the understanding of the human relationship to other species was Charles Darwin's (and, simultaneously, Alfred Russel Wallace's) theory of evolution by natural selection – "transmutation," as it was first known, and later "descent by modification," and occasionally, after 1871, "evolution," as Darwin and his contemporaries called it.

Evolutionary theory was not new in 1858. What was new was the understanding of the method of evolution and the amount of scientific evidence brought to bear. In "An Historical Sketch on the Progress of Opinion on the Origin of Species," appended to later editions of *The Origin of Species* (first edition 1859), Charles Darwin (1809-92) mentioned more than thirty earlier scholars who had contributed to the theory, including Aristotle, Buffon, Lamarck, Goethe, Erasmus Darwin, Geoffroy Saint-Hilaire, Robert Chambers (who claimed humans were descended from frogs), Baden-Powell, Count Keyserling, and Herbert Spencer (who coined the phrase "the survival of the fittest"). Among those whom Darwin did not mention were the Sumerians of the third millennium BC, who taught that originally people walked with limbs on the ground and ate herbs with their mouth like sheep; Thales, Empedocles, and Anaximander among the Presocratics (Anaximander thought humans were descended from fish); Epicurus a little later; and Diderot, Maupertuis, and Herder in the eighteenth century. However, if evolution was not a new conception in itself, no one prior to Darwin had succeeded in making the theory sufficiently convincing to change scientific, philosophical, or public opinion fundamentally. With the publication of *The Origin of Species* almost all were now compelled to take notice of the idea that species were not fixed and immutable, that they had not been created separately and permanently.

Not only were all species formed on the same principles – a fact emphasized as early as Porphyry and Arnobius, repeated by Borelli, Spinoza, and Leibniz, and later advanced by Goethe, Herder, Emerson, and Balzac – but all species were descended from other species. And if all species had evolved from other species, as the transmutationists now argued, kinship could no longer be in doubt – though one might note also that such thinkers as Basil of Caesarea and Plutarch had held firmly to their kinship beliefs without the confirmation of evolutionary theory. Still, it was well into the twentieth century before evolution by natural selection was both scientifically confirmed and generally accepted.

Intellectually, the second half of the nineteenth century centred on the implications of Darwinism but they were not really viewed as issues of animal ethics, despite the exaggerated claims often made for the impact of Darwinism.[2] Rather, they were viewed in relation to religious questions – whether evolutionary theory was essentially atheist or "agnostic," a Huxleyan coinage, and whether it demonstrated the irrelevance of God to human providence, for example – and scientific questions – about the very nature and development of natural history. After all, our responsibilities to other species, often explicitly our kinship with them, were long recognized by the compassionate without the necessity of a well-grounded evolutionary theory, as we have seen in previous chapters. Indeed, many of the most prominent supporters of the humane movement and of animal welfare legislation remained unconvinced by the arguments for natural selection. And the devout and compassionate vegetarian Leo Tolstoy wrote against evolutionary theory with consummate vitriol, both in *Religion and Morality* (1893), where he attacked the morality of evolutionary theory by equating transmutation with its illegitimate offspring Social Darwinism, and in *What is Religion and of What Does Its Essence Consist?* (1902), where he proclaimed the futility of its investigation. He advised his son against "Darwinism" which "won't explain to you the meaning of your life and won't give you guidance for actions."[3]

In fact, Darwinism, like the Great Chain of Being, could be used either to elevate the status of animals or to demean other species. On the one hand, the theory could be used, as it was by Darwin himself, for example, to stress human-animal similarities. On the other hand, it could be used to argue that humans were so much more "evolved," so much more "advanced" – indeed, so much "fitter" – than other species that humans held a very special place in natural history (and, for some, that Caucasians in particular held a very special place in human history). If Darwinism did not significantly alter human attitudes toward animals – the same debates continued in similar moral terms – it did provide a new scientific and even religious context in which the debates took place. For those who argued the case for our kinship with other species, Darwinism could be offered as confirmatory evidence. For those who argued the case for human moral and intellectual superiority, Darwinism could be offered as confirmatory evidence. The difference was that it was no longer God who had granted our pre-eminence. We had achieved it for ourselves. Human hubris was as great as ever – probably even greater.

While Darwin cautioned himself against using the terms "higher" and "lower"[4] – despite very often failing to heed his own warning, it should be added – and referred at least once to animals as "our fellow brethren,"[5] and stressed emphatically human-animal homologies, the same could not be said of some of his evolutionary associates, even the most gifted. The great publicist of transmutation, T.H. Huxley, deemed by some a more profound and brilliant evolutionist than Darwin, emphasized the hiatus between man and the "lower" species.[6] Huxley wrote:

I have endeavoured to show that no absolute structural line of demarcation ... can be drawn between the animal world and ourselves; and I may add the expression of my belief that the attempt to draw a physical distinction is equally futile, and that even the highest faculties of feeling and intellect begin to germinate in the lower animals. At the same time, no one is more certain than I of the vastness of the gulf between civilised man and the brutes; or is more certain that whether from them or not, he is assuredly not of them.[7]

For Huxley, the kinship is no more than skin-deep – human exclusivity is still proclaimed. Nor was Darwin devoid of responsibility in encouraging this view. He stressed "the struggle for existence" in *The Origin of Species,* and minimized, while acknowledging, sociability and cooperation, factors to which he devoted more attention in his later works, especially *The Descent of Man* (1871), though his explicit elevation of Caucasians over lesser humans is even more pronounced there. Darwin provided the ammunition for those far less sensitive even than Huxley – who claimed to care deeply about the sufferings of animals in experimentation, yet initially opposed almost all regulation of vivisection – who would deem humans the superior being for their success in the evolutionary struggle, and Europeans the predominant human. If Darwin himself ridiculed those who claimed his arguments proved "might was right," many of the almighty were happy to avail themselves of the opportunity to employ the unassailable voice of science as a convenient rationalization of their sovereignty.

The dominant animal ethical issues of the Victorian and Edwardian eras were vivisection and vegetarianism, both of which had been matters of dispute for centuries. Now with the general issue of animal welfare firmly settled in people's minds – at least to the degree that more or less everyone with a measure of sensibility concurred that animals were entitled to a modest degree of moral consideration and legislative protection – these became the dominant contentious issues. In fact, without the RSPCA playing its earlier leading role, new legislation was passed in Britain: in 1869, to protect wild birds; in 1876, to give a measure of protection to laboratory animals; in 1878, to animals in transit; in 1900, to wild, zoo, and circus animals, and to outlaw rat-fighting, which had become popular following the restrictions of the 1835 legislation (see pp. 222-3).

Vivisection became a matter of great urgency with the publication of Claude Bernard's *Introduction to the Study of Experimental Medicine* in 1865, a text that established the principle of the laboratory rather than practice as the foundation for medical knowledge. Bernard convinced the medical profession of the benefit of the artificial production of disease by physical and chemical means through reliance on animal models. Such models, according to Bernard, were "very useful and entirely conclusive of the toxicity and hygiene of man from the therapeutic point of view."[8] Prior to Bernard, the argument that vivisection was not only cruel and inhuman but that nothing good ever came of it, even for humans, could be made, and was made, both persuasively and with conviction. After Bernard, the utility of animal experimentation became increasingly evident to many observers – and utility often overrode moral considerations – especially to those with scientific knowledge, though the occasional vociferous scientist would dispute its validity well into the twentieth century, and as late as 1909 the Archdeacon of Westminster could still refer to the "popular superstition that vivisection produces benefit to the human race." The medical fraternity, in general, now viewed vivisection as the most effective means of saving human lives, curing hitherto incurable diseases, and developing the most effective antidotes to disease, as well as promoting scientific knowledge. Moreover, analgesics were increasingly available, and were used at least in some instances to reduce the pain and suffering of the animals, though often the claim was made that the research would lose its validity if anaesthetics were employed. The debate was no longer between those who supported and those who opposed intrusive experiments on animals. A third element was added: those who were dismayed by the harm inflicted on animals, but found the procedures acceptable provided every effort was made to minimize the amount of animal suffering. Unfortunately, the evidence suggests that as often as not every effort was made by the vivisectors to avoid compliance rather than to welcome it in the name of humanity. The resultant vitriol expressed toward the medical profession should not surprise us too greatly. Physicians were not yet the minor deities they were later to become in popular consciousness. It was only in the latter part of the nineteenth century that the patient came to have a better chance of being cured by medical practitioners than killed.

Charles Darwin

Darwin's research was based initially on the voluminous notes he made during his voyage as semi-official naturalist aboard HMS *Beagle* from 1831-36, continuing and advancing in many respects Borelli's and later scientists' studies of homologous structures in different species, but investigating also rudimentary or vestigial organs, as Goethe had done, and the recapitulation of species history in individual embryonic development. He did not, however, distinguish successfully between acquired and hereditary characteristics, nor could he have understood genetic mutation, both of which were necessary before Darwinism could be fully confirmed. What could be confirmed before the theory was established was Darwin's measured respect for his fellow creatures.

Darwin's sensibilities to animals are most pronounced in *The Descent of Man* of 1871, but they are presaged too in his earliest work. He wrote in his *Notebook* for 1838:

Let man visit Orang-outang in domestication, hear expressive whine, see its intelligence when spoken [to]; as if it understands every word said – see its affection. – to those it knew. – see its passion & rage sulkiness, & very actions of despair; let him look at savage [man], roasting his parent, artless, not improving yet improvable & let him dare to boast of his proud preeminence.[9]

In like, but less bigoted, vein: "Man in his arrogance thinks himself a great work, worthy the interposition of a deity. More humble, and, I think, truer to consider him created from animals"[10] and: "[A]nimals whom we have made our slaves, we do not like to consider our equals."[11]

In his first public advancement of evolutionary theory, published in the *Journal of the Proceedings of the Linnean Society* (1858), he presented the view that: "all nature is at war, one organism with another, or with external nature. Seeing the contented face of nature, this may be at first well doubted; but reflection will inevitably prove it to be true ... It is the doctrine of Malthus applied in most cases with tenfold force."[12] Darwin had read Thomas Robert Malthus's *Essay on the Principle of Population* (1798) on his return from the *Beagle* voyage. A part of Malthus's thesis was that war, famine, and disease were inevitable, since they were nature's way of dealing with excess population. Hence struggle and competition were unavoidable.

By the time of *The Descent of Man* (1871) Darwin had come to regret his excesses. There he wrote: "In the earlier editions of my 'Origin of Species'

I perhaps attributed too much to the action of natural selection and the survival of the fittest."[13] Sociability and cooperation were important aspects of animal behaviour too. Still, like Leonardo, Hugo, Thoreau, and others before him, he continued to view nature as the problem rather than the solution, railing against "the clumsy, wasteful, blundering, low, and horridly cruel works of nature."[14]

The Descent of Man charts the progress of Darwin's sensibilities to animals.

It is notorious that man is constructed on the same general type or model as other mammals. All the bones of his skeleton can be compared with corresponding bones in a monkey, bat or seal. So it is with his muscles, nerves, blood-vessels, and internal viscera. The brain, the most important of all the organs, follows the same law ... [15] man and all other vertebrate animals have been constructed on the same general model ... they pass through the same early stages of development ... they retain certain rudiments in common. Consequently, we ought frankly to admit their community of descent; to take any other view, is to admit that our own structure, and that of all the animals around us, is a mere snare laid to entrap our judgment. This conclusion is greatly strengthened, if we look to the members of the whole animal series, and consider the evidence derived from their affinities or classification, their geographical distribution and geological succession. It is only our natural prejudice, and that arrogance which made our forefathers declare that we were descended from demi-gods, which leads us to demur to this conclusion. But the time will before long come, when it will be thought wonderful that naturalists, who were well acquainted with the comparative structure and development of man, and other mammals, should have believed that each was the work of a separate act of creation ... [16]

As man possesses the same senses as the lower animals, his fundamental intuitions must be the same[17] ... the lower animals, like man, manifestly feel pleasure and pain, happiness and misery. Happiness is never better exhibited than by young animals, such as puppies, kittens, lambs, etc., when playing together like our children ... The fact that the lower animals are excited by the same emotions as ourselves is so well established [by others] that it will not be necessary to weary the reader by many details ... [18] animals not only love but have a desire to be loved. Animals manifestly feel emulation. They love approbation or praise; and a dog carrying a basket for his master exhibits in a high degree self-complacency or pride. There can, I think, be no doubt that a dog feels shame, as distinct from fear, and something very like modesty when begging for food ... [19]

Of all the faculties of the human mind, it will, I presume, be admitted that *Reason* stands at the summit. Only a few persons now dispute that animals possess some power of reasoning. Animals may constantly be seen to pause, deliberate, and resolve. It is a significant fact, that the more of the habits of any particular animal are studied by a naturalist, the more he attributes to reason, and the less to unlearned instincts ... [20] man and the higher animals, especially the Primates, have some few instincts in common. All have the same senses, intuitions, and sensations – similar passion, affections and emotions, even the more complex ones, such as jealousy, suspicion, emulation, gratitude, and magnanimity; they practice deceit and are revengeful; they are sometimes susceptible to ridicule; and even have a sense of humour; they feel wonder and curiosity; they possess the same faculties of imitation, attention, deliberation, choice, memory, imagination, the association of ideas and reason, though in very different degrees ... [21]

I fully subscribe to the judgment of those writers who maintain that of all the differences between man and the lower animals the moral sense or conscience is the most important* ... [22] The following proposition seems to me in a high degree probable – namely, any animal whatever, endowed with well-marked social instincts, the parental and filial affections being here included, would inevitably acquire a moral sense or conscience, as soon as its intellectual powers had become as well, or nearly as well, developed, as in man ... the social instincts lead an animal to take pleasure in the society of its fellows, to feel a certain amount of sympathy with them, and to perform various services for them ... [23] In the same manner as various animals have some sense of beauty, though they admire widely different objects, so they might have a sense of right and wrong, though led by it to follow widely different lines of conduct ... [24] Animals of many kinds are social, we find even distinct species living together, for example some American monkeys, and united flocks of rooks, jackdaws and starlings.[25] Man shows the same feeling in his strong love for the dog, which the dog returns with interest. Every one must have noticed how miserable horses, dogs, sheep, etc., are when separated from their companions, and what strong mutual affection the two former kinds show, at least, on their reunion ...[26] The most common mutual service of the higher animals is to warn one another of danger by means of the united senses of all ... [27] It is certain that associated animals have a feeling of love for each other which is not felt by non-social adult animals ... [28] dogs possess something very like a conscience ... [29] All animals living in a body, which identify themselves or attack their enemies in consort, must indeed be in some degree faithful to one another; and those that follow a leader must be in some degree obedient ... [30] Species which are not social, such as lions and tigers, no doubt feel sympathy for the suffering of their own young, but not for that of any other animal ... [31]

Sympathy beyond the confines of man, that is, humanity to the lower animals, seems to be one of the latest moral acquisitions. It is apparently unfelt by savages, except toward their pets. How little the old Romans knew of it is shown by their abhorrent gladiatorial exhibitions. The very idea of humanity, as far as I could observe, was new to most of the Gauchos of the Pampas. This virtue, one of the noblest with which man is endowed, seems to arise incidentally from our sympathies becoming more tender and more widely diffused, until they are extended to all sentient beings. As soon as this virtue is honoured and practiced by some few

---

* This is identical to Goethe's proclamation in his 1785 poem "Das Göttliche." See p. 179.

men, it spreads through instruction and example to the young, and eventually becomes incorporated in public opinion ... [32] Some naturalists, from being deeply impressed with the mental powers of man, have divided the whole organic world into three kingdoms, the Human, the Animal and the Vegetable, thus giving to man a separate kingdom* ... Spiritual powers cannot be compared or classed by the naturalist; but he may endeavour to show, as I have done, that the mental faculties of man and the lower animals do not differ in kind, although immensely in degree. A difference in degree, however great, does not justify us in placing man in a distinct kingdom ... [33] If man had not been his own classifier he would never have thought of founding a separate order for his own reception ... [34] As the class of fishes is the most lowly organized, and appeared before the others, we may conclude that all the members of the vertebrate kingdom are derived from some fish-like animal ... [35] man still bears in his bodily frame the indelible stamp of his lowly origin.[36]

These statements, the conclusions of years of research – and now, incidentally, usually considered gross anthropomorphic exaggeration by scientists – form the foundation of Darwin's ethics, and informed much of the ethics of his era.

Darwin claimed in an 1863 article that the "setting of steel traps for catching vermin" was too cruel a business for civilized people to tolerate, and that "we naturally feel more compassion for a timid and harmless animal such as a rabbit than for vermin, but the actual agony must be the same in all cases." He added:

If we attempt to realise the sufferings of a cat, or other animal when caught, we must fancy what it would be to have a limb crushed during a whole long night, between the iron teeth of a trap, and with the agony increased by constant attempts to escape. Few men could endure to watch for five minutes, an animal struggling in a trap with a crushed and torn limb; yet on all the well-preserved estates throughout this kingdom, animals thus linger every night; and where game-keepers are not humane, or have grown callous to the suffering constantly passing under their eyes, they have been known by an eye-witness to leave the traps unvisited for 24 or even 36 hours.[37]

On the question of vivisection, though, he was more ambivalent. He wrote to a correspondent in 1871:

You ask me about my opinion on vivisection. I quite agree that it is justifiable for real investigations in physiology; but not for mere damnable and detestable curiosity. It is a subject which makes me sick with horror, so I will not say another word about it, else I shall not sleep tonight.[38]

---

* Darwin probably has in mind primarily the German anthropologist and taxonomist Johann Friedrich Blumenbach (1752-1840) and the French pioneer in the science of comparative anatomy Baron Cuvier (1769-1832).

However, in opposition to the relatively modest proposals to control animal experimentation that resulted in the 1876 Cruelty to Animals legislation, Darwin appears rather less opposed to "damnable and detestable curiosity." He wrote to one of his daughters:

I have long thought physiology one of the greatest sciences, sure sooner, or more probably later, greatly to benefit mankind, but, judging from all other sciences, the benefits will accrue only indirectly on the search for abstract truth. It is certain that physiology can progress only by experiments on living animals ... I conclude, if (as is likely) some experiments have been tried too often, or anaesthetics have not been used when they should have been, the cure must be in the improvement of humanitarian feelings. Under this point of view I have rejoiced at the present agitation. If stringent laws are passed, and this is likely, seeing how unscientific the House of Commons is, and that the gentlemen of England are humane, as long as their sports are not considered, which entail a hundred or thousand-fold more suffering than the experiments of physiologists – if such laws are passed, the result will assuredly be that physiology, which has been until the last few years at a standstill in England, will languish or quite cease. It will then be carried on solely on the Continent; and there will be so many the fewer workers on this grand subject, and this I should greatly regret.[39]

In a letter to a Swedish physiologist in 1881, Darwin was even more emphatic. "I know that physiology cannot possibly progress except by means of experiments on living animals, and I feel the deepest conviction that he who retards the progress of physiology commits a crime against mankind."[40] Clearly, if Darwin respected animals, and he did, he respected science much more. In the final analysis, even though he scribbled himself a note against using "higher" and "lower," there can be no doubt that he did think humans higher, and by a significant degree. Yet Darwin's dilemma is one that suffuses all human minds, for in the end choosing what is right often involves choosing between admirable yet competing principles. No wonder that the anti-vivisectionist **Frances Power Cobbe** wrote of the man she once ardently admired: "Mr. Darwin eventually became the centre of an adoring *clique* of vivisectors who (as his biography shows) plied him incessantly with encouragement to uphold their practice, till the deplorable spectacle was exhibited of a man who would not allow a fly to bite a pony's neck, standing before all Europe as the advocate of vivisection."[41]

We should not allow ourselves to imagine, however, that Darwin's ethical principles were derived from the theory of evolution, even though, no doubt, they were informed by it. We can find fairly similar ethical principles being expressed by scientists before the publication of *The Origin of Species*. Thus, for example, in his *Practical Naturalist's Guide* of 1858 **James Boyd Davies** tells us about the nature and use of collections of mammals, birds, nests, eggs, insects, and so on. For Davies, it is quite appropriate, for the sake of knowledge, to kill, stuff, or dissect our fellow creatures. Yet he adds: "In killing animals, the shortest way is always the best. To the humane naturalist, and it is to be hoped that all who pursue the science are really humanized by it, nothing can be more distressing than to see a creature writhing under pain ... It is well in all cases to lean to the side of mercy; to kill only where a decided object is in view, and then in the quickest manner."[42]

Adherence to a scientific theory and professional interests, in the same manner as historical conditions themselves, may alter the context of application of moral intuitions. The truly moral person is the one who can make decisions that counter his or her professional and other interests. And several of the physiologists and other scientists interested in evolution were far more successful than Darwin in transcending these bounds.

In 1879 the Darwinian physician **Lauder Lindsay** offered a stern rebuke to scientists and evolutionists who stressed human mental superiority as a justification for the way they treated animals. "Man's claim to pre-eminence on the ground of the uniqueness of his mental constitution is as absurd and puerile ... as it is fallacious. His overweening pride or vanity has led to his futile contention with the evidence of the facts. He has trusted to a series of gratuitous assumptions."[43]

Writing in 1885, **A. Armitt** pointed out what he saw as the essential paradox of the vivisectionist position. "It is, indeed, the scientists themselves who have proved to us the close relationship existing between man and animals, and their probable development from the same origin. It is they who instruct us to cast aside the old theology which makes men different from the beasts of the field, inasmuch as he was created in 'the image of god,' and yet would arbitrarily keep for their own convenience, the line of division which such a belief marked out between man and animals."[44]

The great American surgeon, **Albert Leffingwell** (1845-1916), asked himself in 1893 how one might determine ethical issues with regard to vivisection. "This is the problem: To what ethical principle or rule of right and wrong may mankind, at all times, confidently appeal for the determination of the quality of conduct toward the lower animals?" In his search for an answer he surveys the possibilities of an appeal to custom, to law, to religion, and to science, but finds no answers; yet he is convinced: "in the end, we are governed by our ideals. What is duty? Simply the highest ideal of action." Relying on Confucius's principle of reciprocity, which predates the similar Christian ideal by half a millennium, he states his conclusion: "Its expression as a formula will perhaps be something similar to this: – 'Our moral duty to all living creatures, from the highest to the lowest form of life, is to treat them precisely as we ourselves should be willing to be treated for the same objects in view, were we instantly to exchange with them every limitation and circumstance of their condition and form.'"[45] Only if those conditions could be met was vivisection justifiable.

Alfred Russel Wallace

The "other" discoverer of evolution by natural selection, Alfred Russel Wallace (1832-1913) acknowledged Darwin's primacy and wrote two books about the theory, one of which he graciously entitled *Darwinism* (1889). His special contribution to the application of the theory was in the field of biogeography: *The Geographical Distribution of Animals* (1876) and *Island Life* (1880). In his maturity he espoused mysticism and socialism. In his *World of Life* (1911) his views on vivisection were substantially opposed to those of Charles Darwin, and on the supposedly humanizing potential of invasive naturalist studies the very reverse of those of James Boyd Davies.

I have a fundamental disgust of vivisection for its brutalizing and immoral effects.

The moral argument against vivisection remains whether the animals suffer as much as we do or only half as much. The bad effect on the operator and on the students and spectators remains; the undoubted fact that the practice tends to produce callousness and a passion for experiment, which leads to unauthorized experiments in hospitals on unprotected patients, remains; the horrible callousness of binding the sufferers in the operating trough, so that they cannot express their pain by sound or motion, remains; their treatment after the experiment by careless attendants, brutalized by custom, remains; the argument of the uselessness of a large proportion of the experiments, repeated again and again on scores and hundreds of animals, remains; and finally, the iniquity of its use, to demonstrate already established facts to physiological students of hundreds of colleges and schools all over the world, remains. I myself am thankful to be able to believe that even the highest animals below ourselves do not feel as acutely as we do; but that fact does not in any way remove my fundamental disgust at vivisection as being brutalising and immoral.[46]

In his correspondence Wallace was even more emphatic. "I have for some years come to the conclusion that nothing but total abolition will meet the case of vivisection. I am quite disgusted at the frequency of the most horrible experiments to determine the most trivial facts recorded in the publications of scientific societies month by month, evidently carried on for the interest of the 'research' and the reputation it gives."[47]

Wallace would have found confirmation of his views in *Heart and Science: A Story of the Present Time* (1883), the anti-vivisection novel of **Wilkie Collins** (1824-89), famed author of *The Woman in White* (1859-60) and *The Moonstone* (1868). Collins describes vivisection practices as "the atrocities of the Savage Science."[48]

"Now about yourself," Lemuel continued. "You won't be offended – will you? Should I be right, if I called you a dissector of living creatures?"

Benjulia was reminded of the day when he had discovered his brother in the laboratory. His dark complexion deepened in hue. His cold gray eyes seemed to promise a coming outbreak. Lemuel went on.

"Does the law forbid you to make your experiments on a man?" he asked.

"Of course, it does!"

"Why doesn't the Law forbid you to make your experiment on a dog?"

Benjulia's faced cleared again. The one penetrable point in his ironclad nature had not been reached yet. That apparently childish question about the dog appeared, not only to have interested him, but to have taken him by surprise. His attention wandered away from his brother. His clear intellect put Lemuel's objection in closer logical form, and asked if there was any answer to it thus:

The Law which forbids you to dissect a living man, allows you to dissect a living dog. Why?

There was positively no answer to this.

Suppose, he said, Because a dog is an animal? Could he, as a physiologist, deny that a man was an animal too?

Suppose he said, Because a dog is the inferior creature in intellect? The obvious answer to this would be, But the lower order of savage, or the lower order of lunatic, compared with the dog, is the inferior creature in intellect; and, in those cases, the dog has, on your own showing, the better right to protection of the two.

Suppose he said, Because a man is a creature with a soul, and a dog is a creature without a soul? This would simply be inviting another unanswerable question: How do you know?

Honestly accepting the dilemma which thus presented itself, the conclusion that followed seemed to be beyond dispute.

If the Law, in the matter of Vivisection, asserts the principle of interference, the Law has barred its right to place arbitrary limits on its own action. If it protects any living creatures, it is bound, in reason and in justice, to protect all.

"Well," said Lemuel, "am I to have an answer?"

"I'm not a lawyer."

Benjulia opens a letter addressed to him, but written in ignorance of his vivisection practices. It reads:

"We all know what are the false pretences, under which English physicians practice their cruelties. I want to expose those false pretences in the simplest and plainest way, by appealing to my own experience as an ordinary working member of the medical profession.

"Take the pretence of increasing our knowledge of the curative action of poisons, by trying them on animals. The very poisons, the actions of which dogs and cats have been needlessly tortured to demonstrate, I have successfully used on my human patients in the practice of a lifetime.

"I should also like to ask what proof there is that the effect of a poison on an animal may be trusted to inform us, with certainty, of the effects of the same poison on a man. To quote two instances only which justify doubt – and to take birds this time by way of a change – a pigeon will swallow opium enough to kill a man, and will not in the least be affected by it; and parsley, which is an innocent herb in the stomach of a human being, is deadly poison to a parrot ...

"Again. We are told by a great authority that the baking of dogs in ovens has led to new discoveries in treating fever. I have always supposed that the heat, in fever, is not a cause of disease, but a consequence. However, let that be, and let us still stick to experience. Has this infernal cruelty produced results which help us to cure scarlet fever? Our bedtime practice tells us the scarlet fever runs its course as it always did. I can multiply such examples as these by the hundreds when I write my book.

"Briefly stated, you now have the method by which I propose to drag the scientific English Savage from his shelter behind the medical interests of humanity, and to show him in his true character – as plainly as the scientific Foreign Savage shows himself of his own accord. *He* doesn't shrink behind false pretences. *He* doesn't add cant to cruelty. *He* boldly proclaims the truth: I do it, because I like it."

Benjulia rose and threw the letter on the floor.

"*I* proclaim the truth," he said: "*I* do it because I like it ..."

"... Am I working myself into my grave, in the medical interest of humanity? *That* for humanity! I am working for my own satisfaction – for my own pride – for my own unutterable pleasure in beating other men – for the fame that will keep my name living hundreds of years hence. Humanity! I say with my foreign brethren – Knowledge for its own sake, is the one god I worship. Knowledge is its own justification and its own reward. The roaring mob follows us with its cry of Cruelty. We pity their ignorance. Knowledge sanctifies cruelty. The old anatomist stole dead bodies for Knowledge. In that sacred cause, if I could steal a living man without being found out, I would tie him on my table, and grasp my grand discovery in days, instead of months ... Have I no feeling, as you call it? My last experiment on a monkey horrified me. His cries of suffering, his gestures of entreaty, were like the cries and gestures of a child. I would have given the world to put him out of his misery. But I went on. In the glorious cause I went on. My hands turned cold – my heart ached – I thought of a child I sometimes play with – I suffered – I resisted – I went on. All for Knowledge! all for Knowledge."[49]

Henry Bergh

Returning from a diplomatic post in Russia in 1865, where he had been appalled by the treatment of transport horses, Henry Bergh (1811-88) stopped en route to confer with John Colam, Secretary of the RSPCA, and his previous acquaintance, the Earl of Harrowby, President of the Society. Persuaded that the existence of such an organization was overdue in the United States, Bergh succeeded in having the American Society for the Prevention of Cruelty to Animals, based on the British model, incorporated by the state legislature of New York on 10 April 1866. Its charter contained a "declaration of the Rights of Animals" which Bergh described as "a species of Declaration of Independence," believing it would eventually receive similar recognition and reverence to Jefferson's monumental pronouncement. Bergh moved quickly to have animal cruelty legislation passed by the state legislature, which provided a degree of protection for both domesticated and wild animals. The ASPCA was quickly followed by the founding of societies in Pennsylvania, Massachusetts, New Jersey, San Francisco, and Minnesota, the last two including children under their protection. The ASPCA made "an unsuccessful attempt in the New York Legislature" in the winter of 1879-80 "to secure the passage of a law which would entirely abolish the practice as now in vogue in our medical schools, or cause it to be secretly carried on, in defiance of legal enactments."[50] The Anti-Vivisection Society was formed in 1883. The Vivisection Reform Society, which sought to restrict vivisection, was incorporated in 1903 and included among its officers in 1907: a US Senator, a cardinal, a bishop, two former college presidents, a former judge, and a smattering of surgeons, professors, and journalists.

Following the pattern of the RSPCA, Bergh's efforts – because it was, in the main, a one-person organization – were devoted to enforcing legislation and educating the public, especially the very young. In an article he contributed to the *Journal of Education* Bergh wrote that: "Undoubtedly, the best way to prevent cruelty to animals on the part of men it is to teach children to be merciful ... the children of America needed to have planted in their minds the seeds of kindness which would flower in manhood and womanhood into a broad humanitarianism."

He continued by appealing directly to the educators.

As the twig is bent the tree's inclined. Children of the tenderest age, even before they can articulate, may be taught through simple pictures to appreciate living creatures. Later on, the schoolmaster can mingle humanity with rudimentary instruction by teaching that knowledge is worthless if undirected by benevolence. Let the children learn that there is no being so insignificant as to be unworthy of protection, be it the worm which crawls on the ground, or the suffering orphan or widow.

The child that serves its apprenticeship to inhumanity by tearing off the wings of a fly, or robbing a bird of its eggs, when arrived at maturity, insults the poor, beats his inferiors, and shows the same cruelty, intensified by age, which characterized his early training.[51]

As to those who complain that such principles are only concerned with animal suffering in order to alleviate human suffering – forgetting that even today the most radical animal rights organizations find the argument that animal cruelty leads to human cruelty the most effective to use with legislators and the judiciary – Bergh had a ready response in his address at Clinton Hall, New York, on 8 February 1866: "This is a matter purely of conscience; it has no perplexing side issues. Policies have no more to do with than astronomy, or the use of globes. No; it is a moral question."[52]

Bergh was aptly eulogized by **Henry Wadsworth Longfellow** (1807-82), although the poet may have had George Angell in mind instead.

Among the noblest of the land
Though he may count himself the least
That man I honour and revere
Who, without favor, without fear,
In the great city dares to stand
The Friend of every friendless Beast.[53]

By the 1870s Bergh was a more fervent proponent of animal rights than any of his British RSPCA counterparts.

Now is it against all these devilish abominations, inflicted on the defenseless brute, and the unfortunate members of our own race – deeds done in the outraged name of Science, and which challenge the iniquities of hell itself to surpass – that this appeal is made to public opinion, for the exercise of its sovereign power to suppress? Is it not time that universal sentiment should put a stop to those horrid operations, which tend to harden the heart, extinguish those instincts which give man confidence in man, and make the physician more dreadful than the disease itself?

It is maintained by the most eminent physiologists of the world that vivisection is not only a cruelty but a scientific failure, since the information sought to be obtained thereby is no more attainable while the body is writhing in agony than the correct hour of the day can be recorded while the clock's machinery is disordered ...

While reading these frightful atrocities, perpetrated on innocent, unoffending animals, the inquiry springs to the lips: can the perpetrators of them be human beings? Can the brain that conceives them, the heart that tolerates, and the hand that executes them belong to the being who, it is said, was made in God's image?[54]

One of the "eminent physiologists" Bergh had in mind was **Henry Jacob Bigelow** (1818-90), Professor of Medicine at Harvard, who claimed: "There will come a time when the world will look back on modern vivisection in the name of Science, as they do now to burning at the stake in the name of Religion."[55]

George Angell

In outraged response to an infamous horse race in which both equine competitors died as a consequence of the cruelty of the riders, wealthy Bostonian lawyer and anti-slavery campaigner George Thorndike Angell (1823-1909) helped found the Massachusetts Society for the Prevention of Cruelty to Animals and became its first president on the granting of a state charter in 1867. Like Bergh, Angell was an advocate of humane education, founding the Bands of Mercy in 1882 and the American Humane Education Society (AHES) in 1889, thereafter devoting his life to the reform of an educational system he found remiss in its lack of emphasis on humanity and compassion. His motto for the AHES was: *Glory to God,*

Peace on Earth, Kindness, Justice and Mercy to Every Living Creature. His *Autobiographical Sketches and Personal Recollections* (c. 1892) is a veritable mine of information on the development of sensibilities toward animals in the United States in the second half of the nineteenth century, and also contains some valuable information on European conditions and developments.

On 22 August 1864, before Bergh's return from St. Petersburg, Angell expressed his dedication in practical reformist terms:

It has long been my opinion that there is much wrong in the treatment of domestic animals: that they are too often overworked, overpunished, and particularly in winter and in times of scarcity, underfed. All these I think great wrongs, particularly the last; and it is my earnest wish to do something towards awakening public sentiment on this subject; the more so, because these animals have no power of complaint, or adequate human protection, against those who are disposed to do them injury. I do therefore direct that all the remainder of my property not hereinbefore disposed of shall, within two years of the decease of my mother and myself, or the survivor, be expended by my trustees in circulating in common schools, Sabbath schools, or other schools, or otherwise in such manner as my trustees shall deem best, such books, tracts, or pamphlets as in their judgement will tend most to impress upon the minds of youth their duty towards those domestic animals which God may make dependent upon them.[56]

No doubt he would have found succour in the words of President **Abraham Lincoln** who avowed: "I am in favor of animal rights as well as human rights ... I care not much for a man's religion whose dog and cat are not the better for it ... An ant's life is as sweet to it as ours to us."[57]

On 4 October 1875, Angell gave the first college-level humane education lecture to the faculty and 400 students at Dartmouth College, a lecture he would repeat at many other academic institutions.

I am sometimes asked, "Why do you spend so much of your time and money in talking about kindness to animals, when there is so much cruelty to men?" And I answer. "We are working at the roots. Every humane publication, every lecture, every step in doing or teaching kindness to them, is a step to prevent crime." – a step in promoting those qualities of heart which will elevate human souls, even in the dens of sin and shame, and prepare the way for the coming of peace on earth and good-will toward men ...

Standing before you as the advocate of the lower races,* I declare, what I believe cannot be gainsaid, that just so soon and so far as we pour into all our schools the songs and poems and literature of mercy towards these lower creatures, just so soon and so far shall we reach the roots not only of cruelty, but of crime ...

[T]he question was asked, "What can we do to stop the growth of crime?" I answered, "Form a Band of Mercy in every public school of your city as quickly as

---

* That is, species.

you can. So you will reach the children at once; and through them, and their cards, badges, and humane literature, you will reach also the parents."[58]

In the January 1884 edition of *Our Dumb Animals*, the Massachusetts SPCA magazine, Angell listed what he regarded as the four greatest contemporary cruelty problems. In order of magnitude they were: transportation of livestock, slaughtering in abattoirs, vivisection, and the treatment of farm animals in winter. On the question of vivisection, he wrote, it

is a question to be squarely met. We have seen it stated in newspapers, that one man in Ohio has already taken the lives of nearly three thousand animals in his various experiments; and we have been told by one of the most eminent surgeons of Massachusetts, a professor of surgery, that not one important useful fact has thus far, to his knowledge, been discovered in America by vivisection. What ought our societies to do? It will probably take years to enact laws in this country prohibiting vivisection, and perhaps years before laws can be enacted to limit it. And, after the laws are enacted, what then?

Animals cannot testify, and no man be made to criminate himself. Under these circumstances, it would be extremely difficult to obtain evidence. If our medical men believe that vivisection is essential to medical progress, we think that students would practise it without regard to what they would consider an unwise law; and animals would not be helped.

What can our societies do? We know of no reason why physicians and surgeons should be less humane than other citizens. Some of them, we know, are among the best and noblest of men. A few words against vivisection from the more eminent would, in our judgment, do more to stop it than any law we can enact. I think, therefore, we should call upon them to do all in their power to stop vivisection, or to confine it within the narrowest and most merciful limits. Let us ask their counsel and advice; and if unscrupulous and unmerciful men of the profession cannot be otherwise controlled, then let us ask a law which shall be approved by the more eminent and humane, and ask them to aid us in enforcing it.

Let our societies in this matter consult the best and the most humane of the profession, and, until it can be plainly shown they are in error, act upon their advice. We think this question should not be ignored by our societies, but, on the contrary, that most carefully selected and judicious committees should be appointed to take it in charge.[59]

In line with his principle of humane education for the young, and his particular passion for the horse, Angell arranged for the publication in the United States of *Black Beauty: The Autobiography of a Horse* by **Anna Sewell** (1820-78), to be sold at a mere 12 cents a copy. He prefaced the edition with the following announcement:

THE "UNCLE TOM'S CABIN" OF THE HORSE
For more than twenty years this *thought* has been upon my mind.
    Somebody must write a book which shall be as widely read as *"Uncle Tom's*

Cabin," and shall have as widespread and powerful influence in abolishing cruelty to horses as "Uncle Tom's Cabin" had on the abolition of slavery.

Many times by letter and word of mouth, I have called the attention of American writers to this matter and asked them to undertake it.

At last the book has come to me – not from America, but from England ...[60]

He printed and distributed a quarter-million copies in the belief that Sewell's treatment of *Black Beauty* would have a profound effect on public attitudes. No doubt Angell was right, as the following short extract – one whole chapter – would intimate. Black Beauty is working as a cab-horse and being treated well.

One day, whilst our cab and many others were waiting outside one of the parks, where music was playing, a shabby old cab drove up beside ours. The horse was an old worn-out chestnut with an ill-kept coat, and bones that showed plainly through it. The knees knuckled over, and the forelegs were very unsteady. I had been eating some hay, and the wind rolled a lock of it that way; – the poor creature put out her long, thin neck, and picked it up, and then turned round and looked about for more. There was a hopeless look in the dull eye that I could not help noticing; and then, as I was thinking where I had seen that horse before, she looked full at me and said, "Black Beauty, is that you?"

It was Ginger! But how changed! The beautifully arched and glossy neck was now straight and lank, and fallen in; the clean, straight legs and delicate fetlocks were swelled; the joints were grown out of shape with hard work; the face that was once so full of spirit and life, was now full of suffering, and I could tell by the heaving of her sides and by her frequent cough how bad her breath was.

Our drivers were standing together a little way off, so I sidled up to her a step or two that we might have a little quiet talk. It was a sad tale that she had to tell.

After a twelve month's run at Earlshall, she was considered to be fit for work again, and was sold to a gentleman. For a little while she got on very well; but after a longer gallop than usual, the old strain returned, and after being rested and doctored she was sold again. In this way she changed hands several times, but always getting lower down.

"And so at last," said she, "I was bought by a man who keeps a number of cabs and horses, and lets them out. You look well off, and I am glad of it; but I could not tell you what my life has been. When they found out my weakness, they said I was not worth what they gave for me, and that I must go into one of the low cabs, and just be used up; that is what they are doing, whipping and working, with never one thought of what I suffer. They paid for me, and must get it out of me, they say. The man who hires me now pays a great deal of money to the owner every day, and so he has to get it out of me too; and so it's all the week round and round with never a Sunday rest."

I said, "You used to stand up for yourself if you were ill-used."

"Ah!" she said, "I did once; but it's no use. Men are strongest; and if they are cruel, and have no feeling, there is nothing we can do but just bear it, – bear it on and on to the end. I wish the end was come; I wish I was dead. I have seen dead horses, and I am sure they do not suffer pain. I wish I may drop down dead at my work, and not be sent off to the knacker's."

I was very much troubled, and I put my nose up to hers, but I could say nothing to comfort her. I think she was pleased to see me; for she said, "You are the only friend I ever had."

Just then her driver came up, and with a tug at her mouth, backed her out of the line, and drove off leaving me very sad indeed.

A short time after this a cart with a dead horse in it passed our cab-stand. The head hung out of the cart tail, the lifeless tongue was slowly dropping with blood; and the sunken eyes – but I can't speak of them, the sight was too dreadful! It was a chestnut horse with a long, thin neck. I saw a white streak down the forehead. I believe it was Ginger. I hoped it was; for then her troubles would be over. Oh, if men were more merciful, they would shoot us before we came to such misery![61]

Angell's analogy between *Uncle Tom's Cabin* and *Black Beauty* was not without relevance, for not only had Angell campaigned against slavery before he became involved in the humane movement but **Harriet Beecher Stowe** (1811-96), the author of *Uncle Tom's Cabin*, was also an enthusiastic supporter of the animal cause, arguing the likelihood of animal immortal souls, writing articles for Angell's American Humane Education Society, and communicating her distress to Henry Bergh in a letter of 6 November 1877 at the treatment of Florida's fauna. In general, those who worked for animal justice also worked for human emancipation.

I and my daughters and husband have been regarded as almost fanatical in our care of animals wherever we have been, and in Florida we have seen much to affect us; not so much in the oppression of useful working animals, as in the starving of dogs and cats and other creatures which people keep and will not feed. Again, we have been distressed by the wholesale barbarity of tourists who seem to make Florida animals mere marks for unskilled hunters to practice upon, and who go everywhere maiming, wounding and killing poor birds and beasts that they do not even stop to pick up, and shoot in mere wantonness. Last year we exerted our-selves to get a law passed protecting the birds of Florida which were being trapped and carried off by thousands to die in little miserable cages ... veritable slave ships. I never happen to have seen any instances of cruelty to working animals, but pre-sume there is much in need of attention. I for my part am ready to do *any* thing that can benefit the cause. I am glad of this opportunity to say with what whole-hearted delight we have watched your noble course, in pleading for the dumb and helping the helpless. May God bless you.[62]

Likewise, her abolitionist theologian brother, **Henry Ward Beecher** (1813-87), urged "all good people to help on [Bergh's] humane mission" to advance "the rights of animals," adding: "For fidelity, devotion, love, many a two-legged animal is below the dog and the horse. Happy would it be for thousands of people if they could stand at last before the Judgment Seat and say 'I have loved as truly and I have lived as decently as my dog.' And yet we call them 'only brutes.'"[63]

John Muir

Following the example of the transcendentalists, John Muir (1838-1914) conceived of the rights of animals in the context of the protection of nature. All life had value, and everything existed first and foremost for itself or the Creator. Like Wordsworth, Emerson, and Thoreau, he thought of animals, vegetation, rocks, and water as what he called "sparks of the Divine Soul."

Would not the world suffer by the banishment of a single weed? ... What good are rattlesnakes for? ... good for themselves, and we need not begrudge them their share of life ... if a war of races should occur between the wild beasts and the Lord Man I would be tempted to sympathize with the bears ... How narrow we selfish, conceited creatures are in our sympathies! How blind to the rights of all the rest of creation! ... A numerous class of men are painfully astonished whenever they find anything, living or dead, in all God's universe which they cannot eat or render in some way ... useful to themselves ... [They have never thought] Nature's object in making animals and plants might possibly be first of all the happiness of each other, not the creation of all for the happiness of one ... I have never yet happened upon a trace of evidence that seemed to show that any one animal was ever made for another as much as it was made for itself ... When we try to pick out anything by else, we find it hitched to everything else in the universe.[64]

Impressed by his reading of *The Origin of Species* in 1867, Muir commented:

[T]his star, our own good earth, made many a successful journey around the heavens ere man was made, and whole kingdoms of creatures enjoyed existence and returned to dust ere man appeared to claim them ... After human beings have also played their part in Creation's plan, they too may disappear without any ... extraordinary commotion whatever.[65]

Edward Payson Evans

University of Michigan modern languages professor, Edward Payson Evans (1831-1917) continued in the tradition of Thoreau and Muir by relating the rights of animals to a respect for nature. In an article entitled "Ethical relations between Man and Beast" in the *Popular Science Monthly* (September 1894) he argued that Judeo-Christianity made humans "a little lower than the angels" instead of recognizing them as "a little higher than the ape." Genesis was, he claimed, in contrast to Oriental religions, the origin of a "tyrannical mandate" over other species. In his 1906 text *The Criminal Prosecution and Capital Punishment of Animals*, Evans wrote of the medieval tribunals that prosecuted animals, partly out of ridicule, but also to show that the Middle Ages treated animals as on a higher plane than did later ages. If animals were responsible for their actions they must be deemed to possess consciousness, intent, and a sense of morality.

It was, however, in *Evolutional Ethics and Animal Psychology* (1897) that he developed what he saw as the ethical implications of Darwinism, insisting that the relationship between all things in the universe was the sole basis for "ethical relations." All living beings, and even inanimate objects such as minerals and vegetation, were included. "Man is as truly a part and product of Nature as any other animals and [the] attempt to set him upon an isolated point outside of it is philosophically false and morally pernicious ... maliciously breaking a crystal, defacing a gem, girdling a tree, crushing a flower, painting flaming advertisements on rocks, and worrying and torturing animals [is unethical]."[66] He followed the reasoning not only of Darwin, who viewed history as progress, but of William E.H. Lecky too.[67]

In tracing the history of the evolution of ethics we find the recognition of mutual rights and duties confined at first to members of the same horde or tribe, then extended to worshippers of the same gods, and gradually enlarged so as to include every civilized nation, until at length all races of men are at least theoretically conceived as being united in a common bond of brotherhood and benevolent sympathy, which is now slowly expanding so as to comprise not only the higher species of animals, but also every sensitive embodiment of organic life ... our children's children may finally learn that there are inalienable animal as well as human rights.[68]

Ernest Thompson Seton

Like Thoreau and Muir, and in contrast with Bergh and Angell, the English-born Canadian-American writer and artist Ernest Thompson Seton (1860–1946; born Ernest Seton Thompson) was primarily concerned with the well-being of wild rather than domestic animals (though he made an exception for his dogs). He wrote standard works of nature study and forest lore. In 1902 he founded the Woodcraft Indians, later the Woodcraft League, a forerunner of the Boy Scout movement organized by Baden-Powell (son of the evolutionist) in England in 1908. His most influential work was *Wild Animals I Have Known* (1898), a compilation of animal stories.

The fact that these stories are true is the reason why all are tragic. The life of a wild animal *always has a tragic end.*

Such a collection of histories naturally suggests a common thought – a moral it would have been called in the last century. No doubt each different mind will find a moral to its taste, but I hope some will herein find emphasized a moral as old as Scripture – we and the animals are kin. Man has nothing that the animals have not at least a vestige of, the animals have nothing that man does not in some degree share ...

Since, then, the animals are creatures with wants and feelings differing in degree only from our own, they surely have their rights. This fact, now beginning to be recognized by the Caucasian world, was first emphasized by the Buddhist over two thousand years ago ... Have the wild things no moral or legal rights? What right has man to inflict such long and dreadful agony on a fellow-creature simply because that creature does not speak his language?[69]

John Howard Moore

Chicago high school teacher John Howard Moore (1862-1916) wrote an impressive number of books on evolutionary biology and ethics that attracted considerable acclaim. The most important of his books were *The Universal Kinship* (1906) and *The New Ethics* (1907). In the latter he expounded his general moral maxim:

Man is simply *one* of a *series* of sentients, differing in degree, but not in kind, from the beings below, above and around him. *The Great Law – Act towards others as you would act toward a part of your own self* – is a law not applicable to Aryans only, but to all men, and not to men only, but to *all beings* ... in the application of this rule human beings restrict it hypocritically to the numbers of their own species ... Our own happiness, and that of our species, are assumed to be so pre-eminent that we sacrifice the most sacred interests of others.[70]

Still, Moore backed away from the ethical conclusions of Muir and Evans. Plants did not possess "consciousness"; they did not "feel"; they were "outsiders ... mere things."

The Universal Kinship is undoubtedly Moore's primary contribution to the field of animal ethics, though he spends rather more of his time condemning his conspecifics than describing the rights of animals. Nevertheless, it is a tour de force defence of the principle of evolution along Darwinian lines, treating it in its physical, ethical, and psychical dimensions.

[M]an is an animal in the most literal and materialistic meaning of the word. Man has not a spark of so-called "divinity" about him. In important respects he is the most highly evolved of animals; but in origin, disposition, and form he is no more "divine" than the dog who laps his sores, the terrapin who waddles over the earth in a carapace, or the unfastidious worm who dines on the dust of his feet. Man is not the pedestalled individual pictured by his imagination – a being glittering with prerogatives, and towering apart from and above all other beings. He is a pain-shunning, pleasure-seeking, death-dreading organism, differing in particulars, but not in kind, from the pain-shunning, pleasure-seeking, death-dreading organisms below and around him. Man is neither a rock, a vegetable, nor a deity. He belongs to the same class of existences, and has been brought into existence, by the same evolutionary process, as the horse, the toad that hops in his garden, the firefly that lights its twilight torch, and the bivalve that reluctantly feeds him ... [71]

Kinship is universal. The orders, families, species, and races of the animal kingdom are the branches of a gigantic arbour. Every individual is a cell, every species is a tissue, and every order is an organ in this great surging, suffering, palpitating process. Man is simply one portion of the immense enterprise. He is as veritably an animal as the insect that drinks its fill from his veins, the ox he goads, or the wild-fox that flees before his bellowings. Man is not a god, nor in any imminent danger of becoming one. He is not a celestial star-babe dropped down among mundane matters for a time and endowed with wing possibilities and the anatomy of a deity. He is a mammal of the order of primates, not so lamentable when we think of the hyena and the serpent, but an exceedingly discouraging vertebrate when compared with what he ought to be ... [72]

Man was not made in the image of the hypothetical creator of heaven and earth, but in the image of the ape. Man is not a fallen god, but a promoted reptile. The beings around him are not conveniences but cousins ...

[I]t is not necessary to be learned in Darwinian science in order to know that non-human beings have souls. Just the ordinary observation of them in their daily lives about us – in their comings and goings and doings – is sufficient to convince any person of discernment that they are beings with joys and sorrows, desires and capabilities similar to your own. No human being with a conscientious desire to learn the truth can associate intimately with them as he himself would desire to be associated with in order to be interpreted, without presumption or reserve, in a kind, honest, straightforward, magnanimous manner; make them his friends and really enter into their inmost lives – without realising that they are almost unknown by human beings, that they are constantly and criminally misunderstood, and that they are in reality beings actuated by substantially the same impulses and terrorised by approximately the same experiences as we ourselves ... [73]

Instead of the highest, man is in some respects the lowest of the animal kingdom. Man is the most unchaste, the most drunken, the most selfish and conceited, the most miserly, the most hypocritical, and the most bloodthirsty of terrestrial creatures. Almost no animals, except man, kill for the mere sake of killing. For one being to take the life of another for the purposes of selfish utility is bad enough. But the indiscriminate massacre of defenceless innocents by armed and organised packs, *just for pastime,* is beyond characterisation. The human species is the only species of animals that plunges to such depths of atrocity. Even vipers and hyenas do not exterminate for recreation. No animal, except man, habitually seeks wealth out of an insane impulse to accumulate. And no animal, except man, gloats over accumulations that are of no possible use to him, that are an injury and an abomination, and in whose acquisition he may have committed irreparable crimes upon others. There are no millionaires – no professional, legalised lifelong kleptomaniacs – among the birds and quadrupeds. No animal, except man, spends so large a part of his energies striving for superiority – not superiority in usefulness, but that superiority which consists in simply getting on the heads of one's fellows. And no animal practices common, ordinary morality to the other beings of the world in which he lives so little, compared with the amount he preaches it, as man ... [74]

If human beings *could only realise* what the hare suffers, or the stag, when it is pursued by dogs, horses and men bent on taking its life, or what the fish feels when it is thrust through and flung into suffocating gases, not one of them, not even the most recreant, could find pleasure in such a work. *How painful* to a person of tenderness and enlightenment is *even the thought* of rabbit-shootings, duck-slaughterings, bear-hunts, quail-killing expeditions, tame pigeon massacres, and the like! And yet with what light-hearted enthusiasm the mindless ruffians who do those atrocious things enter upon them! One would think that grown men would be ashamed to arm themselves and go out with horses and engage in such babyish and unequal contests as sportsmen usually rely on for their peculiar "glory." And they would be if grown men were not so often simply able-bodied bullies. *If human beings could only realise what it means to live in a world and associate day after day with other beings more intelligent and more powerful than themselves, and yet be regarded by these more intelligent individuals simply as merchandise to be bought and sold, or as targets to be shot at, they would hide their guilty heads in shame and horror ...* [75]

All beings are *ends; no* creatures are *means.* All beings have not equal rights, neither have all men; but *all have rights.* The *Life-Process* is the *End* – not *man,* nor any other temporarily privileged to weave a world's philosophy. Non-human beings were not made for human beings any more than human beings were made for non-human beings. Just as the sidereal spheres were once supposed by the childish mind of man to be unsubstantial satellites of the earth, but are known by man's riper understanding to be worlds with missions and materialities of their own, and of such magnitude and number as to render terrestrial insignificance frightful, so the billions that dwell in the seas, fields and atmospheres of the earth were in like manner imagined by the illiterate children of the race to be the mere trinkets of man, but are now known by all who can interpret the new revelation to be beings with substantially the same origins, the same natures, structures, and occupations, and the same general rights to life and happiness, as we ourselves.[76]

Walt Whitman

Among the greatest American poets, Walt(er) Whitman (1819-92) published privately in 1855 a book of twelve poems entitled *Leaves of Grass*. Two larger editions appeared in 1856 and 1860. A further edition in 1871 contained his last lengthy poem, *Passage to India*. The final revised edition came out in 1892.

Emerson described *Leaves of Grass* as "a singular blend of the Bhagavad Gita and the New York *Tribune*," its voice "half song-thrush, half-alligator." Indeed, Whitman had the thoughts of a paradoxical man, as he himself recognized. In *Song of Myself* he captured in verse a substantial measure of what Moore expressed in prose.

I think I could turn and live with the animals, they are so placid and self
   contain'd,
They do not sweat and whine about their condition,

They do not lie awake in the dark and weep for their sins,
They do not make me sick discussing their duty to God,
Not one is dissatisfied, not one is demented with the mania of owning things,
Not one kneels to another, nor to his kind that lived thousands of years ago,
Not one is respectable or unhappy over the whole earth.
So they show their relation to me and I accept them,
They bring me tokens of myself, they evince them plainly in their possession.[77]

Emily Dickinson

Composer of over a thousand poems, only seven of which were published in her lifetime, Emily Dickinson (1830-86) wrote brief, compact lyrics, primarily on nature, love, death, and immortality. Reflective of the increasing American attention to the world of animals, over 300 of her poems touch on this subject.[78]

In a delightful reversal of the customary question about the usefulness of animals to humans, Dickinson queries of the caterpillar:

How soft a Caterpillar steps –
I find one on my Hand
From such a velvet world it comes
Such plushes at command
Its soundless travels just arrest
My slow – terrestrial eye
Intent upon its own career
What use has it for me – [79]

Mark Twain

Famed author of *The Adventures of Tom Sawyer* (1876) and *The Adventures of Huckleberry Finn* (1883), despite not being primarily a children's writer, Samuel Langhorne Clemens (1835-1910) – a Mississippi river pilot, hence the *nom de plume* meaning two fathoms of river depth – possessed animal sensibilities that are only occasionally recognized. In Justin Kaplan's prize-winning biography *Mr. Clemens and Mark Twain* we read in the opening pages that "he was sensitive about animals" and in the closing pages that he "wrote a sentimental story about cruelty to animals."[80] There is no elaboration and nothing in between.

In reality, most of Twain's animal writing is anything but sentimental and always leavened with the spice of unbounded humour. His stories of jackrabbits, mules, and alligators in their authentic characters is nothing if not stark realism. His Swiftian satire is evident in "Man's Place in the Animal World" (1896).

I have been scientifically studying the traits and dispositions of the "lower animals" (so called,) and contrasting them with the traits and dispositions of man. I find the result profoundly humiliating to me. For it obliges me to renounce my allegiance to the Darwinian theory of the Ascent of Man from the Lower Animals; since now it seems plain to me that this theory ought to be vacated in favor of a new and truer one, this new and truer one to be named the *Descent* of Man from the Higher Animals.

In proceeding toward this unpleasant conclusion I have not guessed or speculated or conjectured, but have used what is commonly called the scientific method ...

Some of my experiments were quite curious. In the course of my reading I had come across a case where, many years ago, some hunters on our Great Plains organized a buffalo hunt for the entertainment of an English earl – that, and to provide some fresh meat for his larder. They had charming sport. They killed seventy-two of those great animals; and ate part of one of them and left seventy-one to rot. In order to determine the difference between an anaconda and an earl – if any – I caused seven young calves to be turned into the anaconda's cage. The grateful reptile crushed one of them and swallowed it, then lay back satisfied. It showed no further interest in the calves, and no disposition to harm them. I tried this experiment with other anacondas; always with the same result. The fact stood proven that the difference between an earl and an anaconda is, that the earl is cruel and the anaconda isn't; and that the earl wantonly destroys what he has no use for, but the anaconda doesn't. This seemed to suggest that the anaconda was not descended from the earl. It also seemed to suggest that the earl was descended from the anaconda, and had lost a great deal in the transition.

A number of similar stories follow with the inevitable interpretations.

These experiments convinced me that there is this difference between man and the higher animals; he is avaricious and miserly, they are not ... The cat is innocent, man is not ... Indecency, vulgarity, obscenity – these are strictly confined to man; he invented them. Among the higher animals there is no trace of them. They hide nothing; they are not ashamed. Man, with his soiled mind, covers himself ... man is the Animal that Blushes. He is the only one that does it – or has occasion to ... Man cannot claim to approach even the meanest of the Higher Animals ... I find this defect to be THE MORAL SENSE. He is the only animal that has it. It is the quality *which enables him to do wrong* ... It seems a tacit confession that heavens are provided for the Higher Animals alone. This is matter for thought, and for serious thought. And it is full of a grim suggestion: that we are not as important perhaps, as we had all along supposed we were.[81]

Twain's denunciation of cock-fighting in 1860s New Orleans in *Life on the Mississippi* (1883), while adamant about the inhumanity of the "sport," repeats the argument used in the British debates of the opening decades of the century – cock-fighting is less cruel than fox-hunting.

A negro and a white man were in the ring; everybody else outside. The cocks were brought in in sacks; and when the time was called, they were taken out by the two bottle-holders, stroked, caressed, poked toward each other, and finally liberated. The big black cock plunged instantly at the little grey one and struck him on the head with his spur. The grey responded with spirit. Then the Babel of many-tongued shoutings broke out, and ceased not thenceforth. When the cocks had been fighting for some time, I was expecting them momentarily to drop dead, fore both were blind, red with blood, and so exhausted that they frequently fell down. Yet they would not give up, neither would they die. The negro and the white man would pick them up every few seconds, wipe them off, blow cold water on them in fine spray, and take their heads in their mouths and hold them there a moment – to warm back the perishing life perhaps; I do not know. Then, being set down again, the dying creatures would totter gropingly about, with dragging wings, find each other, strike a guesswork blow or two, and fall exhausted once more.

I did not see the end of the battle. I forced myself to endure it as long as I could, but it was too pitiful a sight; so I made a frank confession to that effect, and we retired. We heard afterward that the black cock died in the ring, and fighting to the last.

Evidently, there is abundant fascination about this 'sport' for such as have had a degree of familiarity with it. I never saw people enjoy anything more than this gathering enjoyed the fight. The case was the same with the old grey-heads and with the boys of ten. They lost themselves in frenzies of delight. The 'cocking-main' is an inhuman form of entertainment, there is no question about that; still, it seems respectable and far less cruel than fox-hunting – for the cocks like it; they experience, as well as confer enjoyment; which is not the fox's case.[82]

"When asked to add pressure for a law fettering vivisection," Louis J. Budd observes, Twain "obliged with 'A Dog's Tale' – and ended up by writing 'A Horse's Tale' to protest against the cruelty to animals that bull-fighting involved."[83] "A Dog's Tale" (1896) – which bears some resemblance to Robert Browning's poem "Tray" of 1879[84] – is told by the dog: "My father was a St. Bernard, my mother was a collie, but I was a Presbyterian." The she-dog is adopted into a good home, save for the physiologist father. The dog has a puppy, the apple of his mother's heart. The mother saves the infant of the house from a fire, but is kicked and lamed by the father who thinks she is harming the child. Eventually the truth is discovered and the dog is heralded.

And this was not all the glory; no, the master's friends came, a whole twenty of the most distinguished people, and had me in the laboratory, and discussed me as if I was a kind of discovery; and some of them said it was wonderful in a dumb beast, the finest exhibition of instinct they could call to mind; but the master said with vehemence, "It's far above instinct; it's *reason,* and many a man, privileged to be saved and go with you and me to a better world by right of its possession, has less of it than this poor silly quadruped that's foreordained to perish"; and then he laughed, and said, "Why, look at me – I'm a sarcasm! bless you, with all my grand intelligence, the only thing I inferred was that this dog had gone mad and was destroying the child, whereas but for the beast's intelligence – it's *reason,* I tell you – the child would have perished!"

They disputed and disputed, and *I* was the very centre and subject of it all, and I wished my mother could know that this great honor had come to me; it would have made her proud.

Then they discussed optics, as they called it, and whether a certain injury to the brain would produce blindness or not, but they could not agree about it, and said they must test it by experiment by and by ...

[O]ne day these men came again, and said now for the test, and they took the puppy to the laboratory, and I limped three-leggedly along, too, feeling proud for any attention shown to the puppy was a pleasure for me, of course. They discussed and experimented, and then suddenly the puppy shrieked, and they set him on the floor, and he went staggering around, with his head all bloody, and the master clapped his hands shouted:

"There, I've won – confess it! He's as blind as a bat!"

And they all said,

"It's so – you've proved your theory, and suffering humanity owes you a great debt from henceforth," and they crowded around him, and wrung his hand cordially and thankfully, and praised him.

But I hardly saw or heard these things, for I ran at once to my little darling, and snuggled close to it where it lay, and licked the blood, and put its head against mine, whimpering softly, and I knew in my heart it was a comfort to it in its pain and trouble to feel its mother's touch, though it could not see me. Then it dropped down, presently, and its little velvet nose rested upon the floor, and it was still, and did not move any more ...

The mother pines for her puppy and dies broken-hearted. "Poor little doggie," says the footman, "you SAVED his child."[85]

Victor Hugo

Late-Romantic novelist, poet, and dramatist, Victor Hugo (1801-85) is today best known for his novels *Notre Dame de Paris* (1831) and *Les Misérables* (1862). He was one of the most adamant animal protectionists. Some of his passages encourage us to place him alongside Plutarch, Porphyry, Leonardo, Goethe, Schopenhauer, Salt, and Shaw.

For Hugo, if not always consistently, as for Leonardo, Darwin, Shaw, and Hardy, among others, Nature is not the standard of the good, but is that which compassion must combat. Nature, he wrote in *Les Misérables* is

pitiless ... There are times when nature seems hostile ..."After all, what is a cat?" he demanded. "It's a correction." Having created the mouse God said to himself, "That was silly of me!" and so he created the cat. The cat is the *erratum* of the mouse. Mouse and cat together represent the revised proofs of Creation ... All the works of God are designed to serve love, and love has the power to change all nature with its messages.[86]

Hugo was an avowed opponent of vivisection, becoming Honorary President of the Société Française contre la Vivisection on its founding in

1883. On accepting the post, Hugo remarked to the members, "Your society is one that will reflect honour on the nineteenth century. Vivisection is a crime."[87] Cruelty to animals may one day, "rebound upon our heads like Nero's cruelties ... God made birds, not game."[88]

In contrast to those who believed God gave us animals for food, Hugo suggests they have a different function for humankind.

> It is our belief that if the soul were visible to the eye every member of the human species would be seen to correspond to some species of the animal world and a truth scarcely perceived by thinkers would be readily confirmed, namely, that from the oyster to the eagle, from the swine to the tiger, all animals are to be found in men and each of them exists in some man, sometimes several at a time.

> Animals are ... the portrayal of our virtues and vices made manifest to our eyes, the visible reflections of our souls. God displays them to us to give us food for thought.[89]

In 1964 the French anthropologist Claude Lévi-Strauss stated famously that Aboriginals think through animals: "they are chosen not because they are 'good to eat' but because they are 'good to think [with].'"[90] Hugo preceded him by over a century (as had Christopher Smart by almost two-and-a-half centuries[91]). Both Hugo and Lévi-Strauss extended the perception to all humans, and Hugo added that the varieties of animal nature live in humanity. By understanding animal natures we come to understand ourselves.

While Hugo treated animals with consummate compassion throughout his works – the representation of the goat Djali in *Notre Dame de Paris* being a notable example – his sensibilities to animals come to the fore in *Les Misérables*.

> Ugliness of aspect and deformities of instinct neither dismayed nor outraged [the Bishop of Digne]. He was moved by them and sometimes grieved, seeming to search, beneath the experiences of life, for a reason, an explanation or an excuse. He seemed to be asking God to rearrange things. He contemplated without anger, rather in the manner of a scholar deciphering a palimpsest, the chaos that still exists in nature, and his reflections sometimes drew from him strange utterances when he was walking in his garden. He thought himself alone, but his sister was a few paces behind him. He stopped suddenly, staring at something on the ground. It was a very large spider, black, hairy and repellent. She heard him say: "The poor creature, it's not his fault."

> Why not record these almost sublime absurdities? They were childish indeed, but it was the childishness of St. Francis of Assisi and Marcus Aurelius. He strained a muscle once in avoiding treading on an ant. Thus did he live ... His heart was given to all suffering and expiation ...[92]

After his reformation, Jean Valjean

> never killed a harmless animal or shot at a small bird.

Although he was no longer young it was said of him that he was immensely strong. He had a helping hand for whoever needed it, would hoist a fallen horse to his feet, put a shoulder to a bogged-down wheel, grasp the horns of an escaped bull ...

Solitude, detachment, pride, independence, love of nature, the absence of regular employment, life lived for its own sake, the secret struggles of chastity and an overflowing goodwill towards all created things – all this had paved the way in Marius for the advent of what is known as passion ...

In the animal world no creature born to be a dove turns into a scavenger. This happens only in men ... [93]

Nothing is truly small, as anyone knows who has peered into the secrets of Nature. Though philosophy may reach no final conclusion as to original cause or ultimate extent, the contemplative mind is moved to ecstasy by this merging of forces into unity. Everything works upon everything else ...

The cheese-mite has its worth; the smallest is large and the largest is small; everything balances within the laws of necessity, a terrifying vision for the mind. Between living things and objects there is a miraculous relationship; within the inexhaustible compass, from the sun to the grub, there is no room for disdain; each thing needs every other thing ... Every bird that flies carries a shred of the infinite in its claws. The process of birth is the shedding of a meteorite or the peck of a hatching swallow on the shell of its egg; it is the coming of an earthworm or of Socrates, both equally important in the scheme of things ... A machine made of spirit. A huge meshing of gears in which the first motive force is the gnat and the largest wheel the zodiac ... [94]

[Cosette] could watch the butterflies, although she never tried to catch them; tenderness and compassion are a part of loving, and a girl cherishing something equally fragile in her heart is mindful of the wings of butterflies ...

"Be generous," said the father. "We must always be kind to animals."[95]

Romain Rolland

Novelist, biographer, musicologist, and playwright, Romain Rolland (1866-1944) won the Nobel Prize for Literature in 1915, primarily for his ten-volume novel *Jean Christophe* (1904-12), a study of contemporary French and German civilization, whence this extract.

Even in the days when he had been happy he had always loved the beasts: he had never been able to bear cruelty towards them: he had always had a detestation of sport, which he had never dared to express for fear of ridicule ... The continual endeavour of man should be to lessen the sum of suffering and cruelty: that is the first duty of humanity ...

He could not think of the animals without shuddering in anguish. He looked into the eyes of the beasts and saw there a soul like his own, a soul which could not speak: but the eyes cried for it:

"What have I done to you? Why do you hurt me?"

He could not bear to see the most ordinary sights that he had seen a hundred times – a calf crying in a wicker pen, with its big protruding eyes, with their bluish whites and pink lids, and white lashes, its curly white tufts on its forehead, its purple snout, its knock-kneed legs: – a lamb being carried by a peasant with its four legs tied together, hanging head down, trying to hold its head up, moaning like a child, bleating and lolling its gray tongue: – fowls huddled together in a basket: – the distant squeals of a pig being bled to death: – a fish being cleaned on the kitchen table … The nameless tortures which men inflict on such innocent creatures made his heart ache. Grant animals a ray of reason, imagine what a frightful nightmare the world is to them: a dream of cold-blooded men, blind and deaf, cutting their throats, slitting them open, gutting them, cutting them into pieces, cooking them alive, sometimes laughing at them and their contortions as they writhe in agony … To a man whose mind is free there is something even more intolerable in the sufferings of animals than in the sufferings of men. For with the latter it is at least admitted that suffering is an evil and that the man who causes it is a criminal. But thousands of animals are uselessly butchered every day without a shadow of remorse. If any man were to refer to it, he would be thought ridiculous. – And that is the unpardonable crime. That alone is the justification of all that men may suffer. It cries vengeance upon the human race. If God exists and tolerates it, it cries vengeance upon God. If there exists a good God, then even the most humble of living things must be saved. If God is good only to the strong, if there is no justice for the weak and lowly, for the poor creatures who are offered up as a sacrifice to humanity, then there is no such thing as goodness, no such thing as justice.[96]

Richard Wagner

German composer and essayist, Richard Wagner (1813-83) based his best-known operas on medieval romances such as the *Nibelungenlied* and *Parzival*. In *Religion and Art* (1880), *What Use is this Knowledge?* (1880), and *Know Thyself* (1881) he formulated a bizarre explanation of the development of human society which his biographer, Barry Millington, has described as "a prodigal seasoning of home-spun biology and anthropology pathetically destitute of scientific merit."[97]

However, no matter how unconvincing Wagner's pseudo-anthropology, which has afforded him the reputation of a racist, one cannot fail to be convinced of his sensibility to animals, which included a thoroughgoing vegetarianism – at least in aspiration, if not in weak-willed reality. After reading Ernst von Weber's *Die Folterkammern der Wissenschaft* (The Torture Chambers of Science), a categorical denunciation of animal experimentation by the founder of the Dresden anti-vivisection society, Wagner told his wife Cosima that "if he were a younger man he would not rest until he had brought about a demonstration against such barbarism."[98] He had in fact displayed compassion toward animals since his youth and now wished to make it a focus of the new religion he was beginning to preach. He treated this at some length in "An Open Letter to Herr Ernst von

Weber" which was published in 1879 in the *Bayreuther Blätter*. He wrote of "pure compassion," cited Schopenhauer, Plutarch, and Pythagoras on more than one occasion, and denounced "the sovereign human beast of prey." Of vivisected animals he wrote:

The thoughts of their suffering penetrates with horror and dismay into my bone; and in the sympathy evoked I recognise the strongest impulse of my moral being, and also the probable source of all my art. The total abolition of the horror we fight against must be our real aim. In order to attain this, our opponents, the vivisectors, must be frightened, thoroughly frightened, into seeing the people rise up against them with stocks and cudgels. Difficulties and costs must not discourage us ... If experiments on animals were abandoned on grounds of compassion, mankind would have made a fundamental advance ... Everyone who revolts at the sight of an animal's torment, is prompted solely by compassion, and he who joins with others to protect dumb animals is moved by nought save pity, of its very nature entirely different to all calculations of utility or the reverse. BUT, THAT WE HAVE NOT THE COURAGE TO SET THIS MOTIVE OF PITY IN THE FOREFRONT OF OUR APPEALS AND ADMONITIONS TO THE FOLK, IS THE CURSE OF OUR CIVILISATION.[99]

Fyodor Dostoevsky

Sentenced to death as a young adult for his radical utopian criticisms of the Tsarist regime, later commuted to four years penal servitude, Fyodor Dostoevsky (1821-81) wrote novels of human pathology that reflected the dark side of life, but in which the flames of hope and liberty were never extinguished. Among the novels that served Dostoevsky's reputation as not merely a great Russian novelist but one of the world's premier writers are *The House of the Dead* (1862), *Crime and Punishment* (1866), *The Idiot* (1875), and by repute one of the finest novels ever written, *The Brothers Karamazov* (1879-80).

Writing of his early youth, he averred: "in all my life nothing have I loved as much as the forest, with the mushrooms and the wild berries, its insects and little hedgehogs and squirrels ..."[100] Nonetheless, his sensibilities were solidified and advanced by his reading of Carl Gustav Carus's *Psyche* (1846) where he encountered the idea that humans are developed by "a love for everything in creation, the earth on which we grow and which nourishes us, the stars that light our way, the air that we breathe, the plants and the trees, the animals."[101] This became and remained a central theme of Dostoevsky's novels.

As with Victor Hugo, evidence of Dostoevsky's sensibility to animals is found throughout his novels. Thus, in the chapter on "Prison Animals" in *The House of the Dead* he demonstrated an awareness that the human-animal relationship may elevate even the depraved soul and that the punishment which forbad the keeping of animals depraved the prisoners further. In *Crime and Punishment* (ch. 5) the unforgettable dream sequence evokes a childhood recollection of a sadistic beating and killing of a horse that arouses a deep sense of sadness. In *The Idiot* a donkey stimulates Prince Myshkin's awareness of the virtues of humility and labour.

Dostoevsky's philosophy is encapsulated in the lines: "The one thing in the world is spontaneous compassion. As for justice – that is a secondary matter" and "Compassion [is] the chief and only law of all human existence."[102] This compassion toward animals and nature, woven within his devout Christianity, is revealed most fully in *The Brothers Karamazov*.

For each blade of grass, each little bug, ant, golden bee, knows its way amazingly; being without reason, they witness to the divine mystery, they ceaselessly enact it ... "all things are good and splendid, because all is truth. Look at the horse," I said to him, "that great animal that stands so close to man, or the ox, that nourishes him and works for him, so downcast and pensive, look at their faces; what meekness, what affection for man, who often beats them mercilessly, what mildness, what trustfulness, and what beauty are in that face. It is even touching to know that there is no sin upon them, for everything is perfect, everything except man is sinless, and Christ is with them even before us." "But can it be that they too have Christ?" the lad asked. "How could it be otherwise," I said to him, "for the Word is for all creation and all creatures, every little leaf is striving towards the Word, sings glory to God, weeps to Christ, unbeknownst to itself, doing so through the mystery of its sinless life. There, in the forest," I said to him, "the fearsome bear wanders, terrible and ferocious, and not at all guilty for that." And I told him how a bear had once come to a great saint, [St. Sergey] who was saving his soul in the forest, in a little cell, and the great saint felt tenderness for him, fearlessly went out to him and gave him a piece of bread, as if to say: "Go, and Christ be with you." And the fierce bear went away obediently and meekly without doing any harm. The lad was moved that the bear had gone away without doing any harm, and that Christ was with him, too ..."[103]

I cried suddenly from the bottom of my heart, "look at the divine gifts around us: the clear sky, the fresh air, the tender grass, the birds; nature is beautiful and sinless, and we, we alone, are godless and foolish, and do not understand that life is paradise, for we need only to understand, and it will come at once in all its beauty, and we shall embrace each other and weep ..."[104]

Love all of God's creation, both the whole of it and every grain of sand. Love every leaf, every ray of God's light. Love animals, love plants, love each thing. If you love each thing, you will perceive the mystery of God in things. Once you have perceived it you will begin tirelessly to perceive more and more of it each day. And you will come at last to love the whole world with an entire, universal love. Love the animals. God gave them the rudiments of thought and an untroubled joy. Do not trouble it, do not torment them, do not take their joy from them, do not go against God's purpose. Man, do not exalt yourself above the animals: they are sinless ... [105]

Dostoevsky is embellishing Jean le Rond d'Alambert's principle in the

section on "Cosmologie" in the *Encyclopédie* (1772): "all things are connected," a proposition also developed by Victor Hugo.[106]

> "I like observing realism, Smurov," Kalya suddenly spoke. "Have you noticed
> how dogs sniff each other when they meet? It must be some general law of their
> nature."
> "Yes, and a funny one, too."
> "In fact, it's not a funny one, you're wrong there. Nothing is funny in nature,
> however it may seem to man with his prejudices. If dogs could reason and criticize
> they would undoubtedly find as much that is funny to them in the social relations
> of humans, their masters – if not far more; I repeat, because I am convinced of it,
> that there is far more foolishness in us."[107]

Leo Tolstoy

Another of the world's greatest novelists, Leo Tolstoy wrote such masterpieces as *The Cossacks* (1863), *War and Peace* (1865-69), and *Anna Karenina* (1875-77). While his sensibilities to animals are not absent from his
novels they are far more pronounced in his later primitive Christian writings. Still, in *Resurrection* (1899), described by Rosemary Edmonds as
"the great imaginative synthesis of Tolstoyism gravid with the fruits of a
lifetime's agony,"[108] we read on the very first page:

> All were happy – plants, birds, insects, and children. But grown-up people – adult
> men and women – never left off cheating and tormenting themselves and one
> another. It was not this spring morning they considered sacred and important, not
> the beauty of God's world, given to all creatures to enjoy – a beauty which included
> the heart to peace, to harmony and to love ... the grace and gladness of spring had
> been given to every animal and human creature.[109]

Even despised hunters, Tolstoy suggests, suffer for their sins.

> [Nekhlyudov] experienced the same feeling he had when he was out hunting and
> had to put a wounded bird out of its misery: a mixture of loathing, pity and vexa-
> tion. The wounded bird struggles in the game bag: one is disgusted and yet feels
> pity, and is in a hurry to put an end to its suffering and forget it.[110]

The character Vera Bogodoukhovska intimates Tolstoy's view: "I think it
is wrong that rich people should bait bears and give the peasants drink"
but it is Simonson who completes it: "the task of man, as a particle of that
huge organism, is to preserve its life and that of all its living parts. Therefore he considered it a crime to destroy life, and was opposed to war, capital punishment and killing of every sort, not only of human beings but of
animals too."[111]

While Tolstoy did not regard animals as possessed of immortal souls and
saw a great distinction between human spirituality and animal animality,
he was nonetheless an opponent of vivisection and an avid proponent of

vegetarianism. His view of vivisection was delivered in a letter in July 1909. "What I think about vivisection is that if people admit that they have the right to take or endanger the life of living beings for the benefit of many, there will be no limit for their cruelty."[112]

Tolstoy's primary vegetarian statement is in *The First Step* (1892), written as an introduction to a Russian edition of Howard Williams's *The Ethics of Diet*.[113]

I had wished to visit a slaughter-house in order to see with my own eyes the reality of the question raised when vegetarianism is discussed. But at first I felt ashamed to do so, as one is always ashamed of going to look at suffering which one knows is about to take place but which one cannot avert; and so I kept putting off my visit.

But a little while ago I met on the road a butcher returning to Túla after a visit to his home. He is not yet an experienced butcher and his duty is to stab with a knife. I asked him whether he did not feel sorry for the animals that he killed. He gave me the usual answer: "Why should I feel sorry? It is necessary." But when I told him that eating flesh is not necessary, but is only a luxury, he agreed; and then he admitted that he was sorry for the animals. "But what can I do?" he said, "I must earn my bread. At first I was *afraid* to kill. My father, he never even killed a chicken in all his life." The majority of Russians cannot kill; they feel pity, and express the feeling by the word *"fear."* This man had also been "afraid," but he was so no longer ...

Not long ago I also had a talk with a retired soldier, a butcher, and he too was surprised at my assertion that it was a pity to kill, and said the usual thing about its being ordained. But afterwards he agreed with me: "Especially when they are quiet, tame cattle. They come, poor things! trusting you. It is very pitiful."

Once when walking from Moscow, I was offered a lift by some carters who were going from Serpuhkov to a neighbouring forest to fetch wood. It was the Thursday before Easter. I was seated in the first cart with a strong, red, coarse carman, who evidently drank. On entering a village we saw a well-fed, naked, pink pig being dragged out of the first yard to be slaughtered. It squealed in a dreadful voice, resembling the shrieking of a man. Just as we were passing they began to kill it. A man gashed its throat with a knife. The pig squealed still more loudly and piercingly, broke away from the men, and ran off covered with blood. Being nearsighted I did not see all the details and watched closely. They caught the pig, knocked it down, and finished cutting its throat. When its squeals ceased the carter sighed heavily. "Do men really not have to answer for such things?" he said.

So strong is man's aversion to all killing. But by example, by encouraging greediness, by the assertion that God has allowed it, and above all by habit, people entirely lose this natural feeling.

On Friday I decided to go to Túla, and, meeting a meek, kind acquaintance of mine, I invited him to accompany me.

"Yes, I have heard that the arrangements are good, and have been wishing to go to see it; but if they are slaughtering I will not go in."

"Why not? That's just what I want to see! If we eat flesh it must be killed."

"No, no, I cannot!"

It is worth remembering that this man is a sportsman and himself kills animals and birds ... [114]

Tolstoy then describes the conditions of the abattoir in gruesome and distressing detail.

But why, if the wrongfulness – i.e. the immorality – of animal food was known to humanity so long ago, have people not yet come to acknowledge this law? will be asked by those who are accustomed to be led by public opinion rather than by reason.

The answer to this question is that the moral progress of humanity – which is the foundation of every other kind of progress – is always slow; but that the sign of true, not casual, progress is its uninterruptedness and its continual acceleration.[115]

John Henry Newman

In the latter part of the nineteenth century, increased sensibility to animals was not restricted to primitive Christianity. Oxford don and Anglican cleric, later Cardinal of the Roman Church, John Henry Newman (1801-90) was one of the founders of the Oxford movement which reformed the Anglican Church in the direction of Anglo-Catholicism. In 1845 he left the Anglican Church for Rome and influenced a number of prominent High Church Anglicans to make the same journey. His *Apologia pro Vita Sua* (1864 onwards) and his *Grammar of Assent* (1870) are his most important religious writings.

In one of his *Parochial and Plain Sermons* he took up the cause of animals.

Now what is it moves our very heart and sickens us so much at the cruelty shown to poor brutes? I suppose this; first, that they have done us no harm; next, that they have no power whatever of resistance; it is the cowardice and tyranny of which they are the victims which makes their suffering so especially touching ... there is something so very dreadful, so Satanic in tormenting those who have never harmed us, and who cannot defend themselves, who are utterly in our power ... It is almost a definition of a gentleman to say he is one who never inflicts pain.[116]

Henry Edward Manning

Fellow member of the Oxford Movement, Henry Edward Manning (1808-92) followed Newman into the Roman Church and also became a cardinal. His greatest accomplishment lay in his support for the striking London dock workers in 1892 and his single-handed settlement of the strike. His best-known publication is *The Eternal Priesthood* (1883). If he followed Newman in his career (and opposed him on almost all major Roman Church issues of his time) he preceded him in the strength of his opposition to vivisection.

In a speech to the Victoria Street Society for the Prevention of Vivi-section, delivered at the Westminster Palace Hotel on 9 March 1887, he assured the audience that vivisection was a detestable practice, that no civilized man could commit or countenance such a practice, and that the time had come to prohibit vivisection altogether.

A literary man of very great reputation, and highly celebrated for his literary powers, but not equally so for his accuracy, I believe, was present at one of our meetings, and he heard out of my mouth this statement: that inasmuch as animals are not moral persons, we owe them no duties, and that, therefore, the infliction of pain is contrary to no obligation. Now he omitted to say that I did make the state-ment only for the purpose of refuting it – but he put it into my mouth, and there it is in a book that is sold to all the book-stalls in the railway stations, and I am cred-ited to this day with what I denounced as a hideous and, I think, an absurd doc-trine. It is perfectly true that obligations and duties are between moral persons, and therefore the lower animals are not susceptible of those moral obligations we owe to one another; but we owe a sevenfold obligation to the Creator of those animals. Our obligation and moral duty is to Him who made them, and, if we wish to know the limit and the broad outline of our obligation, I say at once it is His nature, and His perfections, and, among those perfections, one is most profoundly that of eter-nal mercy. And, therefore, although a poor mule or a poor horse is not indeed a moral person, yet the Lord and Maker of that mule and that horse is the highest law-giver and His nature is a law to Himself. And, in giving a dominion over His creatures to man, He gave them subject to the condition that they should be used in conformity to His own perfections, which is His own law, and therefore, our law. It would seem to me that the practice of vivisection, as it is now known and now exists, is at variance with those moral perfections.

Now there is one other word I will add, and that is, I believe that science consists in the knowledge of truth obtained by the processes which are in conformity with the nature of God, who, the Holy Scripture says, is the Lord of all sciences. I remem-ber Lord Shaftesbury saying at one of our meetings, "I don't believe that science can be attained by processes which are at variance with the perfections of God," and if I have been right in what I have laid down, as it appears to me, that the inflic-tion of torture of the most exquisite kind on the poor animals is at variance with the perfections of God for that reason, my conclusion is that science is not attained by that path, and that those who walk in it are out of the way ...

[A]t the present day we are under the tyranny of the word Science. I believe in science most profoundly within its own limits; but it has its own limits, and, when the word science is applied to matter which is beyond those limits, I don't believe in it, and as I believe that vivisection is susceptible of such excessive abuse – such facile abuse – such clandestine abuse – all over the land, and by all manner of peo-ple, I shall do all I can to restrain it to the utmost of my power.[117]

Manning was one of the earliest members of the Victoria Street Society, as was Anglican Archbishop Thomson of York. The celebrated and brilliant, but surly, Thomas Carlyle was also an enthusiastic supporter. However, he failed to join a delegation to the Home Office in support of proposed anti-vivisection legislation when he discovered that Cardinal Manning – "the chief representative of Beelzebub in England" – was also to be present. Such were the prejudices that plagued the anti-vivisection movement.

Basil Wilberforce
Anglican Archdeacon of Westminster, Basil Wilberforce (1841-1916) was as adamant a critic of vivisection as Cardinal Manning. In a sermon at the abbey on 11 July 1909 he expostulated against contemporary scientific practice.

> For myself I believe that no greater cruelty is perpetrated on this earth than that which is committed in the name of science in some physiological laboratories. I gratefully allow that there is less cruelty in English laboratories than in many laboratories abroad. But in many of those Dantian hells on the Continent there prevails a prying into the movements of life by cutting open and torturing living animals, which, if the general public realized the truth, would be swept away in the torrent of indignation that would pour forth ... The popular superstition that vivisection produces benefit to the human race – a superstition which degrades humanity by exalting physical above moral interest – is breaking down ... The cause which we are championing is no fanatical protest based on ignorant sentimentality, but a claim of simple justice not only on the transcendent truth of the immanence of the divine truth in all that lives, but also upon the irrefutable logic of ascertained fact ...
>
> I believe this practice panders to the very lowest part of human nature, which is our selfishness engendered by fear. There is nothing on God's earth that is so brutally cruel as fear. And when they excite our terrors, and then pander to this fear they have excited, and tell us by the exhibition of a certain amount of necessary cruelty they will be able to relieve us, they are degrading the human race.[118]

It is remarkable how the theory of evolution, deemed by so many to be central to the development of a positive animal ethic, led, in the hands of a Darwin or a Huxley, to opposition to any significant controls on vivisection, whereas Christianity, deemed by so many to be inimical to animal interests, led, in the hands of a Tolstoy, Manning, or Wilberforce (and several other religious leaders) to condemnation of vivisection. Of course, we should not blindly reverse traditional judgments – Alfred Russel Wallace should caution us against that – but we should at least be far more circumspect in our customary conclusions.

Herbert Spencer
In general, philosophers contributed little to the animal ethics discussions of the Victorian and Edwardian eras. To be sure, **Richard Cobden** (1804-65) considered hunting a "feudal sport" while **John Bright** (1811-89) thought vivisection a barbarism, and Henry Salt reported him as writing:

"Humanity to animals is a great point. If I were a teacher in a school, I would make it a very important part of my business to impress every boy and girl with the duty of his being kind to animals. It is impossible to say how much suffering there is in the world from the barbarity or unkindness which people show to what we call the inferior creatures."

However, Cobden and Bright were more economists and statesmen than philosophers. On the whole, philosophers were retreating into the realm of the abstract. Nonetheless, two philosophers, Herbert Spencer (1820-1903) and Peter Kropotkin (1842-1921), did include evolutionary ideas in their works and related them directly to the human-animal relationship. Spencer defined evolution as the interaction of integrative and disintegrative processes in which the more homogeneous structures of nature were broken up to form more differentiated structures. For Spencer, evolution was a movement from the lower to the higher, from the group to the individual, involving "the survival of the fittest." Evolution constituted a natural utilitarian basis for ethics in the adaptation to environmental forces, as a consequence of which there exists "the right of each man to do as he pleases as long as he does not trespass upon the equal freedom of every other man."

In *Social Statics* (1896) Spencer argued:

> Whoever thinks that men might have full sympathy with their fellows, while lacking all sympathy with inferior creatures, will discover his error on looking at the facts. The Indian whose life is spent in the chase, delights in torturing his brother man as much as in killing game. His sons are schooled into fortitude by long days of torment, and his squaw made prematurely old by hard treatment. Among partially civilised nations the two characteristics have ever borne the same relationship. Thus the spectators in the Roman amphitheatres were as much delighted by the slaying of gladiators as by the death-struggles of wild beasts. The ages during which Europe was thinly peopled, and hunting a chief occupation, were also the ages of feudal violence, universal brigandage, dungeons, tortures ...
>
> The same impulses govern in either case. The desire is to inflict suffering, but obtains gratification indifferently from the agonies of beast and human being. Contrariwise, the sympathy which prevents its possessor from inflicting pain that he may avoid pain himself, and which tempts to give happiness that he may have happiness reflected back upon him, is similarly undistinguishing.[119]

If one is dismayed by evolutionary notions that return us to a Hobbesian pessimism (as well as by an alarming interpretation of racial history) one should recognize that, for Spencer, even if our sympathies are grounded in individual self-interest, they do allow for a significant consideration for animals.

Peter Kropotkin

A Russian prince by birth, Peter Kropotkin (1842-1921) espoused an anarchistic philosophy which he spread primarily through pamphlets and journalism. His two major works are *Fields, Factories and Workshops* (1899), in which he advocated industrial decentralization and the combination of the work of hand and brain, and *Mutual Aid: A Factor in Evolution* (1902), in which he argued, as the very antithesis of Spencer's view, that evolution leads to cooperation rather than competition. While Kropotkin is concerned with compassion in general, rather than compassion for other species per se, a primary message of *Mutual Aid* is how much we can learn not merely from the tendencies of evolution but from animal life itself. Kropotkin begins his book with a discussion of the ideas of Darwin, Wallace, Huxley, Spencer, Hobbes, and Rousseau in relation to competition and cooperation. He refers his readers to Tournell, Fée, Houzen, Kessler, Büchner, Perty, Epinas, Lannesan, Romanes, Lubbock, and numerous others, who had demonstrated cooperation among animals. Kropotkin's theme is that "Sociability is as much a law of nature as mutual struggle ... those animals which acquire habits of mutual aid are undoubtedly the fittest." Having elaborated on cooperation among termites, ants, bees, and birds he turned to the mammals and there found the same tendencies.

Life in societies enables the feeblest insects, and the feeblest mammals to resist, or to protect themselves from, the most terrible birds and beasts of prey; it permits longevity; it enables the species to rear its progeny with the least waste of energy and to maintain its numbers albeit at a very slow birth-rate; it enables the gregarious animals to migrate in search of new abodes. Therefore, while fully admitting that force, swiftness, protective colours, cunningness and endurance to hunger and cold, which are mentioned by Darwin and Wallace, are so many qualities making the individual or the species, and fittest under circumstances, we maintain that under *any* circumstances sociability is the greatest advantage in the struggle for life. Those species which willingly or unwillingly abandon it are doomed to decay; while those animals which know best how to combine, have the greatest chances of survival and of further evolution; they may be inferior to others in *each* of the faculties enumerated by Darwin and Wallace, save the intellectual faculty. The higher vertebrates, and especially mankind, are the best proof of this assertion. As to the intellectual faculty, while every Darwinist will agree with Darwin that it is the most powerful arm in the struggle for life, and the most powerful factor of further evolution, he will also admit that intelligence is an eminently social faculty. Language, imitation, and accumulated experience are so many elements of growing intelligence of which the unsociable animal is deprived. Therefore, we find at the top of each class of animals, the ants, the parrots, and the monkeys, all combining the greatest sociability with the highest development of intelligence. The fittest are thus the most sociable animals, and sociability appears as the chief factor of evolution, both directly, by securing the well-being of the species while diminishing the waste of energy, and indirectly, by favouring the growth of intelligence.

Moreover, it is evident that life in societies would be utterly impossible without a corresponding development of social feelings and, especially, of a certain collective sense of justice growing to become a habit. If every individual were constantly abusing its personal advantages without the others interfering in the rights of the wronged, no society-life would be possible. And feelings of justice develop, more or less, with all gregarious animals. Whatever the distance from which the swallows and cranes come, each one returns to the nest it has built or repaired last year. If a lazy sparrow intends appropriating the nest which a comrade is building, or even steals from it a few sprays of straw, the group interferes against the lazy comrade; and it is evident that without such interference being the rule, no nesting associations of birds could exist. Separate groups of penguins have separate resting-places and separate fishing abodes and do not fight for them. The droves of cattle in Australia have particular spots to which each group repairs to rest, and from which it never deviates, and so on. We have any number of direct observations of the peace that prevails in the nesting associations of birds, the villages of rodents, and the herds of grass eaters; while, on the other side, we know of a few sociable animals which so continually quarrel as the rats in our cellars do, or as the morses, [walruses] which fight for the possession of a sunny place on the shore. Sociability thus puts a limit to physical struggle, and leaves room for the development of better moral feelings. The high development of parental love in all classes of animals, even with lions and tigers, is generally well known. As to the young birds and mammals whom we continually see associating, sympathy – not love – attains a further development in their associations. Leaving aside the really touching facts of mutual attachment and compassion which have been recorded as regards domesticated animals and with animals kept in captivity, we have a number of well certified facts of compassion between wild animals at liberty ... Compassion is a necessary outcome of social life. But compassion also means a considerable advance in general intelligence and sensibility. It is the first step towards the development of higher moral sentiments. It is, in its turn, a powerful factor of further evolution.[120]

Happily enough, competition is not the rule either in the animal world or in mankind. It is limited among animals to exceptional periods, and natural selection finds better fields for its activity. But better conditions are created by the elimination of competition by means of mutual aid and mutual support. In the great struggle for life – for the greatest possible fulness and intensity of life with the least waste of energy – natural selection continually seeks out the ways precisely for avoiding competition as much as possible. The ants combine in nests and nations; they pile up their stores, they rear their cattle – and thus avoid competition; and natural selection picks out of the ants' families the species* which know best how to avoid competition with its unavoidably deleterious consequences. Most of our birds slowly move southwards as the winter comes, or gather in numberless societies and undertake long journeys – and thus avoid competition. Many rodents fall asleep when the time comes that competition should set in; while other rodents store food for the winter, and gather in large villages for obtaining the necessary protection when at work. The reindeer, when the lichens are dry in the interior of

---

* That is, the specific types.

306   *The Darwinian Age*

the continent, migrate towards the sea. Buffaloes cross an immense continent in order to find plenty of food. And the beavers, when they grow numerous on a river, divide into two parties, and go, the old ones down the river, the young ones up the river – and avoid competition. And when animals can neither fall asleep, nor lay in stores, nor themselves grow their food like the ants, they do what the titmouse does, and what Wallace (*Darwinism*, ch. v) has so charmingly described: they resort to new kinds of food – and thus, again, avoid competition.

"Don't compete! – competition is always injurious to the species, and you have plenty of resources to avoid it!" That is the *tendency* of nature, not always realized in full, but always present. That is the watchword which comes to us from the bush, the forest, the river, the ocean. "Therefore combine – practise mutual aid! That is the surest means for giving to each and to all the greatest safety, the best guarantee of existence and progress, bodily, intellectual, and moral." That is what Nature teaches us; and that is what all those animals which have attained the highest position in their respective classes have done.[121]

While one may be critical of Kropotkin's account of animal ethology, it should nonetheless be clear from the widely differing interpretations of evolutionary theory, of which Spencer and Kropotkin are diametrically opposing examples, that Darwinism could be, and indeed was, used both to promote competition and individual self-interest, and to enjoin compassion and sociability.

W.E.H. Lecky

If there was one philosophical concept that captivated the Victorian era it was that of "progress," even on occasion "the inevitability of progress." The Irish historian William Edward Hartpole Lecky (1838-1903) expounded the principle of progress in his remarkable *History of European Morals from Augustus to Charlemagne* (1869) – though the scheme he adopts, if not the details, takes us to the nineteenth century rather than the ninth. In *The History of the Rise and Influence of Rationalism* he had argued that greater humanitarian attitudes to animals had been effected "not by any increase in knowledge or by any process of definitive reasoning but simply by the gradual elevation of the moral standard."[122] In *The History of European Morals* Lecky developed that theme, showing that progress is not a simple continuum, for he noted that, in seventeen hundred years, no Christian writer had equalled Plutarch's sensibilities to animals; that, for a time, among the Greeks and Romans it had been a capital offence to kill an ox, a consequence of the attempts to establish agricultural habits; that Quintillian reported a boy sentenced to death for cruelty to birds in the first century; and that, by contrast, cock-fighting was a common pastime among children in twelfth century Europe.[123] In fact,

the general tendency of nations is undoubtedly to become more gentle and humane in their actions; but this, like many other general tendencies in history, may be counteracted by many special circumstances ... The moral duty to be extended in different ages is not a unity of standard, or of acts, but a unity of tendency ... At one time, the benevolent affections merely embrace the family, soon the circle expanding includes first a class, then a nation, then a coalition of nations, then all humanity and finally its influence is felt in the dealings of man with the animal world ... there is such a thing as a natural history of morals, a defined and regular order, in which our feelings are unfolded.[124]

It is scarcely surprising, then, that in Darwin's *Descent of Man* (1871) his footnotes indicate that he drew on Lecky for his general principle of "descent," which, to all intents and purposes, whether or not Darwin actually wanted to avoid "higher" and "lower," is equivalent to "progress." Indeed, Darwin acknowledged that Lecky "seems to a certain extent to coincide" with, in reality to anticipate, his "own conclusions."

However, for Lecky, there is a decided limit to this history of progress.

The duty of humanity to animals, though for a long period too much neglected, may, on the principles of the intuitive moralist, be easily explained and justified ... Yet a man may be regarded as very humane to animals who has no scruple in sacrificing their lives for his food.

Toward the close of the last century an energetic agitation in favour of humanity to animals arose in England and the utilitarian moralists, who were then rising into influence, caught the spirit of their time and made very creditable efforts to extend it. It is manifest, however, that a theory which recognized no other end in virtue than the promotion of human happiness, could supply no adequate basis for the movement. Some of the recent members of the school have accordingly enlarged their theory, maintaining that acts are virtuous when they produce a net result of happiness, and vicious when they produce a net result of suffering, altogether irrespective of the question whether this enjoyment or suffering is of men or animals. In other words they place the duty of man to animals on exactly the same basis as the duty of man to his fellow-men, maintaining that no suffering can be rightly inflicted on brutes, which does not produce a larger amount of happiness in man.

The first reflection suggested by this theory is, that it appears difficult to understand how, on the principles of the inductive school, it could be arrived at.[125]

And Lecky himself does not arrive at it. Animals matter; humans matter a great deal more. Progress, for Lecky, requires us to consider animals, but not to consider them equally.

Frances Power Cobbe

When the 1876 Cruelty to Animals Bill was presented to Parliament, "Darwin vented his spleen in *The Times*, the old patrician targeting those women who 'from the tenderness of their hearts and ... their profound ignorance' opposed all animal experimentation."[126] Uppermost in Darwin's mind was Frances Power Cobbe (1822-1904), who did more than any other individual to bring about the legislation. Cobbe was a journalist and the author of a respectable book on Kantian philosophy: *Essay on the Theory of Infinitive Morals* (1855). She had also contributed an article against vivisection – "The Rights of Man and the Claims of Brutes" – to *Fraser's Magazine* in November 1863.

Together with Dr. George Hoggan[127] and Richard Hutton, editor of the *Spectator*, she founded an anti-vivisection society in November 1875, initially named the Victoria Street Society, later the National Anti-Vivisection Society, whose early membership included Cardinal Manning, Lord Chief Justice Coleridge, Alfred Tennyson, and Robert Browning, and whose president was the Seventh Earl of Shaftesbury.[128]

Writing in the *Contemporary Review* some six years after the legislation had been passed, Cobbe gave her most powerful statement on the issue and on why further legislation was necessary.

The position which we, the opponents of Vivisection find ourselves at present is this: –

We seek to stop certain practices which appear to us to involve gross cruelty, and to be contrary to the spirit of the English law. Our knowledge of them is derived almost exclusively from the published reports and treatises prepared and issued by the actual individuals who carry out those practices; and our arguments are grounded upon *verbatim* citations from those published and accessible reports and treatises.

The persons whose practices we desire to stop, and their immediate associates, now meet our charges of cruelty by articles in the leading periodicals wherein the proceedings in question are invested with a character not only diverse from, but opposite to, that which they were in the scientific treatises and reports containing the original accounts ...

1. ... the *raison d'être* of most experiments appears to be the elucidation of points of purely scientific interest ... every page of these [scientific reports] corroborates the honest statement of [vivisector] Professor Hermann of Zurich: "The advancement of science, and not practical utility to medicine, is the true and straightforward object of all vivisection. Science can afford to despise this justification with which vivisection has been defended in England" ... We can now turn to such articles as the six which have appeared in the *Nineteenth Century* and the two in the *Fortnightly Review* in defence of vivisection, and *mirabile dictu!* Not a solitary vivisection is mentioned of which the direct advancement of healing does not appear as the single-minded object.

2. Again, the *severity* of the experiments in common use, appears from the Treatises and Reports ... to be truly frightful. Sawing across the backbone, dissecting out and irritating all the great nerves ... inoculating with the most dreadful diseases ... baking, stewing ... reducing the brain to the condition of a "lately-hoed potato field." These and similarly terrible experiments form the staple of some of them, and a significant feature in all.

But turning now to the popular articles, we find Dr. Lauder Brunton assuring the readers of the *Nineteenth Century* that "he has calculated that about twenty-four out of every 100 of the experiments ... might have given pain. But of these twenty four, four-fifths are like vaccination, the pain of which is no great moment. In about one-seventh of the cases the animal only suffered from the healing of a wound." Sir James Paget afforded us a still more *couleur de rose* view of the subject. He said: "I believe that, with these few exceptions, there are no physiological experiments which are not matched or far surpassed in painfulness by common practices permitted or encouraged by the most humane persons."

3. Again, in reading these terrible Treatises ... we do not meet with one solitary appeal against the repetition of painful experiments, one caution to the student to forbear from the extremity of torture. One expression of pity or regret – even when the keenest suffering has been inflicted. On the contrary, we find frequent repetitions of such phrases as "interesting experiments," "beautiful" ... cerebral inflammation, and so on. In short, the writers, frankly, seem pleased with their work, and exemplify Claude Bernard's description of the ideal vivisector – the man who "does not hear the animals' cries of pain, and is blind to the blood that flows, and who sees nothing but his idea and organisms which conceal from him the secrets he is resolved to discover." Or, still more advanced, they realized [Elie de] Cyon's yet stronger lecture in his book of the "Methodik" ... [in which we learn:]

The true vivisector must approach a difficult question with *joyful excitement* ... He who shrinks from cutting into a living animal, he who approaches vivisection as a disagreeable necessity, may be able to repeat one or two vivisections, but he will never be an artist in vivisection ... The sensation of the physiologist when, from a gruesome wound, full of blood and mangled tissue, draws forth some delicate nerve thread ... has much in common with that of a sculptor ...

This is the somewhat startling self-revelation of the Vivisector, made by himself to his colleagues. The picture of him in the *Nineteenth Century* and *Fortnightly Review* is almost as different as one face of Janus from the other. We find him talking of the power of "controlling one's emotions," "disregarding one's own feelings at the sight of suffering," "subordinating feeling to judgment," and much more in the same strain, whereby the Vivisector is made to appear a martyr to the Enthusiasm of Humanity.

4. Again, as to the *number* of animals dissected alive ... Schiff is calculated to have "used" 14,000 dogs and nearly 50,000 other animals during his ten years work in Florence. Flourens told Blatin that Magendie had sacrificed 4,000 dogs to prove Bell's theory of the nerves, and 4,000 more to disprove the same ... Dr Lauder Brunton ... told the Royal Commission ... that in one series, out of three on one subject, he had sacrificed (without result) ninety cats in an experiment during which they lingered four or five hours after the chloroform ... with their intestines "operated upon" ... He also carried on another series of 150 experiments on various animals, very painful, and notoriously without results. This is the scale on which vivisections abroad and at home are carried on, if we are to be guided by the Treatises.

Turn we now to the popular Articles; and we find mention only of the very smallest numbers ... every reference to numbers ... being limited to the digits of physiologists.

Again, as regards anaesthetics, throughout the Treatises I cannot recall having once seen them mentioned as *means of allaying the sufferings of the animals,* but very often as convenient applications for *keeping them quiet* ... Nor can haste explain this omission to treat anaesthetics from the humanitarian point of view, for the Treatises contain long chapters of advice to the neophyte in vivisection, how he may ingeniously avoid being bitten by the dogs, or scratched by the yet more *"terrible"* cats, which are, Bernard pathetically complains, *"indocile"* when lifted on the torture trough.[129]

Cobbe's sixth point consists of a denunciation of British researchers' admiration for Bernard. This is followed by an examination of some points on which she had been previously criticized by supporters of vivisection and eleven pages of incriminating evidence of the cruelty of vivisection taken from published descriptions of experiments written by the experimenters themselves.

George Hoggan

However, it is not the redoubtable Frances Power Cobbe, but, instead, a modest physician and former assistant to Claude Bernard, George Hoggan (1837-91), who is honoured as the person who fired the opening salvo in what has been called "the vivisection battle" – though there was certainly some prior sniping, not least from Charles Dickens[130] and Cobbe. The battle was fought bloodily for three decades from the mid-1870s onward, with skirmishes lingering into the second decade of the twentieth century.

Hoggan wrote a letter to the editor of the *Morning Post.* It was reprinted in the *Spectator* on 6 February 1875, together with sympathetic comments from the *Spectator*'s editor, Richard Hutton. Weeks of debate ensued in the Letters to the Editor section of the *Spectator,* and, in part as a consequence of the debate, and in part as a consequence of the urgings of Cobbe and Hoggan who had now joined forces, a regulatory Bill was introduced in the Lords on 4 May 1875, supported by former Home Secretary Robert Lowe and Chief Justice Coleridge. Since a weaker Bill, supported by T.H. Huxley, was introduced in the lower house eight days later, the Government appointed a Royal Commission of Enquiry in June 1875 under the chairmanship of a Vice-President of the RSPCA with Huxley as a representative of the scientific community.

To the Editor of the *Morning Post*

Sir, – If the Society for the Prevention of Cruelty to Animals intend to give effect to the Memorial presented to it on Monday,* and do its utmost to put down the

---

* A plea organized by Cobbe to have the Society become active against vivisection.

monstrous abuses which have sprung up of late years in the practice of Vivisection, it will probably find that the greatest obstacle to success lies in the secrecy with which such experiments are conducted; and it is to the destruction of that secrecy that its best efforts should be directed, in the Legislature or elsewhere. It matters little what criminality the law may clearly attach to such practices. So long as the present privacy be maintained in regard to them, it will be found impossible to convict from want of evidence. No student can be expected to come forward as a witness when he knows that he would be hooted, mobbed, and expelled from among his fellows for doing so, and any rising medical man would only achieve professional ruin by following a similar course. The result is that although hundreds of such abuses are being constantly perpetrated amongst us, the public knows no more about them than what the distant echo reflected from some handbook affords. On the other hand, if special knowledge be not forthcoming, and the public mind be left alone to carry on the crusade against unnecessary vivisection, feelings will be sure to take the place of facts, and the morbid, unreasoning excitement thereby created will either carry matters too far or fail altogether. As nothing will be likely to succeed so well as example in drawing forth information on these points from those capable but hesitating to give it, I venture to record a little of my own experience in the matter, part of which was gained as an assistant in the laboratory of one of the greatest living experimental physiologists [Bernard]. In that laboratory we sacrificed daily from one to three dogs, besides rabbits and other animals, and after four months' experience, I am of opinion not one of these experiments was justified or necessary. The idea of the good of humanity was simply out of the question, and would have been laughed at, the great aim being to keep up with, or get ahead of one's contemporaries in science, even at the price of an incalculable amount of torture needlessly and iniquitously inflicted on the poor animals. During three [military] campaigns I have witnessed many harsh sights, but I think the saddest sight I ever witnessed was when the dogs were brought up from the cellar to the laboratory for sacrifice. Instead of appearing pleased with the change from darkness to light, they seemed seized with horror as soon as they smelt the air of the place, divining apparently their approaching fate. They would make friendly advances to each of the three or four persons present, and as far as eyes, ears and tail could make a mute appeal for mercy eloquent, they tried it in vain. Even when roughly grasped and thrown on the torture-trough, a low complaining whine at such treatment would be all the protest they made, and they would lick the hand which bound them till their mouths were fixed in the gag, and they could only flap their tail in the trough as their last means of exciting compassion. Often when convulsed by the pain of their torture this would be renewed, and they would be soothed instantly on receiving a few gentle pats. It was all the aid and comfort I could give them, and I gave it often. They seemed to take it as an earnest of fellow-feeling that would cause their torture to come to an end – an end only brought by death.

Were the feelings of experimental physiologists not blunted, they could not long continue the practice of vivisection. They are always ready to repudiate any implied

want of tender feeling, but I must say they seldom show much pity; on the contrary, in practice they frequently show the reverse. Hundreds of times I have seen
when an animal writhed in pain, and thereby deranged the tissues, during a deliberate dissection; instead of being soothed, it would receive a slap and an angry
order to be quiet and behave itself. At other times, when an animal had endured
great pain for hours without struggling or giving more than an occasional low
whine, instead of letting the poor mangled wretch loose to crawl painfully about
the place in reserve for another day's torture, it would receive pity so far that it
would be said to have behaved well enough to merit death, and as a reward would
be killed at once by breaking up the medulla, or "pithing," as this operation is
called. I have often heard the professor say, when one side of an animal has been
so mangled, and the tissues so obscured by clotted blood, that it was difficult to
find the part searched for, "Why don't you begin on the other side?" or "Why don't
you take another dog? What is the use of being so economical?" One of the most
revolting features in this laboratory was the custom of giving an animal on which
the professor had completed his experiment, and which had still some time left, to
the assistants to practice the finding of arteries, nerves &c., in the living animal, or
for performing what are called fundamental experiments upon it, – in other words,
repeating those which are recommended in the laboratory handbooks. I am
inclined to look upon anaesthetics as the greatest curse to vivisectible animals. They
alter too much the normal conditions of life to give accurate results, and they are
therefore little depended upon. They indeed prove far more efficacious in lulling
the public feeling towards the vivisectors than pain in the vivisected. Connected
with this there is a horrible proceeding that the public probably knows little about.
An animal is sometimes kept quiet by the administration of a poison called
"droorara," which paralyses voluntary motion while it heightens sensation, the animal being kept alive by means of artificial respiration until the effects of the poison
have passed off ...

[H]aving drunk the cup to the dregs, I cry off, and am prepared to see not only
science, but even mankind, perish rather than have recourse to such means of saving it. I hope that we shall soon have a Government inquiry into the subject, in
which experimental physiologists shall only be witnesses, not judges. Let all private
vivisection be made criminal, and all experiments be placed under Government
inspection, and we may have some clearing-away of abuses that the Anatomy Act*
caused in similar circumstances. – I am, Sir, your obedient servant, George Hoggan,
M.B. and C.M., 13 Granville Place, Portman Square, [London] W.[131]

John Coleridge

Nephew of Samuel Taylor Coleridge, John Duke Coleridge (1820-94),
Solicitor General then Attorney General (1868), became Lord Chief Justice in 1880. He was a convinced anti-vivisectionist at least as early as
1875 and, after becoming Lord Chief Justice, was often rebuked for his

* The Anatomy Act controlled medical experiments on human subjects.

beliefs by his adversaries in the vivisection community. He replied to his critics in a lengthy article in the *Fortnightly Review* in February 1882. Having identified his accusers and acknowledged the limitation of a judge's capacity to comment publicly on a contentious judicial issue, he continued:

> But there are occasions on which it is a duty to speak, and I think this is one ...
>
> In all human action we have to choose and balance between opposing good and evil; and in any change of law to determine whether that which we propose, or that which exists, is *upon the whole* the best. On this principle I do not hesitate to support the absolute prohibition of what for shortness' sake, though with some verbal inaccuracy, I call, as others call it, vivisection ...
>
> Is then the present law reasonable? It is the result of a most careful inquiry by eminent men in 1875, men certainly neither weak sentimentalists nor ignorant and prejudiced humanitarians ... These men unanimously recommended legislation, and legislation, in some important respects, more stringent than Parliament thought fit to pass. They recommended it on a body of evidence at once interesting and terrible. Interesting indeed it is from the frank apathy to the sufferings of the animals, however awful, avowed by some of the witnesses; for the noble humanity of a few; for the curious ingenuity with which others avoided the direct and verbal approval of horrible cruelties which yet others refused to condemn; and in some cases for the stern judgment passed upon men and practices, apparently now, after six years, considered worthy of more lenient language. Terrible the evidence is for the details of torture, of mutilation, of life slowly destroyed in torment, or skilfully preserved for the infliction of the same or diversified agonies, for days, for weeks, for months, in some cases for more than a year ... I think both that the Report of the Commission was at the time and has been since abundantly justified, and that the legislation founded on it did not go beyond very reasonable limits.
>
> But that there exists a statute confining vivisection within reasonable limits, with which some people are dissatisfied, is not, it may be said, any ground for going beyond those limits, and prohibiting the practice altogether. By itself it is not. But the claims of the vivisectors have become so large, the tone they take is so peremptory, the principles on which they base themselves are so alarming and (I think) so immoral, that I have become reluctantly convinced it is only by the strongest law, by absolutely forbidding the practice itself, that the grave mischief which follows from the holding parley with these claims can be stayed or destroyed ... I say, then, that the complete change of tone in the vivisectors, the open scoffing at laws of mercy which not so long ago were honoured at least in words, the broad claim that in pursuit of knowledge any cruelty may be inflicted on animals: these things not only startle me and shock my moral sense, but they convince that a practice which, according to the contention of its best and ablest advocates, involves these claims, is one which it is no longer safe to tolerate.
>
> I do not say that vivisection is useless ... What I ... do say is that very considerable men are not agreed as to the great utility of vivisection, or as to the value of the

results which have followed from it ... I will own a suspicion that if the baked dogs, and mutilated cats, and gouged frogs, and nail-larded guinea pigs, and brain-extracted monkeys, had resulted in anything worth hearing of, I should have heard ...

No fair man, I think, can fail to be struck with the uncertainty, a different point from utility, of the conclusions to which vivisection has conducted those who practise it. The conclusions are doubted, are disputed, are contradicted, by the vivisectors themselves. So that it really is not experiment to verify or disprove theory, which one well-conducted and crucial experiment might do, but experiment *in vacuo,* experiment on the chance, experiment in pursuit of nothing in particular, but of anything which may turn up in the course of a hundred thousand vivisections, and during the course of a life devoted to them. This is the experiment for which liberty is claimed, and the unfettered pursuit of which we are called hard names for objecting to. "Pseudo-humanitarians," "ill-informed fanatics," "true pharisaical spirit," these are but specimens of the language – which the calm and serene men of science find it convenient to apply to their opponents ...

I deny altogether that it concludes the question to admit that vivisection enlarges knowledge. I do not doubt it does; but I deny that the pursuit of knowledge is in itself always lawful; still more do I deny that the gaining of knowledge justifies all means of gaining it ... it is admitted that it is not safe to argue from the ... effects [of poison] on animals to their effects on man. As to man himself, it was not long ago that medical men met with a passion of disavowal, what they regarded as an imputation, viz. the suggestion that experiments were tried on patients in hospitals. I assume the disavowal to be true; but why, if all pursuit of knowledge is lawful, should the imputation be resented? The moment you come to distinguish between animals and man, you consent to limit the pursuit of knowledge by considerations not scientific but moral; and it is bad logic ... to assume (which is the very point at issue), that these considerations avail for man but do not for animals ...

It comes to this, that the *necessity* for vivisection, in order to attain the ends proposed, is not admitted by many persons of knowledge and authority; that its *practical* utility in alleviating human suffering, though not denied, is on the same authority said to be much exaggerated by those who practise or defend it; that even if it be admitted to be a means of gaining scientific knowledge, such knowledge is unlawful knowledge if it is pursued by means which are immoral; and that a disregard of all proportion between means and ends makes both alike unlawful and indefensible ... the amount and intensity of [suffering], as described by the vivisectors themselves, is absolutely sickening. In this world of pain and sorrow surely the highest of God's creatures should not wilfully increase a sum which seems too great already ...

I do not believe that the gentle ladies and refined gentlemen who subject their horses to cruel pain, day by day, or year by year, by means of gag-bits and bearing-reins, have ever seriously thought, or perhaps really know what they are doing ...

So again I should suppose that the vast majority of persons who have white veal brought up to their houses have never seen, as I have seen, a calf still living hung up in a butcher's shop. If they had, and if they knew the process by which veal is made white, I think better of my countrymen to believe that they would bear to see it at their tables. Most men do not reflect; nay, most men do not know these things ...

Why should a venerable osteologist, a world-famed naturalist, or a couple of most illustrious physicians, be any better judges than a man of average intellect, average education, and average fairness, when the question is what is the limit (it being I think certain that there is one) between lawful and unlawful knowledge, and lawful and unlawful means of gaining it; and what is the moral effect necessarily or probably, according to the common facts of human nature, of a certain course of practice? ...

What would our Lord have said, what looks would He have bent, upon a chamber filled with "the unoffending creature which He loves," dying under torture deliberately inflicted, or kept alive to endure further torment in pursuit of knowledge? ... the mind of Christ must be the guide of life. "Shouldst thou not have had compassion upon these, even as I had pity on thee?" So he seems to me to say; and I shall act accordingly.[132]

Seventh Earl of Shaftesbury

Descendent of "the father of sensibility,"[133] Anthony Ashley Cooper, seventh earl of Shaftesbury (1801-85) was a broad social reformer, working to reduce the ill-effects of the Industrial Revolution, especially with regard to housing and education. He introduced legislation to prohibit the employment of women and children in coal mines (1842), to provide care for the insane (1845), and to establish a 10-hour day for factory employees (1847). He was elected first president of the Victoria Street Society in 1875 and spoke eloquently on 26 May 1876 in favour of an act to limit vivisection, in which he suggested, *inter alia*, that animals not only have immortal souls but are more deserving of them than are some humans. He added:

why should [England] not hold her place among the nations of the earth, and be the first to reduce within the closest possible limits, the sufferings inflicted by man on the whole animal kingdom? ... Those ill-used and tortured animals are as much His creatures as we are; and to say the truth, I had in some instances, rather been the animal tortured than the man who tortured it. I should believe myself to have higher hopes and a happier future ... No physical pain can possibly equal the injury caused by the moral degradation of the feelings which such barbarous experiments must naturally induce.

On passage of the Bill on 27 June 1876,

The Earl of Shaftesbury heartily thanked the Government for having brought in the Bill. It was, no doubt, an imperfect measure, and not all that those whom he represented could wish; but it was a marvel that they had obtained so much. He had accepted with much reluctance the introduction of the words permitting vivisection, "for advancement by new discovery of physiological knowledge," but he had done so in the hope of conciliating scientific men, both in the passage of the Bill, and afterwards when it should have come into operation as law.[134]

Shaftesbury's reluctance overrode his compromise. In 1879 he joined with Lord Truro in an unsuccessful attempt to enact legislation to abolish vivisection entirely. He had written to Frances Power Cobbe on 3 September 1878 that: "We are bound in duty, I think to leap over all limitations, and go in for the total abolition of this vile and cruel form of Idolatry; for idolatry it is, and like all idolatry, brutal, degrading, and deceptive."[135] The 1876 compromise satisfied neither the vivisectors nor their opponents. One thing, however, is inexorably clear – those who proclaimed deep-seated Christian principles were much more likely to oppose inflicting pain and suffering on the animals than those who were drawn to a scientific Darwinism.

Lewis Carroll

The list of literary luminaries who took a stand against vivisection is impressive: Charles Dickens (who died before the issue became a major public controversy), Wilkie Collins, Alfred Tennyson, Robert Browning, Thomas Carlyle, Christina Rossetti, Robert Louis Stevenson, John Ruskin, Thomas Hardy, Bernard Shaw, and John Galsworthy, to mention the more prominent among them. None applied themselves to the issue with a greater logical clarity than the author of *Alice's Adventures in Wonderland* (1865) and *Through the Looking-Glass* (1872). Nor should this surprise us, for Charles Lutwidge Dodgson (1832-98) – he based his *nom de plume* on a reversed Latinization of his forenames – was by profession a logician who taught mathematics at Oxford. Among his less famous works – and perhaps no more profound, for the Alice books were subliminal treatises on logic – was *Euclid and His Modern Rivals* (1879).

Already in his childhood, it was said that he numbered certain snails and toads among his intimate friends, and in his youthful poetry he extolled the animals, which set the stage for his later views on vivisection. In a letter to the *Pall Mall Gazette* in February 1875 he depicted "vivisection as a metaphor for the malaise of the age," deploring the "enslavement of his weaker brethren ... the degradation of women ... [and] the torture of the animal world ... the man of science ... shall exult ... that he has made of this fair green earth, if not a heaven for man, at least a hell for animals."[136]

Although Dodgson played no role in the anti-vivisection movement itself – he was not a very public person – his article on "Some Popular Fallacies about Vivisection" which appeared in the *Fortnightly Review* in June 1875 – four months after Hoggan's letter to the *Morning Post* – was grist to the anti-vivisection mill, though some of the ensuing meal must have been a little chewy. Logic, after all, operates within assumptions that may not be universally accepted, as Dodgson himself clarifies at the beginning. An entirely logical argument cannot therefore be fallacious, but it can certainly be wrong if its assumptions are wrong. And some of the more prominent anti-vivisectionists would have had qualms about Dodgson's assumptions, if not about the general tenor of his remarks.

At a time when this painful subject is engrossing so large a share of public attention, no apology, I trust, is needed for the following attempt to formulate and classify some of the many fallacies, as they seem to me, which I have met with in the writings of those who advocate the practice ...

I begin with two contradictory propositions, which seem to constitute the two extremes, containing between them the golden mean of truth: –

1 *That the infliction of pain on animals is a right of man, needing no justification.*
2 *That it is no case justifiable.*

> The first of these is assumed in practice by many who would hardly venture to outrage the common feelings of humanity to state it in terms ...
>
> The second has been assumed by an Association lately formed for the total suppression of Vivisection ... I think I may assume that the proposition most generally accepted is an intermediate one, that the infliction of pain is in some cases justifiable, but not in all.

3 *That our right to inflict pain is coextensive with our right to kill, or even to exterminate a race* (which prevents the existence of possible animals), all being alike infringements of their rights ...*

> The only question worth consideration is whether the killing of an animal is a real infringement of right ... I conclude (and I believe that many, on considering the point, will agree with me) that man has an *absolute* right to inflict death on animals, without assigning any reason, provided that it be a painless death, but that any infliction of pain needs its special justification.

4 *That man is infinitely more important than the lower animals, so that the infliction of animal suffering, however great, is justifiable if it prevent human suffering, however small.*

> This fallacy can be assumed only when unexpressed. To put it into words is almost to refute it. Few, even in an age, where selfishness has almost become a religion† dare openly avow a selfishness so hideous as this! While there are thousands, I believe, who would be ready to assure the vivisectionists that, so far as their personal interests are concerned, they are ready to forego any prospect they may have of a diminution of pain, if it can only be assured by the infliction of so much pain on innocent creatures.

---

* That is, species.
† Dodgson is referring, somewhat exaggeratedly, to the Spencerian Utilitarians and the laissez-faire economists.

But I have a more serious charge than that of selfishness to bring against the scientific men who make this assumption. They use it dishonestly, recognising it when it tells in their favour, and ignoring it when it tells against them. For does it not presuppose the axiom that human and animal suffering differ *in kind?* A strange assertion this, from the lips of people who tell us that man is a twin-brother to the monkey! Let them be at least consistent, and when they have proved that the lessening of *human* suffering is an end so great and glorious as to justify any means that will secure it, let them give the anthropomorphoid ape the benefit of the argument. Further than that I will not ask them to go, but will resign them in confidence to the guidance of an inexorable logic.

Had they only candour and courage to do it, I believe they would choose the other horn of the dilemma, and would reply, "Yes, man *is* in the same category as the brute; and just as we care not (you see it, so we cannot deny it) how much pain we inflict on the one, so we care not, unless deterred by legal penalties, how much we inflict on the other. The lust for scientific knowledge is our real guiding principle. The lessening of human suffering is a mere dummy set up to amuse sentimental dreamers."

I come now to another class of fallacies – those involved in the comparison so often made, between vivisection and field-sports. If the theory that the two are essentially similar, involved no worse consequence than that sport should be condemned by all who condemn vivisection, I should be by no means anxious to refute it. Unfortunately, the other consequence is just as logical, and just as likely, that vivisection should be approved by all who approve of sport ...

5 *That it is fair to compare aggregates of pain.*

"The aggregate of wrong ... which is perpetrated against animals by sports-men in a single year exceeds that which some of them endure from vivisectors in half a century." The best refutation of this fallacy would seem to be to trace it to its logical conclusion – that a very large number of trivial wrongs are equal to one great one. For instance, that man, who by selling adulterated bread inflicts a minute injury on the health of some thousands of persons commits a crime equal to one murder. Once grasp this *reductio ad absurdum,* and you will be ready to allow that the only fair comparison is between individual and individual ...

6 *That the pain inflicted on an individual animal in vivisection is not greater than in sport.*

I am no sportsman, and so have no right to dogmatize, but I am tolerably sure that all sportsmen will agree with me that this is untrue in shooting, in which, whenever the creature is killed at once, it is probably as painless a form of death as could be devised ... Probably much the same might be said for fishing: for other forms of sport, and especially for hunting, I have no defence to offer, believing they involve great cruelty ...

In the seventh proposition, Dodgson argues that the degradation of the vivisector is worse than the animal suffering; in the eighth that vivisection does indeed degrade; in the ninth that "sport" is no more demoralizing than vivisection; in the tenth that selfishness is as logical an explanation as altruism for the practice of vivisection; in the eleventh that the existence of other social evils is no disbarment to controlling vivisection. He continues:

12   *That legislation would only increase the evil.*

The plea, if I understand it aright amounts to this, – that legislation would probably encourage many to go beyond the limit with which at present they are content, as soon as they found that a legal limit had been fixed beyond their own ... the principle of doing evil that good may come is not likely to find many defenders, even in this modern disguise of forbearing to do good lest evil should come. We may safely take our stand on the principle of doing the duty which we see before us ...

We have now, I think, seen good reason to suspect that the principle of selfishness lies at the root of this accursed practice ... [creating] a new and more hideous Frankenstein – a soulless being to whom science shall be all in all.[137]

John Ruskin

Unlike Charles Dodgson, John Ruskin wrote no learned articles on vivisection. However, through his actions, he became renowned for his denunciation of vivisection. The celebrated author of the five-volume *Modern Painters* (1843 on), *The Seven Lamps of Architecture* (1849), and *The Stones of Venice* (1851-53), he was appointed the first Slade Professor of Art at Oxford in 1870. His writings on economic and social reform were perhaps even more influential, profoundly affecting Gandhi, among many others.

His sensibilities to animals had been long known. In drawing up the regulations for the Society of St. George – an association to bring about a just, responsible, and skilled worker society – he wrote as rule 5: "I will not kill nor hurt any living creature needlessly, nor destroy any beautiful thing, but will strive to save and comfort all gentle life, and guard and perfect all natural beauty upon the earth."[138]

As a celebrated proponent of Romantic Toryism (but with socialist leanings), he observed:

The gentleness of chivalry, properly so called, depends on the recognition of the order and awe of lower and loftier life, first clearly taught in the myth of Chiron, and his bringing up of Jason, Aesculapius, and Achilles, but most perfectly by Homer, in the fable of the horses of Achilles, and the part assigned to them, in the relation of the death of his friend, and in prophecy of his own. There is perhaps in all the *Iliad,* nothing more deep in significance – there is nothing in all literature more perfect in human tenderness, and honour for the mystery of inferior life – than the verses that describe the sorrow of the divine horses at the death of Patroclus, and the comfort given them by the greatest of the gods.[139]

A long-time member of the Victoria Street Society he addressed a meeting of the new Oxford branch on 9 December 1884, following earlier addresses against vivisection by Dr. Mackarness (the Bishop of Oxford) and others.

Professor Ruskin said he had learnt much from the speakers, but there were one or two points which he should wish to refer to. It was not the question whether experiments taught them more or less of science. It was not the question whether animals had a right to this or that in the inferiority they were placed in to mankind. It was a question – what relation had they to God, what relations mankind had to God, and what was the true sense of feeling as taught to them by Christ the Physician? The primary head and front of all the offending against the principles of mercy in men and the will of the Creator of these creatures was the ignoring of that will in higher matters, and these scientific pursuits were now defiantly, provokingly, insultingly separated from the science of religion; they were all carried on in defiance of what had hitherto been held to be compassion and pity, and of the great link which bound together the whole of creation, from its Maker to the lowest creature. For one secret discovered by the torture of a thousand animals, a thousand means of health, peace and happiness were lost, because the physician was continually infecting his students not with the common rabies of the dog, but with the rabies of the man, infecting them with all kinds of base curiosity, infecting the whole society which he had taught with a thirst for knowing things which God had concealed from them for His own good reason, and promoting amongst them passions of the same kind. No physician now dwelt in the least upon the effect of anger, upon the effect of avarice, upon the effect of science itself pursued without moral limit; and the rabies of all defiance and contradiction to all the law of God had become the madness abroad, which was without reason at all, and was setting itself against everything that was once holy, once pure, once reverenced among them. For his part, he thought they must not dwell upon minute questions as to whether this or that quantity of pain was inflicted. The question was that here in Oxford their object was to make their youths and maidens gentle, and it seemed to him that they might at least try to concentrate their efforts to prevent these subjects of science being brought into contact with the minds of the noblest youths and maidens who came there to be made gentlemen and ladies. Their noblest efforts and energies should be set upon protecting the weak and informing the ignorant of things which might lead them to happiness, peace, and light, and above all other things upon the relation existing between them and the lower creation in this life. He had always said that the gentleman was primarily distinguished by his fellowship with the nobler animals of creation, and the peasant chiefly by the kindness which he showed to every useful one.[140]

It could be said that words come easily. But the sincerity of Ruskin's convictions was demonstrated when funds were voted by the Oxford Senate in March 1885 to allow for a physiology laboratory in which vivisection would be practised. After some short-lived soul-searching Ruskin resigned his Chair, as he wrote to the *Pall Mall Gazette* (24 April 1885): "on the Monday following the vote endowing vivisection in the University, solely in consequence of that vote." Rarely has principle been so clearly demonstrated through selfless deed.

Robert Browning

Robert Browning (1812-89) was a profound poet whose sense of optimism epitomized the Victorian era. He was the husband of Elizabeth Barrett Browning (1806-61), whose charming poem about her dog was the basis for Virginia Woolf's novel *Flush* (1933). His masterpiece was *The Ring and the Book* (4 vols., 1868-69). As befitting of a vice-president of the Victoria Street Society, he wrote two anti-vivisection poems, in the first of which a dog saves a child's life and is rewarded with the prospect of being vivisected. The idea that animals act from instinct alone is given its due sardonic merit.

"Tray," from Dramatic Idylls, first series (1879)

"A beggar-child" (let's hear this third!)
"Sat on a quay's edge: like a bird
Sang to herself at careless play,
And fell into the stream. 'Dismay!
Help, you standers-by!' None stirred.

"Bystanders reason, think of wives
And children ere they risk their lives.
Over the balustrade has bounced
A mere instinctive dog, and pounced
Plumb on the prize. 'How well he dives!

"'Up he comes with the child, wee, tight
In mouth, alive too, clutched from quite
A depth of ten feet – twelve I bet!
Good dog! What, off again? There's yet
Another child to save? All right!

"'How strange we saw no other fall!
It's instinct in the animal.
Good dog! But he's a long while under:
If he got drowned I should not wonder –
Strong current, that against the wall!

"'Here he comes, holds in mouth this time
– What may the thing be? Well that's prime!
Now, did you ever? Reason reigns
In man alone, since all Tray's pains
Have fished – the child's doll from the slime!'

"And so, amid the laughter gay,
Trotted my hero off, – old Tray, –
Till somebody, prerogatived
With reason, reasoned: 'Why he dived,
His brain would show us, I should say.

"'John, go and catch – or, if needs be,
Purchase – that animal for me!
By vivisection, at expense
Of half-an-hour and eighteenpence.
How brain secretes dog's soul, we'll see!'"[141]

In the second poem, the suggestion is that vivisection is cowardly, haphazard, and directed toward alleviation from the mildest complaints. "Shoots" are corns.

"Arcades Ambo" from *Asolando: Fancies and Facts (1889)*

A. You blame me that I ran away?
    Why, Sir, the enemy advanced:
Balls flew about, and, – who can say
    But one, if I stood firm, had glanced
In my direction? Cowardice?
I only know we don't live twice,
Therefore shun death, is my advice.

B. Shun death at all risks? Well, at some!
    True, I myself, Sir, though I scold
The cowardly, by no means come
    Under reproof as overbold
    I, who would have no end of brutes
Cut up alive to guess what suits
My case and saves my toe from shoots.[142]

Already in 1875 Browning had given support to Cobbe's memorial to the RSPCA encouraging it to oppose vivisection, remarking that "I would rather submit to the worst of deaths, so far as pain goes, than have a single dog or cat tortured on the pretence of sparing me a twinge or two."[143]

Robert Louis Stevenson

Ambivalent about everything to the point of principle, Robert Louis Stevenson (1850-94) was no less ambivalent about his treatment of animals, even if, in the final analysis, he came down firmly on their side. There is relatively little in *Treasure Island* (1883), despite the charm of "Captain Flint," the parrot, *The Strange Case of Dr. Jekyll and Mr. Hyde* (1886), or *The Master of Ballantrae* (1889) to reflect Stevenson's animal orientations. Nonetheless, in his youth he was an avid naturalist and remained a bird-watcher throughout his life. In "The Coast of Fife" he recalled his first day at school: "A benevolent cat cumbered me the while with consolations – we two were alone in all that was visible of the London road; two poor waifs who had each tasted sorrow – and she fawned upon the weeper and gambolled for his entertainment, watching the effect, it seemed, with motherly eyes."[144]

Stevenson's ambivalence is pronounced in *Travels with a Donkey in the Cevennes* (1879), where he practises but abominates an unconscionable cruelty, indicating a recognition that we know what sensibilities we ought to have, but that we are likely to be blind to them when our interests compete with those of the animal. Ultimately, principles can be tested only against practical reality. And it is what one does, not what one says or thinks, that reflects one's humanity. It is an honesty we find only occasionally repeated.

I took in my right hand the unhallowed staff, and with a quaking spirit applied it to the donkey. Modestine brisked up her pace for perhaps three steps, and then relapsed into her former minuet. Another application had the same effect, and so with the third. I am worthy the name of an Englishman, and it goes against my conscience to lay my hand rudely on a female. I desisted, and looked her all over from head to foot; the poor brute's knees were trembling and her breathing was distressed; it was plain that she could go no faster on a hill. God forbid, thought I, that I should brutalize this innocent creature; let her go at her own pace ...

[N]othing but a blow would move her, and that only for a second ... I must instantly maltreat this uncomplaining animal. The sound of my own blows sickened me. Once, when I looked at her, she had a faint resemblance to a lady of my acquaintance who formerly loaded me with kindness; and this increased the horror of my cruelty ... I am ashamed to say, [I] struck the poor sinner twice across the face. It was pitiful to see her lift her head with shut eyes, as if waiting for another blow ... I had now an arm free to thrash Modestine, and cruelly I chastised her ... I promise you, the stick was not idle; I think every decent step that Modestine took cost me at least two emphatic blows ...

They told me when I started, and I was ready to believe it, that before a few days I should come to love Modestine like a dog. Three days had passed, we had shared some misadventures, and my heart was still as cold as a potato towards my beast of burden ... It was my one serious conflict with Modestine. She would have none of my short cut; she turned in my face; she backed, she reared ... I plied the goad.[145]

Finally though, having the finished the journey and having sold Modestine:

It was not until I was fairly seated by the driver, and rattling through a rocky valley with dwarf olives that I became aware of my bereavement. I had lost

Modestine. Up to that moment I had thought I hated her; but now she was gone,
>"And oh!
>The difference to me!"

For twelve days we had been fast companions ... After the first day, although sometimes I was hurt and distant in manner, I still kept my patience; and as for her poor
soul! she had come to regard me as a god. She loved to eat out of my hand. She
was patient, elegant in form, the colour of an ideal mouse, and inimitably small.
Her faults were those of her race and sex; her virtues were her own. Farewell, and
if for ever –

Father Adam wept when he sold her to me; after I had sold her in my turn, I was
tempted to follow his example; and being alone with a stage-driver and four or five
agreeable young men, I did not hesitate to yield to my emotion.[146]

In Stevenson's essay on "The Character of Dogs" he describes the dog in
almost Cartesian terms as "a machine working independently of his control, the heart, like the mill-wheel keeping all in motion." He wrote from
France of his own pet dog Bogue, which he had not bothered to house-
train: "The dog has bogged more than once upon this hostile soil with a
preference for hostile carpets, than could be believed of a creature so
inconsiderable in proportion ... Yet," he added, "we all adore that dog."[147]

His ambivalence went into retreat, however, when he came upon a
Highlander beating his dog. Stevenson remonstrated with the owner. "'It's
not your dog,' was the reply. 'No,' said Stevenson in anger, 'but it's God's
dog and I'm not going to see you ill use it.'"[148] In *Favourite Studies of Man
and Books* (1882) he announced to one who thought immortal souls the
prerogative of humans: "You think dogs will not be in Heaven! I tell you
they will be there before any of us."[149] Of course, the dog's idea of heaven
many not be the same as human conceptions, for, as **Rupert Brooke**
opined in his poem "Heaven": "And in that Heaven of all their wish,/
There shall be no more land, say fish."

Certainly, all ambivalence disappears when we learn from Stevenson's
biographer, Frank McLynn, of his "refusal to fish or hunt on grounds of
cruelty to animals." Most strikingly, he opposed experimentation on the
proverbial guinea pigs, where they were injected with tubercular bacilli,
even though the experiments of Dr. Edward Trudeau were designed to
cure tuberculosis, the illness from which Stevenson suffered and eventually
died. He told the famous and notorious Trudeau: "Your light may be very
bright to you, but to me it smells of oil like the devil."[150]

Whereas Browning proclaimed an honourable principle that was not
put to the test, and Ruskin sacrificed a cherished career for that principle,
the ambivalent Stevenson refused to avail himself of a remote opportunity
to save his life for the same principle. Surely Hobbesians and Spencerians,
even Benthamites, must be compelled to re-think their utilitarian notions
of a sympathy derived from mere enlightened self-interest.

Christina Rossetti

Author of primarily religious verse, much of it melancholy, Christina Rossetti (1830-94) was active in the anti-vivisection movement to the extent that she distributed pamphlets and sent a dozen autographed copies of a poem composed specially for an anti-vivisection fundraising bazaar. Support of the downtrodden was a constant feature of her life and she was a volunteer social worker at the Highgate Penitentiary. Once she found an unfledged thrush fallen from its nest: "so I took it home with me to bring it up till it could take care of itself, when of course I should have returned it to liberty; but the poor little creature refused to eat or drink; so next day I took it out again, and deposited it in a field near a hedge, in the hope that it could manage to maintain itself, or that some parent bird would take care of it. I only hope that neither cat nor cruel boy found it."[151]

Many of her poems reflected her animal sympathies, especially for the insects and the birds, though dogs, cats, crocodiles, sea-creatures, and monsters find their place too. In "Sing-Song: A Nursery Rhyme Book" (1872) the reader is advised:

Hurt no living thing:
Ladybird nor butterfly,
Nor moth with dusty wing,
Nor cricket cheering cheerily,
Nor grasshopper so light of leap,
Nor dancing gnat, nor beetle fat,
Nor harmless worms that creep.[152]

Rossetti's highest estimation of the animal realm came in "To what purpose is this waste?" (1872)

And other eyes than our's
Were made to look on flowers,
Eyes of small birds and insects small ...
The tiniest living thing
That soars on feathered wing,
Or crawls among the long grass out of sight
Has just as good a right
To its appointed portion of delight
As any King ...
Why should we grudge a hidden water stream
To birds and squirrels while we have enough?[153]

Alfred Lord Tennyson

Author of *The Princess* (1847) and *In Memoriam* (1850), Alfred Tennyson, first Baron Tennyson (1809-92), succeeded Wordsworth as Poet Laureate in 1850. Tennyson is sometimes disparaged for having depicted "Nature, red in tooth and claw," but his reputation should be saved by his role as a vice-president of the National Anti-Vivisection Society. He was also a minor authority on birds.

In his notebook for 1820 (he was only eleven years old), he described himself – imaginatively perhaps, but certainly wilfully – as letting wild animals out of traps to the fury of the local gamekeepers. At home he had a pet owl, as a Cambridge undergraduate a pet snake. Later he rescued a hedgehog and fed it on milk and water. Toward the end of his life he kept a wolfhound that he named Karenina out of respect for Tolstoy. His biographer, Peter Levi, tells us that in his poem "The Owl," "he recalls and obviously wants to relive the moment, when the owl really came to the window and sat on his shoulder. Of all the magnificent moments in his life, that one surely must have ranked very high."[154] Yet in the poem itself it is the music not the words that tell us of the affection.

Like Blake, Tennyson subscribed to a kind of pantheism and to Swedenborgianism; and he tried in vain to become a vegetarian. As a student, well before Darwin embarked on the *Beagle*, he adopted a Lamarckian-style theory of evolution and sketched the theory, before the publication of *The Origin of Species*, in both *In Memoriam* and *Maud* (1855). Still, he brooded gloomily on Darwinism: "A monstrous eft was of old the Lord and Master"; now man "is first, but is he the last? Is he not too base?"[155]

Victoria Regina

Constitutionally disbarred from making public pronouncements on contentious issues – though it was a relatively new doctrine only formalized firmly by Walter Bagehot in his 1864 classic, *The English Constitution* – Queen Victoria (1819-1901) used her constitutional right to "advise" and to "warn" her ministers on several occasions on the issue of vivisection. Her granting of the prefix "Royal" to the SPCA in 1840 had been no idle gesture. Already in 1874 – before vivisection had become a major public issue and debate – her secretary wrote to Lord Harrowby as President of the RSPCA: "The Queen hears and reads with horror of the sufferings which the brute creation often undergo, and fears also sometimes from experiments in the pursuit of science."[156]

In 1875 she had a letter written to the prominent surgeon and researcher Joseph Lister, requesting that he desist from his vivisection practices. She urged her premier Benjamin Disraeli in March 1876 to have appropriate legislation enacted and he duly complied. In April 1881 her secretary wrote to the new Prime Minister William Ewart Gladstone: "The Queen has seen with pleasure that Mr. Gladstone takes an interest in the dreadful subject of vivisection, in which she has done all she could, and she earnestly hopes that Mr. Gladstone will take an opportunity of speaking strongly against a practice which is a disgrace to humanity and Christianity."[157]

In the midst of a notorious trial in November 1881 in which the prominent physiologist David Ferrier was accused of horrendous cruelty while vivisecting without a license[158] she addressed Home Secretary Sir William Harcourt:

WINDSOR CASTLE, November 25, 1881. – ... There is, however, another subject on which the Queen feels most strongly, and that is this horrible, brutalising, *unchristian-like Vivisection.*

That poor dumb animals should be kept alive as described in this trial is *revolting and horrible.* This *must* be stopped. Monkeys and dogs – two of the most intelligent amongst these poor animals who cannot complain – dogs, "man's best friend," possessed of more than instinct, to be treated in this fearful way is *awful.* She directs Sir Wm. Harcourt's attention *most strongly to it.*

It must really not be permitted. It is a disgrace to a civilized country.

The Queen was disturbed not only by vivisection, but also by the weakness of the laws against animal cruelty. Two years later her secretary, Sir Henry Ponsonby, wrote to Harcourt: "WINDSOR CASTLE, *July 5, 1883.* – I am commanded by the Queen to ask if men who are cruel to dogs ... cannot be more severely punished than by a fine of £2." Harcourt's biographer, A.G. Gardiner, tells us that on the question of vivisection:

He had already informed the Queen that instructions had been given for rigorous enforcement of the existing law with regard to vivisection and that the limit set to the practice should be restricted rather than extended. Ponsonby was also asked by the Queen (June 20, 1880) to say that she "takes the greatest interest in the protection of wild birds, and trusts therefore that Bill, which I understand is to be brought into the House tomorrow, will receive support." Harcourt replied that he believed it would be a useful measure and a proper correction for the cruelties now so often practised and the destruction of rare and beautiful species by unauthorized persons.[159]

Charles Dickens

In 1740 Henry Fielding chastised and threatened with fisticuffs a coachman mistreating a horse.[160] In 1819 the purportedly effeminate poet John Keats (1795-1821) fought a butcher's lad who was bullying a kitten.[161] By 1838 Charles Dickens (1812-70) had recourse to a smoother path: the legal system. He spoke out heatedly in court against a lout whom he had witnessed savaging his horse.[162]

The most popular novelist of the Victorian era, Dickens wrote such perennial favourites as *A Christmas Carol* (1843), *David Copperfield* (1850), *Little Dorrit* (1857), and *Great Expectations* (1861). The primary focus of his books is the oppressed poor, but he found an occasional place for the animals, as with the sentimental treatment of Florence's little dog in *Dombey and Son* (1848), Dora's "Jip" in *David Copperfield*, and the freeing of the caged birds in *Bleak House* (1853). Perhaps the finest animal elevation came with Putnam Smif's words in *Martin Chuzzlewit* (1843):

"there is a poetry in wildness, and every alligator basking in the slime is himself an Epic, self-contained" – an exquisitely poetical way of saying that each animal is an end in itself.

In his private life, Dickens's animal orientations, although pronounced, were less than complete. He had a particular distaste for snakes and rats, but this was at a time when the infestations of disease-carrying rats helped make London slum life both unsavoury and unhealthy – in 1847 half-a-million Londoners were infected with typhus fever, and the average age of mortality was twenty-seven, twenty-two for the working class.[163] The Dickensian view was that expressed by the Manichean Mr Tulliver in George Eliot's *Mill on the Floss*, where he contrasted the good animals with "rats, weevils and lawyers created by Old Harry" (that is, the devil).

Like Christina Rossetti, Dickens was a frequent visitor to London Zoo. A contemporary tells us that on entering he would: "proceed straight-away to the celebrities of claw or foot or fin. The delight he took in the hippopotamus family was most exhilarating. He entered familiarly into conversation with the huge, unwieldy creatures, and they seemed to understand him. Indeed, he spoke to all the unphilological inhabitants with a directness and tact which went home to them at once."[164] What an original way of avoiding calling animals "dumb!" Like Tchaikovsky at Berlin Zoo, Dickens was revolted by the public feeding of snakes with live guinea pigs and rabbits.[165]

Dickens was especially fond of his horse, but he offends modern sensi-bilities by his instruction that on his death his horse was to be shot[166] – though, in his defence, that was probably to save the steed from the indig-nities and cruelties inflicted on older horses. He kept a variety of pets at different periods of his adult life, including a canary, a bloodhound, a Saint Bernard, and a raven called Grip, whom he admired and to whom he gave a significant role in *Barnaby Rudge* (1841). Through all the slow-witted Barnaby's difficulties during the Popery riots of 1780 to the denouement of 1785 the bird remained a loyal and trusted companion.

The stage for the expression of animal sensibilities is set early in the book: "'The merciful man, Joe,'" said the locksmith, 'is merciful to his beast.'" The raven

listened with a polite attention and a most extraordinary appearance of compre-hending every word, to all they had said up to this point; turning his head from one to the other, as if his office were to judge between them, and it were of the last importance that he should not lose a word.

"Look at him!" said Varden, divided between admiration of the bird and a kind of fear of him. "Was there ever such a knowing imp as that! Oh he's a dreadful fellow!"

The raven with his head very much on one side, and his bright eye shining like a diamond, preserved a thoughtful silence for a few seconds, and then replied in a voice so hoarse and distant, that it seemed to come through his thick feathers rather than out of his mouth ...

"Halloa, halloa, halloa! What's the matter here! Keep up your spirits. Never say die ..."

"I more than half believe he speaks the truth. Upon my word I do," said Varden. "Do you see how he looks at me, as if he knew what I was saying?" ...

"Strange companions, sir," said the locksmith, shaking his head, and looking from one to the other. "The bird has all the wit ... Call him down, Barnaby, my man."

"Call him!" echoed Barnaby ..."But who can make him! He calls me, and makes me go where he will. He goes on before, and I follow. He's the master, and I'm the man. Is that the truth, Grip?"

The raven gave a short, comfortable, confidential kind of croak; – a most expressive croak, which seemed to say, "You needn't let these fellows into our secrets. We understand each other. It's all right."

"I make *him* come?" cried Barnaby, pointing to the bird. "Him, who never goes to sleep, or so much as winks! – Why, any time of night, you may see his eyes in my dark room, shining like two sparks. And every night, and all night too, he's broad awake, talking to himself, thinking what he shall steal, and hide, and bury. I make *him* come. Ha, ha, ha!" ...

The special relationship between Barnaby and Grip is elaborated a little later:

The raven, in his little basket at his master's back, hearing this frequent mention of his name in a tone of exultation, expressed his sympathy by crowing like a cock, and afterwards running over his various phrases of speech with such rapidity, and in so many varieties of hoarseness, that they sounded like the murmurs of a crowd of people ...

"He takes such care of me besides!" said Barnaby. "Such care, mother! He watches all the time I sleep, and when I shut my eyes and make-believe to slumber, he practices now learning softly; but he keeps his eye on me the while, and if he sees me laugh, though never so little, stops directly. He won't surprise me till he's perfect."

The raven crowed again in a rapturous manner which clearly said, "Those are certainly some of my characteristics, and I glory in them."

Grip was not, however, of value to Barnaby alone.

Grip was by no means an idle or unprofitable member of the humble household. Partly by dint of Barnaby's tuition, and partly by pursuing a species of self-instruction common to his tribe, and exerting his powers of observation to the utmost, he had acquired a degree of sagacity which rendered him famous for miles round. His conversational powers and surprising performances were the universal theme: and as many persons came to see the wonderful raven, and none left his exertions unrewarded – when he condescended to exhibit, which was not always, for genius is capricious – his earnings formed an important item in the common stock. Indeed, the bird himself appeared to know his value well; for though he was perfectly free and unrestrained in the presence of Barnaby and his mother, he maintained in public an amazing gravity, and never stooped to any other gratuitous performances than biting the ankles of vagabond boys (an exercise in which he much delighted), killing a fowl or two occasionally, and swallowing the dinners of various neighbouring dogs, of whom the boldest held him in great awe and esteem.[167]

Dickens taught his children to say the following prayer: "Make me kind to my nurses and servants and to all beggars and poor people and let me never be cruel to any dumb creature, for if I am cruel to anything, even to a poor little fly, you who are so good, will never love me."[168] It was, however, in an article entitled "Inhumane Humanity" he wrote for *All The Year Round* in 1866 that he stated his attitudes most directly. The reference to the "Inhumane Society" is not a caustic comment on SPCAs but on the society founded in the later eighteenth century to assist those in peril from drowning.

Will the Society for the Prevention of Cruelty to Animals be good enough to look after the Royal Inhumane Society? I make the request on behalf of the dogs, the cats, the guinea-pigs, and the rabbits who have a very serious charge to bring against the society ...

It claims to be born of respectable parents, to have been repeatedly recommended by the nobility and the clergy, and to be actuated by the purest motives and the best intentions. In its ninety-first annual report of itself, the Royal Inhumane Society states that no serious investigation of suspended animation took place until the middle of the last century ... [Eventually] the work fell into the hands of Dr. Dawes, and that gentleman, moved by [humane] suggestions, formed himself into a Humane Society ... It consisted of thirty-two members, and one of those members was no less a person than Oliver Goldsmith.

There is a magic in the very name. We pause here in our dry history to have a bright vision of the big-hearted, tender-souled, gentle Oliver rushing headlong into the scheme and subscribing his last guinea on the spot. How his face would glow with enthusiasm! ... We may be sure it was from the tenderest and most humane motives that Oliver Goldsmith joined that society. Could he ever have dreamt, even in his surgical philosophy,* of the inhumanities which are now practised in the name of humanity? ...

Now let us hear what the society has done in all those ninety-one years. It has saved and restored thirty-five thousand lives. A great and blessed work truly!

This is undoubtedly a record of great good accomplished by the society, and so far it is fairly entitled to call itself "humane." But even this pure and holy work has its victims. Are the subscribers aware how cruel they are to be kind? I come now to state the hard case of the dog, the cat, the guinea-pig, and the rabbit, and I will produce the society's own report in evidence.

---

* Goldsmith was a physician by training and education.

In the appendix we find a record of nearly a hundred cruel experiments made upon the lower animals, for the purpose of investigating the subject of suspended animation.

At this point, Dickens describes the first of many invasive experiments. "I hope it is not true that the spirits of the departed see and know what we do on earth; because, if Oliver Goldsmith could see such cruelties practised by the society which he helped to found, he would not be happy even in heaven." He then goes on to describe in some nauseous detail several more experiments.

Painful as it has been to me to write the words, and painful as it must be to every person not quite insensate to read them, I have quoted all these records of deliberate cruelty, because the subscribers to the Humane Society may not trouble themselves to read the annual report of their officers, and may, therefore, not be aware of the cruelties which are practised under their sanction. Their experiments were not made long ago, in the infancy of the art of recovering the drowned; but recently after all the symptoms attending such cases had been well ascertained, and a mode of treatment agreed upon and laid down.

No one will go so far as to declare that the slow suffocation of cats and dogs, the cutting of their throats, the piercing of the ventricles of their living hearts with pins, are not acts of cruelty. But no doubt it will be said by some that such experiments are justifiable and necessary in the interests of surgical science for the benefit of mankind. Their necessity I dispute. A set of rules for restoring suspended animation was framed many years ago, and all the experiments recently made on animals have added little or nothing to our knowledge of the treatment of such cases.

In order that the reader may judge for himself, I will quote the old rules laid down by Dr. Silvester, and the new rules recently adopted by the committee of the Royal Medical and Chirurgical Society, as a result of all their experiments upon dogs, cats, guinea-pigs, and rabbits.

Dickens recites the old and new rules, showing little difference between them:

The new method being in all essential respects identical with the old one, it would appear that nearly a hundred animals have been tortured by the Royal *Humane* Society's chirurgical gentlemen to no purpose.

Man may be justified – though I doubt it – in torturing the beasts, that he himself may escape pain; but he certainly has no right to gratify an idle and purposeless curiosity through the practice of cruelty.[169]

Dickens's very early piece on the ills of animal experimentation – nine years before Hoggan's letter to the *Morning Post* – is significant for drawing attention to the fact that these cruelties were practised even by those who proclaimed humanitarianism as their very goal.

Francis Newman

A number of books toward the end of the eighteenth and the beginning of the nineteenth centuries advocated vegetarianism, on both health and ethical grounds. Among them were John Oswald's *The Cry of Nature* (1791), George Nicholson's *The Primeval Diet of Man*, Joseph Ritson's *An Essay on Abstinence from Animal Food* (1802), and John Frank Newton's *Return to Nature* (1811), which we discussed earlier.[170] Already in 1746 Robert Morris had stressed in *A Reasonable Plea for the Animal Creation* that "we have no right to destroy, much less to eat of anything which has life."[171] In *The Ethics of Diet*, Howard Williams mentions many others who contributed to the development of vegetarian thought – Lambe, Shelley, Philips, Metcalfe, and Graham, for example. In 1809 William Cowherd had made vegetarianism compulsory in his Bible Christian Church in Salford, and the social and industrial reformer Robert Owen advocated abstention from flesh for the new society he envisaged. Vegetarianism was becoming more popular, and at a meeting held in Ramsgate, Kent, in 1847 the Vegetarian Society was founded – the term "vegetarian" having been coined in 1842.

Younger brother of Cardinal Newman, co-founder of Bedford College for women, later a part of the University of London, Professor Francis William Newman (1805-97) joined the Manchester Vegetarian Society in 1868, becoming its president from 1873 to 1883. George Eliot attended his lectures on geometry at Bedford College and referred to him as "our blessed St. Francis" whose "soul was a blessed yea."

That the first thought on discovering a new creature should be "Is it nice to eat?" is to me shocking and debasing. What is called the love of sport has become a love of killing for the display of skill, and converts man into the tyrant of all other animals; yet this rose out of a desire of eating their flesh – a desire which cannot be blamed on that state of barbarism in which little other food was to be had. But when with the growth of civilisation other food is easier to get, when bread has won upon flesh-meat, it is evil to struggle for the more barbarous state. Does not the love of flesh inflame the love of killing, teach disregard for animal suffering, and prepare men for ferocity against men?[172]

Howard Williams

Founder of the Humanitarian League with Henry Salt, and board member of the Animal Defence and Anti-Vivisection Society instituted by Lind-af-Hageby,[173] Howard Williams (1837-1931) wrote a profound and influential tome for the vegetarian cause under the title *The Ethics of Diet*. It is primarily an erudite history of vegetarianism over the centuries, dealing at length with the practice in classical Greece and Rome, especially that of Plutarch and Porphyry, and continuing into the nineteenth century. Controversially, Williams argued that Seneca's vegetarianism derived from an authentic disgust at animal cruelty, and that, having abandoned the practice publicly to avoid imperial suspicion, he must have continued it in private.[174] Equally provocatively, he contended that early Greek vegetarianism was the moral cement of the community; and he treated Ovid as a central figure because his golden age arguments (in imitation of Pythagoras) provided the connective unity to vegetarianism, from the eighth century BC Orphics to the Roman eschewers of flesh.

The principles of Dietary Reform are widely and deeply founded upon the teaching of (1) Comparative Anatomy and Physiology; (2) Humaneness in the two-fold meaning of Refinement of Living, and of what is commonly called "Humanity;" (3) National Economy; (4) Social Reform; (5) Domestic and Individual Economy; (6) Hygienic Philosophy ... To the present writer, the humanitarian argument appears to be of double weight ; for it is founded upon the irrefragable principles of Justice and Compassion – universal Justice and universal Compassion – the two principles most essential in any system of ethics worthy of the name. That this argument seems to have so limited an influence – even with persons otherwise humanely disposed, and of finer feeling in respect to their own, and, also, in a general way, to other species can be attributed only to the deadening power of custom and habit, of traditional prejudice, and educational bias. If they could be brought to reflect upon the simple ethics of the question, divesting their minds of these distorting media, it must appear in a light very different from that in which they accustom themselves to consider it ...

The step which leaves for ever behind it the barbarism of slaughtering our fellow beings, the Mammals and Birds, is, it is superfluous to add, the most important and influential of all.[175]

Annie Besant

A controversial social and political reformer, Annie Wood Besant (1847-1933), having separated from her clergyman husband, was deprived of her children by the judicial system in 1879 as a consequence of her atheism and unconventionality. She advocated birth control as a feminist measure, reprinted an old pamphlet on the topic, was charged with immorality, and, famously, acquitted. In 1889 she embraced theosophy, becoming a disciple of the energetic Mme Helen Bavatsky, accepting the doctrine of reincarnation in the form of different animals. Having immersed herself in Hinduism, she founded the Central Hindu College at Benares in 1898, became President of the Theosophical Society in 1907, instituted the Indian Home Rule League in 1916, and became President of the Indian National Congress in 1917.

[People who eat meat] are responsible for all the pain that grows out of meat-eating, and which is necessitated by the use of sentient animals as food; not only the horrors of the slaughterhouse, but also the preliminary horrors of the railway traffic, of the steamboat and ship traffic; all the starvation and the thirst and the prolonged misery of fear which these unhappy creatures have to pass through for the gratification of the appetite of man ... All pain acts as a record against humanity and slackens and retards human growth.[176]

Anna Kingsford

Educated in Paris as a physician, Anna Bonus Kingsford (1846-88) managed to complete her studies successfully, much to the consternation of her professors, without having participated in animal vivisection. She wrote her thesis on *The Perfect Way to Diet*, a vegetarian manifesto. She did not, she wrote, study medicine for the benefit of humankind: "I do not love men and women. I dislike them too much to care to do them any good. They seem to me to be my natural enemies. It is not for them that I am taking up medicine and science, not to cure their ailments; but for the animals, and for knowledge generally. I want to rescue the animals from cruelty and injustice, which are for me the worst if not the only sins. And I can't love the animals and those who systematically ill-treat them."[177]

Raised a Protestant and married to a clergyman, she converted to Roman Catholicism, but found its animal orientations beyond the pale.

The great need of the popular form of the Christian religion is precisely a belief in the solidarity of all living beings. It is in this that Buddhism surpasses Christianity – in this divine recognition of the universal right to charity. Who can doubt it who visits Rome – the city of the Pontiff – where now I am, and witness the black-hearted cruelty of these "Christians" to the animals which toil and slave for them? Ill as I am, I was forced, the day after my arrival, to get out of the carriage in which I was driving to chastise a wicked child who was torturing a poor little dog tied by a string to a pillar – kicking it and stamping on it. Today I saw a great, thick-shod peasant kick his mule in the mouth out of sheer wantonness. Argue with these ruffians, or with their priests, and they will tell you, "Christians have no duties to beasts that perish." Their Pope has told them so. So that everywhere in Catholic Christendom the poor, patient, dumb creatures endure every species of torment without a single word being uttered on their behalf by the teachers of religion. It is horrible – damnable. And the true reason of it all is because the beasts are popularly believed to be soulless. I say, paraphrasing a *mot* of Voltaire, "If it were true they had no souls, it would be necessary to invent them."* Earth has become a hell for want of this doctrine. Witness vivisection and the church's toleration of it. Oh, if any living beings on earth have a claim to heaven, surely the animals have the greatest claim of all! Whose sufferings so bitter as theirs, whose wrongs so deep, whose need of compensation so appalling? As a mystic and an occultist, I *know* they are not destroyed by death; but if I *could* doubt it – solemnly I say it – I should doubt also the justice of God. How could I tell He would be just to man, if so bitterly unjust to the animals?[178] (*Epitre à l'Auteur du Livre des Trois Imposteurs,* CXI)

---

* "If there were no God it would be necessary to invent him."

Kingsford left the Roman Church, founded the Hermetic Society to further the study of religious mysticism, joined the Theosophical Society, and became its president in 1883.

She wrote to her friend, collaborator, and later biographer, Edward Maitland:

when one truly desires a noble end, one does not indulge selfish motives. My real desire is that by some means this horrible stain on humanity [of vivisection] should be wiped away, what matter by whose hand ...

They speak sneeringly of "sentiment." The outcry against vivisection is mere "sentiment." Why, in God's name, what is so great, so noble, as human sentiment? What is religion, what is morality, but sentiment? On what divine feeling are based the laws which bid men to respect the lives, the property, the feelings of their fellow men? Sentiment is but another name for that moral feeling which alone has made man the best that he is now, and which alone can make him better and purer in the future.[179]

Kingsford described her reaction at hearing the screams of dogs being vivisected in Monsieur Béclard's laboratory in Paris:

Much as I had heard and said, and even written, before that day about vivisection, I found myself for the first time in its actual presence, and there swept over me a wave of such extreme mental anguish that my heart stood still under it. It was not sorrow, nor was it indignation merely, that I felt; it was nearer to despair than these. It seemed as if suddenly all the laboratories of torture throughout Christendom stood open before me ... And then and there, burying my face in my hands, with tears of agony I prayed for the strength and courage to labour effectually for the abolition of so vile a wrong, and to do at least what one heart and voice might to root this curse of torture from the land.[180]

She was as adamant about flesh consumption as vivisection:

No man who aims at making his life an harmonious whole, pure, complete, and harmless to others, can endure to gratify an appetite at the cost of the daily suffering and bloodshed of his inferiors in degree, and of the moral degradation of his own kind. I know not which strikes me most forcibly in the ethics of this question – the *injustice,* the *cruelty,* or the *nastiness* of flesh-eating. The injustice is to the butchers, the cruelty is to the animals, the nastiness concerns the consumer. With regard to this last in particular, I greatly wonder what persons of refinement – aye, even of decency – do not feel insulted on being offered, as a matter of course, portions of corpses as food! Such comestibles might possibly be tolerated during sieges, or times of other privation of proper viands in exceptional circumstances, but in the midst of a civilised community able to command a profusion of sound and delicious foods, it ought to be deemed an affront to set dead flesh before a guest.[181]

Kingsford's collaborator **Edward Maitland** (1824-1897) was equally convinced that humans ate meat in defiance of their nature.

We hold that neither by his physical nor his moral constitution does man belong to the order either of the carnivora or of the omnivora, but is purely frugivorous; and in this we have the assent of all competent physiologists ... Hence we consider that in accepting the conditions of Nature as our guide, we do but act rationally. Adding to reason, experience, we have on our side, first, the profoundest wisdom of all ages and countries from the remotest antiquity, – the wisdom, namely, of all those really radical reformers, of whom a Trismegistus, a Pythagoras, and a Buddha are typical examples, whose aim it has been to reform, not institutions merely, but men themselves, and whose first step towards the perfectionment of their disciples was to insist on a total renunciation of flesh as food, on the ground that neither physically, intellectually, morally, nor spiritually can man be the best that he has it in him to be save when nourished by the purest substances, taken at first hand from Nature, and undeteriorated by passage through organisms, and eschewing violence and bloodshed as a means of sustenance or gratification.[182]

Arthur Helps

Clerk to the British Privy Council and amanuensis to *The Friends in Council*, Sir Arthur Helps (1813-75) reported the council's proceedings in book form, one of which was *Animals and their Masters* (c. 1872). The council, Helps tells us, consisted of "Sir John Ellesmere, a lawyer of much renown; Sir Arthur Godolphin, a statesman and a learned man; Mr. Cranmer, an official person; Mr. [Leonard] Milverton [also a statesman], Mrs. Milverton; Lady Ellesmere; and myself Mr. Milverton's private secretary."[183] A certain unintroduced Mr. Mauleverer is also present.

The significance of the book is threefold: (1) it reflects the fact that relatively advanced animal welfare issues of a practical nature were now a matter of serious public debate, even among the exalted, and were not the mere concern of "sentimental" radicals and pioneering essayists; (2) it is in part a very learned discussion of some of the precursors of the modern debate, in some instances quoting authorities I have never seen mentioned elsewhere – though they are often quoted in the original Greek, Latin, French, and German – the last in Gothic script yet! – which restricts the audience today even more than it would have then; (3) Sir Arthur Helps's credentials helped persuade parliamentarians that animal issues were serious moral issues worthy of the attention of even the most eminent. For example, in his 1882 reply to his critics, Lord Chief Justice Coleridge twice referred to Sir Arthur Helps to give authority to his remarks in defence of animal interests.[184]

Milverton. The subject would be divided under several heads; the cruelties inflicted upon beasts of draught and of burden; the cruelties inflicted in the transit of animals used for food; the cruelties inflicted upon the pets; the cruelties perpetrated for what is called science; and, generally, the careless and ignorant treatment manifested in the sustenance of animals from whom you have taken all means and opportunities of providing for themselves.[185]

Unfortunately, the ensuing discussion lacks cohesion, jumps from one topic to another and then back again, and occasionally digresses from animal issues altogether. Despite this, there is much that is enlightening.

Milverton. There is a thing called the bearing rein. It is an atrocity when applied to a draught horse. It contradicts every sound principle connected with this subject ... Pretty nearly half the diseases of the domestic animals are the result of a direct violation of the laws of nature upon the part of the owners of the animals ... The cruelties of this transit [of food] animals have increased, by reason of the changed modes of locomotion. Perhaps, however, it would be safer to say that new forms of suffering have been introduced by this change, to alleviate which the proper remedies have not yet been fully provided. The [Parliamentary] Transit of Animals Committee, of which I was a member, made a beginning in the way of improvement ... But much remains to be done ... [to alleviate] the cruel sufferings which are experienced by animals during transit through overcrowding and faulty ventilation ... steps might be taken to compel shipowners to adopt contrivances which would lessen the amount of ill-usage to which animals are frequently exposed ... Returning to the treatment of beasts of draught and burden, I sometimes think it was a misfortune for the world that the horse was ever subjugated.[186]

Ellesmere ... considering how [the horse] is wronged; he is the most quiet and uncomplaining creature in the world ... [187]

Milverton. It goes against the grain with me, to speak against the keeping of pets; and for this special reason, that the young people who keep pets are generally, in after life, those who are the best friends to animals. But if I must answer the question truthfully, I do think that there is a great deal of cruelty in keeping pets – not so much directly as indirectly. There are the cruel devices by which pets are caught and tamed. Moreover we make pets of creatures which were never meant to be made pets of. I allude to the feathered creation. A miserable creature to my mind, is a caged bird ...

Mauleverer. Going back for a moment to the pets of which Milverton disapproves, I hope that he includes gold-fish. When I see those wretched creatures moving round and round about in a glass bowl, I don't know how it is, but I always think of the lives of official and ministerial people, doing their routine work in a very confined space, never suffered to retire into private life amongst comfortable weeds and stones and mud, but always having the eyes of the public and the press upon them ...[188]

Sir Arthur. I deny that the cruelties inflicted by science upon animals, are equal in number and extent to those that were inflicted by [medieval] superstition; and then, look at the purpose – recollect that in some cases it is to master the diseases of animals that animals are subjected to scientific investigation.

Milverton. Scientific investigation! It is very unlike you, Sir Arthur, to use fine words for the barbarities that go on under the pretentious name of scientific investigation ... I believe a vast amount of needless cruelty is inflicted upon animals under the pretext of scientific investigation. I vow that I think it is a crime to make experiments upon animals for the sake of illustrating some scientific fact that has already been well ascertained ... I go further; I don't believe that a single fact has been discovered by any of the tortures which have been inflicted upon animals.

Sir Arthur. I am not prepared to go that length with you. I have a perfect horror of vivisection; the very word makes my flesh creep. But we shall not carry our point (for I take it we are all agreed upon the point) by suffering any exaggeration to enter into our statements ...

Lady Ellesmere. It would be quite enough reason for refusing to marry any man, if one knew that he practised any needless cruelties upon animals, whether called by any scientific name or not ... if he ill-treated animals, I do not think I could endure him ...

Milverton ... If public opinion were strong in the direction in which we wish it to prevail, no government, no public body could have those cruel and wicked experiments carried on under its sanction. I have looked into the subject carefully, and I have come to the conclusion that the action of this opinion upon public bodies would stop many of the horrors we now complain of. I cannot say any more about this branch of the subject. It is so repulsive ... I distinctly hold that every living creature has its rights, and that justice, in the highest form, may be applied to it. I say that a lame horse has a right to claim that it shall not be worked; and just as I would protect one man from being ill-treated by another, so, to use the principle in its widest form, I would protect any one animal from being ill-treated by any other ... You see [through the window] ... a number of flying creatures, whirling about in a mazy dance, and, as far as we can judge, enjoying themselves very much, and doing us no harm ... If you were to kill any of them at this moment, I think it would not merely be cruelty, but an invasion of right – an illegal transaction ... [189]

Sir Arthur ... I object to a neuter relative pronoun being applied to an animal, and I advisedly say 'who' instead of which ... [190]

Ellesmere. I want the Sunday to be not only the most holy, but the happiest day for all of us. But, as regards rest, animals should be considered first.[191]

Milverton refers to a letter he has received from Scotland, criticizing the use of the "bearing-rein" in England and pointing out that it is not used in Scotland. "It would be quite enough to have on our tombs, 'He was one of those who caused the bearing-rein to be discontinued.'"[192]

The discussion eventually returns to the transportation of animals and instances of cruelty are adumbrated.

Milverton. How I should endeavour to meet this particular case, is by the adoption of some general rules ... in all cases of transit of living creatures a certain space should be allowed, bearing some proportion to the size of the creatures respectively.

Lady Ellesmere ... It horrifies one to think sometimes of what other creatures are suffering ... If you have any regulations for the transport of animals, due supply of water must, indeed, be one of them ...

Milverton ... I sometimes think, when I meet with, or hear of, these cases of cruelty, that what we men run a risk of being damned for, is our barbarity to these creatures who have been given into our complete dominion, and for our conduct for whom we shall be fearfully answerable ... [193]

I can hardly express to you how much I feel there is to be thought of, arising from the use of the word 'dumb' as applied to animals. Dumb animals! What an immense exhortation that is to pity! It is a remarkable thing that this word dumb should have been so largely applied to animals, for there are very few dumb animals. But, doubtless, the word is often used to convey a larger idea than that of dumbness, namely, the want of power in animals to convey by sound to mankind what they feel, or perhaps I should say the want of power in men to understand the meaning of the various sounds uttered by animals.

But as regards those animals which are mostly dumb, such as the horse, which, except on rare occasions of extreme suffering, makes no sound at all, but only expresses pain by certain movements indicating pain – how tender we ought to be to them, and how observant of these movements, considering their dumbness![194]

Edward Carpenter

Toward the close of the nineteenth century, and in the early twentieth century, radical animal advocacy became in significant part the province of those who identified themselves as socialists – notably Edward Carpenter, Henry Salt, and George Bernard Shaw. They were, of course, not adherents of Marxism, which has been, often self-consciously and self-proclaimedly, the most "speciesist" of all political persuasions, to employ Richard Ryder's ugly but apposite coinage. Their Fabian socialism has much more of a spiritual and utopian nature than a materialist determinism.

Edward Carpenter (1844-1929) was born into an upper-middle-class family in Brighton, Sussex, attended Cambridge University, and took holy orders in 1869. In 1874 he renounced both orthodox religion and civilized society. In their place he proposed a simple, primitive way of life that he sketched in his *Civilisation: Its Cause and Cure*, which went through seventeen editions between 1889 and 1921. Indeed, Carpenter, known as "The Noble Savage," became a minor cult figure. The essence of his argument lay in the advocacy of living a rural, vegetarian lifestyle in which we would learn to live slowly and simply, in accord with our natural animal being, as other animals do. His prominent works include *Towards Democracy* (1883-1902), most of which is a lengthy Whitmanesque prose poem, *England's Ideal* (1887), and *Love's Coming of Age* (1896).

In *Towards Democracy*, he asked:

Do you grab interest on Money and lose all interest in Life? Do you found a huge system of national Credit on absolute personal Distrust? Do you batten like a ghoul on the dead corpses of animals, and then expect to be of a cheerful disposition? Do you put the loving beasts to torture as a means of promoting your own health and happiness? Do you, O foolishest one, fancy to bind me together by Laws (of all ideas the most laughable) and set whole tribes of unbelievers at work year after year patching that rotten net? Do you live farther and farther from Nature, till you actually doubt if there be any natural life, or any avenging instinct in the dumb elements? ... [195]

Behold the animals. There is not one but the human soul lurks within it, fulfilling its destiny as surely as within you.

The elephant, the gnat floating warily toward its victim, the horse sleeping by stolen snatches in the hot field at the plough, or coming out of the stable of its own accord at the sound of the alarm bell and placing itself in the shafts of the fire-engine – sharing the excitement of the men; the cats playing together on the barn floor, thinking no society equal to theirs, the ant bearing its burden through the grass –

Do you think these are nothing more than what you see? Do you not know that your mother and your sister and your brother are among them?

I saw deep in the eyes of the animals the human soul look out upon me.

I saw where it was born deep down under feathers and fur, or condemned for a while to roam fourfooted among the brambles. I caught the clinging mute glance of the prisoner, and swore that I would be faithful.

Thee my brother and sister I see and mistake not. Do not be afraid. Dwelling thus and thus for a while, fulfilling thy appointed time – thou shalt come to thyself at last.

Thy half-warm horns and long tongue lapping around my waist do not conceal thy humanity any more than the learned talk of the pedant conceals his – for all thou art dumb we have words and plenty between us.

Come nigh little bird with your half-stretched quivering wings – within you I behold choirs of angels, and the Lord himself in vista.

Crooning and content the old hen sits – her thirteen chicks cheep cheerily around her; or nestle peeping out like little buds from under her wings;

Keen and motherly is her eye, placid and joyful her heart, as the sun shines warm upon them.

Do not hurry; have faith ... [196]

In *Civilisation: Its Cause and Cure*, Carpenter added:

The state of the modern civilised man ... is anything but creditable, and it seems to be the fact that, notwithstanding all our libraries of medical science, our knowledges, arts, appliances of life, we are actually less capable of taking care of ourselves than the animals are ... [197]

Health – in body or mind – means unity, integration as opposed to disintegration. In the animals we find this physical unity existing to a remarkable degree. An almost unerring instinct and selective power rules their actions and organisation. Thus a cat before it has fallen ... is in a sense perfect. The wonderful consent of its limbs as it runs or leaps, the adaptation of its muscles, the exactness of its instincts, physical and affectional; its senses of sight and smell, its cleanliness, nicety as to food, motherly tact, the expression of its whole body when enraged, or when watching for prey – all these things are so to speak absolute and instantaneous – and fill one with admiration. The creature is "whole" or in one piece; there is no mentionable conflict or division within it.

Similarly with the other animals, and even with the early man himself ... [198]

In the animals consciousness has never returned upon itself. It radiates easily outwards; and the creature obeys without law or hesitation, and with little if any *self*-consciousness, the law of its being ... [199]

To-day it is unfortunately perfectly true that Man is the only animal who, instead of adorning and beautifying, makes Nature hideous by his presence. The fox and the squirrel may make their homes in the wood and add to its beauty in so doing; but when Alderman Smith plants his villa there, the gods pack up their trunks and depart, they can bear it no longer ... [200]

It may be noted, too, that food of the seed kind – by which I mean all manner of fruits, nuts, tubers, grains, eggs etc. (and I may include milk in its various forms of butter, cheese, curds, and so forth), not only contain by their nature the elements of life in their most condensed forms, but have the additional advantage that they can be appropriated without injury to any living creature – for even the cabbage may inaudibly scream when torn up by the roots and boiled, but the strawberry plant *asks* us to take of its fruit, and paints it red expressly that we may see and devour it![201]

[In a world at one with nature] men, women and children will come to share in the great and wonderful common life, the gardens around will be sacred to the unharmed and welcome animals.[202]

And when the Civilisation period has passed away, the old Nature-religion – perhaps greatly grown – will come back. The immense stream of religious life which beginning far beyond the horizon of earliest history has been deflected into metaphysical and other channels – of Judaism, Christianity, Buddhism, and the like – during the historical period, will once more gather itself together to float on its bosom all the arks and sacred vessels of human progress. Man will once more *feel* his unity with the animals, with the mountains and the streams, with the earth itself and the slow lapse of the constellations, not as an abstract dogma of Science or Theology, but as a living and ever-present fact.[203]

Henry S. Salt

An outstanding classics scholar at Cambridge, Henry Salt (1851-1939) went on to teach at Eton until he met with disfavour for his advocacy not just of the poetry of Shelley but of "Shelleyism" as a school of thought. He retired voluntarily to a life of simplicity in Surrey where he wrote some forty books, twelve of which were on animal rights and vegetarianism, the most memorable being the caustically entitled *Seventy Years among Savages* (1921), the savages being his fellow Europeans; *A Plea for Vegetarianism* (1886), which persuaded Gandhi to become an ethical rather than a cultural vegetarian; and, his pièce de résistance, *Animals' Rights Considered in*

Relation to Social Progress (1892), *inter alia* an outstanding analysis of the history of expanding humanitarian ideals.

In *Seventy Years among Savages* he wrote: "All sentient life is akin ... he who injures a fellow being is in fact doing injury to himself," a fact of which he reminded his readers in verse.

> The motive that you'll find most strong,
> The simple rule, the short-and-long,
> For doing animals no wrong,
> Is this, *that you are one.*[204]

In *Animals' Rights Considered in Relation to Social Progress*, Salt remarked:

> If we are ever going to do justice to the lower races, we must get rid of the antiquated notion of a "great gulf" fixed between them and mankind, and must recognize the common bond of humanity that unites all beings in one universal brotherhood ...

> To live one's own life – to realize one's true self – is the highest moral purpose of man and animal alike; and that animals possess their due measure of this sense of individuality is scarcely open to doubt ...

> Together with the destinies and duties that are laid on them, animals have also the right to be treated with gentleness and consideration, and the man who does not so treat them, however great his learning or influence may be, is, in that respect, an ignorant and foolish man, devoid of the highest and noblest culture of which the human mind is capable ...

> Oppression and cruelty are invariably founded on a lack of imaginative sympathy; the tyrant or tormentor can have no true sense of kinship with the victim of his injustice. When once the sense of affinity is awakened, the knell of tyranny is sounded, and the ultimate concession of "rights" is simply a matter of time ...

> [A]nimals have rights, and these rights consist in the "restricted freedom" to live a natural life – a life, that is, which permits of the individual development – subject to the limitations imposed by the permanent needs and interests of the community. There is nothing quixotic or visionary in this assertion; it is perfectly compatible with a readiness to look at the sternest laws of existence fully and honestly in the face ...

> Apart from the universal rights they possess in common with all intelligent beings, domestic animals have special claim on man's courtesy and sense of fairness as they are not his fellow-creatures only, but his fellow-workers, his dependents, and in many cases the familiar associates and trusted inmates of his home ...

> To take a wild animal from its free natural state, full of abounding egoism and vitality, and to shut it up for the wretched remainder of its life in a cell where it has just space to turn around, where it necessarily loses every distinctive feature of its character – this appears to me to be as downright a denial as could be well imagined of the theory of animals' rights ...

[T]he sporting instinct is due to sheer callousness and insensibility; the sports-man, by force of habit, or by force of hereditary influence, cannot understand or sympathize the suffering he causes, and being, in the great majority of instances, a man of naturally slow perception, he naturally finds it much easier to follow the hounds than to follow an argument ...

What we must unhesitatingly condemn is the blind and reckless barbarism which has ransacked, and is ransacking, whole provinces and continents, without a glim-mer of suspicion that the innumerable birds and quadrupeds which it is rapidly exterminating have any other part or purpose in nature than to be sacrificed to human vanity, that idle gentlemen and ladies may bedeck themselves, like certain characters in the fable, in borrowed skins and feathers.* What care *they* for all the beauty and tenderness and intelligence of the varied forms of animal life? and what is it to them whether these be helped forward by man in the universal progress and evolution of all living things, or whether whole species be transformed and degraded by the way – boiled down –, like the beaver into a hat, or, like the seal, into a lady's jacket? ...

[M]any of those who wear seal-skin mantles, or feather-bedaubed bonnets are nat-urally human enough; they are misled by pure ignorance and thoughtlessness, and would at once abandon such practices if they could be made aware of the meth-ods employed in the wholesale massacre of seals or humming-birds. Still, it remains true, that all these questions ultimately hang together, and that no complete solu-tion will be found for any one of them until the whole problem of our moral rela-tion toward the lower animals is studied with far greater comprehensiveness ...

The wise scientist and the wise humanist are identical. A true science cannot possibly ignore the solid, incontrovertible fact, that the practice of vivisection is revolting to the human conscience, even among the ordinary members of a not over-sensitive society. The so-called "science" (we are compelled unfortunately, in common parlance, to use the word in this specialized technical meaning) which deliberately overlooks this fact, and confines its view to the material aspects of the problem, is not science at all, but a one-sided assertion of the views which find favour with a particular class of men.

Nothing is necessary which is abhorrent, revolting, intolerable, to the general instincts of humanity. Better a thousand times that science should forego or post-pone the questionable advantage of certain problematical discoveries, than that the moral conscience of the community should be unmistakably outraged by the confusion of right and wrong. The short cut is not always the right path; and to perpetrate a cruel injustice to the lower animals, and then attempt to excuse it on the grounds that it will benefit posterity, is an argument which is as irrelevant as it is immoral. Ingenious it may be (in the way of hoodwinking the unwary), but it is certainly in no true sense scientific ...

[T]he conscientious man, when he goes wrong, is far more dangerous to society than the knave or the fool; indeed, the special horror of vivisection consists precisely

---

* The fable of Hercules and the Nemean lion.

in this fact, that it is not due to mere thoughtlessness and ignorance, but represents a deliberate, avowed, conscientious invasion of the very principle of animals' rights ...

It is not human life only that is lovable and sacred, but *all* innocent and beautiful life: the great republic of the future will not confine its beneficence to man. The isolation of man from Nature, by our persistent culture of the ratiocinative faculty, and our persistent neglect of the instinctive, has hitherto been the penalty we have had to pay for our incomplete and partial "civilization;" there are many signs that the tendency will now be towards that "Return to Nature" of which Rousseau was the prophet.[205]

George Bernard Shaw

A Fabian socialist, who was nonetheless customarily chauffeured in a Rolls Royce, George Bernard Shaw (1856-1950) is perhaps, with the sole exception of Shakespeare, the most popular of all anglophone dramatists. He described himself as "a vegetarian purely on humanitarian and mystical grounds" who had "never killed a flea or a mouse vindictively or without remorse."[206] Meat-eating, he opined, was "cannibalism with the heroic dish omitted."[207] Shaw described his literary "pastime as writing sermons in plays, sermons preaching what Salt practised."[208] In fact, Shaw's "sermons" are to be found rather less in the plays themselves than in their extraordinary Prefaces, which are often more wordy than the plays themselves. Still, in *The Devil's Disciple* (1897) we learn: "The worst sin towards our fellow creatures is not to hate them, but to be indifferent to them. That's the essence of inhumanity." In *The Admirable Bashville* (1901) he castigates both vivisection – "Groping for cures in the tormented entrails/ Of friendly dogs" and the wearing of animal products – "Oh, your ladies/ Seal skinned and egret feathered; all defiance/ to Nature."

The Doctor's Dilemma continues the vivisection theme (Act V).

JENNIFER ... To you he was only a clever brute ... Don't you see that what is really dreadful is that to you living things have no souls.

[DR.] RIDGEON. (with a skeptical shrug) The soul is not an organ I have come across in my anatomical work.

JENNIFER ... If you dissected me you could not find my conscience. Do you think I have got none?

RIDGEON. I have met people who had none.

JENNIFER. Clever brutes? Do you know, doctor, that some of the dearest and most faithful friends I ever had are only brutes! You would have vivisected them. The dearest and greatest of all my friends had a sort of beauty and affectionateness that only animals have. I hope you may never feel what I felt when I had to put him in the hands of men who defend the torture of animals because they are only brutes ... there are doctors who are naturally cruel; and there are others who get used to cruelty and are callous about it. They blind themselves to the souls of animals; and that blinds them to the souls of men and women. You made a dreadful mistake about Louis; but you would not have made it if you had not trained yourself to make the same mistakes about dogs. You saw nothing in them but dumb brutes; and so you could see nothing but a clever brute ... [209]

In *Back to Methuselah* (1922) Shaw shows his contempt for those who claim carnivorousness a prerequisite of strength, courage, and valour: "[One of Adam's sons] invented meat-eating. The other was horrified at the innovation ... With the ferocity which is still characteristic of bulls and other vegetarians, he slew his beefsteak-eating brother, and thus invented murder. That was a very steep step. It was so exciting that all the others began to kill one another for sport, and thus invented war, the steepest step of all. They even took to killing animals as a means of killing time, and then, of course, ate them to save the long and difficult labor of agriculture."[210] And in *Too True to be Good* he soliloquized, somewhat tongue in cheek, as he so often was, on the rights of "a poor innocent microbe."[211]

Strangely, Shaw held to a theory of evolution that was not only pre-Darwinian, but was precisely the kind of creative will theory that Goethe had rejected in his "Metamorphose der Tiere" and elsewhere.[212] Around the turn of the century, Shaw informed his French translator Augustin Hamon that "I am before all things a believer in the power of Will (Volonté). I believe that all evolution has been produced by Will, and that the reason that you are Hamon the Anarchist, instead of being a blob of protoplasmic slime in a ditch, is that there was at work in the Universe a Will which required brains & hands to do its work & therefore evolved your brains and your hands."[213] Darwinian "Natural Selection" he castigated as "no selection at all, but mere dead accident and luck."[214] A true Lamarckian indeed! In fact, Shaw's conception of "Will" was a self-conscious, though certainly misconceived, adaptation of Schopenhauer's philosophy.

His *Preface on Doctors* to *The Doctor's Dilemma* – the preface is 82 pages in length, the play 105! – is reflective of the general tone of his remarks (only a few pages deal at length with animal issues, especially vivisection, the remainder concentrating on the practices of the medical profession in general, which he treated with a measure of scorn).

Scandalized voices murmur that these operations are necessary. They may be. It may also be necessary to hang a man or pull down a house. But we take good care not to make the hangman and the housebreaker the judges of that. If we did no man's neck would be safe and no man's house stable ...

As to the honour and conscience of doctors, they have as much as any other class of men, no more and no less. And what other men dare pretend to be impartial where they have a strong pecuniary interest on one side? Nobody supposes that doctors are less virtuous than judges; but a judge whose salary and reputation depended on whether the verdict was for the plaintiff or defendant, prosecutor or prisoner, would be as little trusted as a general in the pay of the enemy ...

From Shakespeare and Dr. Johnson to Ruskin and Mark Twain, the natural abhorrence of sane mankind for the vivisector's cruelty, and the contempt of able
thinkers for his imbecile casuistry, have been expressed by the most popular spokes-
men of humanity. If the medical profession were to outdo the Anti-Vivisection
Societies in a general professional protest against the practice and principles of vivisectors, every doctor in the kingdom would gain substantially by the immense
relief and reconciliation which would follow such a reassurance of the humanity of
the doctor ... [215]

When a man says to Society, "May I torture my mother in pursuit of knowledge?" society replies, "No." If he pleads, "What! Not even if I have a chance of
finding out how to cure cancer by doing it?" Society still says, " Not even then." If
the scientist, making the best of his disappointment, goes on to ask may he torture
a dog, the stupid and callous people who do not realise that a dog is a fellow-
creature, and sometimes a good friend, may say Yes ... But even those who say "You
may torture *a* dog" never say "You may torture *my* dog." And nobody says, "yes,
because in the pursuit of knowledge you may do as you please." Just as even the
stupidest people say, in effect, "If you cannot attain to knowledge without burning
your mother you must do without knowledge," so the wisest people say, "If
you cannot attain to knowledge without torturing a dog, you must do without
knowledge ..."[216]

[T]he attack on vivisection is not an attack on knowledge ... no method of investigation is the only method; and no law forbidding any particular method can cut
us off from the knowledge we hope to gain by it. The only knowledge we lose by
forbidding cruelty is knowledge at first hand of cruelty itself, which is precisely the
knowledge humane people wish to be spared ... [217]

On one occasion I was invited to speak at a large Anti-Vivisection meeting in the
Queen's Hall in London. I found myself on the platform with fox-hunters, tame stag
hunters, men and women whose calendar was divided, not by pay days and quarter days, but by seasons for killing animals for sport: the fox, the hare, the otter,
the partridge and the rest having each its appointed date for slaughter. The ladies
among us wore hats and cloaks and head-dresses obtained by wholesale massacres, ruthless trappings, callous extermination of our fellow creatures ... Yet we
were all in hysterics of indignation at the cruelties of the vivisectors. These, if any
were present, must have smiled sardonically at such inhuman humanitarians,
whose daily habits and fashionable amusements cause more suffering in England in
a week than all the vivisectors of Europe do in a year ... Vivisectors can hardly pretend to be better than the classes from which they are drawn, or those above them;
and if these people are capable of sacrificing animals in various cruel ways under
cover of sport, fashion, education, discipline, and, even, when the cruel sacrifices
are human sacrifices, of political economy, it is idle for the vivisector to pretend
that he is incapable of practising cruelty for pleasure or profit or both under the
cloak of science ... [218]

[M]any people do cruel and vile things without being in the least cruel or vile,
because the routine to which they have been brought up is superstitiously cruel

and vile ... Let cruelty or kindness or anything else once become customary and it will be practised by people to whom it is not at all natural, but whose rule of life is simply to do only what everybody else does, and who would lose their employment and starve if they indulged in any peculiarity ... [219]

As a matter of fact the man who once concedes to the vivisector the right to put a dog outside the laws of honor and fellowship, concedes to him also the right to put himself outside them; for he is nothing to the vivisector but a more highly developed, and consequently more interesting to-experiment-on vertebrate than the dog ... [220]

Public support of vivisection is founded almost wholly on the assurances of the vivisectors that great public benefits may be expected from the practice. Not for a moment do I suggest that such a defence would be valid even if proved. But when the witnesses begin by alleging that in the cause of science all the customary ethical obligations (which include the obligation to tell the truth) are suspended, what weight can any reliable person give to their testimony? I would rather swear fifty lies than take an animal which had licked my hand in good fellowship and torture it. If I did torture a dog, I should certainly not have the face to turn around and ask how any person dare suspect an honorable man like myself of telling lies. Most sensible and humane people would, I hope, flatly reply that honorable men do not behave dishonorably even to dogs. The murderer who, when asked by the chaplain whether he had any other crimes to confess, replied indignantly "What do you take me for?" reminds us very strongly of the vivisectors who are so deeply hurt when their evidence is set aside as worthless.[221]

The Achilles heel of vivisection, however, is not to be found in the pain it causes, but in the line of argument by which it is justified ... no criminal has yet had the impudence to argue as every vivisector argues ... He not only calls his method scientific; he contends there are no other scientific methods. When you express your loathing and contempt for his stupidity, he imagines you are attacking science ... You do not settle whether an experiment is justified or not by merely showing that it is of some use. The distinction is not between useful and useless experiments, but between barbarous and civilized behavior. Vivisection is a social evil because if it advances human knowledge, it does so at the expense of human character.[222]

Thomas Hardy

If Fabian socialism informs, and indeed prompts, the writings of Carpenter, Salt, and Shaw, a solid Romantic Tory streak permeates the novels and poetry of Thomas Hardy (1840-1928). His most popular works are *The Mayor of Casterbridge* (1886) and *Tess of the d'Urbervilles* (1891). Animals pervade his works, often with more rustic realism than affection. Yet on other occasions he displays a thorough respect for them and an abomination of their mistreatment. As for Leonardo, Hugo, Darwin, and Shaw,[223] so too for Hardy: nature can constitute no moral standard but is that which must be subdued if humans and animals are to be treated justly. In *Two on a Tower* (1883) he referred to, and commented on, "nature's cruel laws" but in *Jude the Obscure* (1895) it is a recurrent theme. Hardy mentions: "the perception of the flaw in the terrestrial scheme by which what was good for God's birds was bad for God's gardener ... Nature's logic was too horrid for him to care for. That mercy towards one set of creatures was cruelty towards another sickened his sense of harmony ... O why should Nature's law be mutual butchery! ... Cruelty is the law pervading all nature and society; and we can't get out of it if we would!"[224]

Hardy's concerns are often with the practical treatment of animals in husbandry. In *Under the Greenwood Tree* (1872) – set around 1820 – he bemoans bee-keeping conditions which, despite constant innovations, did not improve significantly for the bees until the 1850s (though there had long been rather better practices in certain parts of continental Europe).

"Those holes will be the graves of thousands!" said Fancy. "I think 'tis a rather cruel thing to do."

Her father shook his head. "No," he said, tapping the hives to shake the dead bees from their cells, "if you suffocate 'em this way, they only die once; if you fumigate them in the new way, they come to life again, and die o' starvation; so the pangs o' death be twice upon 'em." ...

"The proper way to take honey, so that the bees be neither starved nor murdered is a puzzling matter," said the keeper steadily.

"I should like never to take it from them," said Fancy.[225]

Hardy acknowledged, and welcomed, the increasing sensibilities to nature's constituent parts, however much he may have detested the laws of nature themselves. In *The Trumpet-Major* (1880) – set in the early years of the Napoleonic wars – he indicates: "As Nature was hardly invented at this early part of the century, Bob's Matilda could not say much about the glamour of the hills, or the shimmering of the foliage, or the wealth of glory in the distant sea, as she would doubtless have done had she lived later on."[226] In *The Return of the Native* (1878) he adds: "To dwell on a heath without studying its meanings was like wedding a foreigner without learning his tongue,"[227] and he despairs at the failure to treat the feathered creation as no more than an object of marksmanship:

A cream-coloured courser* had used to visit this hill, a bird so rare that not more than half a dozen have ever been seen in England; but a barbarian rested neither night nor day till he had shot the African truant, and after that event cream-coloured coursers thought fit to enter Egdon no more.[228]

In the same novel he understands, as had Smart and Hugo[229] before him, the importance of thinking through animals.

In her moments, in her gaze, she reminded the beholder of the feathered creatures who lived around her home. All similes and allegories concerning her began and

---

* *Cursorius isabellinus*, a native of North Africa, and an occasional visitor to southern England.

ended with birds. There was as much variety in her motions as in their flight. When she was musing she was a kestrel, which hangs in the air by an invisible motion of its wings. When she was in a high wind her light body was blown against trees and banks like a heron's. When she was frightened she darted noiselessly like a king-fisher. When she was serene she skimmed like a swallow, and that is how she was moving now.[230]

It is, however, in *Jude the Obscure* that Hardy's sensibilities are most clearly voiced, as portended at the opening of the book: "'I shan't forget you Jude,' [Mr. Phillotson, the schoolmaster] said, smiling, as the cart moved off. 'Be a good boy, remember, and be kind to animals and birds.'"[231] Jude is employed as a boy to keep the birds from the farmer's crops.

He sounded the clacker till his arm ached, and at length his heart grew sympa-thetic with the birds' thwarted desires. They seemed, like himself, to be living in a world which did not want them. Why should he frighten them away? They took upon them more and more the aspect of gentle friends and pensioners ...

"Poor little dears!" said Jude aloud. "You *shall* have some dinner – you shall. There is enough for us all. Farmer Troutham can afford to let you have some. Eat, then, my dear little birdies, and make a good meal!" ... A magic thread of fellow-feeling united his own life with theirs.[232]

The event is witnessed by the farmer and Jude is fired.

With this shadow on his mind he did not care to show himself in the village, and went home by a roundabout track behind a hedge and across a pasture. Here he beheld scores of coupled earthworms lying half their length on the surface of the damp ground, as they always did in such weather at that time of the year. It was impossible to advance in regular steps without crushing some of them at each tread.

Though Farmer Troutham had just hurt him, he was a boy who could not him-self bear to hurt anything. He had never brought home a nest of young birds with-out lying awake in misery half the night after, and often reinstating them and the nest in their original place the next morning. He could scarcely bear to see trees cut down or lopped, from a fancy that it hurt them; and late pruning, when the sap was up, and the tree bled profusely, had been a positive grief to him in his infancy. This weakness of character, as it may be called, suggested that he was the sort of man who was born to ache a good deal before the fall of the curtain on his unnec-essary life should signal that all was well with him again. He carefully picked his way on tiptoe among the earthworms, without killing a single one.[233]

Jude grows up, marries, and is constrained by his wife to slaughter a pig for food. "Jude felt dissatisfied with himself as a man at what he had done, though aware of his lack of common sense, and that the deed would have amounted to the same thing if carried out by a deputy. The white snow, stained with the blood of his fellow-mortal, wore an illogical look to him as a lover of justice, not to say a Christian; but he could not see how the matter was to be mended. No doubt he was, as his wife had called him, a tender-hearted fool."[234] Years later in Oxford:

As a sort of objective commentary on Jude's remarks there drove a cab up at this moment with a belated Doctor, robed and panting, a cab whose horse failed to stop at the exact point for setting down the hirer, who jumped out and entered the door. The driver, alighting, began to kick the animal in the belly.

"If that can be done," said Jude, "at college gates in the most religious and educational city in the world, what shall we say as to how far we've got?" ... "I am not a man who wants to save himself at the expense of the weaker among us!"[235]

Finally: "'Ah, yes' said he, laughing acridly, 'I have been thinking of my foolish feeling about the pig you and I killed during our first marriage. I feel now that the greatest mercy that could be vouchsafed to me would be that something should serve me as I served that animal.'"[236] Only thus could universal justice be preserved. Certainly, Hardy understood that the universe was not made for humankind. As Swithin says to Lady Constantine in *Two on a Tower*: "Whatever the stars were made for, they were not made to please our eyes; nothing is made for man."[237]

Hardy was even more committed to animals in his personal life than in his novels. On 13 July 1888, he wrote in his diary: "After being in the street: What was it on the faces of those horses? – Resignation. Their eyes looked at me, haunted me. The absoluteness of their resignation was terrible. When afterwards I heard their tramp as I lay in bed, the ghosts of their eyes came in to me, saying, 'Where is your justice, O man and ruler?'"[238] In the 1850s he was appalled at "the horrors and cruelties" of Smithfield Market, and, during the Boer War, Hardy and his wife Emma organized an unsuccessful campaign to have horse use restricted to transportation. Throughout his adult life he was opposed to the wearing of fur and feathers, but only when he was eighty-five did he finally write about it in a poem he entitled "The Lady in the Furs."

"I'm a lofty lovely woman,"
    Says the lady in the furs,
In the glance she throws around her
    On the poorer dames and sirs:
"This robe, that cost three figures,
    Yes is mine," her nod avers.

"'True, my money did not buy it,
    But my husband's from the trade;
And they, they only got it
    From things feeble and afraid

By murdering them in ambush
  With a cunning engine's aid."

...

"But I am a lovely lady,
  Though sneers say I shine
By robbing nature's children
  Of apparel not mine,
And that I am but a broom-stick,
  Like a scarecrow's wooden spine."[239]

Hardy was an early convert to Darwin's theory of evolution, and to what he saw as its ethical implications, even though he found the theory inadequate as a full explanation of human and animal life. In the summer of 1909 he responded to an inquiry from a New York woman:

The discovery of the law of evolution, which revealed that all organic creatures are of one family, shifted the centre of altruism from humanity to the whole conscious world collectively. Therefore the practice of vivisection which might have been defended while the belief ruled that men and animals are essentially different, has been left by that discovery without any logical argument in its favour. And if the practice, to the extent merely of inflicting slight discomfort now and then, be defended (as I sometimes hold it may) on ground of it being good policy for animals as well as men, it is nevertheless in strictness a wrong, and stands precisely in the same category as would stand its practice on men themselves.[240]

Hardy might have questioned himself why it was that the conclusion he drew from the theory of evolution with regard to vivisection was quite different from that drawn by the author of the theory.

The following year Hardy wrote to the Secretary of the Humanitarian League (10 April 1910):

Few people seem to perceive fully as yet that the most far-reaching consequences of the establishment of the common origin of all species is ethical; that it logically involved a re-adjustment of altruistic morals by enlarging as a *necessity of rightness* the application of what has been called "The Golden Rule" beyond the area of mankind to that of the whole animal kingdom. Possibly Darwin himself did not wholly perceive it, though he alluded to it. While man was deemed to be a creation apart from all other creations, a secondary or tertiary morality was considered good enough towards the inferior races; but no person who reasons nowadays can escape the trying conclusion that this is not maintainable. And though I myself do not at present see how the principle of equal justice all round is to be carried out in its entirety, I recognize that the League is grappling with the question.[241]

However, for Hardy, no mechanistic law in the manner of evolutionary theory could be adequate. In *The Dynasts* (1904-8) Hardy has different spirits voicing alternative philosophical theories of the universe, in order to demonstrate that science alone did not have the appropriate answers. He wrote in his diary for 26 June 1876: "If it be possible to compress into a sentence all that a man learns between 20 and 40, it is that all things merge in one another – good into evil, generosity into justice, religion into politics, the year into the ages, the world into the universe. With this in view the evolution of species seems a minute and obvious process in the same movement."[242] Nature, not evolution, was the problem. In a letter to *The Academy and Literature* (May 1902) he attacked the "sophistry" of Maeterlinck's *Apology for Nature* where, Hardy remarked, nature is treated as having a "morality unknown to us, in which she is just." To the contrary, Hardy insisted, "she is blind."[243]

Hardy made the relevance to animal ethics clear in a letter of 18 May 1910, to Sidney Trist, editor of *The Animals' Guardian:* "[M]y own conclusion – the difficulty of carrying out to its logical extreme the principle of equal justice to all the animal kingdom. Whatever humanity may try to do, there remains the stumbling-block that nature herself is absolutely indifferent to justice, & how to instruct nature is rather a large problem."[244]

The logic of evolution, for Hardy, necessitated equal justice among the animals. The logic of nature prohibited it.

Louise Lind-af-Hageby

In the year before the anti-vivisectionist *The Doctor's Dilemma* was first seen on the London stage, Parliament was once again visiting the great moral issue of the day. Today abolitionists are a fairly rare breed. Ever since the early 1920s when Frederick Banting and Charles Best discovered insulin through the vivisection of dogs, often stolen from the Toronto streets, the medical benefits of animal experimentation have been predominantly assumed, though some continue to argue there are both more effective and more moral ways of achieving those successes. In 1906 the jury was still out – or at least the more circumspect jurors were still deliberating.

Two Swedish women living in Britain, Emilia Augusta Louise Lind-af-Hageby (1878-1963) and Leisa Schartau, with the support of such prominent citizens as the Honourable Stephen Coleridge and the Duchess of Hamilton, led the anti-vivisection movement to strengthen the 1876 Act, while eminent researchers fought to weaken it. Lind-af-Hageby and Leisa Schartau wrote a memorable book, cunningly entitled *The Shambles of Science* (1903) – the initial title was *Eye-Witnesses*, but was changed from the second edition onward – alluding to both the scientific slaughterhouse and the medical discipline's intellectual and moral disarray.

To take but one example, merely an introduction to a far more sickening tale, and not even one of the most horrific, from a book replete with horror stories of what the authors witnessed as students at the Imperial

Institute, University College, and King's College, of the University of London from 1902-3:

> A white fox-terrier has been tied down on the operating table. It is laid on its left side, and its muzzle is kept closely shut by a piece of string tied round it, and a bar placed behind the canine teeth. There is a wound in the head, about six centimetres in diameter, that is bleeding profusely. The skin and the muscular tissue have been removed, and a hole bored through the skull, and a short metal tube, reaching to the flexible membrane, screwed into the bone.
>
> There is also a large incision in the neck, and a canula, attached to a mercury manometer, has been inserted in the carotid. We are now going to study the circulation in this dog's brain by recording the blood pressure ... [245]

Science and medicine had much to answer for. But the Second Royal Commission on Vivisection of 1906 failed to produce any commonly acceptable answers.

In an attempt to change the moral climate, both in Britain and around the world, Lizzie Lind-af-Hageby was instrumental in devising, developing, and distributing *An Anti-Vivisection Declaration* which was signed by many prominent Britons, translated into other languages, and distributed in many countries.

> I declare that I am opposed to the practice of vivisection because it is inseparable from cruelty to animals.
>
> I believe cruelty to animals to be an evil, not only to the victims but to those who practise it, an obstacle to social progress, and contrary to the highest instincts of humanity.
>
> I decline to accept the vivisectors' plea that cruelty is justifiable provided it is "useful."
>
> I am confident that a practice which is morally wrong cannot be scientifically right.
>
> I justify the movement to protect animals from cruelty and injustice by knowledge of the kinship between them and the human race, and I repudiate the assertions made by some vivisectors that animals are incapable of feeling pain or suffering distress.
>
> I know from the published writings of vivisectors, and the accumulated evidence of pain, caused by experiments on living animals, that the use of anaesthetics cannot, and does not, protect the animal from suffering.
>
> I desire completely to dissociate myself from scientific research and medical practice tainted with cruelty, and from all participation in the use of the alleged benefits of vivisection. I shall not knowingly consult any member of the medical profession who supports and defends vivisection.[246]

In the United States there was as yet no legislation to control animal experimentation, though Bills abounded and there was much discussion about the subject. As we have seen, **Dr. Albert Leffingwell** composed a compassionate plea against the excesses of vivisection, *The Vivisection*

Question (1898), which had a significant impact in America.[247] In the 1908 English edition he commented on the Royal Commission before which Lind-af-Hageby, Stephen Coleridge, and others had appeared to encourage new legislation:

No matter what the Report of the Commission may be, much of the evidence it has elicited will be of value for many years to come ... It has demonstrated the uncertainty of the methods in use for securing to vivisected animals an immunity from anguish ... It has made plain the entire uselessness of Government inspections of laboratories by inspectors who are wholly in sympathy with the vivisector, and apparently without the slightest interest in those humane purposes and objects which such inspection, it was hoped, would secure. It has proven the secrecy in which vivisection may now be carried on in English laboratories – a privacy which even Members of Parliament have no right to invade. The Royal Commission of 1906-7 may not greatly change matters as far as legislation is concerned, but the contribution it has made to public enlightenment can hardly be gainsaid.[248]

Unfortunately, the "public enlightenment" to which Leffingwell referred appears to have been of short duration, finally being recovered only in the 1970s, and then less fully and earnestly than in the Victorian and Edwardian eras.

Over sixty years later, and writing of his experiences as a medical student at the University of Basle in the 1890s, the founder of analytical psychology, **Carl Gustav Jung** (1875-1961), expressed the fundamental conviction of the Victorians and Edwardians who found vivisection so unpalatable.

I could never free myself from the feeling that warm-blooded creatures were akin to us and not just cerebral automata. Consequently I cut demonstration classes whenever I could. I realized that one had to experiment on animals, but the demonstration of such experiments seemed horrible, barbarous and above all unnecessary. I had imagination enough to picture the demonstrated procedures from a mere description of them. My compassion for animals did not derive from Buddhist trimmings of Schopenhauer's philosophy, but rested on the deeper foundation of a primitive attitude of mind – on an unconscious identity with animals.[249]

Few appreciated the beauties and depths of Buddhism more than Jung. Few understood as well as he did how potentially liberating modernity could be. But he also knew that his compassion for animals derived neither from a respect for a particular religious doctrine, nor from his educational and cultural environment. It was instead a dictate of his primordial animal soul.

Postscript: The Ensuing Years

It is a startling and disturbing fact, which should serve as a constant warning, that, from the heights of such ardour and moral righteousness, of persuasive advocacy by many of society's most prominent figures in the political, legal, religious, intellectual, and literary arenas, from the Edwardian era to the 1960s, animal well-being and animal rights became largely forgotten issues. The consensual view is that two world wars, and recurring depressions and recessions, focused minds elsewhere. With humans suffering the effects of destruction, fear, the deaths of close relatives, and general devastation, the well-being of animals became again, to use Hardy's words, a matter of "secondary or tertiary morality." Animal sympathies declined to their early-nineteenth-century condition. Lecky's view of "conditional progress" seems to have been confirmed far more in the "conditional" than in the "progress." There is a "tendency" to a greater moral enlightenment and an extension of its application unless "special circumstances" intervene – and special circumstances did, of course, intervene, as they almost always seem to! For Lecky's thesis to be convincing, the parameters and dimensions of "progress," and what is to count as confirming, negating, or nugatory evidence for progress, need to be spelled out. Moreover, one has to ask how Oriental and aboriginal values are to be explained in such terms. Perhaps the most optimistic interpretation of what Lecky's model shows is that if, in a given societal tradition, progress is prevalent as a consequence of certain material and spiritual conditions, nonetheless the arrival of new material and/or spiritual conditions may reverse, or at least arrest, the prior tendency. It is, at best, an "other things being equal" kind of theory.

It would be misleading to suggest that animal interests were entirely forgotten in those largely apathetic years. New legislation, generally of a very modest nature, was enacted throughout much of Europe, and in many of the states of the American union, though, as in the case of Spain, it was not effectively enforced everywhere. Liechtenstein's 1936 Animal

Welfare Act, however, prohibited all vivisection – although a recent amendment allows for experiments conducted by government agencies in special circumstances. John Galsworthy, Virginia Woolf, Jerome K. Jerome, D.H. Lawrence, John Cowper Powys, James Joyce – initially in *A Portrait of the Artist as a Young Man*, but especially, even sublimely, if cryptically, in *Ulysses* – and C.S. Lewis were among those who promoted respect for, and the interests of, animals in their writings. Stephen Coleridge wrote two well-researched books against vivisection and animal cruelty. Dr. Walter Robert Hadwen and Air Chief Marshall Lord Dowding added their professional prestige to the cause. In 1913 Burgers, the forerunner of the Arnhem Zoo, was instituted in the Netherlands in an attempt to allow the animals a greater chance of living as the beings they are; and in 1917 Jack London began the literary critique of circuses. In 1926 Major C.W. Hume founded the University of London Animal Welfare Society, later the Universities Federation for Animal Welfare, and wrote two valuable books on animal ethics.

In the 1960s we began to see evidence of a return to the finer Victorian sensibilities. Rachel Carson wrote her inspiring *Silent Spring* in 1962. The text, though primarily concerned with environmental degradation, turned attention away from a selfish anthropocentrism. "We cannot have peace among men," she wrote, "whose hearts delight in killing any living creature." The Quaker Ruth Harrison wrote *Animal Machines* in 1964, a devastating critique of intensive farming, in which she advocated legislation to provide adequate conditions for battery hens and veal calves. In 1965 the Shavian Brigid Brophy wrote an article for the London *Sunday Times* entitled "The Rights of Animals," which attracted significant public attention.

In 1969 Oxford University became the centre of a group of intellectuals, mainly academic philosophers, devoted to promoting the rights of animals. The group included Stanley and Roslind Godlovitch, John Harris, and Richard D. Ryder, soon joined by Stephen Clark, Andrew Linzey, and Peter Singer – a disparate group of generally excellent minds, with competing religious and secular orientations, but a common cause. In northern England a decade later, Mary Midgley added a subtle voice. In the United States Bernard Rollin, Tom Regan, Daniel Dombrowski, and Carol Adams had a profound, if quite divergent, philosophical impact. Animal welfare science was instituted as a recognized and reputable academic discipline in Europe, North America, and the Antipodes, and is having a modest but increasing impact on improving food animal conditions; for example, through the scientific and ethical work on poultry, swine, sheep, and cattle, among other animals, of Temple Grandin, Marian Dawkins, David Fraser, Ian Duncan, Donald Broom, and John Webster. Ethology – and here one always thinks first of the work of Jane Goodall – has made the real world of wild animals far better understood and appreciated. Donald

R. Griffin's books, most notably *The Question of Animal Awareness* and *Animal Minds*, have done much to give animals a greater scientific respectability. The face of animal welfare and animal rights has recovered much, if not all, of its Victorian bloom.

There are, however, no grounds for complacency, or even satisfaction. After all, Victorian and Edwardian sensibilities receded into a mid-twentieth-century despondency. It can certainly happen again without constant vigilance to protect what has been gained, as well as to promote the advances that justice requires. In his *Essays on Criticism* (1888), Matthew Arnold described Oxford as the "home of lost causes, and forsaken beliefs, and unpopular names, and impossible loyalties!" But perhaps that was because so often in the past Oxford was on the side of reaction rather than moral majesty. In 1969 it became the home of resurrected beliefs, appealing names, and loyalties to all of animalkind – far-reaching yes, but no longer so impossible to achieve. Its message reflects not moral innovation – it asked for nothing that the Victorians had not previously demanded – but an extension and implementation of values that have always had a place in the human moral imagination. And that message is now a worldwide currency, even if it is not yet embodied in any one culture.

Given the Victorian era's reputation as an age of pious pomposity, repression, and oppression, it may be difficult to countenance the fact that it was more enlightened than is the twenty-first century to date. Yet on the issue of vivisection it undoubtedly was more enlightened; and on that of vegetarianism, it was at least more imaginative in its justifications. It is worth recalling that, but for an unfortunate illness, the legislation that almost certainly would have been enacted in 1876 would have prohibited all experimentation on horses, dogs, and cats, and would have required complete anaesthesia throughout all invasive experiments on animals. However, Lord Carnarvon, who was in charge of the Bill, was called away from Parliament by his wife's sudden illness, and subsequent death, immediately before the Bill was to be presented. In the weeks before the Bill could reappear a concerted effort by the medical profession persuaded the Home Secretary to weaken it. As it was, the measure that was enacted in 1876 was still more favourable to the interests of animals liable to experimentation than any legislation in existence today, that of Liechtenstein excepted.

As previously noted, in 1879 Lord Truro, with the support of the indefatigable Lord Shaftesbury, introduced a Bill for the total abolition of vivisection. Even though it stood very little chance of enactment, parliamentary sentiments were far more favourable than they would be today. Should the twenty-first century recapture the spirit of Victorian England, Lecky's theory of progress might seem more convincing.

Let those who bring about wonderful things
in their big, dark books
take an animal to give them strength.

– Meister Eckhart, German theologian mystic, c. 1260 to c. 1328

Notes

Introduction

1 Mary Midgley, *Animals and Why They Matter* (Athens: University of Georgia Press, 1983), 112. Midgley's chapter on "The Mixed Community" is a profound commentary on persons, things, and community, and is one which has received far too little examination and appreciation from scholars interested in the human-animal nexus.

2 C.G. Jung, *Memories, Dreams, Reflections* (New York: Vintage, 1985 [1963]), 101. For Jung see p. 354.

3 This is a primary premise of Rousseau's writings as a whole, but it is first expressed explicitly at the opening of his *Discourse on the Origin and Foundations of Inequality among Men* (1755). See Alan Ritter and Julia Conway Bondanella, eds., trans. Bondanella, *Rousseau's Political Writings* (New York: W.W. Norton, 1988), 7. For Rousseau see pp. 163-5.

4 Francis Bacon, "Of Goodness, and Goodness of Nature" in *Essays, or Councils, Civil and Moral* (London: R. Chiswell et al., 1706 [c. 1597]), 31. For Bacon see pp. 110-11.

5 Henry Salt, *Animals' Rights Considered in Relation to Social Progress* (Clarks Sumit, PA: Society for Animal Rights Inc., 1980 [1892]), 114. For Salt see pp. 341-4.

6 William Wordsworth, "Ode: Intimations of Immortality from Recollections of early Childhood," stanza 10, 1807, in *The Works of William Wordsworth* (Ware: Wordsworth, 1994), 590. For Wordsworth see pp. 183-6.

7 Fyodor Dostoevsky, *The Brothers Karamazov* (1879-80), trans. Richard Pevear and Larissa Volokhonsky (New York: Alfred A. Knopf, 1992), 241. For Dostoevsky see pp. 296-8.

8 Ibid., 238.

9 The point underlines Goodall's work but is expressed most clearly in *Through A Window: My Thirty Years with the Chimpanzees of Gombé* (Boston: Houghton Mifflin, 1990). Of course, she also demonstrates that they possess many other attributes and emotions which exceed the chimpanzees' instincts.

Chapter 1: Animals in Myth and Religion

1 See "Mother Cow" in Marvin Harris, *Cows, Pigs, Wars and Witches: The Riddles of Culture* (New York: Vintage, 1989 [1974]), 11-34. Unfortunately, Harris's account is unduly determinist and cynical but it is a valuable corrective to those who imagine that ideas and values are individually chosen in isolation from the imperatives of culture.

2 See Rod Preece, *Animals and Nature: Cultural Myths, Cultural Realities* (Vancouver: UBC Press, 1999), especially ch. 7, for an elaboration of the point.

3 See Rod Preece and David Fraser, "The Status of Animals in Biblical and Christian Thought: A Study in Colliding Values," *Society and Animals* 8, 3 (2000): 245-63, for an elaboration of the point.

4 For convenience, I have followed traditional usage with regard to "myth" and "religion," though without imagining there to be very much difference between them. Both provide explanations of the human place in a complex world, enjoin moral orientations, promote or prohibit certain behavioural practices, and provide a sense of the holy.

5 See pp. 31-2.

6 *What is Religion and of What Does Its Essence Consist?* (1902) in Leo Tolstoy, *A Confession and Other Religious Writings,* trans. Jane Kentish (London: Penguin, 1967), ch. 14, 119. It is not an unusual perception. It pervades both Unitarianism and the Baha'i faith. Compare also the *Bhagavad Gita,* IX, 23: "[Yet] even those who worship other gods with love (*bhakta*)/ And sacrifice to them, full filled with faith, / Do really worship Me, Though the rite differ from the norm." (R.C. Zaehner trans., *Hindu Scriptures* [London: J.M. Dent, 1966]), 321. For Tolstoy see pp. 298-300.

7 See Ida Zeitlin, *Skazki: Tales and Legends of Old Russia* (New York: Doran, 1926) for the most eloquent expression of the idea. I am indebted to Johanna Kuyvenhoven, a doctoral student in education at the University of British Columbia, for unearthing this source for me.

8 I am indebted to David Fraser of the Animal Welfare Program and the Centre for Applied Ethics of the University of British Columbia for this insight.

9 From a philosophical perspective, one might express it as a reliance on the practical wisdom of *phronesis,* as expounded by Aristotle, rather than on the intellectual wisdom of *sophia,* as expounded by Plato.

10 Rousseau, *Discourse on the Origin and Foundations of Inequality among Men,* First Part. I have employed the traditional stark translation. In *Rousseau's Political Writings,* trans., Bondanella, 13 (note 3), the whole sentence is rendered as: "I venture to affirm that the state of reflection is contrary to nature and that the man who meditates is a depraved animal."

11 Unlike the often-quoted account of creation in the more recent P-narrative (Genesis 1), wherein humans are told to "subdue" the earth and to have "dominion" over other species, the older J-narrative (Genesis 2) presents a strikingly different image of the human-animal relationship. In *The Yahwist's Landscape: Nature and Religion in Early Israel* (New York: Oxford University Press, 1992, 24) Theodore Hiebert explains that the Pentateuch is thought to consist of "a combination of four different sources or documents, authored by four different authors living at different times in Israelite history." He adds (157) that: "P's view is conspicuously hierarchical. At creation humans are commanded by God to rule (rada), to exercise dominion over other animate life ([Genesis] 1.28). Whether one wishes to construe such rule as benevolent or harsh – and both are possible within the limits of the term in biblical usage – there can be no doubt that rada represents control and power, since it is customarily used of kings and always those with authority over others. By contrast, J conceives of this relationship in more communal terms. As animals and humans alike are made from the earth's topsoil, they possess no distinct ontological status, both being referred to simply as living beings."

12 Quoted in Mathias Guenther, *Tricksters and Trancers: Bushman Religion and Society* (Bloomington: Indiana University Press, 1999), 127.

13 See Rudolf Kaiser, "A Fifth Gospel, Almost: Chief Seattle's Speech(es): American Origins and European Reception" in *Indians and Europe: An Interdisciplinary Collection of*

Essays, ed. Christian F. Feest (Aachen: Herodot Rader-Verlag, 1987), 305-36, and Rod Preece, *Animals and Nature,* 18-19.

14 A painting of St. Jerome with the lion by the Limbourg brothers (c. 1410-16) is contained in the *Belles Heures de Jean, Duc de Berry,* fol. 186v., Cloisters Collection, Metropolitan Museum of Art, New York. The painting is reproduced in Janetta Rebold Benton, *The Medieval Menagerie: Animals in the Art of the Middle Ages* (New York: Abbeville Press, 1992), 10.

15 The story of St. Sergey and the bear is retold in *The Brothers Karamazov,* part 2, book 6.

16 See E.S. Turner, *All Heaven in A Rage* (Fontwell: Centaur, 1992 [1964]), 36.

17 Matthew 7:12: "Therefore all things whatsoever ye would that men should do unto you, do ye even so to them"; Matthew 5:39: "Whosoever shall smite thee on the right cheek, turn to him the other also." (King James version).

18 For an entertaining example of a myth influenced by both technology and oppression, see "Iktome Has a Bad Dream," a legend of the Brule Sioux told in 1969, in Richard Erdoes and Alfonso Ortiz, eds., *American Indian Myths and Legends* (London: Pimlico, 1997 [1984]), 381-2.

19 Ibid., 111-14. The story is based on a rendering by George A. Dorsey in 1905 which is entirely consistent with the 1899 American Museum of Natural History account.

20 Ibid., 114.

21 For a discussion of this theme in aboriginal societies, though not of these examples, see "The Myth of the Noble Savage" in Mircea Eliade, *Myths, Dreams and Mysteries* (New York: Harper, 1967), 39-56.

22 See Beni Prasad, *Theory of Government in Ancient India* (Allahabad: Beni Prasad, 1927), 193, 219; C. Northcote Parkinson, *The Evolution of Political Thought* (London: University of London Press, 1958), 20; and Rod Preece, *Animals and Nature,* 251-2.

23 Hesiod, *Works and Days* in *Theogony and Works and Days,* ed. and trans. M.L. West (Oxford: Oxford University Press, 1988), 40-2.

24 Boethius, *The Consolation of Philosophy* (Harmondsworth: Penguin, 1969), translated with an introduction by V.E. Watts, 68.

25 Geoffrey Chaucer, "The Nun's Priest's Tale," *The Canterbury Tales,* trans. Nevil Coghill (London: Crescent, 1986), 137.

26 *The Tempest,* 2. I.

> Gonzalo: All things in common nature should produce
> Without sweat or endeavour: treason, felony,
> Sword, pike, knife, gun, or need of any engine.
> Would I not have; but nature should bring forth,
> Of its own kind, all foizon, all abundance,
> To feed my innocent people.

27 The theme was most popular in France where François Fénelon's *Télémaque* (1699) immediately went into more than twenty editions and Bernardin de Saint-Pierre's *Paul et Virginie* (1788) was reprinted some 150 times. See Stelio Cro, *The Noble Savage: Allegory of Freedom* (Waterloo: Wilfrid Laurier University Press, 1990), 88-9.

28 For a more complete rendering see p. 31. The passages are from The New Jerusalem Bible from which all Biblical quotations are taken hereafter unless otherwise indicated. The New Jerusalem Bible is a translation from the original texts undertaken by the scholars of L'Ecole Biblique in Jerusalem in the 1950s and later revised.

29 John Oswald, *The Cry of Nature; or, an Appeal to Mercy and Justice, on Behalf of Persecuted Animals* (London: J. Johnson, 1791 [reprint: Lampeter: Mellen, 2000, with an introduction by Jason Hribal]); George Nicholson, *On the Primeval Diet of Man* (Poughnill:

Nicholson, 1801 [reprint *George Nicholson's On the Primeval Diet of Man (1801): Vegetarianism and Human Conduct toward Animals,* edited, introduced, and annotated by Rod Preece (Lampeter: Mellen, 1999)]; Joseph Ritson, *An Essay on Abstinence from Animal Food as a Moral Duty* (London: Richard Phillips, 1802); John Frank Newton, *Return to Nature; or a defence of the vegetable regimen; with some account of an experiment made during the last three or four years in the author's family* (London: T. Cadell and W. Davies, 1811); Percy Bysshe Shelley, "A Vindication of Natural Diet" in *The Complete Works of Percy Bysshe Shelley,* eds. Roger Ingpen and Walter E. Peck (New York: Gordian Press, 1965), vol. 6, 6ff.

30 See David Leeming with Margaret Leeming, *A Dictionary of Creation Myths* (Oxford: Oxford University Press, 1995).

31 See, for example, the Apache story of "Creation" and the Chippewa-Ojibwa story of "The Great Serpent and the Great Flood" in Margot Edmonds and Ella E. Clark, eds., *Voices of the Winds: Native American Legends* (New York: Facts on File, 1989), 101-4 and 247-50.

32 "Duties toward Animals and Spirits" in Immanuel Kant, *Lectures on Ethics,* trans. Louis Infield (New York: Harper and Row, 1963 [1930]), 240.

33 "How the Buffalo Hunt Began" in Edmonds and Clark, *Voices of the Winds,* 184-5. According to the compilers, this version is "only slightly altered" from that recorded in 1899 at the Cheyenne Agency in order "to retain the character and flavor" of the original.

34 Rudyard Kipling, *Just So Stories* (Ware: Wordsworth, 1993 [1902]), 1-62.

35 In *An Essay on Humanity to Animals* (London: T. Cadell, Jun. and W. Davies, 1798 [reprint edition: Lampeter: Mellen, 2001, edited, introduced, and annotated by Rod Preece]), ch. 4, Thomas Young argued from a Christian perspective that God has granted humans the right to eat animals, that without that grant we would possess no such right, and that since God gave us no explicit to right to "sport" hunting or fishing we possess no such right.

36 The legend, which was also collected by the American Museum of Natural History in 1899, is included in Edmonds and Clark, *Voices of the Winds,* 185-6.

37 Lines 111-15, book XV, of Ovid, *Metamorphoses,* trans. Mary M. Innes (London: Penguin, 1995), 338.

38 Claude Lévi-Strauss, *Totemism* (London: Merlin, 1964), 89. Both Christopher Smart in 1720 (see p. 141) and Victor Hugo in 1862 (see p. 293) preceded Lévi-Strauss in the recognition and, rightly, did not restrict the application to Aboriginals. Nonetheless, the point is always associated with Lévi-Strauss.

39 See note 12.

40 See p. 30 for the whole of Ecclesiastes 3:19-21.

41 Quoted in Guenther, *Tricksters and Trancers,* 77. Reproduced in accordance with the original.

42 Ibid., 146. Reproduced in accordance with the original.

43 Ibid., 126. Ellipses in the original. There are "approximately seventy variants of this haunting myth of lost immortality" according to Guenther (128). He offers the following as the "stripped-down, generic, and composite form":

> The moon enjoins Hare to go to the village of the people to take to them the moon's message to humankind that henceforth humans, when they die, would not die forever but would, upon their deaths rise again. In this they would be like Moon himself, who dies at day's rise, only to rise again the following night. Upon arriving at the village of the people Hare distorted the message, telling the humans that when they died they would die forever. Hare's distorted message cost humans their

immortality and it brought them also the fear of death. Angered at hare's lying, Moon split his mouth, creating the split hare's lip. Humans have hated the hare ever since and will kill it when they see it in the veld. (129)

44 Ibid., 129.
45 From Jack Mapanje and Landeg White, compilers, with Isidore Okpewho, adviser, *Oral Poetry from Africa: An Anthology* (Harlow: Longman, 1983), 64.
46 Ibid., 66-7.
47 Big Bill Neidjie, *Speaking for the Earth: Nature's Law and the Aboriginal Way* (Washington, DC: Center for Respect of Life and Environment, 1991), 27, 35. Reprinted from Big Bill Neidjie, Stephen Davis, and Allan Fox, *Kakadu Man* (Northryde, NSW: Angus and Robertson, n.d.).
48 For examples, see Rod Preece, *Animals and Nature*, especially 199-1230.
49 G. Naganathan, *Animal Welfare and Nature: Hindu Scriptural Perspectives* (Washington, DC: Center for Respect of Life and Environment, 1989), 2.
50 R.C. Zaehner, trans., *Hindu Scriptures* (London: J.M. Dent, 1966), 185.
51 Juan Mascaró, ed. and trans., *The Upanishads* (London: Penguin, 1965), 49.
52 It is not, however, an uncontested assertion. Thus, for example, Basant K. Lal tells us: "The Hindu recommendation to cultivate a particular kind of attitude toward animals is not based on consideration for the animals as such but on consideration about how the development of this attitude is a part of the purificatory steps that bring men to the path of moksa (salvation) ... Hinduism in all its forms teaches that we have no duties to animals and thus implicitly denies that they have rights." ("Hindu Perspectives on the Use of Animals" in Tom Regan, ed., *Animal Sacrifices: Religious Perspectives on the Use of Animals in Science* [Philadelphia: Temple University Press, 1986], 200-5). Suffice it to say that Professor Lal's view is not the predominant one. Moreover, if consideration for other species is beneficent to purification there must be something seen to be admirable in the act itself. Otherwise the act would be merely ritual. If Lal is right, the striking conclusion must be that the animal-regarding philosophy of Hinduism is identical to that of Immanuel Kant. (See p. 173-4.)
53 *Bhagavatam*, 6, quoted in G. Naganathan, *Animal Welfare and Nature*, 5.
54 Surendra Bothara, ed., *The Yoga Shastra of Hemchandracharya: A Twelfth Century Guide to Jain Yoga*, trans. A.S. Gopani (Jaipur: Prakrit Bharti Academy, 1989), 11-12. Reflective of the fact that very similar principles are contained in different texts, we can read in the *Srimad-Bhagavatam*: "Ahimsa, truthfulness, freedom from theft, lust, anger and greed, and an effort to do what is agreeable and beneficial to all cultures this is the common duty of all castes." Quoted in Jon Wynne-Tyson, *The Extended Circle: A Commonplace Book of Animal Rights* (New York: Paragon House, 1989 [1985]), 121. That nothing in Eastern thought is ever simple, however, is exemplified by p. 41 of the above edition of the *Yogashastra* where the killing of animals for religious sacrifice is expressly permitted.
55 *Mahabharata*, 12, quoted in Naganathan, *Animal Welfare and Nature*, 9.
56 *Mahabharata*, quoted in Wynne-Tyson, *The Extended Circle*, 122. Compare the *Bhagavad Gita* X, 20: "I am the Self established/ In the heart of all contingent beings;/ I am the beginning, the middle and the end/ Of all contingent beings too." (Zaehner, *Hindu Scriptures*, 325). The central message of both passages is, again, of a pantheism in which God exists within all living creatures.
57 *Mahabharata*, 23, quoted in Naganathan, *Animal Welfare and Nature*, 15. For a lengthy list of relevant passages from the *Mahabharata* see Christopher Key Chapple, *Nonviolence to Animals, Earth and Self in Asian Traditions* (Albany: State University of New

York Press, 1993), 16-17. Reflective, again, of the great varieties of translations of the Indian classics (see 32-3), a reading of Edwin Arnold, *Idylls from the Sanskrit of the Mahabharata* (London: Kegan Paul, Tench, Trubner, Taylor, 1893) will yield nothing comparable to the passages cited here, in Naganathan, or in Chapple.

58 *Laws of Manu*, v, 27, quoted in John Mackenzie, *Hindu Ethics: A Historical and Critical Essay* (London: Oxford University Press, 1922; reprint, New Delhi: Oriental Books Reprint Corporation, 1971), 59.

59 *Laws of Manu* in ibid., 60.

60 Ibid., 61-2.

61 *Pancatantra*, 13, quoted in Naganathan, *Animal Welfare and Nature*, 10. It should be noted, however, that Visnu Sarma, ed., *The Pancatantra*, trans. Chandra Rajan (London: Penguin, 1993) has no equivalent passage.

62 *Pancatantra*, 24, quoted in ibid., 15. Again, there is no equivalent passage in Chandra Rajan's translation. See note 61.

63 *Acaranga Sutra*, 1, 1, 3 quoted in Chapple, *Nonviolence to Animals, Earth and Self in Asian Traditions*, 11.

64 *Acaranga Sutra* quoted in Wynne-Tyson, *The Extended Circle*, 141.

65 *Yajur Veda*, 36, 18, quoted in Chapple, *Nonviolence to Animals*, 15.

66 *Dhammapada*, 129, Juan Mascaró, trans., *The Dhammapada* (London: Penguin, 1973), 54. Section 130 is identical to that of 129 with the exception that the words "life is dear to all" replace "all fear death."

67 *Dhammapada*, 142, ibid., 55. The implication is that a holy man is known by his actions rather than by his caste, which was one of the principles of Gautama Buddha. In his *Ahimsa: Gautama to Gandhi* (New Delhi: Sterling, 1973), 31, George Kutturan elaborates the Buddha's principle as: "Him I call a Brahmin who is free from anger, who gladly endures reproach, and even stripes and bonds inflicted upon him without cause. Him I call a Brahmin who slays no living creatures, who does not kill or cause to be killed any living thing. He is born of Brahma, a Brahma-farer, living the God-life."

68 *Dhammapada*, 270, Mascaró, *The Dhammapada*, 74.

69 *Dhammapada*, 405, ibid., 91.

70 *Lankavatara Sutra* quoted in Chapple, *Nonviolence to Animals*, 27.

71 *Mahavagga*, 1, 78, quoted in ibid., 22.

72 *Hitopadesa* quoted in Wynne-Tyson, *The Extended Circle*, 121.

73 *The Yogashastra of Hemchandracharya*, 39.

74 Ibid., 38.

75 *Jaina Sutra* quoted in Wynne-Tyson, *The Extended Circle*, 140.

76 *Sutrakritanga* quoted in ibid., 140.

77 *Sutrakritanga* quoted in ibid., 141.

78 *Bhagavad Gita*, V, 18, in Zaehner, *Hindu Scriptures*, 304.

79 V, 25, ibid., 304.

80 VI, 29, ibid., 308.

81 VI, 31, ibid., 309.

82 XII, 13, ibid., 337.

83 Idanna Pucci, *Bhima Swarga: The Balinese Journey of the Soul* (Boston: Little, Brown and Company, 1992), 84, 98.

84 It has become customary to give dates as c.e. (common era) or b.c.e. (before common era). However, the commonality is restricted to the Abrahamic tradition. The terms may thus be seen to demean all outside that tradition. While BC and AD are also agenda laden, it is now commonly recognized that they do not coincide with the birth of Christ, and are thus artificial, almost arbitrary, and are, in my view, preferable for that very reason.

85 *The Wisdom of Confucius,* ed. Lin Yutang (New York: Modern Library, 1996), 166.
86 Ibid., 109.
87 Quoted in Philip J. Ivanhoe, *Ethics in the Confucian Tradition: The Thoughts of Mencius and Yang-Ming* (Atlanta: Scholars' Press, 1990), 6, citing *Analects,* Harvard-Yenching Institute Sinilogical Index Series (HYSIS) #16: 2/2/7.
88 Quoted in ibid., 13, citing *Mencius,* HYSIS #17: 54/7A/45.
89 Quoted in ibid., 34, citing *Mencius,* HYSIS # 17: 46/6A/19.
90 Tai-shang kan-yingp'ien, pre-fourteenth century, and attributed, probably erroneously, to Ko Hung (AD 284-AD 363). Quoted in Wynne-Tyson, *The Extended Circle,* 56.
91 Yin-chih-wen, probably post-fourth century AD, attributed, again without much evidence, to Wen Ch'ang. Quoted in ibid., 56.
92 Thomas Young, *An Essay on Humanity to Animals (1798),* ed. Rod Preece (Lampeter: Mellen, 2001), 52-8.
93 Anne Brontë, *Agnes Grey* (London: Penguin, 1988 [1847]), 105-6.
94 Victor Hugo, *Les Misérables,* trans. Norman Denny (London: Penguin, 1982 [1862]), 81.
95 See pp. 15-18.
96 See pp. 12-13.
97 Quoted in Juliet Barker, *Wordsworth: A Life* (London: Viking, 2000), 705. Wordsworth used the phrase on several occasions, notably in *The Old Cumberland Beggar.*
98 See pp. 8-10.
99 See Lewis G. Regenstein, *Replenish the Earth: A History of Organized Religion's Treatment of Animals and Nature – including the Bible's Message of Conservation and Kindness toward Animals* (New York: Crossroad, 1991), 201.
100 Quoted in Regenstein, *Replenish the Earth,* 184, citing Rabbi Solomon Ganzfried, *Code of Jewish Law* (New York: Hebrew Publishing Company, 1962), Bk. 4, ch. 19, 184. Compare also Isidore Epstein, *Judaism* (London: Penguin, 1990 [1959]), 27, 153.
101 Quoted in Richard H. Schwartz, "Tsa'ar Ba'alei Chayim: Judaism and Compassion for Animals" in Roberta Kalechofsky, ed., *Judaism and Animal Rights: Classical and Contemporary Responses* (Marblehead, MA: Micah Publications, 1992), 61. The Hebrew phrase is the mandate not to cause pain to any living creature.
102 Quoted in Ronald Isaacs, *Animals in Jewish Thought and Tradition* (Northvale, NJ: Jason Aronson, 2000), 85, citing Even HaEzer 5:14.
103 Quoted in ibid., 85, citing Orach Chayyim 223:6.
104 Quoted in ibid., 86, citing Mechilta to Exodus 23:12.
105 Quoted in ibid., 87, citing Kitzur Schulchan Aruch, 186:1.
106 Quoted in Regenstein, *Replenish the Earth,* 184, citing Richard Schwartz, "Judaism and Animal Rights," distributed by CHAI (Concern for Helping Animals in Israel), Alexandria, VA.
107 *Shabbat* 77b, quoted in Regenstein, *Replenish the Earth,* 189, citing Barry Freundel, "The Earth is the Lord's: How Jewish Tradition Views Our Relationship to the Environment," *Jewish Action,* Summer, 1990, 24-5. By contrast, the Flemish Jesuit Cornelius a Lapide (1567-1627) claimed that "lice, flies, maggots and the like were not created directly by God but by spontaneous generation, as lice from sweat." (Quoted in Seamus Dean's notes to James Joyce's *A Portrait of the Artist as a Young Man* (London: Penguin, 1993 [1916]), 324. Such animalcules were so despicable, Lapide imagined, God would not have deigned to create them.
108 *Shabbat* 151b, noted in Regenstein, *Replenish the Earth,* 190, citing Alan Hertzberg, "The Jewish Declaration on Nature," World Wildlife Conference statement, Assisi, September, 1986, distributed by the International Network for Religion and Animals, Silver Springs, MD.

109 *Yerushalmi Keturot,* 4:8, 291; Yevanot 15, noted in Regenstein, *Replenish the Earth,* 191, citing *Encyclopedia Judaica.*

110 *Sefer Hassidim* 13c, #142, 64, quoted in Regenstein, *Replenish the Earth,* 191, citing *Encyclopedia Judaica.*

111 Quoted in George Boas, *Primitivism and Related Ideas in the Middle Ages* (Baltimore: Johns Hopkins, 1997 [1948]), 187-8.

112 Quoted in W. Youatt, *The Obligation and Extent of Humanity to Brutes, Principally Considered with Reference to the Domesticated Animals* (London: Longman, Orme, Brown, Green, and Longman, 1839), 16, citing Josephus [*Antiquities of the Jews*], vol. 1, b. 4, c. 8.

113 Qur'an Majeed, Sura VI, [aya 38], quoted in Regenstein, *Replenish the Earth,* 249, citing Guy Delon in report distributed by the Animal Welfare Institute, Washington, DC.

114 [Qur'an Majeed], Sura VI, aya 38, quoted in Regenstein, *Replenish the Earth,* 249, citing Abou Bakr Ahmed Ba Kader, Abdul Latif Tawik El Shirazy Al Sabbagh, Mohammed Al Sayyed Al Gleni, and Movel Yousef Samarrai Izzidien, *Islamic Principles for the Conservation of the Natural Environment* (Switzerland and the Kingdom of Saudi Arabia: International Union for the Conservation of Nature and Natural Resources, 1983), 17.

115 Qur'an Majeed 11:6, quoted in Regenstein, *Replenish the Earth,* 249, citing Al-Hafiz B.A. Masri, "Synopsis of Islamic Teachings on Animal Rights," distributed by International Network for Religion and Animals, Silver Spring, MD.

116 Qur'an Majeed 55:10, quoted in Regenstein, ibid., 250, citing Masri, ibid.

117 Qura'n Majeed 55:12, quoted in Regenstein, ibid., citing Masri, ibid.

118 Qur'an Majeed 15:19, quoted in Regenstein, ibid., citing Masri, ibid.

119 Qur'an Majeed 45:4, quoted in Regenstein, ibid., citing Masri, ibid.

120 Qur'an Majeed 5:103 and 4:118, 119, quoted in Regenstein, ibid., citing Masri, ibid.

121 *Hadith,* quoted in Regenstein, ibid., citing Masri, ibid.

122 *Hadith,* quoted in Regenstein, ibid., citing Basil Wrighton, "Animals in Other Religions," *The Ark* (London: Catholic Study Circle for Animal Welfare), April, 1968.

123 *Hadith Mishkat,* 3, 1392, quoted in Regenstein, ibid., citing Masri, ibid.

124 *Hadith,* quoted in Regenstein, ibid., citing Guy Delon, superintendent of the American Fondouk, Fez, Morocco, [in report distributed by] the Animal Welfare Institute, Washington, DC.

125 *Hadith Awn,* 7, 222:2533, quoted in Regenstein, ibid., citing Masri, ibid.

126 *Hadith Mishkat,* Bk. 6, ch. 7, 8:178, quoted in Regenstein, ibid., citing Masri, ibid.

127 *Hadith Al-Nasai,* 7, 206, quoted in Regenstein, ibid., citing Masri, ibid.

128 *Hadith,* quoted in Regenstein, ibid., citing Masri, ibid.

129 *Hadith,* quoted in Regenstein, ibid., citing Guy Delon in report distributed by the Animal Welfare Institute, Washington, DC.

Chapter 2: The Classical World

1 Quoted in George Nicholson's *On the Primeval Diet of Man (1801): Vegetarianism and Human Conduct Toward Animals,* ed. Rod Preece (Lampeter: Mellen, 1999), 203-4.

2 Leporem et gallinam et anserem gustare fas non putant; haec tamen alunt animi voluptatisque causa (G. Iulii Caesaris, *De Bello Gallico* [London: G. Bell and Son, 1965], Bk. V, ch. 12, 45). (Hare and cock and goose they do not think it appropriate to partake of; yet they raise them from desire and for pleasure.)

3 See pp. 45-6.

4 See pp. 50-1.

5 That is, the Body of Civil Law.

6 A. Passerin d'Entrèves, *Natural Law: An Introduction to Legal Philosophy* (London:

Hutchinson, 1970 [1951]), 29, citing *Digest,* I, i, i (Ulpianus: libro primo institutionem). It should be acknowledged that Ulpian confuses the laws of nature (i.e., behavioural laws) with natural law (i.e., universal moral laws), a confusion that was customary until the late Enlightenment. Nonetheless, it is significant that Ulpian saw human and nonhuman animals alike participating in what he regarded as natural law, thereby emphasizing human–animal similarities rather than the differences.

7   *Batrachomyomachia* in *Chapman's Homer: The Iliad, The Odyssey and the Lesser Homerica,* ed. Allardyce Nicoll (New York: Pantheon Books, 1956), vol. 2, 515, lines 9-12. George Chapman's translations were undertaken in the first quarter of the seventeenth century. I have modernized the spelling.

8   Lines 338 and 420 of "A Hymn to Apollo" in ibid., 534, 536. Spelling modernized.

9   Line 382 of "A Hymn to Hermes" in ibid., 554. Spelling modernized.

10 Lines 120-1 of "A Hymn to Venus" in ibid., 571. Spelling modernized.

11 Line 5 of "To the Mother of the Gods" in ibid., 588. Spelling modernized.

12 S.H. Butcher and A. Lang, trans., *The Odyssey of Homer* (New York: P.F. Collier and Son, 1969 [1909]), 235-6.

13 *Anacreon: With Thomas Stanley's Translation,* ed. A.H. Bullen (London: Lawrence Bullen, 1893), XLIII, 111-13. (The Greek text is on even numbered pages). Stanley's translation was originally published in 1651. Abraham Cowley published an entertaining expansion of the grasshopper ode which is reproduced at 221-2 of the Bullen edition; and Goethe's admirable translation into German, "An die Cicade," is reproduced at 223. A modern translation may be found in Willis Branstone, trans., *Sappho and the Greek Lyric Poets* (New York: Schocken, 1988), 254.

14 Ibid., IX, 21-3.

15 See Dominic J. O'Meara, *Pythagoras Revived: Mathematics and Philosophy in Late Antiquity* (Oxford: Clarendon Press, 1992).

16 From Jonathan Barnes, ed. and trans., *Early Greek Philosophy* (London: Penguin, 1987), 86. As we shall see throughout this book, the idea of the transmigration of souls has never quite disappeared from Western discourse. Raised in an Orthodox Jewish family in Poland before the Second World War, Isaac Bashevis Singer reports its then continued existence. He heard and read that the souls of the dead were reincarnated in cattle and fowl and that when the slaughterer killed them with a kosher knife and said the blessing with fervour, this served to purify these souls. (*Law and Exile: An Autobiographical Trilogy* [New York: Farrar, Strauss and Giroux, 1997], 19). The philosopher Stephen R.L. Clark nears the concept in his embracing of the world soul. See Daniel A. Dombrowski, *Not Even a Sparrow Falls: The Philosophy of Stephen R.L. Clark* (East Lansing: University of Michigan Press, 2000), ch. 9. For a discussion of the continuity of the idea in Western thought, see Rod Preece, *Animals and Nature: Cultural Myths, Cultural Realities* (Vancouver: UBC Press, 1999), ch. 8.

17 See p. 58-61.

18 From Jonathan Barnes, *Early Greek Philosophy,* 87.

19 From ibid., 82. For a longer extract, see Diogenes Laertius, *The Life of Pythagoras* in Kenneth Sylvan Guthrie, ed. and trans., *The Pythagorean Sourcebook and Library* (Grand Rapids, MI: Phanes Press, 1987), 144-5.

20 From Jonathan Barnes, *Early Greek Philosophy,* 200.

21 See pp. 56-7.

22 From Jonathan Barnes, *Early Greek Philosophy,* 176.

23 From ibid., 199.

24 See pp. 8-10.

25 From Jonathan Barnes, *Early Greek Philosophy,* 198-9.

26   From ibid., 199-200.

27   See pp. 22-3.

28   From Jonathan Barnes, *Early Greek Philosophy*, 116.

29   From ibid., 262.

30   See pp. 45-50.

31   From Jonathan Barnes, *Early Greek Philosophy*, 291.

32   Plato, *Republic*, trans. H. Spens (Glasgow: Robert and Andrew Foulis, 1763), 427-8.

33   Plato, *Phaedo*, trans. Benjamin Jowett (1875), in *The Trial and Death of Socrates: Four Dialogues* (New York: Dover, 1992), 80-1.

34   Harold Cherniss and William C. Helmbold, trans., *Plutarch's Moralia* (London: William Heinemann, 1957 [1927]), vol. 12, 355.

35   Arthur Hugh Clough, revised trans., *Plutarch's Lives: The Dryden Plutarch* (London: J.M. Dent, 1910), vol. 1, 520-1.

36   Plutarch, *Essays*, trans. Robin Waterfield, introduced and annotated by Ian Kidd (London: Penguin, 1992), 385, 386, 387, 389, 392, 397, 398.

37   Cherniss and Helmbold, *Plutarch's Moralia*, vol. 12, 329, 361, 369, 387, 377. (Sections 960-1, 966, 967, 968-9, 970).

38   Ibid., 547, 550-1. The essay is reproduced at greater length in Kerry S. Walters and Lisa Portmess, eds., *Ethical Vegetarianism: From Pythagoras to Peter Singer* (Albany: State University of New York Press, 1999), 28-34.

39   D. Shackleton Bailey, trans., *Cicero's Letters to his Friends* (London: Penguin, 1967), 81.

40   See, for example, James Lovelock, *Gaia: A New Look at Life on Earth* (London: Oxford University Press, 1979).

41   Lucretius, *On the Nature of the Universe*, trans. R.E. Latham (London: Penguin, 1994 [1951]), 164.

42   Ibid., 46-7.

43   From Elijah Judah Schochet, *Animal Life in Jewish Tradition: Attitudes and Relationships* (New York: KTAV Publishing House, 1984), 160-1.

44   Seneca, *Ad Lucilium Epistulae Morales*, trans. Richard M. Gummere (New York: G.P. Putnam's Sons, 1925), vol. 3, 241-3.

45   Pliny the Elder, *Natural History: A Selection*, with an introduction and notes by John F. Healey (London: Penguin, 1991), 74-6, 108, 149 (7, 1-5; 8, 1; 11, 11-12).

46   A small portion has, however, been included in the section on Alexander Pope (pp. 129-30).

47   Ovid, *Metamorphoses*, translated with an introduction and notes by Mary M. Innes (London: Penguin, 1955), 228. (Book 10, secs. 109-11; 115-18).

48   George Long, trans., *The Meditations of the Emperor Marcus Aurelius Antoninus* (New York: A.L. Burt, n.d. [c. 1900]), 194, 196-7, 200, 219, 262. (V, 16; VI, 23; VI, 36; VII, 65; X, 10).

49   Aelian, *On the Characteristics of Animals*, trans. A.F. Schofield (London: William Heinemann, 1958), vol. 1, 93-7.

50   R.G. Bury, trans., *Sextus Empiricus* (London: William Heinemann, 1955 [1949]), vol. 1, 39-43.

51   Arthur O. Lovejoy, *The Great Chain of Being: A Study of the History of an Idea* (New York: Harper and Row, 1960 [1936]), viii.

52   A.H. Armstrong, trans., *Plotinus* (London: William Heinemann, 1967), vol. 3, 67, 79, 83-5, 117, 119, 133. (3,2,7; 3,2,11; 3,2,13; 3,3,3; 3,3,6).

53   In his *Animal Minds and Human Morals: The Origins of the Western Debate* (Ithaca: Cornell University Press, 1993), 221, Richard Sorabji described *On Abstinence from Animal Food* as "by far the most important of classical texts relating to animals." A new

translation has been completed recently by Gillian Clark under the title *On Abstinence from Killing Animals* (Ithaca: Cornell University Press, 2000).

54 Perhaps Porphyry is referring to the *Historia Animalium* (588, A:8): "just as in man we find knowledge, wisdom and sagacity, so in certain animals there exists some other natural propensity akin to these."

55 Compare Hobbes's words: "I pray, when a lion eats a man and a man eats an ox, why is the ox made more for the man than the man for the lion?"

56 This kind of thinking played a significant role in the Middle Ages when animals were sometimes deemed criminally responsible for their actions and prosecuted in public courts of law. See Edward Payson Evans, *The Criminal Prosecution and Capital Punishment of Animals* (London: Faber and Faber, 1987 [1906]).

57 Porphyry, *On Abstinence from Animal Food,* trans. Thomas Taylor (Fontwell: Centaur, 1965 [c. 1793]), 110, 140-1.

Chapter 3: The Dark Ages

1 One of the consequences of animal experimentation of *ultimate* benefit to the animals was a recognition of the structural homologies between humans and nonhumans. The fact that all animals, including human animals, are basically alike eventually hindered the argument for a human exclusivity.

2 According to Charles Knight, commenting on medical training as late as the fourteenth century, Chaucer provided a catalogue of the books which physicians studied: "Esculapius, Hippocrates, Galen and Discorides are there with Rufus, a physician of Ephesus during the time of Trajan; and we may observe that, in reference to these, all our medical knowledge rests on Greek foundations." (*Old England* [London: James Sangster, 1847], i, III, iii, 326). To be sure, much medical knowledge came via Arab and Moorish sources, but it rested on the Hippocratic concept of humours and the practice of leeching, which were predominantly lacking in medical benefit, and often themselves the cause of suffering.

3 W.E.H. Lecky, *A History of European Morals from Augustus to Charlemagne* (New York: D. Appleton, 1869), vol. 2, 161.

4 Quoted in Dom Ambrose Agius, *God's Animals* (London: Catholic Study Circle for Animal Welfare, 1973 [1970]), 45, citing *Ark*, 18, 6.

5 Quoted in Joyce E. Salisbury, *The Beast Within: Animals in the Middle Ages* (New York: Routledge, 1994), 19.

6 John Passmore, "The Treatment of Animals," *Journal of the History of Ideas,* 36, 1975, 215-16.

7 Lecky, *History of European Morals,* vol. 2, 182-3.

8 Giorgio Vasari, *The Great Masters* (1550), ed. Michael Sonino, trans. Gaston Du C. de Vere (1912) (New York: Park Lane, 1988), 93-4.

9 Andrew Linzey, "Christianity and the Rights of Animals," *The Animals' Voice,* Los Angeles, August, 1989, 45.

10 Dix Harwood, *Love for Animals and How It Developed in Great Britain* (New York: Privately Printed, 1928), 47-9. A new edition is to be published in 2002 in the Mellen Animal Rights Library, edited, introduced, and annotated by Rod Preece and David Fraser.

11 There is a fictional account of such a trial, based on detailed historical research, in Victor Hugo's *Notre-Dame de Paris* (1831), Bk. 8, chs. 1-3. Ninety-three cases of criminal proceedings against animals have been documented, the first in 1266. (Joyce E. Salisbury, *The Beast Within,* 39, citing E. Bonkalo, "Criminal Proceedings against Animals in the Middle Ages," *Journal of Unconventional History,* 3, 2, 1992, 26).

12   Boria Sax, *Animals in the Third Reich: Pets, Scapegoats and the Holocaust* (New York: Continuum, 2000), 162.

13   Richard D. Ryder, *Animal Revolution: Changing Attitudes Towards Speciesism* (Oxford: Basil Blackwell, 1989), 34. Slightly less lengthy lists may be found in E.S. Turner, *All Heaven in a Rage*, 25, Dix Harwood, *Love for Animals*, 11-12, and Rod Preece, *Animals and Nature*, 127. Indicative of the generality of the phenomenon, there is little overlap among the four accounts. A fuller account of saints and animals is to be found in Agius, *God's Animals*, 42-5.

14   Wolfgang Mohr, *Wolfram von Eschenbach: Parzival* (Göppingen: Verlag Alfred Kummerle, 1977 [c. 1200]), 65, 93. This trans. Rod Preece.

15   *The Wars of Alexander: an alliterative romance, translated chiefly from the Historia Alexandri Magni de preliis,* Early English Text Society, extra series, 47 (New York: Kraus Reprint, 1973 [1886]), 3818, 5582ff.

16   William Langland, *Piers the Ploughman,* translated into modern English with an introduction by J.F. Goodridge (Harmondsworth: Penguin, 1959), pt. 2, Bk. xi, 136-8.

17   For the view that the medieval concept of animals was as entirely irrational creatures, see Joyce E. Salisbury, *The Beast Within,* Introduction and ch. 1.

18   Thomas Bullfinch, *Bullfinch's Mythology* (New York: Crown, 1979), 661-3; 708-9; 819-21.

19   See pp. 12-13.

20   See Chrétien de Troyes, *Yvain, or the Knight with the Lion,* trans. Ruth Harwood Cline (Athens: University of Georgia Press, 1975), 94, 100.

21   Bullfinch, *Bullfinch's Mythology,* 537-8; 540-1; 551-3; 622-4.

22   For a selection rendered in modern translation, see Kenneth Hurlstone Jackson, *A Celtic Miscellany* (London: Penguin, 1971).

23   From Joseph Campbell, *The Masks of God: Occidental Mythology* (London: Penguin, 1976 [1964]), 436, 458, citing Egerton MS 112 in the British Museum.

24   See p. 30.

25   Hamilton Bruce and Hugh Campbell, trans., *The Seven Books of Arnobius Adversus Gentes* in *Ante-Nicene Christian Library, translations of the fathers down to AD 325* (Edinburgh: T.T. Clark, 1871), vol. 19, 82-4.

26   Francis McDonald, trans., *The Fathers of the Church: Lactantius, The Divine Institutes, Books I-VII* (Washington: The Catholic University of America Press, 1964), 185-6.

27   From Andrew Linzey and Tom Regan, eds., *Animals and Christianity: A Book of Readings* (London: SPCK, 1989), 98-9, citing Athanasius, *Contra Gentes and De Incarnatione,* trans. Robert W. Thomson (Oxford: Clarendon Press, 1971).

28   Quoted in Daniel A. Dombrowski, *The Philosophy of Vegetarianism* (Amherst: University of Massachusetts Press, 1984), 142.

29   Quoted in C.W. Hume, *The Status of Animals in the Christian Religion* (London: Universities Federation for Animal Welfare Theological Bulletin, no. 2, 1962), 3.

30   See *Book of Needs,* ed. A St. Tikhon's Monastery Monk (South Canaan, PA: St. Tikhon's Monastery Press, 1987).

31   Quoted in Hume, *The Status of Animals,* 21.

32   Quoted in Agius, *God's Animals,* 28, citing Augustine, *De Nat[urz] Bon[i],* 2, 16.

33   St. Augustine, *Concerning the City of God against the Pagans,* trans. Henry Bettenson (Harmondsworth: Penguin, 4th ed., 1980), Bk. xix, ch. 14, 872-3.

34   St. Augustine, *The Confessions of St. Augustine* (London: Longman's Green, 1897), 72.

35   Ibid., 179-80.

36   See p. 58.

37   Quoted in Agius, *God's Animals,* 52.

38 Quoted in Agius, *God's Animals*, 12, citing La Marquise de Rambures, *L'Eglise et la Pitié envers les Animaux* (Paris: Crépin, Leblond, 1908), 22.

39 From Harwood, *Love for Animals*, 65-6, citing John of Salisbury, *De Nugis Curialium*, I, iv. (Harwood cites the piece at greater length than here).

40 Walter Map, *De Nugis Curialium: Courtiers' Trifles*, ed. and trans. M.R. James (Oxford: Clarendon Press, 1983), 5, 7.

41 Quoted in Agius, *God's Animals*, citing Alban Butler, *Lives of the Saints*, revised and supplemented by Rev. Herbert Thurston and Donald Attwater (New York: P.J. Kennedy and Sons, n.d.), II, 362. The quotation in the epigraph from Richard de Wyche is a slightly different translation of the same statement.

42 From Linzey and Regan, eds., *Animals and Christianity*, 124-7, citing *Summa Theologica*, literally translated by the English Dominican Fathers (London: Benziger Brothers, 1918), pt. II, Question 64, Article I, and Question 65, Article 3.

43 Quoted in Agius, *God's Animals*, 10, citing Aquinas, *De Moribus divinis: de cura Dei de creaturis.*

44 René Descartes, *Oeuvres de Descartes* (Paris: Charles et Paul Tanery, 1897), vol. VI, letter cxxxii.

45 See Denis Saurat, *Milton: Man and Thinker* (New York: Haskell House, 1970 [1925]), pt. II, ch. I: "The Zohar and Kaballah," and ch. II: "Robert Fludd (1574-1637)." We are told there is but one great idea of the Zohar which is not in Milton: the idea of reincarnation (283), that the idea of free will within a pantheistic system was the central point of Milton's thought, both in *Paradise Lost* and in *De doctrina Christiana* (286), and that these were derived from unorthodox Jewish antecedents. Likewise, Milton accepts the Zohar doctrine (which is a compendium of prior non-orthodox Jewish traditions, including that of the kaballah) that all souls form one unity with the essential soul (283). Fludd accepts the doctrine of the scale of being, apparently from Zoroastrian and kabbalistic sources (307).

46 See Introduction to Roberta Kalechofsky, ed., *Judaism and Animal Rights: Classical and Contemporary Responses* (Marblehead, MA: Micah Publications, 1992), 4.

47 Quoted from "Sherira Gaon Defends the Rights of Animals" in ibid., 15.

48 Quoted in Lewis Regenstein, *Replenish the Earth: A History of Organized Religion's Treatment of Animals and Nature* (New York: Crossroad, 1991), 184, citing Steven Rosen, *Food for the Spirit* (New York: Basic Books, 1987), 43.

49 Moses Maimonides, *Guide for the Perplexed*, trans. M.D. Friedlander (New York: New Dover, 1956), III, 48.

50 Quoted in Regenstein, *Replenish the Earth*, 185, citing *Guide for the Perplexed.*

51 Quoted in Aviva Cantor (with Barry Rosen and Hillel Besdin) "Kindness to Animals" in Kalechofsky, *Judaism and Animal Rights*, 27, citing *Guide for the Perplexed.*

52 Quoted in Regenstein, *Replenish the Earth*, 196, citing J.H. Hertz, *The Pentateuch and the Haftorahs* (London: Soncino Press, 1958), 855.

53 Quoted in Regenstein, *Replenish the Earth*, 192-3.

54 See pp. 32-3.

55 See pp. 110-11, 129, 132.

56 See p. 58.

57 See p. 126.

58 Quoted in Al-Hafiz B.A. Masri, *Animals in Islam* (Petersfield: The Athene Trust, 1989), xi, citing Syed Amir Ali, *The Spirit of Islam* (London: Chatto and Windus, 1964, 10th edition), 424.

59 Quoted in ibid., 4, citing *Maxims of Ali*, trans. Al-Halal from *Nahj-ul-Balagha* (Lahore: Sh. Muhammad Ashraf, n.d.), 436.

60   Quoted in Regenstein, *Replenish the Earth,* citing Masri "Synopsis of Islamic Teachings on Animal Rights."

61   Regis J. Armstrong and Ignatius C. Brady, trans., *Francis and Clare: The Complete Works* (New York: Paulist Press, 1982), 38-9. One of the many problems of translation is reflected in the fact that the version of the canticle in Marion A. Habig, ed., *St. Francis of Assisi: Writings and Early Biographies* (Chicago: Franciscan Herald Press, 1983, 130-1) makes no mention of animals at all in any of its 37 lines.

62   Armstrong and Brady, *Francis and Clare,* 29.

63   Ibid., 152.

64   Marion A. Habig, ed., *St. Francis of Assisi: Writings and Early Biographies* (Chicago: Franciscan Herald Press, 1983), 227-8, 297, 495.

65   Ewart Cousins, trans., *Bonaventure: The Soul's Journey into God, The Tree of Life and the Life of St. Francis* (Mahwah, NJ: Paulist Press, 1978), 254-9.

66   See p. 30.

67   For an exhaustive account and explanation of the bestiaries, see Ron Baxter, *Bestiaries and their Users in the Middle Ages* (London: Sutton Publishing/Courtauld Institute, 1998). See also Louis Charbonneau-Lassay, *The Bestiary of Christ,* trans. D.M. Dooling (New York: Arkana, 1992 [1942]).

68   From *Fourteenth Century Verse and Prose,* ed. Kenneth Sisam (Oxford: Oxford University Press, 1985 [1921]), 41-2. This trans. Rod Preece.

69   Quoted in Agius, *God's Animals,* 43, citing St. Catherine of Siena's *Letters,* I, 237.

70   Quoted in Arthur Helps, *Animals and their Masters* (London: Chatto and Windus, 1883 [c. 1872]), 124.

71   Quoted in Michael W. Fox, *St. Francis of Assisi, Animals and Nature* (Washington, DC: Center for Respect of Life and Environment, 1989), 3.

72   Geoffrey Chaucer, *The Canterbury Tales,* trans. Nevil Coghill (London: Crescent, 1986), 19.

73   Keith Thomas, *Man and the Natural World: Changing Attitudes in England 1500-1800* (London: Penguin, 1984 [1983]), 153.

74   Quoted in Harwood, *Love for Animals,* 39. The text may be found in Priscilla Barnum, ed., *Dives et Pauper,* Early English Text Society, 1976 reprint, 1, 2, 36.

Chapter 4: The Renaissance

1   Aristotle, *Metaphysics,* Bk. I, ch. I, in Aristotle, *On Man in the Universe: Metaphysics, Parts of Animals, Ethics, Politics, Poetics,* ed. Louise Ropes Loomis (New York: Gramercy, 1971), 5.

2   Fénelon was not, however, as naive as he appears at first blush. As Arthur O. Lovejoy explained in *The Great Chain of Being: A Study of the History of an Idea* (New York: Harper and Row, 1960 [1936]), 162, for Fénelon, "though the gift of speech presumably makes human beings "more perfect" their perfection is not necessarily proportional to their use of the faculty: "il arrive même souvent que je sois plus parfait de me taire que de parler." [It happens equally often that I am more perfect when I am silent than when I speak.]

3   From Irma A. Richter, ed., *Selections from the Notebooks of Leonardo da Vinci* (Oxford: Oxford University Press, 1977), 61.

4   Quoted in Emery Kellen, ed., *Fantastic Tales, Strange Animals, Riddles, Jests, and Prophecies of Leonardo da Vinci* (New York: Thomas Nelson, 1971), 78-9.

5   Quoted in Philip Kaplan, *To Cherish All Life: A Buddhist Case for Becoming Vegetarian,* 2nd edition (Rochester: The Zen Center, 1986), 82, citing "da Vinci's Notes." There is, however, some dispute as to the authenticity of this quotation, some claiming that

the passage is an invention of Merezhovsky in his 1920s novel *Romance of Leonardo da Vinci.*

6   From Richter, *Selections from the Notebooks,* 245-6.

7   From Kellen, *Fantastic Tales,* 116-19.

8   Giorgio Vasari, *The Great Masters,* ed. Michael Sonino, trans. Gaston Du. C. de Vere (New York: Park Lane, 1988), 93-4.

9   Quoted in Arthur Helps, *Animals and their Masters* (London: Chatto and Windus, 1883 [c. 1872]), 157.

10   From Dix Harwood, *Love for Animals and How it Developed in Great Britain* (New York: Privately Printed, 1928), citing *Notes and Queries,* series 8, ii, 233.

11   Desiderius Erasmus, *The Praise of Folly and Other Writings,* trans. Robert M. Adams (New York: W.W. Norton, 1989), 40.

12   See p. 80.

13   Thomas More, *Utopia: Latin Text and English Translation,* ed. and trans. George M. Logan, Robert M. Adams, and Clarence H. Miller (Cambridge: Cambridge University Press, 1995), 171.

14   *The Compete Works of St. John of the Cross,* trans. E. Allison Peers (London: Burns, Oates and Washburn, 1935), vol. II, stanza 5 of "Spiritual Canticle," 50-1. It is found in a slightly different version in Andrew Linzey and Tom Regan, eds., *Animals and Christianity: A Book of Readings* (London: SPCK, 1989), 93-4.

15   Quoted in Keith Thomas, *Man and the Natural World: Changing Attitudes in England 1500-1800* (London: Penguin, 1984 [1983]), 159, citing *Essays of Montaigne,* trans. Florio, ii, 126.

16   In R.A. Latham's translation, *On the Nature of the Universe* (London: Penguin, 1994 [1951]), the phrase is nicely rendered as "each species develops according to its own kind, and they all guard their specific characters in obedience to the laws of nature" (Bk. 5, lines 922-4, 152).

17   "Apology for Raymond Sebond" in Michel de Montaigne, *Selected Essays,* trans. Donald M. Frame (New York: Oxford University Press, 1982 [1943]), 323, 324, 326-7, 330, 342-3, 357.

18   The quotations from Shakespeare are taken from *The Complete Works of William Shakespeare* (London: Ramboro, 1993 [c. 1870]).

19   Stanza 19, lines 281-90, of *Metempsycosis* in *The Complete English Poems of John Donne* (London: J.M. Dent, 1985), 417. Spelling modernized.

20   Quoted in Richard D. Ryder, *Animal Revolution: Changing Attitudes Towards Speciesism* (London: Basil Blackwell, 1989), 51, citing *Century 2,* no. 100. Spelling modernized.

21   Quoted in ibid., 51, citing *Century 3,* no. 23. Spelling modernized.

22   George Wither, "When We Ride for Pleasure," Hymn 22, in *Hallelujah, or Britain's Second Remembrancer* (London, 1641), pt. 1.

23   Margaret Cavendish, Marchioness of Newcastle, *Philosophical Letters* (London, 1664), 40-1.

24   Margaret Cavendish, *Poems and Fancies: Written by the Right Honourable the Lady Newcastle* (London: Martin and Allystrye, 1653), 113. Spelling modernized.

25   Quoted in Denis Saurat, *Milton: Man and Thinker* (New York: Haskell House, 1970 [1925]), 141-2, citing Milton, *Treatise of Christian Doctrine* in *Prose Works,* IV, 195, 198.

26   See pp. 163-4.

27   John Evelyn, *The Diaries of John Evelyn,* ed. E.S. de Beer (Oxford: Clarendon Press, 1955), vol. 3, 549.

28   Samuel Pepys, *The Diary of Samuel Pepys,* ed. Henry B. Wheatley (New York: Random House, n.d. [c. 1893]), vol. 6, 295.

29   I have seen this quoted incorrectly as "parliament men," thereby suggesting it a cus-
     tomary activity among parliamentarians. In fact, this was by most accounts an uncom-
     mon occurrence. By far the majority of the participants came from what was regarded
     as "the lower orders."

30   *The Diary of Samuel Pepys,* vol. 1, 800-1.

31   Quoted in Harwood, *Love for Animals,* 51, citing Richard Butcher's *Survey of Tutbury*
     (1696) as mentioned in Joseph Strutt's *The Sports and Pastimes of the People of England*
     (London, 1810).

32   George Fox, *The Serious People's Reasoning and Speech, with the World's Teachers and Pro-
     fessors* in *Gospel Truth Demonstrated in a Collection of Doctrinal Books Given Forth by that
     Faithful Minister of Jesus Christ, George Fox: Containing Principles Essential to Christian-
     ity and Salvation, Held among People Called Quakers* (Philadelphia: Marcus T.C. Gould,
     1831), vol. 1, 195, 196, 198.

33   George Fox, *To All Sorts of People in Christendom* in ibid., 320-1.

34   From Thomas, *Man and the Natural World,* 170, 155, citing *The Country-man's Com-
     panion* (London, 1683), 171, sig. A2.

35   Quoted in Rod Preece and Lorna Chamberlain, *Animal Welfare and Human Values*
     (Waterloo: Wilfrid Laurier University Press, 1993), 73.

36   See p. 108.

37   Quoted in part in Richard D. Ryder, *Animal Revolution,* 52, and, in part, in Jon
     Wynne-Tyson, *The Extended Circle: A Commonplace Book of Animal Rights* (New York:
     Paragon, 1989 [1985]), 378.

38   William Leiss, *The Domination of Nature* (Montreal and Kingston: McGill-Queen's
     University Press, 1994 [1972]), 48.

39   See p. 94.

40   Quoted in Michael Holroyd, *Bernard Shaw* (London: Penguin, 1990), vol. 1, 87, 218.

41   Francis Bacon, "Of Goodness and Goodness of Nature" in *Essays, or Councils, Civil and
     Moral of Sir Francis Bacon* (London: R. Chiswell et al., 1706 [1597]), 30-1. Spelling
     and punctuation modernized.

42   *De Augmentis Scientarium* in *The Philosophical Works of Francis Bacon,* ed. John M.
     Robertson (Freeport, NY: Books for Libraries Press, 1970 [1905]), 586. The *De Aug-
     mentis* of 1627 should not be confused with the more widely read *On the Advancement
     of Learning* of 1605.

43   There has been a dispute in recent years as to whether Descartes allows for animal
     sensation. See John Cottingham, *A Descartes Dictionary* (Oxford: Basil Blackwell,
     1993), 16, 75; and A. Kenny, *Descartes' Philosophical Letters* (Oxford: Clarendon Press,
     1970), 207, for the case in the affirmative; and Gary Steiner, "Descartes on the Moral
     Status of Animals," *Archiv für Geschichte der Philosophie,* 80, 3, 1998, 268-92 for the
     negative. Whichever view is correct, Descartes clearly treats animals as automata.

44   René Descartes, *Oeuvres de Descartes* (Paris: Charles et Paul Tannery, 1897), vol. V, 243.

45   Pierre Gassendi, *Exercises in the Form of Paradoxes in Refutation of the Aristoteleans,* 2,
     sec. 5, subsec. 4 and 2, sec. 6, subsec. 2 in *The Selected Works of Pierre Gassendi,* trans.
     Craig B. Brush (New York: Johnson Reprint Corporation, 1972), 73, 86.

46   Pierre Gassendi, *Metaphysical Colloquy, or Doubts and Rebuttals concerning the Meta-
     physics of René Descartes,* Rebuttal to Meditation 2, Doubt 7, in ibid., 197-8.

47   Quoted in Howard Williams, *The Ethics of Diet: A Catena of Authorities Deprecatory of
     the Practice of Flesh-Eating* (London: F. Pitman, 1883), 104, citing Gassendi, *Physics,*
     Bk. II, "De Virtutibus."

48   Quoted in ibid., 104. Williams has several pages of interesting and useful material on
     Gassendi, far too much to be reproduced here.

49 See p. 111 for the first part.
50 Descartes, *Oeuvres de Descartes*, vol. 5, 243.
51 Quoted in Harwood, *Love for Animals*, 95, citing John Norris, *An Essay toward the Theory of the Ideal or Intelligible World* (London, 1701), pt. II, ii, 44.
52 Quoted in ibid., 97, citing "Of the Soul of Brutes" in Thomas Willis, *Dr. Willis's Practice of Physick* (London, 1684).
53 The sixteenth-century writer Hieronymus Rorarius was, Bayle tells us, "nuncio of Pope Clement VII at the court of Ferdinand, King of Hungary, who undertook to show not only that beasts are rational creatures, but also that they make better use of reason than men do." Pierre Bayle, *Historical and Critical Dictionary: Selections,* trans. Richard H. Popkin with the assistance of Craig B. Brush (Indianapolis: Bobbs-Merrill, 1965), 213.
54 Ibid., 216-17.
55 Ibid., 226.
56 Ibid., 232.
57 Ibid., 233, 236. In his *Monadology* of 1714 Leibniz developed his conception of the animal soul further, but not in any fundamentally different manner. See the London: Lowe and Brydone edition (1898) 259-60. An extensive extract of Leibniz on animal souls may be found in Paul A.B. Clarke and Andrew Linzey, eds., *Political Theory and Animal Rights* (London: Pluto Press, 1990), 27-32.
58 Pliny the Elder, *Natural History,* trans. Robin Waterfield (London: Penguin, 1992), VIII, I.
59 Richard Overton, *Man's Mortalitie,* ed. Harold Fisch (Liverpool: University of Liverpool Press, 1968 [1643]), 27, 26, 68. Spelling and punctuation modernized.
60 Quoted in Erica Fudge, *Perceiving Animals: Humans and Beasts in Early Modern English Culture* (London: Macmillan, 2000), 170, citing Overton, *Baiting of the Bull,* sig. A4.
61 Quoted in Richard D. Ryder, *Animal Revolution,* 51, citing Stubbes, *Anatomy of Abuses* (Colliers reprint edition [London, 1583]), 177.
62 Quoted in Erica Fudge, *Perceiving Animals,* 14, citing Stubbes, *The Anatomie of Abuses* (1583) sigs. D, Qv, Qvi.
63 Quoted in ibid., 38, citing Thomas Draxe, *The Earnest of Our Inheritance* (London, 1613), 26.
64 Quoted in Colin Spencer, *The Heretic's Feast: A History of Vegetarianism* (London: Fourth Estate, 1993), 228.
65 Matthew Hale, *The Primitive Organization of Mankind* (London, 1677), sec. 4, ch. 8.
66 Quoted in W. Youatt, *The Obligation and Extent of Humanity to Brutes: Principally Considered with Reference to the Domesticated Animals* (London: Longman, Orme, Brown, Green and Longman, 1839), 31.
67 Quoted in Ryder, *Animal Revolution,* 55.
68 Quoted in Thomas, *Man and the Natural World,* 154-5, citing *The Poems of Sir Philip Sidney,* ed. William A. Ringler Jr. (Oxford: Clarendon Press, 1962), 106.
69 See p. 31.
70 Evelyn, *Diary of John Evelyn,* vol. 4, 106.
71 Quoted in Thomas, *Man and the Natural World,* 155.
72 Quoted in Fudge, *Perceiving Animals,* 14-16, citing Robert Bolton, *Some Generall Directions for a Comfortable Walking with God* (1625), 155-6.
73 Quoted in Thomas, *Man and the Natural World,* 158, citing Bolton, *Some Generall Directions,* 157.
74 Quoted in Harwood, *Love for Animals,* 72-3, citing Edmund Ellis, *The Opinion of Mr. Perkins, Mr. Bolton and Others concerning the Sport of Cock-Fighting* (London, c. 1635), vii, 70.

75 Quoted in Thomas, *Man and the Natural World,* 157-8, citing William Hinde, *A Faithfull Remonstrance of the Happy Life and Holy Death of John Bruen,* (London, 1641 edition [c. 1625]), 31-2.

76 Quoted in ibid., 166, citing Thomas Edwards, *Gangraena* (London, 1646), I, 20.

77 Quoted in Spencer, *The Heretic's Feast,* 205, citing Norman Cohn, *The Pursuit of the Millennium* (London: Paladin, 1957).

78 Quoted in Thomas, *Man and the Natural World,* 162, citing Edward Bury, *The Husbandman's Companion* (London, 1677), 222-3.

79 Quoted in ibid., 171, citing John Flavel, *Husbandry Spiritualised* (London, 1699), 210.

80 Lord Thomas Macaulay, *History of England* (London: Longman, 1854), vol. 1, 161.

81 Quoted in Eileen Whitlock and Stuart R. Westerlund, *Humane Education: An Overview* (Tulsa: National Association for the Advancement of Humane Education, 1975), 36-7. Spelling modernized.

82 Lines 1-24 of "The Nymph complaining for the death of her Faun" in *The Poems and Letters of Andrew Marvell,* ed. H.M. Margoliouth (Oxford: Clarendon Press, 1952), vol. 1, 22.

83 See p. 44.

84 *Satyr* in *The Poems of John Wilmot, Earl of Rochester,* ed. Keith Walker (Oxford: Basil Blackwell, 1984), 91, 94, 95, lines 1-11, 114-18, 125-32.

Chapter 5: The Enlightenment

1 John Ray, *The Wisdom of God Manifested in the Works of Creation* (London: Samuel Smith, 1691; facsimile reprint, New York: Garland, 1979), 127-9.

2 John Locke, *An Essay Concerning Human Understanding* (London: H. Hills, 1710 [1690]), vol. II, Bk. III, 49.

3 John Locke, *Some Thoughts Concerning Education* in John William Adamson, ed., *Educational Writings of John Locke* (Cambridge: Cambridge University Press, 1922), sec. 110 of first edition, sec. 111 of subsequent editions, 90-2.

4 Alexander Pope, *An Essay on Man,* 1.8.5-9; 3.1.22-5; 3.4.23-7; 3.4.34 in *The Works of Alexander Pope* (Ware: Wordsworth, 1995), 197, 209, 213.

5 *Guardian,* 61, 21 May 1713, in *The Tatler and Guardian* (New York: Bangs Brother, 1852), *Guardian,* 89-92. Such articles were untitled and the titles now ascribed to them are additions of later commentators.

6 Quoted in Dix Harwood, *Love for Animals and How It Developed in Great Britain* (New York: Privately Printed, 1928), 297, citing Joseph Spence, *Anecdotes, Observations and Characters* (London, 1858 edition), 222. Although the material was collected during Spence's lifetime it was first published in 1820.

7 Quoted in Marian Scholtmeijer, *Animal Victims in Modern Fiction: From Sanctity to Sacrifice* (Toronto: University of Toronto Press, 1993), 17.

8 Lines 111-34 of *Windsor Forest* in *The Works of Alexander Pope,* 28.

9 *Tatler,* 112 (27 December 1709), in *The Tatler and Guardian, Tatler,* 221-2.

10 *Tatler,* 134 (16 February 1710), in ibid., 252-3.

11 *Spectator,* 116 (13 July 1711), in *The Spectator; a New Edition Corrected from the Originals,* by Alex Chalmers (New York: E. Sargent and M.A. Ward, 1810), vol. II, 267.

12 *Spectator,* 120 (18 July 1711), from ibid., 283-4.

13 Quoted in Richard D. Ryder, *Animal Revolution: Changing Attitudes Towards Speciesism* (London: Basil Blackwell, 1989), 59.

14 Henry Fielding, *Joseph Andrews* in *Joseph Andrews and Shamela* (Oxford: Oxford University Press, 1980 [1742]), Bk. I, ch. XI, 44.

15 Henry Fielding, *Amelia* (London: Penguin, 1987 [1753]), Bk. 5, ch. 3, 198.

16 Quoted in Martin C. Battestin with Ruth R. Battestin, *Henry Fielding: A Life* (London: Routledge, 1989), 533, citing *Covent-Garden Journal,* no. 15, 22 February 1751-52, "Covent-Garden."

17 See p. 67.

18 In fact, Miguel de Cervantes's *The Ingenious Gentleman: Don Quixhote de la Mancha* (1605-15) exhibits sensibilities to animals beyond those to Rocinante, not least to Squire Sancho Panza's ass. In ch. 11 Cervantes pays due tribute to the golden age conception and its vegetarian lifestyle.

19 *The Champion: containing a series of papers, humorous, moral, political and critical edited by Henry Fielding,* no. 56, 22 March 1739-40. Microform.

20 Fielding, *Joseph Andrews,* Bk. III, ch. VI, 210-11.

21 Fielding, *Miscellanies by Henry Fielding, Esq.,* ed. Henry Knight Miller (Oxford: Oxford University Press, 1972 [1741]) vol. I, 191-204, Appendix D, 253-9) contains a copy of the edition of the Royal Society's *Philosophical Transactions* which Fielding was parodying.

22 From Nicholson *On the Primeval Diet of Man,* 178. Nicholson offers several other examples of antipathy to animal experimentation, but none with the unparalleled peroration of this piece.

23 From ibid., 178-9, citing *Monthly Review,* September 1770, 213.

24 "To Mr. Congreve, Written November, 1693" in Swift, *The Poems of Jonathan Swift* (Oxford: Clarendon Press, 1937), vol. 1, 43-50.

25 Ricardo Quintana, *The Mind and Art of Jonathan Swift* (Gloucester, MA: Peter Smith, 1951 [1936]), 42.

26 Aristotle announced: "If man be without virtue, he is a most unholy and savage being, and worse than all the other [animals] in the indulgence of lust and gluttony." (*Politics,* 1.2.15-16, trans. Ernest Barker [London: Oxford University Press, 1952], 7).

27 See p. xv.

28 See p. 299.

29 Lemuel Gulliver, *Travels into Several Remote Nations of the World. In Four Parts* (London: Benj. Motte, 1726) reprinted as Jonathan Swift, *Gulliver's Travels* (London: Penguin, 1967), 278-9, 294-5, 309, 315.

30 *"Bipes et implumis"* (two-legged and featherless) refers, one presumes, to Plato's definition of man as a two-legged animal without feathers. Diogenes, it is said, plucked a cock, took it to the Academy, and announced: "This is Plato's man."

31 Lines 1-2, 215-20, of "The Beasts' Confession to a Priest" in *The Poems of Jonathan Swift,* vol. 2, 601, 608.

32 From John Vyvyan, *In Pity and In Anger* (Marblehead, MA: Micah, 1988 [1969]) 26, citing *The Plays of William Shakespeare,* ed. Samuel Johnson (London, 1765), vol. vii, 279. Johnson was commenting on the rebuke against the Queen in *Cymbeline* when she proposed to experiment with poison on animals. With justice, Johnson assumed opposition to experimentation to be Shakespeare's own view, as later did Bernard Shaw (see p. 346).

33 *The Idler,* 17 (5 August 1758), in *The Idler* (London: W. Suttaby, 1810). Microform.

34 Quoted in Arthur Helps, *Animals and their Masters* (London: Chatto and Windus, 1883 [c. 1872]), 193.

35 James Boswell, *The Life of Samuel Johnson* (London: J.M. Dent, 1906 [1791]), vol. II, 36. The conversation took place in 1776 when Johnson was 67.

36 Quoted in Keith Thomas, *Man and the Natural World: Changing Attitudes in England 1500-1800* (London: Penguin, 1984 [1983]), 175, citing Norman Callan, ed., *The Collected Poems of Christopher Smart* (London: Routledge and Kegan Paul, 1949), ii, 990-1.

37   Quoted in Thomas, ibid., 176, citing Callan, ed., *The Collected Poems of Christopher Smart*, i, 290.

38   Christopher Smart, *Jubilate Agno*, ed. W.H. Bond (London: Rupert Hart-Davis, 1954 [1760]), lines 1-4, Fragment A; Fragment B2, lines 717-20; 726; 731-2, 742.

39   See p. 16.

40   Laurence Sterne, *A Sentimental Journey through France and Italy* (London: Penguin, 1967 [1768]), "Nampont: The Dead Ass," 63-4.

41   Laurence Sterne, *The Life and Opinions of Tristram Shandy, Gentleman* (New York: Alfred A. Knopf, 1991 [1759-67]), vol. 3, ch. 32, 58-9.

42   Sterne, *A Sentimental Journey*, "The Hotel de Paris," 96-7.

43   Sterne, *Tristram Shandy* (1759), vol. 1, ch. 48, 176-7.

44   Lines 27-42 of "The Philosopher and the Pheasants" in *Fables* in *John Gay: Poetry and Prose*, ed. Victor A. Dearing with the assistance of Charles E. Beckworth (Oxford: Clarendon Press, 1974), vol. II, 322.

45   "The Wild Boar and the Ram," in ibid., 307-8.

46   "Of Walking Streets by Day," in *Trivia* in ibid., vol. 1, 150.

47   Lines 29-40 of "A Nocturnal Reverie" in *The Poems of Anne, Countess of Winchilsea*, ed. Myra Reynolds (Chicago: University of Chicago Press, 1903), 269-70.

48   Lines 15-29 of *The Fleece*, Bk. II, in *The Poems of John Dyer* (London: Llanerch Enterprises, 1989), 68-9.

49   For eulogies on Thomson, see William Collins, "Elegy on Thomson," in *The Poems of Gray and Collins*, ed. Austin Lane Poole (London: Oxford University Press, 1961 [1749]); Thomas Young, *An Essay on Humanity to Animals (1798)*, ed. Rod Preece (Lampeter: Mellen, 2001 [London: T. Cadell Jr. and W. Davies, 1798]); and Dix Harwood, *Love for Animals*. All three recognize Thomson's vital role in changing the orientation of sensibilities to animals.

50   Lines 358-70 of "Spring" in James Thomson, *The Seasons* in *The Seasons and the Castle of Indolence*, ed. James Sambrook, (Oxford: Clarendon Press, 1991 [1972]), 12-13.

51   Lines 717-28, ibid., 22-3.

52   Lines 1172-1200 of "Autumn" in ibid., 120-1.

53   Lines 326-9 and 334-51 of *The Task*, Bk. III, in *The Poems of William Cowper*, ed. John D. Baird and Charles Cooper (Oxford: Clarendon Press, 1995), vol. II, 171.

54   *Gentleman's Magazine*, lxiv, 1784, 412. The complete article is reproduced as Appendix II in *The Poems of William Cowper*, vol. II, 433-6.

55   Lines 560-7 and 576-80 of *The Task*, Bk. III, in *The Poems of William Cowper*, vol. II, 251.

56   Quoted in Harwood, *Love for Animals*, 197.

57   Quoted in ibid., 325-6, citing Hurdis, 13 June 1791. Hurdis's play *Sir Thomas More* (3, 1) has some interesting comments on cruelty to animals with regard to the kind of animal that is mistreated and how it is obtained.

58   Quoted in ibid., 236-7, citing Goldsmith, *An History of the Earth and Animated Nature* (Philadelphia, 1830 [1754]), i, 166; ii, 20; iii, 149.

59   "The Hermit: A Ballad" in *The Poetical and Prose Works of Oliver Goldsmith* (Edinburgh: Gall Inglis, n.d. [c. 1880s]), 37 (as a separate ballad), 219 (as a part of *The Vicar of Wakefield*).

60   *The Citizen of the World*, Letter XV, in Oliver Goldsmith, *The Citizen of the World, The Bee* (London: J.M. Dent, 1934), 38-9.

61   Quoted in Thomas, *Man and the Natural World*, 178, citing Defoe, *The Complete English Tradesman* (London, 1841 edition), ii, 228-9.

62   Quoted in ibid., 117, citing Smollett, *Travels through France and Italy* (London, 1907 edition), 174.

63 *A Pastoral Ballad: Hope* in *The Poetical Works of William Shenstone* (Edinburgh: James Nichol, 1854), pt. 2, stanza 5, 152.

64 Quoted in Harwood, *Love for Animals,* 203.

65 Quoted in ibid., 288.

66 Quoted in ibid., 211-12, citing Henry Brooke, *The Fool of Quality; or the History of Henry, Earl of Moreland* (London, 1859 edition), i, 11-12.

67 Quoted in ibid., 286, citing *Gentleman's Magazine,* vi, 19, 1736.

68 For Rousseau see p. 164 and for Bentham p. 178.

69 See, for example, Peter Singer, *Animal Liberation* (New York: New York Review of Books, 1990 [1975]), 200; Angus Taylor, *Magpies, Monkeys and Morals: What Philosophers Say about Animal Liberation* (Peterborough: Broadview Press, 1999), 23; Barbara Noske, *Beyond Boundaries: Humans and Animals* (Montreal: Black Rose Books, 1997), 46. For the contrary view, see Rod Preece and David Fraser, "The Status of Animals in Biblical and Christian Thought: A Study in Colliding Values," *Society and Animals,* 8, 3, 2000.

70 See p. 128.

71 Joseph Butler, *The Analogy of Religion, Natural and Revealed, to the Constitution and Course of Nature* (London: Longman, 1834 [1736]), i, l.

72 Ibid., 3.

73 Ibid., 13-14; 16-17.

74 John Wesley, "The General Deliverance" (1788) in *Sermons on Several Occasions,* second series, Sermon LX, in *The Works of John Wesley* (Grand Rapids, MI: Zondervan, n.d. [reprint of the Wesleyan Conference Office edition, London, 1872]), vol. VI, 240, 244, 248.

75 Ibid., 251.

76 From Nicholson, *George Nicholson's On the Primeval Diet of Man,* 113-14, citing Hildrop, *Free Thoughts upon the Brute Creation.*

77 From Harwood, *Love for Animals,* 151, citing John Hildrop, *The Works of John Hildrop,* (London, 1754), vol. 1, 230.

78 From ibid., 155, citing *Notes and Queries,* ser. 2, xi, 342.

79 From Nicholson, *George Nicholson's On the Primeval Diet of Man,* 71-2, citing Richard Dean, *Essay on the Future Life of Brutes, introduced with Observations upon Evil, its Nature and Origins* (Manchester, 1767).

80 Quoted in Ryder, *Animal Revolution,* 68, citing Lawrence Gowing, *Hogarth* (London: Tate Gallery, 1971), 69.

81 Quoted in Helps, *Animals and their Masters,* citing Abraham Tucker, *The Light of Nature Pursued* (London, 1777 [1954]), vol. 5, pt. 3, ch. 19.

82 See p. 29.

83 Robert Burton, *The Anatomy of Melancholy* (London, 1621), pt. III, sec. 3, memb. 1, subsec. 2.

84 James Granger, *An Apology for the Brute Creation, or Abuse of Animals Censured in a Sermon on Proverbs xii, 10* (London: T. Davies, 1772), quoted, in part, in Jon Wynne-Tyson, *The Extended Circle: A Commonplace Book of Animal Rights* (New York: Paragon, 1989 [1985]), 106, in part, on Thomas, *Man and the Natural World,* 176, and, in part, in E.S. Turner, *All Heaven in a Rage* (Fontwell: Centaur, 1992 [1964]), 67.

85 Humphry Primatt, *The Duty of Mercy and the Sin of Cruelty to Brute Animals,* ed. Richard D. Ryder (Fontwell: Centaur, 1992 [1776]), 21, 126.

86 See pp. 193-6.

87 Emanuel Swedenborg, *Angelic Wisdom Concerning the Divine Love and the Divine Wisdom* (New York: Swedenborg Foundation, 1960), 27-9, 184, 190-1.

88   Solomon Stoddard, *Three Sermons Lately Preach'd at Boston* (Boston, 1717), 37, quoted
      in Norman Fiering, "Irresistible Compassion in the Eighteenth Century," *Journal of the
      History of Ideas,* vol. xxxvii, 1976, 204.

89   See pp. 109-10.

90   For Franklin's statement in his brother's newspaper, see Fiering, "Irresistible Compas-
      sion," 204, citing *the Papers of Benjamin Franklin,* eds. L.W. Labaree and W. Bell Jr.
      (New Haven: Yale University Press, 1959), I, 37. For his experiences as a vegetarian
      and his refusal to fish or shoot, see Benjamin Franklin, *The Autobiography and Other
      Writings,* ed. Kenneth Silverman (London: Penguin, 1986), 17, 39, 40, 73.

91   John Woolman, *On the Right Use of the Lord's Outward Gifts* in *Considerations on Pure
      Wisdom and Human Policy: On Labour; On Schools; and On the Right Use of the Lord's
      Outward Gifts* in *The Journal and Essays of John Woolman,* ed. Amelia Mott Gummere
      (New York: Macmillan, 1922), 393.

92   *The Journal of John Woolman* in ibid., 152-3, 156-7, 301-2.

93   Voltaire, "Bêtes," in *Dictionnaire philosophique* (Paris: Garnier, 1961 [1764]), 33. This
      trans. Rod Preece. Also in the dictionary, Voltaire says bees are superior to humans
      because their secretions are beneficial while those of humans are noxious. The section
      on "Âmes" (souls) has also much to say of relevance to animals.

94   Voltaire, *Traité sur la tolérance* (Paris: Flammarion, 1989 [1763]), 170-1. This trans.
      Rod Preece. This extract comes from an endnote to ch. xii, 89, note 73. In Voltaire's
      original text the notes are footnotes and not numbered. René Pomeau, editor of the
      Flammarion edition, has included his own notes sequentially with those of Voltaire, so
      reference should be made in the first instance to the opening of ch. 12 if one is not
      using the Flammarion edition.

95   Montesquieu, *The Spirit of the Laws,* trans. Thomas Nugent (New York: Hafner, 1966),
      3-4.

96   Rousseau, *Discourse on the Origin and Foundations of Inequality among Men,* Preface, in
      Rousseau's Political Writings, eds. Alan Ritter and Julia Conaway Bondanella, trans. Julia
      Conaway Bondanella (New York: W.W. Norton, 1988), 7.

97   Ibid., 28.

98   Ibid., 29.

99   Jean-Jacques Rousseau, *Emile, or On Education,* trans. Allan Bloom (New York: Basic
      Books, 1979), 55.

100   Ibid., 79, 223.

101   Jacques-Henri-Bernardin de Saint-Pierre, *Suites des Voeux d'un solitaire* in *Oeuvres de
      Jacques-Henri-Bernardin de Saint-Pierre,* ed. L. Aimé-Martin (Paris: Chez Ledentu,
      1840), 733-4. This trans. Rod Preece.

102   Howard Williams, *The Ethics of Diet: A Catena of Authorities Deprecatory of the Practice
      of Flesh-Eating* (London: F. Pitman, 1883), 167.

103   From ibid., 166.

104   See Basil Willey, *The Eighteenth Century Background: Studies in the Idea of Nature in the
      Thought of the Period* (London: Chatto and Windus, 1946 [1940]), 58.

105   Shaftesbury, *The Moralists, a Philosophical Rhapsody, Being a Recital of Certain Conver-
      sations on Natural and Moral Subjects* in Anthony Ashley Cooper, third Earl of Shaftesbury,
      Characteristics of Men, Manners, Opinions, Times, ed. Lawrence E. Klein, (Cambridge:
      Cambridge University Press, 1999 [1711]), pt. I, sec. III, 298. See also Thomas, *Man
      and the Natural World,* 69, citing *The Philosophical Regimen of Anthony, Earl of Shaftes-
      bury,* ed. Benjamin Rand (1900), 121-2.

106   Shaftesbury, *An Inquiry Concerning Virtue or Merit* in *Characteristics of Men,* Bk. 2, pt.
      II, sec. 3, 226.

107   Bernard Mandeville, *The Fable of the Bees: or Private Vices, Publick Benefits* (Oxford: Clarendon Press, 1924 [1714-28]), Remark (P.), 178-80.

108   Ibid., 180-1.

109   See pp. 219-20.

110   David Hume, *A Treatise of Human Nature,* ed. L.A. Selby-Bigge and P.H. Nidditch (Oxford: Clarendon Press, 1978 [1739-40]), Bk. 1, pt. 3, sec. 16, 176-9.

111   Ibid., Bk. 2, pt. 2, sec. 12, 397-8.

112   David Hume, *An Enquiry Concerning the Principles of Morals,* pt. I, sec. III, 152, in *Enquiries Concerning the Human Understanding and Concerning the Principles of Morals,* ed. L.A. Selby-Bigge (Oxford: Clarendon Press, 1902), 190-1.

113   Hobbes was just about as denigrating of humans as animals, whereas Descartes singled out animals.

114   Lord Bolingbroke, *Essay the First, Concerning the Nature, Extent and Reality of Human Knowledge,* sec. I, in *The Works of Lord Bolingbroke* (Philadelphia: Carey and Hart, 1841), vol. 3, 66.

115   Ibid., 182.

116   *Fragments, or Minutes of Essays* in ibid., vol. 4, 428.

117   David Hartley, *Observations on Man, His Frame, His Duty, and His Expectations* (London: S.D. Richardson, 1748 [Gainesville, FL: Scholars' Facsimiles and Reprints, 1966]), vol. 2, ch. III, sec. 2, prop. 50, 222-3. A lengthier extract is to be found in Williams, *The Ethics of Diet,* 138-9, and in Kerry S. Walters and Lisa Portmess, eds., *Ethical Vegetarianism: From Pythagoras to Peter Singer* (Albany: State University of New York Press, 1999), 57-9.

118   Adam Smith, *The Theory of Moral Sentiments* (London: G. Bohn, 1853 [1759]), pt. II, sec. III, ch. 1, 137-8.

119   Edmund Burke, *A Philosophical Enquiry into the Origin of Our Ideas of the Sublime and Beautiful* (London: F.C. and J. Rivington, 1812 [1756]), pt. I, sec. 10, 66-7.

120   Williams, *The Ethics of Diet,* 170.

121   William Paley, *Moral and Political Philosophy,* Bk. II, ch. XI, in *The Works of William Paley, D.D., Archdeacon of Carlisle* (Philadelphia: Crissy Markley, 1850), 43-4.

122   See p. 157.

123   Immanuel Kant, "Duties towards Animals and Spirits," in *Lectures on Ethics,* trans. Louis Infield (New York: Harper and Row, 1963 [1930]), 239-41.

124   Soame Jenyns, *Disquisition II: On Cruelty to Animals* in *Disquisitions on Several Subjects,* from Nicholson, *George Nicholson's On the Primeval Diet of Man,* 205-6. A lengthier extract is to be found in Williams, *The Ethics of Diet,* 322-4.

125   Soame Jenyns, *A Free Inquiry into the Nature and Origin of Evil,* 2nd edition (London: R. and J. Dodsley, 1757; facsimile reprint, New York: Garland, 1976), 21-2, 36, 69, 73-4, 76-7.

126   Quoted in Thomas, *Man and the Natural World,* 175, citing Richard Cumberland, *A Treatise on the Laws of Nature,* trans. John Maxwell (1727), 302.

127   Quoted in ibid., 179, citing Hutcheson, *A System of Moral Philosophy* (1755), vol. I, 314.

128   Quoted in Harwood, *Love for Animals,* 163, citing Francis Hutcheson, *A System of Moral Philosophy* (London, 1755), Bk ii, ch. vi, sec. III, IV.

129   Quoted in Thomas, *Man and the Natural World,* 175, citing Wollaston, *The Religion of Nature Delineated,* 5th edition (1731), 139.

130   John Balguy, *The Foundation of Moral Goodness: or a Further Inquiry into the Original of Our Idea of Virtue* (London: John Pemberton, 1728; facsimile reprint, New York: Garland, 1976), vol. 1, 14-15.

Chapter 6: The Utilitarian and Romantic Age

1 See Alfred Cobban, *Edmund Burke and the Revolt against the Eighteenth Century: A Study of the Political and Social Thinking of Burke, Wordsworth, Coleridge and Southey*, 2nd edition (London: Allen and Unwin, 1960 [1929]), passim; and Russell Kirk, *The Conservative Mind from Burke to Eliot*, 7th edition (Chicago: Regnery, 1986), for Wordsworth, 11, 496, for Coleridge 126-7 and 133-49, for Southey 26, 189, 191. For Wordsworth see also Stephen Gill, *William Wordsworth: A Life* (Oxford: Oxford University Press, 1989), especially 108-9, and Juliet Barker *Wordsworth: A Life* (London: Viking, 2000), especially 626. For Southey see also Mark Storey, *Robert Southey: A Life* (Oxford: Oxford University Press, 1997), especially 100 and 290. For Coleridge see also Richard Holmes, *Coleridge: Early Visions, 1772-1804* (New York: Pantheon, 1999 [1989]), especially 179, 264.

2 See, for example, Ann Radcliffe, *The Romance of the Forest* (Oxford: Oxford University Press, 1986 [1791]), passim, but especially Chloe Chard's notes, 336-97.

3 Jeremy Bentham, *An Introduction to the Principles of Morals and Legislation*, ed. J.H. Burns and H.L.A. Hart (London: Methuen, 1982 [1789]), 17, 4, b, 282.

4 Jeremy Bentham, *Principles of Penal Law* in *The Works of Jeremy Bentham* (New York: Russell, 1962 [1843]), vol. 10, 549-50.

5 I find it necessary to put Bentham in an appropriate historical context because there are such exaggerated and unsupportable claims for his significance in the development of animal ethics. For example, we read in the *Oxford Companion to Philosophy* (Oxford: Oxford University Press, 1995), 35, that "other than in the writings of Jeremy Bentham it was not until the 1970s that the rights of animals received recognition." It is to be hoped that the evidence presented in this book will dispel such myths once and for all.

6 See Nicholas Boyle, *Goethe: The Poet and the Age: The Poetry of Desire, 1744-1790* (Oxford: Oxford University Press, 2000), vol. II, *Revolution and Renunciation, 1790-1803*, 33.

7 See pp. 92-5.

8 See Goethe, *Faust: Part Two*, trans. Philip Wayne (London: Penguin, 1959), 150.

9 Lines 3-6 of "Das Göttliche" in Johann Wolfgang Goethe, *Sämmtliche Werke, nach Epochen seines Schaffens* (München: Carl Hanser Verlag, 1986-92), Band 2, 1, 90. This trans. Rod Preece. The poem was revised in 1803 but these lines remained the same.

10 *Faust: Part One*, "Waldhöhle" in Goethe, *Sämmtliche Werke* (1986), Band 6, 1, 629. This trans. Rod Preece.

11 See Nicholas Boyle, *Goethe: The Poet and the Age*, vol. II, 309: "Of all his contemporaries Goethe was, and remained, closest to Kant ..."

12 See ibid., vol. I, *The Poetry of Desire*, passim, and vol. II, passim, but especially ch. 9.

13 "Metamorphose der Tiere" in Goethe, *Sämmtliche Werke* (1992), Band 13, 1, 153-5. This trans. Rod Preece. I am indebted to Mathias Guenther for his telling critique of the first draft of my translation and for his valuable suggestions. In some sources the title of the poem is given as "Athroismos: Metamorphose der Tiere" which would appear to be the title it bore in its 1819 publication form.

14 Boyle, *Goethe: The Poet and the Age*, vol. 1, 399.

15 Goethe, *The Sorrows of Young Werther*, trans. Michael Hulse (London: Penguin, 1989 [1774]), 29 (17 May 1771).

16 *Ideas for a Philosophy of the History of Mankind*, Bk. iii, sec. 6, in F.M. Barnard, ed. and trans., *Herder on Social and Political Culture* (Cambridge: Cambridge University Press, 1969), 255, 257. A fuller extract is to be found in Paul A.B. Clarke and Andrew Linzey, eds., *Political Theory and Animal Rights* (London: Pluto Press, 1990), 34-6.

Since the original allows for it, perhaps requires it, I have used a rather more gender inclusive title translation than that provided by Barnard.

17 Lines 121-4, 133-68, 177-80 of *Hart-Leap Well: Part Two* in William Wordsworth, *Poems*, ed. John G. Hayden (London: Penguin, 1977), vol. 1, 415.

18 Lines 36-41, stanza IV, of *Ode: Intimations of Immortality from Recollections of Early Childhood* in ibid., 525.

19 "Tribute to the Memory of the Same Dog" (that is, Music not Foxey) in ibid., 650-1.

20 Lines 48-64 of "Lines left upon a Yew-tree, which stands near the lake of Esthwaite, on a desolate part of the shore, commanding a beautiful prospect" in ibid., 255.

21 Dorothy Wordsworth, *The Grasmere Journals* in *Journals of Dorothy Wordsworth*, ed. Mary Moorman (London: Oxford University Press, 1971), 136-7, 138, 139, 142, 145, 146.

22 "To a Young Ass: Its Mother being tethered near it" in *The Poetical Works of Samuel Taylor Coleridge*, ed. Ernest Hartley Coleridge (London: Henry Frowde, 1912), 74-6.

23 Lines 272-90 from pt. IV, and lines 610-17 of "The Rime of the Ancient Mariner" in ibid., 193, 209. The lines are from the amended 1800 version, with marginal glosses added by Coleridge in 1815-16.

24 *A Lay Sermon* (1817) in *The Collected Works of Samuel Taylor Coleridge*, vol. VI, *Lay Sermons*, ed. R.J. White (London: Routledge and Kegan Paul, 1972), 183, n.6. The Socinian creed is named for Faustus (1539-1604) and Laelius Socinius (1525-62), who denied the doctrine of the trinity, the natural depravity of humankind, vicarious atonement, and eternal punishment.

25 From stanzas 2 and 5 of "To Contemplation" in Robert Southey, *Poems* (Bristol: Joseph Cottle, 1797), 135, 137.

26 "On the Death of a Favourite Old Spaniel" in ibid., 132-4.

27 Quoted in Celia Haddon, *The Love of Cats: An illustrated anthology about cats and their companions* (London: Headline, 1992), 41.

28 From Keith Thomas, *Man and the Natural World: Changing Attitudes in England 1500-1800* (London: Penguin, 1984 [1983]), 143, citing *Letters of Robert Southey*, ed. Maurice H. Fitzgerald (New York: AMS Press, 1977 [1912]), 33.

29 From ibid., 280, citing Jennings, *Ornithologia*, [1828], 201, n.

30 Lord Byron, *Byron: The Complete Poetical Works*, ed. Jerome K. McGann (Oxford: Clarendon Press, 1980), vol. 1, 391-2. The epitaph is neither titled nor included in the body of the *Works* but as a note. At 224 of McGann's edition the date of death is given as 10 November.

31 "Inscription on the Monument of a Newfoundland Dog" in ibid., 224-5.

32 Lines 854-8, canto xiii, stanza 106, of *Don Juan* in ibid., vol. 5.

33 Thomas Young, *Thomas Young's An Essay on Humanity to Animals (1798)*, ed. Rod Preece (Lampeter: Mellen, 2001 [London: T. Cadell, Jun. and W. Davies, 1798]), 81.

34 From Thomas, *Man and the Natural World*, 177, citing Charles Lamb, *The Letters of Charles Lamb*, ed. Alfred Ainger (London: Macmillan, 1904), i, 106.

35 "The Sea" in John Bidlake, *The Poetical Works of John Bidlake* (London: J. Murray, 1804), 155.

36 John Wolcot, "A Moral Reflection on the Preceding Elegy" in *The Works of Peter Pindar, Esq.* (London: John Walker, 1797), vol. 2, 298. The title of the "Preceding Elegy" is "The Royal Bullocks: A Consolatory and Pastoral Elegy."

37 From Dix Harwood, *Love for Animals and How It Developed in Great Britain* (New York: Privately Printed, 1928), 294, citing Radcliffe, *The Mysteries of Udolpho* (London: J.M. Dent, 1912 [1794]), 8.

38 Plate 16 of *For Children: The Gates of Paradise* in *Blake: Complete Writings*, ed. Geoffrey Keynes (London: Oxford University Press, 1966), 209.

39   Lines 5-22, 27-34, and 37-8 of "The Auguries of Innocence" in Blake, *Poems* (New York: Alfred A. Knopf, 1994), 117-19. The lines are printed there as a separate stanza following each period. I have adopted the practice of, for example, Peter Ackroyd in his *Blake* (London: Sinclair-Stevenson, 1995), 275, of reproducing the poem without the breaks.

40   Ibid., 55.

41   Ibid., 57-8.

42   Ibid., 201.

43   Lines 8-10, *Visions of the Daughters of Albion* in *Blake: Complete Writings*, plate 8, 195.

44   Lines 26-7, *Book of Thel*, pt. II, in ibid., 174.

45   From John Sutherland, *The Life of Walter Scott* (Oxford: Blackwell, 1995), 13.

46   For Newton see pp. 220-1; for Ritson see pp. 219-20.

47   Shelley, *The Complete Works of Percy Bysshe Shelley*, ed. Roger Ingpen and Walter E. Peck (New York: Gordian Press, 1965), vol. VI, 6, 8, 11, 17, 18. For a lengthier extract than provided here, see Kerry S. Walters and Lisa Portmess, eds., *Ethical Vegetarianism: From Pythagoras to Peter Singer* (Albany: State University of New York Press, 1999), 69-74.

48   Shelley, ibid., 338, 339, 340-1, 343-4.

49   Lines 303-5, *Prometheus Unbound*, Act I, in ibid., vol. II, 188.

50   Lines 5-7, "Love's Philosophy," stanza 1, in ibid., vol. III, 299.

51   Lines 526-8 of *The Revolt of Islam*, under the original title of *Laon and Cyntha*, Canto Fifth, 5, in ibid., vol. 1, 325.

52   Lines 1-12 of "To a Mouse, on turning her up in her Nest, with the Plough, November 1785" in Burns, *The Poems and Songs of Robert Burns*, ed. James Kinsley (Oxford: Clarendon, 1968), vol. 1, 127-8.

53   Lines 7-18 of "Poor Mailie's Elegy" in ibid., 34-5.

54   Lines 1-8 of "On Seeing a Wounded Hare limp by me, which a Fellow had just shot at" in ibid., 465.

55   Lines 257-68 of *The Parish Register*, pt. 1, "Baptisms," in George Crabbe, *The Complete Poetical Works*, eds. Norma Dalrymple-Champreys and Arthur Pollard (Oxford: Clarendon, 1988), vol. 1, 220.

56   From E.S. Turner, *All Heaven in A Rage* (Fontwell: Centaur, 1992 [1964]), 138.

57   From ibid., 139.

58   Mrs. Trimmer, *Fabulous Histories, Designed for the Instruction of Children, Respecting their Treatment of Animals* (London: T. Longman and G.G.J. and J. Robinson, 1786; facsimile reprint, New York: Garland, 1977), ch. ix, 72-3.

59   From Harwood, *Love for Animals*, 254, citing Trimmer, *Easy Introduction to the Knowledge of Nature* (Philadelphia, 1846 [1782]), 67.

60   Thomas Day, *History of Little Jack* (London: John Stockdale, 1788), 11-12, 55, 60, 71.

61   Thomas Day, *The History of Sandford and Merton, a Work Intended for the Use of Children* (London: J. Stockdale, 1803 edition; facsimile reprint, New York: Garland, 1977), vol. 1, 4-6.

62   Mary Wollstonecraft, *Original Stories from Real Life, with Conversations, Calculated to Regulate the Affections and Form the Mind to Truth and Goodness* (London: J. Johnson, 1788), 3-4, 4-6, 7.

63   William Godwin, *Fleetwood: or, The New Man of Feeling* (London: Richard Phillips, 1805; facsimile reprint, New York: Garland, 1979), vol. 1, 32-3.

64   Priscilla Wakefield, *Instinct Displayed, in a Collection of Well-Authenticated Facts, Exemplifying the Extraordinary Sagacity of Various Species of the Animal Creation*, 4th ed. (London: Harvey and Darton, 1821 [1811]), 192.

65   Ibid., 171, 254, 220, vii-ix.

66   Jean Paul Friedrich Richter, *Levana; or the Doctrine of Education* (Boston: Ticknor and

Fields, 1863 [1807]), Sixth Fragment, ch. III, sec. 118; 311-12. No translator's name is given.

67 Ibid., sec. 120; 315, 316, 318-20.

68 Wakefield, *Instinct Displayed*, ix.

69 Gilbert White, *The Natural History of Selborne*, ed. W.S. Scott (London: The Folio Society, 1962 [1789]), Letter 9 to Thomas Pennant, Esq., 19.

70 Ibid., Letter 6 to Pennant, 13.

71 Ibid., Letter 13 to the Hon. Daines Barrington, 109.

72 Ibid., Letter 24 to Barrington, 139-40.

73 Quoted in Desmond King-Hele, *Erasmus Darwin: A Life of Unequalled Achievement* (London: Giles de la Mare Publishers, 1999), 351, citing *The Temple of Nature*, IV, 426-8.

74 Erasmus Darwin, *Zoonomia; or the Laws of Organic Life* (London: J. Johnson, 1794; facsimile reprint, New York: AMS Press, 1974), vol. I, 169.

75 Ibid., vol. I, 509.

76 Quoted in W. Youatt, *The Obligation and Extent of Humanity to Brutes: Principally Considered with Reference to Domesticated Animals* (London: Longman, Orme, Brown, Green and Longman, 1839), 34.

77 Anna Seward, *The Poetical Works of Anna Seward, with Extracts from her Literary Correspondence*, ed. Walter Scott (Edinburgh: Ballantyne, 1810), vol. 2, 59-60.

78 Herman Daggett, *The Rights of Animals: An Oration* (New York: American Society for the Prevention of Cruelty to Animals, 1926), from Clarke and Linzey, eds., *Political Theory and Animal Rights*, 129-32.

79 Thomas Paine, *Age of Reason, Being an Investigation of True and Fabulous Theology* (Baltimore: Oppenheimer, n.d. [1794]), pt. 1, 67-8.

80 From George Nicholson, *George Nicholson's On the Primeval Diet of Man (1801): Vegetarianism and Human Conduct Toward Animals*, ed. Rod Preece (Lampeter: Mellen, 1999), 171-2, citing David Williams, *Lectures on Political Principles* (London, 1789), iv, ii, 62.

81 John Oswald, *The Cry of Nature; or an Appeal to Mercy and Justice, on Behalf of the Persecuted Animals* (London: J. Johnson, 1791), ii, 6.

82 Ibid., 29.

83 Ibid., 31-3.

84 Ibid., 36-9.

85 Ibid., 40-2, 44.

86 Ibid., 75-8.

87 Ibid., 81-2.

88 This trans. Rod Preece. The German original is reproduced in Howard Williams, *The Ethics of Diet: A Catena of Authorities Deprecatory of the Practice of Flesh-Eating* (London: F. Pitman, 1883), 327.

89 Quoted in Turner, *All Heaven in a Rage*, 75.

90 John Lawrence, *A Philosophical and Practical Treatise on Horses and on the Moral Duties of Man toward the Brute Creation* (London: H.D. Symons, 1802 [1796-98]), vol. I, 117-20.

91 Ibid., 123.

92 Ibid., 125.

93 Quoted in Nicholson, *George Nicholson's On the Primeval Diet of Man*, 171. The source, not given by Nicholson, is Helen Maria Williams, *Sketches of the State of Manners and Opinions in the French Republic to the Close of the Eighteenth Century* (London: J. Johnson, 1801).

94 See pp. 80, 82, 157, 210-11.

95 Thomas Young, *An Essay on Humanity to Animals* (1798 edition), 6-7.

96   Ibid., 133-4.

97   Ibid., 188-9.

98   Ibid., 199-200.

99   Or, at least, *possibly* his own. While Nicholson acknowledges he has contributed little to the book, it is not always easy to tell where quoting ends and commentary, if any, begins. Moreover, it is often unclear whom, and from what, is being quoted. It would not, I must confess, surprise me unduly to discover at some future date that these are not the words of Nicholson himself.

100   Nicholson, *George Nicholson's On the Primeval Diet of Man.* 182-3.

101   Ibid., 223.

102   See pp. 167-8.

103   Joseph Ritson, *An Essay on Abstinence from Animal Food as a Moral Duty* (London: Richard Phillips, 1802), 226.

104   Compare Hobbes on the man and the ox, epigraph, p. vi.

105   Ritson, *An Essay on Abstinence,* 231-3.

106   John Frank Newton, *Return to Nature; or a Defence of the Vegetable Regimen; with some account of an experiment made during the last three or four years in the author's family* (London: T. Cadell and W. Davies, 1811), 67.

107   Ibid., 154.

Chapter 7: The Legislative Era

1   See pp. 214-16.

2   Myriad edicts, proclamations, decrees, and non-general laws were previously passed in various countries. In England, during the reign of Henry VIII (1509-47), legislation had been passed to protect the eggs of certain birds in the breeding season. In 1616 a proclamation was issued in Bermuda "against the spoyle and havock" perpetrated against the cahows threatened with extinction, but also to protect all birds subject to "stoneing, and all kinds of murtherings." In 1641 the Massachusetts Bay Colony provided protection for working animals. In 1654 the Protectorate in England outlawed public exhibitions of animal fights. Legislation was passed in England in 1670, 1671, and 1722, and in Nova Scotia in 1768, to protect owned animals, but more to protect the interests of the owners than the animals.

3   From Jon Wynne-Tyson, *The Extended Circle: A Commonplace Book of Animal Rights* (New York: Paragon, 1989 [1985]), 111.

4   *Parliamentary Papers,* 18.919, April 1800, Parliamentary, committee, and other formal reporting at this time, was in the third person past tense, I have amended the text to reflect how Sheridan would have spoken.

5   For other material by Southey see pp. 190-1. See also Mark Storey, *Robert Southey: A Life* (Oxford: Oxford University Press, 1997), 53-5 and 88-9 on the relationship between Southey, nature, animals, and the other Lake Poets.

6   Quoted in Richard D. Ryder, *Animal Revolution Changing Attitudes Towards Speciesism* (London: Basil Blackwell, 1989), 84.

7   Quoted in Wynne-Tyson, *The Extended Circle,* 78.

8   Quoted in W. Youatt, *The Obligation and Extent of Humanity to Brutes: Principally Considered with Reference to the Domesticated Animals* (London: Longman, Orme, Brown, Greene and Longman, 1839), 31-2.

9   Lewis Gompertz, *Moral Inquiries on the Situation of Man and of Brutes,* ed. Peter Singer (Fontwell: Centaur, 1992 [1824]), 150. For Thomas Young see pp. 217-19.

10   In his *Remarks on Forest Scenery* (1783), William Gilpin wrote at length against such practices. They are excerpted both in Young's *Essay on Humanity to Animals* (110-25 of

1798 edition) and George Nicholson's *On the Primeval Diet of Man* (165-70 of 1999 edition).

11 Gompertz, *Moral Inquiries,* 21-5.

12 Ibid., 149-50.

13 Quoted in E.S. Turner, *All Heaven in a Rage* (Fontwell: Centaur, 1992 [1964]), 136.

14 Ibid.

15 Quoted in Keith Thomas, *Man and the Natural World: Changing Attitudes in England 1500-1800* (London: Penguin, 1984 [1983]), 176, citing Philips, *Golden Rules of Social Philosophy* (London: Richard Philips, 1826), 42.

16 Quoted in ibid., citing Fletcher, *A Few Notes on Cruelty to Animals* (London, 1842), 4.

17 Youatt, *The Obligation and Extent of Humanity to Brutes,* 30-1.

18 Ibid., 48.

19 Ibid., 53.

20 Ibid., 55.

21 Ibid., 54.

22 John Styles, *The Animal Creation: Its Claims on Our Humanity Stated and Enforced,* ed. Gary Comstock (Lampeter: Mellen, 1997 [London: T. Ward, 1839]), 176.

23 Compare, for example, 133-4 of Young with 167 of Styles.

24 Styles, *The Animal Creation,* 167-72.

25 John Clare, *Selected Poems,* ed. J.W. Tibble and Anne Tibble (London: J.M. Dent, 1965), 231-2.

26 J.W. Tibble and Anne Tibble, eds., *The Prose of John Clare* (London: Routledge and Kegan Paul, 1951), 201-2. To make the unpunctuated prose more readily readable I have left a short space at natural breaks. I have, however, left Clare's idiosyncratic spelling unaltered.

27 John Clare, *Selected Poems,* 309.

28 Quoted in Ryder, *Animal Revolution,* 95-6, citing *Insects and their Habitations: A Book for Children* (London: SPCK, 1833), 48.

29 Mary Shelley, *Frankenstein: The Modern Prometheus* (New York: Dover, 1994 [reprint of third edition of 1831]), 67.

30 Ibid., 81, 94, 105.

31 See pp. 75-6.

32 Mary Shelley, *The Last Man* (New York: Bantam, 1994 [1826]), 328.

33 Ibid., 423.

34 See pp. 233-5.

35 See pp. 328-30.

36 Quoted in Fleur Adcock and Jacqueline Simms, eds., *The Oxford Book of Creatures* (Oxford: Oxford University Press, 1995), 82-3.

37 Quoted in ibid., 36. The poem is quoted in full at 34-6.

38 *Dubrovsky* in Alexander Pushkin, *The Queen of Spades and Other Stories,* trans. Rosemary Edwards (London: Penguin, 1962), 94-5.

39 Charlotte Brontë, *Shirley* (London: Penguin, 1974 [1849]), 225.

40 Ibid., 420-1.

41 Ibid., 314.

42 Ann Brontë, *Agnes Grey* (London: Penguin, 1988), 78-9.

43 Ibid., 105-6.

44 Ibid., 192.

45 E.C. Gaskell, *The Life of Charlotte Brontë* (Edinburgh: John Grant, 1905), 243-6.

46 Alphonse de Lamartine, *Les Confidences* (Paris: Hachette, 1893 [1848]), 77-9. This trans. Rod Preece.

47   George Sand, *Indiana*, trans. Sylvia Raphael (Oxford: Oxford University Press, 1994 [1831]), 17, 77, 190-1.

48   George Sand, *The Master Pipers,* trans. Rosemary Lloyd (Oxford: Oxford University Press, 1994 [1852]), 99, 121.

49   Jules Michelet, *The Bible of Humanity,* trans. Vincenzo Calfia (New York: J.W. Bouton, 1877), 37-8.

50   Jules Michelet, *The Bird,* trans. W.H. Davenport Adams (London: Wildwood House, 1981 [1879]), 18, 52, 67, 148.

51   Ibid., 265-6, 268-9, 271.

52   W.H. Davenport Adams, *The Bird World* (London: Thomas Nelson and Sons, 1878), 15-16, 19-20.

53   Charles Baudelaire, *Selected Poems from "Flowers of Evil,"* trans. Wallace Fowlie (New York: Dover, 1995), 25.

54   Honoré de Balzac, *Père Goriot,* no translator given (London: Daily Telegraph, n.d. [c.1888]), Preface, v-vi.

55   Arthur Schopenhauer, *The World as Will and Idea,* trans. R.B. Haldane and John Kemp, 6th edition (London: Kegan, Paul, Tench, Trubner, 1909), vol. 1, 481.

56   Arthur Schopenhauer, *On the Basis of Morality,* 2nd edition, trans. E.F.J. Payne (Indianapolis: Bobbs-Merrill, 1965), 81.

57   Ibid., 96.

58   Ibid., 141.

59   Ibid., 140, 152, 172-3.

60   Ibid., 179-80.

61   John Stuart Mill, *Utilitarianism* in *Utilitarianism, Liberty and Representative Government* (London: J.M. Dent, 1910), 9.

62   Quoted in Ryder, *Animal Revolution,* 101.

63   John Stuart Mill, "On the Grounds and Limits of the *Laissez-Faire* or Non-Interference Principle" in *Principles of Political Economy, with Some of their Applications to Social Philosophy* in *Works of John Stuart Mill* (Toronto: University of Toronto Press, 1965), vol. 3, 952. For Queen Victoria's comments on the meagre fines see p. 327.

64   John Stuart Mill, "Three Essays on Religion" in *Essays on Ethics, Religion and Society* in *Works of John Stuart Mill,* vol. 10, 185-7.

65   Auguste Comte, *Theory of the Great Being* in *System of Positive Philosophy, or Treatise on Sociology,* trans. Henry Dix Hutton (New York: Burt Franklin, n.d. [c. 1877]), vol. 4, 33, 43.

66   Auguste Comte, *Theory of the Future of Man* in *Système de politique positive, ou traité de sociologie, instituant la religion de l'humanité,* trans. Henry Dix Hutton (Paris: Carilian-Goeuvry, 1854), vol. IV, 359.

67   Ibid., 225.

68   *System of Positive Philosophy,* vol. 1, 495-6, 497-8.

69   *Nature* in *The Selected Writings of Ralph Waldo Emerson,* ed. Brooks Atkinson (New York: The Modern Library, 1992), 5.

70   Ibid., 8.

71   Ibid., 11.

72   Ibid., 12.

73   Ibid., 18, 19, 20, 21.

74   Ibid., 22, 23, 33.

75   Ralph Waldo Emerson, *Poems* in *The Complete Works of Ralph Waldo Emerson* (New York: AMS, 1968 [reprint of Boston: Houghton Mifflin, 1904]), vol. ix, 39.

76   Ibid., 235.

77 See p. 30.

78 Nathaniel Hawthorne, *The House of the Seven Gables* (New York: W.W. Norton, 1967 [1851]), 87-8, 89-90.

79 Quoted in Wynne-Tyson, *The Extended Circle*, 118.

80 Hawthorne, *The Artist of the Beautiful* in *Nathaniel Hawthorne's Tales* (New York: W.W. Norton, 1987), 166.

81 Ibid., 171.

82 Ibid., 177.

83 Quoted in Mason Wade, *Margaret Fuller: The Whetstone of Genius* (New York: Viking, 1940), 4-5.

84 William A. Alcott, *Vegetable Diet* (New York: Fowlers and Wells, 1848), 264-5. Alcott's book is excerpted at much greater length in Kerry S. Walters and Lisa Portmess, eds., *Ethical Vegetarianism: From Pythagoras to Peter Singer* (Albany: State University of New York Press, 1999), 82-8.

85 Quoted in Edwin Haviland Miller, *Salem is My Dwelling Place: A Life of Nathaniel Hawthorne* (Iowa: University of Iowa Press, 1991), 216.

86 See Rod Preece, *Animals and Nature: Cultural Myths, Cultural Realities* (Vancouver: UBC Press, 1999), xxvii, 104-5.

87 Thoreau, *The Annotated Walden: Walden; or, Life in the Woods by Henry D. Thoreau, together with "Civil Disobedience,"* ed. Philip Van Doren Stern (New York: Barnes and Noble, 1970), 192.

88 Ibid., 295.

89 Ibid., 222.

90 Ibid., 223.

91 Ibid., 250-1.

92 Ibid., 279.

93 Ibid., 246.

94 Ibid., 339-44.

95 Ibid., 346.

96 Ibid., 348.

97 See pp. 94, 110-11, 270, 345.

98 Compare Machiavelli, *The Prince* (written c. 1513, published 1532) on the concepts of *virtù* and *fortuna*.

99 See pp. 341-4.

Chapter 8: The Darwinian Age

1 See Richard Ryder, *Animal Revolution: Changing Attitudes Towards Speciesism* (London: Basil Blackwell, 1989), 101-5, for an illuminating account.

2 See p. 351. The view is still widely held. It pervades, for example, James Rachels's otherwise admirable study, *Created from Animals: The Moral Implications of Darwinism* (Oxford: Oxford University Press, 1991).

3 Letter of November 1, 1910. Quoted in William Shirer, *Love and Hatred: The Stormy Marriage of Leo and Sofya Tolstoy* (New York: Simon and Schuster, 1994), 350-1.

4 Noted in Roderick Frazier Nash, *The Rights of Nature: A History of Environmental Ethics* (Madison: University of Wisconsin Press, 1989), 42, citing Francis Darwin and A.C. Seward, eds., *More Letters of Charles Darwin* (London, 1903), vol. 1, 114.

5 Quoted in Nash, ibid., 43, citing Francis Darwin, ed., *The Life and Letters of Charles Darwin* (New York: Basic Books, 1959 [1888]), vol. 1, 368.

6 See, for example, Eric Trinkaus and Pat Shipman, *The Neandertals: Changing the Image of Mankind* (New York: Alfred A. Knopf, 1993), 74ff.

7   T.H. Huxley, *Man's Place in Nature, and Other Collected Essays* (New York: D. Appleton, 1900 [1863]), 152.

8   Quoted in Robert Sharpe, "Animal Experimentation: A Failed Technology" in Gill Langley, ed., *Animal Experimentation: The Consensus Changes* (New York: Chapman and Hall, 1989), 89, citing C. Bernard, *An Introduction to the Study of Experimental Medicine*, trans. H.C. Green (New York: Dover, 1957 [1865]).

9   Quoted in Adrian Desmond and James Moore, *Darwin: The Life of a Tormented Evolutionist* (New York: Warner, 1991), 244, citing *Notebooks*, C79, 1838.

10 Quoted in E.S. Turner, *All Heaven in a Rage* (Fontwell: Centaur, 1992 [1964]), 1. Also in Rachels, *Created from Animals*, 1, citing *Charles Darwin's Notebooks*, transcribed and ed. Paul H. Barrett et al. (Ithaca: Cornell University Press, 1977), 300.

11 Quoted in Rachels, 132, citing Paul H. Barrett ed., *Metaphysics, Materialism and the Evolution of the Mind* (Chicago: University of Chicago Press, 1974), 187.

12 Quoted in Walter Sullivan's Introduction to Charles Darwin, *The Voyage of the Beagle* (New York: Mentor, 1972 [1839]), xvi.

13 Charles Darwin, *The Descent of Man, and Selection in Relation to Sex* (New York: A.L. Burt, n.d. [reprint of 2nd edition of 1874]), 68.

14 Quoted in Rod Preece, *Animals and Nature: Cultural Myths, Cultural Realities* (Vancouver: UBC Press, 1999), 60.

15 Charles Darwin, *The Descent of Man*, 6.

16 Ibid., 28.

17 Ibid., 74.

18 Ibid., 77.

19 Ibid., 80. It has struck me as singularly interesting that at the Stratford, Ontario, Shakespeare Festival Theatre, as of August 2001, one of the few non-drama-oriented books available in the theatre store is Darwin's volume on *The Expression of the Emotions in Man and Animals* (1872). Evidently, it is the view of at least some producers that Darwin captured what is essentially common about human and animal expression over a century and a quarter ago.

20 Ibid., 84.

21 Ibid., 89.

22 Ibid., 110.

23 Ibid., 111.

24 Ibid., 112.

25 See Rev. Gilbert White, *The Natural History of Selborne*, ed. W.S. Scott (London: The Folio Society, 1962 [1789]).

26 Darwin, *Descent of Man*, 113-14.

27 Ibid., 114.

28 Ibid., 115.

29 Ibid., 117.

30 Ibid., 118.

31 Ibid., 121.

32 Ibid., 139.

33 Ibid., 167.

34 Ibid., 170.

35 Ibid., 180.

36 Ibid., 709.

37 Quoted in Rachels, *Created from Animals*, 213, citing "Vermin and Traps" in the *Gardener's Chronicle*, 1863, in *The Collected Papers of Charles Darwin*, ed. Paul H. Barrett (Chicago: University of Chicago Press, 1977), vol. II, 83-4.

38   Quoted in Rachels, ibid., citing *Life and Letters of Charles Darwin*, vol. III, 200.

39   Quoted in Rachels, ibid., citing *Life and Letters of Charles Darwin*, vol. III, 202-3.

40   *The Life and Letters of Charles Darwin*, vol. II, 382-3.

41   Quoted in Rachels, *Created from Animals*, 215, citing Frances Power Cobbe, *The Life of Frances Power Cobbe as Told by Herself* (Boston: Houghton Mifflin, 1894), vol. II, 445.

42   James Boyd Davies, *The Practical Naturalist's Guide, Containing Instructions for Collecting, Preparing and Preserving Specimens in All Departments of Zoology* (Edinburgh: Machlachlan and Stewart, 1858), 4.

43   Quoted in Ryder, *Animal Revolution*, 162, citing Lauder Lindsay, *Mind in the Lower Animals [in Health and Disease]* (London: Kegan Paul, 1879), 125.

44   Quoted in Ryder, ibid., 163, citing A. Armitt, *Man and His Relatives: A Question of Morality* (London, 1885), 67.

45   Albert Leffingwell, *The Vivisection Question*, 2nd edition (Chicago: The Vivisection Reform Society, 1907), 74, 78, 80. From an address before The Humane Congress of the World's Columbian Exposition, Chicago, Oct. 12, 1893.

46   Alfred Russel Wallace, *World of Life: A Manifestation of Creative Power, Directive Mind and Ultimate Purpose* (New York: Moffat, Yard, 1916 [1911]), 411.

47   Quoted in Jon Wynne-Tyson, *The Extended Circle: A Commonplace Book of Animal Rights* (New York: Paragon, 1989 [1985]), 392.

48   Wilkie Collins, *Heart and Science: A Story of the Present Time* (Peterborough: Broadview Press, 1996 [1883]), 136.

49   Ibid., 188-91.

50   Albert Leffingwell, "The Vivisection Question," originally published as "Does Vivisection Pay?" in *Scribner's Monthly*, July 1880, in *The Vivisection Question*, 1.

51   Quoted in Zulma Steele, *Angel in a Top Hat* (New York: Harper Brothers, 1942), 155, 169. See also Whitlock and Westerlund, *Humane Education: An Overview*, 44.

52   Quoted in Roswell C. McCrea, *The Humane Movement: A Descriptive Survey* (New York: Columbia University Press, 1910), 148.

53   Quoted in Francis E. Clarke [Sarah Grand], *Poetry's Plea for Animals* (Boston: Little, Brown, 1927), 280.

54   Quoted in Wynne-Tyson, *The Extended Circle*, 16-17, citing address given as founder of the ASPCA.

55   Quoted in ibid., 56.

56   Quoted in Roswell C. McCrea, *The Humane Movement: A Descriptive Survey* (New York: Columbia University Press, 1910), 12.

57   See Rod Preece, *Animals and Nature*, 133, and *The Life and Writings of Abraham Lincoln*, ed. Philip Van Doren Stern (New York: Modern Library, 1999), 17.

58   George T. Angell, *Autobiographical Sketches and Personal Recollections* (Boston: AHES, undated, probably 1892), Appendix, 32-3. There was an earlier, but less complete, edition in 1884.

59   Ibid., Appendix, 16-17.

60   Ibid., 94-5.

61   Anna Sewell, *Black Beauty: The Autobiography of a Horse* (New York: Thomas Y. Crowell, 1895), ch. XI: "Poor Ginger," 201-3.

62   Quoted in Zulma Steele, *Angel in a Top Hat* (New York: Harper Brothers, 1942), 286.

63   Quoted in ibid., 288, 290.

64   Quoted in Nash, *The Rights of Nature*, 39-40.

65   Quoted in ibid., 42-3, citing Muir, *A Thousand-Mile Walk to the Gulf* (Boston: Houghton Mifflin, 1917 [1867]), 357-8.

66 Quoted in ibid., 51, citing Evans, *Evolutional Ethics and Animal Psychology* (New York: D. Appleton, 1897), 99-100.
67 See pp. 306-7.
68 Quoted in Nash, *The Rights of Nature*, 52, citing Evans, *Evolutional Ethics*, 4. Nash subscribes to a very similar thesis in 3-12 of *The Rights of Nature*.
69 Ernest Thompson Seton, *Wild Animals I Have Known* (London: Penguin, 1987 [facsimile reprint of 1898 edition]), 12-13, 357. Not everyone considers Seton's stories "true." See Ralph H. Lutts, *The Nature Fakers* (Goldon, CO: Fulcrum, 1990).
70 J. Howard Moore, *The New Ethics* (Chicago: S.A. Block, 1909 [London: E. Bell, 1907]), 14, 41.
71 J. Howard Moore, *The Universal Kinship*, ed. Charles Magel (Fontwell: Centaur, 1992 [1906]), 4-5.
72 Ibid., 100-1.
73 Ibid., 107, 146.
74 Ibid., 239-40.
75 Ibid., 308-9.
76 Ibid., 324.
77 Lines 683-91 (stanza 32) of Walt Whitman, *Leaves of Grass*, ed., Harold W. Blodgett and Scully Bradley (New York: New York University Press, 1965 [1892]), 60.
78 See Mary Allen, *Animals in American Literature* (Urbana: University of Illinois Press, 1983), 36-59. "In over 300 poems featuring animals (compared to very few about people) most are no bigger than a robin" (36).
79 Poem 148, *The Complete Poems of Emily Dickinson*, ed. Thomas H. Johnson (Boston: Little, Brown, 1960), vol. 1, 615, c. 1878.
80 Justin Kaplan, *Mr Clemens and Mark Twain* (New York: Touchstone, 1983 [1966]), 18, 373.
81 "Man's Place in the Animal World" (1896) in Mark Twain, *Collected Tales, Sketches, Speeches, & Essays, 1891-1910*, ed. Louis J. Budd (New York: The Library of America, 1992), 207-10, 212, 216.
82 Mark Twain, *Life on the Mississippi* (Oxford: Oxford University Press, 1990 [1883]), 296-7.
83 Louis J. Budd, *Mark Twain: Social Philosopher* (Bloomington: Indiana University Press, 1962), 201.
84 See pp. 321-2.
85 "A Dog's Tale" (1896) in *Collected Tales, Sketches, Speeches, & Essays*, 561, 568-70.
86 Victor Hugo, *Les Misérables*, trans. Norman Denny (London: Penguin, 1982), 995, 804.
87 Quoted in John Vyvyan, *In Pity and in Anger: A Study of the Use of Animals in Science* (Marblehead, MA: Micah, 1988 [1969]), 143, citing *The Zoophilist* (the organ of the Victoria Street Society), December 1884.
88 Quoted in ibid., 143.
89 Hugo, *Les Misérables*, 164.
90 Claude Lévi-Strauss, *Totemism*, trans. Rodney Needham (London: Merlin, 1964), 89.
91 See p. 141.
92 Hugo, *Les Misérables*, 65-6, 69.
93 Ibid., 159, 590, 613.
94 Ibid., 764-5.
95 Ibid., 780, 1032.
96 Romain Rolland, *Jean-Christophe*, trans. Gilbert Cannan (New York: Random House, 1938), 326-8. The piece is excerpted at slightly greater length in both Wynne-Tyson,

The Extended Circle, 279-80, and Kerry S. Walters and Lisa Portmess, eds., *Ethical Vegetarianism From Pythagoras to Peter Singer* (Albany: State University of New York Press, 1999), 136-7.

97 Barry Millington, *Wagner* (Princeton: Princeton University Press, 1992), 104.

98 Quoted in ibid., 103, citing Cosima Wagner, *Die Tagebücher, 1869-1883* (Munich, 1976-7).

99 Richard Wagner, "Against Vivisection" (An Open Letter to Herr Ernst von Weber, *Bayreuther Blätter*, 19 October 1879) in M.R.L. Freschel, ed., *Selections from Three Essays by Richard Wagner* (Rochester, NH: Millennium Guild, 1933), 8-9. Walters and Portmess include additional material on Wagner's views on vegetarianism (*Ethical Vegetarianism*, 93-5). Unfortunately, they imagine he was a vegetarian in practice (89) rather than solely in theory.

100 Quoted in Joseph Frank, *Dostoevsky: The Seeds of Revolt, 1821-49* (Princeton: Princeton University Press, 1976), 29.

101 Quoted in Joseph Frank, *Dostoevsky: The Years of Ordeal, 1850-59* (Princeton: Princeton University Press, 1990), 173, citing Carl Gustav Carus, *Psyche: Zur Entwicklungsgeschichte der Seele* (Pforzheim, 1846), 297-8.

102 Quoted in Joseph Frank, *Dostoevsky: The Miraculous Years, 1865-71* (Princeton: Princeton University Press, 1995), 260, 326.

103 Fyodor Dostoevsky, *The Brothers Karamazov*, trans. Richard Pevear and Larissa Volokhonsky (New York: Alfred A. Knopf, 1992 [1880]), 294-5.

104 Ibid., 299.

105 Ibid., 319.

106 See p. 294.

107 Dostoevsky, *The Brothers Karamazov*, 527.

108 Rosemary Edmonds, Introduction, Leo Tolstoy, *Resurrection*, trans. Rosemary Edmonds (London: Penguin, 1966 [1899]), 8.

109 Leo Tolstoy, *Resurrection*, 19.

110 Ibid., 99.

111 Ibid., 222, 474.

112 Quoted in Wynne-Tyson, *The Extended Circle*, 376.

113 See Howard Williams, *The Ethics of Diet: A Catena of Authorities Deprecatory of the Practice of Flesh-Eating* (London: F. Pitman, 1883). For Williams see pp. 332-3.

114 "The First Step" in *Recollections and Essays by Leo Tolstoy*, trans. with an introduction by Aylmer Maude, 4th edition (London: Oxford University Press, 1961), sec. IX, 124-6. Other extracts from the same piece may be found in Andrew Linzey and Tom Regan, eds., *Animals and Christianity: A Book of Readings* (London: SPCK, 1989), 194-7, and in Walters and Portmess, *Ethical Vegetarianism*, 97-105.

115 Ibid., sec. X, 134.

116 Quoted in Wynne-Tyson, *The Extended Circle*, 228.

117 From Linzey and Regan, eds., *Animals and Christianity*, 165-6, citing *Speeches against Vivisection*, published as a leaflet by the National Anti-Vivisection Society and Catholic Study Circle for Animal Welfare, n.d.

118 Quoted in Wynne-Tyson, *The Extended Circle*, 400-1.

119 Herbert Spencer, *Social Statics* (New York: D. Appleton and Co., 1896), 234-6.

120 Peter Kropotkin, *Mutual Aid: A Factor of Evolution* (Boston: Extending Horizon Books, n.d. [after 1955]; reprint of 1914 edition [first edition 1902]), 5-6, 57-9.

121 Ibid., 74-5.

122 Quoted in Keith Thomas, *Man and the Natural World: Changing Attitudes in England*

1500–1800 (London: Penguin, 1984 [1983]), citing Lecky, *The History of the Rise and Influence of the Spirit of Rationalism in Europe* (London: Longman's Green, 1910 [1870]), vol. 1, 303.

123 W.E.H. Lecky, *The History of European Morals from Augustus to Charlemagne* (New York: D. Appleton and Co., 1869), vol. 2, 244, 173, 185.

124 Ibid., vol. 2, 174; vol. 1, 143; vol. 1, 103.

125 Ibid., vol. 1, 47, 48-9.

126 Desmond and Moore, *Darwin*, 621.

127 See pp. 310-12.

128 See pp. 300-1, 312-15, 315-16, 321-2.

129 Frances Power Cobbe, "Vivisection and Its Two-Faced Advocates," *Contemporary Review*, XLI, April 1882, 610-26. Cobbe also wrote a book on vivisection: *The Modern Rack* (London: Sonnenschein, 1889). While the book contains more pathos than the article and is eminently persuasive, it is less concise.

130 See pp. 330-1.

131 *Spectator*, 6 February 1875, 177-8.

132 Lord Chief Justice Coleridge, "The Nineteenth Century Defenders of Vivisection," *Fortnightly Review*, XXXVIII, February 1882, 225-36.

133 See pp. 166-7.

134 *Parliamentary Debates*, Third Series, 39 and 40 Victoria, 1876, vol. CCXXX (London: Cornelius Buck, 1876), 486.

135 Quoted in Wynne-Tyson, *The Extended Circle*, 320-1.

136 Quoted in Morton N. Cohen, *Lewis Carroll: A Biography* (New York: Alfred A. Knopf, 1995), 5, 110-11, 391.

137 Charles Dodgson, "Some Popular Fallacies about Vivisection," *Fortnightly Review*, XXIII, June 1875, 847-54.

138 Quoted in Ryder, *Animal Revolution*, 129.

139 Quoted in Arthur Helps, *Animals and their Masters* (London: Chatto and Windus, 1883 [c. 1872]), epigraph.

140 John Ruskin, *The Works of John Ruskin*, ed. E.T. Cook and Alexander Wedderburn (London: G. Allen, 1903-12), vol. 34, 643-4. The third-person form of reporting has made it difficult to determine which words Ruskin actually spoke. I have accordingly retained the third-person form.

141 *The Poetical Works of Robert Browning* (London: Smith, Elder and Co., 1896), vol. 2, 596.

142 Ibid., 753.

143 Quoted in Donald Thomas, *Robert Browning: A Life Within a Life* (London: Weidenfeld and Nicholson, 1982), 265.

144 Quoted in Frank McLynn, *Robert Louis Stevenson: A Biography* (London: Pimlico, 1993), 24, citing "The Coast of Fife" in *Works*, Tusitala edition (1924), vol. 30, 9-10.

145 Robert Louis Stevenson, *Travels with a Donkey in the Cévennes* (London: Chatto and Windus, 1986 [1879]), 43-5, 47-9, 50, 69, 91.

146 Ibid., 126.

147 Quoted in McLynn, *Robert Louis Stevenson*, 186, 187.

148 Ibid., 193.

149 Quoted in David Comfort, *The First Pet History of the World* (New York: Fireside, 1994), 123.

150 McLynn, *Robert Louis Stevenson*, 282.

151 Quoted in Jan Marsh, *Christina Rossetti: A Literary Biography* (London: Pimlico, 1994), 145.

152 Lines 78-91 of "Sing-Song: A Nursery Rhyme Book" (1872) in *The Complete Poems of Christina Rossetti*, ed. R.W. Crump (Bâton Rouge: Louisiana State University Press, 1986-90), vol. III, 210.

153 "To what purpose is this waste?" (1872) in ibid., vol. II (1986), 43-4.

154 Peter Levi, *Tennyson* (New York: Charles Scribner's Sons, 1993), 68. Some of the other information in this paragraph is from ibid., 36, 49, 236.

155 Ibid., 54, 223.

156 Quoted in Wynne-Tyson, *The Extended Circle*, 386.

157 Quoted in Vyvyan, *In Pity and in Anger*, 162, citing Gladstone Papers in British Museum.

158 An account of the trial is to be found in Cobbe, *The Life of Frances Power Cobbe*, 672-5.

159 A.G. Gardiner, *The Life of Sir William Harcourt* (New York: George H. Doran, no date), vol. 1, 402-3. The quoted letters are to be found there also.

160 See p. 134.

161 See Andrew Motion, *Keats* (London: Faber and Faber, 1997), 17.

162 See Peter Ackroyd, *Dickens* (London: Minerva, 1990), 263.

163 See ibid., 405.

164 Quoted in ibid., 295.

165 See ibid., 820.

166 See ibid., xii.

167 Charles Dickens, *Barnaby Rudge: A Tale of the Riots of '80* (London: J.M. Dent, 1931 [1841]), 25, 53-4, 132-3. Much lengthier and quite different excerpts are to be found in Cecily Boas, ed., *Birds and Beasts in English Literature* (London: Thomas Nelson, 1926), 23-46.

168 Quoted in Ackroyd, *Dickens*, 553.

169 Charles Dickens, "Inhumane Humanity," *All the Year Round*, vol. XV, 17 March 1866, 238-40.

170 See pp. 212-14, 219-21.

171 Quoted in the Appendix to Henry S. Salt, *Animals Rights' Considered in Relation to Social Progress* (Clarks Summit, PA: Society for Animal Rights, 1980 [1892]), 139. Salt lists and describes a number of books on animal rights in the Appendix, including Henry Crowe, *Zoophilos*, 1819; William H. Drummond, *The Rights of Animals, and Man's Obligation to Treat them with Humanity*, 1838; Rev. J.G. Wood, *Man and Beast, here and hereafter*, 1874; Edward Byron Nicholson, *The Rights of an Animal, a new Essay in Ethics*, 1879; J. Macaulay, *A Plea for Mercy to Animals*, 1881; J.B. Austin, *The Duties and the Rights of Man*, 1887; and Countess Martinengo Cesaresco, *The Place of Animals in Human Thought*, 1909; all published in London.

172 Quoted in Wynne-Tyson, *The Extended Circle*, 227.

173 For Salt, see pp. 341-4; for Lind-af-Hageby, see pp. 352-3.

174 See pp. 52-3.

175 Howard Williams, *The Ethics of Diet: A Catena of Authorities Deprecatory of the Practice of Flesh-Eating* (London: F. Pitman, 1883), vii-ix, xii.

176 Quoted in Philip Kapleau, *To Cherish All Life* (Rochester, NY: The Zen Center, 1986), 81.

177 Edward Maitland, *Anna Kingsford: Her Life, Letters, Diary and Work*, 3rd edition (London: G. Redway, 1913), vol. 1, 45-6.

178 Ibid., vol. 2, 311-12.

179 Ibid., vol. 1, 86-7.

180 Ibid., 1, 76.

181 Anna (Bonus) Kingsford and Edward Maitland, *Addresses and Essays on Vegetarianism*

(London: John M. Watkins, 1912; facsimile reprint, Kiler, MT: Kessinger Publishing, n.d.), 65.

182   Ibid., 170.

183   Arthur Helps, *Animals and their Masters,* 1883 edition, ii.

184   See pp. 312-15.

185   Helps, *Animals and their Masters,* 8.

186   Ibid., 10, 11, 14-15, 20.

187   Ibid., 21.

188   Ibid., 23-5.

189   Ibid., 41-7.

190   Ibid., 56.

191   Ibid., 63.

192   Ibid., 68.

193   Ibid., 116-7.

194   Ibid., 129.

195   Edward Carpenter, *Towards Democracy* (London: Unwin Brothers, 1926 [1883]), 21.

196   Ibid., 174-5.

197   Edward Carpenter, *Civilisation: Its Cause and Cure, and Other Essays* (London: Allen and Unwin, 1919 [1883]), 2.

198   Ibid., 21.

199   Ibid., 23.

200   Ibid., 38.

201   Ibid., 39.

202   Ibid., 39-40.

203   Ibid., 45.

204   Quoted in Ryder, *Animal Revolution,* 127, citing Salt, *Seventy Years among Savages.*

205   Salt, *Animals' Rights Considered in Relation to Social Progress,* 10, 15, 17, 21, 28, 43-4, 68, 83-4, 88, 97-8, 101, 114.

206   Quoted in Michael Holroyd, *Bernard Shaw* (Harmondsworth: Penguin, 1990), vol. 1, 87.

207   Quoted in ibid., 86.

208   Quoted in ibid., vol. 3 (1993), 214.

209   *The Doctor's Dilemma* in *The Doctor's Dilemma, Getting Married, and The Shewing-up of Blanco Posnet by Bernard Shaw* (London: Constable, 1911), 99-100.

210   Quoted in Holroyd, *Bernard Shaw,* vol. 3, 45.

211   Quoted in ibid., 255.

212   See pp. 179-82.

213   Quoted in Holroyd, *Bernard Shaw,* vol. 2, 58.

214   Preface to *The Doctor's Dilemma,* lviii-lix.

215   Ibid., xiii, xv, xlii.

216   Ibid., xlvii.

217   Ibid., xlix.

218   Ibid., l-li.

219   Ibid., liv-lv.

220   Ibid., lix.

221   Ibid., lxi.

222   Ibid., lxi-lxii.

223   See pp. 94, 270, 292, 345.

224   Thomas Hardy, *Jude the Obscure* (Ware: Wordsworth, 1995 [1895]), 8, 10, 284, 294.

225   Thomas Hardy, *Under the Greenwood Tree* (Ware; Wordsworth, 1994 [1872]), 106.

226 Thomas Hardy, *The Trumpet-Major* (London: Penguin, 1996 [1880]), 147.

227 Thomas Hardy, *The Return of the Native* (London: Penguin, 1994 [1878]), 81.

228 Ibid., 100.

229 See pp. 141, 293.

230 Hardy, *The Return of the Native*, 249.

231 Hardy, *Jude the Obscure*, 2.

232 Ibid., 7.

233 Ibid., 8-9.

234 Ibid., 57.

235 Ibid., 303, 353.

236 Ibid., 357.

237 Quoted in Joanna Cullen Brown, *Let Me Enjoy the Earth: Thomas Hardy and Nature* (London: Allison and Busby, 1990), 279.

238 Quoted in ibid., 113-4, citing F.E. Hardy, *The Life of Thomas Hardy 1840-1928* (London, 1928).

239 Quoted, in full, in ibid., 116-17.

240 Quoted in ibid., 290, citing *The Life of Thomas Hardy*.

241 Quoted in ibid., 290-1, citing *The Life of Thomas Hardy*.

242 Quoted in ibid., 295, citing *The Life of Thomas Hardy*.

243 Quoted in ibid., 278, citing *The Academy and Literature*, 17 May 1902.

244 Quoted in ibid., 279.

245 Quoted in John Vyvyan, *The Dark Face of Science* (London: Michael Joseph, 1971), 36-7.

246 Document in the archives of the Ontario SPCA, Newmarket, June 1993.

247 See p. 274.

248 Quoted in Vyvyan, *The Dark Face of Science*, 74, citing *The Vivisection Controversy*, 240-1, of the English edition of 1908. It is not included in the American edition of *The Vivisection Question* of 1907.

249 C.G. Jung, *Memories, Dreams, Reflections* (New York: Vintage, 1985), 101.

Index

Printed and bound in Canada by Friesens

Set in Caslon and Stone by Brenda and Neil West, BN Typographics West

Copy editor: Lesley Cameron

Proofreader: Deborah Kerr